SOCIAL INEQUALITY

SOCIAL INEQUALITY

FORMS, CAUSES, AND CONSEQUENCES

CHARLES E. HURST

The College of Wooster

ALLYN AND BACON

Boston   London   Toronto   Sydney   Tokyo   Singapore

Series Editor: Karen Hanson
Series Editorial Assistant: Laura Lynch
Production Administrator: Annette Joseph
Production Coordinator: Holly Crawford
Editorial-Production Service: Laura Cleveland,
    WordCrafters Editorial Services, Inc.
Cover Administrator: Linda K. Dickinson
Cover Designer: Suzanne Harbison
Manufacturing Buyer: Megan Cochran

Copyright © 1992 by Allyn and Bacon
A Division of Simon & Schuster, Inc.
160 Gould Street
Needham Heights, MA 02194

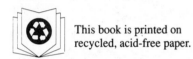

This book is printed on
recycled, acid-free paper.

Library of Congress Cataloging-in-Publication Data

Hurst, Charles E.
    Social inequality : forms, causes, and consequences / Charles E. Hurst
        p.   cm.
    Includes bibliographical references and index.
    ISBN 0-205-12792-4
    1. Equality—United States.   2. United States—Social conditions.
I. Title.
HN90.S6H87   1992
305'.0973—dc20   91-17337
                                                                 CIP

Printed in the United States of America

10   9   8   7   6   5   4   3   2   1   96   95   94   93   92   91

Photo and Cartoon Credits: Page 5 cartoon by David Kordalski; pages 47,
54, 83, 133, 136 by David C. Barnett; pages 60, 314 *The Cleveland Press, The
Cleveland Press* Collection, Cleveland State University Archives; pages 50,
105, 138, 140 by Patrick G. Flanagan; page 325 The Bettmann Archive; page
352 cartoon by Arthur Bok. Reprinted with permission.

To Mary Ellen
with love always for who you are

CONTENTS

PREFACE

Whether it is in the relationships between groups of different income or power, or in those between different races or sexes, social inequality is all around us and infiltrates our lives in innumerable ways. Fluctuations in the economy and government policy, experiences revolving around race and gender, and even the occurrence of international events all impress the consequences of social inequality on each of us. Because of this pervasive impact, it should not be surprising that many of the earliest and most pivotal issues in the social sciences have involved questions of inequality. This makes it important for students of society to understand as much as possible about social inequality, its various dimensions and extent, sources, consequences, and related public policies.

This book is intended as an introduction to the study of social inequality, and its content and organization reflect changes that have occurred in my own thinking after having taught courses on this topic for over twenty years. I have made several fundamental assumptions in developing the manuscript.

1. Social inequality is multidimensional, but not in any simple static or nonrelational way. Class, status, power, race, and sex are each significant segments in the spectrum of inequality, but at the same time are interlinked in a variety of ways. As a result, the book contains several separate chapters on the extent and explanation of these forms of inequality.

2. An understanding of the roots of inequality is crucial to our abilities to deal with its effects on an everyday basis as ordinary citizens and to develop effective policies aimed at curbing its negative effects on our lives. Thus, in contrast to most texts on the subject, three chapters on explanations of social inequality are included, but they are placed at a point in the manuscript where students might be more receptive to reading about them.

3. Consistent with C. Wright Mills's dictum, an understanding of what happens to us as individuals depends heavily on the histories and structures in which we are enmeshed. An understanding of the impact of social inequality on individuals must be embedded in a broader social and cultural framework. Consequently, discussions of the extent and causes of economic, racial, and gender inequality are enlightened by historical summaries and frequent references to social-structural conditions that shape the system of inequality. In addition, while the focus in the text is on inequality in the United States, there are frequent comparisons with conditions in other societies.

4. There are some crucial omissions in many past treatments of the subject. I have tried to rectify this. The most significant addition is discussion of Appalachia as an area where not only social status but economic and political dimensions of social inequality come to bear. Too frequently among scholarly circles, Appalachia is an "other America," that is, it is ignored despite the fact that it constitutes an almost ideal example where many dimensions of inequality have converged and impinged upon the lives of ordinary people.

A second subject that is frequently omitted revolves around questions of fairness, justice, and equity. Despite the association of this topic with philosophy and ethics, an examination of these questions is a legitimate area for social-scientific inquiry. Unavoidably, if social inequality is extensive, and the evidence indicates that it is and that it has real consequences for individuals and groups, then inquiries about the fairness of the system and an individual's position in it almost inevitably arise. These questions come more frequently to the foreground as economic inequality increases, as it has in recent years. In light of these developments, I have included a chapter on the issues of justice and legitimacy in the system of inequality.

A third topic concerns the relationship between social inequality and various social movements. Social movements often are intimately linked with problems associated with being on the low end of the inequality hierarchy, are often central historical events, and are sometimes consequential for the extent of social inequality. Chapter 13 is devoted to a discussion of the working class, civil rights, and women's movements as related to corresponding dimensions of inequality. Finally, an in-depth treatment of social policies aimed at reducing economic inequalities is needed even though an exhaustive discussion of every policy connected to one or more dimensions of inequality is beyond the scope of this book. Consequently, two chapters discuss contemporary income-maintenance programs and alternatives to them.

In addition to these assumptions and beliefs, I have tried to be evenhanded in my discussions, including a variety of both qualitative and quantitative information and a relatively full breadth of theoretical approaches, including some from economics and anthropology. At the same time, I have drawn conclusions about their adequacy. With respect to the placement of theory in the book, it has been my experience that students are not automatically drawn to it, but that their curiosity must first be whetted by demonstrations that the topic of study is worth understanding and that it is important in their own lives. This belief is reflected in the organization of the book, which includes theory only after showing the extent and consequences of inequality in society.

After a brief introduction focusing on an elaboration of several issues that have been at the heart of the study of inequality since its inception, and summaries of U.S. approaches to the subject, the text is divided into four parts that could be moved around depending upon the preferred approach in the class.

Part I deals with the extent of several forms of inequality, including economic, status, racial, sexual, and political inequality. Consequently, most of the statistics are found in this section of the book.

Part II offers a discussion of how inequality affects us intimately as individuals and in the broader society. Central to this discussion is an emphasis on social inequality's implications for basic life chances: physical and mental health, food, shelter, and family relationships. The social phenomena of crime and collective protest also are addressed as related to inequality.

Part III is an in-depth treatment of various theories of economic class, race, and sex inequality. While the emphasis is on sociological theories, a sampling of important anthropological and economic theories also is included, along with comments on each of them. Theories covering a breadth of political perspectives are present, ranging from conservative neoclassical economic explanations to broadly Marxian and feminist explanations.

Part IV deals broadly with the issues of stability and change in the system of social inequality. Mobility and legitimation help to stabilize the system, while social movements and policies attempt either to change or rectify the problems associated with it. This part begins with an overview of social mobility and attainment and then moves to address the thorny question of whether people view the extent of inequality as just or not, and what factors contribute to their viewing the present system as just or unjust. Those groups who view the system as unjust frequently generate movements aimed at changing it, which is the subject of the next chapter. Finally, the last two chapters also deal with the issue of tampering with the system of inequality, but through the development of effective public policies.

I am grateful to a number of colleagues and friends who made valuable comments and suggestions about the manuscript. Most significantly, I appreciate the support, advice, and motivation provided by friends at The College of Wooster. Bob Blair, Terry Kershaw, Karen Taylor, Jim Hodges, Eric Moskowitz, and Dave Guldin provided insightful evaluations or suggestions on various parts of the content. The manuscript is stronger because of their perceptiveness. Haithe Anderson also took the time to read and comment on my discussions of sex and gender.

Outside reviewers provided further detailed and invaluable comments on the manuscript. They include Pranab Chatterjee, Case Western Reserve University; Stephen Green, North Adams State College; Rogers Johnson, College of the Holy Cross; Alice Abel Kemp, University of New Orleans–Lakefront; and Michael Miller, The University of Texas at San Antonio. I took their comments on content very seriously and, in some cases, drastically revised sections because of their suggestions. I hope all of these individuals know how I feel about their assistance and I hope I have done justice to the quality of their comments.

Thanks also go to my research assistants, Robin Cordell and Yalman Onaran, along with Carolyn Rahnema, who did much of the word processing. I also would not have been able to complete this project without support from the Henry Luce III Fund for Distinguished Scholars and The College of Wooster's sabbatical program. My leave a few years ago at Case Western Reserve University and the University of Wisconsin–Madison allowed me to study the relationship of health and health care to class inequality in depth, and I wish to thank Rockwell Schulz for serving as my sponsor in Madison. My discussions with Roger Formisano also proved helpful in this regard.

I am also grateful to my dear wife Mary Ellen for serving as a general sounding board and providing specific suggestions on my treatment of health care in the book. Her own work as a hospital social worker has exposed her to much of the fallout that inequality has on health care. In addition to making my work easier, she and my children—Katie, Brendan, and Sarah—have made the world a better place for me.

SOCIAL INEQUALITY

CHAPTER 1

AN INTRODUCTION TO THE STUDY OF SOCIAL INEQUALITY

It can be argued that the debate over social inequality formed the basis for the emergence of sociology as a modern discipline.
—Bryan S. Turner

Social inequality is not merely an intellectual issue to be debated upon by academics and theoreticians. It is a social fact that impinges on the concrete lives of everyone. In their everyday lives, people are surrounded by social, political, and economic differences that directly affect their feelings and living conditions. Mike Bellamy, for example, works on commission for a small company in Phoenix cleaning sewers and drains ("The Hard Choices" 1987). His monthly income varies greatly since the work is seasonal. In 1986, his annual income was $15,000. Mike and his wife, Vickie, live with their four daughters in a small two-bedroom apartment where the monthly rent is $325. Most months, their expenses for rent, food, medicine and so forth exceed their income, and hard choices have to be made about how to use their money. During a recent Halloween season, Vickie was troubled for days trying to decide whether to purchase a large pumpkin for $1 which she could use later for cookies and bread. She decided not to make the purchase. The family has no medical insurance; Mike's job does not provide any fringe benefits, yet he says, "It's the best job I ever had." Despite debts and obvious needs, Mike and Vickie hate to ask for help. Vickie explains, "I was taught that you don't ask for help. You do for yourself or you go without."

Joe Mendoza is an ambitious working-class youth living in "Cityville," a densely populated city outside Boston (Steinitz and Solomon 1986). His father works in the insulation business, a dirty and tiring job, and Joe feels that his family has little control over their lives. He hopes to go to college and continue pursuing work in the electronics field. At the same time, Joe is angry because he feels that teachers at the high school treat the "college kids" better than those who are in the "general" course of study. He recognizes clear and large differences between classes and believes that large corporations control much of the political life of the country. People, he feels, who commit crimes but have "money and political pull" get off "scot free," but "if you're a poor guy and can't afford a lawyer, you're going to be spending the rest of your life in jail." "Middle-class people have more of a chance at stuff" than poor individuals, who are "probably getting screwed out of something" by the Congress.

Joan Leahy, a resident of the same community as Joe, has applied for entrance into a top-notch private university that is close by, but has decided that she will not go because she feels that she would not fit in with the types of students she thinks she would find there. She says she hates "snobs." Like Joe, she feels that those who have

1

money are better off in a variety of ways. "If you've got money you've got a lot better chance at getting ahead. Your father or your relations back you." But she is still confident about her own prospects. "And if you *don't* have money and connections, well—I'm not going to be a failure. I'll be a success to myself!" Despite their belief in the advantages of the rich, these working-class youth believe in the value of hard work and individual effort.

John Apostle has worked at Trans World Airlines for twenty-six years while leading a middle-class life with his family in their three-bedroom ranch home in Chicago (*Akron Beacon Journal* 1988). He and his wife Bev have lived comfortably, raised three children, had some exciting vacations, and accumulated many wonderful memories. In his job, John has been a workaholic, thinking TWA was family. But times at TWA have gotten worse, and John's wages have been cut by a third and his benefits have been reduced, the result being that John, instead of looking forward to a comfortable retirement, is experiencing downward mobility. He and his wife have had to change their lifestyle and tighten their belts, and John wonders why. "I ask myself, 'what could I have done to prevent this?' and I always come up empty-handed. 'Was I so blind that I couldn't see what was happening to the company? Should I have gotten out? Am I trying to put the blame on someone else? How much of what's happened is my fault? Was it my lack of college education?' Sometimes I stand out in the driveway and I ask myself, 'Where did I go wrong?' " (ibid., p. 5).

While John sees himself falling, the salaries of many chief executives have spiraled upward. "Lee A. Iacocca made enough money last year (1987) to buy a fleet of more than 1,500 Chrysler Le Barons, while his company lost market share to rival automakers and its profit fell 7 percent. Put another way, a worker toiling at minimum wage for 40 hours a week since the birth of Christ probably wouldn't have earned as much as the $38.43 million Iacocca collected in the last two years from salary, bonuses, and exercised stock options, AFL-CIO economists have calculated" (*Wooster Daily Record* 1988, p. 4). Among the thirty companies that make up the Dow Jones industrial average, pay for CEOs sometimes doubled, even though the Dow Jones fell over 22 percent on Black Monday, October 19, 1987.

A SNAPSHOT OF SOME CORE ISSUES

Why are some people so well-off while Mike and Vickie struggle to make ends meet? How much inequality does exist and to what extent do education and background account for these differences? Is one's position due primarily to individual efforts as some of these persons suggest, or is it due more often to the class into which one was born? Are people right in blaming themselves for their own economic failures? Are the discrepancies found between individuals fair or justified? Is this inequality inevitable? Why does Joan Leahy feel the way she does about students from other social classes? How does one's position in the system of inequality shape perceptions and attitudes about others and society? Does inequality in one area lead to inequality in others? The short vignettes raise some interesting issues about inequality, a number of which will be explored in subsequent chapters. Many of these have been a source of controversy among scholars, and a few are briefly outlined in the following sections.

Capitalism versus Democracy

Can free competition, with its resultant inequality, and political equality exist simultaneously? Can capitalism and democracy effectively coexist? Pure capitalism demands that markets be open and free and that individuals be able to freely pursue their economic goals, competing with others within the broad framework of the U.S. legal system. Capitalism's ideal conditions assume *equality of opportunity,* regardless of sex, race, or any other categorical characteristic. Presumably, individual talents and motivations are the prime determinants of how far a person goes in the system. This is how many would explain the high executive salaries noted previously. "My view of executive compensation is like all compensation, it's market driven. The company pays what it has to pay to recruit and retain a person. . . . A person is worth what the market is willing to pay for him" says Charles Peck, an analyst for The Conference Board (*Wooster Daily Record* 1988, p. 4). A system like this presumably would result in the best people being in the highest positions, with the consequence being an efficiently run economy. But if this type of competitive capitalism operates in the United States, then economic inequality is unavoidable, since the talents and motivations of individuals and supply and demand for them vary. There is a potential for economic concentration under these circumstances with a few having much while many may have little.

Alongside this capitalistic economic system exists a political democracy in which everyone is supposed to have a vote in the running of the government. One person, one vote is the rule. *Equality of result* is expected in the political arena in the sense that power should be equally distributed. The question is can equality of political power and inequality in economic standing exist at the same time? Or does economic power lead to inordinate unequal political power, thereby making a mockery of political equality? Can open economic capitalism and political democracy coexist? John Adams, one of the Founding Fathers of the United States, expressed concern that "the balance of power in a society accompanies the balance of property and land. . . . If the multitude is possessed of the balance of real estate, the multitude will have the balance of power and, in that case, the multitude will take care of the liberty, virtue and interest of the multitude in all acts of government (Adams 1969, pp. 376–377). Writes Bryan Turner, "Modern capitalism is fractured by the contradictory processes of inequality in the market place and political inequality at the level of state politics. There is an inevitable contradiction between economic class and the politics of citizenship" (B. Turner 1986, p. 24). Obviously, Joe Mendoza is convinced of the link between economic and political power.

How do individuals who lack economic resources react politically to this situation? Does the contradiction generate resistance?

Is Inequality Inevitable?

The preceding comments are closely linked to another issue, that is, the inevitability of inequality. One side argues that inequality is always going to be present because of personal differences between individuals. If there is an open society and if people vary in their talents and motivations, then this would suggest that inequality is inevitable, a simple fact of society. "Some inequalities come about as a result of unavoidable biological inequalities of physical skill, mental capacity, and traits of personality" argues Cauthen (1987, p. 8) in a recent treatise on equality. Some early philosophers also argued that there are "natural" differences between individuals, and some people, in fact, still maintain that there are differences of this type separating the sexes, resulting in the inevitability of inequality. Aristotle took the position that "the male is by nature superior, the female, inferior; and the one rules, and the other is ruled" (in Kriesberg 1979, p. 12). More recently, Goldberg (1973, p. 133) argued that male dominance and higher achievement are probably inevitable because of the biological differences that he says exist between males and females. An unbroken thread running through several of the vignettes at the beginning of the chapter is the belief that it is differences in individuals that account for inequality between persons. Certainly, we will have to discuss these and other explanations of inequality in detail.

Other theorists have argued that inequality is inevitable because as long as certain kinds of tasks are more necessary for the survival of the society than others, and as long as those able to perform those tasks are rare, social inequality of rewards between individuals is needed to motivate the best people to perform the most difficult tasks. Under these conditions, the argument goes, inequality cannot be eradicated without endangering the society.

On the other side of the fence are those who argue that economic inequality is largely the by-product of a system's structure and not the result of major differences in individual talents, characteristics, and motivations. Rousseau, for example, linked the origins of inequality to the creation of private property (Dahrendorf 1970, p. 10). It is the characteristics of the political economy and the firms and labor markets within it that are primary determinants of differences in income and wealth. Where a person works and in what industry have a major effect on earnings. Essentially, then, this argument states that it is not human nature and individual differences but rather structural conditions that determine where an individual winds up on the ladder of economic inequality. "The theories that say . . . that women are 'naturally' disadvantaged are of use to those who want to preserve and strengthen the dominant political and economic interests. . . . Contrary to the claims of biological determinists, studies of the contributions that biological factors make to human behavior can *at most* give only very limited information about the origins of present differences in human behavior and probably no information about the origins of present social structures" (Lowe and Hubbard 1983, pp. 55–56). Clearly, both Joe Mendoza and John Apostle suspect that their situations may be at least partially determined by forces beyond their control. If the conditions that generate social inequality are artificial creations of human actions, then they can be changed, and economic inequality is not inevitable, nor is it necessarily beneficial for the society and all its members. We will examine this controversy more thoroughly in later chapters.

Are There Classes in the United States?

While we can easily recognize that economic differences exist between families and individuals, does it mean that social classes exist in the United States? The value system stresses the centrality of individualism, liberty, and equality for society. Following these values, it is inconsistent to have *group* inequalities in which a person's fate is largely determined by the group (e.g., sex, race) he or she belongs to, nor is it legitimate to have individual liberty curtailed by the application of structural constraints (e.g., laws, admission requirements) to some groups and not others. Finally, the value of equality in U.S. society is undergirded by a variety of traditions rooted in its historical heritage. The beliefs that they are all one people, that underneath they are all "common folk," that they have no formal titles (e.g., lord, duke, etc.), that mobility is open to all, help to reinforce the basic notion that all Americans are equal. In this view, individual differences in wealth may exist, but underneath Americans are all the same and equally worthy, and classes based on group or categorical differences do not exist. Any individual differences in wealth would be viewed as a continuum along which all individuals and families could be located. Here, the image of a system of inequality is one of a tall but narrow ladder. Discrete, wide, separate layers would not be a part of this perspective.

In fact, some social theorists have argued that the term "social class" has no relevance for the United States, at least in its Marxian definition. Social classes, as unified class-conscious groups with their own lifestyles and political beliefs, do not apply to the United States in this view, while they may still fully apply to European countries that have a tradition of class conflict. Frequently, part of this position is the conviction that there are differences in lifestyle and status between different occupational groups, but these differences are not class-based. Much of the traditional research in the field of inequality, in fact, has focused upon social lifestyle differences between groups rather than on economic-class differences. The focus of research is, of course, conditioned by the historical context in which it occurs, the cultural milieu, and events of the times. As we shall see, this is clearly the case in U.S. research on social inequality.

Some argue that social classes as full-fledged groups antagonistically related to each other do not fit the American condition today,

INEQUALITY

"IT LOOKS LIKE SOCIO-ECONOMIC STATUS TO ME."

Social scientists often have called different aspects of inequality by different names. There is always danger that we may mistake one part of inequality for all of it.

while others suggest that fairly distinct classes exist at the extremes of the inequality hierarchy but not in the middle, which is considered largely a mass of relatively indistinguishable categories of people. A third position is that distinct classes have always existed and continue to exist in the United States, and that *class* conflict has not been absent from its history and continues to this day. Joan Leahy, the young woman cited earlier, seems to feel that there are clear class differences between categories of people.

Is Inequality Increasing or Lessening?

Another issue revolves around whether socioeconomic differences between classes, races, and the sexes are increasing or decreasing. One position is that the United States is largely a middle-class society and that governmental pressures keep the lid especially tight on the upper class's wealth and movement, while at the same time they aid the lower classes through various social programs. The result is a *structural* tendency for most

groups to move toward the middle—a class system with an ever-increasing bulge in the middle. This argument is related to the classlessness position noted earlier in that if, ultimately, the pressure results in a largely middle-class society or middle mass, then in effect there is virtually only one large class. In *cultural* terms, this argument says that different classes come to subscribe to the same value system, and specifically, that lower classes adopt the values of those above them. This has been particularly stressed in some discussions of the working class, which, it is said, takes on the values of the middle class as its economic fortunes improve.

Another version of this homogenizing scenario suggests that race may be becoming less important as a determinant of life chances and that the differences between the races are diminishing. In fact, it is suggested, class differences *within* racial groups may be more significant than those existing *between* such groups. Similarly, as women move increasingly into the labor market, their status moves closer to that of men, and many argue that women have made great strides in reducing the socioeconomic differences between themselves and men.

In sharp contrast to these images of decreasing differences, others have argued that polarization is occurring with respect to the social classes, with the gap between the top and bottom increasing. They cite the number of poor, homeless, and an "underclass" as evidence for this trend, along with changes in governmental tax and poverty policies. In essence, they are saying that the rich are getting richer and the poor poorer. The same general kind of argument has been made regarding race and sex, stating that not only have race and sex continued to be important determinants of life chances but that there has been little reduction in the extent of differences that exist between the races and sexes in the United States. We will examine these issues closely in the next and succeeding chapters. If what is happening to John Apostle and the salaries of chief executive officers is fairly typical of what happens to many as the economy shifts, then perhaps the gap is increasing between the top and the bottom. But if, on the other hand, blacks and women are breaking through the walls of discrimination and moving up, then perhaps the gaps are closing. We shall see.

Equality or Inequality: Desirable or Undesirable?

A variety of recent studies have asked Americans how they feel about equality and inequality, and it is clear that they are ambivalent in their positions. Several years ago, Reissman (1973) suggested this ambivalence when he commented that "there has been a clear preference to think positively in terms of an ideal goal [of equality] rather than to face up to the negative realities of inequality. Illogical as it may sound, many people are adamantly 'for' equality but are without concern for inequality of matching intensity" (p. 1). Part of the problem here is that people think about different things when they think about inequality, and people feel differently about different kinds of equality/inequality. Moreover, there are a variety of inequalities/equalities; thus the meaning of equality/inequality is not self-evident. "Trying to think clearly about equality," writes Cauthen (1987), "is indeed like being tossed naked into a tangled thicket in the midst of a briar patch" (p. 2). For example, Bryan Turner (1986) cites four basic kinds of equality: (1) that pertaining to all as basic human beings; that is, the notion that basically we are all the same and equally worthy as persons; (2) equality of opportunity; the idea that access to valued ends is open to all; (3) equality of condition; that is, that all start from the same position; and (4) equality of results or outcome, or equality of income. The latter is the most radical of the four and the one most likely to incite controversy.

Studies suggest that most Americans are against limiting the amount of income an individual can make, but at the same time they feel that many in high-paying occupations receive more than they deserve (Kluegel and Smith 1986). Americans feel quite differently about equality of opportunity than they do about egalitarianism, and groups feel differently about the fairness of the system. A study of over 2,700 leaders in various areas, for example, showed that they feel any fair distribution of goods should be based on equality of *opportunity* rather than equality of *result*. At the same time, however, black and feminist leaders are much less likely to consider the free enterprise system fair, and are more likely to consider poverty to be caused by problems in the system rather than by deficiencies in the individual (Verba and Orren 1985). We will examine the tangle of American beliefs about inequality and its fairness more fully in Chapter 12.

Scholars also have taken different positions on the issues we have been discussing. Conservatives and radicals generally take different positions on each of these issues. Conservatives tend to praise the virtues of open capitalism and emphasize its benefits for the individual, rather than seeing the internal contradictions between capitalism and democracy. Radicals, on the other hand, view unbridled capitalism as destructive of human beings and stress the interlinkage between economic and political power. Conservatives also tend to consider social inequality as being inevitable, if not necessary and desirable, and perceive the United States as being largely classless, seeing the similarities among Americans as being more fundamental than the differences. In sharp contrast, radicals conclude that inequality is neither inevitable nor desirable, that the United States is a class society, and that basic social, economic, and political conditions create deep divisions within the population.

RACE AND THE STUDY OF INEQUALITY

Race inequality will be considered fully in the text because black/white relations make up part of the system of inequality in the United States and because there has been an intensified examination of intersection of racial with other types of inequality.

Traditionally, inequality among blacks has been analyzed separately, as distinct from the "general American class system" (Gordon 1963, p. 252). Part of the reason for this is that problems of race relations have been considered a part of social psychology. The emphasis on prejudice and individual personality has pushed the study of race relations away from the assumption that the conditions of blacks are related to the manner of their integration into U.S. society. "American sociology has been slow to move beyond an emphasis on individual psychology and behavior in the examination of racial inequality" (Allen and Farley 1986, p. 304). Consequently, the incorporation of race into the field of social stratification has been slowed. Moreover, discussions of the values and attitudes of blacks have usually been couched in a theoretical scheme created by white sociologists, rendering predictions about blacks faulty and unreliable (Yancy et al. 1972). Traditionally, there has been an overemphasis on the *attitudes* of whites toward blacks. At a minimum, social psychological approaches need to be combined with more *structural,* macroscopic explanations of black/white inequality (Pettigrew (1985).

Explanations of race inequality also have been held inadequate because white sociologists have a difficult time in dealing objectively with the black experience (Smith 1972; Record 1972). While understanding that the historical development of race relations is important for a full explanation of race inequality, models based on analogies to white immigrants have been heavily criticized. Adequate explanations need to be more "Afrocentric," that is, take into account and consider the central life experiences of blacks themselves, rather than focusing attention on other groups, and then applying those experiences to blacks (Kershaw 1987). In Chapter 10 we will survey some of the more traditional and more recent structural-power theories of black/white inequality.

As mentioned earlier, there have been investigations on black/white relations that have embraced class. First, Marxism's influence on the study of social inequality has been obvious in recent years, and several of the models used to describe and analyze race relations are influenced by this perspective (e.g., Bonacich 1980). Second, the concept of a permanent "underclass" has become increasingly popular and has been applied especially to blacks in U.S. society (Glasgow 1980; Lemann 1986). Third, and most significantly, there has been a continuing debate about the relative importance of race and class in explaining the life chances of blacks (Wilson 1978, 1987). This is an important issue and will be examined later in detail. It is reasonable to assume that both race and class play roles in determining the fate of individuals; while discrimination operates, it often operates within the class structure (Kerbo 1983). We need to understand what role race plays within different classes as well as the role different class positions play for individuals of the same race (Pettigrew 1985).

SEX AND THE STUDY OF INEQUALITY

As in the study of race inequality, explanations aimed at understanding women's positions in society have been limited because of biases often built into the theories. Most sociologists have been male and have adopted a conservative view of women's roles (Stacey and Thorne 1985). Critics argue that any theory that pretends to be adequate in understanding the situation of women in U.S. society must start with the life experiences of women themselves, rather than from the removed perspective of male sociologists (Farganis 1986).

In addition, some have suggested that sex inequality does not belong in the study of social stratification, thereby trivializing the sex variable even further. Until the early 1970s, sex inequality was not incorporated into the analysis of class and status stratification (Acker 1980). One reason for minimizing its importance has been that the family has been considered the central unit in stratification studies. Generally, when a child is born it is believed that he or she automatically acquires the status level of his or her family. If individuals are to be treated as members of families in which all share a "common rank," then the wife "has to share" the lot of the husband (Bergel 1962, pp. 17–18). However, with the influx of women into the paid labor market, the validity of this position has been severely tested, and new measures of family class positions have been suggested.

Another reason gender traditionally has not been considered a more systematic part of the study of social inequality and stratification was suggested several years ago: "And if the wives and daughters of unskilled laborers have some things in common with the wives and daughters of wealthy landowners, there can be no doubt that the *differences* in their overall situation are far more striking and significant" (Parkin 1971, p. 15). Essentially, Parkin is saying that differences in sex are less important than differences in class as far as consequences for lifestyle and life chances are concerned. The "inequalities associated with sex differences are not usefully thought of as components of stratification" (ibid., p. 14). Hopefully, this situation has changed to the extent that the examination of sex inequality is considered crucial in portraying the system of social and economic inequality in society. General explanations of inequality ought to account as fully as possible for the socioeconomic conditions of all racial and sex groups. Thus, for example, a theory of how the labor market and economy work to explain the differences in earnings, income, and occupational differences should explain the inequalities among all groups, not just those within the white and male populations. At the same time, those seeking to understand the predicament of individuals in the structure of inequality must consider the unique characteristics of each group.

ORGANIZATION OF THE BOOK

The text is divided into four parts that address the issues of (1) the extent of inequality in its various forms, (2) the consequences of inequality for individual life chances and society as a whole, (3) the explanations given for the existence of inequality and individuals' positions within the system of inequality, and (4) the changes that are or are not occurring in the extent of inequality and attempts that have been made to reduce inequality and poverty. In Part I, we survey the magnitude of social, economic, and political inequality in U.S. society. Chapter 2, for example, documents the continuation of extensive income and wealth inequality from early in U.S. history. Despite recent growth in the economy, the poverty rate has climbed since 1980. Income inequality also has grown. Wealth remains highly concentrated. The following chapters show the wide variety of bases on which status is awarded. Often status is based on wealth, but occupation, education, physical appearance, clothes, and region also are used to assess the social status of an individual or a group. Even the kinds of shoes people wear have become a basis for status! Race and sex are also determinants of social status, and the inequality between the races and the sexes is explored fully in Chapter 4. Evidence again suggests that a great deal of economic and political inequality remains among these groups. Part I concludes with a discussion of political inequality. Political power, measured in a variety of ways, is unevenly distributed in society, and the influence of economic power on political power remains despite attempts to limit its effects.

Having shown in Part I the diverse ways in which inequality appears, Part II continues by discussing the pervasive effects it has on everyday lives. Physical and mental health, hunger, homelessness, and the intimate relationships within families are all subject to the influences of individual positions in the hierarchy of social inequality. The chances of getting adequate medical care and living a life unspoiled by the problems of physical abuse are affected by class position. The long arm of inequality reaches far into personal and private worlds, but its effects also extend into the wider society as well. In Chapter 7, we explore the effects of inequality on crime and collective protest. Specifically, the effects of socioeconomic position, race, and sex on criminal justice are examined, ranging from the chances of being arrested to the likelihood of being given a long sentence. Inequality also has played a role in generating high crime rates and in fomenting unrest. We focus on worker strikes as one form of such protest.

Our discussions of the extensiveness and widespread effects of inequality should spur an interest in trying to understand it. Part III deals in detail with several attempts to explain different forms of inequality. Chapter 8 reviews the classical theories of Marx, Weber, Durkheim, and Pareto. The modern theories discussed in Chapter 9 were often built upon the ideas of the classical scholars. There is a separate discussion on explanations of sex and race inequality in Chapter 10. Several of these are of a cross-cultural nature. Again, the ties to earlier theories are clear. The summary of each theory is followed by a brief critique.

The last part of the book examines what has been happening to the system of inequality and what is being done about it. Is there a great deal of mobility in U.S. society? Do rags-to-riches stories provide a typical picture of the careers of most Americans? How does the United States compare with other countries in its rate of mobility? Is it more open than others? Have blacks and women become more upwardly mobile in recent years? What determines how far up people go in the occupational hierarchy? What do Americans think about their system inequality? Is it fair? What's being done about it? What kinds of policies exist to deal with inequality and poverty and how effective are they? Are there any better ways to address the problem of poverty? These comprise some of the central questions addressed in Part IV.

The lines separating the social sciences are often vague, the result being that discussions in the book often will draw upon the work of economists, anthropologists, and others, as well as sociologists. In addition, there is material from other countries and a discussion of inequality between countries. These inclusions, hopefully, result in a more thorough and well-rounded perspective on the anatomy of social inequality.

CHAPTER 2

ECONOMIC INEQUALITY

*The American economy is changing. It is becoming more polarized—
income inequality is increasing.*
—Katherine S. Newman

In the next several chapters we will be considering several forms of inequality: economic, social, and political. In this chapter, we examine economic inequality in the form of social class and income/wealth differences. "Social class" has been defined in a variety of ways by classical and contemporary scholars, and conceptualizations especially vary between more conservative traditional and radical writers.

Traditionally, American researchers have defined social class statistically in terms of occupational status, education, and/or income. Persons or families that fall in the same category on these dimensions are then said to be in the same social class. Generally, persons receive a score depending on their placement on these variables, and in essence, social class is thus determined by a statistical score. Since these scores are continuous, the class hierarchy is frequently viewed as a continuum where the boundaries between classes are not always clear and distinct. Classes may merge imperceptibly into one another and, as a result, boundary determination becomes an important problem. Another characteristic of this approach is that the dimensions used to measure social class are not all purely economic in nature. Occupational status is essentially a measure of the prestige of an occupation; that is, it reflects the subjective judgment of individuals about an occu-

pation. Education is also a noneconomic phenomenon. The result is that this measure of social class is not only multidimensional but mixes economic with social dimensions of inequality. Consequently, this measure is often referred to as *socioeconomic status*. Finally, this measure does not assume any kind of necessary relationship between the classes. There is no assumption, for example, that the upper and working classes are in conflict with each other. Classes are merely the result of scores on a series of socioeconomic dimensions. In sum, the traditional, more conservative American measure assumes that social class, or socioeconomic status, is (1) a continuum of inequality between classes, (2) partly the result of subjective judgments as well as objective conditions, (3) multidimensional, and (4) nonconflictual in nature.

The following are two examples of definitions of class that use this approach. Rossides defines a social class as being "made up of families and unrelated individuals who share similar benefits across the three dimensions of class, prestige, and power" (1976, p. 23). Similarly, Gilbert and Kahl recently defined social class as "a large group of families . . . approximately equal in rank to each other and clearly differentiated from other families. . . . [T]he various stratification variables tend to converge and jell; they form a pattern, and it is this pattern that creates social classes" (1987, p. 16). In other words, these authors are saying that individuals and families who are ranked similarly on several dimensions—income, occupation, and power—are in the same social class.

An interesting variant of this approach is found in the work of Gerhard Lenski who defines a class as "an aggregation of persons in a society who stand in a similar position with respect to some form of power, privilege, or prestige" (1966, pp. 74–75). Note that Lenski uses the word "or" in his definition; this leads him to suggest that there are several class hierarchies, and individuals can be located on different levels in each of them. Thus, for example, there is a political class system as well as property, occupational, ethnic, sexual, educational, and age class systems.

Generally, radical or Marxian sociologists have in mind a conceptualization of class that is quite different, and they object to the mixing of economics, social status, and other socioeconomic variables. This merging of a variety of factors or using "class" to describe noneconomic hierarchies, the argument goes, dilutes what Marx considered to be the core meaning of social class. We will examine in detail his concept of class later, but essentially, for Marx class was basically an economic phenomenon and was defined by an individual's position in the social relations of production, by control over the physical means (property) and social means (labor power) of production. In other words, class is not defined by income or occupation but rather by ownership/control in the system of production. In this view, introducing other socioeconomic variables such as prestige or occupational status only distorts the meaning of social class. Prestige and class are analytically separate phenomena (Staples et al., 1984). Thus, in the Marxian definition, class is much less multidimensional in nature. Moreover, the crucial differences between the social classes are qualitative in nature; that is, the class system is not a continuous hierarchy. The boundaries between the classes are discrete and clear. Finally,

classes in this view are defined by the exploitation that exists between them and by the interconnection of the functions of each class. This means that a given class is defined by its relationship to another class. Workers are members of the working class, for example, because of the nature of their relationship to capital and capitalists. Different classes perform distinct but interrelated functions in capitalist society.

As we have seen, the basic Marxian definition of class sees it as "first of all a place in the system" (Ollman 1987, p. 62). This "place" simply may refer to ownership or nonownership or it may refer to a variety of *structural* conditions that define an individual's place in the system of production. For example, Wright recently defined classes in terms of several "mechanisms of exploitation" based on ownership of property, skills, and organizational tools (Wright and Martin 1987). We will have more to say about this conceptualization later when we examine Wright's perspective on the U.S. class structure. Suffice it to say at this point that his is a *structuralist* definition in the sense that he, like others, stresses the location or position of the individual in the productive system as the crucial determinant of class. Anderson (1974) gives a similar "objective" Marxian definition when he views class position as being "broadly determined by a person's property placement and relationship to the means of production" (p. 124). "If the Marxist concept of class has anything distinctive to offer to the analysis of social cleavage in capitalist society," writes Burris (1988), "it is certainly the notion that material interests rooted in relations of exploitation define the fault lines along which epochal struggles for social transformation take place" (p. 63). These definitions are essentially materialist and objective in nature; that is, they do not consider class consciousness, a sense of "groupness," or similar social psychological components as being crucial parts of the definition of class.

Some Marxian social scientists, however, argue that class consciousness or a similar sense of belongingness and organized opposition must be present for *social* classes to be present; that is, individuals must identify with each other and understand their real relationship to other classes and act upon that knowledge. Ollman states flatly that the concept of class has both subjective and objective dimensions, that subjective element being a sense of unity that develops as a class emerges. People "tend to acquire over time other common characteristics as regards . . . lifestyle, political consciousness and organization that become, in turn, further evidence for membership in their particular class and subsidiary criteria for determining when to use the class label. Here, class is a quality that is attached to people" (Ollman 1987, p. 64). In this approach, people become a real *social* class when they acquire a common culture and political awareness. In addition to occupying the same location or position in relation to the means of production, then, people in the same social class "share the distinctive traditions common to their social position" (Szymanski 1978, p. 26). This common identity, especially when it involves awareness of common exploitation and engagement in class struggle, Marx suggested, is what welds an aggregate of people into a social class, or a "class-for-itself" (Bottomore 1956).

It should be clear at this point that even among Marxists there is lack of agreement on the exact definition and measurement of social class. Marx never gave an explicit, clear-cut definition of class. Moreover, he suggested various definitions and different numbers and types of social classes at different points in his writing. Nevertheless, his approach and that of contemporary Marxian analysts are clearly different from those discussed earlier who define class in broader socioeconomic terms. In sum, Marxists generally view classes as (1) discrete rather than continuous, (2) real rather than statistical creations, (3) economic in nature, and (4) conflictual in their relations. In contrast, traditional conservative approaches define classes as existing along a continuous hierarchy, largely statistically created, and as multidimensional and nonconflictual in their relationships.

THE STRUCTURE OF THE
U.S. CLASS SYSTEM

Americans' perceptions of class structure and class placement are complex and presenting a single "true" portrait of the class structure is next to impossible. People in different categories view that structure and their positions in it differently. Coleman and Rainwater tried, in their Kansas City/Boston study, to piece together what the class structure might look like, based on their interviews in these cities. "Ultimately, [they argue,] to number and name the American social classes is a task for the social scientist. The status structure is too complex to be comprehended fully by average persons from their inevitably narrow vantage points" (Coleman and Rainwater 1978, p. 120). To develop a scheme of the class structure, they (1) asked their respondents in an open-ended way to describe the class hierarchy and (2) presented respondents with the names of different classes and asked them for their attitudes about what kinds of people are found in each class.

In response to the first inquiry, about one-third of their sample said there were three classes in this country, while the rest gave different responses, some saying there were two classes, while others mentioned as many as nine. Some felt they could not even answer the question since there are "too many classes for me to count and name" (ibid., p. 121). The three-class model was especially used by individuals from blue-collar groups, and income was the criterion most often used to distinguish these classes from each other. Among those individuals who volunteered an image of the structure involving more than three classes, there was a tendency to use a variety of criteria in addition to money to differentiate the classes. Source of income, education, place of residence, standard of living, and occupation also were used by them to make cuts or draw boundaries between the classes.

Coleman and Rainwater went on to present the names of several classes, ranging from "the top class" to "the class at the very bottom of the ladder," and then asked respondents for the images that came to mind for each of them. Based on the responses to this inquiry and what they had found earlier about the criteria individuals were using to separate classes, they devised a scheme of the U.S. class structure using their own terms.

In summary form, the class structure, going from the top to the bottom, looks like this:

1. The old aristocratic rich families: "old family money," "bluebloods," "aristocracy"
2. The "new rich success elite": high-level professionals
   a. Upper level: medical specialists, corporate executives, lawyers with incomes in excess of $60,000 (1978), "newer money," "the first generation of achievers"
   b. Lower level: more "run-of-the-mill" professionals, individuals who are "successful but not super-successful"
3. The "college-educated professional and managerial class"
   a. The "average educated business or professional person, including college graduates, some with advanced degrees," incomes at $25,000–$35,000 (1978)
   b. "Marginal" college graduates, "not earning all that much money, maybe $15,000–$20,000" (1978)
4. "Middle Americans of comfortable living standards"
   a. The "socioeconomic elite" of "people who didn't finish college but are making good money," some small businesspeople, top-level craftspeople, salespeople
   b. Lower ranking white-collar and blue-collar workers living comfortably
5. "Middle Americans just getting along": working class, people getting by, paying their own bills, including factory and lower level office workers
6. "People who are poor but not on welfare"
   a. People who are "decent," "barely making ends meet," who live in below average neighborhoods, "but they're not lower class"; "marginal middle Americans"
   b. People making a minimum wage, who

are proud, lack education but not on welfare; common laborers many of whom are members of minority groups; "lower Americans but not the lowest class"
7. The "non-working welfare class"

There were some differences, which we need not pursue here, between the classes in terms of how they interpreted different class labels and the distinctions they made within each of them. But it appeared to be most difficult for individuals to agree on the subcategories of those listed as "middle Americans" (ibid., pp. 126–30).

This model of the class structure was developed as a composite by Coleman and Rainwater based on what individuals in their sample said about it. Other schemes that have been developed are not based on subjective responses from individuals, but rather on objective criteria such as income, employment status, and similar factors. In this case, it is the researcher who directly determines the kinds and numbers of classes in the system. Some of these portrayals use a variety of qualitatively different criteria, following more closely the "socioeconomic" definition of class discussed earlier in this chapter, while others try to be more faithful to Marxian criteria in outlining their perspectives. Neither of these approaches is inherently better than the other, and each focuses on criteria that often have been found to have separate effects on individuals' life conditions. Each approach attempts to identify meaningful breaks in the class system. We will examine an example of each of these two approaches.

Socioeconomic Measures and Images of Class Structure

The class structure of any society is shaped by the historical, structural, and cultural context in which it is embedded. In the United States, a variety of forces have contributed to the development of the present class structure. Clearly, the changes in technology that have occurred in this country since the turn of the century have contributed to the changing composition of classes and to the different distribution of individuals among the classes. For example, the shift from a rural, agrarian economy to one fully industrialized helped form a different kind and size of working class as well as affecting the poverty rate. As both Braverman (1974) and Garson (1988) have demonstrated, computerization and automation also have helped redefine the nature of white-collar work and the social relationships between those in capitalist and managerial classes, on the one hand, and those in lower, working-class positions on the other. Moreover, the mechanization of agriculture and the shift in emphasis in the early 1800s from independent craftsworkers to wage employees helped increase the poverty rate (Katz 1986; Braverman 1974; Garson 1988). The growth of a larger service sector in the economy has led to arguments about the class nature of white-collar positions, sometimes defined as comprising a middle class and other times a new working class. Changes in the rules and resources governing labor/management conflict, including unionization of workers, have had their impact on class relationships as well. Government policy as it pertains to the economy and the distribution of economic rewards also has affected the shape of the class structure, as have broader changes in the world economy. We will discuss the latter more fully in a later section. Finally, cultural values about democracy, equality, and anti-aristocracy sometimes serve to temper the extent of economic inequality.

A variety of multidimensional measures of social class have been developed by researchers in the last several decades, and two of the most famous are Warner's Index of Status Characteristics and Hollingshead's Index of Social Position. With his Index, Warner hoped to provide educators and others with a simple yet accurate means of detecting an individual's class position. This is the way it worked. An individual would obtain a total score on the index, which was made up of scores from four separate subscales: one each on occupation, dwelling area, house type, and source of income (which may or may not be from the individual's occupation). Then the individuals could be placed in given classes based upon their scores. When using this index, there is no necessary or basic reason why certain ranges of scores on the index are significant indicators of membership in a particular social class. "We are not told of any cluster or group of the various score values . . . which would lead one to conclude that there were 'natural breaks' in the series or that certain score values, for some reason, 'belong together' " (Cuber and Kenkel 1954, p. 127). Moreover, given the fact that Warner developed this measure while studying particular small communities almost half a century ago, one has to be careful in assuming that it is equally applicable today and in every setting.

Hollingshead developed similar types of measures of social class, one of which was a two-factor index that involved using an occupational prestige scale and an education scale. The occupational hierarchy ranges from higher executive/major professional positions to unskilled workers, while the seven-level educational scale goes from graduate professional training to less than junior high school. In computing the total score on this index, occupation is weighted more heavily than education. Like Warner's technique, Hollingshead's has been used as a quick and relatively easy way to uncover an individual's class position, but also like it, has been subjected to some criticism. Two criticisms are that it (1) dilutes the economic component of class by incorporating education and (2) introduces age as a confounding factor since age and education are correlated with each other (Haug 1972).

Keeping these factors in mind, let's examine a recent model of the U.S. class structure. Gilbert and Kahl (1987) have suggested a six-class model of the United States using income, occupational, and educational criteria. A condensed version of their model is presented here:

Class Name (% of Households)
1. *Capitalist Class* (1%): Graduates of high-ranking universities who are in top-level executive positions or are heirs who have an

income in excess of $500,000, mainly from assets.

2. *Upper Middle Class* (14%): Individuals with at least a college degree who are in higher professional or managerial positions or owners of medium-sized businesses who have incomes of at least $50,000.

3. *Middle Class* (30%): Individuals who have high school degrees and maybe some college who are in lower managerial or white-collar, or high-skill, high-pay blue-collar occupations who make about $30,000 a year.

4. *Working Class* (30%): Persons with high school degrees who are in lower level white-collar (e.g., clerical, sales workers) or blue-collar positions (e.g., operatives) whose incomes are about $20,000 per year.

5. *Working Poor* (13–15%): Those with some high school who are service workers, or are in the lowest paid blue-collar and clerical positions who have incomes below $15,000.

6. *Underclass* (10–12%): Individuals with only an elementary school education who work part time, are unemployed, or on welfare, and who have incomes under $10,000.

The percentages that make up each of the last four classes are based on the authors' discussions of these classes. The *underclass* is a concept that has received increasing attention in the last ten years or so, and we will discuss its meaning and implications more fully later in this chapter.

In surveying different models of U.S. class structure that use several kinds of socioeconomic criteria, there are some remarkable *similarities* as well as differences between them. For each of them, occupation is crucial in class placement in a variety of ways. The complexity, degree of independence, prestige, skill-level, associated authority, and manual/nonmanual nature of the occupation are involved in determining the class position of an individual. Second, these models usually see the structure as being composed of five to seven classes, rather than as a dichotomy or trichotomy. Finally, the proportion of the population said to be in each class in each model is

very similar. Generally, the working and middle classes, in which the majority of the population is placed, are considered to be about equal in size, while the upper class is generally said to be around 1 percent. Then, depending on whether or not employed as well as unemployed are included in the lower class, its percentage can range from 10 to 25 percent.

Some of the most significant *differences* in the models presented center on the criteria used to place individuals in various classes. This has an impact in that it affects not only the suggested sizes of classes but also the number and kinds of classes said to exist in the United States. One notable difference lies in the distinctions made about the lower class. Some simply include all those who are poor, while others draw a line between those who are poor but work and those who are chronically unemployed and poor for long periods of time. The term "underclass" is frequently used to refer to the latter group. There is some debate about the actual size of the underclass, and the proposed size, of course, depends on the definition given to it. Wilson (1987) suggests that the term should refer to "individuals who lack training and skills and either experience long-term unemployment or are not members of the labor force, individuals who are engaged in street crime and other forms of aberrant behavior, and families that experience long-term spells of poverty and/or welfare dependency" (p. 8). He believes that the term "lower class" does not really capture the substantive meaning of the group he labels the "underclass." Glasgow (1980) describes the underclass as "a permanently entrapped population of poor persons, unused and unwanted . . . a fixed part of the American economy." These people are "persistently poor" and "immobile" (pp. 3, 6). A recent conference of experts on the issue agreed upon the definition of the underclass as "poor people who live in a neighborhood or census tract with higher rates of unemployment, crime, and welfare dependency" (McFate 1987, p. 11). By this definition, the underclass would include 5 to 10 percent of the population.

Lowenstein (1985) suggested that a "new" underclass may be developing which is made up of the youth of working-class parents. He attributes this growth to (1) an increase in the number of teenagers during the 1960s and 1970s, (2) the movement toward a service-based economy, and (3) a surplus of workers for low-wage service jobs. A recent study by the Joint Economic Committee of the U.S. Congress concluded that since 1981 there has been a shift in job opportunities from jobs in the manufacturing sector with high pay to those in the service sector with low pay ("Study Shows Shift" 1988). While more Americans have found jobs in low-paying places like restaurants, bars, and temporary office services, they have lost more lucrative jobs in steel, construction, and chemical industries. Lowenstein also suspects that many of the offspring of working-class parents may wind up having lower statuses than their parents, and as they come to adjust to their lower status, they may adopt attitudes and behaviors that approximate those of the traditional underclass. Like that of other classes, their behavior is "an adaptive response to the conditions they confront. Faced with continually declining prospects for upward mobility, it would be irrational for those people to act as though they will soon be engaging in mainstream economic life" (Lowenstein 1985, p. 41). However, in contrast to the traditional underclass discussed earlier, the behavior of this "new" underclass is more "cyclical" since it fluctuates with changes in the employment status of the individual, and poverty is not likely to be permanent for most in this class.

Another difference among the models of class structure, which also affects conclusions about the number and size of classes, concerns distinctions between particular kinds of white-collar and blue-collar occupations. For example, Kerbo (1983) and Rothman (1978) use the manual/nonmanual factor as one way to separate the working class from the "lower-middle" class, while others, notably Gilbert and Kahl (1987), include routine, low-skill, white-collar jobs in the working class. Qualitatively, the latter see little difference between routine, mechanized, boring, low-pay nonmanual jobs and similar kinds in the manual sector. At the same time, there are well-paying blue-collar jobs that demand a fairly high level of training, are complex, and are similar in these dimensions to certain mid-level, white-collar occupations.

The question of the relative importance of the manual/nonmanual and level-of-complexity criteria is the subject of some debate and has become focused in the debate about the *proletarianization* of some white-collar work and the *embourgeoisement* of some blue-collar work. Briefly, the proletarianization argument states that a significant and increasing number of white-collar jobs are routine and boring, demand little skill, and involve little worker control. Qualitatively, this makes them no different from many blue-collar jobs. Some have described those who occupy these positions as a "new working class," especially as the economy advances and becomes more automated. Generally, radicals tend to view the U.S. class structure in a manner consistent with the proletarianization thesis. Braverman (1973) forcefully argues that office work has become increasingly standardized, more detailed, and subject to more administrative control because of the use of the computer. As the base of the economy changes, so does the composition and nature of the working class. "The apparent trend to a large nonproletarian 'middle class' has resolved itself into the creation of a large proletariat in a new form" (p. 355).

In contrast, the embourgeoisement thesis, embraced more often by those with a more conservative bent, proposes that complex, high-paying blue-collar jobs take on many of the sociocultural characteristics of the white-collar middle class. As society moves into a "postindustrial" phase and its labor force becomes more saturated with white-collar service positions, the size of the blue-collar work force shrinks. Most people become middle class in their standards of living and lifestyles. While blue-collar workers' job situations may be different from lower white-collar positions, many in the higher blue-collar ranks, argue Mayer and Buckley (1970), have a lifestyle that "resembles that of the lower-middle class much more closely than that of the poorer semi-skilled and unskilled manual laborers. . . . Away from the job, they cannot be distinguished from the lower-middle-class white-collar men" (p. 94).

Are working-class individuals moving closer to the middle class in terms of their lifestyles and values as the embourgeoisement thesis suggests, or are many of those in lower white-collar positions being relegated to the working class because of the nature of their work? What does the evidence suggest? It is mixed. Kerbo (1983) argues that in terms of occupational status, bureaucratic authority, and property ownership, "the middle [nonmanual] and working [manual] classes remain distinct class positions" (p. 274). In an early study on this matter, Hamilton (1966) found that most middle-class individuals with working-class backgrounds continue to identify themselves as working-class. His findings suggest that class of origin continues to have a grip on the values of individuals even when they move up in class position. Hamilton's results help sustain the argument that the classes continue to be distinct. It also has been said that the traditional higher status that comes with white-collar work keeps it separate from and perhaps even above the blue-collar level, at least in terms of prestige (Mills 1951; Crozier 1971; Poulantzas 1974; Hamilton 1966). It even has been suggested that if proletarianization exists in these white-collar occupations, people in them can and do frequently move out of those positions, making the proletarianization less consequential for them (Crompton and Jones 1984).

There is some evidence, however, that supports the proletarianization thesis. Earlier studies on class identification suggest that the manual/nonmanual division is not the crucial one in the minds of the majority of Americans. These studies make a distinction between lower and higher white-collar occupations. The authors of one of those studies conclude that their results "could be taken to indicate that instead of an embourgeoisement process among manual workers, what may

be occurring is a proletarianization process among the lower echelons of the nonmanual labor force" (Jackman and Jackman 1983, p. 75). In their study of the content of job tasks, Glenn and Feldberg (1977) found that clerical jobs were being deskilled, especially women's jobs. In terms of their content, Crompton and Jones (1984) also found that clerical positions in banking and other service industries were deskilled and alienative because of increased computerization. However, they did *not* find that this made these workers any more class conscious in any radical sense. Wright and Singelmann's (1982) study indicated that within the U.S. occupational structure, there has been a proletarianization *within* industries, but that there is a simultaneous shift in the overall economy to less proletarianized industries. In this case, they are looking at proletarianization in terms of the replacement of nonworking-class positions with working-class locations in the class structure during the period from 1960 to 1970. In contrast, however, a more recent examination of the proletarianization issue suggests that in the 1970s there was a distinct trend toward *deproletarianization*. There has been an increase in the proportion of the labor force who are managers, experts, or supervisors, providing more support for the postindustrial theories than the Marxist thesis of proletarianization. Wright and Martin (1987) propose that these results may mean merely that capitalism has internationalized itself and has shifted more proletarianized occupations into Third World countries. Thus, the proletarianization issue is still unsettled.

Marxian Measures and Images of Class Structure

Perhaps the most sophisticated recent attempt to analyze the class structure of the United States in Marxian terms comes from Erik Wright. In the last decade, Wright has written extensively about class measurement and structure, refining and altering his scheme along the way. In an early attempt, Wright (1977) defines classes as "common positions within [the] social relations of production." These relations can be divided along three different dimensions: (1) "control over money capital," (2) "control over the use of the means of production," and (3) "control over supervision and discipline within the labor process." More specifically, Wright outlines four specific criteria that, he says, allow one to place individuals in a class position: (1) ownership of the means of production (that is, is one self-employed); (2) purchase of the labor power of others (that is, does one have employees); (3) control of the labor power of others (that is, does one have subordinates on the job); (4) sale of one's own labor power (that is, is one an employee). Notice that these criteria contain both ownership and authority dimensions. In pure capitalism, two major classes exist—those controlling each of these areas (capitalists) and those controlling none (workers). In less pure types, which is what virtually all real capitalist societies would be, other classes appear, such as the *new middle class,* which has control in some areas but not others. Consequently, since their control in one area pushes them in the direction of the capitalist class or bourgeoisie while their subordination in other areas leans them in the direction of the working class, they are essentially caught between two classes. Wright says this means that they occupy "contradictory locations within class relations" (ibid; see also Wright 1976). Based on a 1969 survey of 1,533 individuals, Wright and Perrone (1977) estimated that the class distribution is as follows:

1. Employers (mostly small)   7.4%
2. Managers   37.4
3. Workers   49.2
4. Petty bourgeoisie   4.3
5. Ambiguous   1.8

The ambiguous category consists primarily of response error. This depiction suggests that workers make up almost half of the class structure, with managers being a very significant minority in the United States.

Wright's model has come under close scrutiny and has encountered some criticism. For example, Robinson and Kelley (1979) suggest that Wright is really mixing Marx's criteria of ownership and control with a more recent use of authority as a measure, and if one wants to see what the separate effects of each of these factors are on income or anything else, then it is best to keep them separate. In any case, they argue that Wright's model is not purely Marxian since he does have a composite measure of class rather than one utilizing only ownership criteria. After all, they contend, one can have authority over some subordinates without controlling or owning the means of production (e.g., supervisors). In other words, within Marx's working class, there are those who have more authority than others, and these differences can have an impact in other areas of life (e.g., income). In fact, in their analysis using three national surveys, Robinson and Kelley found that each of these dimensions of class, along with education and occupational status, has a separate impact on income. They suggest that there are really two stratification systems, a *class* system determined by ownership and authority and a *status* system based on education and occupational status.

Recently, Wright has revised his system and used the concept of exploitation as the centerpiece in defining class position. At a concrete level, there are several "mechanisms of exploitation" in capitalist society, specifically, "exploitation based on ownership of 'capital' assets, control of 'organization' assets, and ownership of 'skill' assets" (Wright and Martin 1987, pp. 6–7). So in any given instance, an individual may be an exploiter in one area but be exploited in another. The real difference of this change from his earlier formulation is minimal when we view his revised class structure of the United States. The category of "semiautonomous employee" is replaced by "experts," and the category of employers more accurately means "small" employers since most employers in any national sample would not turn out to be owners of large corporations. "Managers" are distinguished from supervisors, experts, and workers in that they make policy decisions at work while the others do not. Supervisors have authority over others, and this separates them from experts and workers.

Using the revised "exploitation-based" classification in a recent study, Wright and Martin examined changes in the U.S. class structure from 1960 to 1980 and found that there has been an increase in the percentage of managers, supervisors, and experts who make up the labor force, while there has been a decrease in the percentage that can be classified as workers. Still, the working class made up half of the labor force in 1980. Following is their estimate of the proportion of individuals in each class in 1960 and 1980:

Class	1960	1980
Small employers	8.0%	5.0%
Petty bourgeois	5.8	4.3
Managers	14.8	18.4
Supervisors	11.5	13.2
Experts	5.6	8.6
Workers	54.3	50.5

Several critics have raised some questions about Wright's new measure of class position. Meiksins (1988) argues that it is not necessarily true that those with skills or credentials exploit those below them. This is an empirical issue and cannot simply be settled by conceptual fiat. Burris (1988) calls attention to the fact that Wright's revised version identifies basically the same classes as he delineated in his earlier approach, the issue being if different measures identify the same class structure, how much of a real improvement is the new measure over the old one? In addition, Burris says that while calling it a Marxian measure of social class, Wright has "surreptitiously" included both economic and noneconomic components into his measure. Burris feels that a useful and valid measure of class should include not only property, but authority and market situation as criteria. If this results in Marxian measures being closer to other dimensions of inequality such as race or ethnicity, then it may mean that Marxists will be able to deal with other stratification issues more adequately.

Some Generalizations In reviewing both the multidimensional socioeconomic and Marxian models, we can make a few generalizations about U.S. class structure. First, there appears to be general agreement across all these models that the upper or capitalist class makes up only a very small percentage of the population, about 1 to 2 percent. Second, most of these schemes suggest that the working class comprises at least close to half of the population. Third, estimates of the lower class or underclass range from approximately 5 to 12 percent. Finally, most of these models place lower level white-collar occupations in the working class rather than the middle class. This is consistent with the perceptions of Americans in general surveys.

The main reason for the differences in class estimates in the models just discussed, of course, is that they use different measures of social class position. Each model suggests different criteria and axes along which the population is divided and which presumably have significant effects on the lives of those in the various classes. Measurement is always a critical issue when comparisons are being made, and it is a difficult problem, as we shall see shortly, when examining another aspect of economic inequality, that involving the distribution of income.

INCOME INEQUALITY

We now turn to an examination of the actual income distribution as measured primarily by Bureau of the Census data. "Money income," as defined by the Bureau of the Census, includes money from virtually all sources, including wages or salaries, social security, welfare, pensions, and others. There are some advantages to using "total money income" when assessing the extent of economic inequality. In the first place, it is certainly more immediately quantifiable than many other measures such as real estate. Second, income is highly valued in U.S. society and serves as a base upon which people are evaluated by others. Third, income inequalities saturate and are reflected in a number of other economically related areas. Unemployment, inflation, farm and food prices, rent control, women's liberation, racism, and welfare are all areas that involve income-differential issues. Thus, at least at first glance, income would appear to be a more than adequate measure of economic inequality.

However, when interpreting the following statistics, several factors should be kept in mind. First, "income" is only a partial measure of a family or individual's economic well-being. It does not include the value of stocks, real estate, or other noncash economic assets, and if it is *current* income, it does not take into account the income trajectory an individual may be on if, for example, he or she is just beginning in a lucrative career. Second, some of the estimates of income are based on pooled findings from several government studies that are not always identical in methodology or measures of income. Finally, and most significantly, the Bureau of the Census contends that there is an underreporting of income, with some sources of income being more likely to be reported than others. Tax filers tend to underreport their incomes on their income tax forms,

and not all persons are required to file income tax returns. Independent estimates suggest that incomes from unemployment and worker's compensation and property income are among those most likely to be underestimated (U.S. Dept. of Commerce, July 1987).

Table 2.1 presents information on how households are distributed among various income categories. A "household" in these tables refers to "all persons who occupy a housing unit." In other words, families who live together, individuals who live with other unrelated persons, and those who live alone are all considered households. "Money income" includes money from *all* sources before any taxes or other deductions are taken out. In 1970, for example, just over 7 percent of all households had annual incomes under $5,000, while 15 percent had incomes of at least $15,000. In 1988, 6.2 percent had incomes below $5,000, compared to almost 21 percent who had incomes at the $50,000 or higher level. These figures, especially those at the higher levels, suggest that inequality may be lessening since a larger percentage of households have incomes of $50,000 or more. Since these figures are in terms of constant 1986 dollars, adjusting income for changes in the Consumer Price Index, the figures are comparable across the years.

Table 2.2 presents the same kind of data, except that white and black households are listed

TABLE 2.1 Money Income of Households: Distribution by Income Level in Constant Dollars (1988), 1970–1988

	1970	1975	1980	1985	1988
Under $5,000	7.3%	5.7%	6.3%	6.5%	6.2%
5,000–9,999	10.4	12.2	12.0	11.7	10.8
10,000–14,999	9.3	10.6	11.1	10.5	10.3
15,000–24,999	20.0	20.0	20.0	19.7	18.6
25,000–34,999	19.5	17.9	17.5	16.5	16.0
35,000–49,999	18.6	18.3	17.5	16.9	17.3
50,000 or over	15.0	15.2	15.8	18.2	20.8
Median income	$26,630	$25,947	$25,426	$25,967	$27,225

Source: U.S. Bureau of the Census, *Statistical Abstract of the United States, 1990,* Table 716, p. 444.

TABLE 2.2 Money Income for Black and White Households: 1970, 1980, 1988

Money Income	WHITE HOUSEHOLDS			BLACK HOUSEHOLDS		
	1970	*1980*	*1988*	*1970*	*1980*	*1988*
Under $5,000	6.6%	5.2%	5.0%	13.8%	15.5%	15.4%
5,000–9,999	9.6	11.1	9.8	17.8	19.3	18.4
10,000–14,999	8.9	10.6	9.8	13.3	15.0	13.1
15,000–24,999	19.5	20.0	18.6	24.0	20.1	19.4
25,000–34,999	20.1	17.9	16.5	14.6	13.6	12.5
35,000–49,999	19.5	18.4	18.1	10.8	10.2	11.4
50,000 or over	15.8	16.9	22.1	5.7	6.3	9.9
Median income	$27,736	$26,824	$28,781	$16,882	$15,454	$16,407

Source: U.S. Bureau of the Census, *Statistical Abstract of the United States 1990,* Table 716, p. 444.

separately. These figures suggest that not only has there been and continues to be a greater proportion of black households in the "under $5,000" category, but that the percentage in that category has increased among blacks between 1970 and 1988. It has been argued that part of the reason for the increase in income inequality relates to demographic changes in the population. The increase in the proportion who are aged, the influx of youthful workers into the labor force, and the increase in the number of single-parent families all help increase the number of families in the lower income categories (Currie and Skolnick 1988). But these trends are not enough to account for all the inequality in income distribution found in the United States (Harrison et al. 1986). The median black household income in 1988 was only about 57 percent of white median household income.

Table 2.2 also indicates that there is an increase in the percentage of households who have incomes of at least $50,000 among *both* blacks and whites. The median income of black households, however, was lower in 1988 than in 1970. The opposite is the case for white households. Both suffered a decline in 1980. The increasing percentage of households in both of the extreme income categories among blacks suggests a degree of income polarization within the black population. We will return to this question of a "shrinking" middle shortly.

Table 2.3 presents the median *family* incomes based on type of family and number of earners. In contrast to the definition of household given earlier, the Census Bureau defines a family as "a group of two persons or more . . . related by birth, marriage, or adoption, and living together . . . all such persons are considered as members of one family" (U.S. Bureau of the Census, Feb. 1989, p. 174). Generally, families with married couples have higher incomes than those with only one householder present. This is especially true when we consider female-headed households, which had a median family income of $15,346 in 1988 compared to $36,389 for married-couple families. As the data indicate, the discrepancy between these types of families is greater among blacks than among whites. Black female-headed families have a median income that is about 35 percent that of black married-couple families. In contrast, the ratio among white families is 48 percent. Not surprisingly, Table 2.3 also indicates that a greater number of earners has a positive effect on a family's income.

All of the tables use money income as the economic measure. For many families and individuals, most of their income comes from wages and salaries. In 1986, median incomes for both

TABLE 2.3   Median Income of Families by Race and Number of Earners: 1988

	All Families	White	Black
All families	$32,191	$33,915	$19,329
Type of family:			
Married-couple families	36,389	36,840	30,385
Male householders, no wife present	26,827	28,935	17,853
Female householders, no husband present	15,346	17,672	10,657
Number of earners:			
No earners	13,729	15,552	6,108
One earner	23,872	25,993	14,006
Two earners	38,702	39,413	31,875
Three earners	48,977	49,927	42,002
Four or more earners	64,920	65,853	53,635

Source: U.S. Bureau of the Census, *Statistical Abstract of the United States 1990,* Table 729, p. 451.

male and female workers were about three times what they were in 1970. Still the median income of female workers lags behind that of males. In 1970, female workers had incomes that were approximately 59 percent those of males, while in 1986 their incomes were about 65 percent those of male workers.

Comparing the median incomes of black and white workers, we also find discrepancies. Black males who worked full time, year round had a median income that was about $8,000 less than that of white male workers in 1986 ($18,766 vs. $26,617). Among female workers, blacks had a median income of $14,964 compared to $17,101 among white workers. This indicates that the discrepancy among female workers is less than that between black and white male workers. Nevertheless, black *and* white female workers had median incomes below *both* black and white male workers. We will examine the possible reasons for these discrepancies between males and females and blacks and whites in two later chapters.

IS THE MIDDLE CLASS SHRINKING?

Some of the data presented in Tables 2.1 and 2.2 suggest that there may be a trend toward polarization in the income distribution. A number of studies have suggested that the middle class may be getting smaller while the proportion of individuals at the top and/or bottom of the economic hierarchy may be getting larger. How much the middle class is said to have declined and how much larger the extremes have gotten depends on the measures used to define "middle class" and the income measures used. Household and family incomes as well as weekly earnings all have been used to measure class position in these studies, and, as one might suspect, the findings differ. Using household income as his measure, Thurow (1984) defined the middle class as those households that had incomes within 25 percent of the median income of all households. He concluded that between the late 1960s and early 1980s the size of the middle class got slightly smaller, while both the top and bottom income categories got larger. In contrast, Lawrence (1984) used weekly earnings of full-time workers in his study, and while also finding a smaller middle class, he found that most of the influx was into the lower earnings bracket. Different still, Boskin contends that the middle class has not shrunk and probably will not in the near future. "Even if all jobs became high-tech and service related . . . a large shift out of the middle class is not likely to occur" (Boskin 1987, p. 210).

Most of the recent analyses on this matter do indicate a shrinking in the size of the middle-income categories. Horrigan and Haugen (1988) reexamined this issue recently, using family income and two ways of comparing changes in family income distributions over time. They were interested in examining any changes that may have occurred between 1969 and 1986. Regardless of the method used, they found that the middle was being reduced, but whether or not only the top or both the top and bottom are increasing in size depended on the method used in making comparisons over time. "Some economists," writes Ehrenreich (1988), "have even predicted that the middle class, which has traditionally represented the majority of Americans and defined the nation's identity and goals, will disappear altogether, leaving the country torn, like many Third World societies, between an affluent minority and a horde of the desperately poor" (p. F1).

There has been some challenge to the thesis of a shrinking middle class. In their own study, Kosters and Ross (1988) question the measures used in research by others. While they acknowledge that there has been a shift in the economy from manufacturing to service jobs, that these jobs tend to pay lower wages, and that some measures of wages *do* show a decline over earlier years, they believe that *hourly compensation per hour of work* is a better measure of the economic rewards employees receive at their place of work. This compensation includes not only wages, but also private benefits such as health insurance and pensions, as well as public benefits including employer contributions to programs like social security, workers' compensation, and so on. However,

one can realistically question the validity of incorporating the value of all noncash benefits into the compensation measure since many do not take full advantage of the cost of those benefits to the employer and since they do not really raise the level of economic well-being of the worker. For example, having workers' compensation and health insurance does not raise an individual's standard of living unless he or she uses them fully, and even when they are used it only helps him or her *maintain,* not increase, his or her standard of living.

Nevertheless, Kosters and Ross argue that since the early 1950s hourly compensation per hour of work has increased even though in the last decade or so the rate of increase has not been as great as it had been earlier. They admit that real wages have declined, but not because there has been a shift in the job market to lower paying service jobs but for other reasons. These reasons include: (1) an increase in the nonwage compensation package, (2) an influx of women and youth into the job market, depressing wages, and (3) fewer hours worked per week by full-time workers. They also conclude that there has been no movement of middle-earnings workers into the lower categories of the earnings distribution. In fact, they argue that there has been a *decrease* in the proportion of employment in low-earnings categories since 1967 and an *increase* in employment in high-earnings categories.

It should be clear at this point that what one concludes about a "shrinking middle class" depends heavily upon the measures used in the analysis. Most studies, sometimes using different measures, do conclude that such a reduction is occurring, but they differ in whether they believe the movement is toward the top or the bottom. Using *family* income as their measure, Horrigan and Haugen (1988) conclude that the movement has been toward the top. But part of that increase in the proportion of families in the higher earnings categories can be attributed to the presence of two earners, especially with the recent increase of women into the labor force on a full-time basis.

Regardless of where the middle has gone, however, wage figures for full-time workers and census income-distribution data indicate that the gap between the top and the bottom has grown, and that the bottom 20 percent have not shared in any improvements that may have occurred. Table 2.4 shows that there has been a slight decrease in the last several decades in the share of money income held by the bottom 20 percent of families. In 1947, for example, they owned 5 percent. This fluctuated somewhat between 4.5 and 5.1 percent until the mid-1960s, when a slight increase began to appear, so that, for example in the late 1960s and early 1970s, the percentage was approximately 5.6. However, since the late 1970s the percentage of income going to the bottom 20 percent has declined, from 5.3 in 1979 to 4.6 percent in 1989. The share of the top 20 percent, in contrast, had increased from about 43 percent in 1947 to 44.6 in 1989, the highest it has been during the forty-year period. In the interim years, it had declined slightly to around 40 or 41 percent, but since 1980 has increased consistently to its level of 44.6 percent in 1989. Indeed, the *index of income concentration* (Gini coefficient) in 1947 was .376 whereas in 1986 it was .392, suggesting that an increase in inequality has occurred. Basically, the index measures the extent of the discrepancy between the actual distribution of income among proportions of the population and a condition of perfect equality—one in which the bottom 20 percent receive 20 percent of the income, the bottom 40 percent possess 40 percent of the income, and so forth. The index of concentration has a value range of 0 to 1. Zero indicates complete *equality,* while a value of 1 indicates complete *inequality.* Generally, concentration declined during the years 1947–57, increased in 1957–61, fell during 1961–68, and generally increased since 1969. These data suggest that concentration declines in periods preceding an economic peak in the nation, while it increases following declines in business events. They indicate that lower income families do worse during economic declines than do higher income families.

The proportion of households with incomes below $10,000 was almost the same in 1988 as it was in 1970. Moreover, Table 2.5 indicates the poverty rate was higher in 1989 than it was in 1969. The government's official measure defines poverty in terms of all gross money income from any source. In 1989, the average poverty threshold for a family of four was set at $12,675.

Looking at Table 2.5, we find that blacks, female-headed families, and especially black female-headed families have higher poverty rates than whites and families with both parents present. Indeed, over 46 percent of black female-headed families are poor. This is a slight decline over the 53 percent who were listed as being poor in 1969, but it is still much larger than the 5 percent of white and 11.8 percent of black families with husbands and wives present. Almost one-

TABLE 2.4   Percentage Share of Money Income Received by Each Family Quintile: 1947–1989

	1947	1969	1974	1979	1983	1986	1989
Lowest fifth	5.0%	5.6%	5.6%	5.3%	4.7%	4.6%	4.6%
Second fifth	11.9	12.4	12.0	11.6	11.1	10.8	10.6
Third fifth	17.0	17.7	17.5	17.5	17.1	16.8	16.5
Fourth fifth	23.1	23.7	24.0	24.0	24.3	24.0	23.7
Highest fifth	43.0	40.6	41.0	41.7	42.8	43.7	44.6
Top 5%	17.5	15.6	15.4	15.8	15.9	17.0	17.9

Source: U.S. Bureau of the Census, *Money Income of Households, Families, and Persons in the United States: 1986,* Current Population Reports, Series P-60, No. 159, June 1988, Table 12, p. 39; *Money Income and Poverty Status in the United States 1989,* Current Population Reports, Series P-60, No. 168, Sept. 1990, Table 6, p. 30.

third of all blacks are poor, compared to 10 percent of whites in U.S. society. We will explore the characteristics of this poor population more completely in Chapter 14 and also will discuss the various definitions and alternate measures of poverty that have been suggested. In many ways, defining the poverty threshold is a political issue. Depending upon what is included in the definition of poverty, the poverty rate can be raised or lowered.

Within the poor population, some are poorer than others. Some have incomes that are very near the poverty threshold, while the incomes of others fall well below that poverty line. How far one's income falls below the poverty line is referred to as the *income deficit*. The median income deficit among poor families was $4,344 in 1989. This means that the average poor family's income was over $4,000 below the poverty threshold. The income deficit was higher for black families and those with female heads (U.S. Dept. of Commerce, Sept. 1990, p. 77; Horrigan and Haugen 1988).

In addition to those who are poor by government standards, there are those who are among the "near poor," that is, those whose incomes are below 125 percent of the poverty level. For example, if we add these near poor to those who are actually at or below the poverty level, the percentage of the population in these categories in 1986 jumps from 13.6 to 18.2. Among blacks, the percentage increases from 31.1 percent who are poor to 38.7 percent who are poor or near poor. Among whites it moves from 11.0 to 15.2 percent (U.S. Dept. of Commerce, July 1987, pp. 28–29).

TABLE 2.5 Selected Characteristics of Poverty Population: 1969, 1978, 1987, 1989

	NO. BELOW POVERTY LEVEL (in millions)				POVERTY RATE (%)			
	1989	1987	1978	1969	1989	1987	1978	1969
All persons	31.5	32.5	24.5	24.1	12.8	13.5	11.4	12.1
White	20.8	21.4	16.3	16.7	10.0	10.5	8.7	9.5
Black	9.3	9.7	7.6	7.1	30.7	33.1	30.6	32.2
Under 65	28.1	29.1	21.3	19.4			11.0	10.7
65 and over	3.4	3.5	3.2	4.8	11.4	12.2	13.9	25.3
In metropolitan areas	22.9	23.4	15.1	13.1	12.0	12.5	10.4	9.5
Outside metropolitan areas	8.6	9.1	9.4	11.1	15.7	16.9	13.5	17.9
White families with husband and wife	2.3	2.4	2.0	NA	5.0	5.2	4.7	NA
Black families with husband and wife	0.4	0.5	0.4	NA	11.8	12.3	11.3	NA
White families with female head	1.8	1.9	1.4	1.1	25.4	26.9	23.5	25.7
Black families with female head	1.5	1.6	1.2	0.7	46.5	51.8	50.6	53.2

Source: U.S. Bureau of the Census, *Characteristics of the Population Below the Poverty Level: 1978,* Current Population Reports, Series P-60, No. 124, July 1980, p. 2; *Money Income and Poverty Status of Families and Persons in the United States: 1987,* Current Population Reports, Series P-60, No. 161, Table 15, p. 27; *Money Income and Poverty Status in the United States 1989,* Current Population Reports, Series P-60, No. 168, Sept. 1990, Table 18, p. 56.

Note: In 1989, the average poverty threshold for a nonfarm family of four was $12,675.

COMPARISON WITH OTHER COUNTRIES

The way to consider how "bad" the income inequality and poverty levels are in the United States is to compare them with what is found in other countries. Clearly the rate of poverty is much higher in many other countries, especially considering the fact that poverty is measured in less generous terms in these countries. Three-quarters of the populations of some countries live in stark, absolute poverty (Kurian 1979).

Table 2.6 shows the distribution of income among household quintiles for various industrialized countries. One should keep in mind that not all countries collect income data in the same manner, and the data come from different sources, often from surveys conducted for other reasons. Moreover, the data in Table 2.6 were collected in varying years, but all were gathered between 1975 and 1982. Nevertheless, the information in the table will provide us with a general comparison of the United States with other nations on the income measure. A quick glance reveals that the United States has among the lowest percentages of household income going to the bottom 20 percent. In 1980, the bottom 20 percent of households received 5.3 percent of all household income. Only New Zealand had a lower percentage. On the other end of the continuum, in Japan the bottom 20 percent received 8.7 percent of all household income. When examining the percentage of income going to the top quintile of households, however, the United States is roughly in the middle, with 39.9 percent of income having gone to this group in 1980. In contrast, the top 20 percent in Australia received

TABLE 2.6 Percentage Share of Household Income by Quintiles in Industrial Market Countries

	Bottom 20%	Second 20%	Third 20%	Fourth 20%	Top 20%
Australia (1975–76)	5.4	10.0	15.0	22.5	47.1
Canada (1981)	5.3	11.8	18.0	24.9	40.0
Denmark (1981)	5.4	12.0	18.4	25.6	38.6
Finland (1981)	6.3	12.1	18.4	25.5	37.6
France (1975)	5.5	11.5	17.1	23.7	42.2
Germany, Fed. Rep. (1978)	7.9	12.5	17.0	23.1	39.5
Japan (1979)	8.7	13.2	17.5	23.1	37.5
Italy (1977)	6.2	11.3	15.9	22.7	43.9
Netherlands (1981)	8.3	14.1	18.2	23.2	36.2
New Zealand (1981–82)	5.1	10.8	16.2	23.2	44.7
Norway (1982)	6.0	12.9	18.3	24.6	38.2
Spain (1980–81)	6.9	12.5	17.3	23.2	40.0
Sweden (1981)	7.4	13.1	16.8	21.0	41.7
Switzerland (1978)	6.6	13.5	18.5	23.4	38.0
United Kingdom (1979)	7.0	11.5	17.0	24.8	39.7
United States (1980)	5.3	11.9	17.9	25.0	39.9

Source: The World Development Report 1987. Copyright © 1987 by The International Bank for Reconstruction & Development/The World Bank. Reprinted by permission of Oxford University Press, Inc.

Note: The dates in parentheses are the years in which the data were collected.

over 47 percent of all household income in the mid-1970s.

Table 2.7 gives some information for those countries with the greatest and least concentrations of income in the top 10 percent of the population and those in which the poorest 40 percent receive the largest and smallest proportions of income. It is generally the case that the top 10 percent of persons receive a greater percentage of national income in lower income countries while the bottom 40 percent receive less than they do in higher income countries. There has been a consistent argument that the degree of income inequality is linked to the level of development of a country and that, more specifically, the lower the level of development, the greater will be the extent of income inequality.

In trying to account for the varying levels of development of countries, social scientists have created a number of explanations which can be incorporated under three general headings: (1) evolutionary/stage theories, (2) psychological/value theories, and (3) dependency/world system theories. It is not our purpose here to present an in-depth analysis of theories of development, but since they have relevance for international differences in income inequality, they will be briefly outlined. Broadly speaking, evolutionary or stage explanations contend that development results from movement up through a set of stages brought about by processes at work within the society. For example, Rostow (1960) has suggested that societies go through five major stages in their movement to development: (1) traditional stage, (2) preconditions for "take-off," (3) the "take-off," (4) the drive to maturity, and (5) the "age of mass-consumption." In each stage, certain events must occur in order for a society to move on to the next phase of development. Clearly, the fifth stage is modeled after the United States. A cruder version of this approach to understanding development is found in earlier evolutionary theories which portray development as an almost automatic and universal process attendant with increasing population and progressive integration within the society. Leaving aside the ideological issues surrounding this approach to development, Rostow's theory, like others in this school of thought, has

TABLE 2.7   Some International Comparisons of Income Distribution: 1980

PERCENTAGE OF NATIONAL INCOME RECEIVED BY RICHEST 10%

Top 5 Countries		*Bottom 5 Countries*	
1. Zimbabwe	57%	65. Poland	21%
2. Ecuador	57	66. Hungary	19
3. Kenya	55	67. Bulgaria	19
4. Gabon	55	68. Czechoslovakia	17
5. Brazil	51	69. East Germany	17

PERCENTAGE OF NATIONAL INCOME RECEIVED BY POOREST 40%

Top 5 Countries		*Bottom 5 Countries*	
1. Czechoslovakia	27%	63. Brazil	7%
2. Bulgaria	27	64. Peru	7
3. East Germany	26	65. South Africa	7
4. Hungary	24	66. Iraq	7
5. Poland	23	67. Ecuador	5

been heavily criticized as being ahistorical and weak in its consideration of the ties between countries as a partial explanation for "underdevelopment."

The second type of theory stresses the centrality of values in explaining level of development. In this view, in order for development to occur a particular set of values has to be present in a significant proportion of the population. The psychologist McClelland (1961), for example, stresses the importance of "need for achievement" as a value in individuals, and sociologists Inkeles and Smith (1974) argue for the importance of a number of values if development of a "modern man" is to occur. Among the characteristics they list are a "readiness for new experience," a "democratic orientation," a "belief in human efficacy," a "faith in science and technology," and a "disposition to form and hold opinions." These along with others characterize the "modern man" for Inkeles and Smith. Hagen (1962) also emphasized the importance of certain kinds of personalities for development. In contrast to these "modern values," other more traditional values are said to hinder development. A good discussion of this position comes from anthropologist George Foster. Superstition, ethnocentrism, fatalism, norms of pride, dignity, and modesty are viewed as cultural barriers to development (1973). In these theories, the importance of structure and history for development pales next to the significance placed upon personality and values. Both of these sets of theories assume a basic conflict between tradition and modernity. It is assumed that a "gap" exists between the two conditions, a gap that must be bridged if development is to occur.

The final set of theories of development suggests that the degree of development of a country is tied to its position in the system of inequality in the world economy. More specifically, advocates of the dependency theory contend that the principal reason some countries are "underdeveloped" is because they are minor players in the world market and are linked to major nations through ties of exploitation. Large, powerful nations drain less powerful countries of their resources, estab-

lish markets for their own finished products in these countries, "penetrate" their economies with multinational corporations, and largely determine the terms of trade and pricing in the world economy. This leaves weaker, less prosperous countries in a state of seemingly permanent underdevelopment. For example, one advocate of this position, Andre Frank (1969), refers to this dependency condition as one in which underdevelopment is developed.

More recently, there has been a great deal of interest in world-system theory. Wallerstein (1974, 1979) is largely credited with initiating this discussion, but earlier thinkers considered the idea that underdevelopment/development is related to a country's position vis-à-vis other countries in the world economy (Hunter and Abraham 1987; Christ and Hall 1982). Similar to dependency theory, the world-system approach views the world economy as an interdependent system in which countries play different roles and are in different economic positions. In effect, there is a geographic and functional division of labor among all of the countries. Dominance in this world economy is established through state control and legislation, economic penetration of other countries, and a lowering of a country's dependence on external markets. In essence then, this general perspective emphasizes the importance of the structure of the world economy and a nation's position in it as an explanation of development/underdevelopment. Despite these studies, world-system theory has been open to criticism. Most importantly, Brenner (1977) suggests that, in some cases, the general backwardness of a society can lead to its dependent position rather than vice-versa and that Wallerstein ignores the role of technology and class factors in his analysis of development. (For further critiques, see Chase-Dunn 1975; Robinson 1976; Bornschier and Ballmer-Cao 1979; Sullivan 1983; Stack and Zimmerman 1982.)

As suggested earlier, it is not our task here to give a full assessment of each of these approaches as they bear on development. However, in recent years, the dependency/world-system perspective has been linked by many to the degree of income inequality in a country, and studies have been conducted testing the general hypothesis that the degree of dependency is directly related to the extent of income inequality. Similarly, it also has been argued that a greater level of economic development is associated with lower income inequality. Let us look at each of these propositions.

In the language of world-system theory, countries that are in more dependent, less developed positions are considered noncore or "peripheral" nations, while those in dominant positions in the world economy are labeled as "core" nations. Noncore nations are tied to core nations by a dependent relationship. Their economies, labor markets, levels of development, and political structures are partially shaped by the direct and indirect influence of core nations. This dependent position also helps produce greater income inequality within these nations, in part through its creation of uneven development within these economies.

A variety of studies using various measures of economic dependency indicate that greater dependency produces greater income inequality within the dependent country. More specifically, multinational corporate penetration, foreign debt dependency, and export patterns of concentration all have been found to be positively linked with income inequality (Kuznets 1963; Lenski 1966; Jackman 1975; Bornschier and Ballmer-Cao 1979; Stack and Zimmerman 1982). This relationship has been found even when the country's level of development has been taken into consideration in the analysis. The level of development, however, also appears to be linked to income inequality. The lower the level of development of a nation, the more income inequality is present (Stack and Zimmerman 1982). More specifically, it appears that the degree of income inequality increases with development, up to a point, and then decreases. Stack and Zimmerman's analysis of forty-three nations found this curvilinear relationship, which supports the earlier work of Lenski and Kuznets. However, they also found

that the level of development was *not* related to the share of income received by the bottom 20 percent of the population. In other words, this trend toward greater equality in developed nations was only supported for the top 80 percent of the population. No "trickle-down" effect of development was found. "Development does not result in the redistribution of income to low income groups" (Stack and Zimmerman 1982, p. 355; see also Bollen 1983). In essence, these studies are suggesting that both level of development and dependency in the world economy have independent effects on income inequality.

A link also has been found between the level of economic development and dependency on the one hand, and the extent of political democracy on the other. Bollen's (1983) analysis of a hundred nations revealed that political democracy, as measured by the degree of popular sovereignty and the presence of certain political liberties, is hindered by lower levels of development and greater dependency. Muller (1988), in turn, has recently found that political democracy is related to the degree of the income inequality. His study of about fifty countries revealed that the stability of the democratic regime and how long the country has been democratic affect income inequality; that is, the more stable and longer the democratic tradition in a country, the less income inequality there tends to be. Conversely, when income inequality continues for a number of years, political democracy is undermined. These relationships persist even when a country's level of development is considered (Jackman 1975; Stack and Zimmerman 1975; compared to Robinson and Quinlan 1977; Weede 1982; Muller 1988).

In sum, the proposed relationship is illustrated in Figure 2.1. There appears to be a network of relationships between dependency, level of development, political democracy, and income inequality. Of these, the relationship between political democracy and income inequality is the least settled. Some have found little or no relationship between these two factors, while others have found the predicted relationship (Brenner 1977).

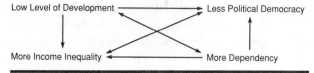

Low Level of Development ⟶ Less Political Democracy

More Income Inequality ⟵ More Dependency

FIGURE 2.1 Macro-Processes and Income Inequality

WEALTH INEQUALITY IN THE UNITED STATES

While there is clearly income inequality in the United States, wealth inequality is even greater. Moreover, wealth is a more complete measure of a family's economic power since it consists of the value of all the family's assets minus its debts. It is all of a family's "stored up purchasing power" (Democratic Staff of the Joint Committee 1986, p. 5). Therefore, it includes the value of homes, automobiles, businesses, savings, and investments. The debt factor is less significant for those in higher wealth brackets because they are less likely to have debts. For example, only about 2 percent of households with annual incomes of $48,000 or more had zero or negative net worth in 1984. Their median net worth was $123,474, compared to a median net worth of just over $5,000 for households with an income of $10,000 or less. Almost 25 percent of the latter households had zero or negative wealth (U.S. Bureau of the Census, July 1986, Table 4, pp. 20–21).

One last point should be made about wealth and the implications it has for an individual's economic ability. Even though the amount of personal wealth gives a fuller picture of an individual's or family's economic position, even it does not fully suggest the fact that the wealthy also have at their disposal a greater number of economic tools that serve to enhance their economic opportunities and market situation. For example, ownership of a great deal of stock in a corporation that is interlocked or directly connected with other corporations may give an individual indirect influence over the economic behavior of the latter organizations. Like poverty, wealth has economic implications beyond the actual size of the holdings. Economic opportunities are at least in part a function of the economic tools a person has at his or her disposal.

The methodology used to uncover the distribution of wealth is not as exact as one would desire. "Thus, the 'general' shape of the distribution of wealth . . . [has] been known for some time," writes Smith (1987), "but because our methodologies have been too crude and too narrow, we have failed to advance much beyond our understanding of 20 years ago. . . . None of these methods is adequate for estimating the total distribution of wealth" (pp. 72, 82). The cost of developing new methods and the comfort of using old ones are two of the reasons old methods persist.

Some of the difficulties associated with present methods are clear. Information about wealth is difficult to obtain. Virtually all data about it come from various field surveys and administrative records. Often individuals are hesitant to be interviewed, and this is especially true of the wealthy who, for several reasons, may be sensitive about their wealth. "As a rule," writes Allen (1987), who has conducted an extensive analysis of the country's richest families, "the members of wealthy capitalist families refuse to divulge even the most rudimentary details of their wealth. . . . In order to maintain their anonymity, the members of corporate rich families typically refuse to disclose even basic biographical information about themselves" (pp. 26–7). What is requested of individuals in surveys and what is given are frequently not the same (Smith 1987). Social scientists in general have produced hundreds of studies of the poor and poverty, even the middle class, but good broad-based information about the wealthy and wealth concentration has always been and remains difficult to come by. Why this has been the case remains an interesting political question (Pessen 1973; Turner and Starnes 1976). Another problem with wealth data is that cash and personal items like jewelry and art are often undervalued. To complicate these matters, researchers use different units of analysis in discussing the distribution of wealth. Sometimes the unit used is the "individual," while in others the "family" or "consumer unit" is the basis of analysis. Keeping these difficulties in mind, we can now turn to the estimates on changes in the distribution of wealth over time in the United States.

Wealth Concentration before the Civil War

If there ever was a time when equality was present, it surely must have been when the United States was first being established. When this nation was being politically formed, many left their European homelands because of oppression of one kind or another to escape to the "land of the free," where the streets were thought to be paved with gold. The Founding Fathers, using "the voice of justice," forged a document that not only enumerated the offenses committed against the then new American people but also demanded freedom and equality for all. While some, such as Hamilton and Jefferson, argued about whether the government should or should not take a strictly egalitarian form, many believed the period was an "era of the common man" (Pessen 1973). The Founders recognized the belief that "all men are created equal" and later devised a constitution that had among its objectives to "establish justice." Wealth inequality may exist today, but the virgin past was surely free from such a condition. In his famous visit to the United States, de Tocqueville (1969) was surprised by the "equality of conditions" that seemed to prevail in the youthful country. And although he believed wealth was certainly present, no one group held a monopoly on it. Indeed, de Tocqueville believed that wealth moved about quite a bit in the country.

Recent studies have simply not borne out these beliefs. Social historians, poring over probate records, tax forms, and old census documents, have found a decidedly different America than one might have expected. The studies of wealth distribution in the early United States consistently point to the fact that wealth inequality was a clear and constant condition during this period. This was especially true for the period between the Revolution and the Civil War, a time in which inequality was on the rise.

Before the Revolution, however, the increases in inequality do not appear to have been as great or as consistent, but differences in wealth were quite noticeable. Studies in Philadelphia and Chester County, Pennsylvania; Boston and Salem, Massachusetts; and Hartford and rural Connecticut point not only to evident variations in wealth among people, but in some cases to increasing differences as time passed (Pessen 1973). In the Chester County study, for example, the richest 10 percent possessed almost one-quarter of all wealth in the early 1700s. In the next century, their portion climbed to 38 percent. Before 1660, the wealthiest 5 percent in Salem held 20 percent of the wealth, and in 1681 they held about half of it. The same kind of trends are present for Boston, but for others, such as Hartford, fluctuations are the rule (Lemon and Nash 1968; Koch 1969; Main 1976). Consequently, uniform evidence about a trend toward increasing inequality before 1776 does not exist. "To put it more cautiously, there appears to be little evidence of a uniform secular drift in colonial inequality. The secular increase in wealth concentration after 1700 seems to be more the result of 'cycle' than trend" (Lindert and Williamson 1976, p. 43). Whether or not a trend was present depends on the base date chosen. After 1776 especially, however, the trend toward increasing inequality is present everywhere.

The years after the Revolution did not produce more equality. In his studies of cities in New England, the Middle Atlantic, the South, and the Midwest, Sturm (1977) found some sobering results for believers in the "romantic hypothesis." Even though these cities may not represent the

America of the time, Sturm felt that "major characteristics and trends can be indicated because
the sample was drawn from important regions
and segments of the population which were crucially involved in development of the national
economy" (ibid., p. 24). Using probate data, he
found distinct and increasing inequality in estate
wealth for the period 1800 to 1850. During this
time, Sturm discovered that the per capita holdings of the very wealthy had gone up about 60
percent (ibid.). An examination by Pessen for this
period in Brooklyn and Boston likewise confirms
the general trend toward inequality. In Brooklyn
in 1810, 1 percent of the population held 22 percent of the private wealth, and in 1840 1 percent
owned 42 percent (Pessen 1973, p. 36).

Figures for Boston and New York duplicate
these findings. In 1820 Boston, the top 1 percent
held an estimated 16 percent of noncorporate
wealth, and in 1833 and 1848 it had 33 and 37
percent, respectively. In New York in 1823, the
top 1 percent possessed 29 percent of private
wealth, and by 1845 that percentage had risen to
40 percent. These trends were evident in other
cities as well (Pessen 1973, pp. 33–34, 39–41;
Lindert and Williamson 1976, p. 18). One also
must keep in mind that these figures probably underestimate the degree of inequality because of
the tendency of the wealthy to undervalue their
property (Pessen 1973).

Concentration of wealth in the nineteenth
century appears to have peaked during the period
from 1850 to 1870. Soltow found that while
wealth inequality remained fairly constant during
this period, it was also very high. Using census
data on real and personal estate holdings among
free adult males, he found that in 1860 the top 1
percent owned almost 30 percent and the top 10
percent owned about 73 percent of estate wealth,
again demonstrating a strong degree of wealth
concentration. During the period 1850 to 1870,
"there very definitely was an elite upper group in
America in terms of control of economic resources" (Soltow 1975, p. 180). A small percentage had great wealth, but large numbers had
little, if any.

In 1850, for example, over half of free adult
males owned no land even though it was quite
cheap. Nor did the situation change much in the
years following 1850 (ibid., p. 175). Given the
period, as one might expect, a person was more
likely to be an owner of real estate if that person
was native born, older, and a farmer (ibid.). In
1860, there were an estimated 41 millionaires,
545 in 1870, and 5,904 in 1922. But if we use
constant 1922 dollars, the real estimate for 1870
would be between 1,800 and 2,600. However, the
main conclusion from all these data is that at least
from the mid-eighteenth to the mid-nineteenth
centuries wealth concentration was high and
tended to increase during that period. Little is
known about the extent of concentration during
1870 to 1922 "except that it was lower after the
Civil War than before and lower in 1922 than it
was to become by 1929" (Lindert and Williamson
1976, p. 31).

Wealth Concentration in the Contemporary United States

Since the 1920s wealth has remained concentrated. In 1929, the top ½ percent of *individuals*
in the United States held about 32 percent of the
personal wealth. After this peak, studies suggest
that this percentage steadily decreased through
1962, when the top ½ percent owned just over 22
percent of all personal wealth (Democratic Staff
of the Joint Committee, 1986, p. 32). Between
1962 and 1972, the percentage owned by the top
½ percent fluctuated only slightly, remaining essentially constant, and then took a dip between
1972 and 1976, only to increase again in 1983.

The total amount of net wealth in the country
in 1983 was estimated to be approximately $10.6
trillion. About 57 percent of personal wealth is in
personal residences and business holdings, while
15 percent is in nonresidential real estate, 11 percent in stocks and bonds, 8 percent in bank accounts, 4 percent in trusts, and 5 percent in other
assets. It is evident that the form of wealth most
often found among the super-rich is different
from that found in the bottom 90 percent of the

population. The kinds of wealth the ordinary person thinks of as major, such as automobile and home ownership, make up only a small percentage of the very wealthy's holdings. Accordingly, Turner and Starnes (1976) have referred to this group of persons as "estate capitalists," since their wealth is concentrated in ownership of capital and property critical to the operation of the economy. The nature of this wealth further permits the continued accumulation of wealth within this group.

A recent survey conducted by the Survey Research Center at the University of Michigan for a congressional committee suggests a continuing heavy concentration of wealth. This study revealed that the top ½ percent of U.S. *families* owned over 35 percent of all net wealth. The study refers to this top ½ percent as the "super-rich." The next ½ percent owns an additional 6.7 percent of the wealth, meaning that the top 1 percent of families is estimated to own almost 42

percent of the private net wealth of the country. The next 9 percent owns almost 30 percent of the net wealth, meaning that, in sum, the top 10 percent owns over 70 percent of the net worth in the United States, while the bottom 90 percent owns just over 28 percent of all net wealth.

Table 2.8 shows that in 1983 the super-rich owned over 15 percent of all real estate, over 46 percent of corporate stock, almost 44 percent of bonds, 77 percent of trusts, and over 58 percent of all business assets. There were about 420,000 households in the super-rich category, and they held an average wealth of just under $9 million per household (see Table 2.9). In contrast, the average household wealth of the bottom 90 percent was $39,584 in the same year. Moreover, the average worth of the super-rich households has accelerated at a much faster pace than that of other households. Between 1963 and 1983, the average household wealth of the top ½ percent increased

TABLE 2.8 Distribution of Major Forms of Wealth among U.S. Households By Percent: 1983

	Super-Rich (Upper ½%)	Very Rich (2nd ½%)	Rich (90–99th%)	Everyone Else (0–90th%)	All Households (100%)
Real estate	15.3%	4.2%	29.5%	50.9%	100% ($5362.3B)*
Corporate stock	46.5	13.5	29.3	10.7	100(981.7B)
Bonds	43.6	7.5	39.3	9.7	100(329.6B)
Certificates of deposit	5.3	6.0	38.9	49.7	100(385.7B)
Trusts	77.0	5.0	13.2	4.8	100(491.6B)
Business assets	58.2	8.0	27.4	6.3	100(3,272.0B)
Money market accounts	17.5	7.3	36.8	38.5	100(265.8B)
Insurance cash surrender	6.5	3.5	20.8	69.2	100(260.8B)**
Gross assets (Total)	32.1	6.3	28.6	33.0	100(12,066.2B)
Net worth (Assets – Debts)	35.1	6.7	29.9	28.2	100(10,587.2B)

Source: Democratic Staff of the Joint Economic Committee of the U.S. Congress, *The Concentration of Wealth in the United States,* Congressional Information Service, Inc., July 1986, p. 24.

*Dollar amounts are given in billions (B).

**The totals of all the listed types of wealth include all but about $700 billion of the $12,066.2 billion in wealth. The $700 billion includes wealth in checking and savings accounts, IRAs, land contracts, and miscellaneous categories.

TABLE 2.9   Average Net Wealth per Household: 1983

Wealth Category	No. of Households	Range of Net Wealth per Household	Average Wealth per Household
Super rich (top ½%)	419,590	$2,509,750 and above	$8,851,736
Very rich (next ½%)	419,590	$1,422,600–$2,509,749	$1,702,376
Rich (next 9%)	7,552,620	$206,341–$1,422,599	$ 419,616
Everyone else (bottom 90%)	75,526,200	$206,340 and below	$ 39,584

Source: Democratic Staff of the Joint Economic Committee of the U.S. Congress, *The Concentration of Wealth in the United States,* Congressional Information Service, Inc., July 1986, p. 27.

147 percent, while that of the bottom 90 percent increased 45 percent (see Table 2.10).

The large amounts of wealth owned by a very small percentage of the population makes one curious about where the wealth comes from and who the wealthy are. Family and inheritance are the major sources of wealth among the corporate rich in the United States. Only a minority have obtained their initial wealth through entrepreneurship or personal saving. While these are important sources for some, "in terms of sheer numbers of people, most of the corporate rich in America are inheritors" (Allen 1987, p. 4). Gift and estate laws have done little to stem the flow of inherited wealth to subsequent generations. Wealth is kept in the family, and this is one reason why the extended family is such an important institution among the rich. The social, cultural, and economic capital passed on to children helps them to maintain and even increase their wealth. The odds of the children of wealthy parents keeping their wealth is probably about 3 to 1 (Currie and Skolnick 1988, p. 106).

Who are these people? A majority of those with assets of at least $300,000 are men, and a slight majority of those with a net worth of at least $5,000,000 are male (U.S. Dept. of Commerce 1988). A greater percentage of those fifty-five to sixty-four years old have a net worth of over $250,000 and over 90 percent are white. A majority of those with a net worth over $1,000,000 live in the South or West. A greater percentage of whites, those fifty-five to sixty-four years of age, those with four years of college,

married couples, and those living in the West have a net worth of at least $500,000, compared with other individuals (U.S. Dept. of Commerce 1986). In contrast, a greater proportion of blacks, those under thirty-five, those with less than twelve years of education, and those living in the Northeast are in the zero/negative wealth category.

A recent *Forbes* survey of the 400 richest individuals in the United States reveals a similar profile of characteristics ("The 400 Richest" 1987). Only 55 of the 400 are women, over 75 percent are married, and 75 percent are in their fifties, sixties, or seventies. Sixty-five of the 400 are in their forties or younger. Over three-quarters have at least attended college or university, but perhaps surprisingly, only 60 percent have graduated. Less than 20 percent have obtained postgraduate degrees. The average number of children for these individuals is 3.1.

The total net worth of these 400 people is estimated to be about $220 billion, the average net worth per individual being about $550 million. The minimum net worth of any of these persons is about $225 million. Roughly, about 40 percent control wealth that is primarily inherited in nature, while the remainder have created fortunes that are mostly not inherited. The wealth of 80 percent of these individuals comes from either manufacturing, media, real estate, or financial activities. The remainder get their wealth primarily from retailing, agriculture, oil/gas, or high technology.

TABLE 2.10 Changes in Wealth Distribution: 1963–1983

	SUPER RICH (UPPER ½%)		VERY RICH (2nd ½%)		RICH (90–99th%)		EVERYONE ELSE (0–90th%)		ALL HOUSEHOLDS (100%)	
	1963	*1983*	*1963*	*1983*	*1963*	*1983*	*1963*	*1983*	*1963*	*1983*
Net worth	$982.6*	$3714.1	$284.2	$714.3	$1247.8	$3169.2	$1350.0	$2989.6	$3864.6	$10587.2
Net worth as % of total net worth	25.4	35.1	7.4	6.7	32.3	29.9	34.9	28.2	100.0	100.0
1963 average wealth per household	$3,588,489		$1,037,543		$253,187		$27,390			
1983 average wealth per household	$8,851,736		$1,702,376		$419,616		$39,584			
Percent change in per household wealth, 1963–83	147%		64%		66%		45%			

Source: Democratic Staff of the Joint Economic Committee of the U.S. Congress, *The Concentration of Wealth in the United States,* Congressional Information Service, Inc., July 1986, pp. 33 and 38.

*All figures are in terms of constant 1983 dollars.

SUMMARY

This chapter has reviewed information on various types of economic inequality. "Social class" has been defined in several ways, most importantly in socioeconomic terms as a multidimensional phenomenon and in Marxian terms as a strictly economic concept. While there are some notable similarities in the perceptions of class structure in the United States using different measures, there are some significant issues that are, as yet, unsettled. Among these are the question of the placement of lower white-collar workers, the issue of the "shrinking" middle class, and the question of proletarianization/embourgeoisement.

Examination of income inequality reveals that the degree of inequality appears to have increased in recent years, with females and blacks lagging behind white males in income, even when occupation and other factors are controlled. The poverty rate also has increased in the last few years. When income inequality in the United States is compared to that in other countries, noticeable differences appear. Part of the explanation lies in the level of development and democracy within a given country.

Finally, wealth inequality in the United States is even greater than income inequality, and data suggest that the top ½ percent is receiving an even greater percentage of the total net wealth today than twenty years ago, while the bottom 90 percent's share has decreased. In sum, this chapter indicates that economic inequality continues to exist along a variety of economic dimensions. But inequality has more than an economic component. In everyday life, invidious distinctions often are made between individuals on the basis of other factors, resulting in a social ranking because of differences in education, lifestyle, and other "social" characteristics. It is to these social-status aspects of inequality that we now turn our attention.

CHAPTER 3

STATUS INEQUALITY

Now, the Star-Belly Sneetches
Had bellies with stars
The Plain-Belly Sneetches
Had non upon thars.
Those stars weren't so big. They were really small.
You might think such a thing wouldn't matter at all.
But, because they had stars, all the Star-Belly Sneetches
Would brag, "We're the best kind of Sneetch on the beaches."
—Dr. Seuss, *The Sneetches and Other Stories*

The previous chapter discussed the various types of *economic* inequality present in U.S. society, namely, class, income, and wealth inequality. But the ranking system is more complicated than that, and experiences in everyday life tell us that invidious distinctions are made between individuals on grounds other than economics. People often are evaluated and ranked on the basis of their education, possession of "culture," type of occupation, and even their speech patterns and clothing styles. Moreover, Stub (1972) has recently suggested that these status differences are becoming increasingly significant in U.S. society, especially in the middle sections of the class system where, he says, distinct classes are not in evidence. Stub and others suggest that within a democracy, where social mobility occurs and class possessions are potentially available to everyone, a leveling of class distinctions and a massification of culture has also occurred. In this view, the weakening of the class factor and the blurring of lines between classes develop in this context; status differences move to the forefront and become more significant (Stub, 1972; Wilensky 1972;

Mayer 1972). In the face of formal legal and political equality, people become more anxious about the status differences between them (Nisbet 1972). While institutionalized inequality continues, the argument goes, Marxian social classes rapidly become "ghost communities" (Wrong, 1972).

However, evidence presented in the last chapter supports the conclusion that classes do exist in the United States. At the same time, however, there is no doubt that inequality includes *social* dimensions as well as the more obvious economic ones. More often than not, we notice these social distinctions in our contacts with others; that is, they become most salient when we interact with individuals with characteristics and lifestyles different from our own. Research suggests that we often rank people differently depending on those characteristics and lifestyles. Indeed, the term "social" stratification suggests that alongside economic inequality we have a system of social inequality, and often these two forms are intertwined with each other as we shall see. Quite often, for example, an individual's economic position will affect his or her social position. In this chapter, we will examine the nature of this social dimension of inequality.

The concept of *social status* has been defined in a variety of ways in sociology. One of the most prominent definitions views it as merely a position within a structure, implying nothing about ranking or hierarchy. In this case, mother, teacher, clergyman, clerk, and so on would all be statuses. In other words, "status" in this sense is essentially a synonym for "position." Each status has a role attached to it—a set of behaviors that are expected of anyone occupying a particular status. Often there are even stereotypes or other general ideas about persons who share a given characteristic, and this conditions how we expect them to behave in given situations (Lasswell 1965). Since each person occupies several statuses or positions, each individual can be said to possess a "status-set" (Linton, 1936; Merton 1957).

Like different positions, groups that have different lifestyles need not be ranked; they merely may be different. Collins (1988) argues, for example, that status groups can be seen as part of the horizontal, rather than the vertical, organization of society. Status groups may only be different cultural groups characterized by different lifestyles. In other words, they need not be stratified into a ranking system. In these cases, the reasons individuals cluster around and interact with each other on a continuing basis are related to the similarities that derive from having a common heritage or culture. That is, status groupings need not derive from differences in power to obtain the resources needed to be attractive to members of a particular group. For example, status groups may be based upon religious beliefs rather than on wealth or income differences. These religious subcultures or status groups may have implications for the ranking system as when different religious communities conflict within a given class, but they can remain essentially horizontal rather than vertical elements in the society's structure.

A good example of this possibility is found in Kephart's (1982) analysis of several different religious groups. As a status group, each has clear restrictions on interaction, behavior, and marriage. For example, members of one of the groups studied by Kephart, the Amish, are not allowed to date non-Amish persons, and are not even allowed to date other Amish from different districts unless there is an established relationship with the group. There are clear rules, rituals, and conventions that are considered sacred. These function to maintain and solidify the group by reinforcing its values. It is fairly typical of the groups studied by Kephart, such as the Shakers and Hutterites, to have frequent social and religious gatherings and common living and eating quarters, all intentionally designed to increase group solidarity and identification with the group. Further, there is a distinctiveness of lifestyle that serves to separate the in-group from the out-group. Tales of past events in the group's history and the legendary charisma of the group's founder further cement the individual's attachment to the group. Violations of conventions and cultural values are punished within the community. Banishment and shunning are two of the more severe forms of punishment found in such groups.

As defined previously, the concept of status is essentially nominal rather than ordinal in nature; it simply suggests differences between individuals without suggesting how those differences are being evaluated by others on some ranking scale. It is closely related, then, to the idea of *social differentiation* in which individuals or groups are viewed as being different on some socially recognizable, and often important, characteristic.

THE THEORY OF SOCIAL STATUS

Since this is a book about inequality, we are more concerned with a second way of conceiving social status, namely one that emphasizes the ranking dimension of statuses and status groups. In this conceptualization, "social status" refers to an individual's ranking with respect to some socially important characteristic; thus, some people are thought to be low in social status, while others are high on this scale. Max Weber, the great German sociologist, stressed the importance of distinguishing between (economic) class and (social) status inequality, while at the same time he pointed out that they could be empirically related to each other, as when social *status* is dependent on *class* position. Weber viewed a person's *status situation* as "every typical component of the life fate of men that is determined by a specific, positive or negative social estimation of *honor.* This honor may be connected with any quality shared by a plurality" (Gerth and Mills 1958, pp. 186–7). This means that individuals are given or not given homage and respect because they possess or lack some characteristic the community considers honorable or dishonorable. That quality is social rather than economic in nature; for example, one's family name, the street where one lives, the kind and degree of education one possesses, or one's race or gender all may elicit such honor or dishonor. Weber argued that this "claim to positive or negative privilege with respect to social prestige" may be based on (a) "mode of living," (b) "a formal process of education which may consist in empirical or rational training and the acquisition of the corresponding modes of life," and/or (c) "the prestige of birth, or of an occupation" (Weber 1964, p. 428).

Whereas economic position can be determined by essentially *objective* measures, for example, amount of money, ownership, and so on, social status is the result of a *subjective* appraisal of people by others in the community. Social status is basically a cognitive phenomenon in which individuals or groups are compared with each other and differentiated from each other on the basis of some characteristic or quality thought to be of significance in the society. In other words, status ranking derives from opinions of others, opinions based on a community value system. A plurality or group of individuals who share some prestige-relevant characteristic, for example, living in a particular area of town or being a member of the same kind of occupation, may occupy a clear place in the social ranking system of a community and thereby form a social stratum. Weber argued that "status groups are normally communities" in the sense that there is greater cohe-

siveness among individuals in the same status position, whereas "'classes' are not communities; they merely represent possible, and frequent, bases for communal action" (Gerth and Mills 1958, pp. 181, 186).

Status groups that are ranked in a certain place on a community's social hierarchy are characterized by (1) a set of conventions and traditions, or lifestyle, (2) a tendency to marry within their own ranks, (3) an emphasis on interacting intimately, for example, eating only with others in the same group, and (4) "often monopolistic appropriation of privileged economic opportunities and also prohibition of certain modes of acquisition" (Weber 1964, p. 428).

A status group that possesses a certain measure of social esteem, or lack of it, then, is characterized by a particular style of life that sets it off from other status groups. "An 'occupational group' is also a status group" (Gerth and Mills 1958, p. 192). Jazz musicians or college professors, occupational groups that are different status groups, often are characterized by the peculiar lifestyles found among individuals in these occupations. To be an accepted member of a status group, a person is expected to follow the normative lifestyle of the group and to have "restrictions on 'social' intercourse" (ibid., p. 187). This means that he or she is expected to associate intimately with only similar kinds of people.

A group tries to set itself apart from other status groups, especially those that might contaminate the "purity" of the group. Status groups try to distance themselves from others "by means of any other characteristics and badges" (ibid., p. 188). To distinguish themselves from outsiders, members of a status group may wear certain kinds of clothes or hairdos, or belong to exclusive clubs. An extreme instance of this process exists when individuals of a particular status group agree to marry only among themselves, that is, to practice endogamy, and to chastise or shun anyone who marries outside the group. Lewis Lapham recently recalled his own experiences in this regard: "At college I knew several boys whose mothers discouraged their sons' acquaintance with anybody who lived in towns not adequately represented in the Social Register. If a boy didn't come from Grosse Pointe or Burlingame or Fairfield County, then his place of origin was listed under the heading *terra incognita*" (1988, p. 160). After all, status honor rests on "distance and exclusiveness." Moreover, "exclusion" is a primary mechanism by which those in powerful status groups keep others from gaining power (Parkin 1979). Residential segregation, to the degree that it is voluntary on the part of a high-status group, might also be an example of an attempt at such separation. Or men may attempt to keep their corporate positions exclusive by preventing women from moving to the top of the ladder. From these examples, it should be apparent that in addition to occupation, status may be based on racial/ethnic or gender "qualities" possessed by individuals, depending on the values of the particular society.

The various conventions, rules, traditions, and rituals of a particular status group help to sustain it over time. Thus, it is not surprising that there are attempts to enforce them within the group. Status groups are the "bearers of all 'conventions' . . . all 'stylization' of life either originates in status groups or is at least conserved by them" (Gerth and Mills 1958, p. 191). So far, we have seen that status groups are (1) associated with different estimations of social honor, (2) based on a variety of socially relevant characteristics such as occupation or ethnicity, and (3) tend toward closure, that is, toward restrictions on contact with those outside the group. In addition, if fully developed, membership in a specific status group may allow an individual to monopolize certain material commodities (e.g., costumes, food, arms, artwork). That is, a community may feel that it is appropriate for only a particular group to be the owner or protector of certain goods.

Weber contended that status groups tend to monopolize particular types of economic opportunities and acquisitions, while at the same time they discourage the possession of other kinds. For example, a status group whose honor or prestige is based on its class position may allow its members to acquire fancy homes in particular neighborhoods, but it may be considered "bad form" to spend money or opportunities acquiring a new bowling ball or a gaudy automobile. In societies where there is extreme *social* stratification, for example, South Africa, this monopolization may be legalized. The *social* privileges of whites are based on their economic and political power. It follows from this view that status groups are "phenomena of the distribution of power within a community" (ibid., p. 181).

When social and economic conditions in a community are stable, Weber argued, stratification by status becomes dominant, and after status has been "lived in" for a while, status privileges can become legal privileges. Moreover, status becomes of central importance in societies where the economy is monopolistically controlled and is of a religious or "liturgical" character. The setting is also one where the needs of groups are based on a feudalistic or patrimonial arrangement, and one that is dominated by "conventional rules of conduct" (Weber 1964, p. 429).

When legalization of status privileges occurs, a society may be on the road toward a full-fledged caste system. According to Weber, the extreme of a caste system developing out of a status system happens only when the "underlying differences . . . are held to be 'ethnic' " in nature (Gerth and Mills 1958, p. 189). Race is a basis for deference/honor, or its opposite, because "it is thought to represent the possession of some quality inherent in the ethnic aggregate and shared by all its members." This "essential quality" is "manifested in . . . external features such as colour, hair form, physiognomy and physique" (Shils 1970, p. 428). Indeed, there is evidence that ranking does take place on the basis of such external features (Lasswell 1965). The existence of varying degrees of "social distance" between various ethnic groups in the United States provides ample evidence of such a ranking system. In this instance, various ethnic status groups that may have been horizontally related are converted into a set of hierarchically arranged groups, those on the top being the most "pure" and those on the bottom being "impure," contaminating, or even untouchable. The latter "pariah" groups may be tolerated only because of economic necessity; that is, the lower castes may perform necessary but "dishonorable," "dirty," and onerous work. For example, lower castes may be the only groups ritualistically permitted to collect garbage or dead carcasses from the street.

In sum, according to Weber, ideal-typical caste systems are characterized by (1) classification into a caste on the basis of some ascribed characteristic such as race, ethnicity, or lineage, and as such it is hereditary; (2) immobility within the system; (3) endogamy and restricted social intercourse; and (4) typically prescribed ranges of occupations associated with each caste. Under a caste system, consequently, the relationships among various status groups have been shaped into a ranking system of superordination and subordination. As we shall see later, some scholars have argued that caste relations exist between the sexes and races in the United States, while others have suggested that the changing, open society is qualitatively different from a society like India, for example, to which the application of the caste system is most often made. We will explore the caste model of race relations in the United States more fully in Chapter 10.

As suggested earlier, quite often status, class, and power systems interact, resulting in the ranking of these status groups on the basis of power or economic factors. Weber (1964, p. 429) noted that class position can provide the resources necessary for the attainment of status, and conversely, social status may affect one's class lifestyle. As we shall see later, Weber emphasized the priority of class in capitalist society.

When ranking does occur among status groups, *deference* is expected to be shown toward those in more prestigious or honored groups. Deference "entails an attribute of superiority (or inferiority). . . . It is an attribution of merit (or of defect); it is an assessment which attributes worthiness (or unworthiness)" (Shils 1970, p. 421). Like Weber, Shils stresses that deference and status are of a different quality than economic phenomena like class and wealth. "Deference-position—or esteem, prestige or status—does be-

long to a different order of events in comparison with events like occupation distribution, income and wealth distribution, etc. It belongs to the realm of values; it is the outcome of evaluative judgments regarding positions in the distribution of 'objective' characteristics" (ibid., p. 436). Consequently, measures of socioeconomic status that mix the subjectively derived deference or status position with more objective measures such as income to form an overall measure of an individual's position, are, according to Shils, "patently unsatisfactory" because social status is a subjective phenomenon, whereas income and wealth, for example, are objective in nature, and therefore, they are qualitatively different (ibid., p. 436).

The presence of a ranking of status groups at the societal level has implications at the individual level, in the behavior between individuals of different status groups. The act of showing deference to persons in higher status positions manifests itself in various "presentational rituals" that essentially indicate to them how they are being regarded. The manner in which the individual is greeted, compliments, or other behaviors of homage are examples of deferential behavior (Goffman 1959, 1967). When a person of lower status approaches one of a higher rank, the interaction may take on a formalistic, ritualistic nature on the surface. That is, in the public setting, each party plays the role that is expected from persons representing each status group. But in private, feelings may be quite the opposite. That private aspect of life is frequently considered more inviolate for those in higher statuses than for those at the bottom, whose privacy/personal space may be more justifiably violated according to social norms. Because of the greater honor given them, the private lives of those in high statuses are more likely to be respected.

While those in lower statuses are presenting themselves in ways that demonstrate respect and deference for those at the top, the latter can use their resources to present themselves in ways that elicit and justify such respect. They typically have the resources and motivation to appear impressive, and so manage situations to obtain the responses they desire. Through their *demeanor,* higher status individuals can suggest that they are worthy of such deference. Demeanor is "that element of the individual's ceremonial behavior typically conveyed through deportment, dress, and bearing, which serves to express to those in his immediate presence that he is a person of certain desirable or undesirable qualities" (Goffman 1967, p. 77).

Deference behavior between individuals in differently ranked status groups can be based on a variety of criteria. An individual may be considered entitled to such behavior from others because of occupation and race or ethnicity as we have already suggested, but also on the bases of level and type of education, gender, lifestyle, political or corporate power or one's nearness to it, family name or kinship network, income, and amount and type of wealth. Service work on behalf of a community or society and formal titles also can serve as grounds for status honor in some locations. All these factors are deference-relevant because they are linked with basic values and/or issues in the society. A region or area can also be the basis of deference because it is thought to be associated with a particular occupational role (e.g., Appalachia with coal mining, Manhattan with the stock market, etc.), with the exercise of power in a society, or with some other valued criterion (e.g., New England with quality education).

CASTE IN INDIA: AN EXAMPLE OF STATUS STRATIFICATION IN ACTION

The caste system in India provides an example of an extreme case of status stratification, exhibiting many of the qualities associated with status inequality just discussed. Ranking and deference behavior are clearly found in the caste system of India, although neither occupational specialization nor ethnicity appears to be the basis of the system. There is a mutual dependence of castes upon each other. The system is a "harmony unifying diversity" (Lannoy 1975, p. 138). Hierarchy,

rather than being solely a divisive element in the society, becomes a source of integration. The caste system in India is related to the four "varnas" described in very early Hinduistic texts. A hymn in the *Rig Veda,* an ancient religious script, describes society as a body in which the Brahmans represent its head, the Kshatriyas its arms, the Vaishyas its trunk, and the Shudras, the feet. As in any organism, all the parts need to work together for the whole system to function properly. Kolenda (1978) has commented that while some western social scientists view the caste system as basically exploitative of those at the bottom, others see it as a system that includes and functions for all. The latter analysts regard the exploitative view as being too narrow and even ethnocentric.

At the top of the varna system, the Brahmans are considered the most pure. They are engaged in teaching as priests, giving sacrifices, and receiving gifts. Brahmans have privileges not open to the members of other castes in classical Hinduism. Theoretically, Brahmans cannot be fined or beaten, for example. Because of their duties and abilities, Brahmans can transmit the sacred and religious element to the king, through whom it then radiates out into the rest of society. The whole caste hierarchy is infused with religious beliefs that tie the various castes together.

As is the case with Brahmans, every other varna is associated with specific duties and tasks (the dharma of the caste). The Kshatriyas, below the Brahmans, are associated with political and top military positions; that is, they function to protect society. The distinction between Kshatriyas and Brahmans is essentially between religious and political functions. The Vaishyas make up the next varna and earn their living from the land as farmers or in grazing livestock or in commerce and usury. The task of the Shudras, the last of the four varnas, is simply to serve those above them. There is a qualitative difference between the Shudras and the three varnas above them. Unlike the other three, the Shudras do not "participate in initiation, second birth, or the religious life in general" (Dumont 1970, p. 67). Members of the first three varnas were said to be "twice-born" in that adolescent boys underwent a particular initiation ceremony when they were just beginning to study the sacred religious texts. Boys in the lower castes were not permitted to read or listen to these writings. A fifth stratum, the Untouchables, are left out of the formal classification system entirely. In a ritual sense, they are outside the caste system.

The four major varnas made up the classic theoretical system of Indian society. But the real, concrete system of castes (jati) was actually more complex. Any given village may have had a few or large number of castes, and these may have varied in nature from village to village. There also may have been kinship or other ties between similar castes in different villages. In other words, in everyday life the operating caste system was very complicated. However, most Indians still associate specific castes in a village with one of the four varnas. In this way, the latter form a sort of "all-India caste system" (Kolenda 1978, p. 94).

Dumont describes an actual caste system as a situation in which "the society is divided into a large number of permanent groups which are at once specialised, hierarchised, and separated (in matter of marriage, food, physical contact) in relation to each other" (Dumont and Pocock 1961, pp. 34–5). Summarizing a number of social-anthropological studies, Kolenda (1978) has distilled what she considers to be the core features of the local caste system in India:

1. It operates as a system only in a confined locality and may consist of a few or many more specific, mutually exclusive castes.
2. A dominant caste or family usually has economic and political control in the area. Its dominance is based on control of land and force.
3. Each caste has an occupational specialty associated with it and offers its services to members of other castes in exchange for food, services, or other products (the jajmani system). This exchange system performs not only an economic function, but

also serves to keep the higher castes pure, allowing those in the bottom castes to absorb pollution.
4. Castes are ranked according to pollution and purity.
5. Each caste segment tends to live in its own area. Untouchables are isolated from the rest of the village, either living in a separate setting altogether or on the edge of a given village.
6. The caste is an endogamous descent group, and the local contingent of a caste are usually kin-related.
7. Efforts to improve caste rank are made by the lower ranks. These include emulating the Brahman lifestyle (Sanskritization) and eliminating certain polluting customs. Mobility is also attempted through (a) arguments that the low rank of one's caste is really the result of an historical error or having really been deprived of one's rightful place, (b) allusions to having been the descendant of a great or high-ranking person or caste, and (c) gaining wealth, allowing a caste to change its name and live an honored lifestyle.
8. Disputes within a village are settled either by a council or by an elder in the dominant caste.

It should be evident that the basic element of separation pervades the system (in associations with others, marriage, and residence). This fundamental trait should not be surprising. In our earlier discussion of Weber's concept of status group, we noted the importance of social distance and exclusivity. The separation underlying the castes is based upon religious and ritualistic notions of purity and pollution. The term "caste," in fact, comes from the Latin root word *castus* which means "pure" (Lannoy 1975). Formally, the caste hierarchy contains the purest castes at the top and the most polluted at the bottom. One must remain ritualistically pure if one is to perform religious duties effectively, and contamination from the outside environment as well as pollutants from the inside (bodily waste) can endanger the purity of the body. One must avoid proximity to the contaminant, because prolonged closeness can mean "permanent pollution" if the contaminant is strong enough. It can then be passed on through one's children. In other words, pollution can be hereditary, even though there are both permanent and temporary types of pollution. Castes associated with polluting jobs (e.g., leather workers, barbers, sweepers, funeral workers—all occupations that involve working with body parts, excrement, or dead organisms) have permanent pollution. Temporary pollution, on the other hand, can be overcome with various rituals of purification. Everyone is exposed to potential contaminants every day because all people eat, go to the bathroom, have sexual relations, and so forth—all activities that bring them into contact with impurity.

Rules determine from whom one can receive food or water without becoming polluted. Thus commensality, eating only with members of one's own caste, encourages the maintenance of purity. Certain foods are believed to be more open to contamination than others or are associated with certain castes. With respect to the latter, for example, some foods are believed to promote lightness and purity, while others supposedly encourage physical strength and passion. There is a concern for maintaining bodily purity because it is believed that spiritual development requires purity through the avoidance of impure relationships and objects, including not only food, but clothing and homes as well (ibid., pp. 145–52). Thus, in this ritual sense, strangers and foreigners are major sources of pollution for the strict caste member. Certainly notions of "racial" purity underlaid many of the justifications for racial inequality early in U.S. society.

There is increasing evidence that the Indian caste system is not the monolithic, simple system it is sometimes portrayed to be. For example, educated, westernized Indians are less likely to believe in the purity/pollution theory (ibid., p. 148). As suggested earlier, there is also some evidence that even in India, there are avenues of social mobility. To move up, for example, some lower caste persons have started their own religious movements, while others have married up-

ward. By gaining political power or mobilizing, a group can also raise (or lower) its caste rank, and some individuals can increase their statuses because of increased economic resources (Kumar 1982; Das and Acuff 1970; Berreman 1960). But these are movements to change one's position *within* the system, not revolutions *against* the system (Kolenda 1978). Moreover, the actual caste system is made up of many subcastes, often varying from region to region. In other words, as we have seen, some have suggested that the manner in which a caste system works in theory is not the same as it works in reality.

In 1975, Richard Lannoy wrote that the caste system is still "the most distinctive feature of Indian culture; it has remained the bedrock of the social structure from ancient times to the present day" (p. 137). Hindu religious beliefs have helped to maintain the stability of stratification in India. Most notably, the emphasis on dharma, karma, and reincarnation have encouraged believers to abide by the status quo. Individuals have been expected to follow the duties of their castes (dharma). They also have been taught to believe that their present behavior has a direct causal linkage with what happens to them in their next life (karma). However, there is evidence that the caste system, while still operative, may be weakening in the face of changes in technology, urbanization, and education; economic and political systems that are increasingly international and competitive in nature also put tradition at risk (Kolenda 1978). These may be creating permanent fissures within the caste system, but at the same time the new formal democracy and constitution have not meant the erasure of real caste inequalities in the Indian system (Sivaramayya 1983).

BASES OF STATUS IN THE UNITED STATES

As suggested earlier, the esteem in which a person is held in the United States can be founded on a variety of factors. Several of the more prominent bases will be discussed here, starting with the traditionally acknowledged criteria of occupation, education, lifestyle, and social class. Less noticed, but also bases of status, physical appearance and region also are analyzed. A brief comment is then made on race and gender as bases for status, which then leads us into the next chapter on race and sex inequality.

Occupation, Education, Lifestyle, and Class

Occupational role, of course, is frequently associated with both social class and social status, but most commonly used measures of occupational ranking tap the prestige/esteem dimension rather than the economic one. Occupation is a basis for deference and honor not only because of its association with valued goals (income, power, etc.), but also because there are often lifestyles associated with particular roles, lifestyles that receive different degrees of honor. Plumbers and professors clearly are accorded different levels of honor because of what people associate with each of these occupations.

A good analysis of a particular occupation as being the basis of status is given in Bensman's (1972) discussion of professional musicians. He argues that musicians form a "status community" in that they adhere to a particular and somewhat unique set of values that shapes their lifestyle. The institutions, behaviors, and practices that organize and comprise their lives, in turn, are based upon those core values. In many ways, this community is like a total institution in that the musician's life is dominated by the community's organization and culture. Insiders are clearly separated from outsiders. There are regularized interactions and rituals that help keep the community cohesive. When the musicians get together informally, they perform, discuss music, or attend concerts, all of which increase their allegiance to the community's values.

In addition to having its own subcultural values, the music community is internally stratified according to a number of musically relevant criteria. For example, Bensman suggests that (1) the instrument one plays; (2) one's role in the community (conductor, performer, critic, etc.); (3) whether one is a soloist, accompanist, or in an orchestra or small group; (4) assessed skill; (5) extent of recording contracts and size of fees; and (6) affiliation with a particular school, conservatory, teacher, or type of music are among the factors that affect one's rank within the community. Thus, for those close to the community, there is an understanding that diverse internal divisions exist within what may appear to the real outsider to be a homogeneous community.

We can, of course, conceive of other occupational groups forming status communities, and Bensman argues that each of us is probably a member of several such communities and organizations in which our particular status may vary. The existence of a large number of such status communities made up of individuals who have positions in several of them creates an image of a societal prestige/status system that is extremely complex. However, some of these status communities may be more central and important than others and, therefore, may have more of an impact on one's status position in the society. How influential one's membership in a given status community is for one's overall status depends upon (1) the prominence and relevance of the community, (2) the extent to which knowledge about it is spread throughout the society, and, perhaps most importantly, (3) the extent to which its values and lifestyle are viewed positively or negatively by the outside society (ibid., p.125).

Generally, status communities based on occupation are socially relevant and prominent. Over the years, there have been several attempts to rank occupations according to prestige or status. Early efforts to measure occupational status suffered from the fact that they generally were based on inadequate samples of respondents, were of a subjective nature, and contained prestige differences within the general occupational categories that were often almost as great as those between such categories (see Counts 1925; Edwards 1943; Smith 1943). It is also difficult to arrange these occupations along a single dimension using one criterion. Although it may seem obvious that skilled blue-collar work would rank above semiskilled in prestige, it is not at all clear why professionals should rank above proprietors using the same dimension of skill.

Several attempts were later made to perfect an occupational status ranking, the most influential being the North-Hatt scale developed in the mid-1940s. It differed from the earlier scales in that a much wider range of occupation types was considered, and it relied less on the creator's judgment of rankings. The "prestige" rankings obtained were based on a 1947 survey of 2,920 individuals who were asked to classify the *general standing* of each of ninety occupations. No mention was made of prestige. The five-point evaluations ranged from "excellent," "good," and "average" to "somewhat below average," and "poor." The most frequently cited reasons for awarding a given occupation an excellent standing, in order of decreasing frequency, were that it paid well (18 percent), served humanity (16 percent), required a lot of previous training and investment (14 percent), and had a high level of prestige associated with it (14 percent).

The North-Hatt scale, which was heavily used in the past, has been criticized for a variety of reasons (Reiss 1961, Chapters 2–3). First, the sample in the survey was a quota sample, meaning that the respondents were not necessarily representative of the population. Second, the list of occupations does not appear to be representative of the U.S. occupational structure; "women's" occupations were dropped because the researchers felt that the continuum already contained occupations of their ranking. Third, the validity of the prestige ratings given by the sample assumed knowledge of the occupations, consensus on the bases for evaluation, and a common interpretation of what was being communicated in the instrument. Fourth, there was ambiguity and variation in the requests being made of respondents, and the reasons given for ranking occupations varied with the respondents' own occupational position. Fifth, some of the occupational categories were more general and internally heterogeneous than others, creating a question about what kind of occupations were really being evaluated. Sixth, it is at least questionable if one can reliably rank an occupation without mention of its organizational context. Finally, given the last three problems, the rankings may not be reliable. How-

ever, a replication of the study in 1963 yielded very similar rankings for the eighty-eight distinct occupation types (Hodge et al. 1964). The rankings appear to be stable over time. There appear to be fairly consistent feelings among Americans in general about the prestige ranking of occupations, a ranking that has not changed significantly since World War II.

As noted, one of the problems with the North-Hatt scale is that not all occupations were included in the list used. Even though it would have been a "formidable task" to get prestige rankings for all detailed occupations, Duncan (1961) felt that there was a need to develop a method to "approximate" such ratings. Accordingly, using the knowledge that occupational prestige was highly correlated with income and education, Duncan was able to develop an equation to estimate the prestige scores of all occupations in the 1950 Census, since data on their required educational levels and income were available from the Bureau of the Census. From these a socioeconomic index (SEI) was developed for all occupations. Several other investigators have used similar information to predict and deduce occupational socioeconomic scores (Charles 1948; Blisher 1958; Bogue 1963).

Occupational scales, especially those in past studies, have virtually always determined the prestige or socioeconomic ratings using only males, the social class of the family using only the husband's occupation, or both. With increased numbers of females in the labor force and the frequent differences in the occupational statuses of the husband and wife, it would not be correct to deduce the wife's status from the husband's. "The family is no longer . . . an adequate unit to accommodate the statuses of the two adult individuals involved" (Nilson 1974).

In addition to occupational role, *education* has been the frequent focus of discussion as a basis of prestige and honor. Level of education is supposed to be related to the level of knowledge and skill one has in a particular field, but in addition to that, education also prepares one for a particular status group and ensures the continuation of status groups. Education helps to create different cultural groups, frequently based on economic class position. At the same time, different *types* of education instill different sets of values and outlooks into those receiving them. The cultural/status effects of education have been analyzed in depth. Bourdieu suggests that higher education helps to reproduce the class structure by functioning to reinforce the value and status differences between the classes. It does this by honoring the *cultural capital* held by those in the higher classes. This capital, which consists of a group's cultural values, experience, knowledge, and skills, is passed on from one generation to the next. In organizing itself around the "linguistic and cultural competence" of the upper classes, higher education ensures that members of the upper classes are successful in school. This legitimates the class inequality that results because it appears that the inequality is largely the result of individual performance in a meritocratic, open educational system. That is, the language used, the cultural knowledge expected for success in school, and the values and behaviors honored are those of the upper class. In short, in the words of one interpreter, "the school serves as the trading post where socially valued cultural capital is parleyed into superior academic performance. Academic performance is then turned back into economic capital by the acquisition of superior jobs" (MacLeod 1987, p. 12). The experiences in school and in the work place of those in the working and lower classes, coupled with the general outlook and specific attitudes they have acquired because of their class milieu, lead them to believe that they cannot succeed in school, thus lowering their aspirations to do so (ibid.).

One of the principal functions of education is to prepare students for the cultural status groups they will be entering upon graduation (Collins 1971). In his biting satire at the beginning of the twentieth century, Thorstein Veblen observed that those elite schools of higher learning had as their primary purpose "the preparation of the youth of the priestly and the leisure classes . . . for the consumption of goods, material and immaterial, according to a conventionally accepted, reputable scope and method." The "reputable seminaries of learning" are conservative and tend to stress the importance of the classics rather than practical and directly serviceable knowledge. The classics, according to Veblen, "serve the decorative ends of leisure-class learning better than any other body of knowledge, and hence they are an effective means of reputability" (Veblen 1953, pp. 239, 256). Similarly, authors of a more recent empirical study of elite prep schools observe that "curriculum is the nursery of culture and the classical curriculum is the cradle of high culture" (Cookson and Persell 1985, p. 74). But they also observe, in sharp contrast to Veblen's emphasis on the nonfunctional learning of the "leisure" class, that the education is deadly serious.

Analysis of the history of U.S. boarding schools supports the conclusion that they were developed to help the established upper class isolate and reaffirm its cultural characteristics. Initially, the founders hoped that these schools would help separate their cultural group from the new wealth developing in industry and from the increasing amounts of lower class immigration. This suggests again the strong impetus toward social closure among the old rich. But the need for financial support of these schools necessitated taking in some of the sons of individuals who had become recently wealthy from industrial, manufacturing, or other enterprises in the latter part of the nineteenth century (Levine 1980). These nouveaux riche, consequently, infiltrated the boarding schools even though the established patrician families winced because the former were often seen as lacking in manners and polish. One of these new-wealth parents, Phillip Armour, once described his occupation as converting "bristles, blood, and the inside and outside of pigs and bullocks into revenue" (ibid., p. 83). This kind of comment is hardly the type that would have won over persons from the established old-wealth families.

Nevertheless, while stressing the rigor and difficulty of attainment within them, studies of elite prep schools confirm the importance of cultural capital and the role of these schools in perpetuating the class system. A large part of the education for students in these "status seminaries" involves learning how to hide or mask their wealth, to acquire "taste," and to prepare themselves to be "soldiers for their class," that is, to occupy and carry out the responsibilities of their class (Cookson and Persell 1985). As Shils (1970) observed, some schools are thought of as more important than others, and "those educated in them acquire more of a charismatically infused culture" (p. 426). The rules of eating, sleeping, and playing together along with peer expectations and formal discipline help forge cohesiveness at the same time that the classical curriculum, the emphasis on dialogue and discussion, and extracurricular activities like sports encourage the development of specific values. The formal and informal curricula of these schools are designed to make sure that these results occur. Even the architecture of the school and demeanor of the headmaster or headmistress conspire to create an atmosphere in which such learning and value development can take place. "The cultural capital that prep school students accumulate in boarding schools is a treasure trove of skills and status symbols that can be used in later life" (Cookson and Persell 1985, p. 30).

For their students, elite prep schools also serve as a major linchpin between parental class position and obtaining positions of power in the wider society. These students tend to get into the better colleges and universities and, ultimately, to obtain positions of influence in the leading political, cultural, legal, and corporate institutions of society. Earlier studies of prep school graduates reinforce the conclusion that these students needed to go on to the "right" Harvard, Yale, or Princeton; that is, they had to get into the appropriate clubs and societies at these universities, and to do this a student had to come from the "right" boarding school. Upon graduating from the university, these students could then take up their memberships in the most exclusive city clubs and become established in a high-status Wall Street law or brokerage firm. This process, covering the youth from their teen years through their attainment of an occupation, helped ensure the exclusivity of this high-status group. A not insignificant reason for this attainment relates to the networks of relationships and values developed during the prep school years. The Cookson-Persell study confirms that going to the "right" schools helps instill those values and aids movement into those positions most highly honored in U.S. society. In this manner, prep schools help to reproduce the values and positions necessary for the legitimation and maintenance of the class structure. In prep schools, class and status intersect.

Many of those who attend elite schools of

Prep schools are crucibles for reproducing elite culture, passing on esteemed cultural capital to new generations of the upper class.

higher learning come from prestigious families whose names are well known. Family name, as indicated, also can serve as a basis for status. The vast majority of those attending prep schools, for example, come, not surprisingly, from wealthy, well-educated, traveled, professional and managerial families. The parents in these families demonstrate the kind of cultural and social capital needed to obtain high status. A recent study of almost 3,000 men and women found that cultural capital, as measured by participation in, knowledge of, and attitudes toward "high culture" (fine art, music, etc.), affects not only the likelihood of attending college, but also college completion, graduate education, and marital selection (Di-Maggio and Mohr 1985).

Lifestyle, by itself, can be a principal source of status honor because the manner in which one lives is a concrete demonstration of one's values and one's degree of "high culture." Lifestyle refers to "expressive behaviors that are observable or deducible from observation" (Sobel 1983, p. 120). In essence, it is a symbol representing what one stands for. Such lifestyles are often internally consistent; that is, they contain behavior or style arrangements that go together by common agreement in the community, or that are found frequently enough to be considered normative. Just as one does not wear sneakers with a tuxedo, one does not mix general stylistic elements. Stylistic unity then becomes the basis of lifestyle (ibid., pp. 123–4).

In his analysis of a 1972–73 survey of consumer spending, Sobel used factor analysis to identify four such style clusters: (1) "prestige acquisition," (2) everyday "maintenance," (3) "high life," and (4) "home life." The first cluster, prestige acquisition, refers to an emphasis in consumption behavior on material acquisitions that traditionally have been associated with social status: "conspicuous luxury items, household decorations, dress clothing, membership fees for clubs and organizations, and vacation expenditures." The second lifestyle cluster, maintenance, refers to the acquisition of more common goods of use in the home, such as items for personal care, food, casual clothes, textiles, dress cloth-

ing, furniture, and so on. The third cluster, high life, as the term implies, relates most heavily to luxury items like the purchase of food away from home, alcohol, and musical expenditures. These behaviors suggest a more "youthful, active, . . . evening oriented, and nonfamilial" lifestyle. Finally, the last cluster identified, home life, signifies a more home-oriented, family entertainment type of lifestyle, involving expenditures not only for food and casual clothes, but also spending on television, camping, health, and sports merchandise.

In his analysis, Sobel found that participation in the prestige acquisition style was positively associated with (a) being from the West, (b) living in a small town or rural area, (c) being married, (d) smaller family size, and (e) higher income, education, and occupational status. Pursuing a "maintenance" set of behaviors is related to (a) living in a nonwestern location, (b) living in a small town or rural area, (c) higher age, (d) having a multiple-person household, and (e) income, especially at the lower levels of the income hierarchy. As they move up the income ladder, individuals spend a smaller and smaller *proportion* of their incomes on such maintenance activities even though the *absolute* amounts increase as they go up the hierarchy. The so-called high-life set of behaviors is especially more likely among those who (a) are younger, (b) have small households, and (c) have higher incomes. Finally, the home life factor is positively linked to (a) being married, (b) larger size of household, (c) western or northeastern residence, (d) smaller locations of residence, (e) higher education and lower occupational status among those at the higher rungs of the socioeconomic ladder, and (f) income. With respect to the latter, while the amount spent on such expenditures increases with increases in household income, the proportion of total income spent on them decreases. Sobel also concludes that the proportion of income devoted to maintenance and prestige-acquisition expenditures is greatest at the lower end of the socioeconomic hierarchy, while that spent on entertainment items is greater at the higher end of the ladder. This suggests that those at the lower end are, proportionately, more concerned with the acquisition of material goods that signify status in U.S. society, while those at the top, who already have a certain amount of these goods, can afford socially to devote more of their incomes to personal entertainment (ibid.). In his witty book on *Class,* Fussel (1983) relates the many ways in which classes differ in lifestyle, including the kinds of furniture they buy, the kinds of vacation spots they choose, and even the way they shop through catalogues.

As the preceding example implies, having a particular amount and type of *wealth* and/or *income* also can be a basis for status. In his time, Weber argued that, in fact, "the class situation is by far the predominant factor [in the formation of status groups], for of course the possibility of a style of life expected for members of a status group is usually conditioned economically" (Gerth and Mills 1958, p. 190). Since each class may form its own status group, it should not be surprising that sociologists have found that certain lifestyles and values are found in each class.

For example, a number of scholars have focused on the status honor of the upper class. The use of inherited wealth, family lineage, club membership, quality of education, and general lifestyle as criteria for membership into the established upper class helps maintain the exclusivity of that class. We have already seen how early boarding schools functioned in this regard. Practicing endogamy within the class helps determine who can get into "Society." Maintaining a closed circle in the face of an ostensibly open democratic society demands that there be mechanisms present to keep just anyone from getting into the circle. E. Digby Baltzell, a member of the upper class himself, has insisted that "there exists one metropolitan upper class with a common cultural tradition, consciousness of kind and 'we' feeling of solidarity which tends to be national in scope." This upper class has been buttressed historically by institutions that serve its members, such as boarding schools, select eastern universities and colleges, and the Episcopal Church (Baltzell 1958; see also Domhoff 1971; Ostrander 1984). The upper class as a status group practices a particular kind of lifestyle with particular kinds of

rules associated with it. Specifically, children are expected to be well bred, with manners and a sense of their importance in society. Boarding schools are a principal source of this training, but family ties are also central. Keeping the family line intact and marrying the "right" kind of person is important. Marriages are not made as facilely as might be the case in other social classes. But some restricted social activities such as debutante balls and fox hunts, which once were prominent elements in the lifestyle of the upper class, have declined in recent years. Acceptable occupations include financier, lawyer, business executive, physician, art collector, museum director, and even architect. Membership in exclusive metropolitan social clubs, most often composed only of males, is also important if an individual is to be part of the upper-class status community. Living in an exclusive residence separate from middle-class and other neighborhoods and maintaining a second summer home are also means by which separation from outsiders is preserved.

Upper-class families tend to be patriarchal, but even the female spouse may be a member of a private social club. Frequently, she is expected to be involved in charitable activities and other social events. There is a division of labor between the sexes in these families. Evidence suggests that members of this upper-status group are concerned with maintaining their separation from others even in death. Their burial customs and sites tend to be different from those of lesser mortals (Kephart 1950). As these characteristics indicate, "members of the upper class not only have *more,* they have *different*" (Domhoff 1971, p. 91).

Weber thought that status groups are ranked according to their patterns of consumption as manifested in their lifestyles (Gerth and Mills 1958, p. 193). It is not so much the economic value per se of the consumed goods that is important, but rather the fact that these goods, especially if owned by a higher ranking status group, serve as symbols of worth and ability. It becomes a matter of self-respect and honor to conspicuously display such goods, not merely to "keep up

What kinds of institutions people can or cannot get into depend heavily upon whether they meet the requirements of entrance, which in many cases include the magnitude of their economic resources. In both of these cases, membership exclusivity is stressed, even though in each case it appeals to a different level of clientele.

with the Joneses," but to surpass them if possible (Veblen 1953).

Veblen's Theory of the Leisure Class   The linkage of class position to status is most clearly seen in the arguments of Thorstein Veblen, an early American sociologist and economist who grew up in rural Wisconsin and Minnesota. His discussion of status applies most directly to the periods up to the early part of the twentieth century. Writing his most important work around the turn of the twentieth century, Veblen contended that manual labor had become defined as dishonorable and undignified, not becoming to one who wished to be considered of high social status. On the other hand, he argued that nonproductive labor, such as that of being a businessman, increased the probability of owning great amounts of property, which in turn, increased one's status honor. Owning property had become, in Veblen's view, the equivalent of possessing honor. In order to show this honor and property to others, one then had to engage in ostentatious displays of wealth and status, namely, various forms of what he called "conspicuous consumption." This display served as a symbol of one's worth and ability. Veblen was well aware of the work of Boas and other anthropologists, and thought of the potlatches of the northwest tribes as a quintessential example of conspicuous consumption. In these ceremonies, the wealthy person would intentionally destroy some prized possessions as a means of showing off his or her wealth. Clearly, in a rational sense, this is unproductive and wasteful behavior, but it is behavior that results in honor for its initiator.

Veblen verbalized a belief in simplicity, functionality, and efficiency, and satirized those goods and conditions that contradicted these characteristics. Yet, the "leisure class" is most likely to engage in activities that are intentionally nonfunctional or unproductive. This class consists of those who are exempt from useful or "ignoble" labor, and evolved with the evolution of society. In the earliest stages of humanity, a period Veblen referred to as "peaceable savagery," there was no system of individual ownership or much "pecuniary emulation," that is, imitation of and competition with others concerning who has more possessions. However, as differentiation between types of labor occurred, as a "predatory" or warlike frame of mind and a system of private ownership developed, the first leisure class appeared. Women were really the first type of private property, owned by men. During this period of "predatory barbarism," according to Veblen, the major class distinction was between men and

women. While women did all the essential, productive labor, men engaged most often in honorific hunting and various types of exploit and plunder, eager to produce "trophies" for themselves. This is the period in which industrious, productive labor came to be defined as dishonorable and "dirty," while the kind of activities in which men engaged were considered to be honorable and praiseworthy. In a manner of speaking, men's work allowed them to avoid getting their hands dirty. In order to show their worth, men led a life of "conspicuous leisure." It was an indication that one is not doing ignoble labor, that is, working. Time was consumed nonproductively. It became a sign of the "decency" of one's life. Men competed with each other in demonstrating their worth by the accumulation of various possessions and trophies, so that they could make an "invidious" comparison of themselves with others. By "invidious," Veblen meant "a comparison of persons with a view to rating and grading them in respect of relative worth or value—in an aesthetic or moral sense. . . . An invidious comparison is a process of valuation of persons in respect of worth" (Veblen 1953, p. 40).

In the "civilized" state of industrial society, really a quasi-peaceable barbarian stage according to Veblen, the cultivation of manners and decorum are a central part of this leisure-class lifestyle. In modern times, the distinction between industry and business parallels the earlier difference between female and male labor. Modern-day businesspeople are industrial society's predatory class, while those directly involved in industrial work are those who are doing the productive labor.

Veblen argued that the modern leisure class of the industrial era not only engaged in conspicuous consumption and leisure, but in conspicuous waste as well. Women, for example, had become in his view not only the "property" of men, but also an ornament with which men could display their wealth and power. Women took on a "ceremonial" function with the rise of the Industrial Revolution and were expected not to engage in industrious, productive work. Rather, in their behavior and appearance, women were to symbolize the status of their husbands. While men, even those in business, could satisfy their "instinct of workmanship," that is, the feeling needed by everyone that one is doing something useful, women were essentially servants of the household head who were expected to be well bred and to use their time cultivating their beauty. Women were in charge of the household, the "woman's sphere," and were expected to engage in conspicuous leisure and consumption, since their behavior reflected the status of the men who owned them. In their dress, they were expected to be especially wasteful, that is, their dresses were to be nonfunctional and waste material. "Special pains should be taken in the construction of women's dress, to impress upon the beholder the fact (often indeed a fiction) that the wearer does not and cannot habitually engage in useful work. . . . [It is] the woman's function in an especial degree to put in evidence her household's ability to pay" (Veblen 1953, p. 126).

As suggested earlier, conspicuous consumption and waste not only occurred in the area of dress, but also in the cultivation of beauty. Indeed, during the nineteenth century, and largely as a byproduct of the Industrial Revolution, the "cult of true womanhood" demanded that a respectable woman refrain from useful work, to be "fragile, idle, pure . . . submissive and subservient to her husband and to domestic needs. Her worth was based on her decorative value, a quality that embraced her beauty, her character, and her temperament" (Fox and Hesse-Biber 1984, p. 19).

We can summarize Veblen's ideas by indicating again that he felt that people's worth and honor, in modern times, were linked to their ability to pay, that is, their wealth and possessions. The more a person can display such resources, the greater the respect attributed to him or her. This leads to an ostentatious show for others in a desire to impress and to a competition to outdo others in such display. Such display covers a wide range of possessions, even such things as better-groomed lawns, ownership of prize horses, and conspicuous dress. Everyone tries to battle in this competition, according to Veblen, but the leisure/business class is most successful.

Since Veblen, there have been other analyses of the lifestyle of the upper class. As noted earlier, status often rests upon class position, and high-class position makes it possible for individuals to pursue desired lifestyles. Brooks (1974) argues that Veblen's ideas must be updated because the lower classes do not revere the upper class as in Veblen's day, nor is leisure strictly the province of the upper class today. More often, people engage in "parody display" of honored status symbols. Just as in a literary parody, people poke fun at possessions that, in the past, have commanded great respect. He views this parody as the result of a mixture of admiration and ridicule by the lower classes. But still he finds that competitive display and conspicuous consumption are alive and well in U.S. society. Speech, clothing, and membership in exclusive clubs, for example, continue to be used in making invidious comparisons. Moreover, even though the contemporary businesspersons cannot use the blatant techniques of a hundred years ago to maintain their seclusion from others, "more devious means are employed . . . to exclude the unwanted. . . . Courteous secretaries explain in detail how the nabob's many vital functions preclude the possibility of adding a new one. . . . In sum, the invidiousness has become gentler in style and equally, or perhaps more, forceful in substance" (Brooks 1979, p. 194).

Physical Appearance and Status

Clearly, physical appearance can provide clues to and is often a basis for social status. In this regard in the next chapter, we will focus in detail on race and gender as a basis for inequality. Along with these variables, physical beauty also serves as a basis for granting status. Fussell (1983) suggests that even one's weight and profile suggest a class position. Beauty, of course, is in the eyes of the beholder, but what the beholder sees and how it is interpreted are shaped by culture's values. Beauty is a social construction, and in U.S. society it has significance. To realize its importance, one need only look at the media to see how it is used to sell everything from automobile transmissions to cologne. It implies that those who possess it have other qualities as well. Research has suggested that individuals who are considered physically attractive also are considered to have happier marriages, better mental health, and to be more confident and likeable than those who are considered unattractive. They also are thought to be more attentive when being interviewed, to be better performers in the classroom, and to deserve more room on the street (Webster and Driskell 1983).

A recent study by Webster and Driskell, conducted among college students who examined photographs of males and females, indicated that people who are labeled as beautiful are considered to be "better at situations in general, things that count in this world, most tasks, and abstract ability" (ibid., p. 158). It is also considered more desirable to be beautiful than to be unattractive.

Status on other grounds, for example, wealth and income, also can affect the way we see the "attractiveness" of the individual. The physical appearance, clothes, and behavioral styles of a person who has wealth may be seen as being more attractive because of his or her wealth, and what is considered attractive may be determined by those who have wealth. As Lewis Lapham acidly put it: "In a rich man's culture, art is what sells and its price determines its worth. If the diamond bought at Tiffany's sparkles more brilliantly than a diamond of equal weight and size bought for $758 on West Forty-seventh Street, the even bad novels by Norman Mailer or Joseph Heller or E. L. Doctorow become masterpieces by virtue of the prices paid for the paperback and movie rights. Once an author or an artist has demonstrated his or her ability to earn money, he or she acquires, as if by court order, a reputation for genius" (1988, p. 67). In the study cited earlier, Webster and Driskell consider beauty to be just as much a status characteristic as sex or race. It is a "status cue" like the latter in that it is associated with particular cultural beliefs and values and has implications for interactions with others.

Of course, the definitions of beauty and other status symbols vary with societies and over time within the same society. The beauty of the human figure portrayed in a Rubens painting is not the same ideal of beauty seen today in the clothing ads of Calvin Klein or Ralph Lauren. Especially in open and democratic societies, the salience and ranking of status symbols waxes and wanes. In one year, having a particular characteristic or possession may result in great status honor or prestige, but a few years later that same possession may be of little social importance, while another has ascended to a position of high prestige.

One of the tasks of those who rank highly is to ensure that they maintain their status. However, over time others in an open society may be able to obtain the objects once held only by those on top. This devalues their worth in the eyes of the higher status group. Mills (1951) argued that, in the middle of the twentieth century, the middle-class, white-collar workers were in a "status panic" because "every basis on which the prestige claims of the bulk of the white-collar employees have historically rested has been declining in firmness and stability" (p. 249). In terms of wages, unemployment rates, education, political power, and ethnicity, Mills felt that the middle class was losing its higher status relative to the working class. This leads to the erosion of status honor for those in the middle class, because "if everybody belongs to the fraternity, nobody gets any prestige from belonging" (ibid.). In order to maintain an edge in prestige, individuals try to increase their status within their own group, purchase as many possessions as possible that serve as status badges, and finally, to temporarily raise their status by living extravagantly on the weekend (ibid., pp. 254–8). Nevertheless, in large and impersonal urban settings where individuals do not know each other personally, displays of status symbols are more common indicators informing strangers *"who"* their owners really are (Form and Stone 1957).

It has been well established that one of the most often-used status symbols in urban settings concerns fashions in clothing. At the turn of the century, Veblen (1953) observed that clothing is particularly well suited to being a status symbol since "our apparel is always in evidence and affords an indication of our pecuniary standing to all observers at the first glance" (p. 119). To be worthy of high status, according to Veblen, clothing must be expensive and clearly not indicative of any productive work. Thus, it must not only be clean and new, but not associated with any form of odious work. Jeans, for example, would not have been statusworthy in Veblen's eyes. Elegant clothes, while appearing to be useful in a broad sense, must give evidence that the individual wearing them is a person of leisure, not one of the working classes. Veblen's ideas on clothing have not always stood the test of time, as indicated by the rise of designer jeans as a status symbol, for example. The wearing of new crisp clothes is not always an indicator of upper-class position. "The upper and upper-middle classes like to appear in old clothes, as if to advertise how much of conventional dignity they can afford to throw away" (Fussell 1983, p. 58).

There is no question that how we dress affects the attitudes and behavior of others with respect to us (Kaiser 1985). "Clothing itself is the beginning and end of human display, touching on one side the skin of the person and reaching out on the other to announce to all what the person inside the skin is or wishes to be" (Brooks 1979, p. 201). Clothing takes on a "moral" character in that people assume that your dress indicates something about the kind of person you are. "A cheap coat makes a cheap man," observed Veblen. The appearance of second-hand clothing stores in Washington, D.C., which cater to the not-quite affluent, for example, testifies to the importance people place on trying to make an impression. Originally expensive suits can be purchased for a low price. Notes one customer: "It pays to shop in a place like this in a town like Washington where clothes are a big part of how you are perceived" (Barringer 1990, p. 10).

Some research suggests that clothing frequently brings out status-related reactions. A study by Stone (1962) analyzed data from over 200 married men and women in a midwestern community to see if they had patterned responses to certain appearances as indicated by clothing. Stone concluded that clothing helps to give individuals social identities with which certain atti-

Clothing is frequently used as a symbol of status. It suggests both occupation and lifestyle.

tudes, values, and behavior are associated. Clothes, like other status symbols, can be used as a device to elicit desired kinds of feelings on the part of others and to manipulate others and their impressions of us.

Alison Lurie recently suggested a number of ways in which clothing can be used to give an impression of high status. She labels these "conspicuous" addition, division, multiplication, and labeling. Conspicuous addition refers to the technique of layering clothes, that is, wearing several kinds of clothing over each other, even though it is not functionally necessary. Scarves and vests, for example, when worn ornamentally, would be a demonstration of conspicuous addition and an example of what Veblen called conspicuous waste. Conspicuous division and multiplication are different forms of the technique of wearing a wide variety of different types of clothing, especially for separate occasions. The point here is that, to indicate high status, a person does not want to wear the same piece of clothing twice consecutively and does want to wear different kinds of clothes for evening, dinner, casual, and other sorts of situations. "Life itself has been turned into a series of fashionable games, each of which . . . demands a different costume—or, in this case, a different set of costumes. . . . The more different looks a woman can assume, the more fascinating she is supposed to be: personality itself has become an adjunct of Conspicuous Waste" (Lurie 1987, p. 129). "The constant wearing of new and different garments is most effective when those you wish to impress see you constantly—ideally every day. It is also more effective if these people are relative strangers" (ibid., p. 127). The latter comment reinforces the notion mentioned earlier that it is in large cities that these symbols become most significant as emblems of status.

A good example of conspicuous multiplication is found in the inner city of Harlem where status among youth is related to the number and kinds of sneakers worn ("The Well Heeled" 1988). One's status is indicated by the use of different sneakers for different occasions and activities. "A man's got to have style, or he's half a man," explains one youth named Mr. Washington. "The fact is, in the inner city you are what you wear—on your feet" (ibid., p. A1). One has to be careful not to wear the wrong brand or style of sneakers in the wrong place or on the wrong occasion. There are regions, sections of cities, even streets, that are closely identified with particular brands of shoes. "In Boston, there are Nike streets . . . and Adidas streets . . . and woe to anyone caught wearing the wrong brand on the wrong street" (ibid., p. A6). Shoes are not only used to identify one's status but turf as well. Some youth are willing to sell drugs to keep themselves in shoes, some of which cost over $100 a pair. The youth quoted earlier, Mr. Washington, owns 150 pairs of sneakers. This recalls Veblen's comment that even those without the resources will go to great lengths, even murder, to practice such "conspicuous consumption." Status-seeking is not a game only among the well-to-do.

Finally, a fourth form of clothing technique mentioned by Lurie, conspicuous labeling, is a way of ensuring that the knowledgeable would be able to distinguish the high-status piece of clothing from an imitation. Otherwise, a status crisis could occur for those who wish to use clothing as a status symbol, since several brand names of clothing may look virtually identical. Labeling on the outside, rather than the inside, of a garment is an obvious way of advertising your status to those around you.

A study at Michigan State University considered "the degree to which clothing is used as a guide in identifying the role and status of unknown persons" and "the various shades of meaning attached to clothing in particular social situations" (Rosencranz 1962, p. 18). The method used involved a modification of the Thematic Apperception Test in which subjects were presented with seven drawings, each of which contained incongruities between (1) clothing and age, sex, or build, (2) clothing of two characters in the same drawing, and/or (3) clothing and the drawing's background. When asked to create stories about each of these pictures, and later asked to explain why they gave the stories they did, respondents frequently referred to the incongruities noted.

Characters in the pictures who were dressed more formally than others were accorded a higher status, while other inappropriately attired individuals were viewed as being of a lower status. Dressing in a manner that was foreign to U.S. culture or considered inappropriate for the gender of the person resulted in a kind of negative sanction. A man dressed in a skirt in one of the pictures, for example, was described as being "dressed like a foreigner" or in particular, "a Chinaman."

Region as a Basis for Status:
The Case of Appalachia

Along with physical appearance and clothing, different parts of the country also conjure up different perceptions and evaluations. There are stereotypes and lifestyles, for example, that have been attributed to Californians, New Englanders, the "Old South," the "New South," midwesterners, and Appalachians. Regions can be and have been the basis for status grouping and ranking, even though the cultural, social, and sometimes even topographical homogeneity attributed to these set-apart places is usually mythical rather than factual. Nevertheless, some of these regions, perhaps most notably Appalachia, have been identified as constituting not only a separate subculture, but a status group that has been consciously ranked as being low in prestige. Let us explore Appalachia as an example of status based on region.

A discussion of Appalachia helps us in at least two ways. First, it allows us to examine economic inequality within a region sometimes described as a colony for more powerful economic interests. Second, it allows us to examine the cultural mystique and folklore associated with a section of the country that has often been thought to be out of touch with the mainstream of U.S. society and its culture. Associated in the public mind with "mountain men," the region has been portrayed as being inaccessible and isolated. As such, it has been viewed in the popular press and mind as constituting a separate and often homogenous culture. It is principally the latter that we

wish to investigate in this section. Does Appalachia constitute a separate subculture and, if so, how is it viewed in terms of social status? What is the origin of this subculture, and how is it linked with the economic inequality that prevails in the region?

As a strip in the eastern part of the United States, the Appalachian mountain area is bounded on the east by the Blue Ridge Mountains and on the west, for the most part, by the Allegheny-Cumberland Plateau. Between these lies the Appalachian Valley. Appalachia covers an area involving parts of thirteen states, bordered on the north by southern New York state; on the south by parts of Mississippi, Alabama, and Georgia; on the west by the eastern sections of Kentucky and Tennessee; and on the east by the western portions of Pennsylvania, Virginia, and the Carolinas. It includes all of West Virginia. Most of the discussion of Appalachia as a subculture, however, is based on material from southern Appalachia (north Georgia, Alabama, North and South Carolina, and parts of Tennessee and Virginia), while discussions of the coal industry focus on central Appalachia (Kentucky, West Virginia, southwestern Virginia and eastern Tennessee). Northern Appalachia is composed of parts of New York, Pennsylvania, Maryland, Ohio, and West Virginia. In their 1985 report, the Appalachian Regional Commission (1985) argued that "Appalachia existed for generations as a region apart, isolated physically and culturally by its impenetrable mountains" (p. 7).

The "Development" of Appalachia   Many of the settlers to the region were farmers from various ethnic backgrounds who had helped develop an agricultural economy there. But in the latter part of the nineteenth century and into early twentieth century, specifically during the period 1880–1930, some major economic changes were occurring in the region. As has occurred in many developing countries, the economic development of the region has always been uneven, and the contrast between rural Appalachia and its industrial areas can be dramatic (Carawan 1975, p. ix). Outside timber, mining, and manufacturing interests were gaining increasing access to and ownership of much of the land and other natural resources in the region. Coal was becoming a major industry, and without understanding all the implications many residents "sold their land and/or mineral rights for pennies an acre to 'outsiders.'. . . Appalachians became not the entrepreneurs but the labourers" (Appalachian Regional Commission 1985, p. 8). The "patterns of corporate exploitation were established that continue to dominate the resource utilization today" (Beaver 1984, p. 82). John Tiller, a former miner from Trammel, Virginia, has described Appalachia as a colony: "It has all the earmarks—the absentee landlords; nothing built of permanence. You can look at the whole area—the poor roads, the poor schools, the lack of facilities—and realize that there's no solutions" (Carawan 1975, p. 26). Hundreds of thousands of acres have been stripped for their lumber and coal resources by absentee owners, individuals who live outside the region but take its resources.

Thus, the region is wealthy in resources, but the native people have been relatively poor. During the late 1950s and early 1960s, about one-third of the families in the area lived below the official poverty level, unemployment was about 40 percent higher than in the rest of the nation, and net migration from the region was over 2,000,000 (Appalachian Regional Commission 1985, p. 13). In many parts of Appalachia, the percentage of persons who had graduated from high school was much lower than the national average, and one in four rural dwellings were considered to have fundamental structural weaknesses. The 1960 presidential election brought many of these problems into the public eye for the first time. In the early 1980s, in many Appalachian counties, less than one-third of the people had a high-school education. Almost as many (30 percent) of all adults in the *entire* region and almost half of the unemployed were functionally illiterate (Darling 1984).

Today, resource ownership in Appalachia is very concentrated. Around 1980, over half of the land was owned by 1 percent of local residents working together with absentee owners, govern-

ment, and corporations. This means that 99 percent of the local people control less than half of the land. Some of the largest owners are multinational corporations. While the 1970s brought some economic growth to the region, the early 1980s brought renewed economic decline fueled by worldwide recession and foreign competition. Coal, oil, electricity, and steel industries all suffered setbacks. Between 1980 and 1983, Appalachia lost more than 500,000 jobs (Appalachian Regional Commission 1985, p. 77). Gaventa (1980) argues that the 1980s brought an intensified attempt to "recolonize" Appalachia, because of the belief in some circles that if we draw our energy resources from within our own country, we will be less dependent upon foreign sources for coal and other minerals. As we will see in a later chapter, the whole process of economic dependence and exploitation of Appalachia fits a general Marxian explanation of the dynamics of economic inequality.

The events and conditions just noted brought attention to the region, and media presentations helped form the images and conclusions outsiders developed about Appalachia. They even helped shape the perceptions of Appalachians about their region. Since the turn of the century, when major changes in the economy and ownership had already begun, the image portrayed of Appalachian culture has been one of stagnation and backwardness attributed in large part to the supposed physical isolation of the region.

But in his recent study of a central Appalachian valley, Gaventa (1980, 1984) argues that the proliferation of the cultural model of Appalachia as being backward, uncivilized, and so on was a creation that helped justify the exploitation (development) of that region by outside interests. The presence of excess investment capital and an ideology that encouraged development of "undeveloped" rural areas led to the purchase and control of Appalachian property by outside investors. Part of the justification of this easy appropriation of resources was couched in the specious argument that the inhabitants were quiescent and backward simpletons. Gaventa points out that the image of Appalachians was molded to fit and justify the exploitation that occurred. While those in his study were not ostensibly aggressive in defending themselves against the domination of outside financial interests, Gaventa demonstrates that this reaction suggesting passiveness and apathy is really a rational response to their condition of powerlessness. Repeated defeats, the greater resource power of outside forces, the construction of various barriers, and the perpetuation of myths and stereotypes about the Appalachian people all have conspired to create less rebellion, even though extensive grievances and discontent on a variety of issues lie just below the surface.

The Subculture of Appalachia Following the Civil War, Appalachia was "discovered" by journalists and others who viewed it as an off-beat place with unfamiliar vegetation inhabited by a people with odd customs. As one popular article of the day described it, Appalachia was "A Strange Land and Peculiar People" (cited in Beaver 1984, p. 86). A variety of values have been associated with Appalachians, many of them negative in nature. "The Appalachian is fatalistic," writes Lewis (1974), "while mainstream Americans believe they can control their environment and their lives. The Appalachian is impulsive, personalistic and individualistic while mainstream Americans are rational, organized, can handle impersonal role relationships and have a social consciousness" (p. 222). Individualism, a love of and dependence upon family and an attachment to home, a belief in personal liberty and independence, fatalism and resignation, a belief in the essential equality of all individuals, a disdain for and suspicion of formal education, the centrality of personal religion all have been characteristics frequently associated with Appalachians (cf., e.g., Erikson 1976; Batteau 1984; Hannum 1969; Turner 1986; Vogeler 1975).

As was indicated earlier in this chapter, the social status attributed to another person or group is derived through a subjective process, one in which the group is portrayed as having a specific lifestyle and set of beliefs that distinguish it from surrounding groups. In most groups, there is more heterogeneity than is suspected by outsid-

ers, but it is the latter's perceptions, whether based on fact or not, that govern their reaction to the group. The fact is that despite the stereotypical view often taken of it, Appalachia is a region with varied resources, differentiated geography, and people with varied ethnic backgrounds.

Alongside the negative image of Appalachia as a stagnant and backward region, another more patronizing image exists. As mentioned earlier, the exploitation of resources by outside interests has caused some commentators to view the area's relationship with the outside as a case of internal colonialism in which the dominant outside group exploits and denigrates the native population and its land (Walls 1978; Lewis and Knipe 1978). This interpretation has helped foster the view of Appalachia as an area of great natural beauty being despoiled by greedy economic interests. Unsullied nature and the rugged individualism of "mountain men" are integral components of this perspective of Appalachia as an innocent victim (Batteau 1984). In this view, the mountains take on a mystical, romantic quality.

Many memoirs and remembrances by individual Appalachians do reveal a continued attachment, a "sense of place," to Appalachia. Mike Smathers, born in Big Lick, Tennessee, says unequivocally that "Appalachia is my land. . . . My roots go deep in the mountains. . . . Mountain people have valued simple adequacy rather than super abundance, overconsumption, and waste. They have a capacity to honor friendship and neighborliness above influence and power. They have a tendency to adapt rather than to manipulate" (Carawan 1975, p. 13). Jean Ritchie, from Viper, Kentucky, proclaims: "I celebrate the fact that this Appalachia has a hold on me. Wherever I go, I'm of these hills. That little cabin at the head of the holler has been in the back of my mind, like an anchor with a long rope . . . here is where I belong" (ibid., p. 77). "Mountain people leave, but some come back," writes Alberta Hannum who has written extensively on the Appalachian Highlands. "They come back, those with their roots deep in these changing mountains that go further than the eye can reach, further than the accounting of time. And others come back who chanced upon the mountains at some magic time or place that took hold on their thoughts and on their lives" (Hannum 1969, p. 204). These are warm memories and attachments, but they also feed the image, not always romantic, of Appalachians as "a separate people," a distinct "race," as Hannum calls them.

A problem with such subcultural descriptions, especially of an area that has been said to be socially, culturally, and physically shut off from the rest of the country, is that they tend to become caricatures over time, ignoring internal differences within the region and changes that have occurred in its relationship with other parts of the world. These subcultural characteristics also have been interpreted as the principal causes for the unusually high rates of poverty found in Appalachia. This constitutes a form of "blaming the victim," however, since evidence suggests that it has not been primarily subcultural values or isolation but rather the nature of a region's ties to the outside that have exacerbated and perpetuated the high poverty rate. Numerous scholars, many from the region, have labeled Appalachia as a rich land with poor people, poor because their resources have been exploited by outsiders (cf., e.g., Eller 1982; Gaventa 1980; Caudill 1962).

Even though Appalachia is a heterogeneous area, where many lead urban and middle-class lives, few have questioned the traditional stereotype associated with the Appalachian. Too often, images of an Appalachian character (1) are derived primarily from descriptions of adult *males,* (2) ignore the fact that many of the characteristics are shared by other Americans, and (3) minimize or deny the inconsistencies and differences found within Appalachian culture (Erikson 1976, pp. 75–8). With respect to the latter, for example, the black ethnographer William Turner (1986) suggests that many Appalachian blacks do not share the values and beliefs of their white neighbors. Rather than being fatalistic, traditional, and so forth, they are attracted to materialism and individual achievement and do not identify psychologically as strongly with the land and the region as white Appalachians do.

Despite the fact that changes have occurred

in the region, many traditional values have become weakened, and many Appalachians are becoming integrated culturally and socially into the wider society, stereotypes still abound. Old images die hard deaths. Berger has cautioned us that "myths are potent enough to survive evidence; they are not disarmed by understanding. Once myths gain currency . . . they become real and function as self-fulfilling prophecies" (cited in Billings 1974, p. 322).

The image of Appalachia as being composed of backward, fundamentalistic, individualistic mountaineers has lowered the status-prestige of this region for most Americans. In the late 1960s, "in some popular and scholarly circles Appalachia was second only to Black America as a repository for social pathos" (Turner 1986, p. 279). Appalachia occupies "the lowest rung in [our] socio-economic ladder" (Coreil and Marshall 1982). Data recently collected in interviews with long-term rural Kentuckians suggest that a large majority of them feel that Appalachians are given "much less respect than other Americans." Many also believe that Appalachians experience greater occupational, educational, legal, and income inequality than other Americans. They also are inclined to view the inequality involving Appalachians as being separate from racial and class inequality, suggesting that they identify themselves as a separate group when it comes to the problems of inequality (Smith and Byland 1985).

How do the elements of this discussion of Appalachia relate to our earlier conclusion that status can be based upon region? Let us review the core factors that determine status and status-group ranking. We noted that status honor/prestige is subjectively given by a community to another person or group. This perception, in turn, depends upon the characteristics attributed to the person or group and on how valued these characteristics are in mainstream culture. Status honor can be based on (1) lifestyle, (2) extent of empirical/rational formal education, (3) family genealogy, and/or (4) occupation, according to Weber. We also said that a distinct lifestyle and isolation from outsiders characterize status groups. Weber further argued that individuals in similar status

Even today Americans adhere to stereotypes that define Appalachians as backward and superstitious, holding them in lower regard than most other Americans.

situations tend to form cohesive communities. This cohesiveness is reaffirmed and maintained through intimate associations among themselves and by their wariness of and distance from outsiders. Status groups also are characterized by some uniqueness in their acquisitions; that is, their possessions may be exclusively associated with members of the group. Finally, higher status groups try to avoid contaminating contact with lower status groups, since they represent "impure" qualities, and in the extreme case, may be considered pariah groups.

The evidence we have reviewed strongly suggests that most Americans have a fairly coherent conception of Appalachians as a group and that they perceive them as having distinctive values and behaviors. Moreover, this "subculture" is more often than not portrayed in negative terms; that is, it is attributed with low status-honor. As Bensman puts it, all status communities make claims for prestige, but "the validation of that claim, however, is based less on the claim itself than on the ability and willingness of others to experience and evaluate favorably the activities, characteristics, and institutions buttressing the claim" (Bensman 1972, p. 126). As we pointed

out earlier, status honor/prestige is subjectively and willingly given.

This subculture of Appalachians is thought to have a unique lifestyle, according to the traditional conception, that includes a denigration of formal education, a genealogy composed of "common folk," and traditional occupations that are usually blue-collar or agricultural in nature. None of these characteristics enhances the status-honor accorded Appalachians. The "mountain people" frequently have been portrayed as being physically, socially, and culturally isolated from the outside world, and conversely, as having close relationships among themselves, especially within families. The qualities assessed as different by the standards of the dominant culture help justify the ridicule and romanticism rained upon mountaineers and "hillbillies" by outside urbanites. In correspondence with the romantic view of mountain culture, some of the artifacts associated with this culture, such as musical styles and instruments, have been viewed as being unique and worthy of preservation, especially by intellectual outsiders. In sum, what exists in Appalachia is an interesting confluence of economic, colony, and status factors that must be understood within their historical context. However, our traditional image of Appalachians, while not consistent with much empirical evidence, has encouraged us to label Appalachians as a separate status group having low prestige.

Race and Gender as Bases for Status

There is no question that individuals of different races and genders are ranked unequally in U.S. society. As mentioned earlier, Weber suggested that ethnicity is one basis upon which status is determined. Both blacks and women have been thought of as separate status groups, and in some cases, even separate castes. Do blacks and women constitute status groups that are distinct from those of whites and males? Does it make sense to view them as being members of a caste? Does this model help us to understand and explain the situation of these groups better than other models? While we will reserve a fuller discussion of this matter for the next chapter, we should briefly address this general issue since we are dealing with the various bases of status in this chapter.

Weber argued that, ultimately, the caste system is based upon ethnicity, and that is also legally sanctioned. Movement between castes is restricted, endogamy is expected, and traditional occupations are associated with each caste. On the surface at least, there would appear to be a parallel between this description and a system in which ranking is based either on sex or race, both ascriptive characteristics. Some U.S. laws, in the past especially, have restricted areas or behaviors on the basis of sex and race, race-mixing has been frowned upon, and both blacks and women are found disproportionately in particular kinds of occupations. Our attitudes toward blacks can be partially understood in terms of the purity/impurity dimension associated with caste systems. The concerns for "social distance," racial purity as typified in extreme form by white supremacist groups, and various forms of segregation suggest that purity/impurity is a fundamental dimension of races as status groups.

While these comments on purity do not apply directly to an understanding of women in U.S. society, it is clear that the difficulty of mobility, assumptions about the basic characteristics of women, and associating these with specific types of skills are relevant to explaining the socioeconomic predicament of women today. Clearly, the histories of women and blacks in the United States have been different, and thus it would be a mistake to assume that the same model can be used in the same manner to understand both. Blacks, for example, have never been expected to refrain from manual work or even participation in the labor market, whereas the nineteenth-century "cult of true womanhood" expected this of middle-class, "respectable" women. We will pursue similarities and differences between these groups in the next chapter.

SUMMARY

This chapter has addressed the topic of social status, a form of inequality that is analytically separate from economic inequality, even though it is frequently based on an individual's economic resources. In their extreme form, status groups can be legally sanctioned and exclusive. The caste system of India approximates such a situation. Status also can be based on occupation, education, lifestyle, physical appearance, region, race, and gender. The prestige of our occupation, the kind of education we receive, the lifestyles we pursue, and the way we appear in public are each badges of status. They affect how others perceive us and how they treat us. Veblen was acutely aware of the invidious comparisons that groups made with each other in the early 1900s, and these continue today. Even the labels attached to various regions of the country suggest that they have implications for social status. We examined Appalachia in depth because differences in economic and political power and social status all converge in this region. By analyzing it, one can see several forms of inequality at work all at once. Because race and gender as bases of status are significantly related to many life chances, inequality based on these dimensions needs to be discussed in greater detail.

CHAPTER 4

RACE AND SEX INEQUALITY

The social problems of urban life in the United States are, in large measure, the problems of racial inequality.
— William Julius Wilson

I believe that not only must the hierarchical nature of the division of labor between the sexes be eliminated, but the very division of labor between the sexes itself must be eliminated if women are to attain equal social status with men and if women and men are to attain the full development of their human potential.
— Heidi I. Hartmann

Race and sex are ascribed statuses in the sense that people have no control over whether they are black or white, male or female. However, while each is a biological condition, race and sex also are given particular meaning within the context of a culture's values and beliefs, which in turn may be based upon dominant economic and political arrangements. What is immediately significant about race and sex, therefore, are not the biological differences in themselves, but the fact that these biological characteristics are socially defined and have meanings attached to them. These interpretations often result in races and sexes being hierarchically arranged in society. An indepth discussion of explanations of race and sex inequality is pursued in Chapter 10. In this chapter, we will be surveying the forms and extent of race and sex inequality in U.S. society, some of the conditions that contribute to this inequality, and the extent to which gender and race inequalities interact with each other and with class in-

equalities. First, we turn to a brief overview of the historical condition of women in society.

THE STATUS OF WOMEN THROUGH HISTORY

While the status of women traditionally has been linked to their centrality in the family, women have always participated in the economies of countries. This has certainly been the case in *hunting and gathering* societies, which have been among the most egalitarian, in part because of (1) the lack of a large surplus, (2) the nomadic nature of life, (3) the minimal presence of private property, and (4) the absence of distinct specialized institutions. Structured classes are not present even though there are differences in prestige based on age, sex, and personal skills. In these societies, the division of labor is organized on the basis of age and sex. While women are not primarily engaged in the more honorific adventure of hunting, they often have been responsible for foraging. More often than not, the economic activities of women contribute more to the daily diet than the animals brought in by hunters. Hunting by males, however, generally carries greater prestige because (1) it involves an element of challenge and excitement, (2) meat has more value than vegetables, and (3) it can be shared with the entire group rather than just the immediate family. The risk involved in hunting, the lower mobility of women due to reproductive and nursing obligations, and differences in physical strength are possible reasons for the domination of hunting activities by men.

In hunting and gathering societies, the degree of inequality between the sexes is much less than is found, for example, in agricultural societies. Generally, where women contribute heavily to the economy, there is less inequality between the sexes, and in hunting and gathering societies, gathering has provided the bulk of the diet in the majority of cases. Among the !Kung in Africa, for example, women are very important economically, and there is a great degree of equality between the sexes (Sanderson 1988). In some societies of this type, however, males are still distinctly higher in prestige and power. In several Australian groups, the Tiwi, for example, men are dominant and use their daughters through a betrothal system to establish economic and political ties. A greater number of wives is an economic asset because it means not only more food but a wider network of support. However, even here, women traditionally contribute more food than men because of their gathering activities (Hart and Pilling 1966).

In *horticultural* societies, the status of women varies with the form of kinship descent and the specific society in question. In societies where lineage is traced through the female line and land is owned matrilineally, women tend to have higher status than in societies where lineage and ownership are linked with males (Martin and Voorhees 1975). Among the Yanomamo, on the other hand, which is a distinctly masculine soci-

ety but one that relies heavily upon garden-grown crops, women are held in low esteem. Female children are given household chores before males are, and women have little prestige and power. Female children are promised to others in marriage at an early age, with little consideration of their own wishes. Once married, women are expected to cater to the desires of their husbands, and a husband can beat his wife ferociously for any infraction, however minor (Chagnon 1977). In stark contrast, Iroquois women held positions of high prestige within their society (Brown 1975).

While the status of women within horticultural societies is mixed, it is low in *agrarian* societies. The invention of the plow, argues Joan Huber, affected gender stratification because (1) wherever it was introduced it was controlled by men, (2) it made land the primary source of wealth, and (3) it made life more sedentary than in horticultural societies where periodic moving was mandatory because of soil depletion. The sedentary nature of life meant that the number of potential inheritors of land had to be controlled, and this translated into greater constraints on the behavior of women (Huber 1989). As men gained greater control over production of food, the status of women fell, and a clearer distinction developed between the familial and economic spheres, or between the domestic (inside) and public (outside) areas of life. The outside life, which entails meaningful involvement and influence in religious, economic, political, and educational institutions, was male dominated, while the more intimate "inside" sphere was more fully the province of women (Martin and Voorhees 1975). To maintain this fundamental separation, women's behavior was strictly limited, and social and ideological beliefs supported appropriate roles for each of the sexes.

In our own agricultural pre-industrial colonial society, women were directly involved in a variety of ways in production. On the one hand, their work contributed significantly to the prosperity of the society, but on the other hand, the nature of the labor was more often than not based on gender (Chafe 1977; Blau 1978; Marshall and Paulin 1987). The cultural norms of that time, as well as for following periods, dictated that first and foremost women should be good wives and mothers; but, in fact, women were involved in the economy and often had difficult lives. They were involved in raising stock, weaving, gardening, and even the running of businesses. While some women took over for their deceased or disabled husbands, most of the unmarried and widowed women went on the market as hired domestic workers (Marshall and Paulin 1987).

While there is some debate about the actual diversity of employment undertaken by women during this period, they made valuable contributions to the local economies, but were deprived of many of the political-legal, economic, and personal rights accorded men. They were attached to their families in a literal way, dependent upon and subservient to their husbands (Matthaei 1982). The woman's identity was defined by her relationship to her husband and children. Moreover, wife beating was fairly common at this time. "The husband had the right to chastise his wife physically, and he had exclusive rights to any property she might have owned as a single woman, to her dower, and to any wages and property that might come to her while she was his wife. In short, like slave or servant women, married women whether rich or poor were legal non-entities" (Foner 1979, p. 11). Thus, the idealized life of the female as someone removed from the harsh realities of economic life was strongly inconsistent with the actual circumstances of her life. As Chafe (1977) puts it, "in colonial America, prescriptive norms about women appeared to exist more as part of society's rituals than as a major force dictating people's daily lives" (p. 21).

Through their economic activities, women helped to contribute to the development of the first significant *industrial* organizations in the United States. The first textile factories, built around 1800 in Rhode Island and Massachusetts, recruited unmarried women from the farms of New England. Land was still plentiful and as a result male laborers were in short supply. Reli-

ance had to be placed upon the recruitment of women and children for work in these factories (Blau 1978). At the same time, however, the proper place for women was believed to be with their families. Francis Cabot Lowell, however, conceived of a way to attract young unmarried women from the family farms in a manner that was compatible with the "moral imperative" that the woman belongs with home and family. In his new mills, he offered supervised boarding houses with strict rules and promised that the skills, discipline, and wages earned would ultimately encourage the development of a "proper" woman and at the same time help the family (Kessler-Harris 1989). The factory in Lowell, Massachusetts, among the most famous of the early ones, was advertised as a place where young, unmarried women could learn good working habits and the qualities necessary to make them valuable wives and mothers. It provided boarding houses nearby where unmarried female employees were required to live.

Despite the promises of a proper place to work, conditions at these early factories left much to be desired. Even though Lowell was considered an advanced factory for its time, women worked an average of thirteen hours a day, seventy-three hours a week, including eight on Saturday (Dublin 1979). Working conditions were stifling. Windows in the plant were nailed shut and the air was periodically sprayed with water to keep it humid enough so that the cotton threads would not break. The vapors from whale-oil lamps and floating lint made the air in the shop quite oppressive (Eisler 1977). The Lowell Corporation paid women mill workers $1.85 to $3.00 per week, depending on abilities, from which $1.25 was deducted for board. Female workers were paid only half of what men were paid, even though they made up approximately 75 percent of the workers at Lowell (Eisler 1977). Wages in the Maryland textile mills in 1831 were also lower for women, averaging $1.91 per week compared to $3.87 for men. In neighboring Virginia, male operatives got $2.73 per week and women $1.58 (Marshall and Paulin 1987).

Jobs in these early plants were also sex segregated. While men held all supervisory positions as well as jobs in the millyard, watch force, and repair shop, women were restricted to particular jobs operating equipment such as the looms and dressing machines. The immediate reasons given for this segregation concerned differences in the skills developed and monopolized by men and women over the years, perceived physical strength and dangers associated with various jobs, and the general cultural values prescribing particular roles for men and women (Dublin 1979). Men also were concerned about the entrance of women into the labor market because they felt that it would have a depressing effect on their wages. They fought to keep women out of the craft unions that later developed. Women held strikes in the 1830s and 1840s to protest reductions in wages, speed-ups in work pace, and working hours (Dublin 1979).

While most of the early women workers were native born and Protestant, by the middle of the nineteenth century a significant proportion of these workers were immigrants, many French Canadian and Irish. Later, a greater number of immigrants from Central and Eastern Europe moved into the labor force. During this period, single, native-born, educated women were becoming less and less likely to work in the factories and were increasingly expected to behave in a manner befitting "ladies" (cf. Chafe 1977; Fox and Hesse-Biber 1984). Class distinctions among women were becoming more distinct, even as the factories solidified the separation between home and economy by taking over many of the tasks, for example, making cloth, shoes, and so on, that formerly had been carried out in the home. Black women had been and increasingly became involved in agricultural and domestic labor.

In 1900, just over 20 percent (5,000,000) of all U.S. women fifteen years of age or older were employed as "breadwinners," but only 15 percent of native white females were, compared to 43 percent of black females and 25 percent of white females with at least one foreign-born parent (U.S. Dept. of Commerce and Labor 1911, p. 262). Many young women ten to fifteen years of age also worked outside the home. In 1900, al-most 6 percent of white, native-born females did so, compared to over 30 percent of nonwhite females ten to fifteen years old (ibid., pp. 256–259). From the end of the Civil War, the percentage of females in the work force had increased (U.S. Dept. of Labor 1947, p. 34).

At the turn of the twentieth century, women made up a disproportionate number of workers in several occupations. For example, in 1900 they constituted 80 to 90 percent of all boarding and lodging-house keepers, servants, waiters, and paper box makers and over 90 percent of all housekeepers and stewards, nurses and midwives, dress makers, milliners, and seamstresses. Men, on the other hand, dominated agricultural, common labor, bookkeeping, clerk/copyist, watch and shoemaker, printer, dye works, and photography positions (U.S. Census Office 1900, Plate 90). Perhaps surprisingly, women composed over 70 percent of the teachers and professors in colleges and over 50 percent of teachers of music, while men made up the majority of artists and teachers of art (ibid.). Black females, however, were more likely to be wage earners than either native- or foreign-born white females.

Those who were "native white of native parents" dominated the higher status professions, with over 50 percent of college teachers and clergy and about 75 percent of lawyers and physicians coming from this group. In contrast, they made up less than 30 percent of those in servant, tailoring, laundering, and textile mill working positions (ibid., Plate 88).

PRESENT OCCUPATIONAL AND ECONOMIC CONDITIONS FOR WOMEN

The preceding discussion indicates that differences in occupations and earnings for men and women are not recent phenomena. Historically, men and women have performed different jobs, have had different levels of authority, and have been paid differently. The treatment in the following sections examines occupational and economic conditions for women today and the extent to which unequal situations still exist in the United States. The discussion begins with an analysis of occupational differences between the sexes and then moves to a look at earnings and income discrepancies.

Occupation and Sex

In the last several decades, the percentage of women in the civilian labor force has increased dramatically, while the percentage of men twenty years of age and over in the labor force has actually decreased. In 1948, for example, about one-third of women in this age group participated compared to 42 percent in 1968 and 57 percent in 1988. This compares to 89, 83, and 78 percent for men in the same years, respectively (U.S. Dept. of Labor, June 1985, Table 5; U.S. Dept. of Labor, March 1989, p. 65). Looking back even further to the late nineteenth century, we find that only about 13 percent of women ten years of age or older were gainful workers, and this rate increased steadily in the following decades (U.S. Dept. of Labor 1947, p. 34). While women tend to work fewer hours each week than men, indications are that their participation will continue to increase to the year 2000, while men's participation will decline further (Shank 1988).

Despite this rise in labor-force participation by women, occupational distinctions between the sexes remain within broad occupational groupings, and more deeply, within more narrowly defined positions within specific organizations. The segregation becomes clearer as one moves from examining general to specific categories in concrete contexts. The analysis of broad occupational categories suggests some recent decline in overall sex segregation, but most of it has been in middle-level white-collar rather than in blue-collar positions, and the major declines have been restricted to a few occupations (Beller 1984). Much of this trend has been due to the decline of some traditionally male occupations in the labor force, such as agricultural, unskilled, and self-employment occupations (Blau and Ferber 1986). Table 4.1 presents current information on the distribution of men and women over broad occupational categories. In general, it shows that the female labor force is especially concentrated in technical, sales, administrative support, managerial-professional, and service occupations, while men are found most often in the broad categories of managerial-professional, operators-fabricators-laborers, precision production-craft, and technical-sales-support occupations. But even among these broad areas, men are more spread out than women (U.S. Dept. of Labor, January 1991, p. 184).

Moreover, the extent of segregation increases as the occupational categories become more detailed. Beller's study using census survey data suggests that while segregation within 262 occupations declined during the 1970s, most of it was due to broad changes in the occupational structure. For example, the numbers of phone operators, servers, delivery and route workers, child-care workers, maids/servants, and private household workers have declined since 1960, and these are occupations in which women have been overrepresented. But while some others also experienced declines in segregation, for example, accountants and elementary school teachers, still others showed an increase in occupational segregation, especially those which traditionally have been dominated by women, for example, registered nurses, bank tellers, and miscellaneous clerical workers (Beller 1984, pp. 11–16).

Table 4.2 presents those occupational categories in which employed civilian women sixteen years of age or older are most and least represented. As the table indicates, women occupy virtually all nursing, data entry, secretarial, receptionist, bookkeeping, child-care, and precision clothing positions. On the other hand, they comprise less than 5 percent of those employed in fire fighting, automobile mechanics, construction trades, tool and die/cabinet making, plant operating, heavy truck and equipment operation, and electrician occupations. These comprise a significant number of the skilled trades and crafts professions, which historically have been male dominated. Parcel and Mueller's recent study suggests that "male" and "female" occupations are differentiated on the basis of "physical activity" and

TABLE 4.1 Percent Distribution of Employed Civilians Aged Sixteen and Over, by Sex: 1990 Annual Average

OCCUPATION	MEN	WOMEN
Managerial and professional specialty	25.8	26.2
Executive, administrative, managerial	13.8	11.1
Professional specialty	12.0	15.1
Technical, sales, and adm. support	20.1	44.4
Technicians and related support	3.0	3.5
Sales occupations	11.2	13.1
Adm. support, including clerical	5.9	27.8
Service occupations	9.8	17.7
Private household	—	1.4
Protective service	2.6	0.5
Service, exc. private and protective	7.1	15.8
Precision production, craft, and repair	19.4	2.2
Operators, fabricators, and laborers	20.6	8.5
machine operators, assemblers, inspectors	7.5	6.0
transportation and material-moving occs.	6.8	.8
handlers, equip. cleaners, helpers, laborers	6.2	1.6
Farming, forestry, and fishing	4.4	1.0
Total Percent	100.0	100.0

Source: Bureau of Labor Statistics, U.S. Dept. of Labor, *Employment and Earnings,* January 1991, Table 21, p. 184.

"interpersonal" criteria (Parcel and Mueller 1983). The traditionally male crafts and trades occupations certainly involve the kind of physical labor associated with being male in the United States, and the interpersonal skills associated with being a secretary, receptionist, or phone operator fit the characteristics that are perceived as being dominant in women.

The occupational profiles are quite similar to those that existed in earlier years. In 1940, almost all of the servants, stenographers/secretaries, housekeepers, and nurses were women, and they comprised over half of the teachers (not elsewhere classified), apparel and accessories operators, waitresses, and bookkeepers. As far back as 1870, women dominated in servant, clothing, certain kinds of teaching, and nursing occupations (cf., U.S. Dept. of Labor 1947, p. 52). One of the implications of the presence of sex segregation is that occupants of "female" positions, whether they are males or females, earn less than their counterparts in positions dominated by males. Jobs of "comparable worth" do not have equivalent earnings because of the sex compositions (England and Farkas 1986; Treiman et al. 1984).

When we look still closer at specific occupations in specific organizations in the private sector, occupational segregation becomes even clearer. Not only are women spread among fewer occupations than men, but within the same occupation, they are employed in different kinds of organizations and economic sectors, tend to have less authority in the same occupation and have different job titles, and make less money in their jobs than men do. Fewer than 25 percent of women workers are in manufacturing firms employing over fifty persons, while about 50 percent of those in nonmanufacturing firms work in organizations having fewer than fifty employees (Bielby and Baron 1984). Part of this overrepresentation in small firms is due to the fact that

TABLE 4.2 Selected Occupations in Which Females Compose More than 90 Percent or Less Than 10 Percent of the Labor Force: 1979 and 1986

OCCUPATION*	1979	1986
Secretaries	98.8	99.2
Typists	97.0	95.7
Receptionists	96.2	97.5
Licensed practical nurses	95.8	98.9
Registered nurses	94.6	92.7
Textile sewing machine oper.	92.9	90.8
Data-entry keyers	92.1	91.1
Bank tellers	91.5	91.7
Telephone operators	90.8	97.7
Child-care wkrs., e.p.h.**	88.9	97.7
Bookkeeping, accounting, & auditing clerks	88.1	93.0
Payroll and time-keeping clerks	82.0	90.0
Misc. material moving equip. operators	15.6	9.3
Painting and paint spraying machine oper.	13.2	8.6
Butchers and meat cutters	9.5	9.2
Industrial engineers	8.8	15.8
Postal mail carriers	8.3	16.7
Farmers, except horticultural	7.1	8.6
Garage & service-station related occupations	6.3	5.5
Police/detectives, public services	4.9	6.8
Welders and cutters	4.9	3.0
Industrial truck & tractor equip. oper.	4.4	4.4
Electrical/electronic engineers	4.4	9.4
Furnace, kiln, and oven oper., except food	3.9	1.0
Machinists, e.a.***	3.8	3.8
Clergy	3.8	7.4
Truck drivers, light	3.8	6.5
Painters, construction & maintenance	3.7	2.7
Supervisors, mechanics, & repairers	2.4	9.3
Construction laborers	2.0	2.5
Electricians, e.a.	1.7	0.6
Tool and die makers, e.a.	1.5	2.7
Truck drivers, heavy	1.5	1.5
Carpenters, e.a.	1.1	0.5
Plumbers, pipe-fitters, & steam-fitters, e.a.	1.0	0.3
Automotive mechanics, e.a.	0.9	0.6
Fire-fighting occupations	0.7	1.3

Source: U.S. Bureau of the Census, U.S. Dept. of Commerce, *Male-Female Differences in Work Experience, Occupation, and Earnings: 1984,* Current Population Reports, Series P-70, No. 10, August 1987, Table 11, pp. 23–26.

*Occupations with at least 100,000 full-time workers in 1979.

**Except private household.

***Except apprentices.

women are more likely to be found in the "peripheral" rather than the "core" sector of the economy. The peripheral sector is largely made up of small, less stable, local, nonunionized organizations lacking a clear career ladder, while the core consists of the larger, stable, multimarket, unionized organizations with career systems. These differences between men and women exist even when experience, education, and other factors are taken into account (Coverdill 1988). Factors that are characteristic of each of these sectors, moreover, appear to contribute to differences in unemployment rates and earnings levels between the sexes (Bibb and Form 1977; Coverdill 1988; Beck et al. 1980). Given the organizations in which they tend to find jobs, it should not be surprising that women are more likely than men to be in occupations with short career ladders and, therefore, have comparatively flat career trajectories.

Data collected from 290 organizations in California for the period 1964–1979 suggest that while a woman may occupy the same census occupation as a man, each is likely to work in a different type of organization and to have a different job title (Bielby and Baron 1986). The authors of this study contend that when using 645 detailed occupations in these institutions, over 75 percent of the incumbents would have to shift positions for equality between the sexes to exist. To have equality in job title, moreover, over 96 percent would have to change position. Most of the workers were not employed in mixed-sex categories. These results at the concrete, specific level imply that there is "a structural basis for sex difference in promotion opportunities, occupational status, and earnings trajectories" (Bielby and Baron 1986, p. 788). A recent Gallup survey indicates that, in fact, a greater proportion of women in 1987 (56%) than in 1975 (46%) feel that persons of their sex do not have the same opportunities as men, and about half feel that they do not have the same chance as a man to become a corporate executive even if they have equality ability. But the same poll shows that a higher proportion of both men and women in 1987 would prefer to work for a male rather than a female boss when taking a new position ("Women's Perception of Job Bias Grows" 1987).

It has been found that women also tend to have different levels of authority and power than men in the same occupations (Wolf and Fligstein 1979; Parcel and Mueller 1983). Using property ownership, labor power, and supervisory authority as criteria, for example, roughly 54 percent of women compared to 40 percent of men in the labor force could be considered to be in the "working class" (Wright et al. 1982). Among full-time faculty at colleges and universities, only 12 percent of the full professors are women while 44 percent of the instructors are women. Forty percent of male faculty members are full professors compared to only 14 percent of female faculty (U.S. Dept. of Education, March 1990). This hierarchical discrepancy between the sexes even exists within those occupations in which there are large numbers of women, for example, social work and public sector positions. Female managers also are underrepresented in Fortune 500 firms (cf., Blau and Ferber 1986; Lapidus 1976). When women are tokens in certain positions within corporations, for example, their position leads to greater pressures for performance and boundary-heightening between the sexes (Kanter 1977).

Our discussion thus far has focused on jobs in the private sector of the economy. When it comes to *public*-sector jobs, occupational mobility has been greater for women, but less than it was in the 1960s and 1970s. Women have increased their share of local governmental positions, with most of these jobs being in social service and health/welfare areas, suggesting tasks and abilities that have traditionally been associated with women rather than men (Moss 1988).

How do these conditions compare with those in other countries? While in many industrial countries the labor-force participation of women has increased, the rates for women in other countries vary greatly. For example, while the participation rate for U.S. women is well over 50 percent, recent rates of Spain, Ireland, and Colombia are between 20 and 30 percent. In 1980, the participation rate for women in Egypt was 7.8 percent and just over 14 percent in Guatemala (cited in Blau and Ferber 1986, pp. 308–313). On the other hand, in the same year the rate was 76.6 percent in Thailand. With respect to occupational segregation, again there are significant differences between the sexes. In 1981, for example, women comprised 81 percent of all clerical workers in the United States, while in 1974 they constituted only 1 percent of all clerical workers in Bangladesh (Blau and Ferber 1986, p. 323). Differences in the level and natures of the economies very likely contribute to these intercountry differences. With respect to earnings, women consistently earn less than men. Treiman and Roos (1983), for example, found significant earnings differences between the sexes in nine industrial societies, and others have found that women make less than men in both socialist and capitalist countries (Cukor and Kertisi 1985, Swafford 1978). In most countries, women also do most of the domestic work, and in the United States this is true for women of all races (Cook 1987; Brewer 1988).

Accounting for Occupational Sex Segregation   What are the reasons behind the sex segregation in the occupations just discussed? Some have suggested that differences in education and skills, experience, and career aspirations may account for women moving into particular kinds of jobs, but recent evidence suggests that individual factors such as these do not fully account for differences in occupations and earnings between the sexes (e.g., Blau 1984; England et al. 1988). Sex-role socialization appears to have affected choice of occupation, but differences based on such socialization have declined in recent years. Younger women now plan for more continuous lifetime employment (England and Farkas 1986). Those who argue that sex-role socialization is an important source of sex segregation also overestimate the incompatibility of home and employment responsibilities.

One should keep in mind that the "free choice" of an occupation takes place within a structure with particular characteristics, among individuals who have been socialized into a particular set of cultural values about their "proper" role in society, and within an historical context in which women traditionally have been employed in certain kinds of positions. The choices women make about jobs and their work at home are conditioned by labor-market discrimination in the first place. This means that labor-market opportunities affect the role and amount of time spent in home labor by men and women. If women spend more time in the home than men because of fewer opportunities open to them in the market, it seems questionable at best to then argue that it is their free choice alone that determines the amount of time spent in accumulating experience and education which in turn affects their occupational positions (Blau 1984, pp. 124–125).

Among the more prominent barriers that have prevented women from obtaining more well-paying occupations are:

1. Less access to training and apprenticeship programs.
2. Appointment to perceived sex-related tasks ("light" work).
3. Nonbureaucratized, patrimonial relationships with males in authority positions.
4. Less access to information about job openings.
5. Less fully developed job and contact network.
6. Seniority systems that limit women.
7. "Protective" laws inhibiting women from pursuing certain positions and restricting the number of hours and time of day they could work.
8. Disproportionate representation of women in lower ranking or smaller industries, firms, and markets.
9. Stereotyping, discrimination, and the consequent "crowding" of women into certain kinds of positions.
10. Lack of internal mobility ladder for many "female" occupations within organizations

(i.e., "dead-end" or "flat-career" jobs) (cf. e.g., Roos and Reskin 1984).

Some factors do appear, however, to contribute to a decline in occupational sex segregation. Among these are the development of new forms of work resulting from broad economic changes and white-collar service employment of an unspecialized nature. On the other hand, it has been suggested that the large size and increased specialization in the core sector, along with the presence of a union and manual work, appear to have fostered greater sex segregation (Bielby and Baron 1984). Greater formalization—that is, increased presence of written rules, tasks, procedures, and so on—has been linked to sex segregation, but also to the greater hiring of women. In a review of research on the kinds of organizations that hire women and blacks, Szafran (1982) concludes that greater formalization, centralization of decision making, and a large number of secondary occupations in an organization lead to a greater proportion of women being hired.

Earnings and Sex

As in occupational distribution, we have indicated that there are also significant earnings differences between men and women. Women, especially nonwhite women, have become less economically dependent on their husbands in the last forty years but they still make less money than men (Sorensen and McLanahan 1987). Table 4.3 shows the median weekly earnings for

TABLE 4.3 Median Weekly Earnings of Full-Time Wage and Salary Workers by Occupation and Sex, Annual Averages: 1990

OCCUPATION	MALE	FEMALE
Managerial & professional specialty	$731	$511
Executive, adm., and managerial	$742	$485
Professional specialty	$720	$534
Technical, sales, and adm. support	$496	$332
Technicians and related support	$570	$417
Sales occupations	$505	$292
Adm. support, including clerical	$440	$332
Service occupations	$320	$230
Private household	*	$171
Protective service	$477	$405
Other service	$273	$231
Precision production, craft, & repair	$488	$316
Mechanics & repairers	$477	$459
Construction trades	$480	$394
Precision production	$508	$300
Operators, fabricators, & laborers	$378	$262
Machine operators, assemblers, inspectors	$391	$260
Transportation and material moving occupations	$418	$314
Handlers, equipment cleaners, helpers & laborers	$308	$250
Farming, forestry, & fishing	$263	$216
Median weekly earnings for all full-time workers 16 and over	$485	$348

Source: Bureau of Labor Statistics, U.S. Dept. of Labor, *Employment and Earnings,* January 1991, Tables 54 and 56, pp. 221, 223–27.

*Data not given where base is less than 50,000.

full-time male and female workers (U.S. Dept. of Labor, Jan. 1991, pp. 223–227). Overall, the median earnings for full-time males at least sixteen years old in 1988 was $485 compared to $348 for females (ibid., p. 221). In each major occupational category, men make more than women. For example, the 1988 median weekly earnings for men in professional/managerial positions working full time was $731 compared to $511 for women in the same general positions. Even in the category of service occupations, men earn more than women. In 1987, the median yearly earnings for males working full time was $26,722, compared to $17,504 for females similarly employed (U.S. Bureau of the Census, Feb. 1989a, Table 27, pp. 104–105). For males with four years of college working full time, the median income was $35,201 compared the $22,412 for women in the same situation (ibid., pp. 136–137).

As indicated earlier, it is more than level of investment in one's "human capital" (e.g., experience, skills, education) that determines one's earnings. Even when these investment factors are considered, women take home less pay than men, as the preceding figures attest. Recent evidence suggests that women's experience has increased even though their earnings relative to those of men in the same kinds of occupations have not gone up proportionately (Lloyd and Niemi 1979). If the argument is true that women and blacks have less attachment to the labor force, then we should expect to find that productivity would be lower in those industries in which a large proportion of the labor force is made up of these groups. Yet this is not the case, and in fact, when other factors are controlled, productivity may actually be higher in those industries in which minorities make up a higher percentage of the labor force (Galle et al. 1985). Moreover, while fertility has an effect on a woman's employment in the *short* run, its effect is negligible in the *long* run because of the increased age of the child (children). In fact, in the *long* run, employment has a greater effect on fertility than vice versa (Cramer 1980).

Nor are differences in work effort or inter-ruptions, which can take one away from the job, significant variables in explaining sex earnings differences. It appears that women may, in fact, give *greater* work effort when at their jobs than men, even when important individual characteristics are controlled. This weakens the argument that women devote less effort to work than men because of family and other social responsibilities (Bielby and Bielby 1988). It also has been found that job characteristics, such as the degree of autonomy associated with it, have much more effect on the extent to which women (or men) get involved with their jobs than do their responsibilities at home or their socialization (Lorence 1987). But a study of over 5,000 men and women found limited effects for differential attachment to the labor force on the earnings of males and females (Corcoran and Duncan 1979). Women are more likely to have limitations on their hours and places of work and have less work experience, while both women and blacks lose more hours of work because of illness and have less on-the-job training than white men. In contrast to men, white women withdraw from work for longer periods and throughout their careers. Despite these differences between men and women in labor-force attachment and continuity of work, they do not account for much of the differences in pay between the sexes. "Even after adjusting the wage gaps between white men and white and black women and black men for differences on an extensive list of qualification and attachment measures, white men earn substantially more than did the other groups—particularly women. . . . That is, those who claim that the labor market treats workers 'fairly' in the sense that equally productive workers are paid equally are likely to be wrong" (Corcoran and Duncan 1979, p. 19).

Some studies suggest that turnover rates are not different for the sexes when relevant individuals and job characteristics are controlled (Blau and Kahn 1981; Osterman 1982). Even census data indicate clearly that differences in earnings persist even when work interruptions are taken into account. Women earn less than men even when their tenure on the current job is the same

(U.S. Bureau of the Census, August 1987, Tables D and F). In sum, differences in work interruptions and work effort do not appear to be major factors in accounting for the earnings differential between men and women.

As explained earlier, one factor that clearly affects these differences in earnings is the fact that the sexes are distributed differently among occupational categories (Treiman and Hartmann 1981, p. 135). Within those categories, women are less likely to be in positions of authority and to be given distinct kinds of tasks, factors that also influence earnings (Parcel and Mueller 1983; Wright and Perrone 1977; Kalleberg and Griffin 1980; Blau 1984). The crowding of women into specific kinds of jobs, of course, increases the supply of women and could thereby reduce the wages associated with those occupations and jobs (Bergmann, Dec. 1970; Stevenson 1978). Evidence also suggests that female-dominant jobs yield lower earnings, even when men are in those jobs. "Net of human capital, skill demands, and working conditions, those who work in occupations with more females earn less" (England et al. 1988; U.S. Bureau of the Census, August 1987). These jobs frequently have shorter career ladders which may further affect long-range earnings. Consequently, in addition to differences in characteristics between individuals, occupational, job, and organizational factors play significant roles in explaining earnings discrepancies.

RACE, ETHNICITY, AND INEQUALITY IN THE UNITED STATES: A BRIEF HISTORY

As in the case of women, the unequal position of blacks goes back to early U.S. history. Beliefs about racial inequality are not a recent phenomenon in this country. Attitudes about "color prejudice," which W.E.B. DuBois called the "problem of the twentieth century," go back to the early years of colonization and even before to English views about blacks.

Anglo-Saxon colonists' earliest contact with a visibly different group were with Native Americans, and took a different turn than those in the ancient world. (The term "Indian" arose because Columbus thought, mistakenly of course, that he had discovered India [cf. Thio 1989].) Ideas and stereotypes of the "savage" had developed in the sixteenth and seventeenth centuries and provided colonists with a framework within which to interpret Native Americans. Rather than color or racial distinction, religious and ethnocentric criteria were used initially to separate groups into superior and inferior categories. Specifically, distinctions were made between "Christians" and "heathens" and between "civilized" and "savage" (Fredrickson 1981). Clearly, the Native Americans were placed in the heathen and savage categories. Thus, distinct attitudes about this group were entrenched by the time the American Revolution occurred.

Despite these beliefs, early contact between colonists and Native Americans was frequently cooperative since both groups were interested in trade and barter. In fact, Native Americans frequently had quite a bit of power when it came to bargaining because of their prowess in the fur trade (Lurie 1982). But this cooperation was short-lived. Relationships with the British became increasingly belligerent, since the British were farmers and interested in obtaining Native American land, whereas the French were primarily traders (Garbarino 1976). The Native Americans whose economy emphasized agriculture and who were located near the coast were the first to be overwhelmed by the colonists (Lurie 1982).

In order for the colonists to spread their "civilization," land held by Native Americans had to be obtained. Many of the latter resided in villages and cultivated crops in a manner not very different from the traditional European way. But the arguments about the savage and heathen way of life of Native Americans were used as devices to justify taking over this land. Many of the arguments were similar to those used to justify black slavery (Farley 1988). The belief was that such action would rescue the earth from these savages and speed progress and Christianity (Fredrickson 1981).

In the period roughly between 1880 and 1930, over 65 percent of the 138 million acres that had been held by Native Americans moved to white ownership (Carlson and Colburn 1972). By the last decade of the nineteenth century, most Native Americans were on reservations where they were forbidden to practice their religions and their children were forced to go to boarding schools run by whites where they had to speak English (Farley 1988). Much of the policy of this period was aimed at forcing Native Americans to assimilate into the dominant white culture (Marden and Meyer 1973). Nevertheless, they were not allowed to vote since they were not considered citizens. The Constitution had never actively incorporated concerns for the rights of these groups, and it was not until the 1920s that Native Americans were granted citizenship. Even as late as the 1920s and 1930s, there was a feeling among some influential individuals that Native Americans were biologically inferior to white Anglo-Saxons (Carlson and Colburn 1972).

In the 1920s, the death rate of Native Americans was actually greater than their birth rate, and in the 1960s their life expectancy was still only forty-seven. The Termination Act of 1953 aimed at removing Native American dependency from the federal government, but it did so by cutting back and eventually eliminating needed health, educational, and other services, which proved to be a disaster for these people (Schaefer 1988). While their numbers have grown to about 1.5 million, Native Americans are considered the poorest group in the nation (Thio 1989). "American Indians have the highest infant-mortality rate, the shortest life span, the poorest housing, the poorest transportation, the lowest per-capita income, and the lowest level of education in the nation. . . . 40 percent of those on reservations lived below the poverty level. . . . No ethnic group in America has lower average income than the Indians. Suicide and alcoholism are epidemic. The rate of alcohol-related deaths among Indians is 5.6 times that of the general population (Williams 1987, p. 29). The reservation system, which is a kind of exile and permanent dependency, has only intensified these problems (ibid.).

In reviewing the history of their relationship with the dominant group, it is clear that not only (1) the nature of the initial contact between them and the latter group, but also (2) the battle over scarce and valuable resources such as land (3) early ethnocentric and prejudicial attitudes, and (4) a discrepancy in the amount of power held by each group contributed to the development of Native Americans as a minority group (O'Sullivan and Wilson 1988; Noel 1968; Barth and Noel 1972). The competition between the groups was over resources, the seizure of Native American land was justified by stereotypes and beliefs about "savages," and the greater power of the colonists served to solidify their ranking as a higher stratum.

Black/White Inequality in History

Land in early America was plentiful but greater labor power was needed to take full advantage of its resources. The absence of large numbers of willing free laborers led to attempts to obtain forced labor that could be justified on ideological or philosophical grounds. Native Americans were difficult to subdue and were a potential major threat since they were familiar with the countryside and could put up fierce resistance. On the other hand, large-scale, prolonged use of indentured white servants was unrealistic because they were freed after a period of servitude. This made the importation of nonwhite slave labor attractive. It created a large labor pool of workers who did not know the land, and it helped to elevate all whites to a higher status (Fredrickson 1981). A major difference in the initial contacts, of course, was that whereas colonists conquered Native Americans and annexed their land, in initial black/white contact, it was a case of involuntary immigration (O'Sullivan and Wilson 1988).

Moreover, this treatment of black Africans could be justified on ideological grounds. Even before the English colonized America, they had a negative view of blacks. "Blackness was synonymous with filth, foulness, and evil" (Feldstein 1972, p. 13; see also Carlson and Colburn 1972). Many of the images that had been associated with Native Americans—viewing them as savages, animalistic, and so forth—were imposed on blacks. It also has been argued that the un-Christian character and what was perceived as the uncivilized nature of blacks may have been more significant in justifying their use as slaves than the fact that they were black. But, late in the seventeenth century, there was a movement to make slaves of all those with a heathen *ancestry,* thus fostering the notion of *race* as a basis for slavery (Fredrickson 1981). The conviction that these were uncivilized heathens promoted the conclusion that blacks were basically different from the colonists. Later, especially in the first half of the nineteenth century, a systematic argument about the *racial* inferiority of blacks developed, even though there was a general feeling about the inferiority of blacks well before that time (Praeger 1987; Fredrickson 1971). Science often lent credence to such views by its insistence on the biological and genetic inequality of the races (Gossett 1963).

Given these views about blacks, it is not surprising that the early colonies passed laws banning sexual mixing and intermarriage. Children of mixed parentage were considered black (Fredrickson 1981). Even though several thousand blacks fought in the Continental Army, at the Constitutional Convention it was decided that a black man was only three-fifths of a man. Although Thomas Jefferson is associated with the belief that "all men are created equal," he "owned" 180 slaves when he died and thought of blacks as inferior to whites: "I advance it therefore as a suspicion only, that the blacks, whether originally a distinct race, or made distinct by time and circumstances, are inferior to the whites, in the endowments both of body and mind" (quoted in Feldstein 1972, pp. 52–53). Beliefs in the different endowments helped to justify slavery. After all, inhuman treatment could be tolerated if the members of a race were not considered fully human.

At the time of the first official census in 1790, the black population was approximately 757,000 of whom almost 700,000 were slaves. The black population grew to almost 4.5 million in 1860, of whom 89 percent were slaves. Between 1790 and 1860, about 90 percent of all blacks in each census were slaves. Even though the slave trade was officially outlawed in 1808, it still flourished along the long east coast of the country (U.S. Bureau of the Census, *Social and Economic Status;* Schaefer 1988). In 1790, 23 percent of all families had slaves, while in 1850 10 percent of families owned them. Most of these owned only a small number, the average being seven to nine slaves per family (U.S. Bureau of the Census, *Social and Economic Status*).

The system of inequality that developed between the races during the heyday of slavery up to the Civil War was essentially a *caste* system. Laws forbade blacks to (1) intermarry with whites, (2) vote, (3) testify against whites in legal cases, (4) own firearms, (5) use abusive language against whites, (6) own property unless permitted by a master, (7) leave the plantation without permission or disobey a curfew, (8) make a will or inherit property, and (9) have anyone teach them to read, write, or give them books (Blackwell 1985; Schaefer 1988; Fredrickson 1981; Elkins 1959; Franklin 1980).

The end of the Civil War, Emancipation, and Reconstruction did not end the misery for blacks, and in fact, appear to have done little to change their caste relationship with whites (Turner et al. 1984). Legal, intellectual, economic, and population changes were occurring that provided support for continued discrimination against blacks. The Jim Crow laws in the South and "scientific" beliefs about the inferior nature of blacks, along with increased labor competition from a continuously rising number of white immigrants from all parts of Europe, conspired to keep blacks in a lower socioeconomic position. Lynchings increased in the latter part of the nineteenth century. I.Q. tests, developed as early as the 1890s, were erroneously used to test native intelligence, and then used to demonstrate the intellectual inferiority of blacks. This occurred even though some of the early inventors of such measures cautioned against using them for this purpose (Gossett 1963). Social Darwinism, an intellectual application of the notions of the "survival of the fittest" and "natural selection" to whole groups and societies, provided another basis to explain the differences in the accomplishments of the races (Turner et al. 1984).

While some early unions, such as the Knights of Labor, included blacks among their ranks in the latter part of the last century, later craft unions and most notably the AFL excluded them on grounds of competition. The United Mine Workers and Timber Unions included blacks in their membership, as did the Congress of Industrial Organizations (CIO) (Fredrickson 1981). Part of this inconsistent union situation was due to the fundamental conflict developing within the labor movement between the often unskilled and semiskilled industrial workers and craft workers (Fredrickson 1981; Brody 1980). Blacks as well as immigrants were used as strikebreakers by industry, which further intensified racial and ethnic divisions within the industrial working class.

Racist feelings were fueled by several events during this period. The rising number of immigrants from Europe, especially eastern Europe, in the latter decades of the nineteenth century and the early twentieth century helped to create a fear on the part of some that the "white race" was in danger of being extinguished. Madison Grant's *The Passing of the Great Race* (1926) argued that the white race was being overcome with "inferior" immigrants. Grant himself had attended Yale, received a law degree from Columbia, and had come from a wealthy New York family (Gossett 1963). The Eugenics Movement of the early twentieth century also argued that blacks could not serve as "builders" of the country, but could only serve to threaten its progress (Carlson and Colburn 1972). World War I and the Russian Revolution of 1917 with its attendant "Red Scare" only helped to bolster a hatred for individuals of different nationalities and races. During and im-

mediately after World War I, membership in the Ku Klux Klan grew dramatically (Johnson 1976). Black southern migration to the industrializing North during and after World War I resulted in severe clashes between black and white workers, and in the years 1917–1919 riots broke out in several cities (Brody 1980; Schaefer 1988). Protectionist nativist feelings ran high, and in the 1920s legislation was passed that restricted immigration.

In the 1920s, anthropologist Franz Boas spoke out forcefully against the racialist theories being propagated at the time, and by the 1930s and 1940s, other important scientists joined him in attacking the idea that blacks were inferior to whites (Gossett 1963). Nazi racism also contributed to a reexamination of race domination in this country (Turner et al. 1984). But discrimination continued with blacks still having problems within unions and industry. Blacks also were segregated within the military. Riots occurred during World War II, which further demonstrated that the United States still had a long way to go to bring about equity between the races. Increasing organization and political power of blacks during the late 1940s and 1950s helped to bring about some legislative changes and, eventually, the Civil Rights Movement.

RACIAL INEQUALITY TODAY

The preceding historical sketch reveals how extensive racial inequality has been in U.S. society. But perhaps recent legislation, affirmative action, and economic expansion have contributed to a lessening of this inequality. How far have blacks really come today? We now turn to an analysis of present-day racial inequality. Despite some clear advances, blacks and whites continue to have significantly different incomes, occupations, and earnings. In a variety of socioeconomic areas, there are conflicting trends, so that in some areas blacks have improved their positions relative to whites, while in others little or no progress has been made (Pettigrew 1985; Allen and Farley 1986). On the one hand, if the emphasis is on comparing the situation of blacks with what it was in the past, then undoubtedly improvements have occurred. In absolute terms, illiteracy among blacks has declined drastically since the turn of the century, educational levels are up, and occupational upgrading has occurred. On the other hand, if we compare the situation of blacks to whites today, then there is still a great deal of inequality in the areas of earnings, income, and occupations.

Income, Earnings, and Race

In 1947, the median income of *nonwhite* families was 51 percent that of white families. In 1957, it was at 54 percent, and in 1967 it was 62 percent of white family income. In 1977, the ratio of nonwhite to white median family income stood at just under 61 percent, while in 1987 it was almost 63 percent. In these figures, "nonwhite" refers to blacks as well as all other nonwhite groups. If we focus only on the black-white distinction, census data do not allow us to go back as far. In 1967, the median black family income stood at $16,595 in 1987 dollars, compared to $28,029 for whites, which means that black families had about 59 percent of the median income of white families. In 1977, it was 57 percent and in 1987 it was 56 percent ($18,098 vs. $32,274). Thus, when considered alone, median black family income has not risen relative to that of whites in the last twenty years, and in fact, has slid downward since the 1960s War on Poverty.

A majority of blacks, compared to a much smaller proportion of whites, worry that their incomes will not be high enough to pay basic expenses and bills, and there are times during the year when almost one-third have not had enough income to pay for necessary clothing, medical care, or food (*The Gallup Report,* Jan./Feb. 1987, p. 14). Table 4.4 gives the percentage of families in various income groups for different racial groups over the last several decades (U.S. Bureau of the Census, Feb. 1989, pp. 38–39). The data for 1967–1987 are for black and white families only. During the years 1967–1987, the

percentage of black families at the lower end of the income ladder rose, while the proportion of such families in the middle ranges of the income scale declined. Using 1987 dollars as the measure, 9.8 percent of black families had incomes below $5,000 in 1967 and 13.5 percent fell into this category in 1987. The percentage of those in the categories covering $5,000–$34,999 declined during that twenty-year period. This also has occurred to a certain degree for white families.

Census data also indicate that the degree of income concentration has increased among both blacks and whites, but especially among blacks. For example, in 1947 the lowest fifth of the nonwhite population held 4.3 percent of the aggregate income, but in 1987 it owned only 3.2 percent of it. In contrast, the top fifth of nonwhites owned 45.3 percent in 1947 and 48.3 percent in 1987. A similar, but less marked shift exists among whites. This trend recalls the earlier discussion of the increasing polarization of the income hierarchy. Generally, the gap between black and white per capita incomes rose during the early and mid-1980s, and economic inequality between the races also increased during this period (Swinton 1987). In sum, inequality *between* the races has not declined in recent years and has increased *within* the populations of both races (U.S. Bureau of the Census, Feb. 1989, pp. 42–43). When overall wealth rather than income is used as a measure, black households own less than 10 percent that of white households. In 1984, for example, black households' median net worth was $3,397 compared to $39,135 for white households (U.S. Bureau of the Census, Feb. 1989a, p. 440).

There are also striking differences in the poverty rates of blacks and whites. Table 4.5 demonstrates that these differences have been long-standing ones. In 1959, before the War on Poverty, over 55 percent of blacks were poor by government standards, compared to 18.1 percent of whites. In 1989, the rate for blacks had been reduced to 30.7 percent and the rate for whites to 10.0. While both rates have declined in the last thirty years, the proportion of black-to-white

TABLE 4.4   Family by Total Money Income in 1947–1987, by Race (in Constant 1987 Dollars)

Income category	BLACK AND OTHER RACES		BLACKS ONLY		
	1947	1957	1967	1977	1987
Under $5,000	28.4	23.6	9.8	8.7	13.5
5,000–9,999	33.1	22.4	18.5	17.8	16.5
10,000–14,999		18.5	17.5	15.6	12.5
15,000–19,999		17.3	14.4	13.0	11.8
20,000–24,999	38.6	7.4	12.1	10.3	10.0
25,000–34,999			14.5	14.3	13.6
35,000–49,999		10.9	8.7	13.2	12.8
50,000 and over			4.2	7.2	9.5
Median income	8,212	11,157	16,595	17,935	18,098
	WHITES				
Under $5,000	8.9	7.0	3.2	2.4	3.2
5,000–9,999	14.6	10.2	7.3	6.3	6.1
10,000–14,999		12.6	8.8	8.9	8.6
15,000–19,999		22.9	10.3	9.5	9.3
20,000–24,999		12.5	12.9	10.1	9.1
25,000–34,999	76.5		24.7	20.0	18.1
35,000–49,999		34.9	19.4	22.8	21.2
50,000 and over			13.4	19.9	24.4
Median income	16,063	20,868	28,029	31,396	32,274

Source: Bureau of the Census, U.S. Dept. of Commerce, *Money Income of Households, Families, and Persons in the United States: 1987,* Current Population Reports, Series P-60, No. 162, February 1989, Table 11, pp. 38–39.

poor remains at about three to one. In 1987, 42.8 percent of black compared to only 12.9 percent white families had female-headed households with no husband present (U.S. Bureau of the Census, Feb. 1989, p. 50). Table 4.5 indicates that female-headed households with no husband present are most likely to be poor, although most of the blacks in these households were poor *before* they became female-headed (Bane 1985). Almost half of such homes among blacks were poor in 1989. Again, while the poverty rates among these families have declined in recent decades, the ratio between blacks and whites has remained fairly consistent. Finally, not only are a greater percentage of blacks poor, but, on average, they are *poorer* than the white poor. The income deficits in Table 4.5 indicate that the average poor black family would have to raise its income by $5,076 to reach the government's poverty line. The median income deficit for poor white families, by comparison, was $4,021 in 1989.

A variety of reasons have been suggested for the income gap that exists between black and white families. Often these reasons involve references to differences in educational levels, labor force participation, family composition, and occupation. Yet even when these differences are taken into account, differences between the races remain. Given the same employment status, size

TABLE 4.5   Poverty Rates of Persons, 1959–1989, by Race

Year	White	Black	White Female Household with No Husband Present	Black Female Household with No Husband Present
1959	18.1	55.1	40.2	70.6
1966	11.3	41.8	29.7	65.3
1969	9.5	32.2	29.1	58.2
1972	9.0	33.3	27.4	58.1
1975	9.7	31.3	29.4	54.3
1978	8.7	30.6	25.9	54.2
1981	11.1	34.2	29.8	56.7
1984	11.5	33.8	29.7	54.6
1987	10.4	32.4	29.6	54.1
1989	10.0	30.7	28.1	49.4

1989 income deficit	White	Black
Median family deficit	$4,021	$5,076
Median per family member	$1,383	$1,499

Source: U.S. Bureau of Census, *Money Income and Poverty Status in the United States 1989,* Current Population Reports, Series P-60, No. 168, September 1990, Tables 19 and 25, pp. 57–58, 77.

of family, sex, and amount of education, blacks still on average have lower incomes than whites. For example, the median family income for married couples in which both spouses worked in 1987 was $41,685 for black families and $46,646 for white families. At each family-size level, black families have lower incomes. For example, among female-headed families with five members, the median income for blacks is $8,570 whereas for such white families it is $13,823 (see Table 4.6).

Another suggested reason for the income differences between blacks and whites concerns variations in their employment statuses. The labor participation rate for black males and males in general has declined in recent years, and added to this is the argument that black males are more likely to be erratically employed. Moreover, in 1990, the unemployment rates for blacks was more than twice that of whites (11.3 versus 4.7 percent) (U.S. Dept. of Labor, Jan. 1990, Table 3, pp. 165–166), and on average they tend to be unemployed for longer periods (ibid., Table 15, p. 178). Thus, it should be expected that black families would have lower incomes as a result of this unstable participation in the labor force.

Despite these facts, however, black males and females have lower incomes than their white counterparts even when they work year-round on a full-time basis (Table 4.7) or have similar amounts of education (Table 4.8). In 1989, the income of black males who worked full time was about 70 percent of white male income. The income gap between black and white female full-time workers has declined over the years to a point where they are more similar. Also, when compared to whites, a greater percentage of black males and females who work full time, year-round are poor. Table 4.8 shows the different median incomes at various educational levels. Again, it is clear that blacks have less income than whites at each level, and females, particularly black females, are especially low when compared to white males.

TABLE 4.6   Median Money Income in 1987 of Female-Householder Families, No Husband Present, by Race and Family Size

	Total	2-person	3-person	5-person	7-person+
BLACK					
Median income	$ 9.710	$11,161	$ 9,101	$ 8,570	$11,646
WHITE					
Median income	$17,018	$17,019	$18,009	$13,823	*

Mean size of families: White 2.79   Black 3.41

Source: U.S. Bureau of the Census, U.S. Dept. of Commerce, *Money Income of Households, Families, and Persons in the United States: 1987,* Current Population Reports, Series P-60, No. 162, February 1989, Table 19, pp. 79–80.
*Less than 75,000.

TABLE 4.7   Median Income of Persons Aged 15 and Over Who Are Full-Time, Year-Round Workers, by Race and Sex: 1989

	MALE	FEMALE
Black	$20,706	$17,908
White	$29,846	$19,873

Source: U.S. Bureau of the Census, U.S. Dept. of Commerce, *Money Income and Poverty Status in the United States 1989,* Current Population Reports, Series P-60, No. 168, Sept. 1990, Table 12, pp. 43–44.

Finally, blacks who work full time also earn less even when they are in the same general occupational categories as whites. Table 4.9 demonstrates this point. This is especially the case when comparing males in each race. Black males who are in managerial or professional occupations, for example, earned an average of $33,020 in 1987 compared to $42,111 for white males. These discrepancies exist at each occupational level. On average, black females make almost as much as white females in different occupations, but recent evidence suggests that a large percentage of this narrowing occurred before 1975 (Fosu 1988).

Occupation and Race

It is, of course, also the case that within each of the broad occupational categories just mentioned there is a wide variety of specific occupations, and blacks and whites are variously concentrated among them. As mentioned earlier, there has been some occupational upgrading for blacks in recent decades. A greater percentage of blacks have moved into white-collar and blue-collar/manufacturing positions since World War II, and a smaller percentage are service and farm workers. For example, in 1940, 32 percent of employed blacks were farm workers, whereas in 1970 that percentage had fallen to 3. In contrast, in 1940 only 6 percent of employed blacks were white-collar workers compared to 24 percent in 1970 and 44 percent in 1990.

These changes are in large part a result of broader changes in the U.S. economy and polity. Principal among the changes that have reshaped the distribution of occupations among blacks have been:

- The shift away from agriculture since 1900.
- A decline in the centrality of unskilled work.
- The movement toward a service-oriented economy.

TABLE 4.8 Median Income of Persons Aged 25 and Over Who Are Full-Time, Year-Round Workers, by Race, Sex, and Education: 1987

	Black Male	Black Female	White Male	White Female
8 yrs. ed.	$15,735	*	$19,566	$12,244
4 yrs. H.S.	$18,920	$15,582	$26,046	$16,674
4 yrs. college	$26,550	$21,140	$35,701	$23,749

Source: U.S. Bureau of the Census, U.S. Dept. of Commerce, *Money Income of Households, Families, and Persons in the United States: 1987,* Current Population Reports, Series P-60, No. 162, February 1989, Table 35, pp. 140–144.
*Less than 75,000 persons.

TABLE 4.9 Mean Earnings of Year-Round, Full-Time Workers Aged 18 and Over, by Race, Sex, and Civilian Occupation: 1987

Occupation	Black Male	Black Female	White Male	White Female
Managerial/prof.	$33,020	$23,434	$42,111	$24,943
Technical, sales, adm. support	22,028	17,453	31,368	17,785
Service occups.	16,333	11,848	20,641	11,713
Farming, forestry, fishing	*	*	15,764	7,121
Precision prod., craft, repair	21,885	18,027	25,992	19,008
Operators, laborers, fabricators	18,314	14,353	22,558	14,373

Source: U.S. Bureau of the Census, U.S. Dept. of Commerce, *Money Income of Households, Families, and Persons in the United States: 1987,* Current Population Reports, Series P-60, No. 162, February 1989, Table 40, p. 166.
*Less than 75,000.

- The movement of industry out of central cities into suburbs, different regions of the country, or even different countries.
- Attacks upon unions, and the general weakening of the power of labor relative to corporate management.
- "Retrenchment of civil rights enforcement." (Wacquant and Wilson 1989; see also Blau and Ferber 1986; Glasgow 1987)

These macrolevel shifts are not only important for understanding the distribution of occupations among blacks and whites, but are also directly tied to unemployment and poverty levels, the "hyperghettoization" of the inner city, and the size of the underclass discussed in Chapter 2. The decline in basic blue-collar jobs, especially those requiring little formal education, and the mismatch between the location of jobs and blacks have intensified the unemployment problems of inner-city blacks (Lichter 1988; Kasarda 1989). These shifts in the economy, however, do not mean that race itself has become unimportant as a factor in accounting for occupational differences between blacks and whites. We will have more to say about the relative significance of economic class and race shortly.

Table 4.10 presents the current occupational distribution for blacks and whites of each sex using broad categories. While the greatest percentage of white males are in upper-white-collar and skilled crafts positions, black males are most disproportionately represented in the operator/laborer category, and black females in the lower-white-collar and service categories. But these general categories mask greater discrepancies among more detailed classifications of occupations. Data suggest that black mobility has been much more restricted than that of whites. Blacks do not become managers very often and have difficulty moving from the poor-paying, unstable jobs in the peripheral sector to the better paying positions in the core sector of the economy (Pomer 1986).

Table 4.11 gives a sampling of the specific occupations in which blacks are over- and underrepresented. In 1990 blacks made up 10.1 percent of employed civilians. As is clear from this list, blacks are most underrepresented in prestigious white-collar or high-paying skilled blue-collar jobs, and overrepresented in a variety of middle-to-low-level service or government occupations and semiskilled manufacturing positions. Blacks and whites also differ, like males and females generally, on (1) the levels of authority they possess in their jobs, (2) the specific kinds of organizations they work for, and (3) in the economic sector in which they work. Currently, for example, blacks are underrepresented in the agricultural occupations as well as in the fields of "mining, construction, durable goods manufacturing, wholesale and retail trade, and finance insurance and real estate," whereas they are disproportionately located in "nondurable goods manufacturing, transportation and public utilities, services, and public administration" (Swinton 1987, p. 64). Similar to the situation for females, human-capital variables do not fully account for these discrepancies in occupational distribution between the races. Rather, structural factors, such as place of employment, along with discrimination appear to be implicated in discrepancies in the occupational structure and explanations for them.

MICROINEQUITIES IN THE TREATMENT OF BLACKS AND WOMEN

Beyond the occupational and earnings differentials just discussed, there are other forms of inequalities experienced by blacks and women. While those forms relating to occupation and earnings have been in the public eye for years,

TABLE 4.10 Occupational Distribution of Employed Civilians Aged 16 and Over, by Race and Sex: 1990 Annual Average

Occupation	White Male	White Female	Black Male	Black Female
Managerial/prof.	26.9	27.2	13.3	18.6
Technical, sales, adm. support	20.3	45.3	17.1	39.1
Service occups.	8.7	16.4	18.2	27.3
Precision prod., craft, repair	20.0	2.1	15.6	2.3
Operators, laborers, fabricators	19.4	7.8	32.7	12.2
Farming, forestry, fishing	4.6	1.1	3.2	0.3

Source: Bureau of Labor Statistics, U.S. Dept. of Labor, *Employment and Earnings,* January 1991, Table 21, p. 184.

Blacks are still underrepresented within corporate executive ranks.

TABLE 4.11　Percentage of Blacks in Labor Force of Selected Occupations: 1990

UNDERREPRESENTED	%	OVERREPRESENTED	%
Pilots/navigators	0.6	Cleaners/servants	35.6
Farmers	0.8	Nurses aides, orderlies	30.7
Architects	0.9	Pressing machine operators	26.8
Precious stones		Health services occups.	26.3
& metal workers	1.0	Short-order cooks	25.5
Cabinetmakers	1.5	Taxi drivers/chauffeurs	25.3
Technical writers	1.6	Postal clerks	25.1
Chemical engineers	1.7	Maids/housemen	24.8
Dental hygienists	2.5	Welfare service aides	24.1
Natural scientists	2.7	Industrial truck/tractor	
Painters, sculptors,		operators	23.5
printmakers	2.8	Bus drivers	23.4
Speech therapists	2.8	Concrete/terrazo finishers	23.1
Managers (marketing,		Vehicle washers/equipment	
advertising, public		cleaners	23.0
relations)	2.9	Correctional institution	
Physicians	3.0	officers	22.8
Real-estate sales	3.0		

Source: Bureau of Labor Statistics, U.S. Dept. of Labor, *Employment and Earnings,* January 1991, Table 22, pp. 185–190.

"microinequities" between the genders and races permeate the everyday world that we take for granted. *Microinequities* refer collectively to ways in which individuals are either *singled out,* or *overlooked, ignored,* or *otherwise discounted* on the basis of unchangeable characteristics such as sex, race, or age" (Sandler 1986, p. 3). These microinequities generally take the form of different kinds of language, treatment, or behavior exhibited toward blacks or women on a regular basis. In this brief section, we merely point to some inequities that appear in everyday language, communication, the media, and education.

In language, the generic term "man," for example, has been meant to include both men and women. Yet when most people think of that term, they think of men rather than women. In other words, this term does not suggest all of humanity to most individuals, but rather men in particular (Richardson 1987; Martyna 1978). Similarly, the pronoun "he" when used in a generic sense is supposed to represent both males and females; yet it is often attached to various kinds of occupations in a way that perpetuates sex-typed career ambitions and expectations (Richardson 1987). For example, the pronoun "she" is used when speaking of occupations in which a majority of persons are women. Nurses, elementary school teachers, and the like are almost always referred to as "she," while mechanics, doctors, and mathematicians are spoken of in terms of "he."

Our language, which reflects our cultural values, helps to undergird the system of social inequality as it pertains to the genders, and yet because it is so much a part of our everyday lives, we seldom step back and look at it in any depth. The derogatory terms used to describe different ethnic and racial groups also suggest the value we place on these groups, and we reinforce this negative imagery when terms referring to these groups are used to describe some behavior we dislike or despise (e.g., "Indian giver," "to Jew down," "to gyp," to "nigger" lip, etc.) (Marger 1985). Language is a powerful tool for shaping the attitudes toward and general beliefs about

groups, and what makes it exceptionally influential is the fact that these terms are part of the matrix of everyday life and often used without intentional thought being given to their implications.

Even the styles of speaking and communication are often different between the races and genders, reflecting their social positions in society. The controversy over the value of Black English demonstrates these differences. Even though it has been shown to have basic linguistic rules associated with its usage, Black English has been criticized as a poor version of the English language (Baratz and Baratz 1970; Fickett 1975). Part of the problem with accepting Black English is the fact that many white teachers do not really understand it (Farley 1988). Women's language also differs in important ways from that used by men. For example, it tends to involve a greater use of qualifiers and to be less direct and forceful than men's language (Parlee 1979). Men also talk more than women, interrupt women more often than other men, and are more likely to initiate conversation on a topic that is then carried on by others rather than on a topic that is subsequently dropped by others (Argyle et al. 1968; Bernard 1972; Zimmerman and West 1975; Eakins and Eakins 1979; Parlee 1979). People in an audience are also more likely to respond in depth to comments made by a man than by a woman, and to be more attentive to a speech by a male (Sandler 1986). It has been suggested that many of these differences are due to differences in power rather than to the sex of the communicators (Kollock et al. 1985).

The images of women in popular literature and music similarly mirror the stereotypes we have of them (Freeman 1975). The media, especially movies and television, also have perpetuated stereotypes of blacks learned in other contexts. Traditionally, blacks and other nonwhite individuals have either been absent from the media or have been portrayed in negative terms, for example, the black as lazy, slow-thinking, and subservient, and the Native American as savage and hostile (Marger 1985). The fact that blacks were not often found on early television was principally due to the fear of offending white viewers in the 1950s and 1960s (Marger 1985). A recent study of a couple of popular magazines revealed that in the years 1952–1982, the percentage of ads including blacks has increased, but blacks are still underrepresented (Humphrey and Schuman 1984). Blacks are still not likely to be presented as high-status consumers or professionals and are disproportionately viewed as being poor, dependent on whites, or involved in sports. "Advertisements usually portray whites as whites like to see themselves and blacks as whites like to think of blacks" (Humphrey and Schuman 1984, p. 563).

There is some evidence that general acceptance of blacks, *in principle,* has increased since the 1940s. Americans are also more likely to endorse the idea of equal treatment for blacks. Most Americans would endorse a qualified woman or black for president. But even on the hypothetical level, acceptance of racial intermarriage is still low. Moreover, in their analysis of data from three national survey sources covering four decades, Schuman et al. found that agreement with the *implementation* or putting into practice of egalitarian principles was much lower than agreement in the abstract, and the uniformity of agreement across different areas of life is also much lower than is the case on general principles. While general attitudes may have improved, America is still as "color-conscious" as it was in the 1940s (Schuman et al. 1985; see also Schaefer 1987).

Scholarly disciplines also have been criticized for approaches and methodologies that are male rather than female-centered or Eurocentric rather than Afrocentric. Sociology's theories and subject matter, for example, have been attacked for incorporating stereotypical images of the genders and including concepts that do not shed much light on the life experiences of women (Stacey and Thorne 1985; Chafetz 1988; Lengermann and Niebrugge-Brantley 1988; Kandal 1988). Similarly, sociology's theories have also been criticized for not taking an Afrocentric

view, that is, one in which social phenomena are viewed from a black rather than white perspective. Like other disciplines, sociology is a product of its time, and thus it should not be surprising if the field reflects most of the beliefs and values of the surrounding culture.

In the field of education generally, the races and sexes receive different treatment. Students' race and class affect the manner in which they are perceived by teachers, what teachers expect of them, and into what curriculum track they are placed (cf., e.g., Harvey and Slatin 1975; Brophy 1983; Boocock 1978; Alexander et al. 1978). Because of stereotypical images and beliefs about particular groups, teachers develop certain expectations about them with respect to classroom performance, and this, in turn, shapes the manner in which they interact with these students, finally causing their expectations to become manifest in the student's behavior. This behavior then reinforces the original image held by the teacher (Rosenthal and Jacobson 1968) and thus a "self-fulfilling prophecy" is realized. In a later chapter, we will discuss more fully how education operates to perpetuate rather than erase inequality.

Most of these problems can even be found in colleges and universities, and the comparatively small numbers of women in top positions increase the chances of their being treated differently from men. A review survey by the Project on the Status and Education of Women reports a wide variety of forms of unequal treatment for women on campuses. For example, women are provided with fewer resources and less desirable offices, are not taken as seriously as male colleagues by students or male faculty, are considered less for their scholarly accomplishments than for their "feminine" characteristics, and are subject to a variety of forms of sexual harassment (Sandler 1986).

In reflecting on her own career in sociology, Alice Rossi remembers that as a child of the Great Depression, she had to learn many of the household chores carried out by her mother. It was an experience which, she argues, forces one to think in terms of "contingency" rather than "continuous" employment. She goes on to recollect that most of the federal funds available for research after World War II most often aided the careers of men rather than women. "Not only did men have wives at home to rear their children, maintain their households, and manage their social affairs, but at their offices, they had an unprecedented array of services as well, with secretaries, large numbers of graduate students, research assistants, and research associates to facilitate their professional work, far in excess of that experienced by their own mentors before World War II" (Rossi 1988, p. 50).

Oliver C. Cox, the famous black sociologist of the World War II generation, had difficulties obtaining a position in a high-status university, despite having a graduate degree in economics and a Ph.D. in sociology from the University of Chicago. Rather, he had to seek employment in black colleges that did not have the level of graduate-student assistance found in some prestigious universities, but had heavier teaching loads and little research support. "Cox was destined to spend his career in both intellectual and geographical isolation, not only working within a framework that removed him from the mainstream of academic sociology but working in institutions where few of his colleagues could match his academic credentials and scholarly accomplishments" (Hunter and Abraham 1987, p. xxii).

Theda Skocpol, a current young sociologist, also reflects on the significance of gender for her career. While some have suggested that conditions may be better for the young than for the middle-aged woman in terms of prospects for equality, Dr. Skocpol has experienced difficulties she attributes to her gender. She notes that in 1984 she "was offered the Harvard tenured professorship that I am convinced would have been mine in 1981 if I had been 'Theodore' rather than 'Theda' " (Skocpol 1988, p. 155). She goes on to comment that in general "ambitious women are still not accepted at the top and, no matter what

their achievements, they still have to endure the worse personal insults and struggle without end against virtually insuperable obstacles to their having real power" (ibid., p. 156).

These examples suggest the variety of problems that groups of lower status face in U.S. society. Benokraitis and Feagin (1986) summarize the kinds of subtle sex discrimination that presently exist. Some are intentional while others are not, but generally they occur on an informal basis. Among the types they cite are:

- Chivalry, which treats women in an overly protective manner thereby encouraging the image of them as nonadults.
- Encouraging women to be ambitious and active but then creating blockages that make it difficult for them to perform effectively.
- Forms of humor and suggestion, which on the surface may appear innocuous, but are demeaning and embarrassing.
- Treating women as objects, that is, as sex symbols or as status objects.
- Devaluating the talents and abilities of women and focusing on stereotypical or superficial characteristics to honor them.
- Overloading or overburdening women in their tasks or jobs under the guise of allowing them full participation or equality with men.
- "Benevolent exploitation" in which women are exploited in an often unnoticed manner, that is, "showcasing" token women, using their talents and then not giving them appropriate credit.
- Portraying dominant males as considerate and concerned with the welfare of women.
- Socially and physically isolating women in professional settings.

This list should serve as a reminder that sex discrimination can occur in several forms, not only in the formal institutional areas of occupation and earnings. The list also parallels the kinds of subtle discrimination that blacks have experienced historically under paternalistic treatment of them as simple-minded children and tokens of their group.

THE INTERSECTION OF CLASS, RACE, AND SEX

In their everyday lives, of course, individuals accumulate experiences as members simultaneously of a particular class, race, and sex. Thus, the effects of these in real lives are interactive in nature. The previous discussions suggest that often race, sex, and class interact with each other. But in recent years, there has been a controversy over the relative primacy of race, class, and sex in affecting an individual's life chances. With the formal elimination of racist legislation and slavery, understanding and explaining the inequality between the races has become more difficult. The arguments typically are couched in "either/or" terms, for example, "class versus race," in affecting the lives of blacks. Part of this orientation to the issue may be the result of social science's belief in studying *independent* variables, factors that are examined as discrete and separate in the lives of individuals. But in fact, these factors *interact* while individual careers are being played out, and it is often difficult, if not impossible, to fully separate out the effects of each of these variables in isolation from the rest. "It is quite common in the social sciences to separate racism from economics, as if race were only a social category and not an economic category" (Beverly and Stanback 1986).

In explaining the historical situation of blacks in the United States, scholars have taken different positions over the years regarding the primacy of race and class in understanding that situation. Around the turn of the century, W.E.B. DuBois suggested in his study of *The Philadelphia Negro* that not only racial discrimination but economic factors as well affected the everyday living conditions of blacks. E. Franklin Frazier also suggested that both race and class play a role in determining what happens to blacks, but finally felt that economics may be more important than race (1937), an opinion later shared by Oliver Cox. Cox viewed race relations in the United States as stemming from and continuously being conditioned by economic class relations. "The fact of crucial significance is that racial exploitation is merely one aspect of the problem of the proletarianization of labor, regardless of the color of the laborer. Hence racial antagonism is essentially political-class conflict" (in Hunter and Abraham 1987, p. 58).

Currently, William Julius Wilson (1978) argues that today class has become more important than race in determining the life chances of blacks (1978). This is because basic political and economic changes in the society have opened up more potential opportunities for blacks, but have also helped to create urban joblessness. One consequence has been an increasing differentiation among blacks in their class positions. Wilson is not arguing that race is irrelevant today and does say that historically racism has had a major effect on the lives of blacks that continues today, but political and economic changes have changed the terrain on which blacks must battle for position. *Historic* rather than *contemporary* discrimination plays a more significant role in affecting blacks' lives, but other political and economic forces have become more immediately important in understanding events and behaviors within the black community (Wilson 1987).

Blacks have been particularly affected, for example, by the shift from a manufacturing to a service economy, by the broadening split between low-wage and high-wage labor markets, and by the movement of industries out of the central cities (Wilson 1987; Bonacich 1985). "I . . . maintain," writes Wilson, "that in the modern industrial period the economy and the state have, in relatively independent ways, shifted the basis of racial antagonisms away from black/white economic contact to social, political, and community issues. The net effect is a growing class division among blacks, a situation, in other words, in which economic class has been elevated to a position of greater importance than race in determining individual black opportunities for living conditions and personal life experiences" (Wilson

1982, pp. 399–400). Others have suggested different means by which economic position affects relationships between the races. Capitalist owners exploit blacks by using racism to create a pool of black laborers whom they can hire for demeaning jobs at low wages, and white workers fight to keep black workers out of their professions because of the fear of labor competition, thereby creating a split labor market (Bonacich 1985).

In sharp contrast to those like Wilson and assorted exploitation theorists, who stress the primacy of economic-class factors in explaining the socioeconomic condition of blacks, others emphasize the greater and, in some cases, increasing significance of race in understanding the economic predicament of blacks. They criticize Wilson for underplaying the role of race and the persistence of racial discrimination (Lichter 1988). The present era is not as egalitarian with respect to race as Wilson believes (Omi and Winant 1986). They also suggest that the gains that blacks have made relative to whites have been blown out of proportion (Willie 1979). Analyses of national surveys over the last decade show that blacks have lower feelings of psychological and physical well-being than whites. "Blacks have lower life satisfaction, less trust in people, less general happiness, less marital happiness, more anomie, and lower self-rated physical health than whites regardless of social class, marital status, age, or year" (Thomas and Hughes 1986, p. 839). What these differences between the races mean is that race is still a significant factor in determining an individual's life chances.

Earlier studies by Myrdal and Davis et al. also suggested that race was more important than class in explaining the living conditions of blacks (1944, 1941). The presence of blacks in many white-collar, middle-class jobs masks the underlying and continuing significance of race for them. The growth of a black middle class as evidence of real and lasting changes within the black community is criticized by Collins (1983) who found that most blacks in white-collar positions are in tenuous government positions and, therefore, are not a stable middle class (see also Hout 1986; Moss 1988). Moreover, the fate of middle-class blacks is still tied to that of poorer blacks through (1) family connections and community living, (2) the need for voting blocs along racial lines, and (3) their middle-class government jobs whose clients are often poor blacks (Omi and Winant 1986). These arguments suggest that class is not as important a factor in dividing the black community as it has been made out to be by some class theorists.

Attempts have been made to find out how important people think race and class is in their lives. But those taking the polls have focused more often on the opinions of white respondents than on blacks. "Especially in social psychological research, there is a gross imbalance of studying race relations by looking only at white reactions to blacks" (Pettigrew 1985, p. 344; see also Schaefer 1988). Studies that have been done with black respondents indicate that while an increasing percentage of blacks have identified themselves as middle class, there is not much evidence to support the notion that blacks from different classes differ much in their opinions on social policies and programs (Cannon 1984; Welch and Combs 1985; Gilliam 1986). Moreover, Jackman and Jackman (1983) found that blacks in the middle class feel closer to other blacks and to those in lower classes than they do to others in their own class. So as blacks climb the social-class ladder, their social class apparently does not become more significant than their race as a basis for identification. It is only when Jackman and Jackman examined the poor class that they found blacks identifying as closely with their class as with their race. While being in a particular class position does not automatically mean that blacks will identify with others in that position, there is some evidence that race is an important predictor of class consciousness, with blacks being more militantly class conscious than whites (cf., e.g., Zingraff and Schulman 1984). Finally, as another indicator of the relevance of race, blacks and women have views of the class system and the operation of equality of opportunity that are different from those of white males (Kluegel and Smith 1986).

Some survey data point to a lessening of

overt prejudice. Research on whites suggests that the percentage of persons who would vote for a black or woman for president is much higher today than it was thirty years ago. A recent survey showed that in 1987 well over three-quarters would do so, while in 1958 only one-half or fewer would vote this way (Gallup 1987). But while there appear to be fewer who are prejudiced against blacks in all areas of life, there has not been a decline in the proportion of those who hold prejudicial views in at least a few areas such as business. Moreover, there was less decline in prejudice in the last decade than in each of the previous two (Schaefer 1988; Tuch 1981). All of this research suggests strongly that race continues to be an important element in understanding the distribution of occupations and perceptions.

One of the unfortunate consequences of the debate about the relative significance of race and class is that there is a temptation to ignore one of them while emphasizing the other. It is not necessarily the case that because one variable may increase in importance, another, by definition, must decline in significance. "The fallacy lies in the belief that an increase in the predictive power of one set of variables (class) requires a decrease in the predictive power of another set (race)" (Pettigrew 1985, p. 336). In this instance, race conditions class while class conditions what a member of any particular race can attain. The same can be said regarding sex. Sex discrimination appears to be an important element in the continuance of occupational segregation, thereby affecting class position. At the same time, class and race divisions among women historically helped to determine the nature of their involvement in the labor market. Almquist (1984) found, for example, that some female minority groups have different occupational patterns than others. The patterns of Asian women approximate those of Anglo women, while those of Native Americans are closer to the patterns found among black and Hispanic women. Educational patterns also vary among these groups. "People's class position at birth, even for those of the dominant ethnic group, is an overarching factor in determining

their eventual wealth, power, and prestige. . . . But for minorities, the chances of winding up at the bottom are much greater" (Marger 1985, p. 40). In essence, we can say that race, sex, and class are each important and often interact in their influence on the individual.

We saw that, historically, economic and racial factors interacted in the treatment of Native Americans and blacks. Economic motives played a role in driving Native Americans from their land and developing black slavery into an extensive labor force. At the same time, we found that class distinctions existed among blacks and women that were important for understanding the differences in life conditions. We also found that racism as a fully developed ideology was used to legitimate and sustain the economic systems that were being constructed. In the same way, ideologies about the sexes and their proper roles have helped to keep occupational sex segregation intact. Economic as well as other conditions helped bring about the migration of blacks to the North and the consequent form of the class structure within the black population.

In contemporary times, Wright (1978) has shown in his studies that race as well as class, measured in largely Marxian terms, has an influence on income. Race plays a different role at different class levels. Among managers, blacks receive less income return for their education than whites, but black supervisors and workers receive returns that are similar to those of whites. Ethnicity, race, and class background all play a role in determining earnings (cf., e.g., Hirschman and Kraly 1988). Blacks and women both earn less than white males, even when they have the same qualifications, but black women are the worst off of these groups. Another recent study by Tienda and Lii (1987) indicates that the earnings of nonwhites, including blacks, suffer when they are derived from participation in a labor market with a concentration of minorities, while the earnings of college-educated whites benefit from association with such a labor market.

What is important to demonstrate, then, is how race, gender, and class interweave and coincide to influence the situations of groups and the lives of individuals within them. The data presented on incomes of full-time workers make it evident that race *and* gender have an influence on income, earnings, and the distribution of occupations. Blacks and whites differ on each of the latter, but within each race males and females are differently situated with respect to income, earnings, and occupation. The social relations of production and distribution in the economy, which create given class positions, are infused with gender's influence. This means that the distribution, nature of tasks, authority, and wages/salaries associated with particular occupations are all affected by gender. Acker (1988) argues that the theory of social class must be broadened to incorporate the influence of gender. Wages, for example, which are influenced by gender as we've seen, are also the primary source of subsistence for many and a major way by which people are tied to the means of production. Gender and class are interwoven in their influence.

Census data clearly show that while blacks and women in general have increased their representativeness in professional occupations, they continue to be severely underrepresented in professions dominated by males (Sokoloff 1988). Even though the proportion of male professionals declined, males continue to dominate certain high-ranking professions. In fact, their overrepresentation in these professions has *increased*. Black men are the next group most represented in these professions, followed by white women and black women, respectively. These findings again suggest the complex interplay of race and gender that affects class position.

Attitude toward the feminist movement is another area that demonstrates the detailed interworking of race, gender, and class. Many black women do not identify with the movement because they associate it with white, middle-class women, a group whose interests and needs differ in many ways from their own (cf., e.g., Davis 1981; Hooks 1981; Reid 1984; King 1988). Historically, black women have been suspicious of white women (Chafe 1977). Many view their class and race interests as separating them from

the feminist movement that has developed in the United States. Hooks writes that "we were disappointed and disillusioned when we discovered that white women in the movement had little knowledge of or concern for the problems of lower class and poor women or the particular problems of non-white women from all classes. . . . Black feminists found that sisterhood for most white women did not mean surrendering allegiance to race, class, and sexual preference. . . . It did not serve the interest of upper and middle class white feminists to discuss race and class" (Hooks 1988, pp. 188, 190). Thus, in discussing the "feminization" of poverty, Burnham (1985) argues that this concept really distorts the roles of race and class in generating poverty. Not all women are equally likely to be poor; it is their race and class origin that have a major impact on who among them will be in poverty. Some argue that the race-versus-gender stance suggested here is unfortunate because it hinders black women from working against *both* racism and sexism (Reid 1984).

Recent studies suggest that during the period between the 1960s and 1980s, there has been an increase in the proportion of persons who support equal roles for men and women (Cherlin and Walters 1981; Thornton and Freedman 1979). However, among women, those who have a higher education and are working are more likely to feel this way (Thornton and Freedman 1979) whereas black men, especially those who identify themselves as middle class, are less likely than white males to have an egalitarian attitude about gender roles (Ransford and Miller 1983).

The influence of race, class, and sex on the life chances of an individual are multiplicative because they interact in complex and different ways depending upon the specific sociohistorical and cultural context and the area of life chances in question (King 1988). In this sense, black women are often in a situation of "multiple jeopardy" because of their racial, sexual, and class positions. It is inappropriate to lump blacks and women into the same category because their current life experiences and past histories are unique, even though, in general terms, the two groups share some characteristics. For example, both (1) are readily physically distinguishable from white men, (2) have endured similar kinds of social control to keep them "in their place," and (3) are assigned characteristics of excessive emotionality and childlike qualities (Chafe 1977; Hacker 1951). But these somewhat superficial and broad similarities disguise what are more specific and deeper differences between the groups in terms of their concrete historical experiences, as our earlier historical summary of these groups indicates. Moreover, whereas the races have been expected to restrict intimacy with each other, men and women have been expected to do the opposite. In this manner, blacks have occupied a castelike position while women have not (Keller 1987). Even more specifically, black women are often left to fall between the cracks when discussions of blacks (usually meaning black "men") and women (usually meaning "white" women) are carried out. The lesson here is that even though the histories of the sexes and races have been unique in many ways, the influences of race, sex, and class interweave when affecting individual lives.

SUMMARY

This chapter documented the historical and continuing inequality that exists between the races and sexes in the United States. Despite having been consistently involved in the economies of their countries, women have generally held lower positions in them. Even in colonial times in the United States, women were paid less than men and jobs were sex segregated in the earliest factories. While there are distinct differences in the historical situations of Native Americans, blacks,

and women, all have been in a lower socioeconomic position than white males. The hostile treatment of Native Americans and the importation of black slaves signaled the beginning of racial inequality in the United States. Historically, the races and sexes have been distributed differently with respect to income, occupations, and earnings even when their educations and experiences have been similar. In addition, minorities and women are treated differently from white males in a variety of everyday activities. Communication, presentations in the media, educational experiences, and rules of common interaction reflect the social inequalities that exist between the races and sexes. While declines in inequality have occurred in some areas, in others there continues to be a significant amount. Debates in recent years have centered around the relative importance of race, sex, and class in producing these inequalities between groups. Some have argued for the primacy of one of these over the others, but it seems clear that all affect the life chances through complex routes. Early racial and ethnic antagonisms helped to justify the economic exploitation of Native Americans and blacks, and sexual stereotypes had the equivalent effect on women. At the same time, class differences within these groups created divisions that were sometimes hard to bridge. Sex and race also interact. For example, women of different races have different occupational and educational patterns. Race has been a source of division within the feminist movement as well.

In addition to their lower economic status, racial minorities and women also have had fewer political power resources. In the last three chapters, we have reviewed economic, social status, race, and sex inequality. In the next chapter, we turn to a discussion of political-power differences as a final form of social inequality.

CHAPTER 5

POLITICAL INEQUALITY

Power is a many-sided thing. In its various forms and multitudinous expressions, it is the agent, indeed the very being, of all that happens on earth and over the whole universe.
— Robert MacIver

Every social act is an exercise of power, every social relationship is a power equation.
— Amos Hawley

Power is considered by many social scientists to be one of the core concepts in their field (e.g., Olsen 1970; Crozier 1973; Martin 1971). Sociologists in particular often pay homage to Max Weber by subscribing to his theory that stratification is multidimensional, that is, it incorporates elements of class, status, and power. Yet the economics of class and the analysis of lifestyle have proven much easier to study than power. "Power, like love is a word used continually in ordinary speech, understood intuitively, and defined rarely" (Martin 1971, p. 241). This chapter begins with a brief look at the meaning of "power," and then moves on to an analysis of the national power structure and the extent of political inequality in the United States.

ELUSIVENESS OF POWER

Max Weber is perhaps the sociologist most frequently associated with the concept of power. In speaking of the distribution of power, Weber defined it generally as "the chance of a man or a number of men to realize their own will in a com-

munal action even against the resistance of others who are participating in the action." "Communal action" is "that action which is oriented to the feeling of the actors that they belong together" (Gerth and Mills 1962, pp. 180, 183). The majority of definitions of power are based on the Weberian one. Authority as legitimate power is a specific type of power and can be based on formal position. Power is such a basic and general phenomenon that Weber referred to the social stratification system of a society as an expression of the distribution of power in that society. Power precedes stratification and creates the institutionalized "differential access of life chances" that make up the system of social inequality (Dahrendorf 1970; Martin 1971).

In more recent years, definitions of power have taken on more radical and social-structural tones, incorporating the ideas of asymmetry and dependence, which further stress the *relational* nature of power and remove the locus of power from the individual to his or her position in the social structure. Both Emerson (1962) and Blau (1964) couch power in terms of independence/dependence relations. Blau (1964, p. 21) outlines several conditions for a power relationship to exist over a given party: The party (1) cannot reciprocate with anything, (2) has no alternative suppliers for the desired resource, (3) does not have power to force the person to give up the resource, and (4) cannot get along without the resource. These four situations assume the importance of the social setting in which power relationships exist. Since government is the major source of laws, policies, and social programs, the average citizen is heavily dependent upon those with formal political power. Whether or not an individual can remove conditions of dependence relies heavily on the way in which the surrounding social environment is structured. Networks of power among organizations and lobbying groups form part of the texture of the political and social environment. Thus, social power is viewed here as not only relational in character but as being embedded in and characteristic of a particular system's structure (Clark 1968). The organization of the social setting must be understood if one is to fully understand the power relationship within it. This is crucial, for example, in the elite studies of Mills (1956), Useem (1984), Dye (1986), and others who examine and demonstrate relationships between events and structures in the economy and the distribution of political power.

PORTRAITS OF NATIONAL POWER STRUCTURE

In characterizing the political power structure of the United States, some argue that the majority are dependent on a minority, that a power elite or ruling class exists. On the other side of the debate are those who believe the evidence supports a more pluralistic interpretation of the national power structure. Basically, the argument boils down to one over the extent of inequality in political power. Some argue that U.S. institutions and cultural values are such that they promote an elite structure, whereas others contend just the opposite.

Most of these theories can be listed under one of the following types: (1) pluralist, (2) power elite, or (3) ruling class. What immediately follows is a brief description and critique of each of these approaches. The principal issue on which these approaches differ is the degree to which they see power as being concentrated in the United States. After the summaries of these perspectives, a survey of the empirical evidence that bears upon them will be presented.

The Pluralist View

Pluralism as a concept became influential in U.S. intellectual circles around the turn of the twentieth century. It was associated with the notions of change, variety, and competition (Solomon 1982). Basically, this position argues that there are a number of competing groups and organizations that hold much of the power in the country, but no one of these groups holds power all of the time. There is no "central" or "inner" circle that dominates or coordinates the connections between these groups, since each is relatively autonomous and self-interested. Each group pursues issues that are of narrow interest to its organization; in those areas it can have influence, while in others it has little or no power. Generally, social inequality is "noncumulative, i.e., most people have some power resources, and no single asset (such as money) confers excessive power" (Manley 1983, p. 369). While there is some contact between organized groups it tends to be inconsistent and deals with specific issues rather than broad orientations (Higley and Moore 1981). The shifting of power from group to group as issues fluctuate keeps power in a rough balance throughout the society. Individuals can exercise power in part by becoming members of these groups which can then represent their interests and serve as a bulwark between the individual and the state. This belief that power is held by different specific elites in different policy domains is "widely accepted" (McFarland 1987).

In sum, although the pluralist approach has spawned a number of specific theories, many of them share core ideas:

1. Power is shared rather than concentrated among a variety of groups and individuals.
2. These groups are relatively autonomous of each other and become politically active primarily when political policies are at issue that directly affect their narrow interests.
3. The average citizen can be politically influential through membership in these groups and through voices of responsible journalists and intellectuals.
4. The consequences of items 1 through 3 is that there really is no single, permanent structure of power. Power is "mercurial" and its distribution is somewhat balanced by the existence of varied competing groups (Riesman 1950; Galbraith 1962; Berle 1959; Rose 1968).

In these theories, *one is given the impression of a society that, although made up of a variety of different groups and categories of people, is fundamentally based on a system of values on which there is a widespread consensus.* In this society, each individual is rational and free, and his or her interests are taken into account in one way or another by those organizations such as government or corporations that might be seen as having greater power. Power and powerlessness do not appear to be problems. The sharing of power actually helps the society to function. This conception of the structure of power and its functions is quite consistent with the broader structural functionalist theory of society in sociology, which has generally been regarded as a conservative perspective.

It is noteworthy that many of these pluralistic arguments were popular during the 1950s, a period in which nationalism was extolled by many and in which political complacency was accepted. This decade also gave birth to the theory that many citizens in U.S. society were becoming gray-flanneled, "organization men," and it was also a period that ended with Daniel Bell's pronouncement that we had come to "the end of ideology." The period was conducive to the development of pluralist theory and inhospitable to power

elite theory. If we assume that our interpretations and perspectives on social conditions are strongly affected by the political and economic context in which they are generated, then we should not be surprised by the connections between the historical period and ideas about power structure.

The pluralist image of power in the United States has been very popular in many quarters. Cunningham (1975–1976) explains much of its popularity by observing that it has something to offer everyone. "On the one hand, pluralists offer their view as a tough, realistic perspective, one that gets down to the power-political guts of society; on the other hand, they paint a 'soft' picture of the community of happy Americans . . . able to get along . . . despite their differences" (p. 388). Since U.S. society is so complex, it is easy to think of cases where different groups were powerful in different situations and to believe that, in the final analysis, some competition exists. Rose (1968), in proposing his "multi-influence hypothesis," says that this position portrays reality as much more complex than does elite theory. Given this complexity, he finds that he "can but suggest the range of the indefinitely large number of groups and categories of the population that exert power on the political scene, aside from the political, economic, and military elites" (p. 152). His findings lead him to the conclusion "that power is somewhat dispersed through the general population and that there is a wide range of class differentiation in the non-leadership general population" (ibid., p. 179).

A variant of the pluralist model has been proposed by Keller (1969). She contends that the increasing complexity and differentiation in modern societies makes the existence of "coordinating elements" essential. The "strategic elites," as she calls these elements, perform the coordinating function for society, and serve as the "guardians and creators of common purpose and . . . managers of collective aims and ambitions. . . . Whether or not an elite is counted as strategic depends not so much on its particular activities than on its scope, impact, and society-wide influence" (Keller 1969, p. 521). These elites are specialized and expert in the performance of their critical roles and what they do has general consequences for the society. Obviously, not all organized groups in the society qualify for this elite status. Included among the strategic elites, Keller states, are leaders in the political, economic, military, cultural, and recreational fields. Other kinds of elites exist (as in various occupations and pastimes), but they have little or narrow social impact and are thus only elites in their small arena ("segmental" elites).

Since the strategic elites are specialized, none of them dominates in the society according to Keller, nor do these elites constitute a ruling class. Unfortunately, this theory does not tell us much about the *degrees* of importance of each of the strategic elites; nor does it tell us what happens when strategic elites, such as those in economic, political, and military domains, collide with each other. As just noted, Keller does suggest that since each is specialized, none can dominate over the others. This conjures up a view of power as being balanced among these elites. Finally, what makes these groups strategic elites is their expert knowledge in critical areas. But a theory that stresses specialized knowledge as the important basis for power neglects the fact that ideology and outlooks frequently are the bases for advancement in power (Prewitt and Stone 1973, pp. 126–27).

In recent years, two of the principal architects of the pluralist position, Charles Lindblom (1977) and Robert Dahl (1982), have argued that corporate groups have become increasingly powerful and even more powerful than other groups in the competition for power. Dahl suggests that what is needed is a changed civic consciousness to increase pressures for equity in the distribution of power and increased control of corporations by workers to decentralize power. The question, of course, is whether one could expect such workers to be more civic-minded than protective of their own narrow interests once they assume greater control of corporations. Lindblom and Dahl have been criticized for trying to maintain the viability of the pluralist model while at the same time ac-

knowledging the inordinate power of corporations, which suggests that class and elite power are not equally distributed in the United States. This position, which Manley labels as "Pluralism II," "now tries to hold in balance severe criticisms of the system's performance, the need for major structural reforms, support for redistribution of wealth and income, and more government ownership of private enterprise, at the same time that it supports social pluralism as necessary for democracy, denies the special importance of class, reconfirms the inevitability and value of incremental change. . . . The problem . . . is that Pluralism II still defends many features of the system that perpetuate the social results it now deplores" (Manley 1983, pp. 371–372). Nevertheless, some still hold the position that the power of corporations can still be incorporated into a pluralist or interest-group approach (Vogel 1987).

Over the last thirty years, pluralism has been roundly criticized (Bachrach and Baratz 1962; Mills 1956; Domhoff 1967; Connolly 1969; Prewitt and Stone 1973; Cunningham 1975–1976). Social and historical events during the 1960s and 1970s helped spur a rise in a "critical stance" in all of the social sciences, especially economics, political science, and sociology. The central criticisms of pluralism frequently reflect skepticism about the reality of democracy in society today and are based on an analysis of current events on the political scene. First, the issues of concern to many people frequently are not dealt with by the government. In large part, this occurs either because these individuals are not in positions to make their interests known or because their interests are of less concern than those of people who hold positions of economic and social power and whose values are represented and reflected in the government (Connolly 1969; Prewitt and Stone 1973). Second, voluntary associations are no longer effective representatives of the average citizen since they have themselves become oligarchical in nature. And individuals in positions of organizational power do not represent the average membership. These members do not have access to power (Presthus 1962; Kariel in Connolly 1969, p. 16). Finally, nondecisions and problems that never become publicly defined as issues must be examined. Pluralism examines issues but ignores "the values and biases that are built into the political system and that, for the student of power, give real meaning to those issues which do enter the political arena" (Bachrach and Baratz 1962, p. 950).

The Power-Elite View

The idea of a power elite differs drastically from pluralist conceptions and Keller's concept of strategic elites, but it is not the same as the "ruling class" concept, which we will discuss shortly. Power-elite theory has a long history in social science, going back to the works of Mosca, Pareto, and Michels. Mosca contended that there could be no such thing as a democracy in which all the people rule, but rather every society has a minority that rules it. Moreover, in large societies this minority tends to be quite small. "It follows that the larger the political community, the smaller will the proportion of the governing minority to the governed majority be, and the more difficult will it be for the majority to organize for reaction against the minority" (Mosca 1939, p. 53). The minority can control the majority because it is organized whereas the majority is not and because its members possess "some attribute, real or apparent, which is highly esteemed and very influential in the society" (ibid.). Michels (1915–1949) similarly argues that there is an "iron law of oligarchy" according to which every organization develops into a type where a minority dominates. This includes "democracies" as well, and the process is inexorable because of the complexity and need for efficiency in society and the unique and irreplaceable skills developed by those in leadership positions. Finally, Pareto developed a theory known as the "circulation of elites," "elites" referring to those who were best in their respective fields. While there is often change in modern societies, there is always a small group that rules, and usually this group

contains both "nonelites" and "elites" in Pareto's sense of the term. We will examine Pareto's theory in greater detail in Chapter 8.

Perhaps the most famous power-elite theory was developed by C. Wright Mills (1956). Mills felt strongly that social science has a responsibility to demonstrate the connections between the "private troubles" of individuals and the "public issues" in society, that is, to elucidate the link between what happens to individuals in their everyday lives and what occurs in the broader structure and history of their societies. His study of power is one attempt to do this kind of "useful" social science.

Because Mills's portrayal of the power elite has drawn an inordinate amount of attention in the years since it was written, and because it represents a prime example of a theory in opposition to the pluralist position, it is presented here in detail. Mills's essential argument is that power is centralized in a power elite. He did not believe that a system of checks and balances, countervailing power, or balance existed in the United States. In fact, he felt that the theory of balance is really an uncrystallized and confused view of power in this country; he argued that to take that position is to assume that all competitors for power are equal and that basically there is more harmony of interest than actually exists.

According to Mills, certain historical changes have brought about the development of a power elite. As the society has grown, institutions have become more complex, and national functions have become centralized in specific institutions, namely, the economic, military, and political institutions. Mills contended that with historical changes, the tasks in top positions in each of these institutions have become so similar that it is now possible for those in top positions in each of them to interchange positions. Consequently, in addition to centralization in institutions, there has been an increasing coalescence, so much so that *three* separate political, military, and corporate elites are now *one* power elite made up of individuals in the highest positions in an interconnected set of institutions. "By the power elite, we refer to those political, economic, and military circles which as an intricate set of overlapping cliques share decisions having at least national consequences" (Mills 1956, p. 18). The nucleus of the power elite includes those who hold high positions in more than one of the three major institutions as well as those, such as prestigious lawyers and financiers, who serve to knit the three institutions together (Mills 1956, pp. 288–289).

The persons within this structure have their power because of their positions. It is not their personal characteristics that make them powerful but their positions in the military, political, and economic institutions. This does not mean, however, that the incumbents of these positions do not have certain kinds of qualifications that make them stand out. On the contrary, they do tend to come from the same kinds of economic, social, and educational backgrounds and do informally intermingle but, ultimately, it is their position that makes them powerful in national decision making.

Mills described the top part of the power structure as possessing a "higher immorality." What he was talking about is not personal immorality (that is, one caused by a corrupt personality) but a structural immorality, in that because of the way society is organized, because of the way its institutions are structured, certain individuals can take advantage of others and their positions. It is similar to what has recently been called "structural corruption," a situation in which structural avenues are open in our society that allow outside money to influence the political and intellectual stance of those in positions of power (Judis 1990). Part of the higher immorality is reflected in the fact that Mills believed that such characteristics as cynicism, personality selling, conformity, and mediocrity (all valuable in a society such as ours) have replaced values based on knowledge, skill, and independent thinking.

Some may feel that Congress is part of the power elite, but Mills did not feel that it was a member. Rather, he referred to the Congress as a "semi-organized stalemate" made up of people who, since they have their eyes on re-election, are concerned largely with the fluctuating local issues of their constituencies back home. In other words, such groups as the farm bloc, labor unions, white-collar workers, and Congress really have little to do with decisions of "national consequence." These groups, specifically Congress, make up a middle level of power in the United States. If the competition of groups in pluralism operates at all it is at this level. Mills further believed that the wealthy and political officers who are entrenched in local interests will not become nationally important. As he put it, "to remain merely local is to fail" (ibid. p. 39). Local society has, by and large, been swallowed up by the national system of power and prestige. This is in part due to increasing urbanization, the increasing satellite status of smaller towns, improved transportation networks, and similar kinds of changes. Again, it has been changes in the structure of the society that have resulted in the appearance of a particular kind of power structure.

On the bottom of the power structure are the large majority of people who are quickly developing into a mass society. Masses are characterized by the fact that they are always on the receiving end of opinions, cannot or do not effectively respond to opinions expressed in the mass media and really have no outlet for effective action in society. Mass media, largely controlled by those on the top of the power structure, have only served to weaken communications between the top and the bottom of the structure. The media tell people what their experiences are or should be and stereotypes them, and an education only serves to help people to "adjust" to a society that is very hierarchical in terms of power. Voluntary associations, although they theoretically might be viewed as a link between the individual and the people at the top, do not perform this function because as they have grown, the individuals in them feel less powerful. Power is distant and inaccessible to average members.

Gusfield's (1962) neat summary of the central characteristics of mass society fits in nicely with Mills's description. In a mass society there is a:

1. Weakening of primary and local associations.
2. Strengthening of impersonal bureaucraticized relationships in large-scale organizations that have replaced smaller and more informal systems of loyalty and affiliations.
3. Homogenization of the population and a leveling of conditions and ideologies that have reduced traditional authority systems characteristic of stratified communities.
4. Lengthening of the chain of organizational authority, which makes local groups less viable and more amenable to control from above.
5. In addition to the structural disintegration indicated, there is a personality disintegration in the individual characterized by alienation, lack of commitment, and malaise.

It should be pointed out that Mills was not saying that there is a conspiracy on the part of a small group of individuals to control political power in the United States. Rather, it has been a sequence of historical and structural events and changes, such as the growth in major institutions, that has led to the development of such a power structure. For example, the military are not powerful because they are conspiring against civilian populations but are in a position of power because the United States as a nation is now within an international military neighborhood, surrounded by allies and enemies. This means that what in the past may have been simply and purely political issues have now become largely military issues. For example, foreign aid is no longer just an economic or political issue but a military issue as well. In any case, it bears repeating that for the most part Mills felt that a series of structural and historical changes have brought about the power elite, not a conscious conspiracy on the part of a tightly knit group of corrupt individuals.

The *current* power elite is a relatively recent phenomenon which, in Mills's view, came into existence only after the New Deal. Before that time, the power structure passed through several other epochs in which either no single institution or one of the three major institutions was dominant. Today, the hierarchy among these institutions is much less clear, and they are much more equal and intertwined.

Assessment of Mills's The Power Elite.   When *The Power Elite* appeared, it was considered to be a provocative and radical interpretation of power in the United States. Over the several decades since its appearance, however, the face of sociology has changed. Today, the thesis of the book is no longer considered radical, and indeed, radical sociologists — especially of neo-Marxist bent — have criticized the work. In fact, some radicals have referred to the Millsian thesis as a variant of pluralism in which the checks and balances have broken down (for example, Cunningham 1975–1976). This is interesting if only because Mills's argument is most often seen as an argument against the pluralist position. Thus, over the years, criticisms have come from conservative and liberal as well as radical quarters.

Several central criticisms have been made of *The Power Elite;* they range from stylistic and conceptual comments to more methodological and substantive remarks.

1. Despite its apparent clarity at first glance, parts of the theory suffer from conceptual vagueness. Mills is not consistent or rigorous in his usage of the term "power elite." The term itself is a compelling one but Mills also alternatively talks about "leading men," "command posts," institutions, domains, higher circles, those who count, and sets of cliques as partial definitions of a power elite.

2. Mills seldom qualifies his statements and has a tendency to phrase them in absolute terms. Rather than talking about events or power as variables or continuous, he tends to present them in zero-sum terms. Events and power are not as simple as Mills's thesis would suggest.

3. Mills concentrates on foreign policy decisions, largely those involving violence or the mil-

itary as examples of national issues and, consequently, tends to ignore important domestic issues that are of national consequence. His analysis, for example, ignores blacks as a separate group and the importance of political parties on the national scene. Prewitt and Stone (1973) contend that Mills has neglected to fully relate his theory to the economic system and neglects to discuss important institutions and their role in decision making.

4. Some argue that Mills was attracted by violence and power and not really concerned with dealing with the issue of authority.

5. Mills's data are often very selective, and it has been argued that contrary evidence could easily be mustered. For example, for every retired general who moves to a top position in an economic or political institution, there are others who do not go into these circles. There also are reputed cases where legislation desired by the power elite has not materialized.

6. Numerous political scientists have criticized Mills's methodology. They doubt that Mills has really tested the actual influence of an elite in a variety of decisions. At best, Mills's elite, say these critics, has only "high potential for control" and *potential* is not *actual* power. They also feel that since Mills does not look at a wide range of issues, the question of broad power is left unanswered. This kind of criticism is related to the general debate that has existed for years between sociologists and political scientists about the best method by which to detect the power structure in a given situation.

7. Mills insists that his is not a conspiracy theory, but it becomes very difficult to believe that a conspiracy does not exist, at least to some extent, given Mills's description of the interrelationship among the different sectors of the elite, the fact that they have come from similar backgrounds and have similar beliefs, and the fact that they interact often. Several critics (such as Truman 1959; Parsons 1968; Crozier 1973) have, in fact, suggested that *The Power Elite* is a conspiracy theory.

8. Mills's emphasis is on power flowing from the top down: those at the top have a great deal of power, those in the middle have little, and those at the bottom have none. The empirical question, however, is whether or not power is really unidirectional or whether, as has often been found, those at the bottom still have influence on those at the top. Moreover, the conclusion that our society is becoming masslike is debatable given the existence of strikes, movements, and organizations created at the grassroots level.

Despite these criticisms and others, however, Mills's analysis is not without its strengths. Among other points, Prewitt and Stone (1973, p. 90) mention that "whatever else it accomplished, *The Power Elite* raised the level of debate to a higher plane" since the author was the "first major analyst of American society" to observe that power relationships can vary with the issue at hand and to anchor his analysis in concrete and major institutions. Mills's study also demonstrated that (1) he could live up to his own view of social science as an attempt to make sense of personal problems in terms of social issues; (2) the sociologist could help identify master trends in society; (3) effective political analysis and practical use could be united in sociology; and (4) sociological analysis could effectively demonstrate the interconnection between social structure and personality.

The Ruling-Class View

As we have seen, Mills's description of the power structure is one in which a group of individuals in high positions in core institutions dominate, while those at the bottom comprise an unorganized, ineffectual mass. They have little power and offer little active resistance. Rather, they are manipulated and educated in a manner that makes them almost willing subordinates in the society. The ruling-class view similarly proposes that a small group has inordinate political power in the society and that there are important interconnections between economic and political institutions.

But, aside from these similarities, it differs from the power-elite model in several ways:

1. Rather than stressing several types of institutions as being involved in the elite, it emphasizes the paramountcy of the economic institution and position within it.

2. It often views the bottom of the power structure as being more active and effectual as a working class. It can organize and bring about change in the society. In the case of the power-elite model, the mass is largely passive in response to its position, whereas in the ruling-class model the working class can be class conscious and organized. Thus, the relationship between those on the top and those on the bottom is characterized more fully by conflict (Bottomore 1964).

3. The relationship between the upper class or bourgeoisie and political power is portrayed as being much tighter than is the case in Mills's power-elite theory where the upper class and celebrities are more tangential to the political process. In Mills's view, it is strictly *institutional position* not *personal wealth* that leads to political power.

A prime example of one version of the ruling-class approach can be found in the writings of G. William Domhoff (1967, 1971, 1979, 1983). Essentially, Domhoff argues that the upper class rules through its power elite, which consists of the politically active core of the upper class. "More formally, the power elite consists of active, working members of the upper class and high-level employees in profit and nonprofit institutions controlled by members of the upper class through stock ownership, financial support, or involvement on the board of directors" (Domhoff 1983, pp. 109–110). And although he does not believe that the power elite is a conspiratorial group, he does believe "that the power elite are more unified, more conscious, and more manipulative than the pluralists would have us believe, and certainly more so than any social group with the potential to contradict them" (1971, p. 299).

The power of this ruling class, Domhoff argues, is found in the fact that members (1) own or control a very disproportionate amount of the wealth in the United States, (2) are significantly better off on a number of well-being scales than other citizens, (3) exercise control over a vast array of social and economic institutions, and (4) dominate the political process in the United States (Domhoff 1979). The upper-class power elite dominate U.S. society by being extraordinarily influential in determining the policy agendas and rules under which others must operate. They also dominate the political process through specific mechanisms discussed by Domhoff. These mechanisms include the:

1. "Special interest process," including the use of lobbyists, lawyers, and membership on regulatory commissions and Congressional committees to insure that the interests of their class are served in the political system.

2. "Policy formation process," in which members of the upper class serve on various blue-ribbon presidential commissions, councils, and other policy-planning groups (e.g. Business Council, Committee for Economic Development, Council on Foreign Relations), and because of this service, develop an overall class consciousness actively working for the general interests of the upper class.

3. "Candidate selection process," in which campaign contributions, political party influence, and media manipulation result in the selection of candidates who serve the interests of the upper class.

4. "Ideology hegemony," in which the media and other socializing institutions, which are controlled and/or owned by members of the upper class, advance the values and outlook of the upper class, thereby maintaining the existing class system (Domhoff 1979, 1983).

These mechanisms illustrate that Domhoff is not merely arguing that political power is class based and traceable to given upper-class individuals, but that the structure of institutions in the United States and their penetration by upper-class persons are implicated in a full understanding of U.S. power structure. Domhoff's analysis attempts to show how economic power can be translated into political power. Figure 5.1 summarizes Domhoff's view of how policies are determined.

DISTRIBUTION OF POLITICAL POWER

Each of the positions just discussed suggests a different distribution of power and political influence. But we have to look at the data that bear on them before conclusions can be drawn about the concentration and dispersion of political power. The degree of power and political participation can be measured in a variety of ways, and each of these measures provides clues concerning the actual distribution of power.

Voting

Though some people feel they have little influence, perhaps they are wrong. To what extent are all individuals really politically influential in the United States? Does being a citizen mean by definition that a person is a participant? One means by which to assess the potential political impact of a group is through its history of participation in the political process. "Participation is a potent force; leaders respond to it. But they respond more to the participants than to those who do not participate" (Verba and Nie 1972, p. 336). A group obviously has to make its desires known if it is to have the possibility of gaining political power under the present system. "Party politicians are inclined to respond positively not to group *needs* but to group *demands,* and in political life as in economic life, *needs* do not become *marketable demands* until they are backed by

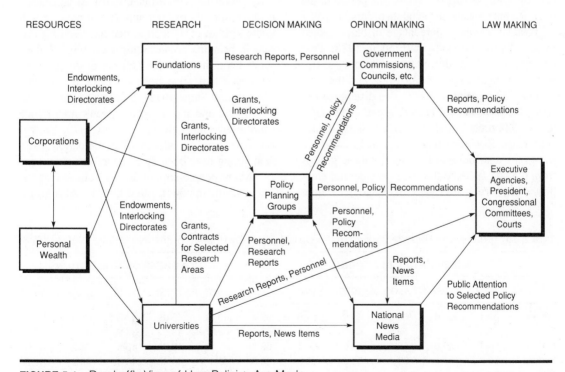

FIGURE 5.1 Domhoff's View of How Policies Are Made

Source: From *The Powers That Be,* by G. William Domhoff. Copyright © 1978 by G. William Domhoff. Reprinted by permission of Random House, Inc.

'buying power' or 'exchange power' because only then is it in the 'producer's' interest to respond" (Parenti 1970, p. 528; emphasis in original).

A frequently used measure of participation in the political process is voting. Voting turnouts for national elections in this country are well below the 80 percent turnouts found in other industrial democratic nations. This lower voting rate is somewhat surprising given the fact that evidence suggests that Americans tend to be more politically aware than adults in other similar countries. The party system's lack of close connection with many other social groups, along with voluntary registration, have weakened participation in the U.S. political process (Powell 1986).

Generally, there are clear relationships between selected social characteristics and voting behavior. Historically, whites have been much more likely than blacks to register and to vote in congressional and presidential elections. The data show that during the 1960s, the period of the Civil Rights movement, racial disorders, and War on Poverty, a greater percentage of blacks voted in presidential elections than did in 1988. That percentage declined during the 1970s only to rise again to almost 56 percent in 1984, and then fall to under 52 percent in 1988. The difference between the sexes has not been as great, and in fact, in the 1988 presidential election a slightly higher percentage of women than men voted. Table 5.1 shows the distribution of voting for these groups from the late 1960s to the 1988 presidential election. Why are blacks less likely to vote than whites? An examination of election data for a twenty-year period (1952–1972) reveals that how supportive a political climate is at a particular time for different groups directly affects voting and registration patterns (Danigelis 1978).

Table 5.2 presents the patterns for registration and voting by education, employment status, and family income. Again, these patterns vary by social characteristic. Those who have higher incomes, are employed, and are more highly educated are more likely to register and to vote. Clearly, a large percentage of some groups do not participate much in the political process, even at this basic level. Verba and Nie summarize their survey of voting and electoral studies with the observation that what is revealed is "a picture of low levels of citizen participation and concentration of political activity in the hands of a small portion of the citizens" (1972, pp. 26–27).

If people did vote, would they be more politically powerful? Unfortunately, if past legislation is any guide, it does not appear that popular will is the kind of participation that has been significant in bringing about political changes. Rather, it has been the organized efforts of groups with resources that have been effective in the past (Prewitt and Stone 1973). Platitudes about popular control and the average citizen's importance simply have not held up (Parenti 1970; Prewitt and Stone 1973). Modes of participation other than voting have been more effective.

Many people simply do not believe that the vote gives them power. But if they do not vote, we

TABLE 5.1   Percentage Reported Voting in the United States by Race and Sex: November 1968 to 1988

	PRESIDENTIAL ELECTIONS						CONGRESSIONAL ELECTIONS				
	1988	*1984*	*1980*	*1976*	*1972*	*1968*	*1986*	*1982*	*1978*	*1974*	*1970*
White	59.1	61.4	60.9	60.9	64.5	69.1	47.0	49.9	47.3	46.3	56.0
Black	51.5	55.8	50.5	48.7	52.1	57.6	43.2	43.0	37.2	33.8	43.5
Male	56.4	59.0	59.1	59.6	64.1	69.8	45.8	48.7	46.6	46.2	56.8
Female	58.3	60.8	59.4	58.8	62.0	66.0	46.1	48.4	45.3	43.4	52.7

Source: U.S. Bureau of the Census. October 1989. Voting and Registration in the Election of November 1988. *Current Population Reports,* Series P-20, No. 440, p. 2.

TABLE 5.2 Selected Characteristics of the Voting-Age Population Reported Having Registered or Voted: November 1988

Characteristic	% Registered	% Voted
Years of School Completed		
0–8 years	47.5	36.7
1–3 years high school	52.8	41.3
4 years high school	64.6	54.7
1–3 years college	73.5	64.5
4 or more years college	83.1	77.6
Employed	67.1	58.4
Unemployed	50.4	38.6
Family Income		
Under $5,000	47.6	34.7
$5,000–9,999	52.8	41.3
$10,000–14,999	57.4	47.7
$15,000–19,999	63.2	53.5
$20,000–24,999	67.4	57.8
$25,000–34,999	71.9	64.0
$35,000–49,999	77.9	70.3
$50,000 and over	81.8	75.6

Source: U.S. Bureau of the Census. October 1989. Voting and Registration in the Election of November 1988. *Current Population Reports,* Series P-20, No. 440, p. 4.

should not conclude that they are apathetic. On the contrary, they may be concerned and even enraged and perhaps believe that alternative avenues provide more effective means of political participation. As suggested earlier, however, a lack of perceived effect leaves people cynical and wary about political processes and their participation in them. Given these conditions, it is not surprising that Almond and Verba (1963) found in their study of five countries that people with higher education are more likely to subscribe to the belief in individual participation. However, it is the nature of participation that makes the difference.

Some groups are at best only minimally involved in the political process. Those who are totally inactive have disproportionate numbers from low-income and low-education backgrounds, whereas "complete activists" have an overrepresentation of high-status individuals in their ranks (Verba and Nie 1972, pp. 97–99).

The complete activists are individuals who participate in a variety of ways (voting, attending meetings, campaign contributions, contacting officials, and so forth). In an investigation of over 3,000 "attentive citizens," Rosenau (1974) found that they were "older, better educated, wealthier, more widely travelled, and composed of more men, whites, Jews, Northeasterners, Far Westerners, and professional and managerial persons than is the population as a whole" (p. 318). Regardless of how it is measured, political inequality is present, and present to a large degree.

Holding Political Office

Holding political office is another and more substantial means by which to wield political power. White males dominate political positions at the federal level. In terms of absolute figures, the number of black elected officials has gone up dramatically since 1970. Table 5.3 indicates the changes that have occurred since 1970. In 1988, there were 6,829 black elected officials in the United States; this comprised well under 2 percent of all elected officials, even though blacks make up over 11 percent of the voting-age population. Roughly two-thirds of these positions were held in the South. Only 23 of the almost 7,000 black officials held office at the federal level, while almost half were at the municipal level and 1,550 held offices in educational institutions (Joint Center 1989). There were no black U.S. senators in 1988. Among blacks, while the proportion of such officials who are male has declined in recent years, black male officials still outnumber black female officials three to one. In 1975, this ratio was almost six to one. Currently, twenty-two of the twenty-three black federal officials are male.

TABLE 5.3 Change in Number of Black Elected Officials

YEAR	N	% CHANGE
1970	1,469	—
1971	1,860	26.6
1972	2,264	21.7
1973	2,621	15.8
1974	2,991	14.1
1975	3,503	17.1
1976	3,979	13.6
1977	4,311	8.3
1978	4,503	4.5
1979	4,607	2.3
1980	4,912	6.6
1981	5,038	2.6
1982	5,160	2.4
1983	5,606	8.6
1984	5,700	1.7
1985	6,056	6.2
1986	6,424	6.1
1987	6,681	4.0
1988	6,829	2.2

Source: Black Elected Officials: A National Roster, Joint Center for Political Studies, Washington, D.C., 1989, p. 8.

Females in general also are underrepresented in elected political positions. In 1988, about 5 percent of members of the U.S. Congress were women: twenty-five were members of the House of Representatives and two were members of the Senate. In contrast, women comprise almost 16 percent of the membership of state legislatures. This is up from the 4.5 percent who were state legislators in 1971 (Rix 1988). Most of these women do not have the seniority that even several blacks in Congress possess. This is in part due to the fact that most blacks in Congress are elected in districts with very large minority populations, whereas "women don't run from districts that are generally women" (*Congressional Quarterly* Nov. 12, 1988, p. 3294).

In addition to sex and race, other studies indicate that socioeconomic background also is tied to the likelihood of holding office. Matthews's (1954) study of the Eighty-first Congress in 1954 suggests that upper-class origin is linked to being a member of Congress. While 63 percent of the employed in 1890 were low-salaried workers, wage earners, servants, and farm laborers, only 4 percent of the senators in the Eighty-first Congress had fathers in any of those categories. As the cliché might put it, the Senate was largely made up of white Protestants, most of whom were born into middle- and upper-class families, and a majority of whom were lawyers. Matthews concluded that his and other findings suggest a class ranking of political office, with those from the higher classes occupying the highest political offices. Moreover, as long as the system of inequality remains intact things are not likely to change: "So long as the system of stratification in a society is generally accepted, one must expect people to look for political leadership toward those who have met current definitions of success and hence are considered worthy individuals" (Matthews in Lopreato and Lewis 1974, p. 341).

Mintz (1975) and Freitag (1975) researched the class backgrounds of *all* Cabinet officers during the period from 1897 to 1973 and found that there were strong ties to the upper class. A full 66 percent of these officers were from upper-class backgrounds and 90 percent had occupied a top corporate position before or after being appointed or had upper-class origins. The particular political party that happened to be in power at the time did not make much difference (Mintz 1975). Freitag's analysis supports Mills's conclusion that there is a clear connection between corporate and political elites and does not support Keller's and other pluralists' arguments about autonomous elites. His study, based on biographical information for all Cabinet secretaries from McKinley to Nixon's first term, involving 358 Cabinet positions, shows that *at least* 76 percent of Cabinet members were tied to the corporate sector by being either corporate executives, officers, or corporate lawyers. Since President Truman's administration, this percent is even higher (86% under Eisenhower, 77% under Kennedy, 86% under Johnson, and 96% under Nixon) (Freitag 1975). Again, neither the political party in power nor the particular Cabinet post make any difference in this relationship. Most of these individuals had connections with their corporations *before* taking office, but over 40 percent had such ties *before and after* appointment. Freitag concludes that the data do not prove that the corporate and governmental elite sectors are unified in terms of policies, but they do suggest that it is a "serious possibility" that the Cabinet may be accountable to large corporations (ibid.).

Top federal officials are not likely to come from working-class or lower-class families. Presidents also tend to come from higher educational and occupational backgrounds, and certain ethnic backgrounds are overrepresented in these positions. For example, twenty of the first thirty-six presidents were of English background, twenty-six were college graduates, and twenty-five were lawyers (Kane 1974, pp. 343–344, 351).

Prewitt and Stone (1973) have explored the issue of recruitment of political elites, initially entertaining the question of whether or not every-

Who has political power? Statistics demonstrate that those in higher socioeconomic statuses make up the vast majority of those who hold high political offices.

one has an equal chance to enter political office, especially in an elite position. They came to the conclusion that although an individual's chances are limited they are not necessarily closed – perfectly closed, that is. They do indicate that "it is not wrong, however, to claim that the wealthiest strata of the population supply a very disproportionate number of those recruited into the elite" (Prewitt and Stone 1973, p. 137). "If you aspire to political-elite status, it is advantageous to be white, well-educated, Protestant (and more specifically of Episcopalian or Presbyterian upbringing), native born and preferably British or Northern European extraction, and successful in a prestigious occupation" (Prewitt and Stone 1973, pp. 137–138).

Over the last decade and a half, Dye (1986) has documented the characteristics, backgrounds, and interconnections of the institutional elite in the United States. He includes in his definition of elites all those who occupy positions of high authority in the governmental, media, educational, civic/cultural, military, financial, industrial, and legal institutions in the United States. Based on this definition, Dye concludes that there are 7,314 such positions. Taking all of the corporate, public-interest, and governmental elite together as a group, Dye estimates that about 30 percent come from upper-class origins, measured in terms of education and occupation of parent (1986, p. 194). However, while that class is disproportionately represented, the remaining 70 percent come from middle-class backgrounds. Less than 5 percent of these institutional leaders are women and only 20 out of 7,314 are blacks (Dye 1986). Considering only the governmental elite – that is, those who occupy the top positions in the executive, legislative, and judicial branches – almost 75 percent have law or other advanced degrees. Over 40 percent are graduates of highly prestigious, private universities or colleges. Women and blacks, as might be expected, are grossly underrepresented.

Finally, a recent study of elites in political, social, and economic institutions found that not only are they nearly all male and college educated, but the largest ethnic group are WASPs (white-Anglo-Saxon-Protestant), comprising 42 to 48 percent of the sample. In Congress and business, this group makes up about 60 percent. "Minority groups bring up the rear," making up under 4 percent of the elite (Alba and Moore 1982, p. 378). The WASPs also tend to have greater amounts of formal education and to have been in the U.S. for more generations. An important qualifier in their study is that while ethnicity may help a person get into the elite, once in, ethnicity has no effect on his or her status *within* the elite. Other research similarly suggests that once in the institutional elite, upper-class background has little impact in determining status within it (Moore 1979).

What is the meaning of these studies in terms of the perspectives on power presented earlier? If the essence of pluralism is the presence of a rough balance of power between constituencies with different interests, then these data clearly do not support the pluralist position. Some groups, most notably women, racial minorities, and working/lower class members are seldom found in offices of political power. To the extent that these offices are a principle means by which to gain and exercise political power, and that incumbents reflect and work for their own interests, then some groups have much less power than others.

INTERLINKAGE OF ECONOMIC AND POLITICAL POWER

Several of the studies discussed suggest that those with economic power are also more likely to be in positions of political power. It is important to know what the actual connection is between economic and political power in a society such as that of the United States, if only because it is widely considered to be a democracy in which every individual counts politically. As noted in Chapter 1, there has been a long-standing concern for keeping economic power from contaminating the political arena and thereby keeping those who are wealthy from controlling the political process.

In addition to the studies just discussed, we have come across the tie between economic and political institutions before. At the world-system level, which we reviewed in Chapter 2, economic order is viewed as being made up of countries that perform different functions and occupy different ranks in the world economic hierarchy. Political power in this network roughly corresponds with the economic power of the countries. World trade, resource development, multinational corporations, and similar entities that tie countries together result in economic and political power being inevitably connected. At another level, we saw that economic development and political democracy often have been found to be related. Economic development also has been linked to a country's position in the world economic system.

Domhoff (1979, 1983) has examined the link between personal wealth and political power in detail. As we said earlier, he believes that the power elite in the United States is but the ruling contingent of the upper class. In this sense, the upper class, which makes up only 0.5 percent of the population according to Domhoff, is a ruling class. Two of the mechanisms by which the upper class rules are in the candidate-selection process and in its control of the media. Domhoff does not believe that recent changes in the law regarding campaign contributions will cut off the funneling of large sums of money to appropriate candidates. Individuals still can contribute as much as they want for advertisements promoting a particular candidate, and there is no ceiling on how much candidates can spend on their own candidacies (Allen 1987). Moreover, Political Action Committees (PACs) still can be created under various names to contribute to and campaign for chosen candidates and issues.

Finally, Domhoff (1979, 1983) argues that the upper class rules through its control of the "ideology process," that is, its position in the media and educational institutions. It has been suggested elsewhere, for example, that the capitalist class helped create and uphold laissez-faire ideology, which argues for the separation of economic and political affairs, in order to promote stringent governmental welfare policies, thereby providing a labor force willing to work for low wages (Piven and Cloward 1982). Control of the major media corporations has become more concentrated in recent years, and the reach of their influence has broadened to reach larger national audiences. "Most of the large media corporations in America are subject to some form of family control. . . . Indeed, several corporate rich families, such as the Hearsts, Scrippses, Pulitzers, Coxes, and Newhouses, own virtually all of the stock in major media corporations. In other cases, corporate rich families, such as the Grahams, Sulzbergers, Chandlers, Medills, Knights, and Gannetts, are major stockholders in publicly owned media corporations" (Allen 1987, p. 286). With respect to education, a recent study argues that elite prep schools are "crucibles" that prepare upper-class students for their positions in the corporate and governmental power elite (Cookson and Persell 1985).

Domhoff's conclusions about the mechanisms through which the power elite rules raise a number of questions. First, does the fact that upper-class individuals occupy positions of political influence mean that they will press for policies that only benefit the upper class? The evidence on this question has implications for several of the mechanisms just discussed. Second, are PACs and lobbying influential in the political process in a way that suggests domination by one class? Does money buy elections and votes? Third, and perhaps most importantly, is the upper class in general and its ruling "power elite" as united as Domhoff suggests? We address each of these issues in the following pages.

With respect to the first question, there are clear dangers in assuming that once in office a person will automatically represent the interests of his or her class:

1. Although most of the elite are from wealthy backgrounds, not all wealthy individuals become members of the elite.

2. Not all of the wealthy who become members of the elite were born into or inherited their wealth. Some are more obviously self-made individuals, although they are wealthy. Those of poor backgrounds may certainly act differently from those who inherited their wealth.

3. The values of the elite can change even though recruitment continues to be from the wealthy (Prewitt and Stone 1973, pp. 146–147).

4. Finally, internal conflicts and competition within the elite among those with different capital interests hinder unity on specific policy content (Poulantzas 1973).

Despite these factors and the possible wide range of specific policies the elite may introduce, these differences are outweighed by the cohesiveness of broader agreements on how policies should be made and by concern for the preservation and protection of U.S. values and institutions (Prewitt and Stone 1973, pp. 148–157).

Candidate Selection and Campaign Funding

Short of actual occupancy in a political office, another substantial manner in which an individual or organization can attempt to have political impact is through direct influence of office-holders. Two forms these attempts can take are the formation of interest groups and campaign contributions. Any mass of people thinking about organizing into an interest group must have access to resources necessary for effective mobilization in support of its interests. Presently, it is much easier for wealthy elites to mobilize political-party support for their interests. Most consumers, for example, "find it hard or impossible to [organize] for obvious reasons—their large numbers, their lack of face-to-face contact or facilities for communicating with each other, and above all, the fact that people do not often think of themselves in the role of consumers" (Dolbeare and Edelman 1971, p. 343). Even when consumer groups are organized, they are usually

of an elite nature and tend, like most groups, to become oligarchical. Consequently, the tendency is for interest groups to become "mass managing" rather than "representing" units (Dolbeare and Edelman 1971, pp. 392–393).

In the recent past, direct lobbying has been carried out by various groups with financial power. The exact amount of political influence these groups possess, however, is a subject of debate. Lester Milbrath (1965) concluded that their political power is evidently not very great, but an historical study done in the late 1960s began by stating that:

> The influence of pressure groups and paid lobbyists on Congressional legislation in recent years has been great. Almost every bill considered by Congress has had its contingent of interested pressure groups which presented testimony, wired or met with Members of Congress, sent delegations or hired lobbyists to meet them, or carried on propaganda designed to sway public sympathy and thus eventually sway the legislators. (Congressional Quarterly *1968, p. 1*)

The report goes on to say that there is "abundant evidence" that during the nineteenth and early twentieth centuries pressure groups were often effective in bringing about the kinds of legislation they sought (*Congressional Quarterly* 1968, p. 2). One obvious avenue by which a group (or person) can tie itself to political power is through campaign contributions. A study of the 1972 national elections by Common Cause revealed that most of the contributions to congressional candidates "came in large sums from well-heeled givers—individuals and special interest and party committees" (Campaign Finance Monitoring Project 1974, p. v). Groups representing economic interests gave a total of $8,267,485 to the campaigns of congressional candidates during the 1972 election. These groups represent unions as well as business, banking institutions, and dairy workers (Campaign Finance Monitoring Project 1974, p. 4), and the amounts are "an effort by the interests to win influence with victorious candidates." One million dollars also was contributed by health organizations, principally the American Medical Association.

In the early 1970s, wealthy individuals figured significantly in the campaign contributions to certain individuals and parties. In 1972, twenty-five contributors gave a total of $11.6 million to candidates at all levels of government. The 1,254 individuals who gave $10,000 or more contributed a total of $51 million to candidates or party committees (Alexander 1976b, pp. 372–375). Money from the super wealthy was more likely to go to Republican candidates than Democratic contenders. The largest campaign contributor in 1972 was insurance executive W. Clement Stone, who gave $2,141,666, the vast majority of which went to Republicans.

In an attempt to limit and make known the sources of contributions, the Congress passed the Federal Election Campaign Act of 1971 to which amendments were added in 1974, but it is still questionable that such legislation affected the system of giving significantly (Alexander 1967a, pp. 11–12). In fact, some feel that the whole emphasis on trying to limit *individuals* is misplaced. These critics argue that what needs changing is the *economic system,* because as it stands the officeholders can do little else but support powerful economic interests. Individual officeholders do not have to consciously attempt to uphold the interests of these groups in order to do so (compare with Block 1977, for example).

Running for political office has become very expensive. For example, the cost of the 1980 presidential campaign was $275 million and for congressional campaigns $239 million (Alexander 1983, p. 104). Succinctly put, "money is essential to elective politics" (ibid., p. 103). With campaign changes, the number of PACs willing to fund campaigns has grown rapidly. The number of PACs and how much they contribute to federal elections have exploded since the mid-1970s. In 1974, there were 608 but by 1984 there were over 4,000. In 1974, PACs contributed a total of $12.5 million to candidates for Congress, whereas in 1984 contributions totaled $132.2 million (Stern 1988, p. 24). In the late 1970s and early 1980s,

the unification and amount of spending by corporate PACs grew significantly. Corporate contributions to federal-level candidates grew from $9.8 million in 1978 to $21.6 million in 1980. Corporate PACs contributed more than any other type of PAC. On the other hand, labor PACs and organized labor in general declined in financial power during the same period (Alexander 1983; Edsall 1984). In 1974, labor PAC money composed 50 percent of all PAC contributions, but by 1980 it had fallen to 24 percent (Alexander 1983, p. 368).

Regarding the issue of PACs and their impact, recent studies suggest that while PACs may increase an individual's access to given members of Congress, they do not systematically affect how these members vote. Senator Russell B. Long once said that "the distinction between a large campaign contribution and a bribe is almost a hairline's difference" (quoted in Stern 1988, p. 146). But in research on twenty labor-related issues in the U.S. House of Representatives, Jones and Keiser (1987) found that the amount of contributions from union-approved PACs was related to voting only on issues that had little media attention. In other words, the less visible the issue, the greater the effect of contributions on voting behavior. A second analysis of 120 PACs connected to 10 different organizations examined the effect of PACs on the voting behavior of members of the House of Representatives and no significant influence on voting was found. However, these PACs and the organizations they represent can influence voting to the extent that they can influence the election process in the districts from which these congressional members originate (Grenzke 1989; see also Sabato 1984). It is not through the amount of the PAC contribution itself, but through other mechanisms that economically powerful groups can influence voting patterns. PACs, however, vary in their approaches to elections and in deciding who will receive contributions. Some PACs support incumbents in office because they are primarily interested in obtaining access to officeholders while others contribute to those who will increase the proportion of officeholders from a particular party. Finally, still others are "ideological" or "adversarial" and promote candidates who are on a particular side of an issue (Eismeier and Pollock 1986). While some are more likely to support challengers, most PAC contributions appear to go to incumbents (Wilhite and Theilmann 1986; Stern 1988; Eismeier and Pollock 1986). Black candidates, however, receive much less PAC support than whites (Wilhite and Theilmann 1986).

PACs represent many different interest groups. Corporations, labor, assorted trade, and nonconnected specific-issues groups are among the organizations with PACs, and each follows different strategies. A study looked at the strategies followed by corporate PACs during the 1980 congressional elections. Pluralists argue that the upper class and corporate elite are not united, but these data indicate that while PACs with corporate affiliations may follow different general strategies, they rarely conflict with each other when it comes to specific races. This analysis of 243 PACs that made contributions of $25,000 or more revealed that while some PACs backed a candidate or incumbent for "ideological" reasons, others followed a more "pragmatic" course by backing the incumbent, assuming his or her re-election. This suggests an internal division within the corporate elite. However, on the level of the individual races there was a great deal of overlap between these types of PACs in terms of which candidate was supported. In almost 75 percent of the races, 90 percent of the corporate money went to only one of the two candidates. In other words, these corporate groups do not tend to conflict with each other when it comes to specific political races (Clawson et al. 1986).

RULING-CLASS UNITY

Several of the studies on PACs bear on Domhoff's argument about the unity of the ruling class, which has been the subject of a recent controversy. Some view the corporate capitalist class as being divided along a variety of dimensions. Varying sizes of the workforces, differences in

regions and in economic sectors (agricultural, manufacturing, etc.) with which organizations are identified, and competition and private property within capitalism make it inevitable to some that this class would be fragmented because of the different short-run specific interests within it (Offe 1973; Poulantzas 1973; Aldrich and Weiss 1981). In this view, the narrow interests of each corporation take precedence over the classwide interests of the corporate economy as a whole. This internal division weakens the power of the corporate class as a whole (for a review, see Useem 1984).

Mills and Domhoff's descriptions of the social backgrounds of the elite and the historical circumstances in which they rule suggest that they are unified. Domhoff describes their common membership in and interaction at exclusive clubs, attendance at elite schools, and frequent listing on the Social Register, while Mills not only describes their social-psychological similarities, but the concentration and coalescence that have occurred among the major institutions involved in the power elite. Domhoff details some evidence of intermarriages, unique schooling, and leisure activities that point, he argues, to the existence of a cohesive upper class of which the public is conscious. He contends that his evidence "suggests that the upper class is now national in its scope and has developed a country-wide net of interrelated social and educational institutions" (1971, p. 28). Baltzell agrees that "there exists one metropolitan upper class with a common cultural tradition, consciousness of kind, a 'we' feeling of solidarity which tends to be national in scope" (quoted in Roach et al. 1969, p. 157). In contrast to Domhoff and Baltzell, Giddens argues that it is not in the interest of the upper class to be visible to the public, but rather "to deny their own distinctiveness as a separate and isolable class" because it functions within a political democracy in which the "class principle" is not supposed to operate (1973, p. 176).

Ostrander's (1984) study of upper-class women suggests that they are highly conscious of their class and their responsibilities in maintaining their social class position. In supporting their husbands' economic activities, and as members of voluntary associations and social clubs, upper-class women work to perpetuate their social class. "A central aim of upper-class women's community volunteer work, as they describe it, is to keep private control over community organizations. Private control comes to be identified as the control of their own class. . . . [T]heir social life is the social life of a class, and their relations weave the fabric of upper-class life. As community volunteers, upper-class women work almost entirely as members of their class. They have little in common, here, with other women" (Ostrander 1984, pp. 148–149). While there are tensions and individual disagreements within this group, as a whole they are united in defense of their class. This not only helps to maintain their class, but because it is male-dominated, the subordinate position of these women within it (ibid.).

The studies cited focus on the unity of the upper class as a whole. Other studies reviewed earlier on political activity, however, also imply unification of the elite as a group, many of whom are not of upper-class background. In his study of elites, involving individuals from a variety of institutional areas, Dye (1986) also concludes that there is general unity of opinion among the elite, even though there is some evidence of rising factionalism within it. "It is our own judgment, based on our examination of available surveys of leadership opinion as well as public statements of top corporate and governmental executives, that consensus rather than competition characterizes elite opinion. Despite disagreements over specific policies and programs, most top leaders agree on the basic values and future directions of American society. . . . Disagreement among various sectors of national leaders . . . is confined to a relatively narrow set of issues—the size of governmental budgets, specific details of tax reform, and the pace of the defense build-up. There is widespread agreement on the essential components of welfare-state capitalism" (Dye 1986, p. 240). Verba and Orren's study of 2,762 leaders from various institutional areas in the late 1970s

also suggests unity on *basic values*. They found that all types of leaders tend to agree, for example, that a fair distribution of economic resources is one in which everyone has equal opportunity to pursue legitimate goals. They do not feel that everyone should have an equal amount, however. This solidarity of opinion included black, feminist, and labor leaders. However, when it comes to opinions on *specific* matters rather than *general* values, or to descriptions of actual rather than ideal situations, there is disagreement among these leaders. For example, only 9 percent of business leaders view poverty as the result of the workings of the economic system, while 86 percent of black leaders and 76 percent of feminist leaders see it this way (Verba and Orren 1985, p. 74). Seider's (1974) content analysis of the speeches of big business executives also indicates that although there are differences among them on specifics, there is fundamental unity on beliefs supporting the capitalist economic system that "is never challenged."

Even though he has concluded that the elite are generally united on basic values, Dye (1986) also goes on to argue that a split has developed within the elite between those he labels the "sunbelt cowboys" and the "established yankees." As the labels suggest, the cowboys as a group are individualistic, conservative, and often from non-upper-class backgrounds. Their wealth has been recently acquired. In contrast, the "yankees" tend to be more liberal and have established family wealth. They have attended the best Ivy League schools and are also likely to have occupied high positions in prestigious corporate, financial, or legal institutions. Thus, as to the issue of how unified the elite or upper class is, it is important to indicate whether one is speaking of the *general* or *specific* level, in *ideal* or *real-situational* terms, and of *social-background* or *behavioral* unity. In some ways, these groups appear unified while in others they do not; the results from attitudinal and positional studies on unity are clearly mixed and one can find statistics to support both positions. Like Domhoff, Dye, and others, Useem has dissected the capitalist class and its unity in detail. His studies concern the structural texture of that class (cf., e.g., 1978, 1979, 1984). Useem defines the capitalist class as "those who own or manage major business firms and their immediate kin" (1980, p. 200). In one analysis, Useem studied 2,843 officers from 200 corporations that varied in size and sector. The officers also differed in the number of corporations to which they were tied through directorships. Generally, Useem found that members of the capitalist class are not equally powerful. Those from larger firms who were also directors at other corporations were significantly more likely to have served on advisory committees for government at the local, state, and federal levels. They are also more likely to participate in national business groups such as the Business Roundtable, Business Council, Council on Foreign Relations, National Association of Manufacturers, and U.S. Chamber of Commerce and to be involved in significant cultural organizations (elite university boards, art, and research organizations) (1980). Useem, however, did not find significant participation differences between major industrialists and financiers.

In other research, Useem directly addresses the issue of the political unity of what he calls the "inner circle" of business, looking at whether members of this group act on behalf of their own separate corporations or on behalf of the capitalist class as a whole. Useem draws his information and conclusions from a wide variety of data sources, including personal interviews and documentary and survey data. The inner circle he describes is a network of leaders from large corporations who serve as top officers at more than one firm, who are politically active, and who serve the interests of the capitalist class as a whole rather than the narrow immediate interests of their individual companies. To be a member of the inner circle, it helps to (1) have been successful in a major corporation, (2) have multiple directorships, (3) have occupied a senior position, (4) be a member of business associations, and (5) have been a consultant or advisor to government.

Members of the inner circle are more often members of the upper class than are other business leaders, that is, they are richer, have attended elite prep schools, and are in the Social Register (Useem 1984, pp. 65–69).

Useem sees capitalism in the United States as having moved from (1) "family capitalism" in which individual upper-class families dominated corporate ownership, through (2) "managerial capitalism" in which managers began to replace the dominance of upper-class owners around the turn of the twentieth century, to (3) "institutional capitalism" in which networks of intercorporate ties characterize the core of capitalism. The increasing control of corporations by their managers rather than owners and the increased concentration and interlocking in the corporate sector during this century have helped lay the basis for the development of this powerful circle (Useem 1984). Indeed, Dye's study of individuals in top institutional positions reveals that 4,000 to 5,000 individuals have formal control over 50 percent of the country's industrial, banking, communications, transportation, and utilities assets and over 66 percent of the nation's insurance assets. The top 100 of 200,000 industrial corporations control over 58 percent of the $1.6 trillion in industrial assets, the 50 biggest banks control almost two-thirds of all banking assets, and 50 insurance companies control over 80 percent of assets in their field (Dye 1986, pp. 16–19). Fifteen percent of the 7,314 institutional leaders studied by Dye occupied more than one top position (i.e., were interlockers) and a smaller percent held as many as six or more such positions. He views this "inner group" as cohesive for a number of reasons, and, like Useem, finds that multiple corporate interlockers were more likely than single directors to participate in governmental and other major organizations.

In addition to these trends in the corporate sphere, the "inner circle" of corporate leaders Useem (1984) describes has also developed as a result of the "disparate" nature of the business community and the uncertain environment that exists for business in capitalist societies. That is, the inner circle unifies the interests of business as a class in a turbulent political and economic setting. The development of this circle is not the result of a conscious conspiracy, but rather is largely the consequence of structural changes and characteristics of capitalist society. Those in the circle serve on several boards, making them sensitive to the interests of business as a whole, that is, to the "classwide" needs of business. The circle's political style is to adopt a "posture of compromise" and accommodation rather than to be directly confrontational on every specific issue. Its interests are in the general protection of capitalism as a whole, not in the interests of specific companies.

There are a number of ways in which this elite group of business leaders gets politically involved. One principal mechanism is through governmental ties. As Useem's and others' research indicates, for example, they are more likely to serve as Cabinet officers. During Ronald Reagan's first term, Weinberger (Defense), Regan (Treasury), Baldrige (Commerce), Haig (State), and Pierce (Housing and Urban Development), as well as Smith (Attorney General) had all been multiple corporate directors. Like Dye and others, Useem also finds that the inner-circle members play crucial political roles by directing nonprofit organizations, serving as political fundraisers, endorsing candidates, giving larger campaign contributions, and influencing media content (Useem 1984, pp. 76–94).

This inner circle is much more politically active than business in general because its members occupy several important positions at once, which (1) creates cohesiveness among its members, (2) helps mobilize economic and other resources, and (3) provides a powerful platform from which to express political positions. Moreover, its members are also closely tied to the upper class which increases the circle's influence (Useem 1984). In contrast to other research, Useem finds that if members of the upper class are in the business elite, they are more likely than

persons from other classes to get into the inner circle. In sum, characteristics of the U.S. political economy create opportunities for the interconnection of political and economic power.

The Structural Tie

A significant part of the reason for the tie between economic and political power lies in the interlocking between private and corporate wealth and political opportunity. It takes wealth, or at least access to wealth, to run a viable campaign for a major national political office. As Gans put it, given the conditions at the present time, "American democracy allows affluent minorities to propose and the majority to dispose" (1968, p. 132; see also Prewitt and Stone 1973). The connection between economic and political power may be deeper than this suggests, however, and may be based not on the characteristics of particular individuals but on the structure and functioning of the society.

The *structuralist* position suggests that given the structure of a capitalist society such as the United States, the government *must* act in a manner that supports the capitalist class and capitalism in general. This occurs regardless of who is in office. The political and economic institutions are so intertwined that the government, while it may be "relatively autonomous," is constrained to support and pass policies that maintain the capitalist economy. Even in the absence of direct influence by the ruling class, the state would find it difficult to carry out anticapitalist policies (Block 1977). It is the structural context in which the government is embedded that directs its policies most powerfully, rather than individuals who hold political office. "The functions of the state are broadly determined by the structures of state power" (Gold et al. 1975, p. 36). This does not mean that every policy will always benefit each individual corporation, but it does mean that in the long run the interests of capitalism in general will be served by these policies. Hicks et al.

(1978), for example, found that the presence of corporations in general has a negative impact on government policies of redistribution to the poor, while the presence in a particular state of labor unions has a positive effect. According to structuralists, this wedding between economic interests and governmental policies exists for several reasons:

1. *The capitalist economy has developed in such a manner that increasing numbers of workers are together under one system.* In other words, capitalism has speeded the *social* nature of labor and production. This creates a greater possibility for "working-class unity," which in turn can threaten the existing nature of the economy. The state works to prevent this worker unity from becoming too strong by endorsing policies that transform general political interests of the working class (such as control of the production system) into narrower economic ones (such as wages and vacation times) (Gold et al. 1975, pp. 36–37). Class antagonisms can endanger the state and, as a result, policies and ideologies are used to mask and reduce class struggle.

2. *The government helps to provide and regulate a labor force for hire through its provision of educational facilities and restrictive welfare policies.* Educational institutions exist to help prepare individuals to fit into their roles in the economy and class structure, while demeaning and meager governmental support through welfare programs helps to insure that any surplus labor force will be eager to take any job at low wages (Bowles and Gintis 1976; Szymanski 1978; Piven and Cloward 1982).

3. *The state needs to maintain a certain level of economic activity if it is to survive; it needs revenue to run itself.* If capitalists do not invest, then government has problems. Consequently, policies are created to encourage investments and capital accumulation (Offe 1975). This takes place even though the state may not be made up of members of the ruling class. In fact, the state can function best to support capitalism in this view if its class character is hidden and it is seen as a legitimate classless state (Offe 1973).

4. *The state has to insure the smooth running of the economy, because if it is not stable, the state will lose public support.* If the state pursues anticapitalist policies, business confidence will decrease; if that occurs, investments will decline and the economy as well as the government will be in danger. Consequently, it is in the state's own interest to pursue capitalist policies, that is, to act "responsibly" (Block 1977, p. 1519). Affluence helps to maintain control over the citizenry. "As long as the economic system provides an acceptable degree of security, growing material wealth, and opportunity . . . for the next generation, the average American does not ask who is running things or what goals are being pursued" (Fusfeld 1972, p. 2).

5. *The development of monopoly capitalism encourages the intrusion of the state into the economy, and thereby the state itself develops an interest in capital accumulation* (Gold et al. 1975, pp. 40–48; O'Connor 1973; Block 1977). One manner in which this occurs is through the creation of unemployment in part because of technological advances in the monopoly sector. The state then steps in to deal with the problem.

The preceding review of studies indicates that both individuals and structural arrangements foster a relationship between economic and political power. Structural ties among institutions make it possible for some individuals to have access to positions of great power. According to some, however, one of the major problems with both these analyses is that they assume that all major policies are made within the government and, therefore, the focus of both approaches is on the state. In fact, it has been suggested, many major policies are created outside the government, principally by the actions of corporations. Industrial change, for example, to the extent that it can be considered a "policy," has largely been the result of actions by the private sector, not the government (Schwartz 1987).

SUMMARY

This chapter began with a brief discussion on the importance and difficulty of conceptualizing power. We then moved to an analysis of pluralist, elite, and ruling-class views of the national power structure, and the data that bear on the validity of each.

There are clear relationships between socioeconomic position and voting, holding political office, and other forms of political participation. Those closer to the bottom of the class hierarchy are less likely than those in the middle and upper classes to vote, be elected to office, and to be represented in powerful lobbying groups. Research indicates that those from higher socioeconomic levels, especially the upper class, are disproportionately represented in elite positions in a variety of institutional spheres.

Each of these measures is characteristic of an approach to understanding the relationship between economic resources and political power that traces the careers and institutional paths of *individuals* rather than focusing on the *structure* of the institutional network itself as a basis for such understanding. The structuralist approach, on the other hand, focuses on the systemic interrelationships between the economy and the state, suggesting that the government is inextricably tied to the capitalist economy and needs to support capitalism in order to maintain itself. This is independent of the particular individuals who may occupy office at the time. A number of the changes that have occurred in the political economy, such as increased concentration, interlocking between institutions, and the like, encourage greater centralization and unity of economic and political power. On balance, the data presented provide evidence of a greater concentration of political power than is suggested by pluralist theory.

CHAPTER 6

THE IMPACT OF INEQUALITY ON PERSONAL LIFE CHANCES

It is the most elemental economic fact that the way in which the disposition over material property is distributed among a plurality of people, meeting competitively in the market for the purpose of exchange, in itself creates specific life chances.
—Max Weber

"Bobbi paused for a moment, then continued: 'I tell you, times ain't easy. I got up at six this morning. We're flat broke. Ain't got no money, no food. . . . Ain't paid no bills, haven't paid the rent. So I got up at six, got dressed, tried to feed the children, and went over to the welfare. I walked all the way down there, all the way down the road. Got there before seven and it was thirteen degrees' " (Howell 1973, p. 62).

Another view from a white-collar worker who is better off but still not well to do: "Like my father used to tell us, it's a mean and rotten world if you don't have any money. And there I am in the bank deciding if people will get money — but I myself don't have very much! We're always behind on bills" (Coles and Erikson 1971, p. 91).

There wouldn't be much point in studying inequality if it had few implications for people. *Inequality is an important subject because, ultimately, its existence affects the day-to-day lives of people.* The social positions that individuals find themselves in help to determine who they are, what they think and do, and where they are going. Most basically, social inequality affects the life chances of individuals. In this chapter, we

will focus on the relationship of inequality to basic life chances: physical and mental health, personality, relationships and abuse in the family. In Chapter 7, the emphasis will be on two of the many social effects of inequality — crime and collective unrest.

The studies reviewed here do not measure social class in any one way, but rather in variable ways in terms of education, occupation, income, and/or racial-ethnic status. Consequently, results are not always strictly comparable because different measures have been used; however, rough comparisons can be made because of the interrelatedness of the measures used. The statement made by Luther Otto in this regard cannot be stressed too strongly: "Failure to use conceptually equivalent measures leads to one of two results: results in conflict with the findings of other investigations, or consistent results without concomitant consistency with what it is that the results are consistent about" (1975, p. 317). As often as possible, we note the kinds of measures used so readers can take this into account in their own assessment of findings.

BASIC LIFE CHANCES: PHYSICAL HEALTH

There is nothing more basic to life than physical health, and it is evident that individuals rate their own health status differently depending upon their race, sex, and income. A 1987 national survey based on interviews with civilian adults across the country showed, not surprisingly, that a greater percentage of men than women, whites than blacks, and high-income than low-income individuals rated their own health as "excellent" (see Table 6.1). For example, while 42 percent of whites rated their health in this manner, only about 29 percent of blacks felt this way. Over 50 percent of those whose family incomes were at least $35,000 rated their health as excellent, compared to only 26 percent of those whose incomes were below $10,000.

The life expectancies at birth of black and whites and men and women have also been consistently different over time. Generally, women of both races have higher life expectancies than men of the same race, but black women have a life expectancy closer to white men than to white women. White women have the highest life expectancy; in 1986 it was 78.8 years. Black males are the lowest; in 1986 their life expectancy was

65.2 years. Since 1900, the gap in life expectancies between the sexes within each race has increased, while that between the races has decreased (see Table 6.2). The average life expectancy for all Americans in 1986 was about 75. This is the same as the United Kingdom and France, but slightly lower than that found in Italy, Canada, West Germany, and the Netherlands.

The infant mortality rate in the United States in 1986 was 10.4 per 1,000 live births. This is higher than that found in Canada and all major western European countries except Italy (United Nations 1988, p. 72). Within the United States, the percentage of infants under one year of age who die continues to be greater for blacks than for whites, even though the rate for both races has declined in recent decades (cf., e.g., Bertoli et al. 1984). In 1986, the rate for whites was just under 9 while that for blacks was 18 per 1,000 live births (U.S. Dept. of Health and Human Services, March, 1989, p. 54). Moreover, the differences in infant mortality rates between income groups also appears to be continuing (Stockwell et al. 1987). Analysis of data suggests that both mother's education and family income are inversely related to child mortality (Mare 1982).

TABLE 6.1 Self-Assessment of Health by Sex, Race, and Family Income: 1987

	ASSESSMENT			
	Excellent	Very Good	Good	Fair or Poor
Male	42.6	27.4	21.0	9.0
Female	38.2	28.2	23.7	9.9
White	42.1	28.2	21.1	8.5
Black	29.5	24.4	29.4	16.7
Family Income				
Less than $10,000	26.4	24.1	28.9	20.5
$10,000–$14,999	31.9	26.9	27.1	14.1
$15,000–$19,999	34.7	28.1	26.3	11.0
$20,000–$34,999	41.1	29.2	22.7	7.1
$35,000 or more	50.9	28.0	16.3	4.7

Source: U.S. Dept. of Health and Human Services, *Health United States 1988,* March 1989, Table 50, p. 95.

TABLE 6.2   Life Expectancy at Birth by Sex and Race: Selected Years 1900–1986

	WHITE			BLACK		
	Both sexes	*Male*	*Female*	*Both sexes*	*Male*	*Female*
1900	47.6	46.6	48.7	33.0	32.5	33.5
1950	69.1	66.5	72.2	60.7	58.9	62.7
1960	70.6	67.4	74.1	63.2	60.7	65.9
1970	71.7	68.0	75.6	64.1	60.0	68.3
1980	74.4	70.7	78.1	68.1	63.8	72.5
1986	75.4	72.0	78.8	69.4	65.2	73.5

Source: U.S. Dept. of Health and Health Services, *Health United States 1988,* March 1989, Table 13, p. 53.

Health Conditions

Differences in health still exist between the classes in the United States, and in other industrial countries such as England and France as well (Susser et al. 1983; Hollingsworth 1981; d'Houtaud and Field 1984; Cockerham et al. 1986). Those with lower incomes generally report more acute conditions and a greater number of days being restricted and confined to bed because of such conditions. But during their lives, whites generally report more of certain acute conditions than blacks and indicate a greater number of restricted days because of them. These conditions include infective and parasitic diseases, respiratory conditions, ear conditions, and injuries. Among those that are higher for blacks are the common cold and digestive conditions (U.S. Dept. of Health and Human Services, September 1988, pp. 17, 35). While "race" in these statistics may not be a very good measure of "class," it serves as a rough index of socioeconomic status.

"Chronic" conditions are those health problems that continue over a long period of time. For those under forty-five, whites in general have higher rates of conditions such as arthritis, ulcers, heart disease, hay fever, and visual impairment, while blacks report higher rates of asthma, high blood pressure, and anemias. With the exception of arthritis, these differences continue among those sixty-five and older. In most cases, those with lower family incomes have higher rates of chronic conditions than those with high incomes (U.S. Dept. of Health and Human

Services, September 1988, pp. 88–93). Among both blacks and whites, the greatest percentage of deaths are caused by heart disease and malignancies, which account for over 50 percent of all deaths. But within both races, those in the poorest social class with breast cancer have the shortest survival period (Bassett and Krieger 1986).

In terms of health habits, recent evidence suggests that the poor may not be significantly different from the more affluent. For example, the 1984 Illinois Health Survey found that there were no differences between various status groups in terms of concern for physical appearance, eating right, and alcohol consumption. They attribute these results to the media's support and promotion of such health-related behaviors as exercise and its influence on individuals from all classes (Cockerham et al. 1986). Smoking has also declined for all groups, but blacks still smoke more than whites and men more than women. However, the rate of decline in smoking for women since the mid-1970s has been slower than that for men (Fiore et al. 1989).

Verbrugge (1985) has recently summarized the evidence on gender differences in mortality and disease from the last ten to fifteen years and draws the following conclusions:

1. In the last 100 years, mortality rates for both sexes have declined, but have declined faster for women than for men. However, in recent years, the difference in mortality rates may have "stabilized," which may be a harbinger of greater gender equality in mortality.

2. There are indications that the health of both sexes has worsened since 1950, but especially since 1970. These indicators include short-term disability rates, rising rates of chronic activity limitation, and increased rates of chronic conditions. Among the possible reasons for these trends are (a) greater willingness to report conditions, (b) earlier diagnosis of illnesses, and (c) the fact that sick people are living longer.

3. The worsening health among women appears to be concentrated among those who have limited roles, whereas women who are married as well as employed have had better health in recent years.

4. The risks of death are higher for males at all ages and for all causes of death.

5. Women suffer from higher rates of acute and nonfatal chronic conditions, such as arthritis and gallbladder problems and also have higher rates of short-term disability and use of medical services and drugs than men.

6. On the other hand, men have higher rates of life-threatening diseases that can lead to serious disability and/or premature death. "One sex is 'sicker' in the short run [women], and the other [men] in the long run" (pp. 162–163).

7. The gaps between the sexes on health status are greatest when they are young adults and decrease when in old age.

8. Many of the chronic conditions that women endure or attend to by themselves are not picked up in the national statistics and, therefore, the latter only cover the tip of the "iceberg of morbidity."

Verbrugge goes on to examine the possible reasons for these differences in health and concludes from the evidence that "acquired risks" are the most important causes, followed respectively by psychosocial factors, prior health care, biological differences, and reporting differences between men and women. Among "acquired risks," she notes that men have used tobacco and alcohol for longer periods, contributing to their cancer, cardiovascular, and liver morbidity, while their more frequent driving and style of driving may have contributed to their higher rate of motor vehicle accidents.

Employment conditions also appear to affect the differential health statuses of men and women. Employed women, especially those who have been employed for a long period, are healthier than those recently employed or housewives. Those who are recently nonemployed are the least healthy (Anson and Anson 1987). In addition, the nature of the employment and social support for it affect perceived health. More enriching work, coupled with support by colleagues and spouses, is related to better health (Hibbard and Pope 1987). Differences on psychosocial factors, such as how individuals react to symptoms, appear to be more important for less serious chronic conditions and much less significant for very serious, possibly fatal conditions. When the health condition is less serious, there is more room for choice and discretion to operate, allowing gender differences on psychosocial measures to surface (Verbrugge 1985).

In terms of health habits, Verbrugge finds no consistent differences between men and women. When they are suffering from the same condition, men and women do not differ in getting help or slowing down their activities, but women tend to take more time off from their jobs when they have a serious illness or other condition. Women are more attentive to their bodies and, therefore, are more sensitive to symptoms. They also take more continuous care of their health problems than men do. Finally, they are better at reporting minor health problems and this might help minimize the seriousness of those problems later in life and help account for their higher life expectancy. Traditionally in U.S. society, men are supposed to be "strong and silent." But this may work against them.

Use of Health Services

Given the differences in health conditions between groups, we would expect parallel differences in the use of physicians, hospitals, and other health facilities. In general, whites see physicians slightly more often than blacks. In 1987, whites had an average of 5.5 physician contacts per person compared to 5.1 for blacks. These include all kinds of contacts, that is, office and clinic visits as well as telephone conversations. Women have more contacts than men, and those with lower incomes also average more physician contacts. When they do meet, blacks and those with lower incomes more often meet with doctors in a hospital outpatient department or emergency-room setting, whereas whites are more likely to meet doctors in their offices. The time interval between physician contacts has declined for both races and all income groups and between these races and groups in the last two decades, so that in 1987 over 75 percent of blacks and whites and over 73 percent of all income groups had contacted a doctor within the last year. A greater percentage of women than men have contacted a physician within the last year (U.S. Dept. of Health and Human Services, March 1989, pp. 106–107).

Of course, the reasons for these contacts can and do vary even though the intervals between visits may be declining. Women, for example, have more frequent contacts largely because of the childbirth process (Rix 1988). It also appears to be the case that those in higher income categories are more likely to see physicians for preventive reasons than those in lower income groups (Cockerham et al. 1986; U.S. Dept. of Health and Human Services 1985, p. 215).

Women, whites, and high-income individuals also have a higher average number of dental visits than other categories of individuals, and the intervals between visits are also smaller for these groups. In 1986, almost twice as many individuals with family incomes below $10,000, compared to those with incomes of at least $35,000, had never seen a dentist (13.4 percent versus 7.1 percent) (U.S. Dept. of Health and Human Services, March 1989, p. 110). Only about one-third of blacks have dental insurance, and only approximately 10 percent of those with family incomes below $10,000 have such coverage. In contrast, over 40 percent of whites and over 60 percent of those with incomes of $35,000 or more have dental insurance. High-income individuals are also less likely than low-income persons to be edentulous (toothless) (U.S. Dept. of Health and Human Services, October 1988, pp. 60–61). In addition to dental and doctor contacts, groups also differ on the time they spend in hospitals. Men, blacks, and low-income individuals have more hospital visits and longer lengths of stay, on average, than other groups.

Why do these differences in the use of services exist? A number of factors appear to be involved. In his survey of various models of service use, Shortell (1984) concludes that "generally, need for care is the best predictor of differences in use, although the availability of a regular source of care, insurance coverage, and sociodemographic characteristics such as age are also associated with various patterns of use" (p. 83). Usage appears to be related to the perceived quality of care an individual receives, and often those who are less well off will not use a service because of this problem (Dutton 1978). Some have contended that the values and characteristics of the poor themselves contribute to a reluctance to use medical services (Stockwell 1968; Rosenstock 1969; Herman 1972). "The poor are . . . less aware of the concepts and practices of scientific medicine, and differences in many beliefs and values make communication between patient and practitioner difficult" (Herman 1972, p. 12). Nevertheless, national statistics indicate that lower income persons have more frequent contacts with physicians. But many of these contacts are not in depth or lengthy (for example, phone calls and emergency room visits).

The greater number of work days lost and physical contacts by lower income individuals may be related to their interpretation of symptoms and determinants of health. They are more likely than those in the higher income categories to feel that given symptoms require a physician visit and to feel that the quallity of their health is primarily affected by factors beyond their control (Cockerham et al. 1986).

Recent polls indicate that almost 90 percent

of Americans feel the health care system needs a basic overhaul. More Americans than British or Canadians say they do not get needed health care because of financial problems (7 percent versus under 1 percent), and over 60 percent of Americans say they would prefer a government-underwritten health care system like that in Canada to the present system (Hevesi 1989). Clearly, Americans as a whole are dissatisfied with the quality of health care in the United States.

A 1986 national survey of over 10,000 persons revealed that access to health care services is worse for blacks regardless of income, that they are less likely to pursue needed medical care, that they were more dissatisfied than whites with their care by doctors and in hospitals, and more likely to believe that their stays in hospitals are too short. The small number of minority physicians, the low ratios of doctors to population in minority communities, the fact that blacks are more likely to live in states with low Medicaid benefits, and the greater percentage of blacks than whites who have no health insurance are some of the possible reasons for the poorer access to health services

for blacks (Blendon et al. 1989). Table 6.3 gives some of the other reasons for significant differences in dissatisfaction between the races in the survey (ibid., p. 280).

Different reactions to health care received are not limited to race, but are related to sex as well. The helping professions have been accused of neglecting the "real needs" of female patients and "encouraging the perpetuation of sexist attitudes. For example, a poor woman who confesses to her social worker that she does not really want the child she is bearing, until recently would be 'counselled' to be more maternal instead of being offered the option of abortion" (Stoll 1974, p. 179). Many women complain about the insensitivity and lack of interest of their physicians in discussions of illnesses and disabilities especially characteristic of their sex (Stoll 1974, p. 177).

The negative image of women's bodies and sexist beliefs about women's nature are longstanding. In the nineteenth and early twentieth centuries, the female body was considered abnormal compared to the male body. Pregnancies, menstruation, menopause, and similar natural bi-

TABLE 6.3 Patient's Perception of Care Given During Ambulatory Visit for New Illness and Satisfaction with Care, by Race

AREA OF CONCERN	% WHITE	% BLACK
Physician did not ask sufficiently about pain	9.0	23.3
Physician did not say how long it takes for medicine to work	31.6	45.0
Physician did not explain seriousness of illness or injury	27.5	44.2
Physician did not discuss test or examination findings	14.0	22.7
Hospitalized too short a time	7.2	18.9
Physician did not discuss prevention	80.6	67.7
Completely satisfied with care during last hospitalization	77.4	57.5
Completely satisfied with care during last ambulatory visit	84.3	79.5
Had to wait for more than a half-hour at last ambulatory visit	18.1	25.1

Source: Blendon, Robert J., Linda H. Aiken, Howard E. Freeman, and Christopher Corey. January 13, 1989. "Access to Medical Care for Black and White Americans: A Matter of Continuing Concern." *Journal of the American Medical Association* 261(2): 280. Copyright 1989, American Medical Association.

ological events were considered conditions to be "treated," and physicians generally thought that it was in women's nature to be sick (Ehrenreich and English 1981; Rothman 1984). The ovaries and uterus were thought by male physicians to be the absolute core of the female body. Thus, the womb often was viewed as the source for many ailments suffered by women (Ehrenreich and English 1981). At the same time, women were encouraged to develop their "maternal instincts" and were not believed to have a sex drive as strong as men.

Because of their greater economic and organizational resources, male obstetricians successfully competed against midwives in the delivery of children, enabling them to gain control of a whole area of women's lives (Wertz and Wertz 1981). A captive group of female patients not only provided fees at a time when the number of clientele was dwindling, but their bodies provided "teaching material" for budding male physicians (Rothman 1984, pp. 72–73). Many of these attitudes still survive. An analysis of twenty-seven general gynecology textbooks published since 1943 in the United States revealed that at least 50 percent of them emphasize that women are "destined to reproduce, nurture, and keep their husbands happy" (Scully and Bart 1981, p. 350). Many of these same texts also stress that women's primary interest in sex is for "procreation" rather than "recreation" and that most females are "frigid." The authors of this study conclude: "Gynecologists, our society's official experts on women, think of themselves as the woman's friend. With friends like that, who needs enemies?" (Scully and Bart 1981, p. 354).

Class differences also have surfaced in the images of women's health and bodies. During the last century, women of the upper class were thought to be more "civilized" and refined than those in the working and lower classes. As a result, they were thought of as more fragile and vulnerable, more susceptible to various maladies. Ehrenreich and English suggest that much of their sickness may have been due to the "sexuo-economic" relationship in their marriages (1981).

Essentially, these women were viewed as providing sexual and reproductive services in exchange for economic support from their working husbands. The ill-fitting, heavy clothes expected to be worn by "ladies" of the upper class were responsible, in fact, for many of the illness symptoms experienced by these women. But as a consequence of these "health" problems, middle- and upper-class women became a "client caste" to physicians, while poor women received virtually no medical attention. Black, Native American, and working-class women were seen as being hearty of constitution in contrast to their upper-class counterparts and, therefore, in need of less attention. This stereotype provided a convenient rationale for giving medical care to those who had the financial resources to pay for it (Ehrenreich and English 1981; Wertz and Wertz 1981).

Even today, those with lower statuses receive poorer health services. One reason is that obstacles of different kinds prevent or at least hinder the use of appropriate medical facilities. Clinics may be difficult to get to for certain groups or may be overcrowded (or both). Costs may be too high for some. It has been shown that if barriers such as these are eliminated, individuals take advantage of important health services regardless of class. Research has demonstrated, for instance, that black individuals in lower socioeconomic groups often take advantage of free health services to a disproportionate degree, especially when their honor and self-worth are respected (Slesinger et al. 1975). This may be related to the previously mentioned greater worry over symptoms among lower income groups.

A study of those who have health insurance revealed a greater probability that blacks would use preventative services more frequently than whites (Slesinger et al. 1975). Blacks with higher incomes are more inclined to get check-ups and whites in similar circumstances are more likely to have had certain medical tests made on them to detect health deficiencies. But in the sample of almost 1,000, no clear or consistent relationship appears between separate measures of socioeconomic status and use of preventative health services. Thus, reduction of personal medical costs because of the possession of health insurance results in a greater proportion of those who need health care taking advantage of it.

HEALTH-CARE COSTS AND INEQUALITY

Health-care costs undoubtedly have an effect on the extent to which individuals pursue preventive and other health-care services. In 1985, the federal government spent almost $100 billion on health care, while state and local governments spent $60 billion and corporations almost $100 billion (Thurow 1985). Traditionally, compared with higher income groups, those with lower incomes spend *proportionately* more on health care (Anderson 1975). Obviously, obtaining health care is an expensive proposition. Rising health-care costs are a matter of great concern, and the reasons for the rise are various, relating in part to (1) changes in the size, sex, and age distribution of the population; (2) increased use of facilities; (3) advances in technology; (4) increases in third-party payments; (5) inflation, (6) changes in the frequency and types of illnesses, (7) malpractice insurance; and (8) increases in the numbers of diagnostic tests being given.

Possessing health insurance can help buffer the costs to the individual and, as just indicated, blacks are less likely to have such insurance. In 1986, 57 percent of blacks had private health insurance compared to 79 percent of whites. Seventeen percent of blacks and 4 percent of whites did have Medicaid insurance, but almost 23 percent of blacks compared to 14 percent of whites did not have any insurance coverage at all (U.S. Dept. of Health and Human Services March 1989, p. 171).

Not only do individuals find insurance costs prohibitive, but businesses as well, especially small businesses, suffer because of the high cost of insurance. "For thousands of small businesses, health insurance has become a nightmare. . . . Small businesses already commonly pay 10% to 25% more than large ones. . . . Small accounts

require proportionately higher administrative costs and their risks are harder to predict, insurers say. And a small company is in a weaker bargaining position. . . . [I]nsurers blame the rate increases on soaring health-care costs" (Ricklefs 1988).

The increased costs of health care take their toll on everyone but especially groups which are less well off and more vulnerable. Like small businesses, small rural hospitals find it more difficult than larger ones to digest the costs of those who cannot pay or whose costs are not fully picked up by insurance. In 1988, eighty-one community hospitals were forced to close, due in part to inadequate payments from Medicaid and Medicare programs, the loss of physicians, and area economic problems. Most of these were small hospitals (Society for Hospital Social Work Directors 1989). Teaching hospitals also suffer because they are more likely than others to take in patients with long-term problems. One analysis recently labeled such hospitals "an endangered species" (Schwartz et al. 1985). Poor individuals, of course, suffer because if they cannot pay, they may be dumped by a given hospital. It is estimated that hospitals dump about 250,000 persons a year for financial, not medical, reasons (Ansberry 1988, p. A1). Obviously, the problem of costs is a vicious one in which a host of interrelated causes and consequences are tangled.

There are even some signs that local governments are considering rationing health care and making priority lists that rank health problems in terms of need of service (Gross 1989). When it comes to costly health care, the question of "who shall live" remains an issue (Fuchs 1983). Clearly, those who are poorest are in the most vulnerable position, and there is some evidence that cuts in governmental support for health care are taking their toll on the worsening health of poor Americans (Mundinger 1985).

One recently hailed proposal to deal with the issue of high health-care costs is the health maintenance organization (HMO). Basically, HMOs provide a variety of care services to individuals for a fixed monthly premium, and there appears to be general agreement that HMO costs are lower than those for more conventional plans, but the exact reasons are not clear (Wolinsky 1980; Luft 1983; Welch 1985). Because the costs are lower, there is some fear that the individuals who join and stay in HMOs will tend to be those who are sicker than most others. The result is that we will end up having at least a two-tier health system, the traditional "fee-for-service" system in which individuals choose their own doctors and are covered by private health insurance, on the one hand, and a second system of "prepaid" health groups that for a flat fee offer a certain range of health care services. The healthier, better-off individuals will gravitate toward the former, while the latter will attract those who are worse off in terms of both health status and income. Under these conditions, there is some concern that the quality of care in the latter will be adversely affected. If costs continue to spiral upward, short of national health insurance, there is some belief that a lower tier of minimal health services will be financed by the government for the poor and older persons, a system that is not likely to attract the highest quality of professionals (Thurow 1985). The ultimate result of these processes would be unequal health care, meaning worse care for the poor and others who cannot afford quality services.

Is it the case that HMO enrollees are indeed lower in income and poorer in health than those who enroll in more traditional health plans? There is a lot of research on this topic of "adverse selection bias." The results tend to be mixed: There are data that support the presence of such a selection bias (Bashshur and Metzner 1970; Berki 1980; Luft 1983; Greenlick 1984), but other findings point in the opposite direction (cf. e.g., Tessler and Mechanic 1975; Juba et al. 1980; Freeborn and Pope 1982; Garfinkel et al. 1986). The weight of the evidence since 1980 points in the direction of a "favorable" rather than an "adverse" selection bias. That is, HMO members are less likely to have had established ties with physicians, more likely to use preventive services, and show greater health concern than

those in more traditional plans (Wilensky and Rossiter 1986). The bulk of the evidence also shows that HMO members have lower hospitalization rates than those in more conventional health plans (Luft 1978, 1983), but may have higher prospective health care costs, as would be the case with young families (cf. e.g., Berki et al. 1977; 1978; Berki 1980; Luft 1983; Schuttinga et al. 1985).

Data on the socioeconomic characteristics of HMO members are also mixed, with some studies showing a greater probability of members to be from financially vulnerable groups, while other research demonstrates the opposite (cf., e.g., Wolinsky 1980; Welch and Frank 1986; Buchanan and Cretin 1986; Scitovsky et al. 1987; Freeborn and Pope 1982). At this point then, we cannot say unequivocally that HMOs contain a disproportionate number of poor, sick individuals. There may, however, be adverse selection for particular HMOs that draw a large percentage of their clientele from particular neighborhoods or occupations, and for those that are government sponsored, for example, for Medicaid patients. In any case, the rising cost of health care has implications for inequality in health care beyond those caused by traditional problems of access and bias.

BASIC LIFE CHANCES: PSYCHOLOGICAL HEALTH

Physical health and conditions are major factors in determining the parameters of life chances in a variety of areas for individuals, for example, in employment, social activity, travel, and so on. Psychological health is also a basic element in contributing to a meaningful life, but are the chances for such health evenly distributed among groups in U.S. society? As we did in our discussion of physical health, let us begin with some statistics.

In 1980, approximately 1.3 million individuals were admitted to in-patient psychiatric facilities. Eighty percent of these persons were white, 18 percent were black, Native Americans/Alaskan Natives made up 1 percent, and 1 percent were Asians or Pacific Islanders (Manderscheid and Barrett 1987). Blacks were more likely to be admitted to state and county psychiatric facilities than to any other facility, and minority group members had higher rates of admissions to such facilities than nonminority groups. For all major groups, males had higher admissions than females to state and county psychiatric and veteran's facilities, but for private and nonfederal general hospitals, admissions rates for each sex were similar. Males and blacks were more likely than females or whites to be *involuntarily* admitted to state and county mental hospitals, and most of these involved a criminal commitment (ibid.).

In terms of diagnoses for the admittants, schizophrenia was a more frequent diagnosis for blacks than for whites, with over 50 percent of blacks in state and county mental hospitals being so labeled. In fact, in every setting schizophrenia was the most frequently entered diagnosis for blacks, whereas the dominance of a particular diagnosis for whites varied with the type of psychiatric facility. Schizophrenia was the most frequently given diagnosis for whites in county and state mental hospitals, but in private psychiatric and nonfederal general hospitals, affective disorders were the most prominent type of diagnosis (Manderscheid and Barrett 1987).

Some research suggests that there is a relationship between race, sex, socioeconomic status, and diagnosis. A recent study by Loring and Powell (1988) aimed at finding out whether the psychiatrist's or client's race or sex influenced the diagnosis given to the client, even though the symptoms presented in each case vignette did not vary. The authors presented a stratified random sample of 290 psychiatrists with two case studies each, in which the sex and race were either disclosed or not. The point was to see whether these doctors would evaluate the client simply on the basis of symptoms classified in a standard manner by the Diagnostic and Statistical Manual (DSM-III) used by clinicians. Some interesting patterns emerged in the research. The authors found that:

1. White male psychiatrists were more likely to classify a given case in the general schizophrenia category if it involved a white male than if the client were a black or female.
2. Black male and black female psychiatrists followed a similar pattern; that is, they were more likely to present the general schizophrenic diagnosis to clients who were of the *same* sex and race as the psychiatrist.
3. Black psychiatrists tended to give the least serious diagnoses to white male patients, and male psychiatrists did not label any white males as having paranoid schizophrenia. In contrast, this was the most frequently given diagnosis for black male clients by every type of psychiatrist.
4. Male psychiatrists tended to diagnose female clients as having depression disorders, but female psychiatrists shied away from this label.

What these and their other results show is that when psychiatrists are not given either the sex or race of the case they are examining, there is widespread agreement among them on the diagnosis. But when such information is provided, if the sex and race are the same as the psychiatrist who is doing the diagnosing, then the diagnosis is basically the same as that which would have been given had no information on sex and race been provided. In other words, the diagnoses appear to be more "objective." In contrast, in those cases where sex and/or gender of client and psychiatrist differ, diagnoses appear more subjective. For example, male psychiatrists on the whole are inclined to perceive females as having depressive disorders and to assign white females to the histrionic category even when the case study itself gives little evidence of such a disorder. It seems that the stereotype of women being emotional is carried over into these diagnoses. Similarly, the diagnoses of black males also appear to be affected by stereotypical views. Black males are more likely to be considered as being violent, suspicious, or dangerous, even when their clinical characteristics are the same as those of whites. White *and* black psychiatrists tend to give such diagnoses, suggesting internalization of these stereotypes to some extent by both types of psychiatrists. If these biases enter into diagnoses, then official rates of such illnesses for different groups may not accurately reflect the incidence of these disorders among the different sex and racial groups (Loring and Powell 1988).

Other research has found that whether an individual is admitted voluntarily or involuntarily into a state hospital is also related in part to his or her socioeconomic status as well as to the severity of the disorder. Briefly put, individuals from lower socioeconomic levels are more likely to be involuntarily admitted when the disorder is not obvious or severe, that is, when there is room for various interpretations of symptoms (Rushing 1978). Schizophrenia, which is more frequently diagnosed among blacks, is also a disorder in which individual interpretation by the caregiver plays a large role. It has been labeled as an "open concept" and "fuzzy natural category" (quoted in Gottesman et al. 1987, p. 41). The importance of this openness to interpretation parallels Verbrugge's conclusion cited earlier that differences between groups in health conditions and how they are dealt with are more likely to appear when dealing with less severe and less clear problems.

The relationship between race, gender, and socioeconomic factors, on the one hand, and mental illness/psychological distress, on the other, has been studied extensively. Several classic studies examined the relationship between social class and mental illness, and each of them raised questions and issues that have continued in the field and found relationships that have since been reconfirmed.

Three Classic Studies

Dozens of studies have been done on the relationship between various measures of inequality and psychological disorders, but the findings and interpretations in them have not always been consistent. Three of the classic studies were con-

ducted by Faris and Dunham, Hollingshead and Redlich, and Srole and associates.

Faris and Dunham   One of the earlier studies of mental illness was conducted between 1927 and 1929 and published in 1939 by Faris and Dunham. Working out of Chicago, these men were members of the so-called ecological school, which stressed the importance of looking at the effects of niches or locations in a social setting on rates of specific behaviors. Cities were believed to be structured as sets of concentric circles with certain functions and populations found in different circles. The important point for our purposes is to indicate that the lower classes tended to live in areas closest to the downtown area. For example, just outside the downtown area of some cities is a region characterized by tenements and run-down large houses. Beyond this section, moving outward, are more stable working-class areas, better residential areas, and the suburbs.

Faris and Dunham looked at the relationship between this concentric structure and various types of social problems, one of which was mental disorder. They wanted to see if a relationship existed between the extent of social disorganization and the rate of mental illness. The extent of disorganization of an area was measured by (1) the number of foreign born, (2) the number of restaurants, (3) infant mortality, (4) percentage of home ownership (5) level of education, and (6) radio ownership. Using these factors, they found that the degree of disorganization increased toward the center of the city. The "zone of transition," surrounding and located on the edges of the downtown area, was a place inhabited by a heterogeneous group of transients, hobos, and lower-class single men.

Faris and Dunham used hospital cases as a measure of mental illness and found that the mental illness rates varied systematically with concentric zones in the city. Specifically, they found that the rates of "general insanity" went up as they approached the center of Chicago. Since the outer circles of the city were populated largely by more middle and upper classes, while the slums in the inner city housed the lower classes, the conclusion was drawn that mental illness and social classes varied inversely; that is, the lower the social class, the higher the rate of mental illness. In looking at more specific illnesses, they found that schizophrenia varied inversely with class, whereas manic-depressive psychoses showed less of a distinct patterning.

The authors proposed that the conditions under which individuals live thus appear to affect the likelihood of their becoming mentally ill. The isolation, seclusiveness, and general disorganization of certain areas in the city help to create mental abnormality. This kind of hypothesis forms the core of the social causation argument of mental illness, and on its face value it seems to make sense and may even appear to be indisputable.

However, there are several weaknesses in the Chicago study that should be mentioned:

1. Characterizing an area in aggregate terms as lower class, middle class, or otherwise means that the measure will be insensitive to class heterogeneity within a given area. Ecological area is not a perfect proxy for class position and, consequently, a correlation between area and mental illness is not the same as a correlation between individual social class position and illness.

2. Using treated or admitted hospital cases to measure the extent of mental illness has some weaknesses. Some mentally ill individuals may not be treated or admitted because of lack of availability or convenience of services or because of what they consider to be public opinion about those who use them (Dohrenwend and Dohrenwend 1969, pp. 5–6).

3. Although a relationship may exist between social class and mental illness, the direction of causality has not been indisputably established by such a correlation. An equally plausible explanation of such a relationship is that those who are mentally ill may be disproportionately selected out into the lower classes. Comparable correla-

tions by Faris and Dunham on alcoholism and drug addiction could be similarly explained. This is an important issue about which there have been many debates and which we discuss in greater detail shortly.

Hollingshead and Redlich   A second major study of the relationship between mental illness and social class was published in 1958 by sociologist August B. Hollingshead and psychiatrist Fredrick C. Redlich. This research improved on earlier work using a detailed list of all those obtaining aid from a psychiatrist, psychiatric clinic, or hospital in the latter part of 1950 in New Haven, Connecticut. They also used a very detailed classification of various types of psychosis and neurosis. Moreover, they used a control sample from the "normal" population against which to compare their mentally ill group. The Index of Social Position, developed by Hollingshead, which included weighted scores for place of residence, occupation, and education, was used to measure social class. Five classes were identified.

Several important relationships materialized. First, an inverse relationship was found between social class and prevalence of treated mental illness. This relationship existed especially for psychosis, with the lowest class having more than twice the rate of those in the two highest classes. No such relationship was found for neurosis, however. It was more prevalent in the middle classes than in the lowest class. The relationship between mental illness and social class persisted even when sex, age, race, religion, and marital status of the respondents were controlled. Second, results also suggested that diagnosis varied by class, with a lower class person more easily classified as psychotic. Diagnosis was determined by a number of factors of the client, the orientation and training of the attending doctor, and the values of the community. In their book, Hollingshead and Redlich propose that the inflexibility of lower class people keeps them from treatment whereas their treatment reinforces their attitudes toward psychiatry. Finally, the authors found that the treatment received varied with social class. Individuals in the top classes were more likely to be treated by private practitioners and the like than in state or veterans hospitals, whereas the reverse was found for lower class neurotics and psychotics. Moreover, when specific types of diagnosis and type of agency were controlled, the type of treatment received varied with social class, with lower class patients less likely to receive psychotherapy and other individually oriented types of treatment. The conclusion was thus drawn that treatment depends not only on medical factors but also on social forces to which the medical profession had not paid much attention. The authors argued that value differences between psychiatrists and lower class patients hinder the effectiveness of psychotherapy. Lower class patients also were found to be given custodial care in state hospitals more often than individuals in higher classes and to be kept in such care for longer periods of time. In sum, relationships were found on where, how, and how long a patient was treated and social-class position.

Despite the care that went into the design of this study, it also suffers from the fact that treated cases were used to measure the prevalence and incidence of mental illness. Other studies have strongly suggested that the extent of mental illness may be greater than that indicated by the number of *treated* cases (for example, Srole et al. 1962; Eaton and Weil 1955). Second, it is possible that, if broken down, the separate elements of occupation, income, and place of residence would have been differentially related to the mental illness variables. Finally, the question of the possible "downward drift" of the psychotic into lower classes was researched, and it was found that little migration had occurred between social classes among schizophrenics. That is, Hollingshead and Redlich discovered that most of the schizophrenics in the higher classes had always lived in higher class areas, and most of those from the lowest classes had always lived in slum-type areas. Most were in the same class as the

families they grew up in. This does not, however, give us evidence that schizophrenia does not prevent a person from moving up in social class. The direction of causality is still not clear.

The Midtown Manhattan Study A few years after publication of the Hollingshead and Redlich study of New Haven, Srole and his associates published *Mental Health in the Metropolis* (1962), a study based on a large sample representing adults in midtown New York. In contrast to the New Haven study, which relied on treated cases, Srole and his associates used a measure of mental pathology that was independent of treatment condition. A number of items were used, "consisting principally of the psychophysiologic manifestations and those tapping the anxiety, depression, and inadequacy dimensions" and other items "bearing particularly on psychosomatic symptoms, phobic reactions, and moods" (Srole et al. 1962, pp. 42, 60). Hence, questions about nervousness, worries, restlessness, upset stomach, headaches, fainting, trembling, and so forth were used to tap the extent of mental pathology. Socioeconomic status (SES), in turn, was measured using education and occupational level.

As in other studies, the researchers found an inverse relationship between SES and mental pathology. The degree of symptom formation increased as the respondents descended the SES scale, and the relationship was even stronger when their statuses rather than their parents' were used. Of all the variables considered, SES was the one most clearly related with mental pathology. There was an especially sharp distinction between those in the highest and lowest strata. Over 30 percent of those in the lowest stratum were considered to have "severe symptom formation" or to be "incapacitated" as compared to only about 6 percent in the highest ranking group. The group with the lowest degree of impairment lived in "a world characterized by a more secure, expansive, and ego-nurturing style of life with larger buffers or cushions against the inevitable abrasions and knocks of human existence" (Srole et al. 1969, p. 410). On the other hand, those with the most extensive prevalence of pathology generally grew up in a world marked by poverty, low education, and menial occupations. The burdens created by this setting together with the "vulnerable personalities" created while growing up created conditions that fostered poor health. In turn, the majority who were impaired produced a community milieu that fostered its own "pathologenic contagion" for all those in it.

Another finding of the Midtown Manhattan Study was that the downwardly mobile had the highest incidence of pathological symptoms and the upwardly mobile the lowest. This study is important because of its attempt to measure mental pathology among the population at large rather than simply among treated patients. However, as in the two other studies mentioned thus far, a definitive test of a causal relationship between social class and mental disorder was not performed.

Current Status of Evidence

A number of more recent studies have again found relationships between socioeconomic status, race, or gender and psychological difficulties. In 1975 Dohrenwend summarized the findings of a large number of studies conducted since 1900 that examined the relationship between class and the prevalence of mental disorders:

1. About 85 percent of the studies found that the highest rates are in the lowest SES group.
2. This relationship is intensified when urban rather than rural groups are considered.
3. This relationship is "consistent for schizophrenia and personality disorders but not for neurosis or manic-depressive psychosis."
4. The exact reason for the relationship is not clear. That is, the relative roles of class, genetics, and disorder in explaining this relationship have not yet been determined.

More recently, using information from over 2,000 Floridians, Ulbrich and her colleagues (1989) found that race and socioeconomic status interact in their effect on psychological distress symptoms. Specifically, in the lower categories of occupational status, blacks show greater distress symptoms than whites, whereas in the middle categories the differences are reduced, and in the higher ranking occupations, the racial differences are reversed, with whites showing a higher rate of symptoms. The authors also found that within the lowest occupational category, blacks are exposed to more economic problems than whites, but these differences do not exist on other occupational levels. "Undesirable life events" such as deaths, divorces, being fired, and so on create greater distress only for blacks in lower socioeconomic positions, but on the other hand, they react less strongly than their white counterparts to economic problems, even though they are more exposed to them. Perhaps this is related to the strong kinship ties among the black families. Perhaps, because of their greater experience in poverty and near poverty, blacks in the lower socioeconomic and underclass categories have developed mechanisms that allow them to adapt better to poor economic conditions.

Other studies also have found a link between low occupational status or unemployment and psychological problems (cf., e.g., Link et al. 1986; Brown and Gary 1988), and it also has been found that educational, income, and occupational level all have independent effects on feelings of psychological distress, but that the relative importance of each depends on the sex and employment status of the respondent. In his analysis of data from eight surveys, Kessler (1982) found that among working men, income is the most important predictor of distress, whereas among women in the labor force and homemakers, education is the most significant, especially among homemakers.

In a nutshell, the relationship between lower socioeconomic status and psychological distress, each measured in a variety of ways, has been repeatedly verified in research. However, the exact nature of this relationship has been a subject of some controversy. Some have suggested a variant of the "drift" hypothesis cited earlier, in which those who are mentally ill, for example, find it difficult to be upwardly mobile. In this view, people with varying levels of psychological distress are "selected" out into different socioeconomic categories. The "social causation" view suggests, in contrast, that socioeconomic status has a direct bearing on mental health. Data from a recent community mental health study in Texas and Mexico, for example, indicate that those in lower socioeconomic statuses are more likely to have (1) a sense of powerlessness, that is, believe that external factors control the direction of their lives, and (2) a sense of mistrust of others, which in turn helps generate the feeling that others are plotting or talking against them (Mirowsky and Ross 1983).

A study of 1,173 Kansas City respondents eighteen years of age and over between 1971 to 1973 revealed a significant relationship between unemployment and depressive mood and the occurrence of stressful life events during that period (Catalano and Dooley 1977). A second study (Brenner 1977) using longitudinal data starting with 1940 and going forward to the early 1970s suggested that changes in unemployment and real income affect a number of stress indicators, including state mental hospital admissions and suicide rates. The author estimates that "the 1.4 percent rise in unemployment during 1970 has cost society nearly $7 billion in lost income due to illness and mortality." These and other recent investigations (such as Lee 1976) strongly imply that the direction of causality is from conditions in the social environment of the individual to mental disorder, rather than vice versa. However, the issue is far from resolved.

There have been some attempts to test the validity of the drift hypothesis among individuals with specific disorders. Turner and Wagenfeld (1967) studied its presence among schizophrenics. Taking a random sample of 214 patients, they found that a certain percentage of them grew up in low-status families. This would support the social causation thesis. On the other hand, it did not account for the very large proportion of schizophrenics they found in that status. Comparing that group with a large sample of the general population, Turner and Wagenfeld discovered that a

much smaller proportion of schizophrenics were upwardly mobile relative to their parents and that a large percentage were downwardly mobile when compared with the general sample. But within their own careers, the large majority did not move at all, suggesting that although some drift is present, it is not an adequate explanation of the low occupational positions of these schizophrenics. Rather, it appears that these individuals simply are not likely to attain high position and disproportionately move downward compared with their parents. The social causation thesis of the schizophrenia/social class relationship seems to make only a minor contribution to explanation of that relationship.

Thus, this controversy over the direction of causation in the relationship between SES and mental distress has not been fully resolved, but some longitudinal data suggest that conditions associated with low status do affect the likelihood of experiencing psychological disorders (c.f., e.g., Wheaton 1978; Turner and Gartrell 1978; Miller et al. 1979; Dooley and Catalano 1980; Link et al. 1986). Kohn (1976a) has tried to summarize the argument about causation of schizophrenia. It has virtually always been found to be inversely related to SES both in the United States and in other countries, but exactly why the two are related is still not clear. Studies of twins and adopted children indicate genetic factors are involved in the generation of schizophrenia, but others suggest that stress and reactions to it are related to the illness (Kohn 1976a, pp. 178–179). Surveying our knowledge up to this point, Kohn concludes that there is enough evidence to say that:

1. Class is related to schizophrenia, but we are not sure why this is so.
2. Genetics plays a causal role, but we do not know in what manner.
3. Stress also seems to be involved.

Implicit is the argument that no single factor accounts for the illness. Rather, Kohn argues, the conditions for life in the lower class make individuals less able to effectively cope with stress.

Together with genetic vulnerability and great stress, the probability of schizophrenia increases. The curved dashed lines in Figure 6.1 serve to indicate that Kohn's primary concern is to show the causal connections between class, genetic conditions, and stress, on the one hand, and schizophrenia on the other. He is less concerned about the interrelationships among the first three variables.

Gender and Distress It already has been suggested that sex is related to the diagnosis of mental illness. Relationships also have been found between gender and psychological problems. The rates of psychological distress are higher among women (Kessler and McRae 1983). Clinically defined major depression has been found to be two to three times as likely among women than among men, although the gap between them may be narrowing because of the recent increase in depression among young men. These trends have been found not only for the United States but for Sweden, Germany, Canada, and New Zealand as well, but not for Korea or Puerto Rico or among Mexican-Americans (Klerman and Weissman 1989). (The reader should keep in mind the possible diagnostic biases discussed previously when interpreting these findings.) It also has been discovered in analyses of data from five general-population surveys that psychological distress among women is more likely to be affected by some undesirable incidents affecting someone close to them than is the case among men. But women are not *generally* more vulnerable than men to all types of undesirable events. Among the possible contributors to these trends in depression listed by the authors are changes in women's roles and alterations in occupational patterns for men and women (Kessler and McLeod 1984).

Interestingly, another review of five national and community surveys concludes that for the period from 1957 to 1976, there was a decline in the differences between genders for certain psychophysiological symptoms, and that part of the reason for this decline was the increased labor-force involvement of women during the period (Kessler and McRae 1981). It appears that a greater breadth of roles for women may have healthy results. There is evidence that individuals with multiple roles display a greater sense of psychological well-being, and that loss of roles is related to increased feelings of distress. People with multiple roles, for example, employed, married and parents, tend to have better health than those with none of these roles (Verbrugge 1983). Sociologically, this makes sense since roles provide people with their identities. "The greater the number of identities held, the stronger one's sense of meaningful, guided existence. The more identities, the more 'existential security,' so to speak. A sense of meaningful existence and purposeful, ordered behavior are crucial to psychological health" (Thoits 1983, p. 175).

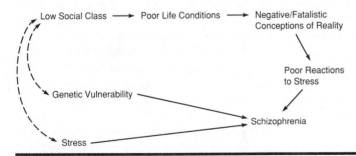

FIGURE 6.1 Melvin L. Kohn's Model of Schizophrenia Etiology

Based on: M. L. Kohn, 1976. "Interaction of Social Class and Other Factors in the Etiology of Schizophrenia." *American Journal of Psychiatry* 133: 177–180.

In her review of the survey evidence over a period of years, Verbrugge (1985) also found that the worsening of physical health among women seems to be concentrated among those with few roles (i.e., those who are unemployed, unmarried, etc.), whereas employed married women have had improving health in the last two decades. Among married persons, unemployed housewives experience more distress and other pathological symptoms than either employed husbands or employed wives (Steil 1984; Gove and Geerken 1977). On the other hand, involvement in responsibility in *too many* areas can increase a person's feeling of loss of personal control and thereby increase stress and depression symptoms (Rosenfeld 1989; Cleary and Mechanic 1983). Another factor probably contributing to the greater distress felt by housewives is their little power in the home compared to their employed husbands (Steil 1984). Employment brings power in the family, and distress may be a function of both lack of power and lack of multiple roles outside the family.

Obviously, some conditions and life events may help prepare and strengthen individuals for stressful conditions. For example, middle-class women who were in or approaching young adulthood during the Great Depression and who suffered serious economic loss because of it, today are less likely to feel helpless, are *more* assertive and in control of their lives than middle-class women who did not experience such losses. Working-class women, on the other hand, who entered the Depression with fewer resources to begin with and experienced serious reductions in economic resources, feel *less* assertive and have a greater sense of being victimized (Elder and Liker 1982). What this suggests is that life's obstacles are more easily overcome and can even have long-term beneficial effects when those experiencing them have had ample resources on which to build a strong life originally.

Treatment and Images of the Mentally Ill

There is a good deal of evidence that the type of treatment sought by individuals also varies with social class, especially measured in terms of education, income, or both. Those from higher SES backgrounds are more likely to seek out psychiatric help rather than help from public hospitals or clinics (Greenley and Mechanic 1974; Kadushin 1969; Gurin et al. 1960). The relationship apparently cannot be explained by different levels of disorder, since it still exists even when level of distress is controlled (Greenley and Mechanic 1974, p. 18). Kadushin (1969) explains this relationship by suggesting that as members of different social networks, individuals are encouraged to seek out different kinds of help.

Most studies also find a relationship between social-class position and admission/commitment for treatment, with lower class clients being more likely to be hospitalized or committed (Wilde 1968; Haney et al. 1969; Rushing 1971). Stern (1977), however, studied 140 publicly funded mental centers in North Carolina and found no relationship between education and either acceptance or length of treatment among clients twenty-five and over and found only a weak relationship between education and the type of treatment. But, as she indicates, such relationships have been found when studies of university clinics have been made, suggesting the type of setting in which treatment takes place is an important factor to consider before reaching any general conclusions about associations between class and admission, treatment, and so forth. Stern says that differences in the composition of staffs, in stress on in-depth psychotherapy, amount of treatment available, and variations in organizational goals help to account for relationships found in some settings and not others.

Attitudes toward the mentally ill also vary by class position. Several studies have shown that psychotherapists usually have training or attitudes that hinder their therapy among lower class patients and that psychiatrists prefer patients from non-lower-class backgrounds (Hollingshead and Redlich 1958; Askenasy 1974; Lorion 1977; Stern 1977). A nationwide study of psychotherapists revealed that a therapist is held in higher regard by his or her colleagues when the patients being treated are of a higher class. Thus, while therapists may not be personally biased against clients who are from the working or lower class, they may realize that to receive the esteem of their colleagues they need to cater to a clientele from the higher classes. One undesirable consequence may be that some who are in need of therapy are neglected (Link 1983).

However, lay individuals with lower education are more likely to have negative stereotypes concerning the mentally ill or former mental patients. Social distance from former patients is greater among those with lower education (Dohrenwend and Dohrenwend 1969, pp. 152–159), and feelings that former patients cannot be trusted vary similarly with education. Askensay (1974), for example, found that a much larger proportion of respondents with less than a high school education felt that mental patients should not be trusted, are dangerous, and are "failures in life" (pp. 241–243). Rejection of the mentally ill seems especially likely if the patient is also thought to be from a lower SES group (Bord 1971).

BASIC LIFE CHANCES: FOOD AND SHELTER

The research on physical and psychological health just discussed clearly shows that economic and status inequality are deeply implicated in the chances of individuals for a healthy life. It does not warrant belaboring that food and shelter, like health, are basic to a decent life, and it is the poor who are disproportionately found among the hungry and homeless. On the international level, poor nutrition is widespread within the countries listed as "low income" by the World Bank. Moreover, within those countries, the poorest and least educated suffer the most from malnutrition, and when food is scarce it is not evenly distributed among family members. The young and females are most likely to suffer in these conditions. Poverty, inequality, the level of economic development, and hunger are closely related (Warnock 1987).

In the United States, hunger appears to have increased in recent years and is widespread among particular groups and regions. In the early

Hunger has become an increasingly serious problem. In the mid-1980s, an estimated 20 million Americans were hungry sometime during any given month.

1980s, the Physician Task Force on Hunger was formed to carry out extensive field studies on hunger throughout the United States. Specifically, the Task Force was to (1) find out how much hunger there is and who is most affected, (2) examine regional variations and similarities in hunger, (3) study the effects of hunger, especially among vulnerable groups like children, older persons, and pregnant women, and (4) try to uncover the sources of the hunger problem and suggest what might be done about it (Physician Task Force 1985).

With respect to its prevalence, the Task Force concluded that about 20 million persons are hungry at some time during each month. Most of these are people who are poor and receive no food-stamp assistance, while the remainder are those who receive inadequate assistance and those who are near poor and cannot afford enough food. The research group also concluded that the problem of hunger appears to be getting worse rather than better, and that recent increases in poverty, flaws in the government's "safety net," and reductions in needed governmental programs are primarily responsible.

The problem of hunger, of course, is linked to the issue of good health discussed earlier. The Physician Task Force argues that inadequate diet has an impact on the health of pregnant women and on the children to whom they give birth. Higher infant mortality rates, low birth weight, slower or deficient brain growth, poorer resistance to infection, and general stunting and anemia are among the conditions related to poor nutrition among children. Other negative effects are found among older persons who are chronically hungry. Many of the health problems among older people, for example, hypertension and weakening of the bone structure (osteoporosis), require careful attention to quality and quantity of diet, and hunger worsens these maladies (Physician Task Force 1985).

The poor also contribute disproportionately to the ranks of the homeless. Along with the increased attention given hunger in recent years, there also has been more media emphasis on the problem of homelessness in the affluent United States. Most recent studies of homelessness have been done on the local or state level, for example, in Los Angeles, Chicago, and Ohio (Redburn and Buss 1986; Ropers 1988; Rossi and Wright 1989). One of the many problems in studying the homeless problem concerns the definition of "homelessness," and studies vary in this matter. For example, Rossi and Wright make a distinction between "the literally homeless" and "precariously, or marginally, housed persons" (1989, p. 134). The former, upon which they focus in their study, are those who have no access to housing of any sort, "and who would be homeless by any conceivable definition of the term" (ibid., p. 134). Even when a definition is decided upon, it is difficult to find out how many are homeless in an area. "Counting the homeless is a social scientist's nightmare." It is difficult because of the relative "invisibility" of the homeless, hostility among them, the mixing of poverty and homelessness, the frequent movement of the homeless from place to place, and the existence of multiple causes that make it difficult to find them (Redburn and Buss 1986, p. 16). As one census worker recently put it, "by its very nature, a site inventory is a moving target" (in Dunlap 1990, p. A16). The estimates of the U.S. homeless population in the country range from about 200,000 to 2,200,000 (U.S. Dept. of Housing and Urban Development 1984; Stefl 1987).

In the *local* studies, results show that a large majority of the homeless, usually about 75 percent or higher, are male. A majority are under forty years old, which is a sharp contrast to the stereotype of the older skid-row homeless. A majority have completed high school, that is, they are not very different from the average for the general population. A majority are white, but blacks are disproportionately represented. Very few are married, and approximately one-half in these local studies have never been married. A relatively small percentage, around 20 to 25 percent, work full or part time. Physical and mental health problems are found in disproportionate amounts among the homeless. For example, 19 percent in the Los Angeles study and 29 percent in the Ohio study had been in a psychiatric hospital (Ropers 1988). Many, though not a majority, have alcohol-related problems. Estimates range from under 20 percent to over 40 percent (Stark 1987).

The *national* study of the homeless by HUD in 1984 estimated that somewhere between 200,000 and 600,000 were homeless, with the "most reliable range" being 250,000 to 350,000 (U.S. Dept. of Housing and Urban Development 1984). This is considered a serious undercount by many, however. It is likely that the actual number of homeless is much larger than the HUD estimate. The HUD study consisted of a phone survey with representatives and a survey of shelters. Their results applied to those who were homeless as of January 1984. HUD defined the homeless as those who slept in some kind of shelter, on the streets, in parks, in subways, in bus and railroad stations, in motor vehicles, or in another space that was not meant for shelter. They found a greater number of homeless in the West (65,500) than in either the Northeast (49,500) or North-Central (45,400) region. This condition is more concentrated in large cities than in small ones. Los Angeles, New York, and Chicago are the metropolitan areas with the highest estimated numbers of homeless. Of those who use shelters, the HUD study estimates that 13 percent are single women, 21 percent are members of families, 44 percent are members of minority groups, and their average age is in the mid-thirties. Only a small percentage are over sixty-five. There are more women, more minorities, and more children represented than was the case in the past. At least 50 percent have either mental or alcohol/drug problems (Peroff 1987).

Why are so many homeless? What are the reasons behind homelessness? The homeless found in the Ohio study were asked to give reasons for their condition. Almost half (48.1%) listed financial or economic reasons. Primary among these were unemployment and difficulty paying rent. Just over one-third mentioned some kind of personal problem such as family turmoil

(13.3%), family break-up (8.0%), or alcohol/drug problems (7.3%). Only 6% said that they preferred a life of homelessness.

A number of other factors have been linked to the rise in homelessness. Primary among these are the lack of unskilled or semiskilled jobs available and lack of affordable housing. Changes in the economy have brought about a decline in low-skilled jobs, making employment a significant problem for many of the homeless. Not being able to afford housing is another source of the problem. In testifying before the Congress in 1988 about homeless conditions in New York City, Charles Schumer said plainly, "There is no mystery to this misery. . . . [I]n 1982 there were 1088 homeless families in New York City alone, many with small children. In 1987 there were almost 5100 homeless families. During that same period the amount of new housing units that HUD has allocated dropped from 2300 in the last year of the Carter administration to 325 in 1987. . . . The administration is ignoring a simple truth: if we take away a poor man's home he becomes homeless" (Schumer in Ad Hoc Task Force, January 21, 1988, pp. 64–65). It appears clear that part of the reason for homelessness is a change in governmental housing policy. Luisa Gonzalez, on the verge of being homeless, testified before the same Committee that while she had received a government voucher to help pay for housing, she was unable to find an affordable apartment in Brooklyn. "So, the situation is really hard for me because I have been looking around for housing, but I haven't been able to find an apartment less than $700. All the apartments are over $800, $1,000." Ms. Gonzalez receives some governmental assistance, but has one child in school and a nineteen-year-old with cerebral palsy (ibid., p. 18).

The homelessness problem is exacerbated by the high cost of what is available. There is evidence that the poor are paying more for their housing. Almost two-thirds of the poor pay more than half of their income for shelter. In sharp contrast, only 8 percent of the nonpoor pay that high a proportion of their incomes for housing. Fed-

There has been a significant rise in the amount of homelessness in recent years.

eral data indicate that whereas in the late 1970s there were many more low-cost housing units available than there were poor needing them, in 1985 that situation was reversed. Immediate causes for this situation include an increase in the number of poor households, a decline in their average incomes, and an increase in the level of rents (Dionne 1989). "Never before in postwar American history have so many poor people competed for so few affordable dwelling units" (Wright and Lam 1987, p. 49). The destruction or conversion of housing units for other purposes, along with gentrification, have worsened the problem.

Other factors then, beyond the characteristics of the homeless themselves, also have contributed to the homeless problem. Deinstitutionalization of those with mental problems, the recession of the early 1980s, the declining value of public assistance benefits, no-fault divorces and increasing numbers of no-children rental rules, the net migration to metropolitan areas, and tighter governmental rules about disabilities have all had an effect on this problem (Hope and Young 1986; Wright and Lam 1987; Carliner 1987; Hoch 1987). Thus, many of the elements that affect the extent of homelessness are "macro-processes" related to the government and market economy (Rossi and Wright 1989). And it is the poor who are especially vulnerable to shifts in these processes. "As long as the distribution of shelter security remains tied to income and social class the poor will bear the burden of going homeless" (Hoch 1987, p. 29).

BASIC LIFE CHANCES: A SENSE OF WELL-BEING

In addition to health, food, and shelter, another condition for an adequate life relates to general feelings of life satisfaction and well-being. Myths about ignorance being bliss and the poor being content in their misery are simply not borne out in research. Not surprisingly, compared with those in higher statuses, lower status groups show less satisfaction with their married lives, economic conditions, and health and physical needs than those in higher categories of income and education. This rather bleak picture is mitigated by the fact that lower status persons *generally* (in contrast to blacks) are not more likely to be critical of governmental and other public institutions. This finding can, of course, be interpreted in a number of ways. In any case, "it is their personal situation that aroused their expressed dissatisfactions. They appear preoccupied and overwhelmed with the clear problems of being poor" (Andrews and Withey 1976, p. 295).

Feelings about life as a whole similarly vary with status. Different measures in various national surveys yielded consistent results: The higher the socioeconomic status, the greater the sense of general well-being in a person's life (Andrews and Withey 1976, pp. 322–323). This does not mean that all those who are low in education and income are dissatisfied with their lives, but it does mean that relative to those in higher statuses they experience lower feelings of well-being. High-status individuals believe they have moved ahead in their lives and will continue to progress more than do lower status persons. Satisfaction and happiness with life show similar relationships (Andrews and Withey 1976). Among those with inconsistent statuses, those with higher income but lower education feel better than those with the opposite combination (Andrews and Withey 1976, p. 322). It appears clear that income and education have real consequences for how people feel about the lives they lead.

Recent surveys further confirm that blacks and those in lower socioeconomic brackets are less satisfied with their lives than whites and those in higher SES categories. A 1988 national Gallup poll asked respondents whether they were satisfied with the way things were going in the country and in their own personal lives. A greater percentage of whites than nonwhites (60 versus 37 percent), college graduates than those with less than a high-school education (64 versus 47 percent), and those with incomes of at least $40,000 than those with incomes below $15,000 (69 versus 43 percent), said they were satisfied

(Gallup 1989). An earlier, more specific poll asked individuals about their satisfaction with various areas of their lives. A greater percentage of blacks than whites were dissatisfied with their housing, standard of living, household incomes, jobs, free time, and personal lives. However, there was little difference in this survey between blacks and whites on their satisfaction with their family lives or health (Gallup 1985).

Results suggest that the relationship between race and feelings of well-being have not changed significantly over the last fifteen years (Thomas and Hughes 1986). It also appears that both race and SES have independent effects on such feelings (Thomas and Hughes 1986; Redmond 1988). In addition, gender appears to be related to feelings of well-being, with men showing a slightly stronger sense of well-being (Haring et al. 1984). However, gender is not more important that social class in explaining level of well-being. Analyzing data from 556 sources and using income, occupational status, or a composite measure of socioeconomic status Haring and her associates found that there is a positive relationship between each of these measures and well-being, and that men have a slightly higher sense of well-being than women, but that gender accounts for little of the variation in feelings of well-being. When men and women are analyzed separately, social-class measures still predict well-being within each group. While women are worse off than men on a variety of *objective* conditions, these conditions are not directly translatable into similar negative *feelings* (Haring et al. 1984). Race and sex interact in their effects on well-being. One recent national study found black females to have the lowest sense of well-being among the race and sex groups (Redmond 1988).

The greater feelings of distress found in the lower socioeconomic groups have been linked to greater feelings of powerlessness and alienation. Research has shown that there is a relationship between general socioeconomic standing and feelings of powerlessness. An individual with a sense of powerlessness has a feeling of little control over his or her life, that he or she cannot

Socioeconomic status sets limits on what people can and cannot do with their lives and on the conditions in which they live.

master or determine the paths that life will take. Rather, the belief is that factors outside the individual, for example, fate or "society," determine what happens to him or her and that there is little he or she can do to change that. Those with lower incomes and lower status occupations are more likely to feel this way, while those in higher positions have a greater feeling of mastery and control (Mirowsky and Ross 1983; Wheaton 1980). This was seen earlier in the relationship between SES and personal control over health. Women, those in lower status jobs, and those who are unemployed have less of a sense of control over their lives (Mirowsky and Ross 1983; Wheaton 1980; Kohn and Schooler 1982; Pearlin et al. 1981).

The Srole Anomia Scale taps feelings of fatalism and pessimism and is virtually identical to some dimensions of alienation that have been studied. Seeman (1961) argued that the subjective feeling of alienation can be separated into five different types of experiences: powerlessness, meaninglessness, isolation, normlessness, and self-estrangement. Given these kinds of vari-

ables, one would expect those low in status to be higher in feelings of anomie and alienation. Individuals with less education are less likely to have a command of the knowledge and resources they need to control and direct their lives and careers. Suspicions and doubts are more likely to find fertile soil under these kinds of conditions. Having a dead-end, low-status occupation is likely to encourage feelings of pessimism and distrust. Cohen and Hodges (1963) propose that values of members of the lower blue-collar class are formed as an adaptation to the concrete conditions under which these individuals live. Their study in California of 2,600 male family heads indicated that those in the lower class have a perhaps realistic but nevertheless pessimistic view of their lives. "In his view, nothing is certain; in all probability things, however, will turn out badly as they generally have in the past" (Cohen and Hodges 1963, p. 322). Kohn's (1969) judgment likewise confirms this conclusion. While members of the upper class are likely to feel that one's life can be shaped and directed by the individual,

"the essence of lower class position is the belief that one is at the mercy of forces and people beyond one's control, often beyond one's understanding" (pp. 189, 192).

Sennett and Cobb's (1973) moving study of Boston working-class men and their families who sense a lack of control reveals the deeply ambivalent attitudes they have about the higher education that might enable them to control their lives. They see higher education as a tool for gaining greater freedom in their lives, but they harbor suspicions that those with higher educations and white-collar jobs really do not work as hard as they do. In a word, education allows people to cheat. At the same time, they are haunted by a lingering belief in the ideologies of individualism and competition which remind them that they have not been as successful as others, and that this may be related to their own lack of efforts and inferior abilities. Figure 6.2 outlines some of the

dynamics involved in their thinking. Recently unemployed executives harbor similar largely unjustified doubts about their own efforts and abilities (Newman 1989).

Most jobs of those in the working and lower classes are characterized by a lack of self-direction, which further leads to a feeling of powerlessness (Kohn 1976b). Those who do repetitive work of little complexity and are closely supervised are more likely to sense a lack of power over their own lives. Blauner (1964) found alienation to be higher in the automobile industry than in an oil refinery, printing firm, or the textiles industry. Work in the automobile industry contains less of the self-direction of which Kohn speaks. The work setting does make a difference; even white-collar workers have been found to be alienated in a very formalized and bureaucratized situation (Lystad 1972).

As a group, however, blue-collar workers

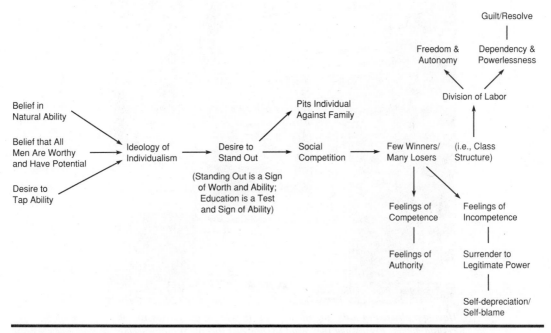

FIGURE 6.2 Ideology, Class Inequality, and Their Effects on Self-Perceptions among Working-Class Men: 1972

Based on Sennett, Richard, and Jonathan Cobb, *The Hidden Injuries of Class*. New York: Vintage, 1973, pp. 58–118ff.

historically have had less control over their work. Numerous studies using national and local samples have found powerlessness and anomie to be inversely related to occupational status (Srole 1956; Bell 1957; Killian and Grigg 1962; Angell 1962; Mizruchi 1964; Simpson 1970; Neal and Groat 1975). Those in lower status groups are more likely to feel that they cannot control their lives. A young electrician apprentice summarizes this feeling well: "See, I feel like I'm being held back, like I'm not on top of things. . . . I don't know what you would call it, maybe sort of powerless, but it's a feeling not about any one thing that's gone wrong" (Sennett and Cobb 1973, p. 34). In summarizing research on this topic, Lystad (1972) comments that black and poor in our society "consider their fate unjust, but they tend to react to it with apathy and show little or no outrage about their situation and little or no hope for its improvement" (p. 99).

Feelings of normlessness and self-estrangement (basic dissatisfaction with one's activities) also have been found to be higher among those in lower occupational statuses (Simpson 1970; Otto and Featherman 1975). However, some research also has found that within occupational groups, education and earnings are *positively* related to powerlessness, but *negatively* related to self-estrangement. The relationship one finds between SES and alienation clearly depends on what specific measures of these concepts are being used. Shepard and Panko (1974), for example, show that the effect of functional job specialization on alienation depends on the form of alienation being examined. Thus, they find that although powerlessness—measured as lack of

Having a physically satisfying life depends in part on the possession of certain goods. Even when they want to, however, people in the working and lower classes cannot always afford to buy quality goods. And when the poor do buy, they are often subject to credit and contractual practices that result in their paying more. This reinforces their low economic position and sense of powerlessness (see Caplovitz, 1963).

control and freedom on the job—is related to specialization, other forms of alienation further removed from the work place are not.

In essence, the objective conditions under which these groups live help to produce particular sets of beliefs. These, in turn, affect levels of distress and the ability of individuals to cope with that distress. If individuals believe that they can do little to change conditions, then they tend to be more distressed, and their feelings of powerlessness discourage the development of coping devices to deal with the distress (Wheaton 1980, 1983). It has been found that lower status persons react more severely to stressful situations, such as physical health problems, death, and divorce (Kessler and Cleary 1980; Turner and Noh 1983). Differences in the psychological distress experienced by different status groups can be accounted for by variations in the degree of social support and feelings of personal control, especially for those in the middle class (Turner and Noh 1983). While there are different levels of problems between the status groups, the various levels of distress are more attributable to differences in the responses to those problems. In summarizing the relationship between socioeconomic status, beliefs, and distress, Mirowsky and Ross (1986) conclude that "people in lower socioeconomic positions have a triple burden: They have more problems to deal with; their personal histories are likely to have left them with a deep sense of powerlessness; and that sense of powerlessness discourages them from marshalling whatever energy and resources they do have in order to solve their problems. The result for many is a multiplication of despair" (p. 30).

FAMILY RELATIONSHIPS AND VIOLENCE

We have been examining the effects inequality has on the intimate lives of people, their health, their chances for the material necessities of life, and their feelings about themselves and their everyday living conditions. The next section continues this theme by analyzing the effects of inequality on family structure and relationships. First, we look at family stability and how it varies by class and race, and then we look inside the family at the important problems of wife and child abuse.

Family Stability

Traditionally, black families and those with parents of low education and/or unstable income and employment have had higher divorce rates than higher status white families (Teachman et al. 1987). A variety of reasons have been offered to explain the higher rate of divorce among lower status groups. It may be that since tradition is stronger in the higher classes, divorce is considered less of a viable alternative and a messier solution to marital problems. For those in the lower classes, on the other hand, it may be a viable alternative. The wider access of those in the upper status to a variety of alternative activities and opportunities may serve to defuse difficulties in the home by turning attention away from it. Finally, the strains, economic and otherwise, on the lower class are greater overall than in the higher classes, making the probability of a longlasting deep marital relationship less likely.

The actual reasons given by individuals for divorce vary by SES. Lower status couples appear more likely to give "physical abuse" as a reason for their divorces than middle-class couples. Levinger's (1966) study of 600 applicants for divorce in Cleveland showed that wives of lower status families more often complained about problems of money, drinking, and abuse, whereas those in middle-status groups more often expressed anger over absence of love, fidelity, and consideration (p. 806). These findings suggest that different levels of needs are not being satisfied in each case. In lower status families, almost by definition, such physical needs as food and shelter are less likely to be met because of higher unemployment, lower income, and the like. It is not surprising that financial complaints would occur more frequently at these levels than at higher ones. Conversely, at higher status levels, the motivators are more psychological in nature. Physical needs of the type mentioned can be much more easily met, and thus such needs as love become more central and problematic. It should be mentioned that the grounds legally allowed for divorce do not always correspond to the real underlying causes for divorce (Adams 1975, p. 361).

Inequality itself, not just low status, apparently can generate stress within the family, especially between husband and wife. Pearlin (1975) found that differences in the status backgrounds of the spouses can create problems in the marriage. Individuals who marry down and consider status important experience much greater stress than equal-status mates or those individuals who marry persons of higher status. His study of 2,300 spouses in urbanized Chicago indicates that this particular form of status inequality leads to breakdowns in reciprocity, affection and communication exchange, and value consensus, which in turn lead to stress. On the other hand, women who are full participants in the labor force and who make high earnings are more likely to divorce than those who are economically dependent on their husbands (Teachman et al. 1987). This suggests that, under certain conditions, an equalization of statuses and economic power between husband and wife can make divorce a realistic alternative.

Segre (1975) contends that family stability in lower status groups can only be maintained under certain conditions. First, the important values in the family must be consistent with and integrated into the value system of the larger society ("ideological integration"). Second, the full-time or usual occupations and work of those in the lower status family must be considered worthwhile and functional for society ("instrumental integration"). Third, the family and its individual members must receive support from outside agencies rather than constantly relying on their own resources to hold it together ("kinship/society integration"). Segre suggests that all three conditions have been absent in lower status families. Thus, not only does traditional instability tend to be prevalent in these families, but the reactions to the strains in them more often tend to take on illegitimate forms, such as desertion and illegitimacy. The factors ultimately responsible for the greater frequency of these problems in the lower status groups do not lie solely within individuals themselves but in the pressures created by the system of inequality itself.

Child and Wife Abuse

The preceding discussion indicates that family problems are related to socioeconomic position. This relationship extends to the areas of child and wife abuse as well. Since the 1970s, there has been a marked increase in the number of reported cases of child abuse and neglect. In 1984, there were 1,024,178 official cases recorded, which represents a 158 percent increase since 1976 (Hampton 1987, p. 3). It is also estimated that 3 to 4 million wives are severely beaten by their husbands (Van Hasselt et al. 1988). The accuracy and stability of these rate statistics, however, have been extensively criticized (Starr 1988; Hampton 1987; Faller and Ziefert 1981; Gelles 1975). Most of the data, for example, show that lower socioeconomic status groups have a higher rate of child and wife abuse than higher socioeconomic groups (cf. e.g., Gil 1971; Lystad 1975; Garbarino 1976; Gelles and Cornell 1985; Biller and Solomon 1986). But the validity or strength of this relationship has been criticized because the abuse in poor families is more likely to come to the attention of officials for a variety of reasons and poverty is associated with a number of other "stressors" such as poor health, housing, and unemployment. Part of the result of this association is to label the abuser as being "poor and uneducated" (Gelles 1975, p. 367).

But the assumptions about abuse that are drawn from these perceptions can be dangerous. Lystad has proposed that upper status persons are more likely to get help from private physicians than lower status persons who are more likely to wind up at a state or county hospital, which has to report the abuse (1975). Moreover, a whole host of individual characteristics, relationship variables, and social-cultural factors have been linked to abuse, with socioeconomic factors being only one of these (cf., Van Hasselt et al. 1988). "While poverty may well be fertile ground for abuse or neglect tendencies to mature, a great deal of variability exists within the poverty population. Ignoring these demographic, ethnic, and functional variations may well lead to faulty conclusions regarding the underlying causes of maltreatment and the most effective interventions" (Daro 1988, p. 65).

Despite these considerations, research has repeatedly found an inverse relationship between lower socioeconomic status and child abuse. Such status, of course, is connected with other factors related to abuse, for example, slightly larger families, unemployment, poorer health and housing, social isolation, and lack of a support network. Lower educational and occupational attainment are among the other stressors related to child abuse (Biller and Solomon 1986). However, poverty is not a necessary cause of abuse, nor is abuse confined to the lower class. Moreover, most poor parents do not abuse their children (Faller and Ziefert 1981; Gelles and Cornell 1985).

The factors associated with abuse suggest that the *social contexts* in which persons of lower SES operate are a "major source" of child abuse (Gil 1975). Thus, parents guilty of child abuse should not be seen as sadists who alone are responsible for their conduct. A "subculture of violence" argument that focuses complete blame on the abuser is misplaced (Erlanger 1974; Giovannoni and Billingsley 1970; Gil 1971, 1975). Rather, the conditions in which individuals live and their lack of meaningful ties to the larger society contribute to stresses that in turn activate abuse. Furthermore, a culture that itself supports familial violence through its reluctance to interfere in the relationship between parents and children and that actively supports competitions in which only the "qualified" survive while many others "lose" contributes to the generation and widespread prevalence of child abuse (Gil 1971; 1975; Giovannoni and Billingsley 1970).

Most of the studies mentioned here specifi-cally point to the fact that abusive or neglectful parents (or both) are frequently cut off from connections to institutions that might help them. "These families are systematically shunted into community systems which are primarily punitive and regulatory, and conversely diverted away from those systems which are supportive and enhancing of parental role performance" (Giovannoni and Billingsley 1970, p. 656). In his report on child abuse in fifty-eight New York counties in 1973, Garbarino (1976) concludes that "such appears to be a major feature of the human ecology of child abuse/maltreatment: economically depressed mothers, often alone in the role of parent, attempting to cope in isolation without adequate facilities and resources for their children" (p. 183). The stresses placed on mothers in poverty seem to be especially important. In addition to the lack of effective "support systems" for such mothers, of course, are the relative and absolute deprivations of "demeaning and debilitating social statuses" (Lystad 1975). Unemployment, overcrowding, dilapidated housing, low incomes, and the frequent presence of only one parent create further pressures and frustrations. Given these conditions, we have to be careful where we point the finger of blame. Gil (1975), in fact, has proposed a very broad definition of child abuse in this regard. He refers to it as "inflicted gaps or deficits between circumstances of living which would facilitate the optimal development of children, *irrespective of the sources or agents of the deficit*" (pp. 346–347, emphasis added). He rightly suggests child abuse can take place on the institutional and societal level as well as in the family.

Consistent relationships between race and likelihood of abuse have not been found. But among abusing families, those that are black tend to be poorer and female headed, with younger parents who have less education and are more likely to be unemployed (Hampton 1987). Some studies have found that a greater proportion of child abusers are women, but these studies often do not control for family type, and within families where both spouses are present, men are more often the abusers. In female-headed families, which are more likely to be poor and subject to many stresses, females of course are more often the perpetrators. But when men are present, they are more often abusive (Gil 1970; Gelles and Cornell 1985; Biller and Solomon 1986). Younger children and children in larger families are more vulnerable to abuse, but the sex of the young child does not appear to make a difference.

Statistics on wife battering suffer from many of the same problems as those on child abuse. Estimates are that about 3.8 percent or 1.8 million wives are beaten by their husbands yearly, with almost half of the husbands beating their wives three or more times (Straus et al. 1980). Many, if not most, incidents of wife battering, however, never come to the attention of authorities. Even confidential reports underestimate the extent of the problem because of the embarrassment and sensitivity of the problem, the belief on the part of some that a certain amount of violence is "normal" and even acceptable, and because many who are abused look for help outside official channels, such as from other couples (Margolin et al. 1988). Finding agreement on what constitutes "wife abuse" also has been difficult, and definitions vary from state to state. Moreover, we should not conclude that physical abuse against women is confined to families. Women who are single, separated, divorced, or are dating are also frequently subjected to abuse. In fact, evidence indicates that compared to these groups, married women are the least vulnerable to abuse (Stark and Flitcraft 1988).

As is the case in child abuse, a large number of factors have been found to be related to wife abuse. While we cannot review them all, we can comment on those that are related to social inequality. Black women are victims of abuse more often than white women, but this may be due in part to the fact that they are more likely to report it and a confounding of race with income and other socioeconomic factors (Casanave and Straus 1979; Hampton 1987; Stark and Flitcraft 1988). While wife abuse may be more prevalent in black families, evidence suggests that blacks are not more likely than whites to be child abusers (Straus et al. 1980).

Most studies, including those done on a national level, have found an inverse relationship between social class and wife abuse. Part of the difference between the classes may be due to the reporting issues on the statistics discussed earlier. Unemployment of the husband also has been found to be related to greater probability of abuse. Men who work part time or are unemployed have rates of abuse that are about twice as high as those for husbands who are fully employed (Straus et al. 1980; Gelles and Cornell 1985). There is also some evidence that the degree of status inconsistency between spouses may be related to wife abuse, although these findings are not firm. Specifically, wives whose educational and occupational statuses are higher than those of their husbands' may be at greater risk than wives whose statuses are consistent with those of their husbands (Hotaling and Sugarman 1984; Gelles and Cornell 1985; Stark and Flitcraft 1988). Domestic violence also seems to be related to the balance of power within families, with democratic, egalitarian families having the lowest rates of violence (Gelles and Cornell 1985).

The preceding discussion indicates that social inequality is implicated in wife abuse. It has been suggested by theorists of patriarchy that as long as a society's values and institutions support male dominance over women, then wife abuse will continue, because such behavior is a manifestation of the greater power and status of men. The institution of the "ideal" family with its male "head," and other legal, economic, political, and social institutions help to maintain the power of men over women. Moreover, women and men are socialized to believe in and accept the inequality between them (Dobash and Dobash 1979; Bersani and Chen 1988). This patriarchy theory of abuse has been criticized for not considering the influence of a number of other factors in domestic violence and by focusing primarily on spouse abuse while ignoring child abuse (Bersani and Chen 1988).

If patriarchy is an important element in the explanation of wife abuse, then we should expect to find that in those societies where women have higher statuses there will be less abuse than in those where women are completely dominated by men. Reports from a study done on ninety small and peasant societies from all over the world indicate that wife beating is the kind of family violence found most often, occurring in almost 85 percent of these societies. It occurs in over 50 percent of the homes in almost half of these societies, but seldom or never in only about 16 percent (Levinson 1988). Evidence from this study suggests that an economic version of the patriarchy theory may be viable. The elements of female status rank that are most closely associated with the economic sphere, that is, labor, wealth, ownership, status of female work groups, are related to the frequency of wife abuse. Abuse is more frequent where men are in full authority in the family and control wealth and labor than in societies where women are in control in the household and can acquire wealth and property on their own (Levinson 1988). Interestingly, other research indicates that wife abuse may be related in a curvilinear manner to status, with women being most likely to be victims in places where they occupy either the lowest *or* highest status (Yllo 1983, 1984).

SUMMARY

This chapter has focused upon a variety of areas concerning personal life chances in different racial, gender, and SES groups. It appears clear that the latter factors are related to physical and mental health in several ways. Moreover, these groups also tend to use health services in different ways, to contact doctors and dentists at different rates, and to differ in the likelihood of possessing health insurance and taking preventive health measures. Inequality also is related to the problems of hunger and homelessness and to general feelings of well-being. Finally, it affects family stability and the probability of family violence. Figure 6.3 summarizes the relationships that have been explored in this chapter.

Two points should be made about the research conducted on these relationships. First, frequently different measures of SES have been used in studies on the same issue, and for the sake of convenience we have generally used the

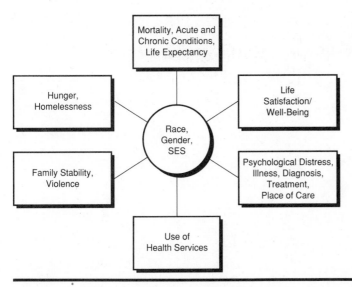

FIGURE 6.3   Summary of the Relationships Examined in Chapter 6

term "social class" in this chapter as if it were synonymous with SES measures. Second, although significant relationships have been found between race, gender, and SES, on the one hand, and health, on the other hand, we do not want to suggest that these are the only variables or always the most important variables in explaining variations. Rather, the question of interest has been whether or not inequality in its various forms plays any role in producing various personal life chances. It seems apparent that they do. Indirectly, the organization of a competitive capitalist society and, more directly, the system of inequality that it creates, results in individuals and families being placed in different positions regarding access to and possibilities of gaining the "good things" in life. At the same time, the lack of economic power of some individuals affects relationships at home. For example, unemployed housewives are more likely to experience various symptoms of distress, and families in which there is a clear imbalance of power between parents are more likely than egalitarian families to contain domestic violence. In many ways, then, the effects of inequality reach inside the intimate lives of families and individuals. In Chapter 7, we turn from these personal effects of inequality to more societywide, macroscopic effects, that is, crime and collective unrest.

CHAPTER 7

CRIME, PROTEST, AND INEQUALITY

The frustrated expectation of equality has been a major factor in all major revolutionary upheavals since Luther posted his Ninety-five Theses on the Wittenberg church door. Indeed, since long before that.
—James Davies

The effects of inequality can be examined in several ways. The last chapter examined individual life chances, while the present one deals with crime and collective protest. These two social effects were chosen because, historically, they have been major "problem" areas in U.S. society and because their relationships to inequality have been studied extensively. These topics can be studied on the macro- and micro-levels, the former focusing on broad *societal* causes and effects and the latter focusing on *individual* causes and effects. Figure 7.1 demonstrates the analysis that can take place at each of these levels. To illustrate, in this chapter the relationship between class and crime will be studied by looking at the

connection between (1) an individual's class position and the likelihood of committing a crime, and (2) class structure/inequality itself and crime rates. The first dissects relationships at the level of the individual, while the latter examines the relationship at the level of social structure. As in the previous chapter, we will be moving between both levels in our search for relationships.

As in that chapter, we do not mean to suggest that inequality or a given dimension of it is the sole or even the most important determinant in producing effects on the individual or the society. But elements of inequality have been significant predictors, as was witnessed in the last chapter and will be again in this chapter.

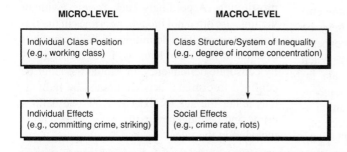

FIGURE 7.1   Levels of Analysis in Studying the Relationship between Inequality and Its Effects

INEQUALITY AND CRIME

Inequality has been linked to the nature and collection of crime statistics, the likelihood of arrest, the social production of crime, and sentencing. In other words, its effect appears to contaminate most phases of the criminal justice process.

The Inadequacy of Crime Statistics

"Now, what I want is Facts. Teach these boys and girls nothing but Facts. Facts alone are wanted in life. Plant nothing else, and root out everything else. You can only form the minds of reasoning animals upon Facts. . . . In this life, we want nothing but Facts, Sir; nothing but Facts!" So exhorts Thomas Gradgrind in Charles Dickens's *Hard Times.* Unfortunately, hard facts about the actual rates of crime and delinquency are not only difficult to come by but are probably impossible to get in the present circumstances. As a result, complete reliance on official statistics will insure that some error will be present in the conclusions drawn about the relationships between social position and crime rate. Statistics can lead away from fact, although they are probably the best means we have to assess the real rate of crime.

Labels and definitions have an impact on what behaviors are defined as "criminal," how much they are enforced, and how individual behavior is interpreted. The definitions of the "crime problem" of some individuals or groups may be favored over those of others. "Groups often vie for control of the definition of a problem. When one group wins, its vocabulary may be adopted and institutionalized while the concepts of the opposing groups fall into obscurity. When terminologies change, when new terms are invented, or existing terms are given new meanings, these actions signal that something important has happened to the career or history of a social problem" (Spector and Kitsuse 1977, p. 8). Defining the crime problem in ways that exclude major white-collar crimes costing citizens billions of dollars while including crimes that are

less costly suggests that some groups may be more favored than others. Similarly, the selective enforcement of particular laws also is a means for insuring that groups are kept in their respective places. "Unequal administration of the law is functional because it keeps the status arrangements of society from being disrupted. When, for example, a drunk appears in public, police often react differently in terms of his social status. If he is lower class, he has a good chance of being arrested. If he is upper or middle class, he will more likely be driven home. Middle- and upper-class people, who control the administration of justice, want these laws enforced only against a certain segment of the population." (Reid 1988, p. 36). Several scholars have suggested that the police are biased against those in the lower class and, thus, are more likely to arrest them than individuals in higher classes who commit the same offenses (Turk 1969; Quinney 1970).

In sum, there are several reasons why current statistics on crime rates are inadequate.

1. *The definition of what constitutes a crime may not be agreed on by all who are in a position to officially define it.* Many people, for instance, do not consider certain kinds of white-collar crimes to actually be criminal in the same sense that more violent acts such as homicide are and, therefore, do not think they should be included under criminal law (Friedman 1959, pp. 200–202). Some also feel that crimes in which no one is visibly harmed are not crimes if consenting adults are involved, as in homosexuality and prostitution. Accordingly such "crimes without victims" are often not thought as crimes in the traditional sense. The definition of delinquency is even more vague and tenuous. Does incorrigibility constitute delinquency, or should the latter be confined to criminal acts committed by individuals under the age of sixteen? How one defines crime and delinquency partly determines who is included in the rates.

2. *An argument has been made that criminal laws are largely a creation of specific interest groups and are not a reflection of the whole soci-*

ety (Quinney 1970). Thus, legally defined crimes are nothing else but acts most often committed by individuals who are not members of the effective interest groups. If the laws were different, the behaviors labeled as crimes would be different. Crime is largely a labeling activity by those in power (Becker 1963).

3. *Even if the definition of crime is clear and the law is a product of consensus in the entire society, crime statistics are still deficient because many crimes go unreported* for a variety of reasons, ranging from embarrassment to lack of concern or knowledge about the law. In addition, police departments use different procedures for recording complaints (Reid 1988).

4. *Official action on the part of the police frequently appears to be dependent not only on the suspected individual's behavior but on his or her attitude, demeanor, and personal characteristics as well.* The latter are related to whether or not crimes will be reported or individuals arrested (Garrett and Short 1975; Green 1970; Black 1970; Piliavin and Briar 1964). Thus, we must question to what extent crime rates are determined by police reports actually based on the commission of criminal acts. As Tittle and Villemez (1977) put it, "It is very likely that official statistics distort the true relationship between social class and criminality" (p. 479).

5. *Plea bargaining and similar judicial opportunities make it difficult to determine what kind of crime, if any, an individual has actually committed.* Crime statistics traditionally include only acts for which individuals have been convicted, not necessarily the ones they have committed. Between the time of a crime's commission and a person's conviction, a lot can happen to make us question the accuracy of the crime rates generated.

In essence, "the most basic shortcoming in criminal statistics is that they can never hope to represent with accuracy the behavior that we are really interested in" (Geis 1965, p. 28). Even self-report studies have potential biases built into

them: (1) respondents may misunderstand the question or understand it differently; (2) persons may wish to shock or impress the interviewer; and perhaps, most important (3) respondents, especially adults, may be unwilling to admit the commission of a crime (see Tittle and Villemez 1977). Self-report studies, in which respondents indicate whether or not they have committed certain illegal acts have been criticized for (1) being less valid for some classes than others, (2) containing primarily trivial criminal acts and excluding more serious crimes, (3) focusing on single sites or areas that are class-homogenous, (4) focusing on continuous socioeconomic status scores rather than discrete classes as measures that are relevant to the commission of crime, and (5) excluding school dropouts and absentees from surveys, thereby minimizing the probability of finding a class effect (Kleck 1982).

Unfortunately, except for some self-report studies, for the most part all we have are the official statistics on which most studies have been based. We must keep both statistical inadequacies and possible shortcomings in mind when drawing conclusions about the relationship between crime rates and SES.

Our discussion of the relationship between inequality and crime/delinquency in the next several sections of this chapter covers both "ordinary" and "white-collar" crime and can be thought of as addressing the issue of criminal justice. Included are discussions of several phases of the criminal justice process, starting with arrests and the commission of crime and ending with sentencing.

Ordinary Crime and Inequality

Crime rates usually are determined by using the FBI Uniform Crime Reports, which lists what the FBI considers the major crimes in society. Currently, the FBI lists eight types of crimes: four serious violent crimes, and four serious property crimes. These are murder and nonnegligent manslaughter, forcible rape, robbery, aggravated assault, burglary, larceny-theft, motor vehicle theft, and arson, which was added in 1978. Together these eight constitute the "Crime Index," which in turn, measures the *known* extent of what is ordinarily called the "crime problem." Hence what is being dealt with in this section is what might be called "ordinary crime."

One of the problems with this list of crimes is that it does not include any serious, costly white-collar or corporate crimes. Since the latter are largely crimes perpetrated by middle or upper class individuals, it would be a mistake to look only at the Index crimes to reach a definitive conclusion about the relationship between race, sex, socioeconomic status, and crime. To do so would bias the conclusion against individuals in lower social and economic rankings. The number of arrests in the statistics also are affected by the probability that a crime will be reported by police when a complaint is made. The likelihood of such a report has been found to be contingent on the status and behavior of the complainant (Black 1970).

Whether or not individuals have encounters with police or are arrested appears to be related to the socioeconomic status of the persons involved. Police generally have particular images of delinquents, stereotypes that result in lower class persons being arrested more often (Sampson 1986). Piliavin and Briar (1964) concluded that how a juvenile was dealt with by a police officer was significantly related to how well the youth fit the stereotype of the officer, a stereotype largely made up of characteristics associated with the lower class. Interviews with police in three diverse cities revealed that police seem to use the "attitude" and demeanor of the youth as a predictor of likelihood of delinquency, a predictor that turns out to be a poor one (Garrett and Short 1975). These police also felt that lower class youth were not only already more involved in delinquency but were more likely to become delinquent if they were not already. In essence, police have certain expectations of the criminal behavior of youth, and these images lead them to monitor and arrest youth in the lower class more often, regardless of the frequency of their actual crimi-

nal behavior (Irwin 1985). Similarly, in studies comparing black and white youths, there is evidence of police stereotypes that results in biases against blacks. Accounts given by police indicate that they develop negative stereotypes of blacks in the course of their work (Waegel 1984).

The negative perceptions of lower class youth by police lead the latter to label whole neighborhoods as being "contaminated" because they are made up of individuals who are considered undesirable (Irwin 1985; Sampson 1986). The result is that the general socioeconomic status of a neighborhood can influence the attention paid to it and its inhabitants by authorities. A recent study by Sampson (1986), using data from the Seattle Youth Study, found that the number of contacts and reports by police is strongly and inversely related to the neighborhood's general SES, independent of the actual extent of criminal and delinquent behavior in the area. He concludes that "for the bulk of offenses typically committed by juveniles (e.g., larceny, fighting, vandalism, burglary, drug violations) official police records and referrals to court are structured not simply by the act itself but by socioeconomic and situational context (e.g., delinquency of friends) as well, a process which may in turn amplify the effect of prior record in later decisions concerning official delinquents" (1986, p. 884).

All of this research strongly suggests that the ecological area and perceptions of law officials affect the relationship between official rates of crime/delinquency and social class. These additional limitations of official statistics should be kept in mind when examining the information in Table 7.1, which presents the arrest distributions for Index crimes by race and sex of those arrested. In 1988, there were 2,122,673 arrests made for such crimes. As the table shows, almost 79 percent of those arrested were males, whereas just over 21 percent were females. The highest arrest rate for females is in the "larceny-theft" category (30.5 percent). In recent years, the arrest rates for women have increased, but the increase has been primarily in the property-crime area (Schur 1984). While the majority of those ar-

TABLE 7.1   Arrests by Index Offense Charged, Sex, and Race: 1988

OFFENSE CHARGED	PERSONS ARRESTED				
	% Male	*% Female*	*% White*	*% Black*	*% Other*[a]
Murder and non- negligent manslaughter	87.7	12.2	45.0	53.5	1.5
Forcible rape	98.8	1.2	52.7	45.8	1.5
Robbery	91.5	8.5	36.3	62.6	1.1
Aggravated assault	86.6	13.4	57.6	40.7	1.6
Burglary	91.6	8.4	67.0	31.3	1.7
Larceny-theft	69.5	30.5	65.6	32.2	2.3
Motor-vehicle theft	89.9	10.1	58.7	39.5	1.7
Arson	86.9	13.1	73.5	25.0	1.6
Violent crime[b]	88.6	11.4	51.7	46.8	1.5
Property crime[c]	76.0	24.0	65.3	32.6	2.1
Total Crime Index	78.7	21.3	62.4	35.7	1.9

Total Index arrests = 2,122,673

Source: Flanagan, Timothy J., and Kathleen Maguire, eds. *Sourcebook of Criminal Justice Statistics—1989,* U.S. Department of Justice, Bureau of Justice Statistics. Washington D.C.: U.S. Government Printing Office, 1990, Tables 4.7 and 4.9, pp. 428 and 430.

[a] American Indian, Alaskan Native, Asian, or Pacific Islander.

[b] Violent crimes are murder, forcible rape, robbery, and aggravated assault.

[c] Property crimes are burglary, larceny-theft, motor-vehicle theft, and arson.

rested in 1988, with the exception of robbery and murder, were whites, blacks were disproportionately represented in the arrest rates for all Index crimes. In fact, the majority arrested for robbery and murder were blacks, and just under half of all those arrested for forcible rape were blacks. Blacks were more overrepresented in the arrest rates for violent crimes than for property crimes. A small percentage of arrests, generally 1 to 2 percent, involve Native Americans, Alaskan Natives, Asians, or Pacific Islanders.

Social-Class Position and the Commission of Crime

The statistics just presented suggest clearly that race and sex are related to the likelihood of being arrested for a crime. The relationship between social class and the actual commission of crime/delinquency, on the other hand, has been the source of a great deal of controversy. Certainly, there are theories which suggest that class and crime rates are inversely related. Broadly speaking, Marxian theory, which proposes that the political and legal systems are organized to serve the interests of the higher classes, would suggest that the working and lower classes are more oppressed and subject to more laws than those in higher classes. Thus, it would not be surprising to find that the definition of crime, enforcement of laws, and judicial and sentencing procedures work against the lower classes, reflected in higher crime rates and more severe sentencing for those groups.

Overviews of studies done on the relationship between social class/socioeconomic status and crime/delinquency have not been consistent. Tittle and his colleagues (1978) concluded after their review of thirty-five studies that the relationship between social status and official crime rates is only weak and that the relationship of status to self-reported crime is nonexistent. They argue that "class and criminality are not now, and probably never were related, at least not during the recent past" (p. 652). However, another review of over a hundred studies by Braithwaite (1981); reached the opposite conclusion, that is, that there is quite a bit of support for the inverse relationship between class and crime.

Early research on the relationship between class and crime suffered from a variety of weaknesses:

1. Ecological rather than individual data have frequently been used, making it unclear if relationships exist between an individual's class position and his or her likelihood of having committed an illegal act.
2. Crude and varied measures of social class or crime/delinquency often have been used.
3. Studies have sometimes included only one sex or race rather than incorporating these as variables.
4. Unrepresentative samples have been used.
5. The analyses of data have sometimes been quite superficial. (Tittle and Villemez 1977).

A large part of the explanation for discrepancies in findings on this relationship appears to relate to the measures used for social class and crime (Kleck 1981). Virtually all of the studies in recent years have used occupational prestige, income, or educational hierarchies as measures of "class," and almost none have used Marxian measures (e.g., ownership, control over labor, etc.). Even within the socioeconomic measures used, there is variation between studies. Hagan and his colleagues (1985, 1987) have suggested that the element of power differences ought to be more fully incorporated into studies of class and crime. This is especially relevant for studies purporting to understand the relationship between gender and crime. They feel that "structural measures of class position, grounded in relations of ownership and authority, speak more directly to the kinds of theoretical issues" that interested criminologists like Edwin Sutherland (Hagan and Pal-

loni 1986). When one considers that power differences frequently separate men and women in families and may be directly linked to the probability of white-collar crime, the request for other measures of class seems more than reasonable.

To test their ideas about the importance of power differences in producing "common" delinquency, Hagan and his associates (1985, 1987) collected data from students in Toronto and used a measure of authority and ownership to determine the position of men and women in the households. The "common" delinquent acts included less serious behaviors like minor theft, fighting, minor vandalism, and the like. The authors hypothesized that in patriarchal families, that is, those in which wives and daughters have little power, there is less freedom and risk taking on the part of women. Hence, they will be significantly less likely than the sons in such families to commit delinquent acts. It is in these types of families that gender differences in delinquency will be most pronounced. On the other hand, in egalitarian families, those in which females have some freedom and can take risks, there will be little difference between the sexes in their delinquency rates. Their analyses supported these hypotheses and also revealed that the gender differences in delinquency declined as one went down the class hierarchy. Gender differences were largest in the employer class. A large part of the reason for this gender difference seems to be that sons in this class have greater power relative to their mothers and are not taking as great a risk in being punished as are daughters. In other words, the authors point out again that gender differences in delinquency are linked to power differences in the family, which in turn are a reflection of power differences in the work place.

In addition to the varied measurement of class, the measurement of crime has also varied between studies. This is especially the case for studies examining delinquency rates. Some studies use official data while others rely on self-reported information. Each of these types of data is subject to different forms of error since the data come from different sources. It is difficult to know how much error of each form has affected each of the statistics. For example, self-report data are subject to errors due to memory loss or embarrassment, while official data are subject to errors related to police-reporting discrepancies. There is also some debate on the relationship between class and validity of responses. Some have argued that lower class children are less honest in their responses than middle-class youth, while others have found no such relationship (Kleck 1982; Hindelang et al. 1979). Self-report studies also tend to stress less serious crimes, while official statistics focus on more serious ones (Thornberry and Farnworth 1982). Many who admit to having committed an illegal offense have never been arrested. Almost 90 percent of the youth interviewed by Williams and Gold (1972) admitted to having committed an arrestable offense, but only a very small percentage said they had even been contacted by the police. Additional studies using self-reporting of delinquent acts also have found little relationship between class and delinquency (for example, Nye 1958), whereas other analyses of "hidden delinquency" still found negative relationships (for example, Clark and Wenninger 1962; Gold 1966). These differences in measures make comparisons across studies difficult.

The Structure of Inequality and the Social Production of Crime

When it comes to the commission of crime, an analysis of its relationship to inequality involves more than just examining it on the micro-level, that is, looking at the connection between the statuses of individuals and the commission of crime. At the social structural or macro-level, the system of inequality itself may be related to the generation of crime rates. In this section, we examine this possibility as it appears in theory and research.

Quinney (1974) takes a broad view and suggests that crime is nothing more than behavior so defined by the powerful in society. Crime then consists largely of behavior inimical to the class interests of the top class in society. Laws are created to maintain their interests, to keep the system intact. The ideas of what constitutes crime and how the definitions of crime are applied arise out of the government and legal agents representing the dominant class.

Gordon (1973) proposes a similar explanation of the production of crime. His thesis pays particular attention to several observations about crime that we have already made and which serve as a partial summary of the preceding arguments:

1. The crime problem ordinarily is considered to consist of the eight FBI Index crimes. White-collar crime is not included, nor is much attention paid to it, although it occurs extensively in U.S. society.
2. Blacks are disproportionately arrested for crimes, and lower SES groups dominate the cells of state correctional institutions and death row.
3. The overwhelming bulk of Index crimes are committed for financial reasons. "Their main purpose is to obtain money or property" (Clark 1970, p. 38).
4. The legal systems of justice are different for ordinary crimes and white-collar crimes; we have separate systems of justice for the rich and the poor.

How can we make sense of all these observations? Gordon (1973) offers "a radical analysis of crime" and it is worth summarizing in depth.

For capitalism to maintain itself, he argues, competition and inequality are necessary. *Without competition,* or a competitive ideology, the individual might not want to work hard to succeed. If he or she fails, the competitive system is not considered at fault since the system does not guarantee success and in it each individual must make his or her own way. After all, that is what free enterprise is all about. *Without inequality,* in turn, it would also be harder to get people to work in unsatisfying environments. "Driven by the fear of economic insecurity and by a competitive desire to gain" wealth, some people will commit crimes, breaking laws created by a previous generation. Crime in this institutional context becomes a rational response to the manner in which society is organized. This applies to crime both in the ghetto and in the corporation. The differences in the character of the crimes committed are based primarily on the differences in the classes and their positions in the society. Some crimes involve violence because those who commit them run a greater risk of being seen, caught, and sentenced. Therefore, they are more likely to use violence to escape because it is these crimes, rather than white-collar crimes, that are focused on by authorities.

As long as white-collar crime harms only those in the lower classes and does not threaten the capitalist system or those in the dominant classes, little heed will be paid to it. Conversely, our concern for crime in the lower classes exists because it does sometimes threaten that system and those in the higher classes. And the system of "selective enforcement" and punishment serves to strengthen the belief that individuals and not society's structure are responsible for their own acts and hence must be punished for them if they constitute violations of certain laws. Punishment further helps to neutralize potential hostility to capitalism by keeping violators imprisoned and out of the primary job market. Given the assumptions stated about the needs of capitalism, it is unlikely that crime can be significantly reduced without basic changes in the society. Gordon's scheme is presented graphically in Figure 7.2.

In Gordon's scheme, inequality plays a central role in creating differential crime rates and degrees of punishment. A core question then arises: If inequality helps create higher crime rates, can reduction of inequality reduce crime? Gordon's explanation suggests that it would. Gordon's is a structural model that concentrates on actual *class structure* as a root factor in crime. Since inequality is needed by capitalism, the consequence is that capitalism itself must be changed or eliminated for crime rates to be affected.

Is there any *evidence* that inequality itself or

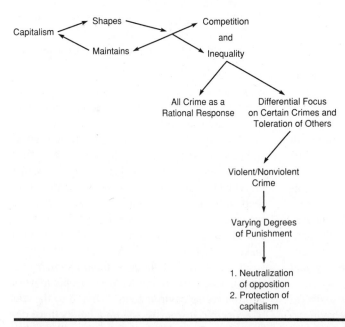

FIGURE 7.2   Gordon's (1973) Scheme of the Relationship between Capitalism and Crime

the manner in which it is structured is related to crime rates? Ehrlich's 1973 analysis of the FBI Crime Index in different states in 1940, 1950, and 1960 found a strong relationship between the degree of income inequality in a state and its property crime rate. The Blaus' (1982) study of inequality and violent crime rates in metropolitan areas is another illustration of research that focuses on the structure of inequality as a source of crime. Basically, they were interested in, "not what kind of individuals tend to commit violent crimes, but what social conditions make it likely that many people commit them" (pp. 114–115). They used official crime statistics from the largest 125 metropolitan areas in the United States to find out if the crime rates varied with the extent of socioeconomic inequality in the area.

Theoretically, they reasoned that in a democracy inequalities based on skill or other achieved qualities are perceived as justifiable, while those based on ascribed characteristics such as race or sex are not. When a nominal or horizontal trait like race is linked to the ranked or vertical structure of inequality, racial and class differences become consolidated, and conflict between groups results in the society. "Ascriptive socioeconomic inequalities undermine the social integration of a community by creating multiple parallel social differences which widen the separations between ethnic groups and between social classes, and it creates a situation characterized by much social disorganization and prevalent latent animosities" (1982, p. 119). One result of this situation is higher violent crime rates. Their findings bear out this theory. Economic inequality generally, and racial socioeconomic inequality in particular, is related to the production of violent crimes. Areas with greater inequality have higher crime rates. Inequality, rather than poverty itself or racial composition of an area, is principally related to violent crime rates.

Messner's (1989) cross-national study of homicide rates supports the Blaus' theory as well. Messner predicted that countries with greater ascribed economic inequality in the form of discrimination would have higher homicide rates.

While his measures of discrimination are rather crude, the analysis of data from fifty-two nation-states confirms this hypothesis and, in fact, demonstrates that inequality in the form of economic discrimination is more strongly related to homicide rates than is the extent of overall income inequality. This suggests that the *form* of inequality may be more important than its *extent* in accounting for homicide rates.

A reanalysis of the Blau data by Williams (1984) suggests that poverty may indeed also be related to homicide rates, especially in areas outside the South. This supports the findings of other studies (e.g., Danziger and Wheeler 1975; Messner 1980; Loftin and Hill 1974; Williams and Flewelling 1988). As Williams and Flewelling state, "it is reasonable to assume that when people live under conditions of extreme scarcity, the struggle for survival is intensified. Such conditions are often accompanied by a host of agitating psychological manifestations, ranging from a deep sense of powerlessness and brutalization to anger, anxiety, and alienation. Such manifestations can provoke physical aggression in conflict situations" (1988, p. 423). Their theoretical model of criminal homicide is presented in Figure 7.3. The influence of violent cultural or subcultural values is restricted to homicides that are the result of interpersonal problems. In fact, few of the studies we have been discussing find much support for the violence-as-a-cultural-value theory of crime.

Gender inequality also has been linked to homicide rates in developed countries. Child homicide rates are higher in developed counties in which there is (1) high female labor-force participation but (2) little child support for them and (3) low female status in the society (Fiala and LaFree 1988). This combination creates greater economic stress which heightens the likelihood for child abuse and homicide. Nations that provide more public assistance to mothers in the form of family allowances or social security programs have lower rates of such homicide. It has been argued elsewhere that not alleviating this kind of stress among women in families increases child

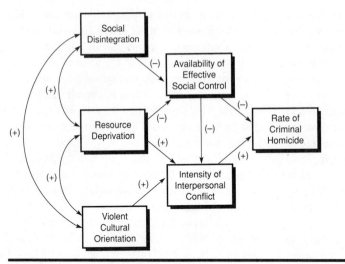

FIGURE 7.3   A Generic Model of the Social Production of Criminal Homicide
Source: Williams and Flewelling 1988, p. 422.

abuse and is part of the reason why the United States has a higher rate of abuse than many other developed countries (Vesterdal 1977; Kamerman 1980; Zigler and Muenchow 1983).

In addition to economic, gender, and racial inequality, unemployment rates also have been found to be related to crime rates. Extensive reviews of studies suggest strongly that unemployment and property crime are positively related (Gillespie 1978; Chiricos 1987). These studies rely heavily upon official rather than self-reported statistics. Tracing homicide, burglary, and robbery crime rates from 1948 to 1985, Devine and associates (1988) found that economic distress in the form of high unemployment and inflation rates is related to higher crime rates. In another longitudinal study, Cantor and Land (1985) examined rates for seven Index crimes from 1946 to 1982. They were interested in trying to account for the sometimes conflicting results of previous studies involving the effect of unemployment on crime. Their results are valuable because they indicate that unemployment can have both positive and negative effects on crime, depending upon the particular crime in question. Specifically, unemployment can have a dampening effect on the

crime rate because it means in part that the *opportunity to be a victim* of a property or violent crime is lower. When people are unemployed, they are at home "guarding" property and also among friends and relatives. The latter means that they are less likely to be victims of crimes by a stranger. On the other hand, unemployment has a positive effect on *criminal motivation,* thereby increasing the probability of crime, especially property crime. Cantor and Land's model of criminal motivation and opportunity is presented in Figure 7.4.

At the individual level, employment has been found to be related to a lower probability of committing a crime. An experimental study of over 2,000 ex-offenders in Texas and Georgia revealed that those who were given employment were less likely to commit a crime after being released than those who were not given employment (Berk et al. 1980). Unemployment is positively related to both property and nonproperty crime commission. Moreover, those who were given some money in the form of transfer payments, which in effect reduced their poverty, were less likely to commit a crime. The latter suggests that there may be a trade-off between

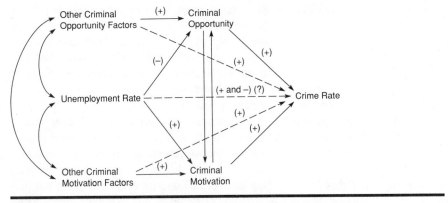

FIGURE 7.4 Unemployment, Motivation, Opportunity, and Crime Rate

Source: Cantor and Land 1985, p. 321.

unemployment/poverty and crime. Among black teenagers, employment and criminal behavior do appear to be used as substitutes. Both are viewed as income-producing activities. Black teenagers who are employed engage in fewer criminal behaviors and vice versa. Involvement in criminal activity, in turn, results in less employment (Good and Pirog-Good 1987; Freeman 1989). Not only unemployment itself, but the quality of employment can have an effect on property crime rates. Among young adults, those with poor-paying jobs having bad hours are more likely to be arrested for property crimes (Allan and Steffensmeier 1989).

There has been some question about the causal direction of the relationship between unemployment and crime. While unemployment may lead to crime, a criminal record can affect an individual's chances of employment. A recent study of this issue using data from Philadelphia indicates that while unemployment can have relatively *immediate* effects on criminal behavior, the reciprocal effect of criminal behavior on unemployment is over a *longer* period of time. These relationships hold up especially well for less-advantaged groups in U.S. society (Thornberry and Christenson 1984).

All of these results suggest that changes in the structures of capitalism and inequality would result in changes in crime rates. Danziger and Wheeler's (1975) research does suggest that income distribution affects crime rates and that reduced inequality is related to reduced crime rates. They contend, as others have, that inequality generates crime both of the ordinary and white-collar variety. Crime also depends on an individual's allegiance to society's norms and the deterrent effect of the justice system. Using national data on crime rates for the United States during the period 1949 to 1970, Danziger and Wheeler found that "higher crime rates are associated with either a higher absolute income gap or with a relatively more unequal distribution of income" (1975, p. 124). Low incomes in themselves do not appear related to high crime rates in this study; it is the distribution that is important. The authors' analysis of fifty-seven large metropolitan areas confirms this finding, even when the educational, unemployment, and size/density characteristics of the areas are considered. Danziger and Wheeler conclude that "levels of criminal activity are responsive to changes in the distribution of income . . . a one percent reduction in . . . inequality was shown to reduce crime to a larger extent than a one percent increase in deterrence" (1975, pp. 126–127).

Inequality and Criminal Sentencing

Once arrested for commission of a serious crime, blacks and those with lower educations are less likely to be "spared the stigma of felony adjudication" (Chiricos et al. 1972). That is, they are more likely to have a felonious decision made about them and to be labeled as criminals. Chambliss (1966) also has suggested that lower class individuals are more likely to be found guilty of crime and to be given more severe punishments than are persons from higher classes. Finally, it has also been proposed that men are treated more harshly than women after being arrested (Stoll 1974).

Certainly, beliefs about the existence of injustice in sentencing vary between groups. Blacks and the unemployed are more likely to believe that criminal injustice exists, especially when it concerns police and law enforcement agencies (Blumenthal et al. 1972; Davis 1974; Hagan and Albonetti 1982). The issue of sentencing goes to the heart of questions about the fairness of the criminal justice system. We have seen that inequality is related to crime at the individual level and to crime rates at the structural level. Next, we ask if, once arrested and convicted of a crime, individuals in different socioeconomic positions are likely to receive similar sentences. Do the populations of correctional facilities represent a cross-section of the American public? Does an individual's position in the system of inequality affect length or type of sentence as the beliefs mentioned suggest, even when the crime and criminal record are taken into account? Certainly, the information in Table 7.2 implies that social class, race, and sex do make a difference.

Table 7.2 presents a profile of those found in U.S. jails and state prisons. Over half of these were in prison for violent rather than property crimes. As the table indicates, in 1989 almost all of those in jails are males and a slight majority are white. However, blacks are disproportion-

ately represented, constituting 47 percent of the jail inmates. In state prisons, again almost all are males, almost half are whites. With respect to socioeconomic status, almost 62 percent had less than a high-school education, about one-third had not been employed just prior to their arrests, and well over half had yearly incomes below $10,000 in the year prior to their arrests. In other words, males, blacks, and lower socioeconomic groups are heavily overrepresented in state prison populations. Recent data also suggest that an increasing number of minority youth are being put into correctional facilities and are more likely to be arrested and charged with crimes than white youths who are similarly delinquent. This applies not only to blacks, but to Hispanic and Native American minorities as well (Krisberg et al. 1987).

How does one account for the disproportionate numbers of lower ranking groups in correctional facilities? If these groups have higher crime rates then we might expect to find them overrepresented in jails and prisons. However, given the issues concerning (1) the definition and creation of crime statistics, (2) the studies of arrest suggesting some bias against lower status groups, and (3) the inconsistency in many studies on the relationship between race, class, and crime, there is reason to be at least minimally suspicious of the conclusion that higher crime rates are the only or even the primary reason for the strong connection between status and being incarcerated.

With respect to gender bias, recent studies are more mixed in their results than earlier ones which suggested a "paternalistic" or "chivalric" reaction to female offenders. Nagel and Weitzman's (1971) often-cited study of national data concerning over 11,000 criminal cases revealed that while the poor and blacks received less favorable treatment than the well-off whites, women were treated more leniently. They were less likely to be held in jail before the trial and to be sentenced to prison. The analysis focused on the crimes of grand larceny and assault. A more recent study by Curran (1983) in Florida supports

TABLE 7.2 Percent Distribution of Jail Inmates, June 1989, and State Prison Inmates, 1986

	JAIL INMATES	PRISON INMATES
Male	91	95.6
Female	9	4.4
White	51	49.7
Male	46	
Female	5	
Black	47	46.9
Male	43	
Female	4	
Other	2	3.4
Male	1	
Female	<0.5	
Less than 12 years education		61.6
12 years or more education		38.4
Prearrest employment		
Employed full-time		57.4
Employed part-time		11.6
Not employed, looking		18.0
Not employed, not looking		13.0
Annual income prior to arrest		
No income		1.6
Less than $3,000		24.7
$3,000 to 9,999		33.7
More than $10,000		39.9

Source: Flanagan, Timothy, J., and Kathleen Maguire, eds. *Sourcebook of Criminal Justice Statistics – 1989,* U.S. Department of Justice, Bureau of Justice Statistics. Washington, D.C.: U.S. Government Printing Office, 1990, Tables 6.28 and 6.50, pp. 573 and 590.

the leniency argument. She found that at the sentencing stage of the criminal process women received lighter sentences even when relevant legal (e.g., prior arrests, etc.) and other nonlegal factors (race, age, occupational status) were taken into account. Other studies, however, have suggested that the courts have become less chivalrous in their behavior toward women, and that if the criminal act for which a woman is arrested is considered a "manly" crime, she may receive a longer sentence than a man (Simon and Sharma 1979; Kruttschnitt and Green 1984). Research by Ghali and Chesney-Lind (1986) on 5,226 Hawaiian arrest records found that the importance of

gender in the justice process depends upon the stage of the process being examined. Specifically, after controlling for pertinent sociodemographic characteristics of the defendants, the authors found that females were more likely than males to be prosecuted, but in the final stage they were more likely to be given probation than to be sentenced to prison. It was only at this last stage that the leniency hypothesis was supported.

There is also suspicion that racial and ethnic minority members receive harsher sentences than whites for the same crimes. Historically, blacks have been heavily overrepresented on death row, along with others with low socioeconomic status

(U.S. Department of Justice 1976, pp. 2–3). Of the 455 rapists who were put to death between 1930 and 1975, 405 were black; of the convicted murderers, 49 percent were black. No executions were recorded for the period from 1968 to 1975, but since 1930 blacks have been more likely to be executed than whites.

Suggestive as these statistics are, however, they do not constitute conclusive evidence that blacks or those in poorer circumstances are more harshly sentenced than those in higher ranking groups. The findings from research on this issue are mixed. A number of studies lend support to the belief that those in lower statuses receive more severe sentences (Bedau 1964; Judson et al. 1969; Nagel 1969; Thornberry 1973). But some do not. Investigations in some cities have shown that race is not important in court disposition (e.g., Burke and Turk 1975; Clarke and Koch 1976).

Chiricos and Waldo (1975) have criticized the methodology, operational definitions, and the small number of offenses considered in prior studies of severity of sentence. Most of them, for example, utilize only gross categories to measure status, a dichotomy to measure severity of punishment (such as death penalty or not; probation or not), and do not control for the effects of other potentially influential factors such as prior record and other pertinent demographic variables. Chiricos and Waldo (1975) attempted to overcome these shortcomings in their study of all felon inmates in three states in the late 1960s and very early 1970s. Using a measure of SES tapping income, occupation, and education, measuring sentence in terms of number of months sentenced, and considering seventeen different offenses, the authors found little support for the thesis that lower SES is related to more severe punishment. They did not include those convicted of first-degree murder because "virtually all penalties received are life or death sentences" (p. 758).

However, since the sample includes only those in prison and not those on probation, the full relationship between status and sentencing is not examined. Chiricos and Waldo readily admit that "the present research must be regarded as but a partial test" of the proposition that those in the lowest status categories receive the most lengthy penalties (ibid., p. 758).

Data on about 10,000 male defendants in Los Angeles in the late 1970s also suggest that there is little difference in the dismissal, conviction, and incarceration rates of Hispanic, Black, and Anglo defendants (Welch et al. 1984). These results stand up even when the type of offense, prior arrest record, employment status, type of attorney, and aggravating circumstances during the crime are controlled. However, the study does not deal with other stages of the justice process or the *length* of sentence if incarcerated, and the authors suggest that the western locale of the study may help account for the lack of discrimination found.

In fact, research carried out in other parts of the country reveal that discrimination is operative. National research on a variety of crimes has found that black defendants who have no previous record receive stiffer sentences even when the type of offense and other factors are taken into account (Tiffany et al. 1975). A study of 1,265 convicted rapists in the South demonstrated that when a number of factors are separately controlled for, blacks are much more likely to receive the death penalty (Wolfgang and Riedel 1973). Another study of almost 900 sexual assault cases between 1970 and 1975 in a large midwestern city confirmed that black men who assault white women (1) have more serious charges leveled against them, (2) receive more severe sentences, (3) are more likely to have their offenses listed as felonies, (4) receive sentences that are executed, and (5) are more likely to be sent to a state penitentiary (LaFree 1980). These relationships were found even when controls for past record, age, and other factors were taken into account. On the other hand, LaFree found no relationship between race and the probability of being arrested or found guilty. Finally, in their study of all recorded offenders who were sentenced in a western state, Hall and Simkus (1975) found that Native Americans were more likely than whites to be put in prison and less likely to receive a deferred sentence. This is despite controlling for differences in background characteristics and type of offense.

Although Hall and Simkus's results indicated that ethnicity does not account for much of the variation in sentencing, ethnicity was significantly related to it. Their results tentatively suggest that the lack of power and stereotyping of this group do not explain the differences in the sentencing, but rather the interviews with judges imply that the defendant's attitude in the courtroom and the report of the probation officer are significant in determining the type of sentence given. Hall and Simkus propose a circular process: The low status individual knows his or her group receives more severe sentences, which in turn leads to a "poorer attitude" in court, which then leads to a prison term.

Like the research on rape mentioned earlier, evidence from a study of "capital murder" in South Carolina also strongly suggests that the race of the victim plays a role in determining whether the defendant is given the death sentence. "Capital murder" refers to homicides that are committed in conjunction with another serious felony, such as rape, burglary, kidnapping, or robbery. The information from 300 homicides shows that, when other relevant factors are controlled, homicides involving white victims result in death penalties being given significantly more often than when victims are black. This discrepancy in penalty was found to be especially operant when there were fewer aggravating circumstances associated with the murders. The relationship becomes much weaker when multiple felonies are associated with the homicides (Paternoster 1984). Otherwise, blacks were found to be given the death penalty more often than whites regardless of number of victims or offenders, sex, age, or acquaintanceship of victim involved in the crime. Table 7.3 summarizes some of the basic results from Paternoster's study. Basically, this table shows that the probability of requesting the death penalty for homicide was about two-and-one-half times as great (2.51) when the victim was white. Just under one-half (.432) of the homicides involving white victims were associated with such a request, compared to fifteen out of eighty-seven (or .172) when the victim was black. This is a significant difference. Racial biases of this type have been found in other studies of homicide disposition (e.g., Wolfgang and Cohen 1970; San Marco 1979). Radelet (1981) also found in his study of 600 homicide indictments in Florida that indictments for first degree murder and imposition of the death penalty are more likely when the victim is white.

Finally, an analysis of data spanning several decades and involving over forty specific studies concludes that:

TABLE 7.3 Probability of Prosecutor Requesting Death Penalty in Felony Homicides, According to Race of Victim and Offender

	No. of Homicides Events	No. of Death Requests	Probability of Death Request	Ratio of Probability
White victim	213	92	0.432	2.51[a]
Black victim	87	15	0.172	
White offender	119	46	0.386	1.12
Black offender	178	61	0.343	

Source: Paternoster 1984, Table 3, p. 451. Reprinted by permission of the Law and Society Association.

[a] $p < .001$

- Black homicide offenders have been less likely than whites to receive a death penalty or to be executed, except in the South.
- Of the executions that have been carried out in the past for rape, there is substantial discrimination in the South against blacks who were convicted of raping whites.
- There appears to be a general pattern of less harsh punishment when the crimes involve black victims, especially when the death penalty is involved.
- With respect to noncapital sentencing, there does not appear to be widespread discrimination against blacks, although there is evidence for this in certain jurisdictions.
- Although crimes involving black offender/white victim combinations usually have heavier sentences attached to them than other combinations, this seems to be due to other legally relevant factors associated with the crimes (Kleck 1981).

Kleck states that in some cases blacks receive more lenient sentences than whites for the same crimes. He cites as possible reasons for this that (1) most involve black victims who are devalued and considered less important; (2) white paternalism toward blacks is present; (3) white guilt about blacks is present; and/or (4) blacks are perceived as being less responsible for their crimes since they are exposed to more pressures beyond their control than whites. Finally, Kleck makes the point that his study addresses only one stage of the criminal justice process and that discrimination may exist at any or several other levels. What all these results suggest is that discrimination during different phases of the criminal justice process has not been eliminated, particularly in certain parts of the United States.

In addition to gender and race, income also has been found to be related to sentencing in some studies. Even when such factors as the type of offense and previous criminal record are controlled, income appears to affect whether or not a defendant receives a prison sentence, with lower income persons getting more severe sentences.

Clarke and Koch (1976) argue that such persons have less of a chance for pretrial release on bail and for a private rather than a court-appointed attorney, and this may explain why income is related to severity of sentence for burglary and larceny, which their study examined.

The Other Kind of Crime

All the adult crimes we have been discussing involve those listed on the FBI's Crime Index. We have noted issues revolving around the definition of "crime," the probability of arrests and reporting of complaints, and the process of sentencing. These issues raise questions about fairness in the criminal justice system and the validity of crime rates in different groups. The prevalence and magnitude of white-collar crime cast further doubt on the completeness of crime-rate statistics.

White-collar crimes are not part of the FBI's Crime Index. Generally, though not always, white-collar crime refers to crimes committed by white-collar persons in the course of their occupations. It is the latter part of the definition that is critical; thus, blue-collar workers who steal or defraud in the course of their jobs might be considered guilty of similar crimes, but ordinarily the focus has been on those in the higher status occupations (Newman 1958). The classic definition and usual usage of the term are given by Edwin Sutherland: "A crime committed by a person of respectability and high social status in the course of his occupation" (1949, p. 2).

Edelhertz (1970, p. 12) suggests that several ingredients are found in most white-collar crime:

1. Intent to commit a nonlegal act.
2. Concealment of the real intent of the act.
3. Reliance on the ignorance or laxness (or both) of the victim.
4. Compliance of the victims in what they think is the real nature of the behavior.
5. Hiding the crime by making the victim think he or she has not been taken.
6. Making plans for those few who realize they

have been victimized in the event they try to retaliate.

Since the crime occurs in the context of a job, white-collar crime usually involves violation of trust. Thus, such acts as misadvertising, price fixing, credit card abuse, computer fraud, and other kinds of duplicities and misrepresentations are a large part of white-collar crime.

White-collar crime, including corporate crime, is costly for economic and social reasons. Recent estimates are that it costs society between $40 and $100 billion annually (Reid 1988). When price fixing, trade restraints, and health and safety violations are incorporated into those figures, the costs for occupational crime may run as high as $231 billion (Kramer 1984). These costs are incredibly high compared to the estimated $4 to $5 billion costs attributed to robbery and burglary (Michalowski 1985). But in addition to the economic costs, depending upon the type of crime, white-collar crime also has detrimental effects on the health of individuals and their trust in institutions.

Corporate crime appears to be extensive. A recent survey of 1,043 large corporations searched for evidence of bribery, fraud, illegal political contributions, tax evasion, and antitrust violations (Ross 1980). The examination revealed that 11 percent of them were guilty of at least one violation. In terms of domestic violations, there were ninety-eight cases of antitrust violations and smaller numbers of the other crimes.

A recent case of criminal fraud involved the investment giant E. F. Hutton. It was found that individuals in the company were taking advantage of funds available before checks were cleared at the banks. This is parallel to an individual writing checks on money that has been deposited but not yet registered in an account. Essentially, E. F. Hutton employees intentionally did this for a period of about one-and-a-half years. In effect, E. F. Hutton was getting the free use of money on which it earned interest. The government determined that about two dozen employees were involved in the fraud, but no one was prosecuted.

Instead, the company was ordered to pay $2,750,000 in fines and costs (Barlow 1987). Numerous other corporate crimes have occurred in a variety of other fields: computers, credit cards, health, repairs, sales promotions, advertising, drugs, real estate, and securities.

In early 1990, Michael Milken pleaded guilty to six felonies concerning securities fraud. In return for his cooperation and plea, more than ninety charges pending against him were dropped by federal prosecutors. These charges included allegations of racketeering and insider trading in the stock market. Thus far, Milken has been fined $600 million, a large part of which is supposed to go toward compensating those investors he swindled. But it is likely that he will be able to consider at least that portion a business expense, and thereby write it off as such on his taxes. Lest one consider this $600 million fine exorbitant, we should also consider that Milken made almost that much in one year, and between 1983 and 1987 made $1.1 billion ("Sniping" 1990, p. 48).

In sharp contrast to many past cases of white-collar abuse, Milken was sentenced to ten years in prison but could be eligible for parole after serving about one-third of that sentence. The judge and U.S. attorney for the case cited abuse of his talents and leadership position as well as deterrence as justifications for the sentence (Fatsis 1990). Milken was viewed by many as the epitome of abusive practices on Wall Street during the 1980s.

But white-collar crime is not a new phenomenon. A study of white-collar crime during World War II by Marshall Clinard (1946), a sociologist who held an important position in the Office of Price Administration (OPA) at the time, uncovered well over 300,000 violations of the price and rationing rules of the OPA in 1944 alone. In the vast majority of cases, only warnings, dismissals, or minor reprimands were used as punishments. In 1961, a major antitrust violation was taken to court involving General Electric and Westinghouse. Behind closed doors, using hidden codes and meetings, the conspirators negotiated with each other, deciding how the market should be divided among themselves. "A low price would be established, and the remainder of the companies would bid at approximately equivalent, though higher levels" (Geis, 1967, p. 122). A newspaper account recorded by Geis describes the high-status defendants as they appeared in court as "middle-class men in Ivy League suits— typical businessmen in appearance, men who would never be taken for lawbreakers" (ibid., p. 117). One defendant's lawyer called the government's recommendation of a jail sentence "cold-blooded" and said that the government did not realize what would happen to "this fine man" if he were put in jail in which there were "common criminals who had been convicted of embezzlement and other serious crimes" (ibid., pp. 117–118). One of the witnesses referred to his actions as "illegal . . . but not criminal."

Milken's lawyer similarly described his client's behavior as "deviations from an otherwise admirable life" and asked for a sentence of community service instead of prison (Fatsis 1990, p. 113). Such crimes involving the manipulation of money and stocks often involve much larger sums than those associated with most robberies or burglaries. One need only think of recent scandals on Wall Street to realize the sums involved. Despite the high costs associated with such violations, few have involved individual prosecutions. Most white-collar criminals, it appears, do not really think of themselves as criminals but as just trying to advance or gain promotions. The public's reactions have been mixed at best since many of these acts exhibit a cleverness and ingenuity that Americans prize. Moreover, most Americans do not directly experience the crime as is the case in robbery, rape, or other crimes against the person or private household. Corporate officials who commit corporate crimes are also usually subject to civil rather than to criminal law, and such violations are handled by agencies rather than by the criminal courts. This is because "corporations" have not, traditionally, been considered "persons" who commit criminal acts with "intent" (Reid 1988).

The manner in which white-collar crime is treated—namely, the special kind of legislation, the special kind of enforcement groups used, and the usual minimal types of punishment meted out—indicate that white-collar crime is treated differently than ordinary crime in the U.S. justice system, even though its cost to victims is much greater. Geis (1974) states the point bluntly: "Upperworld crime portrays the manner in which power is exercised in our society. A review of upperworld violations and the manner in which they are prosecuted and punished tells who is able to control what in American society and the extent to which such control is effective" (p. 114). "Whether he likes it or not, the criminologist finds himself involved in an analysis of prestige, power and differential privilege when he studies upperworld crime" (Newman 1958, p. 56).

Some systematic studies have been done of the relationship between individuals' characteristics and their punishment for white-collar crimes. Wheeler and associates' (1982) study of several white-collar crimes over a three-year period in seven federal districts suggests that socioeconomic status is positively related to being incarcerated and to the length of sentence given those convicted of these crimes. The crimes included in the study were eight federal crimes: "antitrust offenses, securities and exchange fraud, postal and wire fraud, false claims and statements, credit and lending institution fraud, bank embezzlement, IRS fraud, and bribery" (Wheeler et al. 1982, p. 642). The authors found that not only was SES as measured by occupational prestige *positively* related to imprisonment and length of sentence, but that the "impeccability" of the person's past life was *inversely* related to both of the latter variables. They suggest that a "paradox of leniency and severity" runs through a judge's decisions on these matters, impeccability and SES pulling in opposite directions. Other factors, of course, also were found to be related to imprisonment, such as the severity and scope of the crime and the sex of the offender. Men were much more likely to be sent to prison than women, but it is not the role of motherhood that accounts for the differences in treatment. Rather, the authors suggest, "the answer lies deep in the history of sex-role relationships in American society. . . . There is something about the specter of women behind the bars and walls of the prison that leads many judges to a kind of protective paternalism" (ibid., p. 656). In making their decisions, judges consider (1) the seriousness of the crime, (2) the "blameworthiness" of the criminal, (3) the category of the offense and the district in which it is committed, and (4) the offender's sex.

Following up on Wheeler et al.'s model of sentencing, Benson and Walker (1988) studied sentencing for a sample of white-collar criminals in one federal court over a ten-year period. Basically, the crimes examined were the same as those in the previous study, with the addition of embezzlement by a public employee. In contrast to the Wheeler study, Benson and Walker found that SES and impeccability had little to do with the decision to send an offender to prison. They also found that nonwhites were more likely than whites to be imprisoned even after SES was taken into account. With respect to length of sentence, the researchers found that SES was not related to it, but that being nonwhite and scoring high in "impeccability" were related to longer sentences. In essence, most of their results contradict those of Wheeler et al. They attribute much of this variation to differences in the distribution of crimes among the sample, the differences in the districts studied, and perhaps different values among judges in large urban settings, and those in smaller rural areas. They suggest, in sum, that "contextual" factors may affect the findings in different studies. The districts studied in the Wheeler et al. research "have larger caseloads, are more urbanized, and are more racially mixed than most federal districts" (Benson and Walker 1988, p. 301). They included the Atlanta, Los Angeles, Dallas, Manhattan and the Bronx, Chicago, and Seattle areas. In contrast, the Benson and Walker study was based on one district in a midwestern state.

What makes such white-collar crime possible? Newman (1958) suggests that the economic growth and changes in the economic organization of U.S. society have created a need for new means of social control. The widespread availability of sophisticated computer systems has made possible a wide variety of fraudulent acts (Halloran 1977). Moreover, U.S. society stresses the goodness of competition, success, and getting ahead, which nurture such activities. After all, free enterprise and the right to make a profit are part of the "American Way" (Newman 1958, pp. 58–60). Society encourages the clever fellow who can "pull the wool" over someone else's eyes (Schur 1969). And no one likes to admit that he or she has been duped or defrauded (read as "stupid"). Most of those caught do not even consider themselves criminal, even though their acts are clearly illegal and should be treated as crimes (Clinard 1946; Geis 1974).

With respect to corporate crime, a capitalist society in which corporations must successfully compete to survive creates pressures to violate the law. The uncertainties in the social, political, and economic environments in which corporate profits must be obtained make success problematic (Box 1983). Corporations, like other large organizations, try to control their environments in order to create a level of certainty in their operations, and they have become powerful actors in their own right (Thompson 1967; Coleman 1982). One of the means to create predictability in the resource and consumer markets is to behave in an illegal manner. When legitimate means to obtaining organizational goals are either difficult to use or unavailable, pressure exists to obtain legitimate goals such as profit by illegitimate means (Sherman 1987). This argument again suggests that capitalism helps to generate corporate and other white-collar crimes.

INEQUALITY AND COLLECTIVE UNREST

Crime rates are only one social phenomenon related to inequality. Social reactions to inequality take many forms, and even though strikes and movements are not caused simply by inequality, it helps to nurture invidious comparisons and discontent, and the existing structure of inequality can speed the success or failure of such collective actions. The history of the United States is replete with examples of deprived groups that have become conscious of their conditions and the causes for them and have acted to try to change them. On the other hand, the "class consciousness" of a collection of individuals is shaped by specific historical, cultural, and social-structural conditions. In this section, we will focus on an analysis of strikes and the conditions that give rise to them. We will also briefly detail the social-structural conditions associated with collective actions by "underdog" groups in U.S. society.

Workers, Unions, and Strikes

Working-class consciousness is measured in part by the collective organization of workers. This collective power, in turn, affects the economic benefits workers receive. Historically, the earnings of union members have been higher than those of nonunion workers. When unions have been well established, they have had a significant effect on wages, independent of the effects of supply and demand in the market. When unions have not been institutionalized in a particular economic sector or period, wages have been more vulnerable to fluctuations in the economy (Rubin 1986). In 1988, the median weekly earnings of union members was $480 compared to $356 for nonunion workers (U.S. Dept. of Labor, Jan. 1989, p. 227). The discrepancy in wages is especially clear in occupations below the professional level. At that level, there is little difference in median earnings.

Despite the benefits of union affiliation for many workers, only a small percentage of workers are union members. In the late 1940s, about one-third of all nonagricultural employees belonged to unions. In contrast, in 1988, just under 17 percent of the employed wage and salary workers in the United States were members, and a large majority of these were white males. But a larger percentage of blacks than whites are members (23 versus 16 percent) (ibid., p. 225). In general, workers in blue-collar, machine, transportation operator, and laborer positions, along with those in protective service work and professional specialties, are the most unionized. Overall, unions appear to be becoming less important as representatives for labor, which may be a sign that the traditional understanding between labor and management to collectively bargain peacefully through unions may be disintegrating (Rubin 1986).

In addition to unionization, strikes sometimes are used as a measure of the degree of class militancy among workers. Strikes are part of the "class struggle American style" (Rubin 1986). But in 1988, there were only forty work stoppages (strikes). Since 1980, when there were 187 strikes, the number has declined dramatically, along with the declining power of unions. In the years immediately following World War II, there were many more strikes. The numbers of workers involved in strikes have also declined significantly. Table 7.4 shows the number of work stoppages and numbers of workers involved over the period from 1947 to 1988. Almost all of the strikes involved members of unions, with the AFL-CIO affiliates accounting for well over half of all workers involved in strikes. Among the largest strikes in 1989 were those against Eastern Airlines, which involved 28,000 workers, and the Los Angeles Board of Education, in which 27,000 employees participated (U.S. Dept. of Labor, June 1989, p. 23).

The reasons for strikes vary, of course, and Table 7.5 presents the percentage of strikes that were instigated by selected issues in 1980. As the table shows, over two-thirds of the strikes involved concerns over wages. This concern was followed by plant administration, union organization, and contract-related and job security issues in order of frequency. Work hours were least likely to be the central issue in strikes. These figures suggest that workers are primarily concerned with changing their position within the system rather than with changing the system itself. "Workers have used neither their strikes nor their unions to question capitalism itself" (Rubin 1986, p. 619).

Most observers seem to agree that the U.S. working class and most of its unions have been

TABLE 7.4 Work Stoppages Involving 1,000 Workers or More: 1947–1988

Year	No. of Stoppages Beginning in Year	No. of Workers Involved Beginning of Year
1947	270	1,629,000
1949	262	2,537,000
1951	415	1,462,000
1953	437	1,623,000
1955	363	2,055,000
1957	279	887,000
1959	245	1,381,000
1961	195	1,031,000
1963	181	512,000
1965	268	999,000
1967	381	2,192,000
1969	412	1,576,000
1971	298	2,516,000
1973	317	1,400,000
1975	235	965,000
1977	298	1,212,000
1979	235	1,021,000
1981	145	729,000
1983	81	909,000
1985	54	324,000
1988	40	118,000

Source: Ruben, George, and Olivia G. Amiss. June 1989. *Current Wage Development,* U.S. Dept. of Labor, Bureau of Labor Statistics. Washington D.C.: U.S. Government Printing Office, Table 1, p. 22.

reformist rather than revolutionary in character. A few exceptions have existed, of course, such as IWW (Industrial Workers of the World). Rather than trying to change society, most unions are viewed as being concerned with improving the market situation of working-class people (Perlman 1923; Bottomore 1966; Parkin 1971; Giddens 1973). This contrasts with the historical situation in some European countries, notably France and Italy. "Certainly it is the case," writes Giddens, "that the labour movement in the United States has been . . . disconnected from socialist political objectives or cooperative experiments; there has not really been a 'narrowing down' of industrial conflict to economism, because this has been the predominant characteristic of the labour movement from the nineteenth century onwards" (1973, p. 208). He goes on to say that "the primacy of an orientation towards economism is

maintained . . . because workers are prepared to trade off 'alienating' work experiences for economic rewards" (ibid., p. 210).

That this reformist perspective is a permanent one for U.S. workers (not necessarily unions), however, should be questioned for several reasons:

1. Trade unions and leaderships generally have grown to be integrated into capitalist society, but the last four decades of unionism have not increased equality of income, nor is there evidence of a trend toward economic equality (Bottomore 1966; Aronowitz 1974; Taussig and Danziger 1976).
2. There is evidence of an increased polarization and proletarianization of the lower nonmanual ranks into the working class.
3. Many young workers are aware that "most

TABLE 7.5   U.S. Work Stoppages by Major Issue

MAJOR ISSUE	PERCENT
General wage change	66.9
Supplementary benefits	2.0
Wage adjustments	1.3
Hours of work	0.2
Other contractual issues	5.3
Union organization and security	5.3
Job security	5.2
Plant administration	9.9
Other working conditions	1.4
Interunion or intraunion matters	1.7
Not reported	0.8
Total no. of stoppages = 3,885	

Source: U.S. Dept. of Labor, Bureau of Labor Statistics, *Analysis of Work Stoppages, 1980,* Bulletin 2120. Washington D.C.: U.S. Government Printing Office, March 1982, Table II, pp. 24–25.

work in our society is deadening and much of it unnecessary" (Aronowitz 1974, p. 261). Simply getting better wages will not permanently alleviate these conditions.

4. The perfection of technology and an increasing division of labor, coupled with an increased polarization and proletarianization of sections of the manual ranks into the working class, may serve to refocus the concerns of the working class on control rather than narrow economism.

Some have cited evidence that this is already occurring. "The struggle of American industrial workers to improve the conditions under which they perform their labors," writes Weir (1977), "is not an effort simply to obtain a better physical work environment. . . . Of equal, if not greater importance, is the drive to obtain formal contractual control over the methods whereby they are forced to perform their productive duties and to control their relationship to the machines with which they live" (p. 506). Moreover, many of these grievances have been made without the sanction of union leadership. Despite Giddens

(1973) remarks, strikes during the 1930s not only reflected deep dislocations in the society but involved radical, not merely reformist, demands by workers over the economic and political/organizational aspects of their working conditions (Piven and Cloward 1977, Ch. 3).

Historically, unions and workers in the United States have not always joined hands. Before full unionization was legalized in the 1930s, labor protests were frequently violent, caused by problems created during the Depression. A central grievance of workers was their demand for the right to organize. While the early policies of the Roosevelt administration encouraged unionization, established unions at the time tended to be antagonistic toward unionizing all workers (Piven and Cloward 1977, pp. 115–116). This split between unionized and nonunionized workers highlights what many feel to be a central characteristic of U.S. economy, namely, a dual labor market. Because of government policies, in large part forced by the threat and presence of disruption by labor, labor unions were sanctioned but failed to satisfy the needs of workers because of the growing conservatism and accommodation policies of union leaders.

Unionism was not the reason workers frequently protested their conditions. Workers fought for the right to organize long before the Depression, but "that does not mean that established unions played a central role in these uprisings. In fact, some of the fiercest struggles in the nineteenth and early twentieth centuries occurred when the unions were weakest and sometimes despite the resistance of established union leadership" (ibid., pp. 147–148). Many of the leaders were from the rank and file and were often political radicals. They had to tone down their complaints about ownership and political arrangements and express concerns in terms of "working conditions." Unions agreed to act as intermediaries between labor and management and head off disruption; consequently, unions, industry, and government had entered into an alliance (ibid., pp. 159–167). There were times when unions were contented, while workers were not.

But in assessing the overall significance of union for workers, however, Piven and Cloward conclude that American workers have still been better off with than without them "because unions still lead strikes; they still use some disruptive leverage" (ibid., p. 174).

The findings that most strikes involve unions and that unionization is related to higher worker compensation suggest that collective actions by workers and their success depend in large part upon the collective power of labor. Simply put, the greater the power of labor, the less vulnerable it is and the more likely it is to strike and be successful. Thus, the success of labor is intricately tied to its position in the wider power structure of the production process. Perrone (1983) recently proposed a new measure of positional power that takes into account the location of workers in the production process. If the workers' performance significantly affects the production process both "upstream" and "downstream," then workers are in a crucial or pivotal position and thus have great power. In this sense, they are indispensable to the success of the overall production process. Evidence from the period from 1963 to 1977 suggests that power measured in this manner has an important positive effect on (1) unionization, (2) striking or labor militancy, and (3) wages (Wallace et al. 1989). Power provides opportunity for collective action and increases the likelihood of its success through the provision of resources necessary for a successful battle. In essence, the structure of power in a society or industry helps determine the amount of collective protest by groups within it. Historical studies of the determinants of strikes confirm the importance of economic and political structural factors.

Inequality and the Occurrence of Strikes

What kinds of economic and political conditions promote strikes? Do conditions of severe inequality enhance or dampen the chances for worker strikes? Before unions were well established, strikes and other uprisings frequently occurred, many involving demands for rights to organize. But initially the worker protests of the Depression era grew out of the economic and related strains of the Depression. High unemployment rates and a drastic drop in wages caused agitation among the ranks of workers, and accompanying political instability and attempts by the government to improve the economic situation served to legitimize worker unrest (Piven and Cloward 1977, p. 172). The latter point is significant because it suggests that the possible gains for labor during these periods were greater because of unstable political conditions. It afforded the workers a chance to show their dissent in their voting, as they did in the national elections of the early 1930s.

Snyder (1975) has proposed that in a setting such as that which existed before the 1930s, where unions are not well institutionalized, have erratic and small memberships, and are considered an illegitimate interest group, strikes are more likely to focus on political rather than economic goals. Long-term "political ends such as polity membership are more salient to labor than are short run, strictly economic costs and benefits" (p. 266). Indeed, as Piven and Cloward point out, many of the strikes by labor involved the right to organize and to have more influence in industry and society. The reactions of laborers to their conditions were at first political and tame: "The first large-scale expression was to occur not in the streets, but at the polls, in the dramatic electoral realignment of 1932 when masses of urban working-class voters turned out against the Republican Party to vote for a president of 'the forgotten man' " (1977, p. 110). When Roosevelt was elected, the workers felt a sense of "righteousness." "The impact on workers was electrifying. . . . Felt grievances became public grievances, for the federal government itself had declared the workers' cause to be just" (ibid., p. 113). Labor legislation increased the confidence of workers, and from 1935 through 1937, strikes increased, often again involving demands for union recognition (ibid., p. 133). In the pre-World War II period, it does not seem that laborers made careful economic calculations of short-run costs and benefits of their strikes (Snyder 1975, p. 268).

Snyder (1975) argues that during this period, a government sympathetic to labor abetted labor's demands. He finds in fact that in the United States during 1900 to 1948, the percentage of Democrats in Congress and the party of the president were positively related to the number of strikes occurring. Strikes are more likely to be successful when supported by the government. Before the Depression, strikes were often crushed by the state (Piven and Cloward 1977, pp. 102–104). When union membership was up, strikes also increased during this period, though Piven and Cloward indicate that in the mid 1930s worker militancy went up when employers, established unions, and initial government wavering discouraged new unionization and union membership fell.

All this suggests that under conditions of a lack of political and economic power, labor will protest for greater organization and political power, and that once it has unions and a sympathetic government behind it, institutionalized strikes are more probable. Under these conditions of political stability and organizational power, the costs of strikes to labor become lower, and the probability of strikes becomes more responsive to short-run economic changes affecting workers, such as unemployment rates and wage trends.

Under conditions when labor is in demand and unemployment is low, the risks involved in a strike to entrenched labor are low, and strikes over wage changes are more likely. When prosperity is generally present and demand for labor is high, worker solidarity and success is more probable (ibid., p. 98). Thus, Snyder (1975) found that political and organizational factors were significant predictors of strikes during 1900 to 1948 and that after 1948 economic factors were more important. As indicated earlier, in 1974 virtually all strikes were in unionized industries, often during periods of contract negotiation and involving wage changes.

Kaufman's (1982) research on strikes since 1900 indicates that the relative impact of economic and political conditions on strike activity varies with the period. Prior to 1948, both economic and political factors were predictors of strikes (see also Skeels 1982). Specifically, union membership, price inflation, and the New Deal were positively related to strike prevalence, while greater unemployment and welfare capitalism during the 1920s were associated with less frequent strikes. "Welfare capitalism" refers to benefit programs, especially among large companies, which attempted to placate potentially disruptive workers (Brody 1980).

For the period from 1949 to 1977, however, Kaufman found that only unemployment rates and price inflation were related to the number of strikes. Other single political events or legislation are not, nor is union membership or the particular political party in power. In sum, like Snyder, he concludes that while economic factors were important predictors of strikes for the entire period, political conditions were relevant only in the pre-1948 period. Since then, economic issues have become the major factor in strike activity. He argues that inflation and unemployment affect the relative bargaining *power* of labor and management. Other research suggests that the lower the vulnerability of labor and the greater the vulnerability of the firm involved, the higher the probability of strikes. This again emphasizes the crucial role of the structure of power in determining strikes. Tracy (1986) found that smaller firms with more unpredictable profits and with more educated workers who are in demand are more likely to have strikes than firms that are larger and more powerful and who have a larger labor pool from which to draw.

In sum, economic and political arrangements are intricately related to strikes and worker protests. During the late 1920s and 1930s, when economic conditions were bad and the organizational power of workers was low, but political and organizational power were anticipated, strikes were likely to occur. Once the economic and political power of organized labor was established after World War II, strikes were more likely to be successful and, accordingly, the occurrence of strikes has become less responsive to changes in political officeholders and more attuned to fluctuations in wages and other short-run economic trends.

The growth of unions, the organizational power of labor, and the integration of organized labor into the U.S. political economy have similarly affected the form that strikes have taken, generally making them more institutionalized and less violent. The specific shape taken by strikes also depends on industry, plant, and union characteristics. Britt and Galle (1974) analyzed data from the Bureaus of the Census and Labor Statistics to look at the "structural antecedents of the shape of strikes" in the United States. The study led to several conclusions:

1. Larger industries are more likely to have short but more frequent strikes.
2. The more workers in an industry, the more strikes "would be expected by chance alone" (Britt and Galle 1974, p. 648).
3. Unionization and union size are both related to more frequent strikes, but unionization is related to broader and shorter strikes.
4. Concentration of workers (as measured by plant size) was related to *fewer* strikes during 1968 to 1970, but concentration is related to "broader" and shorter strikes (as measured by number of workers involved and number of work stoppages).

In essence, the context for potential strikes is important not only in determining whether or not they will take place but in influencing the shape they will take. Plant and industry size and unionization are related to the shape of strikes but not always in the same manner. Larger industries may be more alienating because of their more mechanized and advanced technologies and thus may be more likely to experience strikes. Unions provide a "capacity for organization" for "effective collective action" when grievances are present and are, therefore, positively related to strike frequency. Larger plants may be associated

with fewer strikes, on the other hand, because they allow for more frequent *individual* demonstration of discontent, such as quitting a job (Britt and Galle 1974, p. 650).

EXPLANATIONS OF COLLECTIVE PROTEST

It is perhaps inevitable that inequality would be linked with social protest as a significant element in the formation of major unrests. "Whether the language was Lutheran, Wesleyan, Calvinist, Jefersonian, Rousseauan, or Marxian, the frustrated expectation of equality has been a major factor in all major revolutionary upheavals since Luther posted his Ninety-five Theses on the Wittenberg church door. Indeed, since long before that" (Davies 1971, p. 7). But the exact manner in which inequality is related to political unrest has been a subject of continuing debate. By stressing "expectation of equality," Davies is in effect saying that it is an injured sense of justice and violation of what is felt as deserved that connect inequality with protest. As a result, his is a social-psychological perspective, one allied to explanations emphasizing relative deprivation as a cause of unrest. As we have seen from previous studies of strikes, however, deprivation alone does not produce protest. The more concrete structural aspects of inequality and the social framework that affects the probability of protest also have to be considered.

Structural Shaping of Disorders and the Role of Inequality

The research on strikes has clearly indicated the importance of structural characteristics within the economy and society for the frequency and shape of strikes. Deprivation and/or position in a deprived group are not enough to produce collective action, nor may they even be the most significant predictors of such disorders.

In fact, relative deprivation theory as it applies to the generation of social movements, has been severely criticized for its psychological emphasis and vagueness. Specifically:

1. The relationship between *objective* conditions and subjective perceptions is not clear in the theory.
2. The empirical evidence supporting the relationship between psychological distress and social movements is weak.
3. Attitudes taken alone have not been found to be good predictors of behavior.
4. Using a *psychological* mechanism to explain a social phenomenon like protest or movements reduces sociological theory to psychology.
5. The theory focuses too much on relative deprivation as a cause of collective action without giving much attention to the causes of relative deprivation itself.
6. The theoretical and operational definitions of "relative deprivation" vary widely.
7. The causal order of the relationship between relative deprivation and collective action is still at issue, especially because of the lack of longitudinal data testing the relationship (Gurney and Tierney 1982).

Collective protest depends in large part on conditions that affect the mobilization possibilities of a group and on political conditions in the wider society. Even when frustrations do exist, as they usually and consistently do for deprived groups, one must still explain how individual frustrations develop into collective protests (Snyder and Tilly 1974, p. 612). Deprivation and feelings of powerlessness may instigate dissatisfaction and even willingness to use violence, but they are not enough to generate actual protest of a collective nature. "The occasions when protest is possible among the poor, the forms that it must take, and the impact it can have are all delimited by the social structure in ways which usually diminish its extent and diminish its force" (Piven and Cloward 1977, p. 3).

The immediate characteristics and requirements for collective protest are clear: (1) the system being attacked has lost legitimacy in the eyes of the protestors, (2) individuals begin to feel more acutely that they have rights, and (3) they begin to think that their desperate, deprived situation is no longer inevitable but can be changed. Groups of people then collectively defy laws and arrangements that undergird established institutions (ibid., pp. 3–5). The critical issue is what and how conditions in the wider society, especially those relating to the system of political and economic inequality, affect these characteristics in such a way as to enhance the probability of collective disorder.

At least seven elements pertaining to societal conditions have been related to the frequency and form of protest. The first of these is the presence of wrenching changes in the society—not merely severe inequalities, but "profound changes in the larger society" (ibid., p. 7). The transformation of institutions in a society leads to a clash between old and newly developing rules and frameworks for everyday behavior. Under these conditions, political leaders are more vulnerable, and new opportunities to protest can easily surface, especially if the dislocations are severe and last long enough. *"Only under exceptional conditions are the lower classes afforded the socially determined opportunity to press for their own class interests"* (ibid., p. 7, emphasis in original). Dislocations, then, can create both deprivation and opportunities to protest. Among the basic transformations that would most readily have implications for protest would be drastic fluctuations in the business cycle, shifts in the nature of technology such as the continued trend toward automation, and basic changes in the content of the labor market, such as the influx of women into the market.

A second societal condition for protest is related to the first. The ideology of the state and its agents can and usually tries to symbolically lighten the burden of deprivation or encourages the belief that the individual is responsible for his or her own fate, not the system against which reaction might otherwise take place (ibid., pp. 6–7). A maintaining ideology is essential: "The willingness of mass publics to follow, to sacrifice, to accept their roles is the basic necessity for every political regime. Without a following there are no leaders." Such sacrifice and willingness to be loyal are legitimized by policy rationales, such as those that appeal to "national security" and similar symbols (Edelman 1977, p. 5). Severe dislocations can shake adherence to ideologies, and the latter are necessary to maintain "peace" in the system as it stands. The role of ideology in maintaining inequality is discussed further in Chapter 12.

The third condition relates directly to the power of the state and political inequality in the society and concerns the power and likely use of repression in dampening unrest. Repression is most likely to be used when the central institutions of the society are being attacked and when concessions have been made, but some continue to protest. Repression raises the cost of protest for those with grievances and thus lowers the odds for successful protest. Snyder and Tilly's (1972) analysis of collective violence in France from 1830 to 1960 found evidence that some measures of the government's repressive action were negatively related to the extent of collective violence.

The fourth structural factor is the power of the government to create opportunities and grant concessions. By doing these, government can defuse protest. One of the first responses of a government to protest is to in some way co-opt leaders or channel protest into legitimate routes. If legitimate opportunities are available, protest, if it occurs, is not likely to be violent. Violence is usually a last resort and involves a great many risks for the group (Coser 1967; Piven and Cloward 1977, p. 19). Government can create opportunities by developing "acceptable and responsible" programs to deal with grievances, and thereby can, in effect, reshape the stated demands of the group. In this way, the government can weaken public support of the continued protest and present itself as "a benevolent and responsive government that answers grievances and solves problems" (Piven and Cloward 1977, p. 34). Then when protest dies down, concessions can safely be diluted or taken away; concessions that are not withdrawn can often be made to serve powerful groups as historically has often been the

case with unions (ibid., p. 35). "Protestors win . . . what historical circumstances has already made ready to be conceded" (ibid., p. 36).

The structure of opportunities also affects the tactics protestors must use and the duration of protest. When protestors devise tactics to attain their goals that are then counteracted by successful tactics by the other side, protest is neutralized unless protestors create new tactics and approaches to continue the protest. The life of a movement depends upon the ability of its members to constantly develop innovative tactics against those in power. Analysis of the civil rights movement during the years 1955 to 1970 demonstrates this process (McAdam 1983). In other words, the maintenance of protest depends upon the power structure and opportunities in the social setting.

The fifth condition is connected to the fourth and concerns the political position of government vis-à-vis the aggrieved group. If the government is suspected of being supportive or actually does actively support potential protestors, protest is more likely. Jenkins and Perrow (1977) found in their historical study of farm-worker movements that some were successful while others failed because of changes in political circumstances in the society. Their success in the late 1960s and early 1970s was heavily due to the fact that government was not solidly against them, and liberals united with workers in publicly denouncing agribusiness. Success requires tolerance or support from those in power or a lack of unity among those who would discourage protest.

The resources of the group gleaned from inside and outside constitute a sixth way in which outside social and economic circumstances affect protest. In discussing strikes, Korpi (1974) suggests that their probability and likelihood of success increase with the strength of resources a group possesses. Relative deprivation may intensify the wish for change, but strikes are more likely if a group has ample power resources from which to draw. These resources can come from individuals or be collective in nature. Coalition formation, for example, can serve as a type of collective resource that can strengthen the position of a discontented group. Since deprivation is usually constantly present for many groups, it is external resources that are needed to organize them and create viable protest. "Disorders do not arise from disorganized anomic masses, but from groups organizationally able to defend and advance their interests" (Jenkins and Perrow 1977, p. 250).

Finally, the shape of protest is influenced by the structure, function, and ideology of the institutions in which protesting groups are immediately located. They determine the composition of groups that will protest, the avenues of protest, and the terms in which demands are phrased. Students protested war in Vietnam while in college and did so by symbolically attacking the system through their assaults on college administration offices and company interviewers. Factory workers protest through strikes; the unemployed cannot go on strike because they are outside the institution. It is the institutions in which the people are immediately involved that help shape protest. "People cannot defy institutions to which they have no access, and to which they make no contribution" (Piven and Cloward 1977, p. 23).

To sum up, in a number of ways the probability and form of protest are determined by political and economic factors other than feelings of deprivation and powerlessness. Several of those previously listed clearly implicate the system of inequality in the likelihood of protest. For example, the factors of resource availability and likelihood of repression reflect to a large degree the extent of economic and political inequality in society.

SUMMARY

Inequality can affect behavior and social events in several ways. At the outset it was stated that not only individual position in the system of inequality but the system as a whole can have such effects, and in this chapter concern was expressed for both aspects. We looked at the relationship between class, race, sex, and crime rates, as well as the relationship between capitalism/inequality and crime rates in general, and found that in each

case inequality is implicated in the generation of crime. Official statistics reveal a relationship between being black and of low income and the probability of being arrested. The bulk of the studies on sentencing suggests a bias against groups of lower socioeconomic standing. This is especially borne out in cases of rape and homicide when the victim is white. A variety of data, then, raise questions about the fairness of the criminal justice system. The definition of the crime problem in terms of FBI Index crimes, which do not include white-collar crimes, and the special treatment given to white-collar crime, the frequent discovery that SES is related to likelihood of arrests, official reporting of crimes, and type of punishment strongly suggest that justice is not evenly meted out in U.S. society. Moreover, the findings of a relationship between income inequality and property crime rates further suggest that inequality helps produce crime and that reductions in inequality may produce reductions in property crime.

If inequality and deprivation are clear and severe enough, they also can foment collective protest. Deprivation, however, is insufficient to produce such protest. The lower class often has been found to be more willing to use violence or see it as necessary for progress, but feeling a need to be violent and actually engaging in protest are two different things. Wider structural conditions also must be considered when explaining protest. Studies of the riots and strikes during the 1960s suggest that the structure of inequality affects the social factors that generate collective protest. The power to mobilize resources, to avoid repression from official sources, to gain concessions, to successfully counter the tactics of those in power, and to discredit official ideology all depend heavily upon power arrangements in the society at large.

The last two chapters have made it clear that inequality has an impact on both individuals and social conditions. It is this pervasive impact that makes it important to understand its origins. The next three chapters discuss various theoretical attempts to explain inequality in society. We begin with an analysis of some of the classical theories.

CHAPTER 8

CLASSICAL EXPLANATIONS OF INEQUALITY

Being poor is a matter of their own choice. Some people would rather live in Harlem than Fifth Avenue.
—Quote from a Rich Man*

The rich? Got to be a certain amount of crook in 'em or they wouldn't be rich.
— Quote from a Poor Man*

Because inequality is related to the lives of individuals in a multitude of ways, both directly and indirectly, it is important to understand it. In this chapter, the ideas of four classical theorists are introduced, those of Marx, Weber, Pareto, and Durkheim. Karl Marx is discussed first because virtually all of Marx's central ideas were formulated before Weber and Pareto wrote their major works and before Durkheim's work on the division of labor. Moreover, the works of both Pareto and Weber are often seen as reactions to Marx's own theory. Few social scientists have had as great a political and economic impact as Karl Marx. His perspectives on society have been used by social scientists and idealogues, and his influence on modern sociology, particularly in areas such as conflict theory, has been pervasive.

*From Huber, Joan, and William H. Form. 1973. *Income and Ideology: An Analysis of the American Political Formula.* New York: The Free Press, pp. 102–103.

KARL MARX (1818–1883)

The ideas of all scholars are in large part shaped by the historical events and life situations they experience. This appears clearly in the case of Marx, as well as Weber and Pareto. Karl Marx was born on May 5, 1818, in the city of Trier. His family was of Jewish background and provided a bourgeois setting for Marx in his youth. His father and a neighbor, Ludwig von Westphalen, introduced him to the thinkers of the Enlightenment. Ludwig von Westphalen in particular became an intellectual companion with whom Marx discussed philosophy and literature. Marx later married von Westphalen's daughter, Jenny.

While studying at the universities of Bonn and Berlin, Marx became a friend of a group known as the Young Hegelians. Although Hegel was dead, his ideas survived as an intellectual force at Berlin. The Young Hegelians helped to convert Marx from the study of law to the study of philosophy. The increasing radicalism of his ideas encouraged his departure for Paris in late 1843. It was in Paris, a center of invigorating intellectual activity, that Marx began his close association and collaboration with Frederick Engels, the son of a manufacturer who acquainted Marx more fully with the real conditions of the working class. Marx's writing again caused his expulsion, and he moved from Paris to Brussels in 1845. By then, Marx already considered himself a socialist and revolutionary. He had aligned himself with several workers' organizations, and in 1848 he and Engels produced the *Manifesto of the Communist Party.*

After some moving around, Marx left in 1849 for London, where he stayed for most of the remainder of his life. It was there that he produced most of his major writing. During his stay, his life and that of his family were marked with poverty, which was relieved only by his occasional employment as a European correspondent for the *New York Daily Tribune* and periodic help from his friend Engels. He became a leader of the *International,* a radical movement made up of individuals from several European countries and in 1867 published the first volume of his monumental *Capital.* In the last decade of his life, Marx was already an honored figure among socialists and was able to live somewhat more comfortably than in his earlier years in London. He died on March 14, 1883, only one year after the death of his elder daughter and two years after the death of his wife Jenny (Coser 1971).

Despite the familiarity of Karl Marx's name to most, many of his ideas are still not properly understood by many students. Two of these are especially relevant to his statements concerning class relations. First, Marx did not believe that everything is determined by the economic structure, that all other institutions are merely reflections of the economic system and are without causal influence. Although Marx considered the economic aspect the *"ultimately* determining element in history" and the "main principle," he did not think it was the only determining one. In a personal letter, while admitting that he and Marx had probably contributed to the confusion on this

point, Engels put the matter succinctly: "The economic situation is the basis, but the various elements of the superstructure . . . also exercise their influence upon the course of the historical struggles and in many cases preponderate in determining their *form.* There is an interaction of all these elements in which, amid all the endless host of accidents . . . the economic movement finally asserts itself as necessary" (Marx and Engels 1970, p. 487, emphasis in original). Thus, political, religious, and cultural factors play a role, though the "ultimately decisive" one is economic.

A second misconception is that Marx argued that only two classes exist in any society. On the contrary, Marx was aware of the diversity of classes that can exist at any one time, as well as the "factions" that can be present within a given class. His discussions in *The Class Struggles in France* and in the third volume of *Capital* make this abundantly clear. We will explore further comments on Marx's ideas after a discussion of the core elements of his theory.

Marx's Conception of Class

According to Marx, the earliest societies were classless, being based on a "common ownership of land" (Marx and Engels 1969, vol. 1 pp. 108–109). But all known subsequent societies have been class societies, and the engine of change in history has been class struggle. Private property spurs the development of classes. Although societies change and the specific names given to the various classes may change, the presence of dominant and subordinate classes remains. The particular *form* that relations take between the classes depends on the historical epoch and the existing economic mode of production. The "mode of production" refers to the particular type of economic system in operation, for example, feudalism, capitalism, and so on. Within every mode of production are (1) means of production and (2) social relations of production. The "means of production" refers to the tools, machines, and other resources used in production, while the "social relations of production" refer to the property and power relationships among individuals in the economic system. Marx contended that up to his time there had been four major "epochs in the economic transformation of society" (1969, vol. 1, p. 504). These were the Asiatic, ancient, feudal, and capitalist modes of production. Our primary focus is on the last of these.

Generally, classes are defined by their relationship to the means of production. Hence, in the capitalist mode of production, "by bourgeoisie is meant the class of modern capitalists, owners of the means of social production and employers of wage-labour. By proletariat, the class of modern wage-labourers who, having no means of production of their own, are reduced to selling labour-power in order to live" (Marx and Engels 1969, vol. 1, p. 108). But when specific treatment is given, Marx's definition of class appears loose, and a variety of criteria are used differentially in different places. A full-fledged class that satisfied the criteria suggested by Marx would be one that possessed:

1. A distinct relationship to and role in the mode of production (in terms of ownership of means of production, employment of wage labor, and economic interests).
2. A clear consciousness of its existence as a unified class with objective interests that are hostile to those of other classes.
3. An organization of the class into a political party aimed at representing and fighting for its interests.
4. A distinct set of cultural values and a separate style of life (Ollman 1968).

"The owners of mere labour-power, the owners of capital, and the landowners, whose respective sources of income are wages, profit, and rent of land . . . form the three great classes of modern society based on the capitalist mode of production" (Bottomore and Rubel 1956, p. 178). Other "transition classes" exist, such as the petty bourgeoisie and small land-owning peasants, but these would disappear as capitalism inexorably reached its peak as a mode of production. Marx

believed that in his day of the "two great hostile camps," the "two great classes" that were being polarized, were the bourgeoisie and the proletariat (1969, vol. 1, p. 109). However, his use of such terms as "strata," "gradation," "middle classes," and "dominated classes" makes it clear that Marx was aware of the complexity that can characterize a concrete system of inequality. What is also apparent is that mere occupation or source of income is not the criterion used by Marx to define a class. Each class has within it a hierarchy of strata. Thus, within the proletariat, for example, individuals vary by specific occupation and income.

Because of the classes' different relationships to private property, that is, owners versus nonowners, conflict is inherent in class society. Class antagonism is built into the very structure of society. Marx's theory is one of class struggle. The existence of a given class always assumes the existence of another hostile class. " 'Who is the enemy?' is a question that can be asked whenever Marx uses 'class' " (Ollman 1968, p. 578). When the economic bases for classes are eliminated, they will disappear since the proletariat will be without the enemy, the capitalist.

In the process of class struggle, however, the proletariat develops from an "incoherent" mass (a class in itself) into a more organized and unified political force (a class for itself). The conditions that bring about this change are discussed in detail later.

Maintenance of Class Structure

The system of inequality—class positions, the given relations of production, and the profits of capitalists—is maintained and protected by a variety of mechanisms. The *state,* of course, is the ultimate arbitrator and represents "the form in which the individuals of a ruling class assert their common interests" (Bottomore and Rubel 1956, p. 223). "The executive of the modern State is but a committee for managing the common affairs of the whole bourgeoisie" (Marx and Engels 1969, vol. 1, pp. 110–111). The state has used its force and legislation to maintain capitalist class relations (Marx 1967, pp. 734–741). Struggles that do occur within the state are always class struggles.

A second mechanism used to maintain class relations is *ideology,* and the dominant ideology supports and legitimizes the position of the capitalist. "The ideas of the ruling class are in every epoch the ruling ideas: i.e., the class which is the ruling *material* force of society is at the same time its ruling *intellectual* force." Just as the ruling class has control over "material production," so too does it control "mental production," and the form these ideas take is clear: "The ruling ideas are nothing more than the ideal expression of the dominant material relationships" (Marx and Engels 1969, vol. 1, p. 47, emphasis in original.). Of course, the ideas generated can and have been mentally separated in their association with the dominant class and hence can appear as "eternal laws" (such as the "free market") or rules generated by all of the society. Members of the ruling class have themselves believed that. The ideas that support class relations are frequently promoted by bourgeois intellectuals who are often nothing more than "hired prize-fighters" for capitalism (Marx 1967, p. 15). Religion as an ideological institution similarly helps maintain the class system by preventing labor from seeing its real situation.

A third factor serving to bolster the set of economic relations is much less obvious than the two just mentioned. The *capitalist structure itself* strengthens its seeming inevitability by creating a working class that because of custom and training comes to view "the conditions of that mode of production as self-evident laws of Nature. The organization of the capitalist process of production . . . breaks down all resistance. . . . The dull compulsion of economic relations completes the subjection of the laborer to the capitalist . . . . [a dependence] guaranteed in perpetuity by the conditions of productions themselves" (Marx 1967, p. 737). As Miliband puts it, "the capitalist mode of production . . . veils and mystifies the exploitative nature of its 'relations of production'

by making them appear as a matter of free, unfettered, and equal exchange" (1977, p. 45).

Development of Capitalism

The meaning and utility of Marx's central concepts bearing on inequality are embedded in his analysis of historical changes in the mode of production. To fully understand Marx's concept of class, one cannot legitimately remove it from his theory of capitalism but must view it in the context of capitalist development.

Several factors aid in bringing about early forms of capitalism. One of these is the accumulation of capital by some individuals. Increased trade and the opening up of the New World fueled the accumulation of capital. When feudal serf groups were broken up in the fifteenth and sixteenth centuries, "great masses of men [were] suddenly and forcibly torn from their means of subsistence, and hurled as free and 'unattached' proletarians on the labour market" (Marx 1967, p. 716). The direct motivations behind these expropriations of land were most often economic and political in nature. Larger tracts of land then became owned by fewer individuals. By the end of the sixteenth century, England had a group of rich capitalist farmers (Marx 1967, p. 744). The forcible expropriation of all this land through various means "made the soil part and parcel of capital, and created for the town industries the necessary supply of a 'free' and outlawed proletariat" (Marx 1967, p. 733).

The newly developing capitalism required a stable labor force, but it could not possibly absorb all those thrown off the land. Many became "beggars, robbers, vagabonds." Laws were then passed against such individuals and against laborers who tried to organize. Capitalists found it necessary to use legislation to mold these workers into a compliant but disciplined labor force (Marx 1967, pp. 737–742).

Moreover, the means of production they brought with them, which had been scattered in individual homes (spindles, looms, and so forth), could then be brought together under one capitalist's roof. And the raw materials freed up by the expropriation of this population provided a fuller basis for the production of goods by capitalists. The need of these people to work for the capitalists to produce the capitalists' goods rather than their own converted collective labor into a consumer, a mass market. The products that the worker would have developed at home as a means of subsistence became commodities of the capitalist. In sum, freed labor power, raw materials, means of production, and a new market became available to capitalism as a result of the removal of part of the agricultural population from the land.

Capitalists then did all they could, including resort to force, to speed up the fuller development of capitalism in "hothouse fashion." "Force is the midwife of every old society pregnant with a new one" (Marx 1967, p. 751). The increasing prominence of the colonial system in the seventeenth and eighteenth centuries aided capitalist development by providing slave labor power, raw materials, and markets. Systems of trade protection and taxes further strengthened capitalism, as did the increasing use of children and women in the factories. Capital and its accumulation, then, were not attained by owners through careful saving and hard work, according to Marx, but rather came into the world "dripping from head to foot, from every pore, with blood and dirt" (Marx 1967, p. 760).

As capitalism develops, in Marx's view, larger capitalists swallow up the smaller ones; centralization occurs and with it the increasing inclusion of a broader and broader circle of peoples in the world market. Capitalism takes on an international character. The problem of creating a secure, collective labor force in the new colonies, where land is available and where potential laborers might otherwise labor for themselves through their acquisition of such land, is dealt with by placing artificially high prices on the land, which then means that the laborer has to work longer to earn the wages needed to buy the land. The money obtained from the purchase of land can then be used to bring more laborers to

the colonies to keep the labor supply full (Marx 1967, pp. 771–772).

As centralization of capitalism grows, so does the misery and manipulation of the working class. But this misery is not without consequence, because the capitalist system of production serves as a crucible that perfects the discipline and unification of the expanding working class. Eventually, the control of capital by the few hinders the production system and speeds the dissolution of capitalism. "Centralization of the means of production and socialization of labour at last reach a point where they become incompatible with their capitalist integument. This integument is burst asunder. The expropriators are expropriated" (Marx 1967b, p. 763). Individual private property had been taken by the capitalists; now capitalistic property is expropriated by the masses. It becomes "socialized property."

Stages of Capitalism According to Marx, capitalism as a mode of production has gone through three principal stages: (1) cooperation, (2) manufacture, and (3) modern (machine) industry.

Cooperation. Capitalism begins when a large number of laborers are employed in one place working together to produce a given product. "A greater number of laborers, working together, at the same time, in one place . . . in order to produce the same sort of commodity under the mastership of one capitalist, constitutes, both historically and logically, the starting point of capitalist production" (Marx 1967, p. 322). It is when workers are thus brought together that "the collective power of the masses" for the individual capitalist can be realized. Workers become more productive and efficient under these conditions, resulting in greater profit for the capitalist. This and each successive change in the mode of production are motivated by the desire to increase the surplus value of labor power and, therefore, the level of profit.

Manufacture. "While simple cooperation leaves the mode of working by the individual for the most part unchanged, manufacture . . . converts the laborer into a crippled monstrosity, by forcing his detail dexterity at the expense of a world of productive capabilities and instincts" (Marx 1967, p. 360). The period of manufacture begins in the sixteenth century and extends to the last part of the eighteenth century. Its characteristic is a strict and detailed division of labor among workers who have been brought together to cooperate in the production of the capitalists' products. Everyone has a specific function to perform; no one carries out all the tasks. Thus, with this change there no longer exists a group of independent artisans cooperating, but rather a group of individuals performing minute tasks dependent on each other. . . . Its final form is invariably the same—a productive mechanism whose parts are human beings" (Marx 1967, p. 338).

Weber's later description of work under rationalized capitalism is strikingly similar, as we shall see. In manufacture, each person performs the same task over and over again until the job becomes routine and the laborer becomes a mere mechanism, but efficiency and perfection in production become reality. Skills that had been learned in apprenticeship become less necessary, and manufacture creates a set of unskilled laborers. The collective laborer, when organized in this fashion, increases production, and as a result, the surplus value of his labor power to the capitalist; "everything that shortens the necessary labour-time required for the reproduction of labour-power extends the domain of surplus-labor" (Marx 1967, p. 350). The profit for the capitalist goes up, and conditions for him could not be better. Larger manufacturing factories develop different departments that produce different products, with each having their own division of labor: To further speed production and the growth of profits, some workshops produce the new tools of labor—machines.

For the laborers, however, conditions worsen. Under the capitalist mode, their labor is no longer their own, because to increase capital each worker must be "made poor in productive powers" (Marx 1967, p. 361). They become unfit

to produce independently, and their labor power becomes productive only within the factory. They need the factory. Working on minute operations rather than whole products, they become "a never failing instrument," "a mere fragment of his own body . . . a mere appendage" (Marx 1967, p. 349, 360). And the constant regularity and monotony of the task "disturbs the intensity and flow of a man's animal spirits, which find recreation and delight in mere change of activity" (Marx 1967, p. 341).

In essence, the workers become alienated from their own labor. The work being done (1) is not an end in itself but a *means* to an end, (2) is not voluntary but *forced,* (3) is not part of human nature (that is, it is *external*), (4) is not work for the workers but for *someone else,* and (5) is *not spontaneous.* The object of their labor does not belong to the workers even though they have put a part of themselves into it. Rather, the product "becomes an object, takes on its own existence . . . exists outside him, independently, and alien to him, and . . . stands opposed to him as an autonomous power" (Bottomore and Rubel 1956, p. 170). As appendages, workers become alienated from themselves, each other, and nature.

Under manufacturing, therefore, capitalists prosper as workers' conditions deteriorate, and the real nature of capitalism as a mode of production becomes clear. *Capitalists prosper because laborers suffer.* The two classes are not merely different levels but are inextricably interlinked in the capitalist mode. People and their labor power become commodities, things of use value to the capitalist, who owns and controls the instruments of production, the raw materials—everything. The laborers, in turn, have nothing but their own labor power to sell, and even that becomes twisted into a form suitable for maximum production.

Modern (Machine) Industry. Like other forms of capitalist production, the development and use of machines are aimed at reducing the cost of commodity production for the capitalist by reducing the part of the day when the worker is working for himself or herself, and increasing that part when he or she is working for the capitalist. That is, it is a way of increasing surplus value for labor. "The machine . . . supersedes the workman" (Marx 1967, p. 376). In modern industry, machines are organized into a division of labor similar to that which existed among laborers during the manufacture period. Since machines replace labor power, physical strength becomes less important, and capitalists seek to hire children and women. The result is a decrease in the value of the man's labor power, and a concomitant increase in the general exploitation of the family overall. When the value of the workman's labor power vanishes, laborers flood the market and reduce the price of labor power. Supply then outweighs demand for labor. Machines are in effect a means of controlling the collective laborer. "It is the most powerful weapon for repressing strikes, those periodic revolts of the working-class against the autocracy of capital" (Marx 1967, pp. 435–436).

With the advance of machines, production becomes more and more centralized, forcing many small bourgeoisie who cannot compete or find little use for their skills into the proletariat (Bottomore and Rubel 1956, p. 188).

Crises in Capitalism and Class Struggle The increased competition for profit among capitalists generates crises at both the top and bottom of the class structure, ultimately leading to the polarization of large capitalists and the massive class of the proletariat. The initial result of the introduction of machinery is to increase profit, but problems arise. Employees are thrown out of work or work for low wages because they are not in demand. The proletariat increases in number and becomes more concentrated, and life conditions among members become equalized at a level of bare subsistence.

Competition among capitalists produces commercial crises, an "epidemic of over-production," which in turn leans to increased concentration of capital, since many go bankrupt (Marx and Engels 1969, vol. 1, p. 114). Overproduction

serves as an indication that the forces of production have become too strong for the property relations by which they are controlled ("fettered"). The capitalist responds by destroying productive forces and by trying to find new markets, but these "solutions" are at best stopgap measures and crises recur, each more serious than the previous. "Modern bourgeois society . . . is like the sorcerer, who is no longer able to control the powers of the nether world whom he has called up by his spells" (Marx and Engels 1969, vol. 1, p. 113). The means of production that the bourgeoisie originally brought into existence to benefit their own position and that permitted them to supplant feudalism now become the means that destroy them.

Bourgeois society becomes the stage for the impending class struggle between the capitalist and the collective laborer, between the bourgeoisie and the proletariat. As capitalism improved from simple cooperation through modern industry, the bourgeoisie became more powerful and entrenched, their ideology and ideas became dominant, and the organization of the state more evidently reflected their power. But so too did the proletariat develop as a class with the progress of capitalism. Initially, struggle against the bourgeoisie takes the form of individual protests, then protests by larger groups—not against the relations of production, but against the forces of production: Workers smash tools, machines, and so forth in order to maintain their status as workers. At this point, they are still just a mass rather than an organized whole. But as conditions for them worsen, that is, as they become increasingly massed together on an equal basis in a minute division of labor under conditions of extreme alienation and emiseration, and as their livelihood becomes more uncertain, their actions become more those of a united class and less those characteristic of individuals competing among themselves. The conditions under which the proletariat labor forge it into a class.

During the struggle that has its roots in the domination of the means of production and appropriation of its products (that is, in a peculiar set of property relations), the proletariat becomes honed as a class, and the struggle takes on a greater political character. Ironically, the bourgeoisie has created the conditions that develop the class that revolts against it. As the decisive hour approaches, and the class and crisis nature of the society becomes increasingly evident, those in the bourgeoisie who see what is happening on the historical level also join the working class (Bottomore and Rubel 1956, pp. 184–188).

Marx argued that a given social order is not replaced until all the *forces* of production that can be produced under it have been developed, and new *relations* of production (that is, new social orders) do not appear until the material basis for their existence has been formed in the old society. This is essentially what happens, according to Marx, when revolution occurs. Revolutions do not take place until the material conditions for their appearance are present. The mode of production shapes all other aspects of social life, and "at a certain stage of their development, the material productive forces of society come in conflict with existing relations of production. . . . From forms of development of the productive forces these relations turn into their fetters" (Marx and Engels 1969, vol. 1, p. 503–504).

With proletarian revolution, the bases for the class system are removed and the proletariat is emancipated. In the interim, between the capitalist and classless society, a "dictatorship of the proletariat" exists, paving the way for a communistic society and the beginning of truly human rather than class history. Figure 8.1 summarizes some of the key elements of Marx's model that we have been discussing on the last several pages.

Some Comments on Marx

There are few areas in social science that have not had to confront the work of Marx. The sheer number of analyses and critiques of Marx's theory of class struggle and capitalism is voluminous; (e.g., Bottomore 1966; Dahrendorf 1959; Mills 1962; Giddens 1973; Miliband 1977). Consequently, only a few of the recurrent comments and criticisms about that theory are presented here.

Marx's theory has had a significant impact not only on the contemporary analysis of class structures but on the orientation taken in the study of society in general. Marx's approach allows us to see at once the simultaneous existence of organization and conflict and their historical roots. In this sense, Marx's theory is a comprehensive one, in many ways unparalleled in social science. Individual actions and emotions, such as alienation, organizations, and class structure, are analyzed against the backdrop of societal settings and historical change. Marx was aware of their mutual interaction and should not be considered as a simple economic determinist. His impact radiated beyond social science to philosophy and the study of morals and to the political arena. That his work continues to generate not only discussions but explanations and analyses built on his own is a tribute to the continued cogency and relevance of his theory.

Marx's theory of class is based to a large extent on the work of others, notably Saint-Simon, and Marx was well aware of his debt to others: "And now as to myself, no credit is due to me for discovering the existence of classes in modern society or the struggle between them. Long before me bourgeois historians had described the historical development of this class struggle and bourgeois economists the economic anatomy of the classes" (Marx and Engels 1969, vol. 1, p. 528).

Still, his conception of class is often vague and inconsistent, though the main thrust of his criteria—relationship to means of production, employment of labor, and class consciousness—is clear. His description of the classless society and the problems associated with the dictatorship of the proletariat as an interim period are not clear and precise. The state and bureaucracy in what are called communist societies have certainly not withered away. On the other hand, it is doubtful that Marx, who believed in uniting theory, practice, and human needs to help bring about a more humane society, would have considered these societies to be the kind he had in mind. Neverthe-

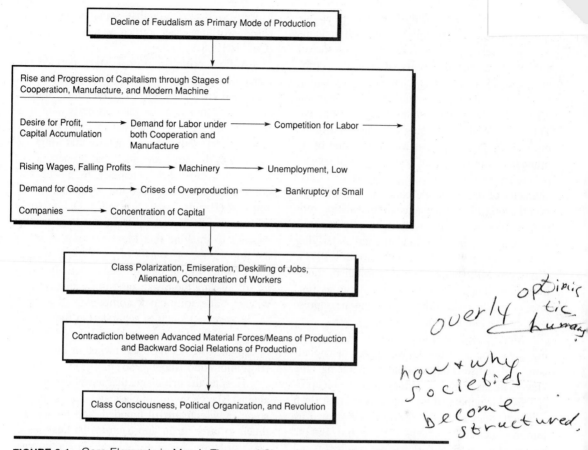

FIGURE 8.1   Core Elements in Marx's Theory of Class Struggle within Capitalism

less, that these societies have turned out as they have suggests a basic flaw in Marx's view of how and why societies become structured as they do. Some have traced this fault to Marx's perspective on human nature which, they argue, is overly optimistic and does not consider the selfishness of people. "The most monumental error in Marx's thought," write Lopreato and Hazelrigg (1972), "is his failure to accept the fact . . . that man is by nature a fallible and 'sinful' animal" (pp. 40–41). Moreover, Marx appears to have "seriously underrated" the ability of individuals to adjust to inequality (Duke 1976, p. 34).

It certainly seems true that Marx also underestimated the strength of nationalism as a force

inhibiting the international union of classes, and the "right to self determination" is something on which many early Marxists could not disagree. Miliband observes that " 'nationalism' has proved a much more enduring and therefore a much more difficult problem to confront than early Marxists thought likely" (1977, p. 105).

Another criticism that has some validity is that the extent of pauperization and polarization of classes that Marx expected has not, as yet, come about. How much one makes of this comment depends heavily on the time frame one selects, because certainly there are indications that the extent of relative economic inequality has not declined and that corporate concentration has increased over the last seventy-five years. Capitalism has proved exceptionally resourceful in maintaining itself and forestalling widespread revolution. Being able to internationalize has provided capitalism with a mechanism for obtaining wider and wider markets and, therefore, has put off a crisis caused by its internal contradictions. The capitalist state, in being reformist and offering welfare programs, has assuaged some of its immediate problems. But, according to Marxists, reformism serves only to disguise the real class character of the state, and concrete reforms support the long-run maintenance of the existing economic order and are meant to solve only immediate problems rather than fundamental underlying ones (compare with Piven and Cloward 1971). Moreover, Miliband contends, "capitalism, however many and varied the reforms it can assimilate, is unable to do without exploitation, oppression, and dehumanization" (1977, p. 39).

Marx thought that the members of the working class would be the "gravediggers of capitalism." But, to use Giddens's colorful phrasing, "the grave remains undug, a century later; and its prospective incumbent, if no longer in the first flush of youth, does not seem seriously threatened by imminent demise" (Giddens 1982, p. 63). But the fact that the working class has not revolted is not conclusive proof of the inadequacy of Marx's theory or that capitalism is not a class society. An effective class society can contain a number of conditions — ideological, political, and otherwise — that serve to minimize the chances of such revolt and maintain conditions of "false consciousness" among workers. Sooner or later (and he believed sooner), however, Marx thought that workers would become aware of their situation and act accordingly.

While Marx's main predictions have not turned out exactly as he thought, many of the phenomena that he foresaw do exist to a degree. As we have seen in an earlier chapter, there has been a consistent trend toward more concentration of corporate power. There is also quite a bit of wealth inequality and there are business fluctuations, ups and downs, that capitalism follows.

Moreover, every capitalist society has "class-based, working-class politics" to a certain degree (Collins 1988).

A final criticism is that Marx defined the concept of property too narrowly and misread its role (Dahrendorf 1959). To Dahrendorf, authority is a broader concept than property, and it is really authority that is the basis of class position. "Dahrendorf would have us believe that Marx, *of all people,* did not understand that property relations refer most fundamentally to power and domination with respect to the production of resources" (Hazelrigg 1972, p. 480). Dahrendorf's criticism on this count is weak; it is hard and erroneous to imagine that Marx was not aware of the importance of *control* of property as well as sheer ownership or of their separation. In *Capital,* discussing the organization of capitalism, he writes: "The joint-stock companies in general . . . have a tendency to separate the function of management more and more from the ownership of capital, whether it be self owned or borrowed" (Bottomore and Rubel 1956, p. 153).

Despite the criticisms that have been leveled against Marx's theory of class and class struggle, some of which are ill-founded, the theory has much to offer as an approach to the analysis of class structure. Moreover, to use Marx's propositions in his general theory of capitalism as "predictions" about concrete capitalist societies without reference to a specific historical society is a mistake. The exact operation of a society depends on a variety of factors other than the abstract characteristics of capitalism (Giddens 1973, p. 37). "Marx should be read today with understanding rather than with misplaced pedantic precision" (Reissman 1959, p. 44).

MAX WEBER (1864–1920)

Many of those who immediately followed Marx in time, and especially the major social theorists of the period, were engaged in a "debate with Marx's ghost" (Zeitlin 1968). Among those most evidently aware of Marx's work and some of its shortcomings was Max Weber.

Weber is often considered to be the greatest sociologist who ever lived. His "shadow falls long over the intellectual life of our era," writes Mitzman (1971, p. 3). Much of what he contributed to social science still remains intact and even those of his ideas that have proven weak or been discarded still provide a foundation from which further analysis can begin. Indeed, it is difficult to imagine what sociology would have been like without his influence. Like Marx and other great theorists, whose specific theories fit into a coherent whole, Weber's formulations regarding inequality must be considered in the context of his broader theory of the rationalization of the modern world. We will examine what Weber had to say about inequality, how U.S. sociologists have interpreted his work in this area, and if and how he added to Marx's own analysis of class structure.

Max Weber's life was quite different from Marx's, but like Marx's, his life experiences were clearly related to propositions about society that he developed. Weber was born in Erfurt, Germany, in 1864, sixteen years after the publication of the *Communist Manifesto* and three years before the publication of the first volume of *Capital*. His family was upper middle class. His father was a fun-loving conformist who disliked and feared upsetting existing political arrangements. In sharp contrast, Weber's mother was an extremely religious person of Calvinist persuasion, who often suffered the abuses of her much less moralistic husband, a fact that later became central in Max's repudiation of his father.

Despite its drawbacks for Weber, his parents' home was the site of frequent and diverse intellectual discussions featuring many of the well-known academicians of the day. So from the beginning, Max was exposed to a potpourri of ideas. Though he was a sickly child, he was very bright, becoming familiar with the writings of a variety of philosophers before setting off at the age of eighteen for the University of Heidelberg, where he studied law, medieval history, economics, and philosophy. At nineteen, Weber left for Strasbourg to put in his military service. It

was there that he developed a lifelong and deep friendship with his uncle Hermann Baumgarten, an historian, and his wife, who was a devout Protestant and was effective in putting her religious fervor into action. Consequently, Weber developed a greater respect for those religious virtues found in his mother and less of a regard for the worldly and cowardly qualities of his father.

A year later he returned to live with his parents and to study at the University of Berlin, where he wrote his dissertation on medieval business. Carrying on a very disciplined and rigid life, he served as a barrister in the Berlin court system and as an instructor at the university and wrote several works on agrarian history and agricultural laborers. These investigations included discussions of the social and cultural effects of commercialization and the role of ideas in economic behavior.

After getting married and serving at the age of only thirty as a full professor of economics at the University of Freiburg, Weber and his wife Marianne left for Heidelberg, where he took a professorship, became more politically involved, and quickly developed a close circle of intellectual friends. During this period, Weber suffered a severe emotional breakdown and was able to do little of anything, even reading. He was only thirty-three at the time, and it was a number of years before his energy was restored. The breakdown may have been precipitated by a harsh confrontation with his father, very shortly after which the father died.

In the early 1900s, Weber's health was restored, and it was between this time and his death that Weber produced most of the works for which he is best known. He became enmeshed in German politics, volunteered for service during World War I, but later became disillusioned by it and the German government's incompetence. Weber, unlike Marx, was accepted in polite society and was not a political radical, but he was generally a liberal and participated in the writing of the Weimar Constitution. There were many occasions when he fought bigotry and close-mindedness. Weber died of pneumonia on June 14, 1920, his broad knowledge leaving an unmistakable mark on social theory (Coser 1971; Mitzman 1971).

Rationalization of the World

Much of what Weber wrote had an undeniable unified theme. His discussions of bureaucracy, the Protestant Ethic, authority, and even class, status, and party fit into his overall concern for social change and the direction in which he thought the western world was moving. Thus, as is the case with Marx and many of the other nineteenth-century theorists, Weber's work on stratification must be understood in the context of his general perspective.

In contrast to Marx, who believed that capitalism and its accompanying denigration of the human spirit were necessary conditions that would eventually lead to a communistic, more humane society, Weber contended that alienation, impersonality, bureaucracy, and, in general, rationalization would be permanent societal features. Weber agreed with Marx that modern modes of technology have dehumanizing effects, but he contended that bureaucracy and alienation are not temporary or peculiar to a passing period, but rather are at the core of the "disenchanted" world. What the future promised in Weber's view was not a wonderful free society where people are reunited to themselves and nature but rather an "iron cage"; what we have to look forward to is not "summer's bloom," but rather a "polar night of icy darkness and hardness." Bureaucratization and technical rationality are not likely to decrease but to increase under socialism.

A bureaucracy is characterized by its impersonality, hierarchy of rational-legal authority, written system of rules, clear division of labor, and career system. According to Weber, it is technically more perfect than other methods of organization and is the most efficient. "Precision, speed, unambiguity, knowledge of the files, continuity, discretion, unity, strict subordination, reduction of friction and of material and personal

costs—these are raised to the optimum point in the strictly bureaucratic administration" (Gerth and Mills 1962, p. 214). Bureaucracy is the perfectly rational system. Business is carried out "without regard for persons," under "calculable rules." The lack of regard for persons is a central characteristic of all purely economic transactions. Since status honor and prestige are based on who the person is, the domination of the bureaucratic organization and a free market mean "the leveling of status 'honor' " and "the universal domination of the 'class situation' " (Gerth and Mills 1962, p. 215). The leveling of status strengthens the rule of bureaucracy by weakening status as a basis for position and encouraging the equal treatment of all regardless of background.

Capitalism and bureaucracy support each other; bureaucracy hastened the destruction of feudal, patrimonial organizations and local privileges. Whereas feudalism was characterized by ties of personal loyalty and was grounded in small local communities, bureaucracy denies or destroys personal loyalty and demands loyalty to position and thereby equalizing individuals. Capitalist production requires it. Conversely, capitalism can supply the money needed to develop bureaucracy in its most rational form (Roth and Wittich 1968, p. 224). Bureaucracy and capitalism are characteristics of the contemporary modern society.

Bureaucracy and capitalism increase the prevalence of authority based on rational-legal as opposed to charismatic or traditional grounds. In the rational-legal form, authority is based on the acceptance of rules regarding the right to issue commands as they apply to formal position in the organization. Authority is attached to the office, not the person; it is impersonal.

Putting all of this together, we see that capitalism and the secularized Protestant Ethic, class, bureaucracy and rational-legal authority are mutually supportive and are integral parts of the increasingly rationalized modern society that Weber saw emerging. They stand in stark contrast to feudalism, the personalism of status honor, tradition and charisma, and premodern forms of organization. An adequate understanding of Weber's perspective on class and status, their relationship, and their distinction can be obtained only if his broader theory of historical development and its associated concepts are incorporated in the analysis. Wrenching them out of this context distorts the meaning of what he had to say about inequality. Keeping his broader theory in mind, we turn to discussion of his more specific ideas on inequality.

Tripartite Nature of Inequality

Weber argued that power can take a variety of forms. "Power," in general, refers to "the chance of a man or of a number of men to realize their own will in a communal action even against the resistance of others who are participating in the action" (Gerth and Mills 1962, p. 180). Power can be manifested in a person's status, class, and party. That is, power can be socially, economically, or politically conditioned. Class, status, and party are all aspects of the distribution of power within a community, and each refers to an order within the society.

The "social order" of a society refers to its distribution of social honor (prestige). The different levels of prestige make up the various *status groups* in that society. The "economic order" in turn consists of the general distribution of economic goods and services, which determines and organizes the *classes* of that society. Finally, the "political order" relates to the distribution of power in influencing communal decisions, re-

gardless of their content, and determines the *parties* in the society. Weber's general scheme for inequality is presented graphically in Figure 8.2.

Although these are presented as three distinct and separate orders, it is a mistake to see them strictly as such since all of them are manifestations of the distribution of power and can and usually do influence each other, often in a quite predictable manner. The inclusion of the social and political dimensions are ordinarily seen as a "rounding out" of the economic determinism of Marx (Gerth and Mills 1962, p. 47). But as has already been pointed out, Marx was not a simple economic determinist; he viewed causal relationships in a more complex fashion. Moreover, Weber's own writing suggests that he did not view the three dimensions as being equal in salience in capitalist society. Parkin (1971) persuasively argues that neo-Weberians have stressed the independence of these dimensions of stratification and thereby ignored, where Weber did not, the *systematic relationship* between the dimensions of inequality. Weber did not fully develop his political dimension, and the economic factor, as we shall see, outweighs the status element in the capitalist system of inequality. But at this point, it is necessary to examine each of Weber's three dimensions in greater detail.

Class More so than Marx, Weber deliberately set out a number of formal definitions for his concepts (Roth and Wittich 1968). In this sense, Weber's work appears and reads more like an academic treatise than does the work of Marx. But Weber acknowledged his debt to Marx: "Whoever does not admit that he could not perform the most important parts of his own work without the work that those two [Marx and Nietzsche] have done swindles himself and others" (Mitzman 1971, p. 182). Weber's own conception of class parallels Marx's in several ways. Class at its core is an economic concept; it is the position of individuals in the *market* that determines their class position. In the last analysis, "the generic connotation of the concept of class" is "that the kind of chance in the market is the decisive moment

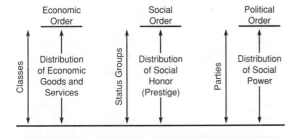

FIGURE 8.2 Weber's View of the General Distribution of Power

which presents a common condition for the individual's fate" (Miller 1963, pp. 44–45). Just as Marx indicated that capital begins when capitalist and laborer meet "freely" in the market, when the laborer is free to sell his or her labor and form a relationship with the capitalist, Weber points out that persons are members of a class only if they have "the chance of using goods or services *for themselves* on the market" (Miller 1963, p. 45, emphasis added). Consequently, slaves are not members of classes.

Weber distinguishes three types of classes: property classes, commercial (acquisition) classes, and social classes. Individuals belong to the same class if they are in the same "class situation," which refers to the probability of individuals obtaining goods, position, and satisfactions in life, "a probability which derives from the relative control over goods and skills and from their income-producing uses within a given economic order" (Roth and Wittich 1968, p. 302).

Property classes are "primarily determined by property differences." There are those who monopolize costly goods and status privileges, such as education, and those who control the bulk of wealth, capital, and sales in the society. Such classes usually are composed of "rentiers," who get income from a number of sources including people, land, factories, and bank securities. Those who are not privileged are those who are unfree or are paupers. Weber stresses the distinction between the top and bottom classes but does mention that in each set of classes there are "middle classes" (Roth and Wittich 1968, pp. 302–303).

Weber is not clear, but he does not appear to make a complete separation between property and commercial classes. Rather, he has a broad conception of property in terms of ownership, and it is " 'property' and 'lack of property' " that are "the basic categories of *all* class situations" (Miller 1963, p. 44, emphasis added). These general categories in turn can be broken down "according to the kind of property that is *usable for returns;* and, on the other hand, according to the kind of *services* that can be offered in the

market" (Miller 1963, p. 44, emphasis added). In a manner of speaking, one can own and dispose of property as well as skills and services.

Commercial-class position is determined by "the marketability of goods and services," in other words, by the opportunity to exploit the market (Roth and Wittich 1968, p. 302). Commercial classes, then, are determined by the skills and occupational characteristics members bring into the market. Hence, those who are privileged in this regard may monopolize management and exercise influence over government political policies that affect their interests. Merchants, industrial and agricultural employers, bankers, ship owners, professionals, and workers who have cornered certain skills are examples of the *entrepreneurs* who are members of privileged commercial classes. In contrast, those who are unprivileged are usually laborers (skilled, semiskilled, and unskilled) (Roth and Wittich 1968, p. 304). Again, there are middle classes, but these are treated more as residual categories when compared with the other classes.

Social classes make up all class situations "within which individual and generational mobility is easy and typical" (Roth and Wittich 1968, p. 302). That is, a social-class structure is one in which there is fluidity and movement of individuals between class situations. Upward mobility is most likely, however, between adjacent classes. Examples of such social classes are the "working class as a whole," "the petty bourgeoisie," "the propertyless intelligentsia and specialists," and "the class privileged through property and education" (Roth and Wittich 1968, p. 305).

Class Consciousness and Class Struggle. According to Weber, classes of whatever kind need not be class conscious as Marx conceived them; they are not necessarily unified "communities." Class organization can occur in any one of these three types of classes, but class consciousness and class (communal) action are likely only under certain conditions. Weber argued that just because there are different property classes, for example, does not mean that they will necessarily engage in class struggle, although they may when circumstances are right. And when struggles do occur, they may not be over a basic change in the entire economy but may be more superficially over the distribution of wealth.

Class-conscious action is most likely if, first, "the connections between the causes and consequences of the 'class situation' " are transparent, or clear. If individuals can plainly see that there is a connection between the structure of the economic system and what happens to them in terms of life chances, class action is more likely. Weber believed this had happened among the proletariat. A second condition for class unification exists if there is an immediate opponent upon whom the class can focus. Hence, workers will react against their immediate employers rather than those who are more distantly and perhaps even more profitably involved (such as stockholders). Third, class organization is also more likely if large numbers of individuals are in the same class position. The increasing growth of the proletariat would increase the chances of class action by them. Fourth, if all of the individuals are in one place and therefore are easier to organize, class unity is more probable. Finally, if the goals they have are directed and interpreted by a group of intelligentsia who are actually outside their class, class organization is more likely (Henderson and Parsons 1947, pp. 427–428; Roth and Wittich 1968; p. 304; Miller 1963; p. 46). These are not inconsistent with the conditions that Marx thought would forge a mass of individuals in the same class situation into a "class for itself." However, Weber cautions us about the belief that fully developed classes are never wrong, that is, "falsely conscious," about their own interests. They can be.

Class struggles have changed in content throughout history, according to Weber. The focus of conflict has altered from struggles over debt and credit in antiquity, to struggles over the availability of consumer goods and their prices in the market during the Middle Ages, to struggles over the price of labor in the modern world. Historically, class struggles begin when a credit market exists in which debtors pay high and often increasing rates of interest to the wealthy, who monopolize the credits (Miller 1963, pp. 45, 48). But in each case, by definition, the struggle is of an economic character.

Status Standing in theoretical opposition to the "market principle" of class, which "knows no personal distinctions" and "knows nothing of 'honor,' " is the principal of status. Traditionally, status groups are ranked in terms of the *"consumption* of goods as represented by special 'styles of life,' " whereas classes are determined by their relations to the production system and acquisition of goods (Miller 1963, p. 56, emphasis in original).

In addition, then, to being ranked in terms of market situation, individuals can be ranked on the basis of honor or prestige. A person's "status situation" consists of all aspects of his or her "life fate" determined by a "social estimation of honor" (Miller 1963, pp. 49, 54). Status groups are based on a particular style of life, formal education, and/or inherited or occupational prestige. Certain groups may lay claim to (or, in other words, may usurp) a certain level of honor because of their hereditary background or family tree (such as "First Families of Virginia"), because of their peculiar lifestyle (such as liberal arts professors, perhaps), or because of their power. The existence of status groups most often shows itself in the form of (1) endogamy or a restricted pattern of social intercourse, (2) sharing of food and other benefits within groups, (3) status conventions or traditions, and (4) monopolistic acquisition of certain economic opportunities or the avoidance of certain kinds of acquisitions. Thus, because of their formal education and occupational prestige, liberal arts professors might tend to socialize only among themselves and might have certain unwritten rules about how a member of the group should act or what kinds of goods and services are suitable for use in the status group and what kinds are not. The conventions associated with the status group control the kind of lifestyle allowable. (Roth and Wittich

1968, pp. 305–306). It is clear that some of the bases of class and status may concern the same factor, such as occupation. However, their characteristics mean that status groups are usually cohesive communities. They tend toward closure, that is, restriction of their memberships (Collins 1988; Grabb 1984).

The stability of status groups is linked to political and economic conditions in a society and is one way in which the latter two aspects of inequality are related to the social dimension. The likelihood of a conventionally recognized status group developing into a *"legal privilege,* positive or negative, is easily traveled as soon as a certain stratification of the *social order* has in fact been 'lived in' and has achieved stability *by virtue* of a stable distribution of *economic power"* (Miller 1963, p. 51, emphasis added). Weber is saying that status groups can be legalized and, therefore, become bases for political power differences when they have been around for some time and are buttressed by parallel differences in the distribution of economic resources. A belief in the long-run consistency between economic and social power is clear in his writing.

Where such stability exists, *caste groups* develop. Castes become supported by ritual (of purity, for example), convention, and law. Separate castes may even develop their own religious beliefs. Usually, the status structure approaches this extreme form only when the fundamental differences between the groups are considered ethnic in nature (for example, Jews). Caste is more than just simple ethnic segregation because, whereas the latter still permits each group in question to consider its own values (honor) to be high, a caste system arranges these groups hierarchically, allotting one more honor than the rest. Any sense of dignity a lower caste group might have would derive from its belief in a *future* beyond present conditions in which it would have an elevated status. In contrast, the privileged caste groups can and do derive their own sense of dignity from their *present and/or past* situation (Miller 1963, pp. 51–52, emphasis added).

Weber stressed that class, status, and political power can be reciprocally related, with each

affecting the others. Status can influence and even determine class (Roth and Wittich 1968, p. 306). However, his writing emphasizes the effect of class on status in capitalist society. "Property as such is not always recognized as a status qualification, but in the long run it is, and with extraordinary regularity" (Miller 1963, p. 49). Frequently, the richest person has the greatest prestige, and those in similar economic situations normally socialize with each other rather than with persons from different classes. Equality of status among individuals in unequal classes can "in the long run become quite precarious" (Miller 1963, p. 49). Weber observed that although race, political power, and class have all been bases for status in the past, "today the class situation is by far the predominant factor, for of course the possibility of a style of life expected for members of a status group is usually conditioned economically" (Miller 1963, p. 53). Despite the controlling importance of the class factor, Weber emphasized that status and class are not necessarily connected. Individuals who are low in class position can be high in prestige and vice versa. Analytically, status is opposed "to a distinction of power which is regulated exclusively through the market" (Miller 1963, p. 54). If individuals who were high in class automatically received high status, "the status order would be threatened at its very root" (Miller 1963, p. 55). Groups who base their high status on their lifestyle rather than crass property are likely to feel threatened when the basis for honor shifts to the economic order.

Weber says very little about the conditions under which stratification by class or status predominate. In fact, his whole definitional classification of class and status is too brief. Parkin (1971, Ch. 1) argues that there was greater justification for seeing class and status as distinct and separate orders in the Middle Ages than is the case today, when status seems increasingly to be based on occupational and economic considerations. Weber maintained that "when the bases of the acquisition and distribution of goods are relatively stable, stratification by status is favored" (Miller 1963, p. 56). If a status order is entrenched by virtue of a monopolization of certain goods by particular groups, then the free-market principle is hindered; it cannot operate. Under these conditions, "the power of naked property *per se,* which gives its stamp to 'class formation,' is pushed into the background." But "every technological repercussion and economic transformation threatens stratification by status and pushes class situation into the foreground" (Miller 1963, pp. 55–56). In contrast to commercial-class societies, which ordinarily operate in market-oriented economies, "status societies" are economically organized around religious, feudal, and patrimonial factors (Roth and Wittich 1968, p. 306). In capitalist societies, classes play a more important role than status (Giddens 1973).

Parties Political power generally is considered to be a third dimension of inequality included by Weber, though some interpret Weber to be saying that class, status, and party are each different forces around which the distribution of power can be organized (Giddens 1973). Although Weber's entire specific treatment of class and status is brief, vague, and sometimes even ambiguous and confusing, his treatment of parties is even briefer.

Parties are associations that aim at securing "power within an organization [or the state] for its leaders in order to attain ideal or material advantages for its active members" (Roth and Wittich 1968, p. 284). Thus, Weber is not referring narrowly to what we think of as political parties (such as the Democrats) but to political groups more broadly conceived. Instead of parties being an outgrowth of class struggle, they can represent status groups, classes, or merely their own members and may use a variety of means to attain power. Since parties aim at such goals as getting their programs developed or accepted and getting positions of influence within organizations, it is clear that they operate only within a "rational" order within which these goals are possible to attain and only when there is a struggle for power. Parties themselves, however, can be organized around a charismatic or traditional leader as well as being structured in a rational way with formal positions to which members are elected. Formally recognized political parties are not the only

kind that exist; parties also can be organized around religious issues or those that concern the traditional rights of a leader in an organization (Roth and Wittich 1968, pp. 285–286).

Marx and Weber

Weber's theory of stratification has traditionally been hailed in U.S. sociology as a major improvement over the supposed narrowness of Marxian theory. Why is this so? To some extent, it reflects the nature of U.S. sociology and the interpretation of Weber by U.S. sociologists. The vagueness in parts of Weber's treatment has encouraged multiple interpretations of what he said on the subject of inequality and the unintentional shaping of what he said to fit the peculiar characteristics of one version of sociology. U.S. sociology has tended to focus on the individual and has, until very recently, tended to ignore the role of the market in generating and perpetuating inequality. Weber's incorporation of noneconomic (status, party) and more general economic elements (such as "market situation") is more appealing to a sociology rooted in a society that has been antiradical and staunch in the belief that individuals can distinguish themselves in a variety of ways other than economic. Despite superficial measures such as income and occupational status, until recently U.S. sociologists have generally neglected the development of measures of Marx's concept of class and an adequate measure of Weber's "market situation." Another reason for Weber's appeal may lie in the belief that many sociologists have "an idealogical aversion to the ideological aspects of Marx's theory" (Lopreato and Hazelrigg 1972, p. 92). A third reason for his appeal in U.S. sociology, and the one most often found, is the argument that Marx developed only the economic aspect of inequality, whereas Weber included social and political dimensions as well. Thus, his approach has been interpreted as being multidimensional.

It is very easy to exaggerate the differences between these two men. Lopreato and Hazelrigg (1972, p. 90), in fact, argue that Weber added little to what was at least already implicit in

Marx's theory. For example, certainly the assignment of prestige (honor) to given positions can be viewed as one way in which the dominant ideology maintains the class system.

There are two basic similarities between Marx and Weber. First, both argued that capitalist society is a class society. Capitalism is characterized by laborers and capitalists meeting freely in the market; it creates a large pool of dehumanized workers of all types and it broadens the market. Second, even though Weber talked about status and party as well as class, he argued that in a rationalized market society, such as capitalism, class becomes predominant, and there is a "leveling of status honor." This distinct separation of status honor from the market principle and property is most characteristic of traditional or premodern societies (Parkin 1971, p. 38). Thus, on the importance of class in capitalist society, Marx and Weber appear to agree.

In light of these core similarities, a good argument can be made that many U.S. sociologists have accepted Weber because they have trivialized his ideas by latching onto the multidimensional aspect of his theory and minimizing the systematic nature of the relationship between those dimensions. Their interpretation of Weber is that class, status, and party are separate, independent dimensions along which each individual can be ranked. By abstracting these concepts while ignoring their systematic interrelationship and the historical context in which they are embedded, Weber's theory becomes seriously distorted.

Of course, there are some basic differences between Marx and Weber. As mentioned earlier, Marx had a more optimistic view of the long-term future than Weber, who believed society would become increasingly rationalized and bureaucratized even under socialism, because bureaucracy once established was virtually "escape proof" (Grabb 1984). Socialism only would intensify the bureaucratic characteristics of the state. Thus, future society would not see the removal of alienation and impersonality but rather their enhancement. A second major difference between the theorists is that because Weber was

concerned with status and party and defined class generally in terms of market situation, the system of inequality contained within it many more groups than are suggested by a class society in which only a few groups dominate. Market situation, for example, if defined broadly enough and in detail, could ultimately mean that each individual is in a distinct class position, meaning that there are as many classes as there are persons. Perhaps the greatest weakness in Weber's discussion is the brevity and ambiguity in his treatment of class, status, and party.

VILFREDO PARETO (1848-1923)

Most scholars generally agree that Marx and Weber had major impacts on sociology. Reactions to Pareto, however, are quite mixed; some argue that he contributed little if anything of lasting value, whereas others are convinced that he had a great deal of importance to say and has been unjustly neglected (e.g., Meisel 1965; Lopreato 1965; Zeitlin 1968; Powers 1987). Part of the reason Pareto is a controversial figure is that he was a counterrevolutionary who stressed the importance of residues (sentiments) as causes of behavior, developed a battery of now curious-looking concepts, and was not always successful in remaining detached in his analyses.

With respect to his being a counterrevolutionary, some argue that he was a theorist of fascism and an early supporter of Mussolini, whereas others have proposed that he was an old-fashioned liberal who detested government intervention of any kind, including socialist intervention. Even though he was something of an elitist, Pareto also disliked and distrusted monarchies and elites (Powers 1987). His theory of residues has been equated to an instinct psychology, and his devotion to certain ideologies sometimes overran his concern for scientific objectivity. Pareto himself was aware of the difficulty in remaining objective:

Pointing out this general human failing, I well know that I am not exempt from it. My sentiments draw me toward liberty, so I took care not to be swayed by them. But in so doing, I may have gone too far and, afraid of being too partial to the arguments for liberty, it is possible I did not give them quite their due. Equally, in order not to be grossly unfair to sentiments of which I disapprove, I may have valued them too highly. (Meisel 1965, p. 11)

So why include a discussion of Pareto here, given all the controversy about him? A summary of Pareto's theory is included here for several reasons. First, although it bears on Marx's explanation and demonstrates a recognition of his work, the factors viewed as basic causes of behavior and structure are quite different from even those stressed by Weber. Second, Pareto focused on political rather than economic classes and was concerned with the interminable shifting of groups between the bottom and the top of the political structure. Third, he is one of the founders of elite theory, which provides another perspective from which to examine inequality.

Having been trained in engineering, mathematics, and economics, Pareto hoped to develop a sociology based on the method that had proved so successful in the sciences. He proposed to get behind the *apparent* reasons for social phenomena to the *real* causes of such events. In this way he is similar to Marx.

Vilfredo Pareto was born in Paris to a well-to-do family on July 15, 1848, the same year in which the *Communist Manifesto* was finished. His father, who had liberal political ideas, had fled to France, where he was a civil engineer. Pareto's own early efforts also consisted of work in engineering and mathematics, study that later fueled his interest in social equilibrium. Politically, he started out as a liberal like his father, but he eventually turned conservative when the leftist parties that came to control Italian politics showed themselves to be corrupt, wheeling-dealing clubs. Pareto ran for political office but lost to the government's candidate. The views and concepts he developed regarding the cycle of "foxes" and "lions" in office were surely influenced by what he saw happening in Italy.

After the death of his parents, Pareto changed his lifestyle and devoted himself to the study of economics. An ardent advocate of free trade and anti-interventionism, Pareto wrote numerous papers attacking the government in Italy. His perception of what the government was like turned his liberal idealism sour. He turned against the policies marked as humanitarian and progressive and became permanently cynical and skeptical about human nature and political affairs.

In 1893, Pareto became a professor of political economy at Lausanne. At this time, his theoretical work became more important in his thinking. Although he still considered himself a liberal at this point, he soon became antidemocratic: "This almost pathological hatred for the ideas of the left would mar all his subsequent writings," writes Coser (1971). "Pareto became a cynical, rancorous, utterly disillusioned loner, at variance with all the dominant tendencies of the age, hating all of them without discrimination" (p. 405). Although this may be an exaggeration, it suggests the kind of position toward which Pareto was leaning at the time. He was a man who tended to be intolerant of people who believed differently than he did (Powers 1987).

Pareto became financially independent after inheriting money and then began to lead a somewhat pleasure-seeking existence. He wrote a treatise attacking the policies of socialist regimes and the weaknesses in socialist theory. On the basis of his own experiences, he increasingly came to believe that it was not rational, logical reason that moves individuals to behave as they do but rather nonlogical factors such as sentiments and beliefs.

During his final years, he lived as an isolate at his private villa. When Mussolini came to power, he praised Pareto, and although Pareto initially was favorably disposed toward some of fascism since it seemed to bring strength and order back to the Italian government, it is not likely that he would have espoused its later policies which suppressed basic freedoms. Pareto died on August 19, 1923 (Coser 1971; Meisel 1965).

As is the case with Marx and Weber, Pareto's theory of elites and their circulation is embedded in his larger theory of human behavior and society. Accordingly, at least a passing acquaintance with some of his central ideas is necessary to fully appreciate what he said about elites and what he accomplished in that regard.

As a forerunner of contemporary functional thought in sociology, and drawing on physical-scientific models, Pareto argued that society is made up of basic elements that are interdependent, each reacting on the others. These elements include the surrounding natural environment, other societies, and forces within the given society (such as race, sentiments, and interests). These elements interacting with each other give a particular *form* to the society and create a *social system,* which should be examined both at given points in time and over time as it changes if it is to be understood. Systems tend to remain in a state of "dynamic equilibrium"; they react to attempted modifications by returning to what would have been their states under normal change (Pareto 1935, pp. 1435–1440). His concern for circulation of elites reflects this more general interest in social equilibrium.

One of the elements determining the form of a society is *residues,* which refer to underlying basic human propensities or basic drives. Pareto discussed six different classes of residues and a large number of specific residues in each of these classes. These residues represent basic sentiments found in every individual. But only two need concern us here: the "instinct for combinations" (Class I) and "group-persistences" (Class II). While each sentiment is present in individuals, one tends to dominate over the other. Class I is "intensely powerful in human species" and is "one of the important factors in civilization" (Lopreato 1965, p. 50). In the economic realm, those dominated by Class I residues are "usually expansive personalities, ready to take up with anything new, eager for economic activity. They rejoice in dangerous economic ventures and are on the watch for them" (ibid., p. 150). This class of residues is, therefore, dominant in persons who are cunning, clever, imaginative, adventuresome, and so forth. On the other hand, Class II residues manifest themselves in individuals who are con-

servative. In the economic arena, this would include individuals "who neither directly nor indirectly depend on speculation and who have incomes that are fixed . . . or at least are but slightly variable." They "are, in general, secretive, cautious, timid souls, mistrustful of all adventure" (ibid., pp. 149–150). Those who are strong in traditional religious faith or who rely on strength rather than cleverness would be high in sentiments of "group-persistencies." In the political sphere, Pareto used Machiavelli's terms of "foxes" and "lions" to label those dominated by one or the other residue; in the economic system, those dominated by Class I were "speculators" and those dominant in Class II residues were "rentiers." How and to what extent societies change depend in part on the distribution of these residues among the different groups in society. On the general level, societies also tend to be dominated by one or the other sentiment and fluctuate between the two.

Individuals frequently give explanations or rationalizations for their behavior that may or may not accurately reflect the real causes for their actions. Such explanations, which Pareto called *derivations,* are not major causes for the form of a society. "For us . . . they figure only as manifestations, as indications, of other forces that are the forces which really determine the social equilibrium" (Pareto 1935, p. 891). A given sentiment or residue may give rise to any number of derivations. Thus, one should be skeptical of the justifications and ideologies people promote even if they embrace a belief in equality. What they say only conceals real motives: The equalitarian ideology used by would-be reformers "is the means commonly used . . . to get rid of one aristocracy and replace it with another. . . . History teaches us that the governing classes have always tried to speak to the people not in words they believe are the most true, but in those which best suit the objectives they have in mind" (Pareto 1971, pp. 93, 98). Like Marx, Pareto recognized the role of ideology in social life. But unlike him, Pareto took a skeptical and distrustful view of human

nature and was driven to conclusions about inequality that were quite different from those of
Marx.

Elite Circulation and the Fluctuation of Power Structure

Pareto is widely accepted as a founder of elite
theory, although there is some question whether
he actually originated the concept. A shadow has
been cast over his work by the debate over the
originality of his ideas on this topic. The argument has been made more than once that Pareto
borrowed freely from the work of others without
giving them due credit (Coser 1971). He and
Gaetano Mosca, a contemporary who also developed a ruling-class theory, were intense enemies
precisely because of this point.

Pareto defines the term *elite* very broadly. In
every area of human life, be it education, burglary, swimming, governing, or others, there are
individuals who stand out. An elite is that "class
of people who have the highest indices in their
branch of activity" (Pareto 1935, p. 1423). In the
political arena, this elite can be divided further
into a "governing elite," who are persons who play
a significant role in government, and a nongoverning elite, who make up the remainder of the
elite. Within the governing *class* are individuals
whose capacities and characteristics make them
qualified to govern and others "who have found
their way into that exalted company without possessing qualities corresponding to the labels they
wear" (ibid., p. 1424). So, there are individuals
who participate in governing even though they are
not qualified to do so (that is, they are nonelite).
Pareto observed that "the governing class is not a
homogeneous body"; rather, within it is a smaller
group that effectively rules (ibid., p. 1575). And,
of course, among those who do not govern at all,
there are those who are capable and those who
are not. The result is a fourfold classification related to ruling, as shown in Figure 8.3

In contrast to Marx, Pareto focused on inequality of political power, although he also dealt

Governing Class	Governing Elite	Governing Nonelite
Governed Class	Governed Elite	Governed Nonelite

FIGURE 8.3   Elites and Nonelites Inside and
Outside the Governing Class

with different groups in the economic arena.
Those who are high in political and social power
are usually the wealthiest. "The classes called *superior* are also generally the richest" (Lopreato
and Hazelrigg 1972, p. 53, emphasis in original). Those who are economically dominant are
maintained in their position by greed, by the apathy and complicity of the dominated, by ideology,
and by sentiments favoring inequality in the society linked to a desire for order and organization
(Lopreato and Hazelrigg 1972, pp. 47–50). On
the societal level, economic conditions influence
the kind of political regime that is present, and
together they are related to the degree of social
equality in the society. For example, favorable,
expanding economic conditions lead to a more
liberal regime and both result in less inequality
(Turner and Beeghley 1981).

The extent to which a society is stable, that
is, in equilibrium, depends in large part on the
circulation of elites. And it is under conditions of
perfect competition that circulation is greatest.
Circulation of elites from the governed to the governing class keeps the latter vigorous and capable
of ruling. It is circulation from the *elite sector,*
not the whole governed class, however, that is
critical. This pattern of circulation is shown
graphically in Figure 8.4. The governed class becomes a source for the continued viability and
strength of the governing class. It is "the dark
crucible in which the new elites are being
formed. They are the roots which feed the flower
blossoming into elites. The blossoms fold and
wilt, but they are soon replaced by others, if the
roots remain inviolate" (Meisel 1965, p. 12).

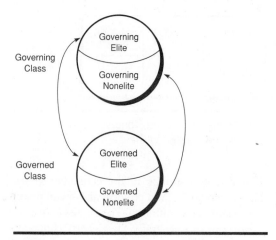

Governing Class

Governed Class

FIGURE 8.4   The Circulation of Elites

Over time, one elite is replaced by another. The process is endless: "Aristocracies do not last . . . after a certain length of time they pass away. History is a graveyard of aristocracies" (Pareto 1935, p. 1430). The significance of the circulation lies in the fact that the governed elite have qualities needed for a governing class. These qualities concern the sentiments and basic predispositions of individuals that affect their ability to rule effectively and, therefore, the distribution of these sentiments within and between the governing and governed classes is important for the stability of government. Regular circulation prevents the formation of a rigid class system.

A number of conditions affect the circulation of elites, bringing about the decline of one and the gradual rise of another. Pareto points out that, after a while, (1) elites degenerate in quality, "in the sense that they lose their vigor, that there is a decline in the proportions of the residues which enabled them to win their power and hold it." They are "restored" by individuals coming from the governed elite (ibid., pp. 1430–1431). The extent of circulation is also determined by (2) "the supply of and the demand for certain social elements." As conditions in a society change, different kinds of qualities will be demanded of those who would competently govern (ibid., p. 1426).

The gap between the *capacity* of the group to govern and its *label* as part of the governing class becomes wider over time (ibid., p. 1430). A final condition is (3) the ability of members of the governing class to biologically replace its members (in other words, fertility rate).

Changes in the governing class also are affected by its own policies. Attempts to slow circulation by trying to hold onto power promote revolution because with slower circulation there is a "disturbance in the equilibrium . . . [because of] the accumulation of superior elements in the lower classes and, conversely, of inferior elements in the higher classes [and a] shrinking from the use of force" on the part of the governing class (ibid., p. 1431). A governing class may seek to maintain itself by recruiting only those who are in agreement with it or are like its present members. But this only hastens the imbalance between Class I and Class II residues in the classes, with each becoming concentrated in one or the other class (ibid., p. 1797).

When free circulation is hindered, clear patterns appear in the ruling and ruled classes that signal the decline of one elite and the rise of another. Force (strength and will), intelligence, *and* consent are needed to maintain power. "If intelligence were to be combined with force, the dominion of the [present governing class] would be perpetual" (ibid., p. 1531). Moreover, governing classes keep themselves "in power partly by force and partly by consent of the subject class, which is much more populous" (ibid., p. 1569). Unfortunately, such happy combinations are not very frequent.

The decline of a governing class begins when it no longer has the force to defend its authority. Hence, instead of using its strength and power, the government position "is maintained by bargainings and concessions, and people are so deceived into thinking that that policy can be carried on indefinitely" (ibid., p. 1432). This means that a group of individuals who are willing to use force (that is, be strong) can impose their ideas and policies on a government unwilling to use force. The larger the proportion of "degenerated individuals, with feeble intelligence" (humanitarians), the more easily this is done. The character and behavior of the classes are shaped by the kinds of sentiments that dominate each of them. If Class I sentiments are dominant enough in the governing class, that is, if members are crafty enough, they will resort to diplomacy, ideology, fraud, and similar nonviolent devices to maintain their power. "Governmental authority passes, in a word, from the lions to the foxes" (ibid., p. 1515). To continue use of these techniques, only foxes are recruited from the governed class. Recruiting a person who would use force, who was high in Class II sentiments, would only "stimulate open resistance" because he "does not know how to crook his spine at the proper times and places" (ibid., pp. 1515–1516). In this manner, Class I residues become concentrated in the governing class and Class II sentiments in the governed class. The politics of government become suffused with greed, more concerned with everyday survival and enjoyment and the individual and less with the long-run survival of the nation. "People who lose the habit of applying force, who acquire the habit of considering policy from a commercial standpoint and of judging it only in terms of profit and loss, can readily be induced to purchase peace" (ibid., p. 1518). Under these conditions, a nation becomes indefensible and the political structure ripe for revolution. A new elite rises from the governed class that is more willing to use force (in other words, it has backbone) and develops policies based on a greater faith in the future, replacing the skepticism of those it supplanted.

The theory of the circulation of elites relies substantially on the distribution of sentiments in groups. In his later writing, Pareto essentially replaced his heavily psychological theory of elite circulation with a more structural theory of centralization and decentralization of political power. While there are some parallels with the earlier work, the emphasis is on the effects of structural characteristics on the decline and rise of political elites. Specifically, centralized power leads eventually to an inordinate reliance on force and per-

sonality as instruments for controlling the populace. This hinders innovation, flexibility, and change, leading to instability and ultimately to decentralization. The decentralization of power, in turn, leads to the diffusion of power, cooptation of many different elements in the society, and ultimately to a lack of control. Extreme centralization or decentralization leads to instability and a decline in power. The most stable regime is one that lies somewhere between these extremes. Generally, societies are involved in a constant fluctuation over time between centralization and decentralization (Powers 1987; Turner et al. 1989).

As mentioned earlier, Pareto was skeptical of those in positions of power. He was especially suspicious of what they *said* they were doing or why they were doing it. Derivations (ideologies) are used in the process of elite circulation by both classes to justify their actions and positions. The governing class may argue that it rules by divine right and that the use of force against it is a "crime" and is "unjust." Members may even bring up a "national security" argument. In effect, the class is using its cunning and intelligence to effectively rule. However, the elite in the governed class who aspire to rule also tailor ideologies to justify their own actions (Pareto 1935, p. 1534). One should not be swayed that their motives are unselfish. "A new aristocracy which wants to supplant another one ordinarily gives battle, not in its own name, but in the name of the greatest number. A rising aristocracy always wears the mask of democracy" (ibid., p. 318).

Pareto does not, however, define the governing class as a cohesive group of conspirators plotting against the general society. "The chief element in what happens is in fact the order, or system, not the conscious will of individuals, who indeed may in certain cases be carried by the system to points where they would never have gone of deliberate choice." "Speculators," for example, "hold no meetings where they congregate to plot common designs, nor have they any other devices for reaching a common accord" (ibid., p. 1576; see also Zuckerman 1977).

Pareto and Marx

Pareto differed from Marx in a number of significant ways. His convictions, based on his own training and experiences in Italy, led him to conclude that Marx's arguments were faulty on a variety of grounds.

1. Individuals do not act solely on logical or economic grounds; rather, the nonlogical sentiments are the prime motivators.

2. Human beings are basically selfish, not altruistic; thus, proletarians are likely to act on the basis of *private* motives, not *class* interests.

3. Given the first two items, private property is not likely to be permanently abolished; the classless society is a myth, only "wishful thinking." The distribution of wealth is not likely to ever be changed significantly. In Pareto's view, "history is an interminable struggle for control" (Meisel 1965, p. 13).

4. Class struggle does not take place only or primarily between the bourgeoisie and the general proletariat. Rather, it occurs between a multiplicity of groups, primarily between the elites of the governing and nongoverning classes. However, in general terms, Pareto felt that Marx and his followers were "entirely right to attribute great importance to the 'class struggle' and to call it the great factor dominating history" (Meisel 1965, p. 10).

5. It is wrong to lump all capitalists together. They vary in their sentiments. It is necessary to distinguish between (a) "owners of savings and persons who live on interest from property" and (b) "promoters of enterprise—entrepreneurs.'" Often these two have quite different interests (Pareto 1935, p. 1558; emphasis in original).

Comments on Pareto

What we see in Pareto, then, is a perspective of society as a social system tending toward equilibrium and a view of behavior as being motivated primarily by sentiments. The distribution of these sentiments affects the circulation of elites, which in turn affects the equilibrium of the society.

Pareto's theory of elite circulation should be viewed in terms of this network of interrelationships. Later, Pareto viewed circulation essentially as a cycle of centralization and decentralization.

Like Marx and Weber, Pareto examined societies and their political and economic components from a broad perspective. Unlike either of them, Pareto first sought the roots of political inequality and mobility in basic psychological characteristics. But like both of them, he realized that social conditions and historical events affect a society's social structure. Like Marx, he viewed class struggle as a significant mover of history, but like Weber he did not believe that classes would disappear. Even though detailed aspects of the contents of elite circulation are not always clear and some of the concepts are vague, Pareto's study of elites and their circulation, and the interrelationships among sentiments and political and economic phenomena laid some groundwork for others working in this area. Finally, the skepticism revealed in his discussions of ideologies alerts the researcher to the distinction between what people say and what they do and to the functions underlying nationalistic ideologies for those in power.

EMILE DURKHEIM (1858-1917)

In contrast to theorists we have discussed, Emile Durkheim was not principally concerned with social equality. Rather, his emphases were establishing sociology as a scientific discipline, uncovering the sources and forms of integration and moral authority, and tracking and understanding the place of individualism in modern industrial society (Giddens 1978). Most of his works revolve around issues of integration and cohesiveness, that is, the question of order in society. Although liberal and reformist in outlook, Durkheim is a central founder of the functionalist school of thought in sociology, which views society as a social system tending toward equilibrium. The organic analogy of society is clear in his writing. Despite his preoccupations with questions of order and the evolutionary growth of societies, however, Durkheim had something to say about social inequality, and it is for that reason that his brief discussion is included here.

Emile Durkheim was born in 1858 in Alsace-Lorraine into a Jewish family, which expected him to become a rabbi. Later, as a young man, he turned away from religion and became an agnostic, even though his study of the "elementary forms of religious life" is one of his major works. Durkheim was a terrific student in his early youth, but was not entirely happy with the lack of scientific and moral emphases at the normal school he attended (Coser 1971). Later, he was to become a highly successful teacher at the high school and university levels.

Durkheim wanted to study a subject that would directly address issues of moral and practical guidance for society, and he wanted to use a scientific approach in the analysis of issues. He turned to sociology as the discipline of choice and, to the disdain of many colleagues, became an imperialistic advocate of sociology rather than the other social sciences (Giddens 1978). It is not surprising that topics related to order, development, and the relationship between the individual and the society would run as a common thread through Durkheim's body of work because of conditions in French society at the time. The early years of the Third Republic in France, when Durkheim was a young man, were filled with instability and conflicts between the political right and left. While events calmed down briefly in the late 1800s, conditions were shaken again by the Dreyfus affair in which a Jewish officer was wrongly accused and convicted of selling sensitive information to Germans. The affair pitted right against left again. At the same time these political events were occurring, France was moving toward more industrialism and a socialist movement was developing. In sum, French society was not experiencing complete stability; it was a time of change.

Durkheim was a defender of Dreyfus and became actively involved in public affairs, including aiding in the restructuring of the university system and helping early in the World War I effort by completing articles attacking Nationalist German writing (Coser 1971). Durkheim's major sociological works did not begin to appear until the end of the nineteenth century. *The Division of Labor,* the source we will be concerned with here, was completed in 1893, followed by *The Rules of Sociological Method* in 1895 and *Suicide* in 1897. Later, in 1912, he finished *The Elementary Forms of Religious Life.* Durkheim died in 1917 at the age of fifty-nine.

Durkheim and Inequality

In *The Division of Labor,* Durkheim developed his theory of the movement of society from "mechanical" to "organic" solidarity. A society based on mechanical solidarity is homogeneous, with a simple division of labor, and based on the similarity of the individuals in it. There is a strong "collective conscience" that serves as a principal source of moral cohesion. The individual ego is not prominent in this kind of society. In sharp contrast, societies organized around the organic form of solidarity are characterized by differences and interdependence in their division of labor. This specialization, along with the increased individualism, can threaten the cohesiveness and stability of society. Corporate groups, according to Durkheim, are to serve as means for integrating individuals in this kind of society. They stand midway, as it were, between the state and individual.

While the "normal" division of labor serves to interconnect a variety of individuals performing specialized functions in an organic society, under certain circumstances the division of labor in modern society can take on "pathological" characteristics. Durkheim argues that this occurs when individuals' positions in it are forced or determined without moral regulation. Individuals must recognize the rights of others in the division of labor and their duties to society as well as to themselves. Each person must have the opportunity to occupy the position that fits his or her abilities (Grabb 1984). When these conditions are not present, "abnormal" forms of the division of labor develop. Two of these are the "anomic" and "forced" forms of the division of labor.

In the first type, relations between people in

the workplace are not governed by a generally agreed upon set of values and beliefs. Two of the developments that divided people were the split between "masters and workers" in which the organization is privately owned by the masters and the arrival of large-scale industry in which workers were each given very narrow and different functions to perform. Both of these factors served to drive a wedge between employers and workers. With large industries, "the worker is more completely separated from the employer." And "at the same time that specialization becomes greater, revolts become more frequent" (Durkheim 1933, p. 355). In smaller industries, in contrast, there is "a relative harmony between worker and employer. It is only in large-scale industry that these relations are in a sickly state" (ibid., p. 356). Large industry develops as markets grow and encompass groups not in immediate contact with each other. Producers and consumers become increasingly separated from each other. "The producer can no longer embrace the market in a glance, nor even in thought. He can no longer see its limits, since it is, so to speak, limitless. Accordingly, production becomes unbridled and unregulated" (ibid., p. 370). Economic crises develop but industry grows as markets grow.

With the growth of industry and an increasingly minute division of labor, the individual worker becomes more "alienated," to use a Marxian term. Like Marx, Durkheim concluded that the worker becomes a "machine" performing mind-numbing, routine, repetitive labor without any sense of the significance of his or her role in the labor process.

> *Every day he repeats the same movements with monotonous regularity, but without being interested in them, and without understanding them. He is no longer anything but a living cell of a living organism which unceasingly vibrates with neighboring cells, . . . He is no longer anything but an inert piece of machinery, only an external force set going which always moves in the same direction and in the same way. . . . [O]ne cannot remain indifferent to such debasement of human nature." (ibid., p. 371)*

While this description may sound intriguingly Marxist, Durkheim's view of the division of labor in modern society was quite different from that of Marx. Because of its nature, Durkheim viewed the division of labor as a central basis for integration in modern industrial society. It is only in certain "abnormal" forms that it becomes a problem. But basically, a complex division of labor is a necessity in *industrial* society. It is expected that as societies develop they become increasingly complex. In contrast, Marx viewed the division of labor as a source of basic problems in *capitalist* society. Class conflict was over fundamental issues in the property and social relationships involved in the division of labor. For Durkheim, class conflict was a surface symptom of an anomic state in which the employers and workers conflicted because of the absence of a common, agreed upon set of moral rules. The problems of the modern society are not due to contradictions within capitalism, "but derive from the strains inherent in the transition from mechanical to organic solidarity" (Giddens 1978, p. 36). While Marx sees regulation in capitalist society as stifling human initiative, Durkheim sees moral regulation as necessary for individual liberty and happiness.

However, the mere presence of rules is not enough to prevent problems in the division of labor because "sometimes the rules themselves are the cause of evil. This is what occurs in class-wars" (Durkheim 1933, p. 374). The problem here is that the rules governing the division of labor do not create a correspondence between individual talents or interests and work functions. The result is that the division of labor creates dissatisfaction and pain instead of integration and cohesiveness. "This is because the distribution of social functions on which [the class structure] rests does not respond, or rather no longer responds, to the distribution of natural talents" (ibid., p. 375). When the rules regulating the division of labor no longer correspond to the distribution of true talents among individuals, then the organization of labor becomes forced. Durkheim felt that inequalities that were not based on "internal" differences between individuals were unjust. "External" inequality, which is based upon inheritance, must be eliminated according to Durkheim because it threatens the solidarity of society. Superiority that results from differences in the resources of individuals is unjust. "In other words, there cannot be rich and poor at birth without there being unjust contracts" (ibid., p. 384). The sense of injustice associated with the significance of external inequalities becomes greater as labor becomes more separated from employers and the collective conscience becomes weaker.

Despite his realization of the injustices suffered by workers in the division of labor, Durkheim was not an advocate of class revolution. As mentioned, he did not feel that there is anything *inherently* wrong with a complex division of labor and, consequently, only reformist change was needed to eliminate the problems associated with it. Durkheim felt that complete revolution would destroy the delicate and complex membrane that made up society. "I am quite aware when people speak of destroying existing societies, they intend to reconstruct them. But these are the fantasies of children. One cannot in this way rebuild collective life: once our social organization is destroyed, centuries of history will be required to build another" (quoted in Fenton 1984, p. 31). Durkheim felt that deep, lasting change would take place gradually and through ameliorative reform rather than through drastic conflict. In this way, he also differed from Marx. Nor did he feel that the state was an instrument of oppression, but rather felt it could serve as an instrument of reform for a better society (Giddens 1978). However, like Marx and in contrast to Weber, he had an optimistic view of future society. Fundamental class conflicts would be minimized once problems in the division of labor could be ironed out with appropriate policies and moral regulations over time.

SUMMARY

It was mentioned at the outset of the chapter that a thorough understanding of what Marx, Weber,

Pareto, and Durkheim had to say about inequality depends on seeing and analyzing that work in the context of their broader theories and perspectives on society and human beings. Too often, as a reflection of our specialization and departmentalization as students, we wrench out only those segments of an individual's theory in which we have an immediate interest. This is not the way in which these theories were developed, and so taking them out of context can lead to distortions and at best only superficial understanding. Consequently, the specific observations made by these individuals on inequality should be couched in the broader frameworks of their overall perspectives and life experiences. Hopefully, this leads to a fuller comprehension of what each of the given theorists was trying to convey.

It is clear from the discussion in this chapter that the theorists covered differed significantly in their views on human nature, the forms that inequality could take, and the bases and future of inequality. Both Pareto and Weber saw human beings as self-seeking, whereas Marx viewed them in more selfless terms. Durkheim felt that individuals required regulation and guidance. Marx focused on economic classes, as did Durkheim in *The Division of Labor,* while Pareto focused on political classes and Weber examined economic classes as well as status groups, and to some extent, parties. Marx sought the source of inequality in an individual's relationship to the means of production, whereas Pareto looked to basic psychological characteristics and structural configurations for an understanding of classes and circulation among them. Weber saw inequality arising from a number of sources, including market situation, lifestyle, and decision-making power. Durkheim traced the problems of inequality to abnormalities in the division of labor. Weber, like Pareto, did not see inequality disappearing in the future. Marx was more optimistic on this point as was Durkheim.

Marx, Weber, and Pareto agreed that classes, class struggle, or both are significant elements in societies. Weber and Marx both felt that capitalism has dehumanizing effects and is class structured and that class is a predominant factor in modern society. Their conceptions of the effects of class anticipated many of the specific effects discussed in the previous two chapters on life chances, crime, and protest. Similar conditions for class consciousness and protest were outlined by Marx and Weber.

The theories of Marx, Weber, Pareto, and Durkheim were presented here because their perspectives have helped to shape modern sociology. Their impact has not always been obvious, but it has been pervasive.

CHAPTER 9

MODERN EXPLANATIONS
OF INEQUALITY

*Social inequality is thus an unconsciously evolved device by which
societies insure that the most important positions are conscientiously
filled by the most qualified persons.*
　—Kingsley Davis and Wilbert Moore

*[The poor] are also separated from the non-poor in the positive sense
that they have economic value where they are and hence that there are
groups interested, not only in resisting the elimination of poverty, but in
actively seeking its perpetuation.*
　—Michael Piori

This chapter consists of a discussion of some of
the more recent explanations of social inequality.
One of the earliest and most controversial of
these theories is the one developed by Davis and
Moore. These scholars provide a functionalist
perspective on inequality, a perspective which is
generally interpreted as being conservative when
compared to those developed by conflict-oriented
or radical theorists. The functionalist theory of
inequality is presented in detail because it occupied an important place in discussions and controversies concerning the origins of inequality,
and because the general framework of functionalism dominated social thought in the United States
for several decades.

Social reproduction theories are fairly recent
conflict or Marxian models aimed at furthering
understanding of the mechanisms that keep inequality intact over time. Lenski's theory, in turn,
is an overt attempt to combine both conservative/
functionalist and radical/conflict assumptions

and propositions into a coherent theory of social
stratification.

Finally, economic labor-market theories of
inequality have, in a broad way, mirrored conservative and radical perspectives in sociology.
Yet they are distinct enough to warrant separate
discussion. Thus, the analysis of Lenski's syn-
thetic theory is followed by a presentation of various versions of labor-market theory as they per-
tain to inequality. This includes a discussion of
more recent radical models.

This chapter is not an exhaustive treatment
of all contemporary theories of inequality. The
work of Erik Wright, for example, a prominent
American Marxist scholar, is not discussed in
this chapter. Wright's principal publications have
been concerned with the Marxian conceptualization and measurement of class and their application to understanding the shape of class structure
in capitalist societies. As a result, his view of the
class concept and class structure were reviewed

in Chapter 2 along with other perspectives on class structure.

FUNCTIONALIST THEORY OF STRATIFICATION

Few contemporary theories of stratification have received the attention and criticism that the Davis-Moore (1945) article, "Some Principles of Stratification," has received. This theory is based on a "structural-functional" view of society, which in an abstract way appears to make a great deal of sense. Its hold on the discipline of sociology has been tenacious.

The functional perspective views societies as social systems that have certain basic problems to solve or functions that have to be performed if the society is to survive. Talcott Parsons refers to the four basic problems as adaptation, goal attainment, integration, and pattern maintenance. In order to survive, a system must somehow glean what it needs from the environment and establish some mechanism by which those goods are distributed. This is the problem of *adaptation*. *Goal attainment* refers to the need to establish goals and their priority and to devise legitimate means to attain them. *Integration* refers to the problem of coordination and maintaining smooth interrelationships among the parts of the system. Finally, *pattern maintenance* refers to the problem of ensuring that new members in the system display characteristics and behavior appropriate for system members and thwarting situations in which the smooth running of the system is threatened.

Another group of functionalist theorists also provided a list of the kinds of problems that have to be solved if a society is to continue. One of these problems concerns the motivation of society's members; if that motivation is absent, a society will not survive (Aberle et al. 1950, p. 103). If a society is to continue, important tasks must be specifically delineated and some means for their assignment created; for a society, "activities necessary to its survival must be worked out in predictable, determinate ways, or else apathy or

the war of each against all must prevail" (ibid., p. 105). And since certain goods of value are scarce (property, wealth, and so forth), "some system of differential allocation of the scarce values of a society is essential" (ibid., p. 106). The result of this differential allocation (stratification) must be viewed as being legitimate and "accepted by most of the members—at least by the important ones—of a society if stability is to be attained" (ibid.). The authors go on to list other "functional prerequisites" for the survival of a society, but it is their view of the necessity of stratification that concerns us here.

The most celebrated and damned theory of stratification using the functionalist perspective was formulated by Kinsley Davis and Wilbert Moore in 1945. Their ideas are quite simple to grasp and, on the surface, may appear to be common-sensical and even self-evident. One should keep in mind that the kind of thinking that is represented in their theory dominated sociology throughout the 1950s and much of the 1960s in the United States. Let us take a closer look at their reasoning.

They indicate at the outset of their argument what they are trying to do:

1. "To explain in functional terms, the universal necessity which calls forth stratification in any social system."
2. To explain why positions, not persons, are differentially ranked in the system of rewards in any society. (Davis and Moore 1945, p. 242).

Assuming that structure is at least minimally divided into different statuses and roles, that is, a division of labor, Davis and Moore begin by arguing that every society has to have some means to place its members in the social structure. A critical issue is the problem of motivating individuals to occupy certain statuses (full-time occupations) and to make sure that they are motivated to adequately perform the roles once they occupy those positions. Since some tasks are more onerous, more important for the society, and more difficult to perform, what is required is a system of rewards (inducements) to make certain that these tasks are performed by the most capable individuals. "The rewards and their distribution become a part of the social order, and thus give rise to stratification" (ibid., p. 243). Like Durkheim's view of the ideal industrial society, Davis and Moore assume that the society will run smoothly because the distribution of rewards to individuals will reflect the "internal inequalities" of their skills and capabilities.

Every society has a variety of rewards that it can use: (1) those "that contribute to sustenance and comfort" (money, goods of different kinds), (2) those related to "humor and diversion" (vacations, leisure plans, and so forth), and (3) those that enhance "self-respect and ego expansion" (psychological rewards, promotion). Consequently, Davis and Moore are not simply talking about the distribution and system of economic rewards but all kinds of inducements that can promote motivation to perform tasks in the society. Not all positions have equal rewards attached to them, of course, and since that is the case, "the society must be stratified because that is precisely what stratification means. Social inequality is thus an unconsciously evolved device by which societies ensure that the most important positions are conscientiously filled by qualified persons" (ibid., p. 243). According to this approach, since every society has tasks that are differentially important to its survival, every society is stratified.

Davis and Moore specify two criteria that determine the amount of rewards that accrue to given positions: (1) functional importance of the task, and (2) the "scarcity of personnel" capable of performing the task, or the amount of training required (ibid., pp. 243–244). Together, these determine the rank of a given position in the system of rewards, that is, in the stratification system. Consequently, "a position does not bring power and privilege because it draws a high income. Rather it draws a high income because it is functionally important and the available personnel is for one reason or another scarce" (ibid., pp. 246–247). The exact contribution of each of these criteria, singly and in combination, to the level of rewards is not spelled out, so one can only guess as to how rewards would be affected if one of these criteria ranked high but the other low on a given position (Abrahamson 1978).

Davis and Moore imply that a third and more radical factor also is involved in determining an *individual's* (as opposed to a position's) rank and reward: economic power or control over resources. They recognize that having a great deal of money can give an individual an advantage in seeking a higher position. Power and prestige can be based on ownership, and "one kind of ownership of production goods consists in rights over the labor of others. . . . Naturally this kind of ownership has the greatest significance for stratification because it necessarily entails an unequal relationship" (Davis and Moore 1945, p. 247). These comments are repeated in Davis's revised version of the theory. Kemper (1976) states that it is remarkable that, given all the critics of the theory, none seems to have noticed that economic power also is considered a cause of distribution in the reward system by Davis and Moore. Clearly, however, it takes a secondary place alongside functional importance and training or talent, especially since it is more clearly a determinant of why *individuals* and not *positions* are distributed as they are in a reward system.

Societies differ in their stratification systems because they contain different conditions that affect either one or both of the principal determinants of ranking, that is, either functional importance or scarcity. The "stage of cultural development" and their "situation with respect to other societies" vary between societies, causing different tasks to be more important in one society than in another, and in personnel being more scarce for certain tasks than for others.

Figure 9.1 outlines the essential argument of the Davis-Moore thesis. Davis and Moore conclude their presentation by noting several dimensions along which stratification systems in different countries can vary. Among others, these include how fine the gradations are between ranks (specialization), the degree of social dis-

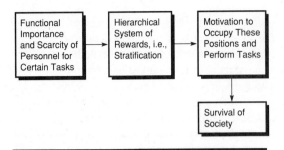

FIGURE 9.1 The Davis-Moore Theory of Stratification

tance from the top to the bottom, the extent of mobility in the system, and the extent to which classes are clearly delineated in the society. What could be more logical? Certain tasks are more important than others, and some are more difficult to carry out. In order to make sure they are performed, more rewards are attached to them. Thus, people are motivated to perform them, and the society continues to function.

Critique of the Functionalist Theory of Stratification

The functionalist theory and the Davis-Moore article in particular have precipitated a storm of criticism and counterattacks. The vehemence with which some of the arguments are made and the tenacity with which this debate has held on for over four decades suggests that a number of fundamental issues are involved. Of the host of criticisms that have been made of the theory, we will focus on four: (1) the issue of the differential functional importance of positions, (2) the question of whether the functionalists are addressing themselves to real societies, (3) the neglect of the dysfunctions of stratification, and (4) the issue of the inevitability of stratification.

Differential Functional Importance A central problem of the Davis-Moore theory is how to establish the "functional necessity" of a task for a society. Davis and Moore acknowledge that it is difficult to define functional necessity, but they

suggest two indicators of importance: (1) "the degree to which a position is functionally *unique*," that is, there are no functional alternatives to the position, and (2) "the degree to which other positions are *dependent* on the one in question" (Davis and Moore 1945, p. 244, emphasis added). They are not saying that individuals may attribute different importance to a given occupation, for example, using different values and criteria, but that in an *objective* sense, certain tasks are more important because they more significantly contribute to the continuance of the society. Davis's later comment, however, that some roles obtain a "high evaluation of the functions" and a "high status," whereas others receive lower ones, suggests that it is the *evaluation* of such roles as being functionally important that is the significant determinant rather than simply the actual functional importance to the society (1948–1949, p. 370).

It is not clear from the Davis-Moore argument whether they are speaking of the *evaluation* of positions as being differentially important or of positions being differentially important by some more objective standard. In the 1945 version, the indicators for measuring functional importance suggest that they are speaking of "functional importance" in an objective sense. Lopreato and Hazelrigg (1972, p. 102) make the interpretation that "the concept of functional importance of a given position is allegedly determined not by actual members of a society but by the 'functional necessities' of the society as a whole." They go on to say that Davis and Moore "do not seem to be sufficiently appreciative of the fact that . . . some individuals and groups . . . may have the power, legitimate or otherwise, to define 'functional necessities' and to impose on others the standards" (ibid., p. 103). If it were clear that Davis and Moore were speaking of functional importance in these terms and were ignoring the role of power in maintaining an individual's position, the criticism would be a powerful one. But, in fact, at one point Davis and Moore use an objective standard and at another appear to focus on the importance of evaluation of positions as being functionally important. As noted earlier, in his revision of the theory Davis observes that some roles obtain a "high evaluation of the functions" and a "high status" while others receive lower ones, suggesting that it is the evaluation of such roles as being functionally important that is the significant determinant of ranking. Moore (1970, pp. 145–146) also takes a more evaluative position later when he notes the importance of evaluating performance, qualities, and achievement in determining rewards.

A second more serious question about the issue of functional importance concerns the possibility of measuring it. Most of the major critics of this theory, including Tumin (1953), comment on this point. Simpson (1956, p. 137) and Huaco (1963, p. 804) similarly conclude that "unequal functional importance is a complete unknown." Davis has reacted to this criticism by saying that just because a given concept is difficult to measure does not make it useless and, in fact, judgments are made during war, for example, about the functional importance of different industries and occupations. But here Davis is implicitly referring to the *subjective* evaluation by some that certain occupations are more important than others, whereas, in fact, if we were to know the *objective* importance of those occupations, we might discover that they are not important at all.

An interesting attempt at escape from the difficulty of measuring functional importance is to substitute the concept of supply and demand in its place (Simpson 1956; Grandjean 1975). The two determinants mentioned by Davis and Moore, scarcity of talent and functional importance, are comparable in many ways to supply and effective demand, respectively. That is, the smaller the supply, the greater the scarcity of talent, and the greater the demand, and the greater the evaluated importance of a position. Simpson (1956) suggests several factors that affect the supply for filling a given position: (1) the amount of talent and training needed for a position, (2) the power of some groups to restrict the supply of workers for positions (such as labor unions), (3) the alleged uniqueness of a given position, (4) the

factors that affect choice of career (values, background, and so forth), (5) and the ease with which workers can move from position to position if desired. The factors that affect the demand side of the equation include cultural values, technology and changes in it, and the power to hire and allocate rewards. In general, we might argue that the higher the demand (functional importance) and the lower the supply (available talent), the higher the rewards.

Two studies attempted to test the functionalist hypothesis that the rewards associated with a given occupation are directly related to its functional importance. In 1963, Lopreato and Lewis examined the intercorrelations among (1) skill, (2) perceived functional importance, (3) rewards, and (4) prestige in a group of occupations. The functional importance of an occupation was determined by asking the respondents which among the list of occupations were the most necessary and which were the least necessary for the life of the community. However, the authors had a difficult time getting across the meaning of the term "functional importance" to the respondents. Their results showed that the first three variables were intercorrelated but that the intercorrelations involving functional importance, rewards, and prestige were not high at all. Thus, the results of their study did not support the functionalist argument.

A second study by Abrahamson (1973) attempted to test the hypothesis that in times of war, the incomes of war-related occupations would go up relative to those of other occupations, the assumption being that in times of war, such occupations are more important than others. Abrahamson looked at these occupations over the 1939 to 1967 period, thus covering the World War II, Korean War, and Vietnam War periods and the peacetime intervals between them. It is significant to mention that he used the percentage of the GNP spent on military activities as an index to determine the existence of wartime and peacetime because the assumption is that a greater percentage of the GNP will be spent on the military during war than peace. His results were in accordance with the functionalist argument: Incomes of war-related occupations went up during wartime, relative to those of other occupations, but they fell during peacetime.

Abrahamson's study is not really an adequate test of the functional theory of stratification because the draft was present during war and hence, the free open market assumed by Davis and Moore was not operative for these positions (Leavy 1974). Nor do the data demonstrate that higher salaries are needed to recruit or motivate people to join the military. What they do show is that when the government decides to step up its military activities, it will also spend more money on the military. It also is possible that the military can use its power to increase the amount given to its budget. In other words, the results might be interpretable in terms of other theories as well as functionalism (Vanfossen and Rhodes 1974). Until better measures of functional importance are developed, or until the concept is recast in other terms, the exact role of functional importance in generating differential rewards will have to await more thorough testing.

The Issue of Dealing with Real Societies   One of the principal criticisms of the functional perspective is that it deals with highly abstract social systems (utopias) while ignoring the operation of real societies (Dahrendorf 1958a). As it applies here, the criticism means that if stratification of rewards is the means by which a society ensures that the most qualified people fill the most important positions, then it is crucial that there be free flow of talent throughout the society. But, in fact, as Tumin (1953) makes plain, this is not the case in real societies. People in the lower strata usually have restricted opportunities, the society is not freely competitive, and we probably are not taking full advantage of the talent we may have. Davis (1948–1949, p. 370) says, however, that even where family influence and so forth play a role in allocating positions, some competition is still involved. Davis tries to further handle this criticism by pointing out that what the theory is concerned with is not the free mobility of *individ-*

uals up and down the reward hierarchy but the assignment of differential rewards to different *positions.* He argues that even if a person's parents are instrumental in getting him or her a position, the influence of the parents still does not explain why the "functions" of that position are evaluated as they are. For example, "the low estate of the sweeper castes in India, as compared with the priestly castes, cannot be explained by saying that the sons of sweepers become sweepers and the sons of Brahmins become Brahmins" (ibid., p. 370). Thus, even in a noncompetitive society, the issue is why a given position is so rewarded or ranked, independent of which person occupies it. This response is not entirely satisfactory, however, because the theory is in fact concerned with the movement of individuals if a society wants to make sure the best people fill the crucial positions. Both the Davis-Moore and Davis treatments of the issue bring in the individual, despite the fact that they insist that what is being ranked are positions. This occurs because of their insistence that "it does make a great deal of difference who gets into which positions, not only because some positions are inherently more agreeable than others but also because some require special talents or training and some have more importance than others" (ibid., p. 367). Concerns over motivation and scarcity of talent necessarily implicate people in the theory.

In criticism, Dahrendorf also argues that any theory of real societies must consider the roles of conflict and constraint. As the content of their argument shows, Davis and Moore are not completely oblivious to the role of power and wealth in societies in determining and maintaining positions, but they do not stress these as major determinants, instead being content to devote their attention to functional importance and scarcity of talent. According to both Parsons and Barber, both of whom are functionalists, although there must be some congruency between the evaluation of positions and the rewards attached to them, this congruency is never perfect since no society is perfectly integrated. According to Parsons, therefore, power also plays a role in stratification in real societies, but his stress is clearly on the role of a common value system in determining rewards. The ability of some groups, such as the AMA, to exercise inordinate political and economic power and restrict entrance into particular occupations, thereby maintaining their high incomes, is not considered by Davis and Moore to any extent.

Neglect of the Dysfunctions of Stratification
Tumin (1953) was the first major critic to point out that stratification can have numerous dysfunctions for society and the individual, a point ignored in the original Davis-Moore argument. Among the dysfunctions he notes are that stratification (1) inhibits the discovery of talent, (2) limits the extent to which productive resources can be expanded, (3) provides those at the top with the power to rationalize and justify their high position, (4) weakens the self-images among those at the bottom and thereby hinders their psychological development, (5) can create hostility and disintegration if it is not fully accepted by all in society, (6) may make some feel that they are not full participants in the society, and, therefore (7) may make some feel less loyal to the society, and may also make some (8) less motivated to participate in the society.

It is somewhat surprising that the original argument by Davis and Moore would neglect the question of dysfunctions, given their comments about power and wealth affecting the reward system. In his reply to Tumin, Davis (1953, pp. 396–397) comments that it is actually the family and the problem of inheritance that may result in most of the dysfunctions noted by Tumin, not the system of differential rewards (stratification).

In his rebuttal, Moore (1970) states that Tumin apparently is a champion of equality of opportunity and equality of rewards but does not deny the need for differentiation of positions. Thus, we would have different positions receiving the same reward, a situation that Moore believes would "require a somewhat greater extension of martyrdom than any religious system has yet achieved" (1970, p. 146). Nor does he think

that "equality is intrinsically more equitable than inequality" (ibid., p. 146). Wrong (1959), in fact, has indicated that many critics of the Davis-Moore theory point to the dysfunctions of stratification and the role of power and so forth in determining rank, but they neglect the dysfunctional effects of equality of opportunity. In a society where individuals can freely move up on the basis of their talent, would not the failures then suffer even more acutely, knowing that they and not the system are to blame for their low position in the system of rewards?

Inevitability of Stratification All of the functionalists stress to greater or lesser degrees that stratification is found universally. Davis indicates that this does not necessarily mean that it is "inevitable." He says that the theory is "not concerned with the indefinite or utopian future but with societies as we find them. No proof or disproof of a proposition about inevitability is possible" (Davis 1953, p. 397). However, his colleague Moore later says in a reply to Tumin that he is repeating "the thesis that 'functional differentiation' of positions will *inevitably* entail unequal rewards" (1970, p. 145, emphasis added). This position is consistent with that of Barber (1957, p. 16), who argues that as long as a society is internally differentiated and has a value system, there will be stratification. He concludes that it is not possible to eliminate it; in other words, it is inevitable. In general, regardless of the rejoinders and replies to the critics, the thrust of the functionalist arguments about stratification is that since it serves to solve basic problems or ensure the performance of crucial functions, and since individuals differentially value the activities carried on by others, stratification is not only universal, but very likely inevitable.

In addition to the problems of the functionalist approach just discussed, Davis's (1948–1949) attempted revision still leaves a number of measurement and definitional problems. He indicates that the family is the basic unit of stratification; everyone in the family has "the same rank. This is because one of the family's main functions is the ascription of status" (1948–1949, p. 364). "Between members of the same family class antagonisms are felt to be inappropriate. This is why all wives do not constitute a social class opposed to all husbands" (ibid., p. 364). Davis goes on to indicate that the wife is certainly "closer to her husband in loyalty and interest" than to other women and "closer to her social class than to the feminine sex as a whole." However, whether this is the case is a matter for empirical testing, not for theoretical fiat. Evidence has been presented in previous chapters that demonstrates that men and women have different social positions, even in the family.

A second problem with his revision is that Davis uses the terms class, stratification, system of differential rewards, and social inequality interchangeably. The uncertainty about exactly what phenomenon is being addressed is suggested by the comment that while "no society is 'classless,' that is, unstratified," in small primitive communities "no class strata appear . . . but even here [there is] an incipient stratification" (ibid., p. 366). Buckley (1958), defining stratification in terms of inherited status, contends that the Davis-Moore theory does not deal with stratification at all. Moore himself later felt that equating unequal rewards with stratification was "unfortunate" (1970, p. 145).

CONFLICT ALTERNATIVE: SOCIAL REPRODUCTION THEORY

During the mid- and late fifties, the functionalist perspective came under a barrage of criticism in sociology. Dahrendorf criticized structural-functionalist theory as being too complacent about the status quo and as being concerned with abstract "social systems" rather than with real societies. Any good theory of society, Dahrendorf (1958a) argued, should be problem conscious and must account adequately for the presence of conflict, change, and constraint in society.

Social reproduction theories are generally built on a conflict model of society and are often aligned with Marxian views on inequality. But rather than focusing on the explanation of the *original appearance* of inequality, these theories focus on outlining the process by which the social class structure is *maintained*. Specifically, they are concerned with the question of how the class structure "reproduces" itself generation after generation. As MacLeod (1987) puts it, "social reproduction theory explains how societal institutions perpetuate (or reproduce) the social relationships and attitudes needed to sustain the existing relations of production in a capitalist society" (p. 9). Thus, even though they are concerned with the reproduction of inequality over time, these theories are in sharp contrast to those that emphasize a "culture-of-poverty" approach, that is, blame the perpetuation of inequality on the values and other characteristics of poor individuals and their families. Recent case studies of such individuals make this point unequivocally. "The view that the problem resides almost exclusively with the children and their families, and that some sort of cultural injection is needed to compensate for what they are missing, is not only intellectually bankrupt but also has contributed to the widespread popular notion that the plight of poor whites and minorities is entirely their own fault" (ibid., p. 99). Of the families she studied, Rubin (1976) writes:

> These families reproduce themselves not because they are somehow deficient or their culture aberrant, but because there are no alternatives for most of their children. Indeed, it may be the singular triumph of this industrial society . . . that not only do we socialize people to their appropriate roles and stations, but that the process by which this occurs is so subtle that it is internalized and passed from parents to children by adults who honestly believe they are acting out of choices they have made in their own lifetime. (p. 211)

Needless to say, there are a number of specific theories of reproduction, but only a couple will be summarized here to leave the reader with the basic outlines of this approach to understanding inequality. These theories tend to focus on the educational institution as the agency of reproduction. As indicated previously, some of these theories borrow heavily from Marx. Bowles and Gintis's theory is a case in point. They are interested in how the educational system helps to reproduce class relationships in capitalist society. While the educational institution has been studied and considered as an avenue to upward mobility and a means for developing the human personality, according to Bowles and Gintis it has not been seen as an institution to perpetuate the capitalist or class system in U.S. society. But, even early in its development, education was a means "to help preserve and extend the capitalist order. The function of the school system was to accommodate workers to its most rapid possible development. . . . Since its inception in the United States, the public-school system has been seen as a method of disciplining children in the interest of producing a properly subordinate adult population" (Bowles and Gintis 1976, pp. 29 and 37). A higher level of education for most people has not reduced economic inequality, nor has it developed their full creativity. Its structure rewards those who conform to its rules and obey authority.

As in the workplace, obedience to authority and rules is expected. There is a "correspondence," Bowles and Gintis argue, between the structure of educational institutions and the workplace. Specifically, there is a similarity between the two spheres in (1) the nature of their authority structures, (2) the student's lack of control over his or her classes and the workers' lack of control over the work process, (3) the role of grades and other rewards (e.g., colored stars on papers in grade schools) and the role of wages as extrinsic motivators in the workplace, (4) ostensibly free competition among students and similar competition among workers, and (5) the specialization and tracking of courses in school and the narrow functional specialization and career paths in the workplace (Bowles and Gintis 1976; MacLeod 1987). These correspondences between the school and workplace reflect a parallelism between them.

In going through the educational process,

consequently, individuals are prepared for their respective roles in the economy. In performing this function, "schools are constrained to justify and reproduce inequality rather than correct it" (Bowles and Gintis 1976, p. 102). By providing a setting in which success appears to depend solely on the individual and his or her talent and effort, schools give the appearance of rewarding those who are most meritorious. The school rewards certain attitudes and behaviors and penalizes others. It rewards those who act and think in a manner that will serve them in the jobs they will perform in the division of labor. Not all who go to school will move on to higher white-collar professional jobs, but will perform the tasks of blue-collar work. As we noted in an earlier discussion of prep schools, education prepares each class differently depending upon the roles they will play when they collectively leave school. This means not only teaching the appropriate skills, but inculcating the appropriate values and demeanor for each class. Schools in different class neighborhoods differ in their organization and value structure.

Parents from different classes and school administrators expect different characteristics from schools. For example, parents from the middle class expect a more open school structure in which autonomy and creativity are valued. This reflects their image of what is needed in middle-class jobs. In contrast, working-class parents know from their job experiences that obedience and discipline are important. This is reflected in the organization and value structure of schools which are made up primarily of working-class students (ibid., pp. 131–134). As Rubin (1976) found in her study of the working and middle classes, "for the working-class parent, school is a place where teachers are expected to be tough disciplinarians; where children are expected to behave respectfully and to be punished if they do not; and where one mark of that respect is that they are sent to school neatly dressed in their 'good' clothes and expected to stay that way through the day" (p. 126). In contrast, the "professional middle-class" parent expects school "to be relatively loose, free, and fun; to encourage initiative, innovativeness, creativity, and spontaneity; and to provide a place where children . . . will learn social and interpersonal skills" (ibid.). In this view, students are perceived as empty vessels that must be filled up with appropriate "knowledge" and attitudes. To use Freire's (1986) colorful phrase, this is the "banking concept of education" in which teachers and students are seen as being on opposite sides. The teacher is the actor and the student is the object that is acted upon.

This one-way form of education serves the interests of those in the dominant group. It is not liberating to those who receive it. Instead it serves "to minimize or annul the students' creative power and to stimulate their credulity [which in turn] serves the interests of the oppressors, who care neither to have the world revealed nor to see it transformed" (Freire 1986, p. 60). It launches a "cultural invasion" in which "those who are invaded come to see their reality with the outlook of the invaders rather than their own; for the more they mimic the invaders, the more stable the position of the latter becomes" (Freire 1986, p. 151). The educational experience, then, reproduces different workers for the economy and the social relationships upon which the economy is based.

In sum, schools are not only interested in producing appropriate laborers for the economy, but also serve the long-term goal of perpetuating the institutions and social relationships that will ensure the continued profitability of capitalism. An educational system accomplishes these goals in four ways: (1) It provides some of the skills needed to perform jobs for each class adequately. Curriculum tracking channels individuals from different classes into appropriate courses. (2) Through its structure and curriculum, the educational system helps to justify and legitimate the economic and occupational inequality present in society. It fosters a belief that individuals wind up in different positions solely because of differences in merit. (3) It encourages the development and internalization of attitudes and self-concepts

appropriate to the economic roles individuals will perform. Those who conform to prized values (e.g., those of the upper or middle class) are rewarded, while those who do not are negatively labeled. (4) By helping to shape the continuing class and status stratification of society, the educational institution "reinforces the stratified consciousness on which the fragmentation of subordinate economic classes is based" (Bowles and Gintis 1976, pp. 129–130).

MacLeod (1987) has criticized the Bowles-Gintis theory as being too mechanistic and simple. Its image is one of capitalism and the educational system reproducing human products for the workplace. Its portrait of the human being is passive. It does not give adequate attention to the possible individual differences in reactions to structures that constrain the person. Nor does it take into account cultural or subcultural variations in values and lifestyles that may shape unique adaptations to structural barriers. Giroux has similarly criticized Bowles and Gintis for ignoring the active element in the individual within the structural framework of the school and economy. People *experience* the authority structure of the school and its teachers and they react to them, sometimes through acceptance and sometimes through resistance. In Bowles and Gintis's theory, "the subject gets dissolved under the weight of structural constraints that appear to form both the personality and the workplace" (Giroux 1983, p. 85). The complexity of school life, the varied ways and levels in which structural constraints operate and curricula are taught in varied school sites is reduced, in Bowles and Gintis's approach, to "a homogeneous image of working-class life fashioned solely by the logic of domination" (ibid.).

A more culturally oriented theory of reproduction is suggested by the work of Pierre Bourdieu. In this perspective, culture is a mediating element between class structure/interests and everyday life and behavior. By appearing to be objective and a source of knowledge, schools that produce successful and failing students can justify the inequality that follows. Since schools represent the interests of the dominant culture, Bourdieu argues, they value the "cultural capital" of the dominant class more than that of the lower classes. "Cultural capital" refers to all the sets of beliefs, practices, ways of thinking, knowledge, and skills passed on from one class's generation to the next. Schools, especially those in higher education, espouse the cultural capital that is most characteristic of the privileged classes, thereby denigrating that which is characteristic of the working and lower classes (Bourdieu 1977a, 1977b). Since this occurs in the "objective" setting of the school, those in the latter classes who do not do well in classes develop an attitude in which they blame themselves and "actively participate in their own subjugation (Giroux 1983, p. 89).

Bourdieu also develops the concept of "habitus" which consists in simple terms of the general outlook (beliefs, attitudes, orientation, etc.) of an individual. The habitus, in turn, is a product of the individual's structural situation. It is through the mediating influence of habitus that the structure affects the individual's experience and behavior. The behavior that follows only reproduces the same social structure. Briefly, the skeletal model looks something like this:

Social structure → Habitus → Behaviors and practices → Social structure

As an example, an adolescent who lives within a structure with poor job opportunities as evidenced by the experiences of his or her parents will develop a view that the chances of success are slight and that school makes no difference. This leads to behavior that accommodates him or her to a menial job, which in turn reinforces the existing job opportunity structure. Nothing changes.

Such an image of reproduction of social structure does not lend itself to reconstructing the social order, nor does it acknowledge the possibility of resistance or rebellion on the part of dominated groups (Giroux 1983). In Bourdieu's theory, the prospect of radically altering the educational institution or the system in general, seems dim indeed (MacLeod 1987). MacLeod believes that while Bourdieu has incorporated an important cultural element into his theory of reproduction, a necessary corrective to the structural-correspondence theory of Bowles and Gintis, his theory is still too deterministic. To have an adequate theory, "we must appreciate both the importance and the relative autonomy of the cultural level at which individuals, alone or in concert with others, wrest meaning out of the flux of their lives" (MacLeod 1987, p. 139). Too often, as well, reproduction theories have ignored the separately lived experiences of women and minority groups, an omission that can seriously limit the theories' ability to understand the "habitus" of these individuals.

MacLeod's (1987) case study of the conditions and behavior among two groups of adolescent males in a public housing development reveals much about the process by which social positions are reproduced. The "Brothers" are a black group, while the "Hallway Hangers" are white. Over time, the adolescents in these groups develop lower aspirations about their futures. MacLeod's research vividly demonstrates the specific and sometimes different factors that produce these "leveled aspirations." Among the Brothers, for example, there is some evidence that success is possible when they look at the occupations of their siblings. Their parents also believe that conditions have gotten better for blacks, and thus they encourage their children in their school work. They have been exposed to tenement living for a shorter time, on average, than the Hallway Hangers, and they are antagonistic to the views of the latter group which regards the blacks with disdain. These conditions lead the Brothers to *accept* the dominant achievement ideology that opportunity exists and success is possible with the proper effort. What ultimately leads the members of this group to lower their aspirations is a combination of the devaluing of their cultural capital by school officials, lower teacher expectations, tracking, discrimination, and their own self-blame. The school's treatment of them leads to relatively poor performance, and since they subscribe to the achievement ideology which says that it is the individual's own characteristics and efforts that determine how far he or she can get, poor performance leads to self-blame. The combination of self-blame and poor performance results in a lowering of expectations and aspirations. Figure 9.2 outlines the basic processes present in the development of leveled aspirations among the Brothers.

In contrast to the Brothers, the Hallway Hangers do not subscribe to the achievement ideology even though they are white. The conditions of their lives are such that they see little evidence for its validity. Their parents and siblings have not done well even though they are white; their parents believe things are stacked against them; they have lived (or been trapped) in the tenements

longer than the Brothers and have a longer history of welfare. They have not seen that education produces many successes in their immediate surroundings. These conditions have bred a feeling of cynicism about the achievement ideology. Their own subculture exerts peer pressure that encourages the rejection of raised aspirations. These experiences and feelings lead to leveled aspirations and a negative attitude toward school. The latter, in turn, results in poorly rated performance and tracking, which reinforce the leveled aspirations and results in a negative evaluation of them from others. The lowered self-esteem that derives from this negative evaluation leads these adolescents to turn to their own subculture with its own values. But it provides only an imperfect haven from the shame of failure in school, an area

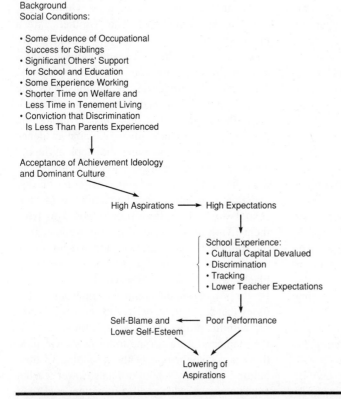

FIGURE 9.2 Basic Dynamics Involved in Lowering of Aspirations among Brothers
Source: Based on MacLeod (1987), pp. 42ff.

highly valued in the wider society. MacLeod states that "the mechanisms of social reproduction" are "well-hidden," and thus these adolescents partially blame themselves for their predicament. The Hallway Hangers also resort to racism as a convenient scapegoat. Neither of these interpretations by them, however, results in a full and accurate understanding of their situation or to a radical consciousness on the part of the Hangers. In the last analysis, the conditions that perpetuate their lower class position are repeated. The basic process leading to leveled aspirations among the Hallway Hangers is laid out in Figure 9.3.

GERHARD LENSKI'S SYNTHESIS

In 1966, Gerhard Lenski published a much heralded attempt at a synthesis of the functionalist and conflict, or as he put it, the conservative and radical traditions in the study of inequality. Lenski selected assumptions from both traditions and tried to build an explanation of inequality based on them. Rather than simply focusing on the fact of inequality, Lenski was concerned with the question of how scarce resources come to be distributed as they are, that is, with the *process* of inequality.

He bases his theory on several postulates, which he takes as givens:

1. Humans are social by nature and therefore live with others as members of society. Cooperative behavior is essential for survival.
2. Unselfish behavior occurs most often when only minor issues are involved. When important decisions are at stake and there is a conflict of interests, individuals virtually always make decisions that benefit themselves rather than others.
3. Most of the items of value that individuals strive for are in short supply, especially given the fact that a fixed satiation point does not exist for many of them (such as money and status). Thus, they are always in demand.
4. From the preceding postulates, it follows that there will be *"a struggle for rewards . . . in every human society"* (Lenski 1966, pp. 31–32, emphasis in original).
5. Humans are "unequally endowed by nature" with the tools needed to be successful in the struggle for rewards.

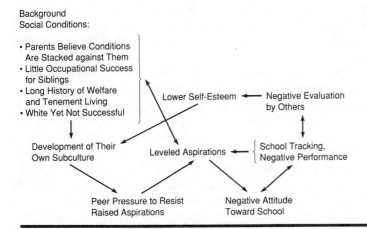

Background
Social Conditions:

FIGURE 9.3 Basic Dynamics Involved in Leveled Aspirations among Hallway Hangers
Source: Based on MacLeod (1987), pp. 23ff.

6. Humans are powerfully influenced by habit and custom, giving stability to the distribution system.

In addition to these postulates, Lenski argues that humans are basically goal seeking in their behavior. Their fundamental goal is survival, followed by health, self-respect (prestige), comfort, salvation, and affection. Money, office, and education as *instrumental goals* help individuals obtain their fundamental goals. And resources of whatever kind an individual starts out with at birth or gains from society help him or her to attain those instrumental goals.

Starting → *Instrumental* → *Fundamental*
resources   *goals*   *goals*

Societies, like individuals, are also self-seeking units whose primary goals are *"the minimization of the rate of internal political change"* and *"the maximization of production and the resources on which production depends"* (ibid., p. 42). The system of distribution in a society reflects both societal and individual needs.

Principles and Structure of Distribution Systems

Using principally his postulates about human nature, especially the first two, Lenski generates his "first law of distribution." Since humans are selfishly motivated but also need others in order to satisfy their principal goal of survival, "men will share the product of their labors to the extent required to insure the survival and continued productivity of those others whose actions are necessary or beneficial to themselves" (the law of need) (ibid., p. 44).

But after that minimum is so distributed to ensure survival, what of the goods and services left over? If we assume that they are in short supply, as in the third postulate, and that there will be struggles for their possession, then the "second law of distribution" is "that power will determine the distribution of nearly all of the surplus possessed by a society" (the law of power)

(Lenski 1966, p. 44). Power, following Weber, is "the probability of persons or groups carrying out their will even when opposed by others" (ibid., p. 44). Privileges then are primarily a result of power, and prestige is largely a function of both.

Lenski goes on to argue that the conditions of the first law of distribution must be satisfied before power, the determinant specified in the second law, becomes operative as a determinant of the distribution of goods and services. Hence, in societies where goods and services are extremely scarce, as in hunting and gathering societies, distribution is based largely on the processes specified in the first law. It is only when, because of changes in technology, a surplus develops that a greater and greater proportion of the goods and services are distributed on the basis of power. As a consequence, the nature of distribution will vary with the level of technology in societies.

Of course, other factors affect the specific character of distribution in any given society, but they are secondary to the technological factor. They include peculiarities in the physical environment, the proportion of the male population who participate in the military, and the specific variations in the technologies that may exist even among societies at the same level of technology. Distribution systems also may vary because of political conditions in a society.

As technology advances, power becomes a more important determinant in the distribution process. Power as coercion and power as right defined by law, public opinion, and propaganda can create and protect the system of inequality that has developed. The law can be phrased to protect those who make it and to punish those who are outside the ruling elite. But, argues Lenski, the shift from the rule of might to the rule of law means a greater decentralization of power, since alternate centers of power can proliferate as long as they stay within the law. In advanced industrial societies, some types of power become shared, such as political rights and education (Milner 1987). Lenski says that under might, the elite need not worry about what the average citizen thinks, but under the rule of law there is at least the pretense that no one is above the law; thus the elite cannot do fully as it pleases. "Thus, even though the laws promulgated by a new elite may be heavily slanted to favor themselves, there are limits beyond which this cannot be carried if they wish to gain the benefits of the rule of right" (Lenski 1966, p. 55). Under the rule of law, power becomes institutionalized, legitimated, and can be based on position or ownership of property.

In addition to describing the *process* of distribution, Lenski discusses the *structure* of distribution systems. This structure is composed of "power classes," power that can be manifested as force or as institutionalized power (based on property or position). The distribution of individuals into prestige and privilege classes is largely determined by their "power-class" positions. Hence, Lenski says that the focus should be on the latter. In essence, he is saying that there are three major hierarchies in distribution systems: privilege classes, prestige classes, and power classes. It is the last that is the most fundamental. Nevertheless, stratification is essentially multidimensional, especially in modern industrial societies.

In reality, since individuals vary quite widely in their prestige, privileges, and power, the stratification hierarchies are also best viewed as continua rather than sets of distinct classes with clear boundaries. These classes need not be class conscious in a Marxian sense, although members of the same class share interests that may or may not result in conflict with other classes.

We can now see that to Lenski the distribution system of a society taken as a whole consists of a number of analytically separate class hierarchies. Each of the separate class systems can vary in (1) its overall *importance* in the distribution of power, (2) its internal *complexity,* (3) its *span,* that is, the range from the top to the bottom, (4) its *shape,* that is, the distribution of power, privilege, or prestige within it, (5) the degree of *mobility* in the system, (6) the amount of *hostility* that exists between classes, and (7) the degree to which the positions in the class structure are *institutionalized,* that is, stabilized on some basis. Individuals can vary in their position within each of the class systems, that is, their rankings can be consistent or inconsistent across each of the hierarchies.

To test his general theory of inequality, Lenski examines inequality in societies at different technological levels, ranging from simple hunting and gathering societies, to horticultural and agricultural societies, to mature industrial societies. Generally, Lenski finds as expected that the degree of inequality increases along with advances in technology until the advanced industrial stage is reached. At this point, there is a "significant reversal in the age-old evolutionary trend toward ever increasing inequality" (Lenski 1966, p. 308). As two examples of this trend, Lenski notes that there is less extreme income inequality in industrial than in agrarian societies and that the government is more responsive to the needs of those who are outside the political elite. This reversal obviously flies in the face of his observation that inequality varies directly with the size of the surplus (ibid., p. 85).

To explain the shift, Lenski cites a number of causes for the trend toward greater equality. First, because of the greater complexity of knowledge in the modern world, there is a greater need to delegate power and authority. Second, the vastly greater productivity of industrial society allows greater concessions to those in the lower classes without a necessary concomitant decrease in absolute gains for those in higher classes. In industrial societies, more often than not, the struggle between those at the top and those at the bottom has benefited those on the bottom, leading to less political, economic, and social inequality (Lenski and Lenski 1982). Third, the creation of effective birth control methods has resulted in a tighter labor supply and therefore greater bargaining power for the working class. Fourth, the greater amount of knowledge and accompanying specialization result in individuals becoming experts and therefore less dispensable in the labor force. Advanced technology has upgraded the occupational structure by creating more white-collar jobs resulting in more upward mobility. "Nearly every industrial society has eliminated the excess of downward mobility" (ibid., p. 337). Fifth, more widespread education and higher levels of living have made it easier to participate in the political process, thereby strengthening the democratic nature of political institutions. "The rise and spread of *the new democratic ideology"* has made those in political power more vulnerable to pressure from the majority (emphasis in original). The state is believed to belong to the people. Thus Lenski links political democracy with less inequality. All of these factors have contributed to a reversal of the trend toward greater inequality.

Assessment of Lenski

In generating his proposed synthesis, Lenski selected parts of both the conservative and radical traditions in the hope that the right blend would result in a more effective and universally applicable explanation of inequality. Certainly, Lenski's (1988) theory fits the type that he feels social science should be developing. It is "multilayered" in the sense that there is a broad basic theory, stressing technology, which then leads to more specific "layers" involving levels of societies and analyses within each of them. He also incorporated consideration of human nature and physical-environmental factors into his theory. To omit these elements or not even take them into account isolates social-scientific theory from the benefits that could be derived from the other sciences. Unfortunately, his attempt suffers from several serious weaknesses. His usage of the terms "power" and "class" leads to a watering down of their meaning, a sapping of their unique content. He argues that the distribution of rewards, especially in advanced societies, is based primarily on power, but his perspective on power leaves something to be desired. He defines power in Weberian terms as "the probability of persons or groups carrying out their will even when opposed by others," but in a concrete setting, what does this mean? Power, as Lenski admits, can refer to force as

well as to institutionalized power; the latter can be based on position or property. But the crux of the matter still is how property and position themselves are distributed. To say that power is based on property and position and that property and position are based on power would not be too illuminating. Power, in Lenski's hands, still remains a much too vague and broad concept to serve as a viable foundation for the explanation of inequalities in privilege and prestige.

His treatment of the concept of class is also disturbing in two basic ways. First, he argues that the stratification system of industrial societies is fundamentally multidimensional, since classes refer to aggregates of individuals who are similar in their power, privilege, or prestige. Since each of these three can take a variety of forms, there are numerous class systems; there are occupational classes, property classes, political classes, educational classes, racial classes, religious classes, age classes, sex classes, and ethnic classes. Earlier in his argument, Lenski stated that privileges and prestige were largely based on power, but by presenting a long list of *separate* class systems, he is watering down the historical meaning of the term "class" and underestimating the systematic interrelationships among power, privilege, and prestige.

The second way in which he weakens the concept of class in his analysis is by defining caste and estate as classes of a particular type. He defines both of them in terms of class and by so doing ignores the historical and societal uniqueness of these systems. In essence, the term "class" is used to cover too much, and when spread so broadly it comes close to being meaningless.

One of the strengths of Lenski's theory is its application to a variety of cultures. By reviewing situations in different *types* of societies, Lenski tries to demonstrate how inequality changes through time as the levels of technology in societies change. But by taking such a broad evolutionary sweep, he underplays the uniqueness of particular societies and their history. A cross-cultural view is not the same as an historically specific one. His postulation of *universal* propositions about human nature and societies forces a neglect of crucial differences in the cultures and histories of societies. Fallers (1966) complains that Lenski has not given enough weight to variations in values and cultures in understanding differences in stratification. He "assumes that the ends of action are objectively given and universal" (p. 718). Moreover, so much attention to stages or levels of evolution leads to an underemphasis on the interdependence of societies on different levels and an explanation of international stratification based on dependency relations and exploitation.

Finally, some comments ought to be made about Lenski's view on industrial society and its progress toward equality. His conclusions about the extent of equality in such societies, even the United States, about which he cites data to support his claims, can leave one too optimistic. Data on income and wealth in the United States, we have seen in Chapter 2, still indicate a high and stable degree of inequality. In fact, there is evidence that earnings inequality has increased in recent years. Lenski's optimism flows largely from the fact that he is comparing industrial with agrarian societies. But by doing so, he is led into the conclusion that U.S. society is more democratic and equalitarian than it actually is. His arguments that industrial societies are much more democratic because of increased knowledge, widespread education, and so forth are not convincing. Clearly, Lenski's view of evolution parallels Durkheim's march from mechanical to organic solidarity. He is a theorist of *industrial* rather than *capitalist* societies. One gets the impression that Lenski is caught up in his own internal logic regarding an evolution that inexorably leads to progress. The result is an underemphasis on the realities of stable inequality in U.S. society.

Despite these shortcomings, Lenski's theory is one of the most detailed and carefully developed in recent years. His work has led to numerous areas of inquiry. Most notable among these is *research* on the interrelationship of economic development, political democracy, and income in-

equality and attempts at developing general *theories* of stratification and societal evolution (e.g., Angle 1986; Leavitt 1986; Milner 1987).

LABOR-MARKET THEORIES OF INCOME AND EARNINGS DISTRIBUTION

All of the theories addressed thus far in this and the previous chapter are macroscopic in nature. They focus on the issue of inequality on a very general level, often trying to generate principles of inequality that apply cross-culturally, through historical periods, or both. Despite their generality, some ideas can be gleaned from them about what factors are important in creating inequality and, therefore, what kinds of elements would have to be affected if economic inequality is to be reduced. Such theorists as Weber and Pareto and the functionalists, however, do not believe it is possible to eliminate inequality, although for very different reasons. Since these theorists often deal with such questions on a global level, it is sometimes difficult to see the intricacies of the process of inequality in concrete societies and thus even more difficult to derive specific policies for dealing with the inequality issue.

In recent years, a set of economic theories regarding income and earnings inequality has been crystallizing, some of which are based on rather old explanations of the working of the marketplace, whereas others are quite different. The treatment that follows is general and aimed at drawing out the *core elements* of the approaches. Consequently, specific theorists using a given approach may differ on specific elements in the approach. What is immediately appealing about these theories is that they put some meat and teeth into explanations by making the detailed process of inequality more testable. Whereas it might be extremely difficult to satisfactorily test a theory of inequality based on the distribution of sentiments or the functional necessity of inequality, it is possible, for example, to see what the effects of various kinds of "human capital investment," such as education and training, are on an individual's earnings.

Most of the theories presented here are principally concerned with explaining poverty and unemployment, but they can easily be used as explanations of the extent of inequality. Each of them focuses on one or another aspect of the labor market in generating inequality.

Neoclassical Labor Market Theory

Part of the capitalist ideology indicates that each individual ought to put something into the society if he or she expects to get something out of it. A person should be rewarded to the extent that he or she contributes to the society (Schiller 1976, p. 45). *In a society in which free competition exists, persons who contribute equal resources in the society receive a wage commensurate with their contributions.* This "is one way of saying that you take out what you put in" (Okun 1975, p. 41). The productive contribution of individuals depends on their (1) acquired skills and assets, (2) their natural abilities, (3) the extent of their efforts, and (4) the demand for and supply of individuals who can perform services similar to those offered by these individuals (Okun 1975, p. 42). "Given a perfectly functioning, competitive labor market, and all people and jobs being alike, there would be no differences in earnings" (Atkinson 1975, p. 79). The first assumption of this approach is that the system is a purely competitive one in which all individuals freely jockey and compete with one another for higher wages. Productivity, of course, also depends on the technology and capital of the firm in which the worker is employed. Thus, otherwise equivalent workers may produce different amounts or quality because of variations in firms.

In this perspective, the factors that determine wages concern supply and demand in the market and the resources (human capital investments) and choices that individuals bring into the market (Cain 1976, p. 1216). The market tends to work so as to balance out the supply and demand factors and wages consistent with the resources each person contributes. The more resources and the greater their value to any potential employer, the greater the demand for the individual's services and the higher the wages (Leftwich 1977; Thurow 1969, p. 26). Thus, traditional analysts would focus on such factors as education, training, skills, and intelligence as "productivity components" to explain an individual's wages. Thurow summarizes this view succinctly: "If an individual's income is too low, his productivity is too low. His income can be increased only if his productivity can be raised" (1969, p. 26).

If a disequilibrium occurs between what the individual contributes and the wages he or she receives, then supply and demand forces are set in motion to restore equilibrium in the market. If the wage is less than is due, the supply becomes smaller, and in the long run the demand for the smaller supply becomes greater. With the greater demand comes an increase in the wages employers are willing to pay these workers, and equilibrium is restored. If the opposite occurs, that is, individuals are paid too much for the resource(s) they offer, a large supply of potential workers will appear, too large for the demand for them in the market. In order to ensure getting jobs, they will lower the wages for which they are willing to work. With the lower wages, employment expands, thus leading to a clearing of the labor market and a balancing between supply and demand. Again, equilibrium is restored (Leftwich 1977, p. 76). So in addition to assuming a competitive market, this approach assumes that automatic mechanisms operate in the market to regulate it toward equilibrium. This tendency toward equilibrium, according to some critics, implies that there is a basic "harmony" between employers and employees (Gordon 1972, p. 33).

An extreme version of this approach would assume that *individuals are free to choose* their own occupations and the amounts of their human capital investments, such as education. Thus, blacks and women might be considered to have lower and relatively nonchanging levels of income because they have invested less in education and have less or interrupted work experience (Gordon 1972, p. 40; Mincer and Polachek 1974). For those individuals who choose to get more education, it is assumed that they will be able to borrow the money needed to procure such education. Given these costs to individuals, the wages they later make should make up for these costs. This is compensation for the training required. Thus, controlling for the probability of unemployment in given jobs, the amount of non-monetary rewards, and the uncertainty of earnings in some occupations, those with greater training should be expected to make more in earnings than those with less (Atkinson 1975, p. 82). Of course, it often doesn't work that way.

Remaining within the broad orthodox framework, we can view income differences as being determined by three factors: "(1) differences in labor resources owned, (2) differences in capital resources owned, and (3) restrictions placed on the operation of the price mechanism" (Leftwich 1977, p. 81). The orthodox view is more concerned with wage differentials than with occupational differences and thus is less equipped to deal with sex segregation, for example (Blau and Jusenius 1976).

Differences in the kinds of labor resources owned can refer to both vertical differences (that is, differences in skill *levels*) or horizontal differences (that is, differences in the *kinds* of skills). Certain kinds of occupations are more in demand than others, and within each of these there are individuals who are better at their jobs and who are more experienced (in other words, are older), and thus receive higher wages. Vertical differences result from differences in physical and mental characteristics between individuals and because some have the opportunity to gain such skills while others do not. Thus, the lack of vertical mobility to the top and the scarcity of individuals at the top creates a greater demand for their services, whereas the greater abundance of individuals at lower skill levels keeps the demand and wages low. Differences in capital resources result from inheritance processes, luck, and "psychological propensities to accumulate" (Leftwich 1977, pp. 77–79).

In view of these determinants, if one wants to reduce inequality, one has to attack the prob-

lems of human capital investment and the factors that give rise to inequality in capital resources. Thus, solutions might, for example, stress more education and training opportunities and changes in the tax system to bring about some adjustment in the distribution of capital resources.

The general economic model just discussed, which in its ideal-typical form posits a freely competitive market tending toward equilibrium, has some fundamental similarities to the functionalist theory of Davis and Moore discussed earlier in the chapter. Like that explanation, orthodox theory aims at simplicity and universality, "hypotheses which transcend institutional and historical variations within or among societies" (Gordon 1972, p. 34). Under conditions of free and open competition in the labor market, causes and effects can ramify throughout the market, becoming universal. Like the kind of society conjured up in the functional approach, Dahrendorf would consider the open, non-conflict-ridden society of the orthodox theory to be a utopia. The image of society conjured up by this model is more fully explored in the critique of status attainment in Chapter 11. Indeed, most of these economists are aware of this issue and make adjustments to account for some of the imperfections of real societies. For example, most realize perfectly well that discrimination exists and that competition is not as free as suggested by the model.

Dual-Labor Market Thesis

It has become increasingly obvious to some in recent years that explanations of income and earnings distribution that rely on images of the free market and investments in human capital as the primary or sole factors in understanding economic inequalities are inadequate. The conviction that those who do not work or are poor are just lazy and are not seeking out employment simply has not been borne out by the evidence. Even those who do not work "do work if and when they are able" (Schiller 1976, p. 47). "Millions of individuals are poor, not because they never work, but because they do not work as much or as often as others" (Schiller 1976, p. 59).

Critics of the orthodox view say that the market simply does not work the way that pure traditionalists say it does. Much of the orthodox research points to flaws in the individual (lack of education and so forth) as a cause for low income, but the major reasons for inequality lie deep within the workings and cleavages of the capitalist economy.

A number of observations about continuing difficulties in the market have made many analysts skeptical about the orthodox approach and its potential effectiveness in reducing inequality. Among those observations that have precipitated a reaction against orthodox theory are (1) the continuation of poverty, (2) continued income inequality, (3) the ineffectiveness of educational and training programs in reducing inequality, (4) the use of education as a screening device by employers to procure only *culturally acceptable* rather than qualified individuals, (5) discrimination against minorities in the labor market, (6) the power of labor unions, employer monopolies, and government intervention to weaken the competitive market, (7) bad attitudes toward work that result from the market itself and not outside the market, and (8) extensive alienation among workers, suggesting that the competitive, equilibrating economy is not working as smoothly as the orthodox model suggests (Cain 1976).

In the face of these alleged anomalies in the economy, some have tried to devise alternate explanations for continued poverty and income inequality. One of the more prominent of these is the dual-labor market approach. Briefly, it consists of four basic elements or assumptions: (1) the private economy is split into two major sectors; (2) the labor market is similarly divided into two parts; (3) mobility, earnings, and other outcomes for workers are contingent upon place in the labor market; and (4) a systematic relationship exists between race/ethnicity, gender, and position in the labor market (Hodson and Kaufman 1982).

On observing labor-market processes in the ghetto, a number of economists have come to the conclusion that two markets operating by different rules exist. In effect, the argument is that the poor are members of a separate market that is largely outside the central economy and as such do not participate in the effects of increases in demand, since those demands usually refer only to certain types of occupations. Researchers have found that the kinds of characteristics usually considered as qualifications (such as education) often seem to have little connection with the type of job the person occupies. In effect, some jobs are "race typed" (Reich et al. 1977, p. 109). The range of jobs available to minority members, in spite of their qualifications, seems to be quite narrow, and consequently many prefer not to work, or in other words, turn down jobs that are not consistent with their qualifications.

As a result of these observations, more attention has been focused on the kinds of jobs these individuals are actually offered and perform. The tasks seem to be menial, not intellectually demanding, with poor working conditions and low wages. They are isolated and have no internal structures or career system. In other words, they appear to be qualitatively distinct from the other kinds of jobs in the market.

Because of the poor nature of the work, workers in this "secondary" market often quit their jobs, which only encourages the belief that these jobs are unstable, and that performing these types of jobs to the exclusion of others encourages instability in the habits of the workers themselves. This *secondary labor market,* as it has come to be known, is set off from the *primary labor market* in which jobs are characterized by stability, high wages, good working conditions, greater degree of internal job structure, and unionization (Gordon 1972, pp. 43–48).

Within firms in the primary sector, there is an *internal labor market* in which individuals from the outside may enter only at selected points. For example, an outsider may get a job at the bottom of a career ladder in an industrial firm because all other jobs higher up the ladder are being filled from within the firm through promotion. These latter jobs are, in effect, protected from outside competition, resulting in a segmentation of the market into competitive and noncompetitive jobs (Doeringer and Piori 1971). Since the skills taught to employees are frequently important, necessary for higher status jobs, and specific to the firm, there will be an attempt by the firm to keep these employees, since training new ones would be costly to the firm. In this protected environment, employees can then work up from the bottom toward the top. In this setting, employees can more easily find security and a lifetime career. Unions also favor the resulting stability for employees, and the employers similarly benefit from retaining trained employees. Given the career system, workers and employers dealing in the primary labor market are less concerned with the perfect balance between earnings and productivity *at a given point in time* than they are with equity over the long run (Doeringer and Piori 1971).

By and large, the primary labor market, with its stability, unionization, career systems, and high wages, is limited to a certain sector of the private economy, sometimes called the *core* or *monopoly sector,* whereas the secondary market exists primarily within the *peripheral* or *competitive sector* of the private economy. In the monopoly sector, firms tend to be large, capital intensive, with high productivity per worker, and to possess large, often national and international markets. Examples of firms in this sector would be those in the automobile, railroad, steel, electric, and airlines industries. On the other hand, firms within the competitive sector are much smaller, more labor intensive, with low productivity per worker, more local in their markets, and not in control of any stable product market (O'Connor 1973, pp. 13–16). Examples of firms in this sector would be local restaurants, gas stations, grocery stores, garages, and clothing stores. *Peripheral*

Despite the fact that conditions are generally worse for the workers in the secondary market and competitive sector, the tasks performed,

though often irregular, are needed in the economy. Consequently, an effort was made historically to stabilize this market and sector; employers worked toward creating a separate market for these workers and these kinds of jobs. Some kinds of workers are in that sector even though they may have the characteristics that would qualify them for work in the primary market. Blacks and women, for example, are usually disproportionately found in the secondary market because of statistical discrimination and other reasons (Gordon 1972, pp. 46–47). Secondary workers were then left with little alternative but to work as part of the secondary labor market in the competitive sector.

The movement toward separate markets has been strengthened by (1) the desirability of retaining individuals who have been carefully trained in large established firms, (2) the presence of unions in some and not other industries, and (3) federal legislation. The trends toward greater job specificity, more on-the-job training in the primary job sector, and the power of custom within given firms have tended to increase the structuring of the internal labor markets within the primary job sector, setting it off more from the unstructured, noncareer patterned secondary job sector (Doeringer and Piori, 1971).

Dual-Labor Market and Income Inequality

The existence of segmentation in the U.S. economy, especially in the form of a dual-labor market, helps to perpetuate income inequality and poverty. Generally, there is little intermarket mobility. The market in which individuals are presently working is generally the one in which they began (Jordan 1982, p. 50). Blacks and women are disproportionately found in the lower wage, secondary market and generally do not move up much over their careers. Wolf (1976) found that women have relatively flat career occupational statuses. She observes that occupations are sex segregated and "we speculate that, at least for most women, these 'women's jobs' are not stepping stones to other more prestigious occupations" (p. 20). Sell and Johnson (1977) also found a great deal of stability in occupational distribution among women across age groups, suggesting that when women leave the labor force, they often reenter the same types of jobs. They also found that changes in the occupational distribution were slight at best during the period 1960 to 1970 (pp. 10–12). Wolf's research further indicates that contrary to what might be expected, it is not the interruptions in employment ("career contingencies") that primarily account for the occupational attainment of women. Rather, as we observed in an earlier chapter, women simply do not get the same kinds of jobs as men, even when their qualifications are similar.

Being in either the secondary or primary labor market has an initial impact on an individual's wages. As already mentioned, jobs in the secondary market generally have lower wages than those associated with the primary market. But once in either the secondary or primary market, the determinants of earnings vary. In the primary market, earnings are affected by seniority and whether a person is in a career job hierarchy. O'Connor (1973) stresses that in the monopoly sector, wages and prices are not primarily determined by market forces; prices are largely "administered" since the corporations in this sector usually have considerable market power. With respect to wages, when the demand for labor is low and the supply is large, monopoly industries, because of their attractiveness to workers, can choose from the oversupply at the going rate. In this way, they have an advantage over competitive industries. When labor is in demand, union power, "pattern bargaining," and productivity have major impacts on wages and wage movements. But many of the wage increases in the monopoly sector do not trickle down to workers in the competitive sector, which results in a further bifurcation of the working class (O'Connor 1973, pp. 19–22).

In the competitive sector, that is, for most of those in the secondary labor market, wages are largely determined by market forces. Since the workers in this market are generally considered homogeneous in nature and have little, if any, union power, their wages are primarily the product of supply and demand forces. If the supply of labor is particularly small and the demand consequently high, their earnings are likely to go up because they will work more. Thus, the differences in earnings among those in the secondary labor market are probably due more to differences in the hours worked than to other factors. But because of the homogeneous nature of the work force in this market, wage differences are not likely to be great (Gordon 1972, pp. 50–51). Moreover, in the competitive sector, the raging competition among firms and the poorer and more unstable economic environment in which they operate often mean that they are less able to raise wages compared with the large firms in the monopoly sector that are relatively free from the extremes of competition (Bluestone 1977).

Osterman's (1975) analysis of a national sample of male workers bears out the hypothesis that the determinants of earnings vary with the labor market in question. His results indeed show that earnings in the secondary market are tied significantly to the numbers of hours worked, with neither experience, race, nor education being important. This supports the view that workers in this market are seen as being interchangeable. In the higher ranking jobs in the primary market, education, age and hours worked are important, whereas in the lower tier in the primary market education is important although less so than in the higher jobs. Age and hours worked are also significant for the lower ranking jobs in the primary market, as is race. In sum, the human capital argument seems much more viable in the primary than in the secondary market. Osterman's conclusion is that "an individual's income is greatly affected by the segment of the labor market in which the individual works" (1975, p. 21).

In applying the dual-market theory to poverty, the central conclusion is that many individuals are poor not because they are unemployed or do not participate in the economy but because of the *way* in which they participate in the economy. Not only are they *excluded* from certain kinds of activities and organizations, they are *included* in the economic structure at particular places because "they have economic value where they are and hence . . . there are groups interested, not only in resisting the elimination of poverty, but in actively seeking its perpetuation" (Piori 1977, pp. 95–96).

Radical Perspective Many of the notions of dual-market theory have found their way into a radical denunciation of orthodox theory. Basically, the radical argument is that capitalists have found it beneficial to segment the labor market and to stratify the working class so as to prevent its unification and to stabilize the labor market. In this view, if we are to understand the creation of poverty and a particular income distribution, we must understand the historical development and conditions that underlay such distributions.

During the late nineteenth century, the U.S. labor force was becoming increasingly homogeneous and proletarianized; having been herded into factories, the separate craft talents became merged into a mass of semiskilled jobs. The potential threat of a unified working class, especially given the increasing evidence of their militancy, had to be met by employers. To deal with this problem, argue Reich and his associates (1977), employers actively promoted labor-market segmentation in order to effectively split up what might otherwise have been a unified work force.

If employers could successfully stratify the working class, it would not only splinter its unity but also, if it could be legitimized, ensure that less desirable (secondary) jobs could be filled. As the clusters of workers were separated from each other, each would develop its own habits and lifestyles consistent with the kinds of jobs they performed. The result would be stability in the labor market for the capitalist class. "To the extent that employers could accomplish this stratification, it became more likely that blue-collar workers would accept their poorer working conditions (relative to those of white-collar workers) because they did not have the necessary credentials and education to move on to jobs with better opportunities" (Gordon 1972, p. 73).

The rise of monopoly capitalism and of large corporations necessitated the existence of a stable labor force. New techniques of division and control were developed to restructure and stabilize relationships within industries (Edwards 1979). The rigid bureaucratic organization of firms served this purpose admirably. The clear and minute division of labor and hierarchy of authority associated with this form of organization encouraged the development of an "internal labor structure" of the kind discussed earlier. Education increasingly became a means of justifying division of the workers, since it became a regularized credential for obtaining certain jobs (Reich et al. 1977, p. 111). Those most readily looked down on by unions and the public, namely, women, blacks, and youth, could more easily be used to fill less desirable jobs. Stereotypes and dislikes of these groups were used to further segment the labor market (ibid.).

Alongside the "conscious efforts" of employers to segment the labor market were systemic forces that furthered the segmentation. Racism was and is used to strengthen the hold of employers by weakening the bargaining power of the working class. The result is lower incomes for both blacks and the white working class and higher profits for the capitalists (ibid., p. 185). Evidence does suggest that white *workers* do not gain from racism against blacks but lose while capitalists gain; even income inequality *between white capitalists and workers* is *increased* when racism is present (Reich et al. 1977; Szymanski 1976). Racism also benefits capitalists by preventing or at least forestalling the unification of black and white workers into strong and more broadly based unions. Research on the period between World War I and the New Deal indicates that employers fought white worker gains by using available blacks as strikebreakers and in place of white workers. This served to help split the working class along racial lines (Bonacich 1976).

As different industrial organizations grew, historically, they advanced at different rates, and a fundamental division developed between them. In one sector were the large, monopoly, capital intensive, technologically advanced, high-profit, and growth industries, whereas in the other were the more competitive, smaller, lower profit, more labor intensive organizations. The large organizations required a stable labor force, given their continuous and ongoing production. This sector could not handle, to its benefit, those areas where the work was seasonal or otherwise erratic. Production of those goods and services in which the demand was unstable demanded a certain kind of labor and was "subcontracted" or "exported" to the smaller more competitive firms. Thus each sector demanded and evolved specific kinds of labor forces, namely, the primary and secondary labor markets, just as the dual-labor market thesis suggested (Reich et al. 1977, p. 111). The overall result of this segmentation process has been the segmentation of the economy into monopoly and competitive sectors, segmentation of primary and secondary markets, segmentation within the primary sector into routine and creative jobs, and segmentation by race and sex (ibid., pp. 108–109).

The existence of segmentation of various types in the labor force has been widely accepted, although the dimensions along which that segmentation takes place have not always been agreed on (Osterman 1975). Results reported in Chapter 4 show black/white and male/female differences in occupational allocation. Blacks are still underrepresented in the high-reward occupations that involved the exercise of authority, domination by whites, and/or equal-status contact with customers. But they are overrepresented in lower status occupations even though some improvement has apparently occurred in recent years.

Gordon (1972, p. 78) suggests that employers will continue to find it beneficial to fill secondary-market jobs with members of minority groups since (1) they are easily distinguishable physically and have been discriminated against before, (2) because more than other groups they have become more resigned to such jobs, and (3) because they are least likely to identify with nonminority groups and unite with them against the capitalists. Such segmentation certainly appears to perform certain functions for capitalists. Reich and associates (1977) outline three of these:

1. It divides the workers and thus prevents unified movements against employers.
2. It establishes qualitative breaks across job hierarchies through the creation of different sets of "criteria for access," thereby discouraging mobility aspirations among workers.
3. The division of workers legitimizes the differences in authority between superior and subordinate position holders (p. 112).

Assessment of Labor-Market Theories

In assessing these labor-market theories, it is clear that there are inadequacies in the orthodox explanations, but given the lack of a "fully embellished theoretical system" by radical theorists, it is not clear how powerful their explanations of occupational and income inequality really are. In fact, perhaps the most valuable contribution of the dual-labor-market approach to understanding economic inequality is its emphasis on a textured economy and labor market, that is, on its insistence that these are not homogeneous in nature and that this texture affects rewards for workers (Hodson and Kaufman 1982). The orthodox approach is most likely to be acceptable when it incorporates some of the elements of dual-labor-market theory and information about imperfections in the market. Some evidence appears to support radical arguments, as was indicated in our discussion, whereas other critics (such as Cain 1976) do not see it as being able to replace orthodox theory. The support for the viability of the radical perspective is clearly split.

Dual-market theory has its evident weaknesses. Within broad sectors, there is a large variety of firms. How are differences among them to be explained? For example, the dual-market theory does not explain differences and sex segregation within each market and differentiation within the female sector (Blau and Jusenius 1976, p. 197). Moreover, within each sector of the economy, there are firms that cater to both the primary and secondary labor-markets. Evidence suggests that the tight link assumed by the approach between the primary labor market and core sector on the one hand, and the secondary labor market and peripheral sector on the other, is much looser than suggested by the model. Moreover, the assumption that blacks and women are concentrated in the peripheral sector is also questionable (Hodson and Kaufman 1982; Kaufman and Daymont 1981; Wallace and Kalleberg 1981). The "theory" has also been said to be largely of a descriptive rather than explanatory nature, and its concepts to have been improperly measured (Hodson and Kaufman 1982). Finally, splitting the private economy into two parts results in too "coarse" an image of the real economy within which there are continuous variations among organizations along a variety of dimensions (Baron and Bielby 1984; Hodson 1984). Despite weaknesses, however, the dual-market and radical perspectives have properly forced us to address the role of market and economy variations in generating inequality.

SUMMARY

The focus in this and the previous chapter has been on the explanation of inequality. Each of the theories covered views the concept of inequality in a different way and is suggestive of different measures of it. Nevertheless, all of them are concerned with the distribution of scarce resources in society, principally political power, economic power, or both. One of the primary values in looking at the classic theorists is that each of them suggests different ways of viewing inequality and makes us sensitive to different aspects of it.

All of these theories organize the phenomenon in diverse ways and evoke different images of how the society is to be seen. "The theory molds an attitude and sets a stance that predetermines how class is seen. . . . The conception and the orientation that a theory invariably creates of the class structure . . . hold direct consequences for the way that the organization and operation of society as a whole is viewed" (Reissman 1959, pp. 35–36). Indeed, it was mentioned earlier that it is inappropriate to assess what the classic theorists had to say about inequality outside of the context of their more general theories of society. This perhaps is less true of more contemporary theories of inequality, which appear to be narrower in their focus, but it is nevertheless true. Some of these, for example, the functionalist and labor-market theories encompass broad assumptions about the nature of society. Because this is so, each of the theories provides us with alternative tools and concepts with which to approach the study of inequality; together they anticipate the kinds of questions and issues that significantly can be raised about inequality.

Each of the theories covered has been primarily concerned with answering the question, "How do we explain the existence of inequality and the form or shape that it takes?" Indirectly, several devote some attention to a second question of how given individuals become placed in positions in the system of inequality.

The next chapter delves more specifically into explaining inequality based on sex and race. Only theories that address the origins of inequality rather than its maintenance will be included. Since the accounts of dual-labor market and radical theories presented in this chapter have included a brief statement on their applicability to job segregation by race and sex, they will not be discussed again in Chapter 10.

CHAPTER 10

THEORIES OF SEX AND
RACE INEQUALITY

It is their [women's] differential role in the reproduction of labor power that lies at the root of their oppression in class society.
—Lise Vogel

When I try to explain American relations to Indians, I describe and analyse America as a caste stratified society, with attention to the similarities and differences in comparison with India.
—Gerald Berreman

Several of the theories discussed in the last two chapters were concerned with explaining social inequality *in general.* Those that were more specific usually dealt with economic or class inequality. In contrast, this chapter deals specifically with explanations of sex and race inequality. There is a wide variety of these theories, ranging from biological and psychological to cultural and structural. In many ways, these theories parallel the kinds of explanations given for poverty and for inequality between nations. Table 10.1 suggests that many of the explanations given for inequality in each of these areas can be incorporated under the same labels.

The table is intended only to demonstrate the broad parallels that exist between many of the explanations of each form of inequality and to give examples of the kinds of theories that fall under each broad category. Some of the specific theories also have been used to explain inequality of several types. Several economic/labor-market theories, for example, were discussed in the last chapter, including how they apply to race and sex

inequality. Consequently, they will not be repeated here. Also, because of the broad range of theories available, the discussion in this chapter will be limited to theories that are more sociological or anthropological in nature. That is, the focus will be on explanations that emphasize the importance of social structure, ecology, or cultural configurations rather than biological or psychological factors. Biological explanations of sex inequality that suggest basic genetic, hormonal, or physical differences determine sex inequality are inadequate for several reasons. First, while there are some hormonal and physical differences between the sexes, they do not mandate that men will dominate women. These differences and any behaviors associated with them still have to be culturally and socially interpreted. For example, aggressiveness is related to domination only if it is interpreted in a particular way. In some societies, such behavior may be not only tolerated but admired, while in others it may be considered deviant and those who engage in it may be assigned low status (Coontz and Henderson 1986).

228

TABLE 10.1 The Classification of Explanations for Inequality between Countries, Blacks and Whites, Men and Women, and Rich and Poor

	BROAD CATEGORIES OF EXPLANATION OF INEQUALITY			
Between:	*Biological*	*Individual flaws*	*Cultural*	*Structural*
Countries	Distribution of races	Lack of achievement, motivation, e.g.	Tradition vs. modernity	World system; dependency
Races	Basic biological deficiencies	Laziness, present orientation, e.g.	Subcultural family values	Internal colonialism; caste, class dynamics
Sexes	Natural differences, strength, aggressiveness, reproduction, e.g.	Fear of succes, lack of ambition, e.g.	Gender-role scripts, patriarchal values	Capitalism; industrialism; ecological conditions
Classes	Genetic or biological differences Social Darwinism	Fatalism, lack of ambition, work ethic, e.g.	Culture of poverty, cultural capital	Capitalism; industrialization

Even in limiting the section below to cultural and social explanations of sex inequality, only samples of each type of theory can be presented. Moreover, in some cases, such as in theories involving patriarchy and capitalism in their explanations, the reader should be aware that there are differences among specific theorists about details. Our goal here is to present a general picture of the kinds of explanations that exist to account for sex inequality.

THEORIES OF SEX INEQUALITY

Largely for the sake of convenience, the theories on sex inequality are divided into four general categories: (1) cultural, (2) social/structural, (3) ecological, and (4) capitalist/patriarchal. This set of categories does not, of course, exhaust all the types of theories of sex inequality that have been developed, nor are they mutually exclusive. Certainly, for example, Marxist theories are social/structural in nature, and some structural theories point out the importance of ecological factors. But while the categories in the list overlap to some degree, they also serve to separate theories whose foci and thrusts differ from each other.

One other point should be made. The theories discussed are principally concerned with addressing the *origins* rather than the *maintenance* of sex and race inequality. Theories involving socialization and the role of education in inequality, on the other hand, shed light on the maintenance of such inequality across generations.

Explanations of inequality between the sexes have been plagued by a number of difficulties (Mukhopadhyay and Higgins 1988; Schlegel 1977; Chafetz 1984). First, it has become increasingly evident that discussions of "women's status" are often too broad. That is, women can be unequal or equal with men on a variety of dimensions, such as public power, prestige, type of work, education, and access to other services and goods that make life more enjoyable and meaningful. Moreover, the status of women on these dimensions is not identical across all cultures. How the genders and their appropriate roles are defined varies among cultures. Second, some have attempted to develop a universal explanation of sex inequality, but because of the variation in cultural beliefs and settings, the development of such a generally applicable theory of sex inequality has been hampered. Without resorting to biological universals that distinguish men from women, it is difficult to identify other core factors that can explain the nuances and peculiarities of inequalities in different cultures. This is assuming that such a universal ahistorical theory is even possible let alone desirable. Third, many of the data from ethnographic studies upon which explanations have been built were collected by anthropologists who were most likely male, and they perceived and interpreted those cultures using a Euro-American gender model (Mukhopadhyay and Higgins 1988). One of the unfortunate biases with which we have approached other cultures is that we make judgments about women's status using our own measures of what is good, prestigious, and desirable. In essence, we end up defining positions of the sexes in terms different from those used by the groups in the cultures in question. Finally, several theories, especially earlier ones, have relied upon simplistic dichotomies in trying to understand sex inequality. The dichotomies include "nature" and "culture," "natural" and "artificial," and "private/domestic" and "public/social" as being embodied in "women" and "men," respectively, to name but a few.

Cultural Values and Sex Inequality

When we speak of a person's "sex," we ordinarily are referring to the biological status of being female or male. However, cultures assign different meanings to the definitions of "male" and "female." To differentiate it from the term "sex," the term "gender" frequently is used to denote the definitions and assignments that different groups and cultures associate with the sexes. In other words, "gender" is a "cultural construct" (Caplan 1987; see also Ortner and Whitehead 1981).

Cultures expect different attitudes and behaviors from members of each sex, but those expectations vary among cultures. In some cultures, what we consider "masculine" behavior is expected of women while in others it is not. In some cultures, men engage in what we would consider to be "feminine" (i.e., "effeminate" in

the U.S. value system) behavior. All this is to say that whereas "sex" is a term used to describe a biological constant, "gender" is a term used to describe socially and culturally approved expectations, and these vary between societies. For example, while we might argue that being a bouncer at a night club is quintessentially a male role, among the Dahomeyan of Africa rulers used women as bodyguards because they considered women to be excellent fighters (Light et al. 1989). Among the Tchambuli of New Guinea, women were the dominant figures, the principal "breadwinners," wore no jewelry, and kept their heads shaved. Margaret Mead's research uncovered some societies where both sexes were expected to be nurturant and gentle, and others where men and women were expected to be aggressive and arrogant (Mead 1963).

So while women are members of the same sex and, therefore, are biologically the same across cultures, their gender roles may be markedly different among those same cultures. Since we are concerned with the inequality of the sexes, the term "sex inequality" will ordinarily be used with the realization that the definition and interpretation of the appropriate roles and values (i.e., gender) directly affect the ranking of men and women.

There is a temptation to think of "sex" and "gender" as being synonymous, but this can lead to serious errors in understanding inequality between the sexes. One pitfall has been to define the gender roles given to each sex as being "natural." This conclusion indicates that there is and should be an invariate relationship between sex and gender, that by their nature men and women perform particular roles and have particular characteristics. The old phrase "men are men and women are women" captures this belief. In this view, there is a consistency between sex and gender that cannot or should not be changed. For example, in U.S. culture, "male homosexuality threatens male solidarity and superordination because some men take on what are thought of as female characteristics. Lesbianism is likewise seen as threatening to male superiority because the women who engage in it appear not to need men." We assume that there needs to be a "correct fit between sex, gender, and sexuality" (Caplan 1987, p. 2). "Cross-gender," the situation of one sex performing and acting like the other sex on a regular basis has been found in a number of cultures, thus raising serious questions about the necessary connection between particular roles and the sexes (Schlegel 1977; Coontz and Henderson 1986; Blackwood 1984). Nor is there sufficient evidence to conclude that basic natural differences in aggression and "strength," even if they were unequivocably demonstrated to exist, and differences in reproductive abilities are adequate explanations of sex inequality or the division of labor between the sexes (Schlegel 1977; Mukhopadhyay and Higgins 1988).

In eighteenth- and nineteenth-century Europe it was common to associate women with "nature." Women's nature was thought to reflect "natural laws" and their behavior to reflect a basic emotionalism and passion. "The opposed categories of nature and culture (or society) arose as part of a historically particular ideological polemic in eighteenth-century Europe; a polemic which created further contradictions by defining women as natural (superior), but instruments of a society of men (subordinate)" (MacCormack 1980, pp. 6–7).

Ortner (1974) has argued that because of women's reproductive role, they have been and still are viewed as being closer to nature than men, who "lacking natural creative functions, must . . . assert [their] creativity externally, 'artificially,' through the medium of technology and symbols. In doing so [the man creates] relatively lasting, eternal, transcending objects, while the woman creates only perishables—human beings" (p. 75). Women are also seen as mediating between nature and culture, while men are divorced from nature. Since nature is generally interpreted as being lower than culture and subject to the constraints of culture, Ortner argues, men are accorded more prestige and women less. While realizing that not all cultures neatly divide the sexes in terms of nature versus culture, Ortner says that

in most the differences between the sexes are seen in dichotomous terms, nature/culture being one of them. Others of a similar kind involve the notion that women's activities and values are circumscribed by the domestic sphere or self-interests, while men's roles are in the public domain or for the social good. Since the public or social sphere of life "encompasses" the narrowly focused domestic sphere, higher value is attached to it (Ortner and Whitehead 1981, pp. 7–8).

The proposals that these dichotomies are central to the explanation of sex inequality have been severely criticized in recent years. Why are women necessarily seen as more "natural" than men when the procreative role of men and many of their other activities (eating, sleeping, etc.) are just as natural as those of women? Moreover, many of the forms taken by "natural" behaviors surrounding reproduction are limited by cultural constraints and are not, therefore, purely natural (MacCormack 1980).

While incorporating the element of cultural beliefs into her theory, Ortner appears to ignore the structural constraints placed on behavior by the social and natural context of the society (Schlegel 1977). Not all cultures devalue what is natural either, and the meaning of "natural" changes historically rather than remaining timeless and static as it appears in Ortner's view (Coontz and Henderson 1986; Yanagisako and Collier 1987). Perhaps the most serious deficiency of the nature/culture dichotomy is that it simplifies the complex reality of diverse cultures. Research indicates that even where such a dichotomy can be derived, nature and culture may be defined in a manner different from western society, or males may be viewed as being closer to nature than females, or the dichotomy may not be associated with the sexes at all (Gillison 1980; Harris 1980; Strathern 1980).

The importance of Ortner's work is that it calls attention to the significance of symbols and cultural constructs in understanding how individuals interpret the sexes and the relations between them. What distinguishes most of the theories discussed below from Ortner's is that they emphasize the centrality of social structure in the process of inequality development between the sexes. Moreover, Ortner and Whitehead proclaim the universality of prestige inequality: "In every known society, men and women compose two differentially valued terms of a value set, men being as *men,* higher (Ortner and Whitehead 1981, p. 16). In contrast, most of the following scholars view distinct sex inequality as an outcome of particular kinds of social or economic structures, and not, therefore, historically universal.

Social/Structural Explanations

Rather than focusing on basic cultural dichotomies as the sources of sex inequality, this group of theories focuses on the importance of the positions and roles of individuals, and general social/structural characteristics of a society for generating sex inequality. These theories are usually universalistic in nature; that is, they propose to explain the degree of sex inequality for societies that are radically different in terms of technology, size, culture, and so forth. In other words, these theories pay particular attention to the social/organizational peculiarities of societies in explaining the varying degrees of sex inequality found in them. Several of the most significant of these theories emphasize the importance of women's work activities and kinship structure as contributors to the overall status of women in a society. Janet Saltzman Chafetz's explanation is a good example of a social structural theory.

Chafetz's Theory of Sex Stratification   Parts of Chafetz's theory of sex stratification are similar to some other structural theories (e.g., Blumberg 1978, 1984). These theories emphasize the importance of the type of labor and kinship structure in understanding sex inequality. However, Chafetz's includes some additional variables and incorporates a number of feedback loops which suggest that the relationships between important variables are not always unidirectional.

This theory is supposed to be applicable cross-culturally. The variable Chafetz is trying to explain is the "degree of sex stratification" in a given society. She faults previous theories for looking at sex stratification in a simplistic way, as if it were a dichotomy rather than a variable that can vary in degree. She observes that there has never been a situation where women dominated men on a systematic and long-term basis, so that societies vary "from near equality to radical inequality favoring males" (Chafetz 1988, p. 51). Stratification is defined as "the extent to which societal members are unequal in their access to the scarce values of their society" (Chafetz 1984, p. 4). In this case, of course, Chafetz is addressing the extent to which men differ from women in their access at a given point in time in a society. She notes that these "scarce values" include a variety of possibilites—not only access to material goods and services, but to prestigious roles, political power, interpersonal decision making, freedom from unwanted constraints, and access to educational and other opportunities. The result is that she views stratification as multidimensional rather than merely economic in nature. She also acknowledges that a number of these dimensions may not be correlated with each other, so that women's position on any one of them may vary independently from the others.

The major part of Chafetz's theory is made up of a variety of intervening variables that connect several independent variables with sex stratification. The most important set of intervening variables relates to the *nature of work organization.* The work organization of a society includes (1) its sex division of labor, (2) the extent to which the labor ordinarily done by one sex can be done by the other, (3) the extent to which sex roles are sex segregated, (4) the "attention span" required for various labor activities, and (5) ownership and control of the means and products of production (ibid., pp. 12–14). When women contribute significantly to highly valued tasks, when they cannot easily be replaced, when occupational tasks are not sex typed, when attention span is not an important variable in a valued task, and when women have ownership and control over the means and products of their production, then sex inequality will be low in a society.

The work organization itself is affected by

several other factors such as the proportion of women's time that is spent on reproduction and childrearing, the distance between places of work and the home, the need for physical strength and mobility in the work tasks, and the relative emphasis a society puts on production for exchange with other groups versus production for their own use. The less time women have to spend on childrearing activities, the smaller the distance between workplace and home, the less the need for physical strength and/or mobility, and the more emphasis that is placed on sustenance rather than surplus production for exchange, the more women can be meaningfully involved in valued work tasks and, consequently, the lower the degree of sex stratification will be.

A second set of intervening variables involves *kinship structure*. Work organization affects family structure and vice versa. Family structure also is affected by the religious and environmental characteristics of a society. When the kinship structure is matrilocal/matrilineal and there is no sex division of labor within it, then sex inequality will be low.

Finally, Chafetz includes both the *degree of ideological/religious support for sex inequality* and the *degree of gender stratification* as additional intervening variables. Briefly, the first of these variables refers to the extent to which there are dominant religious values or other kinds of ideologies that support or promote sex and gender differentiation. For example, some societies may support the notion that "women's place is in the home." Gender stratification, in turn, refers here to a society and culture's view of the known (or believed) and appropriate personality and behavior traits of the two genders. For example, cultures usually contain stereotypes of "male" and "female" characteristics. These two intervening variables are much less important in Chafetz's model than are the work organization and kinship structures.

Up to this point, we have been discussing the factors that intervene between the basic causes of sex stratification and stratification itself. Of those included, Chafetz considers work organization to be the most significant determinant of sex stratifi-

cation. She considers the most important independent variable or determinant of work organization to be the level and type of technology present in a society (Chafetz 1988, p. 54). In this, she follows Lenski who has argued that technology has a major impact on the structure of the distribution in any society. Technology's importance lies in its ramifying influence on most of the intervening variables covered in the theory. *"It is likely that technological level and type are indirectly but powerfully responsible for the shape of most major social institutions, and it is thus very likely that changes in family structure, work organization, and ultimately the system of sex stratification are often, if not usually, rooted in technological change"* (Chafetz 1984, p. 19, emphasis added).

Other independent variables included in her model are (1) the sex ratio, (2) population density, and (3) the degree of harshness and threat in the physical and sociopolitical environment. The level and type of technology affects and is affected by the population density and environment of a society. The sex ratio has obvious implications for the population density. All of these variables are at least indirectly related to the work organization of a society, as well as to some of the other intervening variables in the theory. In concluding a general presentation of it, Chafetz argues that "this model includes all variables with a significant impact on degree of sex stratification and all the important linkages between these variables" (ibid., p. 21). As to the issue of whether women could ever concentrate solely in nondomestic public labor, Chafetz concludes that this would be impossible because of the biological factors relating to reproduction and physical strength. *Some* of women's labor will always belong to the domestic or private sphere (Chafetz 1984). Figure 10.1 portrays a *simplified* version of Chafetz's explanation of sex stratification showing the main relationships among the variables in the model.

There have been conflicting reactions to Chafetz's argument. In a discussion of his view of how sociological theory should be structured, Gerhard Lenski praises her model for being pre-

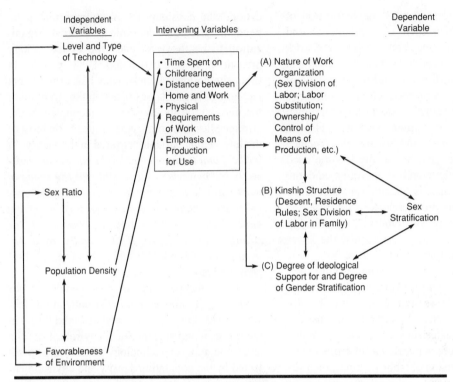

FIGURE 10.1 A Simplified Interpretation of Chafetz's Theory of Sex Stratification
Source: Based on Chafetz (1984), pp. 10–22.

sented in a diagrammatic and essentially proposi-
tional form. Lenski believes that this makes the
theory clearer and more amenable to empirical
testing. It is more difficult to hide in verbiage because the theory is explicitly stated. Lenski believes that this is the kind of approach social science should use in developing and presenting
theory. It appears more systematic and more in
tune with the positivistic posture of the natural
sciences. That is, her model is aimed at providing
an explanation that can be applied independent of
time and place. In doing so, however, it wrenches
the explanation out of specific cultural contexts.
In sharp contrast to the praise of Lenski, Pierre
Van den Berghe is quite critical of Chafetz's formalistic approach to theory, which appears to be
becoming more dominant in the field. In assessing her theory, he bluntly states that "an exercise
in loosely linking a grab bag of 'variables' does

not constitute anything that a real scientist would
recognize as a theory" (1985, p. 1350). However,
this is an extreme reaction to what is a useful predictive model. It brings together variables that
have been cited as important by others into a
somewhat coherent and testable package. One
variable minimized by Chafetz, which is considered central for Sanday's theory to be considered
next, is the role of cultural factors in explaining
and maintaining sex stratification.

Ecological Explanations

The structural theories of Chafetz and others often rely upon the cross-cultural evidence and
ideas of anthropologists who have developed theories of sex inequality. The latters' theories
usually focus upon societies that are simpler in
technology, while sociological theories usually

emphasize complex industrial societies when trying to explain inequality (Chafetz 1988).

Sanday's Theory of Male Dominance Peggy Sanday's theory is based on her analysis of information from over 150 societies, most of them not known to the average reader and many of them extinct. But they provide clues to the origins of male dominance. Sanday defines male dominance in terms of the "exclusion of women from political and economic decision-making" and "male aggression against women" (1981, p. 164). Her principal question addresses the origins of male dominance. Where does it come from? *The basic generating cause for male dominance relates to the nature of the environment in which a society operates.* If that environment is one in which risk is great, danger is present, or resources are uncertain or in scarce supply, then the society is more vulnerable to male dominance over women. For example, when a society's ability to feed itself is dependent on hunting large migrating animals, its continuity is not as certain. This means that people's tie to the environment is more negative than positive under these circumstances. Survival is at risk. This contrasts with situations in which the immediate environment supplies abundant food without risk or uncertainty, as for example, among the Mbuti, an African forest people.

These two different environments generate different stresses for the people exposed to them, their relationships to the environment are defined differently, and the general cultural orientations and consequent sex-role plans they develop also differ as a result (Sanday 1981). In other words, a people develops its "sense of peoplehood" and cultural orientations as responses to its environmental circumstances. When those circumstances involve risk, uncertainty, and so forth, as in the case of societies that rely heavily upon the hunting of large animals, then there is a greater reliance on the aggression of men. These societies, in which animals must be killed, in which "death and destruction" predominate, develop what Sanday calls an "outer orientation" in their world

view. "Men hunt animals, seek to kill other human beings, make weapons for these activities, and pursue power that is *out there*" (1981, p. 5). On the other side are societies whose environments produce abundantly and with certainty, cultures that rely upon the surrounding plants for sustenance. Nature is viewed in a friendly manner, as freely satisfying human needs. In many cases where this situation is present, a basic affinity is seen between women and nature. As women produce so does nature. Women are seen as being more in tune with nature and men are largely extraneous to this relationship. In these cultures, an "inner orientation" is dominant.

The cultural system that develops in a society not only contains "scripts" for the relationships between humans and the natural environment, but between the sexes as well. In societies in which the environment is potentially hostile, men spend much of their time in activities in the outer environment, outside the family, wrestling with forces beyond the family. In these kinds of societies, the ultimate source of power is believed to reside either in animals or in a supreme being of some kind who lives in a place beyond human beings. In these societies, because of their hunting activity, men are "distant" from their children and do not engage much in nurturing activity. The myths surrounding origins of the culture or world are imbued with masculine characteristics. The opposite is the case when a society, especially a technologically simple one, relies upon plants in plentiful supply. Here the earth supplies the food and men are close to their families and children. Growth and life are an inherent part of the culture. Like women, the earth provides and creates life. Tales of life origins have a feminine quality to them. Under both these circumstances, "the phrases 'man the animal' and 'mother earth' make a great deal of sense" (Sanday 1981, p. 73). There is a close connection between the economy of a society and the role of the sexes in myths and childrearing.

A strict sex-based division of labor is more likely when the society depends heavily upon hunting as its means of subsistence, whereas a society that depends equally upon hunting and gathering or inordinately upon the latter for food is more likely to produce a division of labor that is sexually integrated. Cooperation rather than competition is likely to be emphasized. Females *achieve* power when a society has to depend upon their economic activity for survival. This makes men more dependent upon them. Women are *given* power when they are associated closely with nature and the society's continuity as in the origin myths just mentioned (ibid., pp. 89, 114).

With western colonialism, women lost much of the higher status they held in traditional societies. The infusion of new weapons, new technologies (such as the horse), and the increased importance of aggression helped to redefine the roles of the sexes, with male activity becoming more highly valued. In many cases, the increased complexity of economic technology also led to the decline of women's status. In her survey of societies, Sanday concludes that "[m]ale dominance is associated with increasing technological complexity, an animal economy, sexual segregation in work, a symbolic orientation to the male creative principle, and stress" (ibid., p. 171). Sex inequality is much more likely when the environment is "unfavorable" and unstable than when the opposite is the case.

To summarize Sanday's explanation, the nature of the surrounding environment gives shape to the economy and the stress in society and determines the relative worth of men's and women's behavior. Cultural orientations, myths, and sex-role plans develop that are consistent with these conditions. When environmental conditions create stress because they involve risk, danger, or uncertainty, greater reliance is placed on the economic efforts of men. An "outer" cultural orientation develops along with origin myths in which men dominate and create, sex-segregation of roles follows, ultimately leading to male dominance. Sanday's basic model is suggested in Figure 10.2.

Sanday's theory has been criticized for overemphasizing the role of the environment in determining cultural beliefs and for ignoring the internal sources of stress in society. Nor does it take into account the fact that different cultures may react differently to similar environmental circumstances (Coontz and Henderson 1986). Her theory also neglects the possibility that the difficulties men encounter in dealing with a harsh environment may strengthen them enough to dominate women directly. Randall Collins has suggested, for example, that the form of the economic system and the hospitality of the surrounding natural and political environments influence the extent to which warfare is an important element in the society. When the economic system is advanced enough and involves the protection of private property or settled territories, warfare is often part of a society's existence as it tries to defend itself against outside encroachment. Men are generally larger and stronger than women and are, therefore, more likely to control the fighting that occurs. In this kind of a potentially hostile environment, political alliances become important, and males use the exchange of females through marriage with surrounding groups as a means of establishing

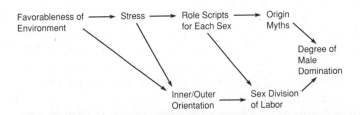

FIGURE 10.2   Sanday's Basic Model of the Genesis of Male Dominance
Source: Based on Sanday (1981), pp. 11–12, 64–75, 163–72ff.

political, economic, and social ties. This control of females by males results in separate cultures and roles developing for each of the sexes (Collins 1971, 1986, 1988). In other words, the need for the mediation of the environment's impact on male domination through the intervening factors of cultural scripts and orientations may either not be necessary or the mediation may involve the operation of other variables like warfare.

The causal nature of the relationships outlined by Sanday also needs to be more fully examined (England and Dunn 1985). One would suspect, for example, that cultural orientation and beliefs would have an impact on the degree to which the environment is *interpreted* as being hostile or friendly. In other words, the environment may not only affect the culture, but the culture may affect the definition of the environment as well.

Capitalism, Patriarchy, and Sex Inequality

Generally, structural theorists, as well as many anthropologists, recognize the significance of broadly defined economic factors for sex inequality. Many point to the significance of labor, work organization, and family structure in shaping inequality. In a general way, then, their perspectives have been affected by Marxian thought as well as by perspectives that focus upon the family structure and the sex/gender divisions within it. Some explanations, however, explicitly focus on the effects of capitalism and patriarchy on sex in-

equality. Figure 10.3 gives a basic model showing some of the alleged major impacts of capitalism/class on sex inequality.

Again, there are a large number of individuals who present such explanations (e.g., Sacks 1975; Leacock 1986; Vogel 1983). Some of them address the adequacy and insights of Engels's theory of the origins of sex inequality, so we will begin with an overview of his position.

Engels's Theory of Sex Inequality   Engels contended that early in human history, people lived together communally and engaged in tasks together to produce goods principally for their own use. Since all resources were communally owned, individuals worked for the group as a whole. Separate nuclear families as we know them, as distinct productive units, did not exist. Rather than being *wives* within separate families, women were *members of society* and contributed fully and equally to society (Sacks 1975, p. 213). Being a mother was a central role in those societies, according to Engels. Since all members of both sexes were involved in producing goods of direct value and use to their own communities, the work of both sexes was considered equally valuable. Women were full participants in the society. While there was a division of labor based on sex, each sex was a "master" in its own sphere of work.

This situation changed, according to Engels, when certain material conditions changed. *Specifically, the development of privately owned pro-*

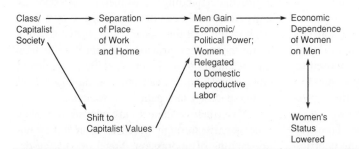

FIGURE 10.3   The Relationship of Class/Capitalism to Sex Inequality

ductive resources in the form of domesticated animals and land laid the groundwork for the differentiation of the sexes and the subordination of women to men. These resources appeared on a continuing basis when the technology and natural resources accessible to the group made possible the development of the abilities necessary to domesticate animals and make productive use of the land. Herding and the use of land made possible greater surpluses than were possible under mere hunting. Engels felt that once domestication and land use were stabilized and part of the society, then private ownership would also be stabilized. He also believed that men were the earliest owners of property (Sacks 1975, pp. 215–256).

Once private property was entrenched in society, economic and other divisions developed between individuals and families; that is, the "preclass" days were over. The extensive domestication of animals and land use made possible greater surpluses, allowing individuals to produce not only for themselves and their families but for others as well. That is "production for exchange" began to become more dominant than "production for use" by the households themselves. With private property owned by men and the increase in production for exchange, the kind of work that dominated the lives of women changed, and with it their status in society (Sacks 1975, p. 217; Leacock 1986). Because men now had property they could pass on to *their* children, men became more concerned about making sure they had children. This encouraged them to usurp more control in the nuclear monogamous family and the procreation process. Women were reduced to being the private servants of men.

Instead of remaining "social adults" who actively contributed to all of society, women became (1) propertyless, (2) involved in work for their own families and their heads as opposed to working for the social group as a whole, and (3) concerned with the maintenance of their own families and support of their heads who were now in competition with the heads of other families. Essentially, women changed from being contributing adults equal to men to "wards, wives, and daughters" in a subordinate and increasingly domestic position. Their reproduction of children was now for producing heirs and workers for their own families rather than for producing another child for the societal group. Individual families and their economic statuses could then be preserved generation after generation. This domination of men over women in the nuclear family setting is, for Engels, the first instance of class domination and struggle in history. "In the family, he is the bourgeois; the wife represents the proletariat" (Engels 1973, p. 247). This class conflict is "a picture in miniature" of what appears later in the society as a whole (Engels 1973). Eventually, property owners joined together to defend their goods against those who owned nothing. This was the beginning of class society and class state (Sacks 1975, p. 217).

Vogel's Reproduction Theory Lise Vogel reviews and assesses Engels's analysis of women's oppression, but comes to the conclusion that his theory is seriously flawed. Among other comments, she argues that Engels assumes that the domestic sphere is the exclusive province of the woman and will continue to be so in the future. Vogel sees this neither as natural or necessary in the future. Second, she says Engels does not clearly trace and explain the development of a separate domestic arena out of class or capitalist society. Third, he does not elaborate on the subordination of women in precapitalist class societies (Vogel 1983, p. 86). These problems lead Vogel to attempt development of her own theory based on Marxian concepts. She recognizes that a full understanding of women's oppression in any given society can only be obtained by a thorough analysis of that society and its history; that while theory may provide "guidance" in general understanding of societies, specific programs of change and policies can only be based on concrete, specific examinations of societies.

Nevertheless, theories are needed to provide a perspective through which to approach an understanding of oppression. Vogel begins the development of her theoretical framework by reviewing several Marxian concepts: production, reproduction, and labor-power. "Labor-power" refers to the capacities, mental and physical, an individual exercises whenever he or she produces something of use. "Production" is a result of labor-power. But every act of production is also an act of "reproduction," since whatever is produced lays the basis for its being reproduced as well. For example, if an individual produces food or other necessary products, these products are at the same time conditions needed for social reproduction to continue. Specifically, a society needs a labor force to continue to produce products and this labor force, in turn, needs food to maintain itself. In other words, part of the reproduction process involves reproducing the laborers who are involved in the labor process. These workers must be maintained and, when necessary, replaced. "Some process that meets the ongoing personal needs of the bearers of labor power as human individuals is therefore a condition of social reproduction, as is some process that replaces workers who have died or withdrawn from the active work force" (ibid., p. 139). Another part involves reproducing the other general conditions that make production possible, or the technology required in the labor process. Sex becomes a significant factor in the discussion of the "generational replacement of bearers of labor power." It is only women who can perform this function. But this regeneration or replenishment of the labor force does not have to occur within the family. Other sources, such as migration, enslavement, and the enlistment of nonworkers within the family, also may serve as potential sources of labor power.

In order for the capitalist system of production to continue then, labor power must produce the conditions necessary for the constant renewal of the labor process. The labor needed to reproduce the workers and their replacement is *necessary* labor. For example, a certain minimum amount of labor is needed to provide basic subsistence to the workers and to produce new workers. Part of this necessary labor is done at the workplace and is paid for by wages, with which the worker can buy those necessities needed to reproduce himself or herself and other nonworkers in the working class. Since it takes place in the social or public sphere, it is the *social* aspect of necessary labor. But as mentioned, biological reproduction and the rearing of children are also needed, and as such constitute a second *domestic* component of necessary labor. In addition to necessary labor, there is *surplus* labor. This is the labor time that is left over after socially necessary labor has been subtracted from the total labor time spent on the job. It provides the profit to the employer.

It is the unavoidable performance of the domestic component of necessary labor by women that creates a basic sex division of labor. "If children are to be born, it is women who will carry and deliver them. Women belonging to the subordinate class have, therefore, a special role with respect to the generational replacement of labor power. . . . It is their differential role in the reproduction of labor power that lies at the root of their oppression in class society" (ibid., p. 145). But their involvement in this activity creates a dilemma for capitalists and constitutes an internal contradiction in the capitalist system. On the one hand, this domestic labor reduces any time women could spend in the labor force producing profit for employers. So in the *short* run, capitalists suffer because of the smaller direct contribution of women to profit. On the other hand, if capitalism is going to continue over the *long* run, replacement and reproduction are necessary. So in these terms capitalism benefits.

In order to benefit both ways, capitalists try to minimize the amount of necessary domestic time needed for reproduction in order to maximize the surplus value of labor, thereby increasing their profit. At the same time, however, male workers try to get the best conditions and wages they can for themselves, their families, and their wives. This may mean more and better-quality domestic time for their wives. So while employers may be trying to enlist wives in the marketplace, husbands are trying to create conditions that will make it more possible for them to stay comfortably at home. In trying to resolve this contradiction, according to Vogel, what almost invariably occurs is the involvement of men in the labor force and the production of surplus labor on the one hand, and the involvement of women in the reproduction of the labor force in the domestic site, on the other. Accompanying this resolution is a male supremacy based on males as the laborers who produce the means of subsistence and receive a wage. "While exceptions exist, . . . the historical legacy remains one that has been characterized, for better or worse, as patriarchal" (ibid., p. 149).

It is in capitalism that a distinct and strong division is accentuated between the arena in which surplus labor is carried out and that in which domestic labor is performed. In order to increase profit, separate factories in which workers are concentrated are needed which are socially and culturally isolated from the home. "Capitalism's drive to increase surplus . . . forces a severe spatial, temporal, and institutional separation between domestic labor and the capitalist production process. . . . Wage labor comes to have a character that is wholly distinct from the laborer's life away from the job" (ibid., p. 153). Men are clearly associated with the social, "working" sphere while women are associated with the domestic sphere. This is a carryover from earlier class societies.

Of course, depending upon the specific historical circumstances of a given society, either the importance of women's power of reproduction or their involvement in the labor force may be stressed. Migration and natural or other disasters may tip the scales in such a way that the participation of females in the work force is more important than their domestic labor. But the usual division of labor consists of men and women being associated with distinct spheres of labor. This clear division of labor, when accentuated in a situation of male supremacy, is the source for ideologies that serve to "explain" and maintain the sexual basis of the division of labor. Since this division of labor is so prominent and obvious, it comes to be viewed as "natural" even though it is

rooted in the capitalist mode of production (ibid., p. 154).

As noted previously, according to Vogel, women's involvement in and relegation to domestic labor is the basic source of their subordination. In fact, she suggests that in advanced capitalist societies, sex sometimes is more important than class in determining differences between individuals. Men support women by working and receiving wages, and this gives them economic power over women. *"It is the provision by men of means of subsistence to women during the childbearing period, and not the sex division of labor in itself, that forms the material basis for women's subordination in class society"* (ibid., p. 147, emphasis added). Moreover, while women of any class may be subordinated to the males in their class by legal and other traditional practices, it is only women of the working class that reproduce the labor force needed by capitalists. Vogel's assumption is that women of the capitalist class do not reproduce workers, but only new members of that class. Vogel includes in her definition of the "working class" all past, present, and potential workers, along with those who must be supported by the wages of those workers. In a particular situation in a specific society, women may be members of the "industrial reserve army," that is, potential employees or only members of the nonworking surplus population.

In discussing the problems of the working class and other oppressed groups within capitalism, Vogel observes that "equality" takes on a particular form within capitalism. By and large, it consists of considering the labor-power of different individuals as equal in the sense that the products produced by it are weighed in terms of the same standards of value. That is, the same standards are used to measure the significance of the products produced. Second, "equality" also refers to freedom in the "sphere of circulation" where capitalists and laborers meet each other to exchange wages for labor-power. Individuals buy and sell labor openly and freely. It is on the level of circulation that political equality exists. However, in the "sphere of production," great disparities in economic power and exploitation occur. Thus, within capitalism there are elements of both political equality and economic inequality, which creates inherent problems for it. Capitalism may provide freedom to sell one's labor, but not freedom from exploitation.

Because of their unique contribution to capitalist reproduction, women hold a special position within the society, one that is different in its problems from those of other oppressed groups. Their particular oppression relates to their role in domestic labor and their lack of equal rights (ibid., pp. 162–168). Since many of the immediate conflicts take place within the context of the family, it is easy to conclude that it is the sex division of labor within it that is at the source of the problems experienced by women. But Vogel reminds us again that it is the nature of the relationship of men and women to the capitalist system of production and women's role in reproducing it that is the basic cause. As long as capitalism remains unchanged, inequality between the sexes will continue.

One of the problems with Vogel's theory is that she dates the beginning of women's oppression with the advent of class societies. Many would argue that male domination predated class society (Nicholson 1984). Vogel's theory also heavily stresses economic factors to the exclusion of cultural, psychological, and other possible contributors to male domination.

The Role of Patriarchy   Vogel acknowledges the division of labor and inequality that exist between the sexes in capitalist society, but Sacks (1975) notes that in many nonclass societies the sexes were also unequal. This suggests strongly that sex inequality preceded capitalism and indeed is a form of domination distinct from class inequality. Unfortunately, we cannot in this space pursue in depth all the variations and nuances of the arguments pertaining to the relationship between patriarchy and capitalism. We can only present some of the main points stressed about that relationship.

Many feminists argue that "patriarchy" not

only preceded capitalism, but existed even in the earliest societies. The term "patriarchy" has been defined in a variety of ways, but basically it refers to a whole complex of structured interrelationships in which men dominate over women. It is a "system of sexual hierarchical relations" (Eisenstein 1981, p. 19). Just as capitalism is based on the relationship between capitalists and workers, so patriarchy is a system based on the unequal relationship of men and women (Phelps 1981). Because of its early appearance, patriarchy is considered by most radical feminists to be the most fundamental of all forms of social inequality, as one in which "men learn how to hold other human beings in contempt, to see them as nonhuman and to control them" (Lengermann and Niebrugge-Brantley 1988, p. 306).

In other words, in this view, sexism and the domination of women did not appear with class societies as some Marxists would have it (e.g., Sherman and Wood 1989), but rather existed long before capitalism came on the historical scene. The roots of patriarchy have been tied to the reproductive function of women in society (Chafetz 1988; Eisenstein 1981; Phelps 1981; Firestone 1970). "On the basis of this capacity she has been excluded from other human activities and contained within a sphere defined as female" in western society (Eisenstein 1981, p. 14). The division of labor between the sexes in this respect is ancient: "Where there is society, there is gender, and the gender division of labor is pervasive" (Smith 1987, p. 4). There was no primordial matriarchal society preceding class society. Table 10.2 suggests some of the basic elements tied to patriarchy and some of the forms it has taken under precapitalist and capitalist societies.

Once men dominate in areas outside the family and gain the economic and political resources attendant with those activities, they can use these resources to maintain patriarchy. The maintenance of patriarchy over generations is clearly in the interests of men. Women serve the material interests of men by serving not only as sexual partners, but as potential laborers, childbearers, ornaments, and status enhancers.

TABLE 10.2 Patriarchy and Sex Inequality

GENERAL FEATURES OF PATRIARCHY	UNDER PRE-CAPITALIST SOCIETIES	UNDER CAPITALISM
a. Power, force of men	Men engage in status-enhancing hunting; men control domesticated animals	Radical separation of home and work; women cheap labor for market, women largely confined to home, women economically dependent on men
b. Control of outer resources by men	women used as exchange, women purchased (bridewealth), men control military	
c. Separate work spheres		
d. Division of labor based on sex		
e. Reproductive capacity of women critical		

The social institutions dominated by men then influence not only the shape of society and relations within it, but the cultural values and ideas that dominate in society. Thus, in present-day society, education and socialization agents instill those values consistent with patriarchal structure. Under capitalism, the culture consists largely of the ideas and values sanctioned by those in power, that is, men. This "ruling ideology" provides an "official" version of social reality, including beliefs about the real nature of men and women. Eventually, among women living under capitalism a "line of fault" or disjuncture occurs between this official version of reality and how the system works and the concrete everyday experiences of women. But this experience is difficult to articulate because the symbols, language, and organization of thought in the society are those of men not women (Smith 1987).

The separation and inequality of men and women is reflected in dichotomies that go back to ancient times. The distinctions between rationality and passion, city and household, and public and private all derive from a belief in the basic differences and inequality between the sexes. In feudal and in capitalist societies, the public sphere is associated with the male, while the private sphere is the designated place for the female. In feudal society, females were considered private

property of the male heads of families, and in capitalist society women are largely relegated to the private sphere of the family. In other words, while the economic system may change, basic patriarchal relationships remain intact and only change form.

One of the difficulties with patriarchal theories is that the original source of patriarchy is not always clearly spelled out. Sometimes it is associated with the differences in the reproductive function between the sexes, sometimes with the physical force of men over women, and other times its source is left undescribed. Collins (1988) argues that basic problem with theories that propose patriarchy as the fundamental, original cause of sex inequality is that they are merely restating the question using a different label. That is, if "patriarchy" *refers* to male domination of one sort or another, then how can it be used to *explain* male domination? This seems to be too severe a criticism given that many of those proposing such theories do attempt to locate the sources of patriarchy itself. Since that source is often viewed as being tied to the elemental function of reproduction, the task remains to identify the exact conditions under which such distinctions in the division of labor do *not* lead to patriarchy. For example, can socializing or spreading a large part of the childrearing function free women to a degree from the "destiny" of remaining in the domestic sphere, thereby potentially raising their status in society?

Socialist-Feminist Theories of Sex Inequality

The role of capitalism and/or patriarchy in producing sex inequality has been the subject of a great deal of debate. There are at least three groups of theories in this area: (1) those that view capitalism as the source of both class and sex inequality; (2) those that consider patriarchy, which preceded capitalism historically, as the ultimate source of continued domination of men over women; and (3) those that view capitalism and patriarchy as being mutually supportive and reinforcing.

Marxian theories generally emphasize the role of capitalism in generating inequality. For example, sex inequality within the household is seen as being derived from the economic demands of capitalism. The lower status of women is due to capitalist demands for reproduction of the labor force and the consequent relegation of women to the domestic sphere. According to Eisenstein (1977), Engels saw both domestic and wage slavery in the marketplace as products of capitalism's push for greater profit. The theories of Sacks and Vogel are examples of Marxian theories of sex inequality.

Some of the most influential recent theories of sex inequality, however, have come from socialist-feminist scholars who analyze the complex interrelationships between capitalism and patriarchy in producing and maintaining sex inequality. While a Marxian analysis of power and the use of the historical method may be important for understanding women's oppression, they are not sufficient. Women's oppression by men cannot be reduced to a matter of class exploitation, according to these scholars. "Exploitation" of women, Eisenstein (1977) argues, exists when men and women are wage laborers. But women are *also* in a lower sexual hierarchy in their roles as mothers and housewives.

The Marxian approach needs to be stretched in order to understand the low status of women under capitalism. "The st... sion, then, must deal wit... nomic material conditions... oppression rather than r... nomic exploitation" (Eise... we will see, those who use an internal-colonialism model in explaining black/white inequality in the United States make a similar argument about understanding racial oppression. At the same time that acquaintance with capitalism and Marxian perspectives may illuminate the conditions of women in present-day society, it must also be understood that the domination of women by men occurs in other kinds of economic systems as well.

Patriarchy predates capitalism, existing in agrarian, feudal, and other kinds of societies. In contrast to capitalism which was a "relative latecomer" on the historical scene, patriarchy "was an early arrival" (Hartmann 1990, p. 147). Within patriarchy, men developed the techniques of control that they could later use to control women in capitalism. In order to understand the social, economic, and political position of women in contemporary societies, one must examine how patriarchy operates in the context of capitalism, because its form may vary with the economic system (Eisenstein 1977).

Eisenstein and Hartmann both emphasize the mutual reinforcement between capitalism and patriarchy. On the one hand, patriarchy supplies capitalism with generations of laborers it needs at minimal costs and with the techniques of control needed to keep oppressed women in their place. All the tasks carried out and raw materials worked on by housewives (e.g., children, husbands) are "future worker-commodities" (Secombe 1973, p. 19). In turn, capitalism reinforces patriarchy by only hiring women for certain low-paying positions, thereby encouraging job segregation, women's relegation to the domestic sphere, and their continued economic dependence upon males.

"Job segregation by sex, in my view, is the primary mechanism in capitalist society that maintains the superiority of men over women, be-it enforces lower wages for women in the ⌐r market. Low wages keep women dependent on men because they encourage women to marry. Married women must perform domestic chores for their husbands. Men benefit, then, from both higher wages and the domestic division of labor" (Hartmann 1990, pp. 147–148; see also Eisenstein 1990).

The domestic division of labor is the "linchpin" that connects capitalism and patriarchy (Philipson and Hansen 1990). Patriarchy defines the role of women as being in the home, while capitalism defines men's role as being in the wider economy and women's role as reproducer of workers in the economy. The division of labor, as it were, brings the private/domestic and public/economic spheres into contact. This has raised a number of questions about the nature of the relationship between the marketplace and the home.

One issue pits the obvious contributions of domestic work to the continuance of capitalism against the fact that domestic labor is basically "unpaid" low-status work "outside" the economy. If such work contributes to the economy by providing functioning laborers, why isn't it paid labor? Because it is not paid, it has lower status in a society in which the amount of money labor brings in is a measure of its status (Benston 1969).

A second issue relating to the relationship between family and marketplace concerns the basic character of domestic labor. In contrast to work in the marketplace, which is seen by some as being alienating and rationalistic, work in the home is sometimes seen as much less alienating and more leisurely (Vogel 1983; Sontage 1973). The home and family life are viewed as the areas in which love, warmth, spontaneity, cooperation, and fun have a central place. In sharp contrast, the public sphere of paid labor is interpreted as one where work is forced, competitive, and rational. It is, of course, questionable whether those who feel "trapped" in the home would describe it in the glowing terms just used. But part of our socialization is aimed at fostering the belief that these terms accurately describe family life in modern society.

A third issue among scholars concerns the effects of involvement in the marketplace upon women. Engels viewed industrialization as providing women with a means of escape from the drudgery of housework and the oppression of domestic life. Work outside the home was interpreted as a liberating experience. However, if capitalism creates work that is fundamentally alienating, a legitimate question can be raised about how liberating and beneficial such an escape would be for women. Are they not just escaping into work that is also alienating and compounding their alienation by doing not only paid labor but unpaid domestic labor as well?

A final area concerns the family's role in socializing new members of society into a dominant set of values and ideas that perpetuate patriarchy and capitalism (Hartmann 1981). The traits attributed to the ideal male—competitiveness, rationality, coolness—are those valued in the marketplace, while those attributed to the ideal female under capitalism—emotionality, sentimentality, and so on—are those valued in the family. These are values that keep patriarchy and capitalism intact.

The last point demonstrates that the concerns with profit in capitalism and with social control in patriarchy are "inextricably connected" and "cannot be reduced to each other." Capitalism and patriarchy, being mutually reinforcing, become an "integral process" (Eisenstein 1990, p. 134). The conditions in the marketplace affect what goes on in the family in terms of production, reproduction, and consumption; conversely, production, reproduction, and consumption in the family affect the production of commodities in the marketplace (Eisenstein 1979, pp. 29–30).

The centrality of the sexual division of labor in maintaining both patriarchy and capitalism has caused both Eisenstein and Hartmann to call for its elimination. Eisenstein argues forcefully that it is this division of labor that must be changed because it is the principal means by which men maintain control. It suggests that the roles and activities that divide men and women are rooted in nature (Eisenstein 1990, p. 140). Eisenstein states that for conditions to change, women must organize and they can do so by becoming conscious of what they have in common with each other. While they may differ in their ties to the marketplace, their "commonality derives from the particular roles women share in patriarchy. From this commonality begins the feminist struggle" (ibid., p. 140). Similarly and even more pointedly, Hartmann believes that both men and women will be better off and more equal only when "we eradicate the socially imposed gender differences between us and, therefore, the very sexual division of labor itself" (Hartmann, 1990, p. 170).

One of the great values of seeing capitalism and patriarchy as "dual systems" is that it encourages us to examine the interlinkage between class and sex in trying to understand the relative roles of men and women in society. Clearly, an individual's position in the general system of inequality is an outcome of the confluence of economic, sexual, and racial/ethnic factors. Understanding the nature of this intersection and its origins will provide us with a more comprehensive and exact explanation of sex inequality. There is no question that women as a group, like blacks, are in a unique position in contemporary society. The data provided in Chapter 4 demonstrates this. Race, of course, also plays a role in determining the unique position of a group in society.

It is clear from the array of different explanations just presented that there is no agreement upon the basic source(s) of sex inequality. One group also suggests that male violence against women is the basic cause of sex inequality (e.g., Goode 1971; Brownmiller 1976). However, it also has been argued that such violence is itself based on patriarchal relationships in general (Walby 1986). It may be asked if there even is a basic set of causes; perhaps the causes vary from culture to culture. Coontz and Henderson (1986) may be right: "The search for origins will never

be definitively settled" (p. 27). We turn now to a discussion of the dominant explanations for race inequality.

THEORIES OF RACE INEQUALITY

As is the case for sex inequality, there have been a variety of attempts to explain race inequality, ranging from biological to cultural and structural. Attempts to anchor an adequate explanation in biology have been widely criticized and largely discredited. We commented on some of the earlier theories of this kind in the historical survey of black/white relations in Chapter 4. Recent research by the psychologist Arthur Jensen, who argued that there are significant differences between blacks and whites in native intelligence, also has been heavily criticized. Using culturally biased IQ tests as a measure of general intelligence makes his results highly suspect (Block and Dworkin 1976). Moreover, even if such differences could be demonstrated, their relevance for social and economic inequality between the races would still be problematic given the fact that numerous studies we have discussed demonstrate that individual characteristics do not fully explain such inequality. Finally, the whole idea of racial differences in biology is based on the assumption that we can accurately, indisputably, and objectively identify different races.

But the fact is that, like gender, "race" is largely a political and cultural creation rather than a biological one. Defining someone as black who has only a small percentage of black ancestry, as we have done in the United States, hopelessly blurs the biological distinctions between individuals. Mixed ancestry is widespread, making the delineation of discrete racial categories an impossible task. The mixing of ethnicity and race for political purposes, as in the concept of "Aryan race," makes it clear that the concept itself is often merely an ideological weapon used to demonstrate superiority and justify unequal treatment. Moreover, some groups that we would define as members of a black race are not consid-

cultures. For example, many who live in Paris would be defined as black by Americans but are not so defined by the French. Rather they are identified according to their cultural background such as African, Brazilian, West Indian, or North American (van den Berghe 1967). Even the U.S. Bureau of the Census has moved racial categories around, making it more obvious that race is a social rather than an immutable biological concept. "Groups such as Japanese Americans have moved from categories such as 'nonwhite,' 'Oriental,' or simple 'Other' to recent inclusion as a specific 'ethnic' group under the broader category of 'Asian and Pacific Islanders.' . . . Viewed as a whole, the census's racial classification reflects prevailing conceptions of race, establishes boundaries by which one's racial 'identity' can be understood, determines the allocation of resources, and frames diverse political issues and conflicts" (Omi and Winant 1986, pp. 3–4).

Race, then, like gender, is ultimately a social creation. It is significant because it receives a certain meaning and interpretation in society. It is this social dimension that makes race significant when discussing it in relation to inequality. This raises the important question of how race and race relations have been interpreted, that is, how they have been conceptualized. In the sections that follow, various interpretations of race relations and explanations for racial inequality will be presented. Most will focus on the United States even though they are frequently based upon analyses developed for the characterization of intergroup relations in other countries such as India and Third World countries in general. The caste model is one of these.

The Caste Analysis of Race Relations

The application of the caste concept to race relations in the United States has not served to fully "explain" those relations as much as to "describe" them. While one can use the history of such relations to help explain the existence of an alleged caste system in the United States, the principal advocates of the caste analogy have been concerned primarily with the characterization and analysis of race relations rather than an explanation of them. It will be recalled from Chapter 3 that caste relations are generally argued to fall under the category of status relations; that is, caste structure is an extreme form of status inequality in that relationships between the groups involved are said to be fixed and supported by ideology and/or law. Membership in a particular caste is hereditary, mobility is virtually impossible, marriage within one's caste is mandated, and occupation is strongly related to caste position. These are the fundamental characteristics of a caste structure.

In *An American Dilemma*, Gunnar Myrdal described black/white relations in the United States as constituting a caste system. Caste characteristics are largely a remnant from the slavery system and are to be distinguished from the class distinctions found within each racial caste (1944, pp. 221, 667–668). One can move *within* one's caste but not *between* castes. "The boundary between Negro and white is not simply a class line which can be successfully crossed by education, integration into the national culture, and individual economic advancement. The boundary is fixed. . . . It is a bar erected with the intention or permanency . . . against the whole group" (ibid., p. 58). Like most caste theorists who followed him, Myrdal argued that a caste system was incompatible with the characteristics of democracy. The ultimate result of both existing alongside each other is not only a conflict in values but a "split in American personality," creating the "American dilemma."

The caste model has continued to be used in recent times (van den Berghe 1967; Berreman 1960, 1972; Willie 1979). Van den Berghe (1967) views race stratification as *"an extreme case of status ascription making for rigid group membership,"* one that is comparable to the Hindu caste system and stratification by sex (p. 24). But he says that before the Civil War, race relations were "paternalistic" in nature, while afterwards they could be described as being "competitive."

Under a paternalistic system of master and servant, the socially dominant group treats subordinate group members as if they were children with an "ideology of benevolent despotism." Members of both castes are expected to abide by a code of race relations in which appropriate behavior and position are expected by each group. In virtually all areas of life there is a wide gap between the races and government is tyrannical. While conflict is present, the uneasy stability is maintained partly by the constant undercurrent of force, but also by the enforced complementarity and "acquiescence" of the subordinate group (van den Berghe 1967). This type of system, according to van den Berghe, is most likely to be found in complex agricultural systems, especially those that produce cash crops on a large scale, such as in slave plantations.

In contrast, a "competitive" system of race relations is more characteristic of industrial societies and developed abruptly in the United States after the Civil War, according to van den Berghe. Briefly, under this system, while caste relations remain, class positions within each caste become more elaborated and more important. In industrial societies, human-capital factors take precedence over race in determining position, and competition characterizes the relationship between blacks and working-class whites. Mobility is more likely, with the result that relationships between the races are more aggressive than accommodative. The stereotypes of blacks change from being perceived as easy-going immature children to that of an aggressive, "uppity" and dangerous people (van den Berghe 1967).

A further distinction has been made by William Wilson between a "rigid" and "fluid" competitive system (1973, 1978). The former is one in which many caste elements still remain and discrimination is formalized even though there is open competition conflict between the races, while the latter exists when discrimination has been outlawed but still occurs informally, and the class system competes with the caste elements in society. In both of these, conflict occurs openly but especially in the latter since members of the minority race are free to compete with majority members.

One of the implications of van den Berghe's description of the conditions under which caste or class predominates is that the former is more likely in a static agricultural society while the latter becomes more important with the advance of industrialization and industrialism. Caste is viewed as being associated with rural areas (e.g., the early twentieth-century South) and class with industrialization (e.g., the North). Frazier (1957) takes a similar position when he says that the conflicts surrounding blacks' status in the United States are symptomatic of the attempt to "force into the mold of a static agricultural society the dynamic economic and social relations which characterize an industrial urban society" (p. 268). The general image of the structure of race relations in a society in which a dominant agricultural economy is in the process of being supplanted by an ever-growing industrialism is one in which caste and class are both a component, as described by Warner, Dollard and others (e.g., Willie 1979).

The caste model of U.S. race relations has come under severe attack from both conservative and more radical scholars. On the conservative side, there is the belief that race either is or is becoming largely irrelevant in modern industrial society. Position in the system of inequality is allegedly based on achieved rather than ascribed characteristics, and movement is based on results of an open "contest" between individuals rather than on the "sponsorship" of influential others. Critics have commented on the inappropriateness of comparing U.S. race relations with the Indian caste system, arguing that in contrast to the Indian situation, black/white relations are (1) not stable, but changing, (2) characterized by mobility for blacks, (3) conflictive and pathological, and (4) characterized by upward aspirations on the part of blacks. Other significant differences between India and the United States, it is argued, are that whereas each caste in India is tied to a particular occupation, in the United States blacks are not relegated to a single type of occupation.

Furthermore, whereas the Indian caste system is legitimized through religion, in the United States racial inequality has been justified on the basis of biological or subcultural differences (Simpson and Yinger 1965; Cox 1942, 1948; Barrera 1979). The caste tradition's treatment and definition of social class also has been criticized for being inconsistent. Finally, as mentioned earlier, the caste model has been used more as a descriptive device than as an historical explanation of racial inequality.

Not all of the preceding criticisms are valid, however. There is evidence that as in the United States, the caste system in India has been challenged by those in the lower groups. There is no consensus on the part of all to see it as a legitimate system (Berreman 1960, 1972). Despite the Constitution in India guaranteeing certain rights and outlawing castes, caste relations still operate and contrast sharply with Constitutional provisions, creating an inconsistency between what is on paper and what really exists in society (Sivaramayya 1983). Similarly, in the United States a distinction has been made between de jure and de facto segregation. In other words, this condition is not unlike the internal contradiction between the tenets of American democracy and the reality of racial inequality, what Myrdal called the "American dilemma." Moreover, as in the U.S. case where classes are divided by race, in India the "primordial loyalties" of caste have weakened the unity of classes and prevented poorer classes from organizing (Chakravarti 1983, p. 170). What several of these comments suggest is that it is not acceptable to compare an *idealized* model of the Indian caste system with a *realistic* view of the U.S. race structure (Berreman 1960; Das and Acuff 1970).

Domination Theories of Race Relations

A variety of specific theories are included under this general category, but all of them incorporate the historically crucial role of power and/or domination in shaping racial inequality. Thus, they tend to be more dynamic and historically rooted than caste approaches. In addition, as will become clear, they are more closely aligned with the conflict perspective in sociological theory. They do not anticipate the eventual automatic assimilation of minorities, nor do they emphasize the stability of the system of inequality or the active complicity of the minority group as is often suggested in caste analyses. Three of these approaches are (1) Noel's theory of ethnic stratification, (2) imperialist/colonial explanations, and (3) class-based explanations of racial inequality. Because of the focal role of power in each of these explanations, these theories are not incompatible and attempts have been made to synthesize them (Barrera 1979; Bonacich 1985).

Noel's Theory of Ethnic Stratification Noel (1968) generated a broad theory of the origins of ethnic stratification which he then tested by applying it to the development of slavery in the United States. By "ethnic stratification" he means "a system of stratification wherein some relatively fixed group membership (e.g., race, religion, or nationality) is utilized as a major criterion for assigning social positions with their attendant differential rewards" (p. 157). He begins with the assumption that before the possibility of such stratification even exists there must be a period of prolonged *contact* between the groups involved. Whether or not contact results in stratification depends upon the existence of (1) *ethnocentrism,* (2) *competition,* and (3) *differential power.* All three of these factors must be present for ethnic stratification to emerge.

"Ethnocentrism," of course, refers to the belief that one's culture is the best, the center of the universe so to speak. All others are judged according to it. Cultures that are similar to one's own are ranked highly, while those that are radically different are looked down upon. Consequently, ethnocentrism fosters an "in-group/out-group" or "us/them" orientation toward others. Since people are so classified double standards may be applied to the groups involved. What one expects of oneself may not be what is expected of those "others." It is important to note that each group is ethnocentric, thinking of the other in terms of mild or severe disdain. Each group measures the other in terms of its own values and beliefs, and of course, the other group is always found to be wanting to some degree. Each group also remains separate and autonomous from the other.

However, mere ethnocentrism is not enough to create ethnic stratification according to Noel. Groups can remain independent and relatively equal with a mutual and healthy respect for each other even though both are ethnocentric. Thus, it is also crucial that competition exist between the two or more groups in question. "Competition," as defined by Noel, refers to the interaction between groups who are trying to attain "the same scarce goal." What is important about this interaction is that the goal is the *same* and that it is *scarce*. If the groups were after different goals, there would be no sense of competition and perhaps even lack of concern over the goals of the other group. If the goal is easily attainable and in abundant supply, there is no reason for one group to try to exploit or stratify the other. There is plenty for all.

If, on the other hand, the desired object or goal is actually or believed to be in scarce supply, then stratification may be seen as functional by each group. The intensity and terms of the competition along with the "relative adaptive capacity" of each group will affect the probability and form of ethnic stratification. Competition is more likely to be highly intense if there are *many valuable, scarce* goals that are shared by both groups, and will be less intense if those shared goals are few in number and relatively unimportant. The more intense the competition, the greater the likelihood of ethnic stratification, other factors being equal. The "terms of the competition" concern the values, rules, and structural opportunities present in the setting. If competition is regulated by agreed-upon rules and some basic humane values are shared by the two groups, then ethnic stratification is far less likely to occur than if the competition is essentially a "free-for-all" and the groups had no values in common. More-

over, if there are few structural outlets in the form of opportunities, then competition is more likely to lead to stratification.

Finally the adaptive capacity of a group relative to its competitor also has an impact on ethnic stratification. Basically, the group that has more cultural and other internal resources to call upon when problems of adaptation and adjustment arise will be more likely to be able to dominate the other group. The chances of stratification occurring are lower when both groups are equal in their adaptive capabilities.

According to Noel, in addition to ethnocentrism and competition, a third variable, "differential power," is also necessary for the emergence of ethnic stratification. "Highly ethnocentric groups involved in competition for vital objects will not generate ethnic stratification unless they are of such unequal power that one is able to impose its will upon the other" (Noel 1968, p. 112 in Yetman). Ethnic stratification simply will not appear in the absence of differential power. Once the greater power of one group is established, the more powerful group initiates measures to subordinate and regulate the other group and to institutionalize the distribution and system of differential rewards.

In sum, Noel is arguing for an interactive model in that all three variables – ethnocentrism, competition with particular characteristics, and differential power – are needed to produce ethnic stratification. In applying this theory to the development of slavery in the early English colonies of the United States, Noel concludes that it adequately explains ethnic stratification. "Given ethnocentrism, the Negroes' lack of power, and the dynamic arena of competition in which they were located, their ultimate enslavement was inevitable" (Noel 1968, p. 117 in Yetman). Earlier in Chapter 4 we saw how these factors also were implicated in the subjugation of the Native American. While Noel's theory does not identify all the specific historical and societal factors that might affect stratification in specific settings, his theory does identify in broad brush strokes three core factors that make it likely.

The next two theories, which also focus on differential power, have a great deal in common. The colonial model of race relations owes a significant amount to the Marxian class framework, and early architects of that model generally acknowledge their debt to Marx (e.g., Fanon 1963; Memmi 1965). In recent years there has been a lot of cross-fertilization of both the colonial and class perspectives with each using concepts from the other. But since the primary impetus that gave rise to each was not the same, they will be presented as if they are distinct approaches. However, their overlap in general orientation will become clear as each is discussed.

Internal Colonialism and Race Inequality This approach to understanding the domination of whites over blacks in the United States is based on discussions and analyses of relationships between colonizing countries in the First World and those who have been colonized in the Third World. In this way, it bears a striking resemblance to world-system and dependency theories which were discussed briefly in Chapter 2. The popularization of the internal-colonial perspective arose during the tumultuous 1960s when the War on Poverty, Civil Rights Movement, and major urban racial confrontations were at their height. Militancy and discussions of "Black power" and "Black Nationalism" made the parallel between the black predicament and that of other oppressed racial groups seem viable. In other words, the times were ripe for a colonial theory of U.S. race relations. Fanon and Memmi, who wrote about colonial relationships in the Third World, had their writings adapted to the U.S. racial setting. Following them, a large number of scholars suggested and elaborated upon what they felt was a basic parallelism between the dynamics in those relationships and those that occur in black/white relations (cf. e.g., Carmichael and Hamilton 1967; Allen 1969; Blauner 1972).

One of the noted differences between classic colonial relationships and the "internal colonial" relationship said to exist between blacks and whites in the United States is that the former generally involves groups from one territory invading and dominating the territory of another group, whereas in the latter case both groups are from and occupy the same country. What can be said in response to this difference is that it is the *character* of the relationship rather than the factor of geography that defines a relationship as colonial (Bonacich 1980; Barrera 1979).

While acknowledging that the analogy is not perfect, Carmichael and Hamilton argue that blacks in the United States "stand as colonial subjects in relation to the white society. . . . That colonial status operates in three areas—political, economic, social" (Carmichael and Hamilton 1967, pp. 5–6). *Politically,* while blacks are technically just as free as whites, whites dominate the power structure of society, holding the most influential positions. Moreover, they exercise "indirect rule" by coopting and controlling selected influential blacks to help maintain the black community in a subordinate position. *Economically,* blacks are more likely to be poor and unemployed and to pay exorbitant prices for shoddy goods. In this manner, the black ghetto is sapped of its resources, which are transferred to the dominant part of society. *Socially,* blacks are looked down upon and demeaned in everyday contacts with whites. Racial ideologies arguing their basic inferiority and presenting negative stereotypes help justify and maintain control over blacks. This interpretation presents all whites as benefiting from the colonial structure rather than only those from a particular class.

Perhaps the most often-cited architect of the colonial model of race relations in the United States is the sociologist Robert Blauner. Blauner argues that assimilationist theories do not accurately explain or describe the conditions of blacks because they draw an analogy between the present situation of blacks and that faced by white ethnic immigrants over half a century ago. He points out that this analogy cannot hold up because the histories and circumstances of their arrival in the United States were qualitatively and highly different. Not only the slavery experience, but the nonvoluntary nature of their ghettos and entrance into the country and the more permanent control of their lives by those outside their communities, distinguishes blacks from earlier white-ethnic immigrant groups. Blacks are not merely the latest batch of immigrants who are waiting to be assimilated and who will be upwardly mobile.

While there are some differences between classic colonialism and internal colonialism, Blauner argues that they share several basic characteristics. First, the political domination and advanced technological level of the West was the basis for both slavery of blacks and the colonization of many countries by Europe. Second, the economic and political superiority of the dominant group encourages a feeling of racial superiority used to justify the exploitation of the other group. In other words, since both types of colonialism have similar roots, Blauner says that they share "a common process of social oppression" (Blauner 1972, p. 84).

He suggests that there are five basic characteristics in the "colonization complex":

1. The dominant-subordinate relationship begins with "forced, involuntary entry"; that is, blacks were brought here as slaves and ghettoes are controlled from the outside by the dominant group. White settlers also, of course, forceably took over Native American lands.

2. The indigenous culture and social organization of the dominated group is altered, manipulated or destroyed; that is, black culture and institutions are undermined. Native American culture also has been subjugated.

3. Representatives of the dominant group control the subordinate group through their legal and government institutions; that is, white institutions control much of the lives of blacks. The placement of Native Americans on reservations also serves as an example of control by the dominant group.

4. Racism as an ideology is used to justify the oppression of the subordinated group; that is, blacks and other racially or ethnically distinguishable groups are seen as biologically or otherwise inferior to whites.

5. The colonizers and colonized occupy different positions in the labor structure and perform different roles; that is, blacks are relegated by and large to menial, nonprestigious jobs while whites dominate in higher ranking positions. The dual-labor market characterizes the occupational positions of dominant and subordinate groups.

The listed characteristics suggest that the black ghetto, instead of being isolated from the rest of society in some kind of autonomous "culture of poverty," is in fact tied to white society by bonds of exploitation and dependency. The educational, political, economic, and legal institutions of the dominant society infiltrate and permeate the dominated colony. Then racism is used to maintain and justify the lower status of blacks.

In addition to these structural characteristics, there are also cultural and psychological ramifications to the colonial relationship. In the colony, individuals cannot break through the racial-ethnic barrier. "Theoretically at least, a worker can leave his class and change his status, but within the framework of colonization, nothing can ever save the colonized" (Memmi 1965, pp. 73–74). Colonized individuals can move up in class but cannot change their position of being colonized except through successful revolutionary movements that transform the structure of society. They may try to gain entrance into the larger society but "everything is mobilized so that the colonized cannot cross the doorstep, so that [they understand and admit] that this path is dead and assimilation is impossible" (ibid., p. 125).

In attempting to assimilate, colonized persons may initially admire aspects of their oppressors, but when it is realized that full structural assimilation is not possible, they begin to reassert themselves in part through resurrecting old traditions and through the advocacy of violence. "Those who understand their fate become impatient and no longer tolerate colonization" (ibid., p. 120).

Most of these stages appear to apply to

blacks and their movements in the United States, although some of the protest behaviors of blacks could be interpreted in ways other than through the colonial model (Omi and Winant 1986). Among the strengths of this model are its historical and comparative dimensions and the fact that it can account for a relatively large number of factors within a fairly straightforward theoretical framework (Barrera 1979). Among the weaknesses of the internal colonial model is one that Blauner recognized himself:

> When the colonial model is transferred from the overseas situation to the United States without substantial alteration, it tends to miss the total structure, the context of advanced industrial capitalism in which our racial arrangements are embedded—a context that produces group politics and social movements that differ markedly from the traditional colonial society. . . . It lacks a conception of American society as a total structure beyond the central significance that I attribute to racism. (1972, p. 13)

To effectively deal with this shortcoming, Blauner suggests that an adequate theory must incorporate elements dealing with characteristics of both colonialism and capitalism. Indeed, several of the attempts to develop a class-based theory of race inequality include references to both of these (e.g., Bonacich 1980; Hunter and Abraham 1987). Omi and Winant (1986) also point out that the internal colonial model does not take into account class differences within the colonized (black) group or relationships between minority groups. Despite these difficulties, the colonial model probably provides a more accurate analysis of black/white relations in the United States than either the assimilationist or caste perspective (Wilson 1970; Barrera 1979).

Class-Based Explanations of Race Inequality

Wilson has argued that economic and class dynamics are becoming more important for determining the life chances of blacks. We discussed his argument in Chapter 4 and there is no need to repeat it here. But well before Wilson developed his theory, others also argued that economic fac-

tors lie behind the inequality between blacks and whites in the United States. One of the most sophisticated class-based theories of race relations in the United States was developed by Oliver C. Cox in the late 1940s. Cox was very critical of the caste model presented earlier, arguing that the structural, cultural, and historical conditions in India were radically different from those characterizing U.S. black/white relations. For example, he contended that a caste structure is ancient, "nonconflictive," static, "nonpathological," status oriented, and contains caste-fixed occupations. In contrast, he said, race relations and racism are relatively recent, conflictive, and pathological, do not usually involve narrow occupational restrictions, and are rooted in political-class conflict and capitalism (1942, 1945, 1948).

Cox views race relations and inequality in the United States as a product of economic exploitation. Forcefully bringing slaves to the United States was essentially a way of getting labor to exploit the natural resources of the country. Racial exploitation is only one form of the proletarianization of labor according to Cox. Racism as an ideology was not the root of exploitation; rather it followed from it and was used to justify economic exploitation of blacks. Racism, therefore, is a relatively recent phenomenon. Given its character and economic basis, "racial antagonism is essentially political-class conflict." Racial antagonism is used by employers to divide black and white workers, and racial ghettos are maintained because they facilitate control over blacks and perpetuate a self-defeating lifestyle. Blacks may want to assimilate but it is not in the interests of dominant whites for them to do so (1948, 1976).

What is attractive about Cox's arguments is that he intermingles elements of racism, colonialism, class inequality, and capitalism in a comparative framework. Racial inequality is bound up with the development and expansion of European empires and the rise of capitalism and its labor needs. Much of Cox's later writing anticipates many of the ideas associated with world-system and dependency theory. Cox traces the development of Venetian commerce and trade as an early major center of capitalism. Trade is the lifeblood of international capitalism. The need to control potential markets and sources of raw materials strengthens the tendency of capitalism to colonize and exercise political control in the world economic system. Loans, raw materials, markets for manufactured goods, and imperialism each play a part in creating and fastening ties (chains) between dominant and subordinate nations in the worldwide capitalist system. Race prejudice is then used to justify imperialism. But the system itself has helped to galvanize "backward" peoples in opposition to the system, even though the working classes in advanced capitalist nations are rather conservative and frequently stand in opposition to people in backward countries (1959, 1964).

One of the thorny areas of disagreement among class-based theorists of race relations concerns who benefits from racism and the nature of the relationship between blacks and the white working class. From one point of view, racism is used by employers to drive a wedge between whites and blacks in the working class, and nationalism is used to divide members of the working class from different ethnic/racial groups in different countries. White workers come to view foreign workers who labor for low wages as unfair competitors, and their racism, which is ultimately rooted in the worldwide development of capitalism, is an attempt to protect their own jobs (Bonacich 1980). But while white or dominant workers may benefit from this racism in the short run, in the long run the inequality within the working class creates divisions that weaken its collective power against employers. Employers exploit members of the minority for greater profits and money with which to pay the dominant working class. Accordingly, the principal beneficiaries of racism are employers rather than all whites (Szymanski 1976; Reich 1977).

In general, having an ethnic/racial working class provides capitalism with a surplus army from which to draw poorly paid workers to perform jobs that are necessary but that no one in the dominant group wants to perform. But as the capitalist economy advances and the revolutionary potential of minority groups grows, many large employers begin to feel that the long-run costs of race inequality may be too high and that it should be eliminated (Baran and Sweezy 1966). One obvious cost of racism to employers is the loss of bright minority members to employers who could use them to increase productivity.

Edna Bonacich (1980) attempts to integrate and synthesize many of the arguments in class-based theories of race inequality. She begins by commenting on the motivations for imperialism abroad. One important source for this movement is the desire to find more malleable and cheaper labor since the cost of labor rises as capitalism develops within a country. Wages rise because (1) the absorption of the entire labor supply into the expanding economy creates increased demand for it; (2) workers have a need for higher wages to purchase the increasing number of commodities produced in the economy; (3) large factories create social conditions conducive to the political organization and greater union power among workers; and (4) increased state support of workers "cushions" them and enables them to hold out for higher wages (see also Piven and Cloward 1982).

Because of these pressures for higher wages by domestic workers, then, employers look outside national boundaries for new sources of cheap labor. Wages are lower in "less developed" countries because of the existence of additional sources of subsistence (production for use) and a traditionally lower standard of living. Members of the domestic working class then see themselves as competing with cheap laborers in Third World countries, and may (1) react with nationalist and racist fervor against such groups or (2) may see both themselves and other working-class groups from around the world as victims of capitalist development. Which of the two reactions is pursued by the domestic working class depends in part upon the extent to which capitalists can control the colonized working class and manipulate the domestic working class, on how imminent the experience of competition with outside cheap labor is in the domestic working class, and on how proletarianized this class is itself (Bonacich 1980).

In terms of their relationship with upper class elements in the host country, outside capitalists can try to use the native elite classes in the colonized countries for their own benefit as a sort of intermediary between themselves and the local labor force. This causes some of these elite to benefit in the short run from this arrangement while others lose by foreign capital's intervention into their country. Those who receive short-run gains will encourage native workers to work for outsiders for nationalist reasons, while those who are themselves immediately exploited will attempt to eliminate foreign intrusion into the home economy and press for the development of their own national industries.

The essential theme of Bonacich's argument is placing class and race dynamics in an international context and tracing racism and race inequality to the expansion of capitalism. Basically, the logic of this international adaptation is similar to the class-based theory applied at the national level. *That is, material economic interests lead, under particular conditions, to the development of structured inequality between racial groups, which in turn leads to the formation of racial ideologies to justify and perpetuate inequality and to divide elements within the working class.* The value of Bonacich's synthesis of class-based theories is that it attempts to illuminate the complexity of the relationships among various class groups and the bases for those relationships and incorporates elements from both the colonial/imperialist and class approaches.

It should be obvious by now that there are several similarities between the Marxian/class and colony theories of race inequality. First, both have as central themes the notion of the exploitation (especially economic) of a lower group, blacks, and/or the working class. Both perspectives view top and bottom positions in relational terms, that is, consider the position of one group to be inextricably linked to that of the other group. Second, in both models justifications (ide-

ologies) are crucial for legitimating the power relationships that exist. But in both the relationship is both "destructive and creative" (Memmi 1965). Third, both perspectives emphasize the polarization of society and the importance of rising consciousness among the exploited. In general theoretical terms, these basic congruences between internal colonial and class theories outweigh their differences (Wilson 1970; Tabb 1970; Blauner 1972; Barrera 1979).

SUMMARY

This chapter has surveyed a variety of sociological and anthropological explanations of sex and race inequality. In the case of sex inequality, the role of women in the division of labor is focused upon as a crucial element fostering and perpetuating inequality between the sexes. In various ways, the differences in the reproductive capacities of men and women, their respective associations with "culture" and "nature," the role of women in reproduction, and their relegation to the private familial sphere are mentioned by several scholars as being linked to inequality. At the same time, the lower status of women in the division of labor has been linked to the needs of capitalism and the rules of patriarchy. The favorableness of the political and natural environment also has been suggested as a root cause of sex inequality.

In the case of race inequality, a variety of theories also have been developed ranging from the caste model to more radical internal-colonial and class explanations. In general, the latter are more sophisticated and focus on the centrality of differential power and economic domination in accounting for race inequality. As is the case with some sex inequality theories, several of these theories are couched in a comparative framework, which lends them some depth. Several of the race and sex theories, especially more recent ones, combine an analysis of economic processes with sexism/racism to provide an explanation of subgroup inequality. Two examples of such theories are the capitalist-patriarchy explanation of sex inequality and the colonial model of race inequality. Both suggest the need for a theory that incorporates an understanding of the economic and political context in which races and sexes meet.

The last three chapters have analyzed attempts to explain different forms of inequality. The theories covered in these chapters contain some broad similarities. Most generally, one can see the influence of Marxian thought in several of them, such as social reproduction theory, radical labor-market theory, Vogel's theory of sex inequality, and the class-based theories of race inequality. On the more conservative side, the functionalist tradition has been carried through most fully in neoclassical economic and human-capital theories of inequality, and to some degree in the adaptive emphases of ecological theories. Several others reflect more than one theoretical tradition. These include Lenski's synthesis, capitalist-patriarchy, and internal colonialism. Each is heavily imbued with Marxian or radical elements while borrowing elements from other traditions as well.

The next chapter begins a discussion of what is happening to inequality in the United States, specifically its openness and changes in positions for members of groups. Following that is a discussion of reactions toward the system of inequality, its justice, and its fairness. The final three chapters concern the different means by which people have attempted to change the system of inequality.

CHAPTER 11

TRENDS IN MOBILITY AND STATUS ATTAINMENT: OPENNESS IN U.S. SOCIETY

We found scant evidence that the system of occupational inheritance is growing more rigid.
—Elton G. Jackson and Harry J. Crockett, Jr.

There is no indication of increasing rigidity in the class structure.
—Peter M. Blau and Otis Dudley Duncan

The strata are becoming more rigid; the holes in the sieve are becoming smaller. Status is crystallizing.
—J. O. Hertzler

Children in U.S. society often are told that if they work hard enough and want something badly enough, they will obtain it. The achievement of desired goals depends on the effort individuals are willing to put out. The opportunities are there to be grasped if a person has the aspirations and perseverance required to take advantage of them. The United States as a storied land of opportunity and freedom is chronicled in many myths and fables about how the individual, no matter how humble and lowly, can succeed. The Horatio Alger stories are but one example.

The United States as a country in which rapid change is occurring is believed by many to provide a variety of opportunities for individuals to advance themselves socially and economically. Always dynamic, always changing, individuals in this portrait are seen as constantly moving up and down and across occupational categories. The traditional belief has been that it is a very fluid society in which individuals frequently rise and fall on hierarchies of inequality.

U.S. society is one in which achievement is believed to take precedence over ascription. Mobility is seen as resulting from a "contest" with others rather than from "sponsorship" by the powerful. The importance that has been placed on education not only by the public but often by social scientists in their theories of achievement suggests the significance that is attributed to individual effort in the attainment of socioeconomic rewards.

In light of these values concerning the individual and achievement, it is not surprising that a central question raised in the study of inequality has concerned the extent to which the United States has been and continues to be an open society. One important aspect to examine in any system of inequality is its characteristic patterns of mobility.

QUESTIONS CONCERNING OPENNESS

Any conclusions about the openness of a society depend on how the question is posed. Openness has meant different things to different researchers, and the concern for openness has been expressed and studied in a variety of ways. Consequently, it is possible to approach the issue of openness with several different and specific questions:

1. In terms of sheer amount, how much mobility has there been and is there now in the United States? How does the United States compare with other countries on mobility?

2. What is the nature of the mobility that has occurred? Is it more often long-distance or short-range mobility?

3. Has the mobility that has occurred been more characteristic of some part of the inequality hierarchy than others? Are there some parts in which little mobility takes place?

4. What have been the trends in intergenerational inheritance? Are individuals more or less likely to have the same occupations as their parents?

5. What has been the pattern of mobility as it pertains to the recruitment and dispersion of individuals into particular occupational strata? When individuals in a given stratum do move, into which strata are they most and least likely to move?

6. What role does socioeconomic background play in determining an individual's present status and has this role changed significantly over time?

Each of these questions poses a separate issue, but all of them are relevant to the general question of how open U.S. society is, and each of them has been addressed in research. The first five questions have been the concern of traditional mobility studies, while the last one has been a main focus of status-attainment research. We will review both of these areas in later sections, but first we need to clarify some basic definitions and methods in the study of mobility.

STUDY OF MOBILITY

Definition of Terms

Pitirim Sorokin (1959) was the first to systematically discuss a number of the central concepts associated with the study of mobility. The distinctions and conceptualizations he made half a century ago are still used in social science in large part because they refer to such basic aspects of mobility. Sorokin distinguished between "horizontal" and "vertical" mobility. *Horizontal mobility* refers to movement into another role or place that does not involve a change in an individual's position in the system of inequality. For example, an individual might change from one occupation to another, even though they yield essentially the same incomes, status, and authority. But our concern here is with vertical rather than horizontal mobility. *Vertical mobility* refers to "any change in the occupational, economic or political status of individuals which leads to a change in their social position" (Sorokin 1959, p. 414). Of course, that change can be up or down; we can have "social climbing" as well as "social sinking." Thus, vertical mobility can be *upward* or *downward*. Most sociologists have focused on the extent of upward rather than downward mobility in the United States, even though some feel the latter is a better indicator of the openness of a society.

A study of mobility also can focus either on the movement of *groups* or *individuals*. Whole categories of individuals can and have sometimes changed positions, or *new* groups of positions, e.g., occupations may come into existence causing a shift in the positions of other groups. Most often, however, studies of mobility have concentrated on the individual and his or her movement up or down an occupational hierarchy. Occupation is seen as the core variable in the system of inequality.

Sorokin also pointed out that mobility can vary in what he called its *intensiveness*. This refers to the amount of vertical distance traversed in the mobility that occurs. Another way of putting this is to say that social mobility can be short or long range, that is, can take place over small as well as large distances. The *generality* of mobility, in Sorokin's terms, concerns the number of persons who are involved in the mobility. For example, it has been suggested that only a limited number of blacks have moved up in recent decades, with many being left behind as an underclass. A final distinction is made between *intra*generational and *inter*generational mobility. The former refers to movement that occurs to individuals during their own careers and thus deals with the effects of their own efforts and experiences since the time of their first social position. Intergenerational mobility, on the other hand, deals with changes in social position that have occurred between generations, usually comparing the father's position with that of the son in some way. Consequently, the study of intergenerational mobility directly addresses the issue of inheritance of position.

Open societies generally have been considered to be those in which a maximum amount of mobility takes place and, more crucially, those in which individuals in different strata can move without being encumbered or aided by the status of their parents. In other words, the most open societies are thought to be those in which there is no relationship between the status of the parents and that of the offspring. Independence exists between these two statuses in the sense that individuals from any socioeconomic background can move into any other positions depending solely on their achievements (Goldhamer 1968). *Closed societies,* of course, are of the opposite kind. Little mobility occurs and position in the system of inequality is entirely dependent on the position in which an individual was born. The caste system of India approaches a closed system of inequality.

Issues and Tools

Understanding the nature of mobility is hindered by difficulties in the methodologies used in mobility studies. First, different studies often use different measures of occupational status. Some use occupational-status scores that measure prestige or socioeconomic rankings of occupations along a continuum, whereas others use discrete categories of varying numbers. Second, the quality and method of sampling is not always comparable between studies. This can lead not only to misjudgments about trends in mobility but to mistaken conclusions about the distribution of occupations at a given time. Finally, in drawing conclusions about social mobility, we should keep in mind that in all studies, we are talking about mobility of a very specific kind, namely, mobility in occupational status.

Miller (1956) has observed, like others, that mobility has a multidimensional character; that is, there are a number of hierarchies in which an individual can potentially move up or down. Wilensky (1966) consequently suggests what he calls a "consolation prize" theory of mobility in which individuals who fail to move up in one hierarchy have available to them other hierarchies in which they can try to move. Of course, a person's potential for movement on one hierarchy is very likely to be dependent on his or her position on another. For example, movement up an income or power hierarchy is very probably dependent on a person's position on an occupational hierarchy.

Most of those who have studied mobility have concluded that the occupational hierarchy is the central one in industrial societies. Blau and Duncan (1967), for example, contend that an adequate understanding of the occupational structure of an industrial society is needed because (1) it is the basis for most other central aspects of social stratification, such as prestige, economic power, and political power and (2) it "serves as the connecting link between different institutions and spheres of social life" because the occupational structure impinges on so many types of relationships (pp. 6–7).

Despite the general acceptance of the centrality of occupation in modern society, we still must address the question of what it is about occupation that makes it important in the study of inequality and mobility. Some have found it rather curious that studies since the early 1960s have not focused on mobility in income, which is the core reward in industrial society (Crowder 1974).

Understanding Mobility Tables The standard tool used to detect the extent and nature of mobility between two generations is the mobility table (sometimes called a "transition matrix"). These tables show how the percentages of sons from given occupational origins distribute themselves in the occupational structure. Thus, in a table where all the data are available, the rows add up to 100 percent. These "outflow" tables show the

pattern of movement of the sons out from the origin position of their fathers. Table 11.1, based on 1962 and 1973 national data, is a good example. This table shows, for example, that in 1962 about 54 percent of sons whose fathers were in upper-white-collar occupations were in similar kinds of occupations. This suggests quite a bit of occupational inheritance. Under conditions of perfect inheritance, the occupational distribution among the sons would be identical to that among the fathers. Table 11.2 is an example of a situation in which inheritance is at its maximum.

Figure 11.1 shows where to look on a mobil-

TABLE 11.1 Mobility from Father's (or Other Family Head's) Occupation to Current Occupation: U.S. Men in the Experienced Civilian Labor Force Aged Twenty to Sixty-four in 1962 and 1973*

Year and Father's Occupation	SON'S CURRENT OCCUPATION						Father's Percentage Totals
	Upper White Collar (%)	Lower White Collar (%)	Upper Manual (%)	Lower Manual (%)	Farm (%)	Total (%)	
1962							
Upper white-collar	53.8	17.6	12.5	14.8	1.3	100.0	16.5
Lower white-collar	45.6	20.0	14.4	18.3	1.7	100.0	7.6
Upper manual	28.1	13.4	27.8	29.5	1.2	100.0	19.0
Lower manual	20.3	12.3	21.6	43.8	2.0	100.0	27.5
Farm	15.6	7.0	19.2	36.1	22.2	100.0	29.4
Son's percentage totals	27.8	12.4	20.0	32.1	7.7	100.0	100.0
1973							
Upper white-collar	52.0	16.0	13.8	17.1	1.1	100.0	18.2
Lower white-collar	42.3	19.7	15.3	21.9	0.8	100.0	9.0
Upper manual	29.4	13.0	27.4	29.0	1.1	100.0	20.5
Lower manual	22.5	12.0	23.7	40.8	1.0	100.0	29.7
Farm	17.5	7.8	22.7	37.2	14.8	100.0	22.6
Son's percentage totals	29.9	12.7	21.7	31.5	4.1	100.0	100.0

Source: Adapted from David L. Featherman, "Has Opportunity Declined in America?" Institute for Research on Poverty Discussion Paper No. 437-77, University of Wisconsin-Madison, Table 2. The basic source of information about this study is from David Featherman and Robert Hauser, *Opportunity and Change* (New York: Academic Press), 1978.

*Data are from March 1962 and March 1973 Current Population Surveys and Occupational Changes in a Generation Surveys. Occupation groups are upper white-collar: professional and kindred workers and managers, officials and proprietors, except farm; lower white-collar: sales, clerical, and kindred workers; upper manual: craftsmen, foremen, and kindred workers; lower manual: operatives and kindred workers, service workers, and laborers, except farm; farm: farmers and farm managers, farm laborers, and foremen.

TABLE 11.2   Example of Maximum-Inheritance Model

FATHER'S OCCUPATIONAL STATUS	SON'S OCCUPATIONAL STATUS			
	HIGH	MEDIUM	LOW	TOTAL *N*
High	100%	0	0	20
Medium	0	100%	0	120
Low	0	0	100%	60
Total *N*	20	120	60	

Summary of mobility measures: total; mobility = 0; structural = 0; circulation = 0.

ity table for the extent of inheritance and the nature and amount of upward and downward mobility. If one were interested in the amount of mobility into different positions independent of the influence of the father's occupational status on the sons, one might want to compute the *mobility ratio* (also called the "index of association"). If statuses of origin (fathers) have no influence on statuses of destination (sons), one would expect to find that the proportion of sons from a given origin status who wind up in that status is exactly equal to the proportion of men who are in that status in the labor force. For example, if professionals made up 30 percent of the labor force, under conditions of no relationship between status of origin and status of destination, one would expect to find that only 30 percent of the sons of professionals are in that occupational category. The mobility ratio, then, is computed by dividing the percentage of sons of fathers in a given occupational category who are in the same category by the percentage of the labor force that is in that category. Thus, in this example, when everything is proportional, the mobility ratio would be 1.0 (that is, 30/30 = 1.0). Generally, the mobility ratios tend to be above 1.0 along the diagonals in the mobility table, which means that sons are more likely to be in positions identical or similar to their fathers than in any others.

Despite its widespread use, there have been some problems with the mobility ratio as it has been used in the study of mobility trends. The most significant and important has been the assumption that the occupational distributions found in the studies for the father's generation are in fact a replica or at least a very good proxy for the actual occupational distribution that existed during the father's generation. This, unfortu-

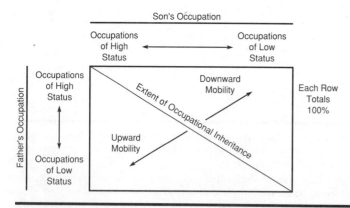

FIGURE 11.1   Where to Look in Reading a Standard Outflow Mobility Table

nately, is not necessarily the case (Duncan 1966; Ramsøy 1966).

As Ramsøy pointedly indicates, "the occupational distribution of the fathers of members of the current generation is indisputably a poor indicator of the true occupational distribution a generation earlier" (1966, p. 215). This is so for several reasons:

1. Some of the fathers who worked in the earlier generation did not produce sons who are currently in the labor force. Only if a father did produce a son would he appear in the sample. Consequently, the chances of a given group of fathers being represented is directly related to their fertility rates. One of the central criticisms Duncan (1966) makes of Kahl's (1957) attempt to assess mobility trends is that he assumes "that all men in the labor force in 1920 have been replaced by their sons by 1950" (p. 56). Obviously, this is a questionable assumption.

2. Some of the fathers who participated in an earlier labor force continued to participate in the present one. That is, since the fathers of sons being studied vary in age, it is very likely that while some participated in only the earlier labor force, others have been in both. Moreover, some fathers may not have entered the labor force at the earlier date.

3. Some of the sons now participating in the labor force may have had fathers who were immigrants and did not participate in the labor force at the earlier date being studied. Duncan puts the whole matter succinctly: "The transformations that occur via a *succession of cohorts* cannot, for basic demographic reasons, be equated to the product of a *procession of generations*" (ibid., p. 59); emphases in original).

Duncan suggests that "instead of thinking of the classification of father's occupation as conveying information about a 'generation' of 'fathers,' think of it as describing the origin statuses of the sons" (ibid., p. 62). Thus, one can still use mobility tables for different periods to discover something about trends in the mobility between fathers and sons and in changes in the extent of inheritance over time. Blau and Duncan (1967) believe that "a direct comparison of . . . outflow tables . . . may well be the best strategy for measuring trends in mobility, though perhaps not for investigating hypotheses about their causes" (p. 97).

COMPARATIVE STUDIES OF MOBILITY

Having discussed some of the basic issues involved in studying mobility, we turn to an analysis of some of the studies that have been conducted. During the late 1950s, concerted attempts were made to compare social mobility rates among western industrialized countries. Unfortunately, most of the analyses were done using extremely general occupational categories of nonmanual, manual, and farm. In different countries, specific occupations are not always classified into the same general category, and this creates problems of comparability between studies (Matras 1980; Goldthorpe 1985).

Most notable among the analyses was one made by Lipset and Zetterberg (1959). A total of nine countries were analyzed, including the United States. On the basis of their research, Lipset and Zetterberg (1959) concluded that (1) the rates of observed mobility in industrialized societies were quite similar; (2) the United States is not higher in upward mobility from manual occupations than all other industrialized nations; and (3) mobility into the elite from manual categories was higher in the United States than in the other nations studied.

This study gave rise to increased interest in the apparent relationship between industrialization/development and mobility rates. Several explanatory versions of this relationship have appeared (Goldthorpe 1985). Essentially, Lipset and Zetterberg (1959) suggested that general social mobility will become increasingly similar in industrial countries because of shifts in the occupational structure. "The overall pattern of social mobility appears to be much the same in industrial societies of various Western countries" (p.

13). Specifically, rises in the proportion of urban occupations coupled with the decline of agricultural work, and the growth of service industries, white-collar occupations, and bureaucracy all provide impetus for greater social mobility. The argument is that industrialization "tends to standardize social structures through the operation of common occupational imperatives" (Archer and Giner 1971, p. 2). This renders as irrelevant to mobility the role of other factors that may be unique to a given industrial country. According to this argument, industrialism has an "inner logic" that, when introduced into countries, overshadows the cultural and social characteristics that distinguish them from other industrial nations. In this sense, industrialism is believed to have a leveling effect. Earlier, we came across another component of this general perspective in the discussion of the "postindustrial" view of society.

Others also have argued that there will be greater mobility with industrialization and development, not because of "occupational imperatives," but primarily because of shifts from more traditional values and orientations to more modern outlooks. In this second interpretation, the belief is that position will be based more on achieved than ascribed characteristics; that is, fewer barriers will prevent talented individuals from moving up. This is an evolutionary/functionalist view that sees development as being associated with greater cosmopolitanism and openness. The expectation is that specific cultural elements will accompany industrialism, such as the greater significance of relevant qualifications over social background in obtaining occupational positions. A third version of the relationship between mobility and development interprets circulation or exchange mobility as being a necessary factor in the development process. If economic development is going to occur, a certain amount of fluidity is needed to distribute talent in the most effective manner (Goldthorpe 1985).

The argument that there is a clear, systematic, and positive relationship between the level of development or industrialization and social mobility, however, has been severely criticized by the British sociologist John Goldthorpe (1964, 1985). According to him, the thesis proposes that industrialism (1) reshapes the occupational structure in such a way as to produce a large middle class; (2) crystallizes positions across various status hierarchies (prestige, lifestyle, etc.) so that they become more consistent with status rankings in the occupational structure; and (3) creates greater mobility or openness in the society. With respect to the first point, the belief is that the political system also becomes more democratic, since a monolithic power structure is thought to be incompatible with industrialism. On the second point, it is believed that high-ranking occupational categories will be associated with high income, prestige, and a particular lifestyle. The third point is self-explanatory.

Goldthorpe takes issue with each of these three points. First, he argues that there is nothing inherent in industrialism to ensure greater equality, and whatever trend toward equality did exist may have been stalled in recent decades. He cites Kolko's 1962 data to indicate that there has been no long-term trend toward income equality in the United States. Second, he argues that there is not a tendency toward greater crystallization of statuses. For example, blue-collar individuals frequently have higher earnings than those in lower white-collar positions. Finally, he suspects that in some ways industrial societies may be less rather than more open than in the past. He suggests that as education becomes a more important basis for attainment of high position, those who are less likely to get it, that is, those in the lower class, will have less chance to move up in occupational status.

Many recent studies also do not support the "industrialism thesis." Comparative studies suggest that *overall* observed mobility rates in western industrial nations are not that similar (Miller 1975; Featherman et al. 1975; Grusky and Hauser 1984; Kurz and Muller 1987). The idea that mobility increases with development in a continuous manner has not been supported by recent research (e.g., Erikson, et al. 1983; Hazelrigg and Garnier 1976). Nor is the *pattern* of mobility the same in all industrial countries (Jones 1969; Blau and Duncan 1967). It also is apparent that the process of industrialization does not follow the same course in all countries. Thus, historical and political conditions help shape the occupational structure and mobility within the country (Hauser and Grusky 1988). Finally, it also has been proposed that any relationship that might be found between industrialization and mobility is due to the shape of the system of inequality in a country, specifically the degree of income inequality. The greater the income inequality, the greater effect an individual's social origins have on his or her occupational destination. In other words, greater equality is linked to greater mobility (Tyree et al. 1979).

In altering the industrialism hypothesis and trying to account for the differences in observed mobility between industrial nations, Featherman and his colleagues (1975) have suggested that (1) while western industrial societies may have similar amounts of *openness* ("social fluidity," "circulation mobility"), (2) they differ in their occupational structures through time, and thus the observed differences in mobility rates between countries are due primarily to historical and cultural variations in the occupational structure. This underscores the importance of the distinction between "structural" and "circulation" mobility. The former is generally thought of as mobility that results purely from changes in the occupational structure, while the latter is ordinarily interpreted as the mobility that results from other sources and is an index of the openness or "fluidity" of the society. This has been a crucial distinction in studies of mobility since the 1950s, but there is some argument whether it is possible, methodologically, to sustain such a distinction (Sobel 1983). Indeed, the usage of a variety of terms among social scientists from various countries to describe "circulation" mobility has not helped consistency or communication among them.

Research generally supports the conclusion that circulation mobility has been quite consistent and constant in most industrial countries. For ex-

ample, not much difference in openness or mobility has been found between Canada and the United States. There appears to be no major discernible trend in mobility at all in these countries (McRoberts and Selbee 1981). Research on Great Britain and the United States has not revealed any significant differences in openness or downward mobility between the countries, even given the suggested differences in values of the two societies (Kerckhoff et al. 1985). The comparative stability in the amount of openness or circulation in western capitalist societies has been attributed to its class structure. "For systems of class stratification, as ones essentially of differential advantage and power, must be regarded as possessing important self-maintaining properties. The general expectations would therefore be for continuing stability in relative rates [i.e., openness]" (Erikson et al. 1983, p. 339).

A number of studies also have found support for the conclusion that occupational-structure changes/composition are largely responsible for variations in mobility between countries (Grusky and Hauser 1984; Kerckhoff et al. 1985; Hope 1982; Erikson et al. 1983; Simkus 1981). Kerckhoff et al. (1985), for example, found that the differences in mobility between Great Britain and the United States are due to historical differences in the occupational structures and career paths taken by men in each society. Specifically, the decline in farming and the rise in professional occupations have been more accentuated in the United States than in Britain, and the routes taken by Britons and Americans while pursuing their careers are different. Americans are more likely to begin their careers in professional occupations, while Britons, in part because of the availability of apprenticeships, are more likely to have crafts positions as their first jobs.

One of the principal changes in the U.S. occupational structure has been the decline in the number of those in agricultural occupations. This change in the *composition* of the occupational structure has increased mobility in the United States since the farming occupations have been among those most likely to be passed on through generations (Kurz and Muller 1987). On the other hand, other changes in the occupational structure may slow mobility. Goldthorpe (1985) suggests that the trend in advanced industrial societies toward more high-status service occupations may increase inheritance and the stability of the class structure since most mobility takes place in the middle of the class structure rather than at its extremes.

U.S. MOBILITY OVER TIME

The extent and future of mobility in the United States have been the subject of many debates extending back decades. Serious mobility research began in the 1940s, and even then there was concern about what the future held. Changes in mobility studies since the 1940s have been driven by changes in the data bases used and increases in the sophistication of techniques for analyzing them.

Estimate of Mobility Trends from World War II to the 1960s

One of the first attempts to arrive at some conclusions regarding post-World War II mobility trends using national sample data was carried out by Jackson and Crockett (1964). The authors compared data for intergenerational mobility between father and son collected in 1957 by the Survey Research Center at the University of Michigan with national data collected in 1945, 1947, and 1952 to determine trends in mobility from 1945 to 1957. The authors noted that none of the earlier surveys had been originally carried out with the specific purpose of examining mobility. Moreover, the sampling designs in these four surveys were different from each other. However, the small variations that occurred in the kinds of occupational questions put to respondents in each of the surveys do not, in the opinion of Jackson and Crockett, seriously jeopardize their comparability.

The results suggest that greater mobility occurred in 1952 and 1957 than in 1947. Some amount of mobility would have occurred simply because of changes in the occupational structure between generations. In other words, between any two periods of time some mobility is bound to occur if the occupational distributions in the two generations in question are different. The difference between that minimum amount of *expected* mobility and what *actually* occurs is often referred to as the amount of "circulation" mobility. As noted earlier, most consider this to be a better measure of the openness of a system of inequality than the total amount of mobility because it allegedly already has taken into account changes that have occurred because of alterations in the occupational structure. A greater proportion of the total mobility in 1947 appears to have been due to "circulation" than to "structural" conditions, whereas in 1952 and 1957, the reverse is the case.

From their data, what general conclusions can we draw from the Jackson and Crockett analysis? Several are suggested. First, in 1957, only a moderate amount of discrepancy from the full-equality model existed. "Full equality" in this context means that the occupational statuses of the fathers and sons are unrelated. Second, comparison with studies going back to 1945 suggests that no major changes occurred in the rates and patterns of mobility since that time, though some increase in mobility occurred. What change has occurred appears to be in the direction of the full-equality model. The authors concluded by stating that their analysis yields "scant evidence that the system of occupational inheritance is growing more rigid" (Jackson and Crockett 1964, p. 15).

Blau and Duncan (1967) added 1962 data to those used by Jackson and Crockett. Their data suggest that circulation has increased since 1957 and that the son's occupation is less dependent on that of the father (p. 104). In other words, the system of inequality as measured by the amount of circulation appears to have been more open in 1962 than in the earlier years.

Some of the principal findings from the national study on intergenerational mobility by Blau and Duncan (1967) revealed some clear patterns:

1. Despite a good deal of mobility, especially of the short-range variety, occupational inheritance was higher than would be expected if no relationship existed between the father's status and the son's 1962 occupational status.

2. Upward mobility was much more prevalent than downward mobility, most of it being structurally induced.

3. The occupational categories that contained the greatest proportions of occupational inheritance and self-recruitment were those involving self-employment: independent professionals, proprietors, and farmers. The authors suggest that being an owner made it hard for the son to leave the occupation (inheritance) and also made it less likely that sons from other origins would enter that occupation (self-recruitment).

4. The highest rates of *inflow into* an occupational category from other categories occurred among the lower white-collar and lower blue-collar occupations. That is, they recruited individuals from a wide variety of occupational backgrounds.

5. The highest rates of *outflow from* an occupational category occurred among the two lowest white-collar, blue-collar, and farm groupings. That is, a greater proportion of these sons went to other occupations, suggesting that they had greater chances for mobility. In the salaried professions, on the other hand, just the opposite situation occurred. The sons were much less likely to outflow to other occupations, suggesting a high degree of inheritance.

6. An increasing proportion of men with non-farm/manual *origins* moved up into the white-collar occupations. But men who started *their own careers* in a blue-collar occupation were less likely to be mobile than those who began their careers as white-collar workers or farmers (pp. 28–41).

Current Mobility Patterns in the United States

Mobility in the United States, as in most industrial countries, tends to be greatest in the middle of the occupational hierarchy and limited at the extremes (Featherman and Hauser 1978; Grusky and Hauser 1984). The top and bottom of the occupational structure are fairly closed, suggesting "barriers to movement across class boundaries" (Featherman and Hauser 1978, p. 180). In contrast, mobility in the middle is more extensive. Men in upper blue-collar occupations are as likely to have come from or be on their way to any lower or higher occupation as their present occupation. "There is no evidence of 'class' boundaries limiting the chances of movement to or from the skilled manual occupations" (ibid., p. 180).

Featherman and Hauser's (1978) replication of Blau and Duncan's national study of American men reached a variety of conclusions about the openness and mobility in the U.S. occupational structure in the 1970s:

1. There was a great deal of movement both within and between generations. Well over half of sons moved out of the occupational strata of their fathers and out of the strata of their own first jobs.

2. Rates of mobility were "far larger" than would be suggested by transformation of the occupational structure alone. There was an increase in mobility from son's first to current occupation which is independent of changes in the composition of the occupational structure.

3. If there was a trend at all, it was toward greater mobility. But there was greater short- than long-distance mobility, and more mobility in the middle of the occupational structure than at the extremes. Upward mobility was more prevalent than downward mobility.

4. There was still a "moderate" correlation between occupational origins and destinations both within and between father's and son's generations, but there has been a decline in this correla-

tion. "Thus, among American men a reduction of obstacles to occupational change appears to be a long-term and continuing tendency" (ibid., p. 136). Background seems to have become less important in determining occupational position. This has been substantiated for the period from 1972 to 1985 as well. "Socioeconomic status has become less important for men's and women's occupational mobility since 1972" (Hout 1988, p. 1389). The decline in the association between an individual's social background and where he or she ends up occupationally appears to be linked to the rise in the proportion of workers who have higher education. This is the case for both men and women (Hout 1988).

5. Race, farm background, and paternal occupation were still important predictors of occupational status and mobility, but recent changes moderated their impact. On the one hand, the educational level of blacks increased, black fathers were more able to pass on their status to sons, and the growing "rationality" of the economy created pressures to reduce discrimination. On the other hand, discrimination did not appear to be any less significant than in the 1960s, racial differences in returns to human-capital investments still remained, and the likelihood of young blacks being in the labor force was smaller in the 1970s than in the 1960s.

6. Stratification within the black community became more visible and clear. Blacks became more differentiated with respect to socioeconomic status, creating more distinct classes and greater inequalities among them.

7. Overall, on balance, there appeared to be "declining status ascription and increasingly universalistic status allocation" (Featherman and Hauser 1978, p. 481).

With respect to the last point, results from the analysis of several national surveys conducted between 1972 and 1985 indicate that the openness of the U.S. occupational structure may be increasing, while changes in the composition of the occupational structure may have slowed in the last fifteen years or so. "In a manner of speaking, the force of structural mobility has declined because a growing proportion of the labor force is second-generation postindustrial; that is, more and more workers are the offspring of the first postindustrial generation" (Hout 1988, p. 1382). This means that, overall, the extent of observed mobility remains unchanged because the increase in openness has been offset by a reduction in mobility resulting from changes in the occupational structure. In the 1980s, women were more likely to have had parental heads with similar occupational status than was the case even as recently as 1970. The same was true for men. For example, the share of men and women whose origins are upper middle class has grown while those with farm backgrounds have declined in proportion. While for most of this century, the extent of mobility in the United States was due primarily to changes in the occupational structure between generations, more recently mobility shifts may be due especially to increases in openness and related factors.

The preceding discussion of mobility within industrial societies and the United States deals primarily with intergenerational mobility, that is, changes in position from parent to child. Social mobility, however, also occurs over time in the careers of individuals, that is, between first job and present occupation. With respect to this "worklife" or "career" mobility, several similarities exist among industrial nations. First, generally there is less worklife mobility than intergenerational mobility, and worklife mobility usually decreases with the age of the individual. Second, most mobility within the careers of individuals is upward rather than downward. Third, a large proportion of worklife mobility is mobility from an initially lower position back to one on a par with one's class of origin. Fourth, the highest class has the least mobility out of it. Fifth, patterns of career mobility tend to be more unstable over time and across countries than intergenerational mobility (Kurz and Muller 1987).

CHANGING NATURE OF MOBILITY STUDIES: FROM MOBILITY TABLES TO STATUS ATTAINMENT

While providing clues about the extent of mobility, mobility tables cannot tell us fully what the causes of mobility are. A number of events made it possible to redirect the study of mobility in the early 1960s. First, up to 1962 the studies of intergenerational mobility in the United States had been based on data that was either local in nature or had been collected for reasons other than the specific study of mobility. That was to change. There was a shift from local to national research on mobility, and from a focus on given occupations to one on prestige strata and determinants of individuals' positions among those strata. Second, new statistical tools were being examined and were considered adaptable to the study of intergenerational mobility. The development of national prestige scores for occupations was among those changes (Goldman and Tickameyer 1984). Finally, it had become clear to many that mobility tables did not allow one to get at the causes of rigidity/openness in systems of inequality to examine them systematically and to assess their relative impacts. The study of openness in the U.S. system of inequality was to shift from the assessment of how much mobility was present to an examination of the relative impact of socio-economic origins on the status attainment of individuals. But still, the focus was to remain on individual rather than group mobility and on upward rather than downward movement.

The U.S. Occupational Structure

The first large-scale set of national data specifically collected for the study of intergenerational mobility in the United States became available with the study of "Occupational Changes in a Generation" (OCG), later published by Blau and Duncan under the title *The American Occupational Structure*. The data were obtained as part of the Current Population Survey (CPS) of the

Bureau of the Census in March 1962. The Bureau regularly carries out surveys of the population on selected issues. At this time, 35,000 households were contacted for participation in the data collection. The regular CPS interview was supplemented on this occasion with a leave-behind questionnaire that the adult male respondents in the household were asked to fill out. The questionnaire contained a number of items on socio-economic background and familial status of the individual. Of the roughly 25,000 men in these dwelling units, 20,700 responded and formed the basic sample for the OCG study by Blau and Duncan. This sample represents about 45 million men between twenty and sixty-four years of age who were in the *civilian, noninstitutionalized* population in March 1962 (Blau and Duncan 1967, pp. 10–19). Thus, this study says nothing about changing economic conditions among women, youth, or the aged. Nevertheless, the data considered to be of unusual reliability and completeness because they were collected by trained individuals using established techniques and working for an institution that had been carrying out such surveys for decades.

Some of the findings of this study have already been alluded to because much of the early discussion in the analysis concerns the interpretation of mobility tables secured from the data. But the real innovativeness in *The American Occupational Structure* lies in its attempt to determine the relative effect of socioeconomic background on occupational attainment. To do this, Blau and Duncan made use of a statistical approach, known as *path analysis,* that would allow them to get at such determination.

Path analysis is a statistical and diagrammatic technique that allows an investigator to analyze the relationships among variables in a causal fashion (ibid., pp. 163–177). Ultimately, it is a form of regression analysis that allows the analyst to get an estimate of the relative contributions or impacts of given variables on others. Very often the impacts occur *directly* between a given factor and the phenomenon to be explained, and at least just as often the effect of a variable occurs *indirectly* through its impact on other intervening variables. In other words, the connection may be direct or it may be mediated by other factors. Path analysis allows one to separate out the direct and indirect impacts while controlling for the effects of other variables involved in the explanation.

Blau-Duncan Findings on Status Attainment With these basic points in mind, we can now look at the findings of Blau and Duncan pertaining to occupational status. Their basic attainment model is presented in Figure 11.2. They are concerned with the relative role of socioeconomic origins in the determination of the son's occupational status. From the diagram, it can be observed that the greatest direct effects on the occupational status of the son in 1962 come from education (.394) and status of first job (.281). Father's education has an indirect effect on 1962 status through its effect on education, whereas father's occupation has a direct as well as an indirect effect through its connections with the son's first job and education.

This is a very basic and simple example of a path model. At a certain point, such models can become so complex, so difficult to grasp, that their utility is questionable. If one can imagine a path model in which there are many more variables, it is easy to see how complex such models can become. At the same time, it is easy to see why such models are often portrayed as having laid out the *causal process* connecting a group of variables.

Factors Affecting Occupational Success. In summarizing the findings of Blau and Duncan, social origin, education, and first job account for less than 50 percent of the variation that occurs in 1962 occupational attainments. The main factor that affects the chances of individuals moving up are the socioeconomic levels from which they begin. The lower the position from which a person begins, argue Blau and Duncan, the greater the probability that he or she will be upwardly mobile, if only because there are more occupational categories above the individual than below. As men get older and move through their careers, their social origins appear to have less effect on

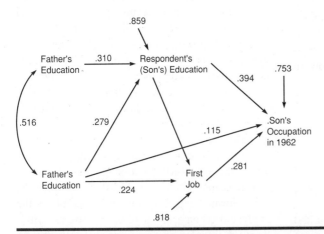

FIGURE 11.2 Path Coefficients in Basic Model of Occupational Attainment

Source: Reprinted with permission of The Free Press, a Division of Macmillan, Inc. from *The American Occupational Structure* by Peter M. Blau and Otis Dudley Duncan. Copyright © 1967 by Peter M. Blau and Otis Dudley Duncan.

their attainment than past experience and career accomplishments.

Working in an urban area is more conducive to occupational success, and urban migrants tend to do better than nonmigrants. Migrants from urban areas to other urban areas do better than the urban nonmigrants. It seems that there is a self-selection process involved in which those with high potential for occupational success migrate. Rural migrants, on the other hand, attain higher status than those rural individuals who do not move, but they do not attain higher positions than those urbanites who are nonmigrants.

The Blau-Duncan findings also suggest that having a stable family life, having fewer siblings, and being the youngest or oldest male are positively related to occupational success. But those who come from large families *and* overcome obstacles are also likely to move up occupationally more readily than others who have not had such problems.

Blau and Duncan conclude that there is no evidence of an increase in rigidity in the occupational structure; upward mobility seems to have increased slightly since World War II, and there has been no change in the dependence of the son's occupational status on that of his father. Moreover, evidence suggests that the role of education, which Blau and Duncan view as an achievement variable, has become increasingly important to occupational attainment. They suggest that this indicates an increase in the importance of universalistic factors in attainment.

In the past, some of the principal sources of mobility were differential fertility, immigration, and technological changes. Today, the main sources consist of (1) internal migration to areas of greater occupational opportunity, (2) continued differential fertility, which Blau and Duncan do not believe will be completely eliminated, and (3) technological improvements that have expanded occupations at the higher status levels and continually eroded those at the bottom. Like Porter (1967), they suggest that such improvement requires the expansion of a larger pool of trained personnel in the labor force. Blau and Duncan

see an increased stress on rationality and efficiency in industrial societies like the United States, which indicates to them that perhaps more objective criteria are being used in the evaluation of individuals. It should be duly noted that Blau and Duncan indicate that they are just speculating on these matters, but these are the speculations that they feel are suggested by their study (Blau and Duncan 1967, p. 431).

Blau and Duncan conclude by indicating that increased industrialization and changes in the occupational structure have given the United States a higher rate of upward mobility from the manual and lower white-collar ranks than most other countries. Hazelrigg's analysis of data from twelve different countries, including data for the United States from Blau and Duncan's OCG study, suggests that much of the mobility in the United States is structurally determined and that when such differences are taken into account, the United States ranks about fourth from the top in free circulation mobility. And despite the fact that the upward-mobility chances for an individual from the manual ranks may be greater in the United States than elsewhere, the chances of such a person moving up into the highest nonmanual occupations is still less than 10 percent when structural factors are controlled (Hazelrigg 1974, pp. 484–486).

Blau and Duncan point out that the United States does not do as well compared with some other countries when it comes to the dependence of the son's occupational attainment on the father's. They also perceptively observe that *a high degree of mobility can be consistent with extensive inequality and can even help to perpetuate that inequality.* The possibility for mobility may make individuals more complacent about the inequality they observe. Mobility also means changes between generations. Thus, "although high rates of vertical mobility may preserve the status differences observable between *some* individuals, they undermine the status differences between the *same* families that are inherited from one generation to another" (Blau and Duncan 1967, p. 441, emphases in original).

The American Occupational Structure opened the door to a whole new way of examining the problem of the openness of the system of inequality, gave impetus to scores of studies, and made some valuable contributions to our understanding of movement in the occupational hierarchy, but it has its limitations. Since most of the basic ones relate to limitations in the status-attainment approach generally, comments on this matter will be deferred until after the discussion of more recent status-attainment research.

A replication of the March 1962 OCG study done in March 1973 suggests that "Americans today enjoy at least as much opportunity for socioeconomic mobility as in earlier periods of this century. For some, especially blacks in the labor force, opportunities seem to have expanded, even though large inequalities in opportunity persist" (Featherman 1977, p. 15).

Explanations of Status Attainment

The first OCG study by Blau and Duncan gave rise, as we saw, to a simple model of status attainment based on characteristics of the individual at different stages of the life cycle. Basically, the Blau-Duncan model relies on *structural* factors as explanatory variables, and it has been elaborated in recent years (Duncan et al. 1972). Fundamentally, this model argues that parental status influences the occupational attainment of the son in part through direct channels, but its main effect occurs via its effect on the education of the son, which then affects his occupational attainment. Education has an effect on both the son's first as well as his present job, and the first job has a major impact on the present one.

It is clear that this model does not consider social-psychological factors, such as aspirations and the influences of parents and peers, which may have a significant effect on attainment. To put it in the words of Haller and Portes (1973), it does not lay out "the finer mechanisms through which status attainment takes place" (p. 58).

To deal with the issue of the effect of varied social-psychological factors on educational and occupational attainment, Sewell and others developed what is known as the "Wisconsin model" of socioeconomic attainment (e.g., Sewell and Shah 1967; Sewell et al. 1970). The large volume of studies produced on this model grew out of an initial survey in 1957 of over 10,000 high school seniors in Wisconsin. Most of the early research was devoted to studying the influence of socioeconomic background and social-psychological factors on aspirations. The follow-up surveys were done in 1964 and in 1975, with a response rate among the original sample of about 90 percent.

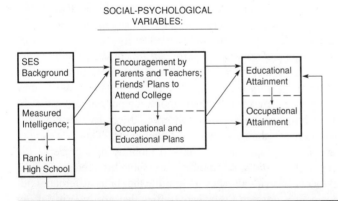

SOCIAL-PSYCHOLOGICAL
VARIABLES:

FIGURE 11.3   A Simplified Version of the Wisconsin Model Showing the Mediating Role of Social-Psychological Factors in Individual Attainment

Source: Adapted from Sewell, Haller, and Ohlendorf (1970), p. 1023.

Wisconsin Model A basic version of the Wisconsin model of early occupational achievement is presented in Figure 11.3. Essentially, it shows that the socioeconomic background (father's and mother's education, father's occupational status, and parental income) does not affect grades and is independent of academic ability but has a sizable ultimate effect on educational and occupational attainments through its influence on the mediating variables of significant others' influences and educational and occupational aspirations. Overall, the model explains about 57 percent of the variation in educational and about 40 percent of the variation in early occupational attainment for the men in the sample. The percentages are somewhat smaller for women (Sewell and Hauser 1976). The model has been applied to individuals with both rural and urban backgrounds, although it was first applied to a sample of farm residents and then later applied to groups from a variety of residential backgrounds.

The Wisconsin model is more effective in explaining the variation in educational and occupational attainment than the basic Blau-Duncan model. The earlier structural model accounts for 26 percent and 33 percent in educational and occupational attainment, respectively. It seems clear from the Wisconsin model that a variety of social-psychological factors play mediating roles linking socioeconomic background and ability to attainment (Haller and Portes 1973, p. 68).

The Wisconsin model has been tested on a variety of samples around the Untied States, and generally the results have been quite similar. Wilson and Portes (1975) tested the model's explanation of educational attainment using a national sample of 2,000 tenth-grade boys from whom data had been collected in 1966, 1968 to 1969, and 1970. Some of the measures of variables used are slightly different from those used in the original studies, but the core variables of the model—SES, mental ability, academic performance, aspirations, and significant others' influence—are included. They found that the results fit the Wisconsin model fairly well, although social-psychological factors play less of a role in

explaining attainment than in the Wisconsin research. Their results, the authors say, "suggest a lesser role for the subjective or social psychological intervening processes linked with social influence and the formation of status aspirations. Conversely, they also point to the greater importance of mediate and more objective factors: socioeconomic background, recorded ability, and school performance" (Wilson and Portes 1975, p. 354). The authors found that the "objective" factors of academic performance and socioeconomic background had stronger direct than indirect effects on educational attainment.

In 1975, another replication of the Wisconsin model was published, this time looking at both educational and occupational attainment. As their data source, the researchers used a national sample of males who had first been surveyed as high school sophomores in 1955 and then followed up in 1970. The results support earlier research, and the authors concluded with respect to educational achievement that what is important about these models is that they demonstrate that attainment is affected by a variety of influences, including social-psychological factors, no one of which has an overwhelming dominance. Their findings on occupational attainment corroborate the earlier findings that indicate that education is the most significant factor in the model affecting occupational attainment, although the total amount of the variation in attainment it explains is in itself quite small (9 to 11 percent) (Alexander et al. 1975).

What is revealing in the other findings is that none of these models explains very much of the variations that exist among individuals in earnings and income, and what small proportion they do explain (under 20 percent) is due primarily to the effect of objective factors, such as SES, rather than to social-psychological variables.

Explanation of Earnings and Income. The discovery that neither the Blau-Duncan nor the Wisconsin model of attainment accounts for very much of the variation in earnings and income has given rise to a variety of speculations about what the really significant factors might be. A large majority of Americans believe that education is the key to socioeconomic success. After all, as the saying goes, "if you want a good job, get a good education." But the connection between education and economic achievement, as we have seen, has not been strong. These models leave almost half of the variation in occupational achievement and much more of the difference in earnings and income unexplained. "Neither family background, cognitive skill, educational attainment nor occupational status explains much of the variation in men's incomes" (Jencks et al. 1973, p. 226).

The Role of Education in Attainment

Hauser's 1969 study of data from 17,000 white public school students in grades seven to twelve in Davidson County, Tennessee, collected in 1957, uncovered that the quality of the high school attended did not make much difference for ultimate educational attainment. Jencks and his colleagues (1973) observe that "school resources do not appear to influence students' educational attainments at all" (p. 159). Alwin (1974) found similar results for educational and occupational attainment using data from the Wisconsin surveys. In essence, he found that the quality of the college attended, measured in a variety of ways, had little effect on either educational or occupational attainment. Earlier research had come up with the same results (Sewell and Hauser 1972).

Most of those concerned with the extent of upward mobility have assumed the importance of equality in education. But the level of its importance has been called into question (Grusky and Hauser 1984; Kaelble 1977). The nature of the connection between educational and occupational achievement also has been the subject of debate. The role of education in affecting attainment varies from country to country. Education appears to have its greatest impact when it provides specific skills for specific occupations or is tied to an apprenticeship program (Kurz and Muller 1987). The traditional argument has been that advances

in technology and upgrading of the occupational structure have resulted in a need for greater skills and training that education is supposed to supply.

Collins (1971) challenged this conclusion, saying there is evidence that what is important about education is not the training it provides but the fact that it represents an introduction into a particular "status culture." Many individuals, argues Collins, are overeducated for their jobs, and those who are better educated do not necessarily perform better on their jobs than the less educated. In fact, he says, U.S. schools generally are not very good at providing students with the vocational skills they need to be successful in the performance of their jobs. What is important about schools for early occupational achievement is that they teach the person a particular set of values and ways of acting and defining things. Employers then select those who would fit into the status culture of the elite and those who might be willing to serve under them because of their adherence to the prescriptions of a particular status culture. In this manner, schools can be used to control membership in economic institutions. Thus, what is important about schools for employment, argues Collins, is not their passing on of knowledge, but the fact that in a variety of ways they instill in students certain kinds of status-cultural values. We do not know at this point whether the training effect of education on mobility is more important than its role in maintaining class positions across generations (Bielby 1981).

If the variables we have discussed, including education, do not fully explain earnings and income, what else does? Sex, race, labor market, industry, and economic sector of employment are involved. Another suggestion is that factors associated with an individual's current experiences may be better predictors of earnings. These might include on-the-job training, job performance and satisfaction, and the nature of the job and labor markets (Sewell and Hauser 1976). The amount of time spent in the labor force also affects an individual's earnings (Spaeth 1976a).

In addition to these, networking and "luck"

may play important roles in the explanation of earnings and income. Some people just happen to be in the right spot at the appropriate time. For example, you happen to be in a community that has a greater range of jobs than others, or the weather may destroy your job in construction, or you happen to be in a city where a new plant locates (Jencks et al. 1973, p. 227). Some of these kinds of events may be appropriately labeled as "luck," but others are factors that are systematically related to earnings but have not yet been incorporated into attainment models. The real job of the analyst, as Featherman puts it, "is to reduce the size of the residual component toward the limits of 'luck's' imprint on the various occupational accomplishments of workers" (1977, p. 16). Luck may certainly play a role, but many of the factors that pass for luck we know are probably elements that are actually systematically related to economic inequality. It may, however, be very difficult to separate the latter factors from luck. Spaeth (1976b) concludes that "there is no way to separate the effects of chance from those of variables or forms of functions of which we are currently unaware" (p. 162).

Spaeth suggests that income is a different kind of variable than occupation or education. Income is a reward for job performance, but most of the factors considered in these models are items that are aimed at explaining entry into the job market, not earnings (Spaeth 1976b).

MOBILITY AND THE ATTAINMENT PROCESS AMONG BLACKS

In their landmark study of American men in the early 1960s, Blau and Duncan (1967) argued that blacks generally start out from a lower position, but instead of moving up in a manner commensurate with their education and other human capital, they become involved in a vicious circle in which they are hindered at each step along the way in the attainment process. That is, their disadvantages are *cumulative*. They have a hard time getting a higher education, and when they do, the occupational returns for that education are less

than those received by whites. Knowledge of this fact may lower the incentive of blacks to obtain such education, and thereby reinforce the negative stereotype of blacks as unwilling to be educated. Although southerners and immigrants are disadvantaged, their problems are not of this cumulative nature.

The replication of this national study in the 1970s found that both blacks and whites have gained in educational attainment, but the gains in recent years have been greatest for blacks and the economic returns to their educations have increased. Moreover, blacks gained in occupational status relative to whites. Recent changes have moderated the effects of racial barriers, according to Featherman and Hauser, and black fathers who are in white-collar positions are able to a greater degree to pass on their occupational statuses to their sons. More blacks had white-collar positions in the mid-1970s (22%) than in 1962 (12%) (Featherman 1977; Featherman and Hauser 1978).

Occupational inequality between blacks and whites, as measured by broad occupational categories, declined between 1950 and 1980. In the South, in contrast to the nation as a whole, the decline in occupational inequality began in the 1960s. It appears to have been governmental policies rather than economic growth that was linked to this decline (Fossett et al. 1986). Declines in family income inequality since World War II, especially for vulnerable groups (e.g., female-headed families) are more closely related to the growth of social welfare programs than to upswings in the business cycle (Treas 1983).

Despite the positive tone of the preceding conclusions, the greater inheritance of occupational status among upper white-collar black fathers and sons has helped to create greater economic inequality and more "visible" classes within the black community (Featherman and Hauser 1978; Hout 1984). Blacks who moved up have been disproportionately drawn from more favored socioeconomic backgrounds, and those who had a privileged occupational position, especially in the public sector, were more likely to be able to hold onto it than individuals in manual positions. In other words, "class" factors became more important for blacks' occupational attainment during the 1960s and 1970s (Hout 1984).

Research on eminent black Americans listed in *Who's Who Among Black Americans* also has found that they are more likely to come from privileged backgrounds. Specifically, they are more likely than the average black to have had parents who are professionals and are highly educated. Further back in their lineage, their ancestors were more likely to have been "free" blacks with lighter skin (Mullins and Sites 1984). However, the paths to eminence and the occupations that characterize eminent black Americans have differed historically from those that distinguish eminent white Americans (Lieberson and Carter 1979). Of course, an increase in the impact of class origins among blacks does not necessarily mean that race has become *less* significant in their lives. While this research may *suggest* that class is becoming more important than race in determining occupational attainment, blacks do not *perceive* it this way. Data from national surveys conducted from the mid-1970s to the mid-1980s show no significant decline in the effects of race on feelings of despair. Blacks are significantly more likely than whites to feel that things are getting worse rather than better for the average person. In fact, the strength of the relationship between race and such feelings increased between 1980 and 1984 (Austin and Stack 1988).

While middle-class blacks may be more able to retain their positions, blacks who were in low-paid jobs were less likely than comparable whites to be upwardly mobile (Pomer 1986). Movement from the peripheral to the core sector of the economy is especially difficult for blacks. Mobility into the higher paying core sector or into a higher status occupation may be hindered by residential segregation which limits access and opportunities to move up, especially in the private sector (Hirschman and Wong 1984; Hout 1986). If blacks do move up, it is most likely to an adjacent category rather than to an upper nonmanual position. Blacks seldom advance to managerial posi-

tions, and in contrast to whites, most of the movement into the "mainstream" is in the public rather than private sector.

The black middle class has grown in recent decades. "In a period of slightly more than one hundred years (1865–1970), the black middle class increased from a small group of 'free Negroes' to a sizable stratum of the black population" (Durant and Louden 1986, p. 254). A variety of factors have been linked to this growth, including industrialization, urbanization, increased education and collective action, and occupational differentiation. However, much of the growth of the black middle class can be attributed to the appreciable number who have assumed public or governmental white-collar jobs, rather than managerial or upper level technical positions in the private sector (Collins 1983; Hout 1984). This makes the black middle class more potentially vulnerable to shifts within government and its budget.

Thus, there is some debate about exactly how much progress there has been for blacks as a whole. Blacks still lag significantly behind whites in median family income, which has not improved relative to whites since the 1960s. The poverty rate for blacks is still three times the rate for whites, and it has been that way for decades. While there has been some occupational upgrading for black men, it is in broad occupational categories. There are greater differences between the races when specific, narrower occupational categories are examined and mobility is more restricted (see Chapter 4).

Race and the Status-Attainment Process

There has been research to determine if the models that have been developed to explain educational and occupational attainment apply to blacks as well as they do to whites. Since race has an effect on a variety of areas in U.S. life, it may be suspected that what applies to whites does not apply to blacks. Since race is an ascribed characteristic, a model based on achievement norms may not fit blacks as well as whites. Also, race affects mobility, and the relationship between many of the variables that are included in these standard models differ from one race to another. Finally, the nature of the socialization process in the two races may be different (Porter, 1974).

A study by Portes and Wilson (1976) suggests that the process of educational attainment does differ among blacks. Analyzing a nationwide sample of boys who had been surveyed over a period of several years, and using a variant of the Wisconsin model of status attainment described earlier, they found several differences between blacks and whites:

1. The variables in the model are better at explaining attainment among whites than among blacks, which suggests that factors not traditionally considered are more important for blacks.
2. The more objective factors of socioeconomic background, mental ability, and academic performance are more important for white attainment, whereas among blacks, the later and more subjective variables of self-esteem and educational aspirations are the significant ones for blacks.
   a. There is a much stronger connection between mental ability and academic performance and between the latter and educational attainment among whites than among blacks. Among blacks, there is no significant *direct* connection between academic performance and attainment.
   b. Conversely, the ties of mental ability to self-esteem and the ties of self-esteem to attainment are much stronger among blacks than whites.

In summarizing their findings, Portes and Wilson suggest that the results imply a distinction among whites and blacks as insiders and outsiders in the U.S. achievement system. In an open society, we would expect that performance and ability would be quite important, and they are for whites. But for blacks, educational attainment is more dependent on self-reliance and ambition. In a manner of speaking, then, while blacks have

had to rely on these qualities, whites "have at their disposal an additional set of institutional 'machinery' which can, in effect, carry them along to higher levels of attainment" (Portes and Wilson 1976, p. 430).

Porter (1974) examined early occupational as well as educational achievement among blacks and whites and also found significant racial differences in the processes involved. His study of a large sample of males suggests that among blacks, grades are largely a function of personality factors, such as conformity and ambition, whereas among whites both personality and intelligence play roles. As in the Portes and Wilson (1976) findings, subjective rather than objective conditions appear to play a greater part in the attainment process for blacks. "It would appear that the official sanctions of the school system operate primarily with reference to the visible being of the pupil, and only secondarily, and on the condition that he is white, with reference to academic ability" (Porter 1974, p. 311). Another interesting finding of this study is that in contrast to the results among whites, grades have no direct effect on either educational or occupational attainment.

Porter does note that there are similarities in the attainment process between the races. Among both, educational attainment is strongly affected by intelligence, and occupational attainment is more affected by educational achievement than by any other factor in the model. Despite these similarities, Porter states that the main results are those that bring out the differences in the attainment process between the races. It must be kept in mind that the major national studies of status attainment were conducted on males, most of whom were white.

PATTERNS OF MOBILITY AND ATTAINMENT AMONG WOMEN

The major national studies done on intergenerational mobility during the 1960s and 1970s concentrated on the occupational statuses of *men*. Thus, most of what we have been reviewing about social mobility has really concerned only the mobility of men. It is difficult to think of the results of national mobility studies as being representative of the entire mobility structure of the United States when at least half of the population is not represented in those studies. Part of the reason for the omission of women in these studies is that they are based on the assumption that women's positions are dependent on those of their husbands or fathers, and that to know the mobility patterns of men is, therefore, to know the patterns for the entire society. Thus, intergenerational mobility studies involving women most often will compare a woman's position with that of her father rather than her mother, or with her husband or brother(s). The latter is done in studies of "marital mobility," as we will see. If the husband's position is higher than that of the wife's brother, then upward mobility through marriage is said to have occurred. This is the same bias that exists when one argues that a woman's class position can be measured by her father's or husband's position, which is an assumption that pervades much traditional stratification literature (Acker 1973).

The central problem with all this is that women are not considered as independent persons, some even unmarried, with their own occupational, educational and income resources. From our discussions earlier in this book, we know that sex inequality exists along a variety of dimensions, and yet our concepts (like class position) reflect a concern primarily for the attributes of males. The fact of sex inequality needs to be taken into fuller account in measures and studies of mobility (Acker 1973). The reader should take these limitations into account in discussions of how mobile women have been in U.S. society.

Evidence varies on the extent to which the socioeconomic position of women has improved. In *absolute* terms there appears to have been improvement in the occupational, educational, and income attainments of women, but in *relative* terms little change seems to have occurred since the late 1960s (Richards 1986). Women still tend to be concentrated in certain kinds of jobs, although there is some evidence that, especially

since the 1970s, there has been a decline in occupational segregation between the sexes (Jacobs 1989). An examination of national data from 1910 to 1986 suggests that while the extent of such segregation remained fairly constant in the period from 1910 to 1970, since that time there has been a measurable decline, especially in nonfarm occupations. Jacobs suggests that part of the reason for the perceived lack of decline in desegregation during the first seventy years of this century relates to the decline of child and agricultural labor, both of which were among the most integrated kinds of work. Had these remained as large relative to other *general* occupational categories as they were at the turn of the century, desegregation would have been more obvious.

Other evidence, however, suggests that some traditionally "female" occupations, such as phone operators, servers, and maids/servants, also have declined in numbers over the last several decades, helping to account for any desegregation that has occurred (Beller 1984). Thus, structural shifts among more *narrowly defined* occupations also contribute to changes in sex segregation. Moreover, while some have suggested that the movement toward more openness in the broadly defined occupational structure is indicative of a long-term trend, others believe that the movement of women into certain traditionally male occupations may be the first step toward a resegregation of women (Reskin 1988). At one time, for example, school teaching was a predominantly male occupation, but since early in this century it has increasingly become defined as a "female" occupation. In more recent years, this trend has occurred for other occupations such as bank-telling and residential real estate. This is important because, as we have seen, the earnings associated with an occupation are related to the proportion of women in it. A greater percentage of females in an occupation is associated with lower earnings.

What causes this shift of males out of an occupation, creating an opportunity for women to move into it? Several factors are involved. First, the decline in rewards attached to an occupation can motivate males to leave the occupation espe-cially if other more lucrative positions are open to them. Second, changes in the nature of the work in an occupation, such as the work becom-ing more monotonous, also can cause them to move to another occupation. Third, a lack of op-portunity to advance or move up increases the probability of movement out of an occupation. Finally, the larger the supply of women available in the labor force, the more likely they are to move into these vacancies, eventually becoming the majority proportion within these occupations (Reskin 1988). The chances of the latter happen-ing are enhanced by the fact that fewer numbers of occupations, especially male occupations, are open to women. The redefinition of an occupa-tion as "female," coupled with the crowding of women into it, then fosters a decline in the wages of workers in that field (Bergmann 1974; Strober and Arnold 1987). "Is resegregation the inevita-ble outcome of occupational integration? The an-swer is probably yes as long as only a small num-ber of traditionally male occupations become open to the large number of women who want and need better paying jobs" (Reskin 1988, p. 263).

What can be said about the occupational mo-bility of patterns of women? The intergenera-tional mobility of women is characterized by spe-cific characteristics (Roos 1985). Large numbers of daughters move into clerical positions regard-less of differences in their fathers' occupation. Overall, daughters are less likely than sons to "in-herit" their father's occupation, that is, to be in the same kind of job as their fathers. While men and women may come from the same status ori-gins, they tend to go to different destinations. The likelihood of working in a professional occupa-tion is greatest for daughters from professional or managerial backgrounds, and lowest for those who have fathers who are in farm or production work. This suggests that most of the mobility is short range in nature. Women who have parents with service occupations are more likely to move into white-collar than blue-collar jobs. Women with urban backgrounds who go into farming are most likely to be daughters of fathers who are la-

borers or farmers, whereas comparable men are likely to come from a wider variety of nonfarm backgrounds. In other words, among women the inflow into farming is more restricted than it is among men (Tyree and Treas 1974). Finally, while there is a relationship between class of ori-gin and class of destination among both men and women, in general women tend to move into cler-ical, low-status professional, and service occupa-tions, while men go into professional and produc-tion occupations. This is the case not only in the United States but in many other industrial coun-tries as well (Roos 1985).

While it has not been extensively examined for men, mobility through marriage for women has been studied. This itself is a telling commen-tary on the manner in which women have been incorporated into mobility studies. *Marital mo-bility* refers to the mobility for the daughter that results from movement from the father's status to the occupational status of her husband. A wom-an's status is considered as being defined entirely in terms of the position of her husband and father. Studies using national data indicate that women who do not work but marry tend to marry men whose statuses are like those of their brothers; on the other hand, women who do work move into occupational statuses quite unlike those of their brothers (Tyree and Treas 1974). In other words, since the women who do marry adopt the statuses of their husbands, and since the patterns of mo-bility for the latter are similar to those of the brothers of these women, it is probable that they will attain statuses similar to those of their broth-ers, especially if they marry into the same social class. When these women are married but not working, their statuses are tied directly to the processes of mobility operant among males. If one is using the husband's occupation as the mea-sure of status, women appear to have slightly greater mobility through their marriage than men have through their employment (Kurz and Muller 1987; Chase 1975).

Men are more likely to stay in the occupa-tional statuses of their fathers than are women who marry but do not work. The latter are more likely to cross major class boundaries, as from blue-collar origins to the white-collar status of their husbands. Chase suggests that the greater mobility of daughters who marry as compared with the intergenerational mobility of men may be due in part to two factors: (1) It is easier to obtain the requirements needed to be maritally mobile (such as attractiveness and charm) than it is for men to obtain the requirements to be occupationally mobile (such as skills and education). (2) Sons are more likely to inherit the businesses of their fathers than are daughters, leaving the latter freer to marry higher or lower than their fathers' statuses (Chase 1975). Of course, these are only suggested reasons. It may very well be that the first is not accurate, and as far as the second is concerned, a son can always sell the business and marry whomever he pleases.

For women who work and thereby derive their statuses from their own work, what they accomplish occupationally depends on the processes of attainment that apply to women. The relative importance of the factors that affect occupational attainment are different for men and women as we shall see shortly. As a result, marital mobility among women is closer to the pattern found in occupational mobility among men than it is to occupational mobility among women (Tyree and Treas 1974).

Obstructions in the Context of Mobility

The preceding discussion covered social mobility between generations in broad terms: the movement from the occupation of an individual's parents (almost always the father's rather than the mother's) to his or her current occupational position. What is missing from such a sweeping discussion is any recognition of the concrete context in which the mobility of individuals occurs. We must consider that mobility for men and women, like that for the races, takes place in a context in which (1) there are different expectations of each sex, (2) occupations are sex segregated to begin with, (3) internal labor markets and hierarchies exist within the organizations in which persons are employed, and (4) firms are differentiated in

terms of formalization, complexity, size, market, and other characteristics. What this all means is that mobility does not take place in a vacuum. Rather, there is a particular texture in the paths to mobility that exist in different countries. The structuring of the private economy into different industrial sectors, for example, creates explicit barriers and avenues for career mobility (Tolbert 1982). For women especially, part of this texture consists of obstacles and dead ends (Diprete and Soule 1988).

For men, part of the texture is related to the autonomous nature of an occupation and/or the specialization of the education associated with it. Barriers to mobility appear to exist between the autonomous and less specialized jobs, on the one hand, and those that are less autonomous or require less specialized education, on the other. In a study of 20,000 men in the civilian labor force, Snipp (1985) found that there is a particular class structure to career mobility. The most difficult barriers to cross in the path to mobility are those that divide manual from nonmanual labor, professional from nonprofessional, and skilled crafts from semi- or unskilled labor, respectively. Thus, while on an abstract level, mobility in an industrial society like the United States would appear to depend solely on merit, at a more concrete and specific level mobility depends on a variety of contextual elements in the setting.

In terms of variations in expectations between the sexes, in the absence of knowledge about a person, external characteristics such as sex and/or race are used to provide clues to what might be expected (Berger et al. 1972, 1977). Traditional U.S. culture contains beliefs about the usual behavior and personality characteristics of each sex. At the same time, the occupational structure is sex segregated. Women, for example, are much less likely than men to be corporate executives, meaning that when someone below or outside the organization is being considered for a top executive position, most of those involved in making the decision will be men who have been socialized into having particular expectations about male and female candidates.

In her study of an industrial corporation,

Kanter (1977) found that at the top is an inner circle of individuals who have to be counted on to share a similar view of the organization and to behave in a manner consistent with that view. There are distinct pressures for homogeneity and conformity at the managerial level. A large part of the reason for this pressure to conform arises from the open nature of organizations and the managerial positions within them. Since position tasks are not well defined at that level and the organization operates in a "turbulent" environment with other organizations, the conclusion is that executives have to be able to trust each other, see each other's behavior as predictable. "Women were decidedly placed in the category of the incomprehensible and unpredictable" (Kanter 1977, p. 58). What Kanter's study suggests is that the external characteristic of sex is used as a criterion to conclude that it may be too much of a risk to have women and other "unpredictable" individuals within the management of the corporation. By continually recruiting men into those positions, the inequality in occupational positions between the sexes is perpetuated.

A study by Wiley and Eskilson (1983) focused on another aspect of expectations about women and its implications for mobility within a firm. They conducted research among employed middle-level managers who were involved in an MBA program. Most were male, had an average of six years experience, and averaged thirty-three years of age. They were asked to respond to various scenarios in which a person was promoted. In each of these scenarios, the individuals had the same background (e.g., education, experience, etc.), but the person promoted was sometimes male and sometimes female. In some scenarios, it was said that there was affirmative action pressure to promote a given person, while in others there was no mention of it. These respondents were asked to give what they thought was the most important reason for the person's promotion (i.e., luck, ability, sponsorship, affirmative action, effort). They also were asked to state their expectations for the person in the future. Results indicated that the men who were promoted were thought to have been more supported and spon-

sored by others in the organization than the women being considered. As a consequence, the respondents also felt that the promoted men would have more power, influence, and mobility in the future than the women. It was believed that the men would be considered more successful than the women who also had been promoted even if their performance levels were equal.

Women, of course, have traditionally been socialized into the same general beliefs about the sexes as men, and their beliefs can have an impact on the probability of their being upwardly mobile. For example, the willingness to move is an important factor in career mobility, but generally women are less willing to move than men. Research among white-collar employees in a federal agency, for example, found that regardless of their education and other factors, women express less desire to move (Markham et al. 1983). Part of the reason may be that women see more family conflict arising as a result of moving. Perhaps this sensitivity is due to the socialization among women to have the family as a central focus of their lives. A significant factor in the reluctance to move is that while most men consider themselves to be the "primary providers," most women do not. Women who *do* see themselves in these terms are just as willing to move as men in similar circumstances (Markham et al. 1983).

All of this suggests that the expectations individuals have of women affect their mobility chances. These expectations also interact with the sex segregation of occupations and the internal structure of the organizations in which men and women work. The segregation creates barriers between occupations that are difficult to overcome, and the structure of the internal labor market within organizations as it applies to men and women also affects mobility. Generally, it has been argued that women are found in disproportionate numbers in the secondary labor market (see Chapter 4). But even within the primary labor market there is a division of labor by sex (Hartmann 1987). Certain jobs are labeled as "female" or "male" in both markets. Within each, women occupy certain kinds of positions that are qualitatively different from those of men not only in terms of the tasks involved, but, most significantly for mobility, in terms of their location in the social structure of the organization.

When women are in a position that is part of an internal labor market, they benefit less from that position than men do, in large part because a majority of them do not make job changes within a firm but move to other employers. Thus, women do not participate as fully as men in the career ladders available in many organizations, and this contributes heavily to the wage differences between the sexes (Felmlee 1982). In other words, "women's" positions are less likely to be linked to apprenticeships and career ladders and more likely to be surrounded by "dead space," that is, not connected to a distinct career-promotion ladder (Seidman 1978). Moreover, when women are in "female" white-collar positions, such as that of secretary, and perform admirably because of their accumulated but very specific job expertise, they may have less chance to be occupationally mobile within an organization (Kanter 1977). Being promoted or not promoted is not always based on merit at the level of the concrete organization (Hartmann 1987). These obstacles in the attainment process for women may provide some of the reasons past research has shown that the career trajectories of women are relatively flat when compared to those of men.

In other words, the entry-level jobs and job families are structured, often even in large firms, to maintain sex segregation. Moreover, if a position is a dead end, it will have consequences on the behavior and demeanor of the individual in that position. "Opportunity structures shape behavior in such a way that they confirm their own prophecies. Those people set on high-mobility tracks tend to develop attitudes and values that impel them further along the track: work commitment, high aspirations, and upward orientations. Those set on low-mobility tracks tend to become indifferent, to give up, and thus to 'prove' that their initial placement was correct. . . . It is graphically clear how cycles of advantage and cycles of disadvantage are perpetuated in organizations and in society" (Kanter 1977, p. 158). Once

in a low-status, "female" job, it is difficult to move out. This result only reconfirms the position as a "female" one and, therefore, one with certain characteristics. "It may be because the jobs are done by women that they are viewed as unskilled and are lower paid, not just that low-wage (low-skills) jobs are created and women are channeled into them" (Hartmann 1987, p. 63).

Sex and the Process of Status Attainment

Some studies have suggested that the basic attainment process is similar for working males and females (Featherman and Hauser 1976a; Treiman and Terrell 1975; McClendon 1976). Among both men and women, education is the most important factor of those included in models of occupational attainment. Socioeconomic background has a much weaker direct effect on such attainment. Education appears to be the critical variable in the occupational attainment models used in most industrial countries. However, among men in those countries, it is one of several factors that are important, while for women, education is the only factor or by far the most important element in attainment (Roos 1985).

A second similarity between the sexes is in the average prestige of their occupational statuses. Occupational *prestige* has been the dimension most often used in studies of occupational attainment, even though there are a variety of other ranked aspects of occupations, such as power, earnings, autonomy, and so on. In other words, while the average prestige of the occupations held by the sexes may be similar, this does not mean that they are similar on other dimensions, as we have seen. Attainment studies that focus on prestige scores as their dependent variable do not, of course, effectively capture the full multidimensional nature of sex inequality in occupations because sex segregation in occupations does not neatly follow prestige lines. Rosenfeld (1978) puts the matter bluntly: "Use of prestige or status scores seems to hide sex differences in occupational location and mobility" (p. 39). In her study of twelve industrial countries, Roos

(1985) found that when "occupational wage hierarchy" is substituted for "occupational prestige" as the dependent variable, then differences between men and women surface. Men receive more income returns on each of the determinants in the models. Moreover, as we indicated in Chapter 3, the development of prestige scores did not include occupations in which women were dominant.

Another consequence of the focus on men and occupational prestige in most studies of attainment have been the omissions of the role of the mother's occupation in explaining attainment and housework as a form of occupation. The exclusion of housework as an occupation because it is not formally defined as part of the labor force means the exclusion of a significant percentage of people, mostly women, from studies of attainment. When one considers that housework contributes to the maintenance of society and capitalism, it appears obvious that it should be considered valuable work and incorporated into the occupational hierarchy in a meaningful and measurable way (Acker 1973). In other words, a class analysis that involves women should include housework as an occupation as well as other occupational differences among women (Eisenstein 1990). "Class categories are primarily male-defined categories. . . . What does it mean to say that a middle-class woman's life is different and easier than a working-class woman's life when her status as such is significantly different from that of her middle-class male 'equivalent'? What of the woman who earns no money at all (as houseworker) and is termed middle class because her husband is? . . . [W]e must develop a vocabulary and conceptual tools that deal with the question of differential power among women in terms of their relations to men *and* the class structure" (Eisenstein 1990, p. 138). Moreover, most studies of intergenerational mobility and attainment have used the father's rather than mother's occupation as a predictor of offspring's attainment. Much of the reason for this involves the debate about what is the most appropriate measure of an individual's class position (Kurz and Muller 1987). When mother's and father's occupational statuses are included as possible determinants of attainment, mother's status is found to be more important in accounting for a daughter's attainment (Rosenfeld 1978). In a national study of almost 3,000 Canadian women, while mother's occupational status "strongly influences" the occupational attainment of the daughter, information about the father's status proved to be "superfluous" (Stevens and Boyd 1980).

There are other differences between the sexes in the status-attainment process. While women have been found to have a higher class standing in their high schools and a higher academic self-concept, being female appears to have a negative effect on the likelihood of being in the college preparatory curriculum in high school (Alexander and Eckland 1974). Ability appears to be more important for males while status background has more effect among females (Sewell and Shah 1967). It may be that males get more encouragement and are expected to be successful academically so they can get good jobs. A study of Wisconsin high school students suggests that hindrances to female achievement occur early in the attainment process. Males get more information and encouragement for their career aspirations than females (Saltiel 1985).

SOME OBSERVATIONS ON STUDIES OF STATUS ATTAINMENT

In recent years, the study of status attainment in U.S. sociology has played a dominant role in research on social stratification and mobility. A large proportion of the research published in the major journals on inequality has dealt with one or another aspect of status attainment. Indeed, among many of those doing this research, the "process of stratification" has come to be defined largely in terms of status attainment.

There is no question that the research in this area has been remarkably coherent, consistent, and cumulative—a feat rarely achieved in sociology. Moreover, the statistical techniques that have been brought to bear on issues concerning mobility and achievement processes have become increasingly sophisticated in the last twenty-five years. Finally, the conclusions of these studies, which are often quite similar, are stabilized by the fact that data from a variety of national samples have been used in reaching them.

Yet the research discussed here and the orientation to inequality or stratification as status attainment have distinct limitations. Some of these are more evident than others, but all are worth mentioning so that the reader is not led to the conclusion that the study of stratification and inequality has become the study of status attainment.

1. *The study of status transmission is not coterminous with the study of stratification or inequality.* It is true that the study of mobility has, in recent years, been defined almost solely in terms of mobility processes over generations, but it is not the case that the study of the degree to which an offspring's status is dependent on that of the parents is the only way in which stratification can be or has been defined. Changes in the occupational structure can occur, and some think are occurring, in which positions may become more clearly distinguished and even polarized in terms of the rewards associated with them. These processes can come about independently of the movement of son's from father's status. Moreover, there are very likely nonachievement factors other than parental origin or socioeconomic background that may just as easily hinder the free movement of individuals in the occupational hierarchy. Yet, about ten years ago, Duncan (1968) argued that "the degree of stratification—or the degree of 'rigidity' in the stratification system . . . refers to the extent to which the level of status achievement depends upon the level of social origin" (p. 696). The more statuses are transmitted between generations, the greater the stratification; if there is little connection between the father's and son's status achievement, then stratification is minimal. In light of this definition, Duncan then says that there can be inequality between positions in terms of rewards without much

stratification as he has defined it. The focus of his definition of stratification is on the extent of movement of individuals out of their statuses of origin.

The definition Duncan and his followers offer appears to be an excessively narrow one, and one that is at variance with more traditional treatments in which stratification refers to the existence of clear social classes or groupings of categories of individuals. "Social stratification means the differentiation of a given population into hierarchically superposed classes. It is manifested in the existence of upper and lower social layers" (Sorokin 1959, p. 11).

This element of stratification is missing from the status-transmission portrayal. The population could be similarly distributed among income categories over a period of time even in the absence of status transmission. If we were to follow only the attainment approach, we would wind up missing, as someone with blinders, a great deal that is of interest to the student of stratification and inequality. There are several ways to view inequality and stratification, and status attainment is just one of these. Status attainment occurs *within* a system of inequality. Moreover, as we have seen, occupational inequality can be measured in a variety of ways, and "prestige" differential is only one of these.

2. *Status-attainment models are inadequate explanations of economic inequality.* They help illuminate part of the process involved in bringing about varying levels of educational and occupational success, but they do much more poorly in explaining income distribution, which some feel to be the major component of the system of inequality. As indicated earlier, large amounts of the variations in socioeconomic attainment are left unexplained by these models, although in contrast to many other theories, they have developed out of rigorous examination of data. Nevertheless, as explanations of economic inequality, status-attainment models founder for several reasons.

One of these is suggested by Blau and Duncan's assessment of the utility of "grand" theories of stratification for the study of mobility. After very briefly addressing the theories of Marx and Durkheim, Blau and Duncan (1967) observe that most studies of mobility do not even refer to these kinds of theories and that "the design of mobility research is not suited for the study of the problems posed by stratification theory, for it centers attention . . . on the differential conditions that affect occupational achievements and mobility within any one [society]" (p. 3). Yet it would seem clear that the latter issues are examples of the very kinds of issues of central interest to the classical and contemporary theorists of stratification who were discussed in earlier chapters. Attention to the types of factors these individuals stressed might give us better attainment explanations.

3. *Status-attainment models tend to ignore the effect of nonindividual factors on attainment.* Much of the unexplained variance in these models may be due to the operation of wider societal and institutional contexts that are not incorporated in these explanations. It seems evident that one cannot explain inequality or stratification by reference solely to characteristics of the individual or his or her background—even if some of these are ascribed and others achieved in nature. Crowder (1974) believes that much of the inequality unaccounted for may be "to a large extent produced by a combination of constraints generated by an occupational system . . . which exists *independent of and prior to* any person entering it whose achieved and familial ascribed characteristics we might measure" (p. 37, emphasis added). He argues that just demographic data on the individual are not enough and that we need knowledge about "social facts" on the nature and origin of the normative system in which rewards occur and the institutions that affect the distribution of income.

An excellent assessment of the limitations of the status-attainment models dealing with the matters just mentioned is presented by Spilerman (1978). Among the factors he contends are important for an understanding of socioeconomic inequality that are neglected by attainment re-

search are (a) the linkages that very often exist among jobs in career lines and branches, (b) the nature of and changes in the labor market over generations—over time supply and demand factors that affect individual attainment fluctuate, (c) the type of industry in which the person is employed that can affect career and promotion possibilities, as well as earnings, and (d) the sector of the economy in which the individual works— the janitor in the competitive sector will not be as economically well off, generally, as a janitor in the monopoly sector. The kind of career line chosen by the individual may also affect the elements involved in the process of attainment.

All of these factors relate in one way or another to the nature of the larger market. "A major difficulty with current models of the socioeconomic achievement process . . . is that they ignore the rich texture in labor market structure" (Spilerman 1978, p. 584). Finally, Spilerman observes that whether or not an individual's first occupation is part of a career line affects the "true value of the entered position." Two occupations of the same status and earnings may not be equal in value if the long-run prospects are much better in one than in the other.

These observations indicate the need to incorporate elements of the theories cited in the last two chapters into any explanation of socioeconomic inequality that claims to be adequate. Some of those most closely associated with status-attainment research are doing just that (Bielby 1981). An increasing number of scholars have incorporated labor market, economic sector, race, sex, and region into their models of attainment.

4. *The theoretical implications of status-attainment research have been a subject of debate.* The research has been said to be dominated by a method "in search of a substance," in essence as being without theory (Coser 1975). Its sophisticated quantitative methodology has been interpreted as symptomatic of the broader rationalization and atomization characteristic of contemporary capitalist society. It has characteristics "like the system it seeks to describe" (Gold-

man and Tickameyer 1984). On the other hand, the status-attainment approach also has been assailed not for being without a theoretical orientation, but for having a conservative one. Horan (1978) contends that it is imbued with a functionalist theoretical orientation regarding the conceptualization of occupational inequality and its implicit interpretation of the attainment process. Occupational inequality is conceived in terms of positions graded on a continuum according to prestige, rather than in terms of discrete groups making up social classes. The attainment process itself is assumed to take place in an open and homogeneous market in which individuals compete freely. Horan argues that the impact of extra-individual contextual factors is minimized in individualistic models of attainment. However, as has been mentioned, such factors have been more likely to be included in attainment models in recent years.

Another more considered and deeper theoretical criticism states that classical status-attainment research, such as that typified by Blau and Duncan, is undergirded by a particular image of society. Specifically, as was hinted at earlier, the image of U.S. society in which occupational attainment takes place is one akin to the "postindustrial" model described before. "A picture emerges of a social structure that is technologically progressive, has an advanced division of labor, an increasing middle mass of workers (many in tertiary, white-collar positions), strong educational institutions, and a stable and open social, political, economic order. This structure is characterized by high rates of mobility, a high standard of living, and increasing equality of opportunity for all" (Knottnerus 1987, p. 116). It is a society in which universalistic values and standards (e.g., ability, knowledge) have increasingly displaced the role of ascribed and other particularistic values (e.g., family ties, race, sex) in determining attainment. While status-attainment research has been voluminous, more and more methodologically sophisticated, and contributed to an understanding of attainment, acceptance of its ade-

quacy as an explanation for inequality rests in large part upon acceptance of the theoretical assumptions it makes about society. In other sections, we have indicated the weaknesses of the image of society upon which much attainment research rests.

SUMMARY

We have surveyed some of the research that has dealt with the trends in the nature of the openness of industrial societies, including the United States. These areas of research concern occupational mobility and status attainment.

After a review of some of the basic concepts developed early in the study of mobility, some of the basic problems in studying mobility were considered. Summaries of various studies of mobility were presented which, up until 1962, relied either on local data or research that had not been specifically designed for the study of mobility. Generally, the findings of mobility studies suggest that the trend in mobility has not been altogether uniform in U.S. society. Most of the mobility that has occurred in this century appears to have been brought about by changes in the occupational structure over time rather than through greater democracy and freedom in the society. The United States has more upward than downward mobility, but most of the upward mobility is of short distance. There does not appear to have been much significant change in the last seventy-five years in the extent to which the occupational status of the son is dependent on that of his father. Some broad socioeconomic advances have occurred for blacks and women in recent years, but they still lag significantly behind white males.

The second major part of the chapter concerned status-attainment research, originally given its impetus by the research of Blau and Duncan. This area of investigation was extensively covered because it has dominated much of the stratification research over the last twenty years and has reshaped the study of mobility. Two basic models of status attainment surfaced: the Blau-Duncan model, which emphasizes the importance of structural factors for attainment, and the Wisconsin model, which incorporates social-psychological elements into its explanation. Both models explain occupational and educational attainment better than they account for differences in earnings and income. Other factors are clearly involved; some of these were discussed near the end of the chapter.

The process of attainment among blacks and females varies from that found among white males. Finally, although status-attainment research has made some valuable contributions, it has limitations, some of which were noted. Both mobility and attainment studies have suffered from this emphasis on males and measures based on male data. The weaknesses of status-attainment models also suggest that wider systemic factors are involved in the generation of inequality, as recognized by some of the theorists covered earlier. The social and economic structures in a particular society provide a context in which barriers and opportunities are created. The organization of these structures can help us understand why some are rich and others poor, or why some occupy positions of high status or power while others are stuck farther down the social ladder. The continued presence of these inequalities raises the possibility that many may consider them unjust. Chapter 12 explores the issue of legitimacy and perceived fairness in greater detail.

JUSTICE AND LEGITIMACY: ASSESSMENTS OF THE STRUCTURE OF INEQUALITY

The issues of social inequality and distributive justice are joined when individuals come to believe that they deserve what they get and get what they deserve.

—Norma J. Shepelak and Duane F. Alwin

The richest one-half percent in the United States own, on average, over two hundred times as much wealth as the average household in the bottom 90 percent of the population. In fact, this small group has more total net wealth than 90 percent of the population put together. It should be apparent at this point that not only is there extensive economic, social, and political inequality in the United States, but that it has consequences for all of the people, and that not all people have an equal possibility of being mobile in the stratification system. In the face of these conditions, individuals develop attitudes and feelings about the extent and bases of economic and other kinds of inequality. It is these reactions that are of concern in this chapter. How do people feel about the present distribution of economic rewards? Do they feel that the distribution is just or fair? Their responses depend in part upon what factors they think are primarily responsible for determining the extent of a person's wealth or income and his or her position in the income/wealth hierarchy. Responses also depend upon the "norms of distributive justice" or criteria that individuals use

when making their assessment about the extent of inequality. Finally and ultimately, they depend upon the effectiveness of national ideologies and institutions in justifying extensive inequality.

When individuals come to the conclusion that a given distribution of rewards is fair, then they also tend to believe that it is legitimate. Beliefs in the fairness and legitimacy of the structure of inequality in a society are two elements that contribute to its stability and continuity over time. Thus, when trying to account for its perpetuation, it is important to know how people feel about it and what factors underlie its legitimacy. Believing that a given distribution is unfair and therefore illegitimate, however, does not necessarily mean that individuals will rise up against it by initiating riots or social movements. We will explore the conditions behind these reactions fully in the next chapter. Here we are concerned only with individuals' attitudes toward the structure of inequality and the conditions that foster legitimation. We begin with a discussion of attitudes about the fairness of economic inequality, proceed to a survey of the various theoretical and empirical definitions of a "just distribution," and finish with factors that contribute to the legitimation of inequality.

U.S. ATTITUDES ABOUT THE DISTRIBUTION OF INCOME AND WEALTH

As was noted in the first chapter, Americans often have ambivalent attitudes about social and economic inequality. This ambivalence is reflected in the way many Americans react to the extent of inequality and the living conditions of people in different economic positions and their feelings about the causes of inequality. Their ambivalence is manifested in their sporadic anger, confusion, and inconsistent attitudes about these matters (Sennett and Cobb 1973; Hochschild 1981).

Lengthy telephone interviews with over 2,200 Americans confirm the operation of an "underdog" principle in reactions to equality and inequality (Kluegel and Smith 1986). As a group, blacks are more likely than whites to consider economic equality as unjust, to desire more equality, and to feel that income should be based more on need than on skills. Women also are more likely than men to see occupational inequality and their own personal income as being unfair. Conversely, whites with higher incomes are more likely than others to endorse the present unequal distribution of income, to believe that income should be based more on skills than on needs, and to be skeptical about the positive outcomes from a more equal distribution. Despite these findings supporting the underdog principle, there is still widespread support, even among "underdogs," for the present system of inequality. The *majority* of blacks in this study, for example, still believe that inequality can be just in principle and believe that a person's income ought to be based more on skills than on need. Only among those in poverty does there appear to be clear support for need as a dominant criterion in determining income distribution (Kluegel and Smith 1986).

Overall, a majority of Americans appear to support the idea of income inequality as being just *in principle,* but do not see the present system as necessarily equitable. This is corroborated by a Gallup poll which reveals that a solid majority of Americans believe that income and wealth should be more evenly distributed. Seventy-two percent of those with incomes below $10,000 supported a more even distribution, but even among those with incomes above $40,000 (which admittedly includes a wide range of incomes) 45 percent feel it should be more evenly distributed than it is at present (Gallup, 1986). A majority of those surveyed by the National Opinion Research Center during the mid to late 1980s also feel that the income differences in the United States are "too large" (Davis and Smith 1989).

WHAT IS A JUST DISTRIBUTION?

The question of what constitutes a just distribution of scarce and desired goods is an issue that has been wrestled with for centuries. While a discussion of justice and fairness may appear to be a relevant topic of concern only for those interested in philosophy and ethics, it is a significant social-scientific concern for several reasons:

1. Since individuals carry around in their heads ideas about what constitutes equity, justice, and fairness, these ideas make up part of the normative orientation that influences their attitudes about social reality, and potentially, their behavior.

2. As social phenomena, theories about what is just often are part of the basic ideologies that influence stability and change in a system of inequality.

3. Definitions of justice and fairness are politically important since they can influence public policy.

4. The definitions embraced and the policies implemented have direct consequences for all

people, regardless of their place in the system of inequality.

What all this means is that a discussion of justice and its possible meanings is appropriate in an analysis of social inequality. In this section, we will explore a variety of interpretations of justice as it applies to inequality, while in the following section we will discuss the criteria that Americans use when deciding whether a given distribution is just or not.

The specific "norms of distributive justice" used to define a just distribution can be grouped under two broad principles. One basically argues that a just distribution exists when equal people are treated equally and unequal people are treated unequally. It is assumed that people start out with different abilities and traits and, therefore, can make different claims on scarce resources and rewards. This is what Hochschild (1981) calls the "principle of differentiation" and it approximates what Ryan (1981) calls the principle of "fair play." Given that individuals vary in their talents, abilities, and interests, it is predictable that they also will vary in their socioeconomic success, and that those with high levels of appropriate talents will assume higher positions in the hierarchy of inequality (Ryan 1981). "Identical treatment must be justified" (Hochschild 1981, p. 51). Generally speaking, this position is most closely aligned with a conservative theoretical perspective such as functionalism and human-capital theory.

A second broad principle, the "principle of equality," argues that people are of "equal value and can make equal claims on society. Differences in treatment must be justified" (ibid., p. 51). This conception approximates Ryan's (1981) notion of "fair shares" as a basis for a just distribution. People ought to have equal rights and equal access to society's resources in order to live decent lives. This principle is consistent with more radical, Marxian views of inequality and its roots, such as those that consider private property to be a major source of exploitation. There are a number of specific variations of each of these principles; let us explore some of them.

Justice under the Principle of Differentiation

The extreme interpretation of a just distribution under the principle of differentiation argues that individuals should receive different rewards because of some ascriptive characteristic on which they differ, such as, race, sex, class or caste of origin, kinship membership, or age. The assumption is that simply because an individual possesses a particular characteristic, he or she is entitled to a given level of rewards. Since people vary on each of these factors, rewards will vary accordingly. It is the way things "were meant to be." There is assumed to be a natural or even supernatural order to the world that dictates a particular hierarchy of inequality. The "Great Chain of Being" in which each lower order of human being receives rewards and duties from those above it is an example of such a belief in a hierarchy based on ascription (Hochschild 1981). The body metaphor mentioned in an earlier discussion of the caste system in India provides another, similar example of a natural order justifying social inequality (see Chapter 3).

One version of the principle of differentiation focusing on the process and assuming that people are initially different is embodied in the ideology of Social Darwinism. Social Darwinism, developed by the English sociologist Herbert Spencer, was transferred to the American context principally by the Yale sociologist William Graham Sumner. Basically, this belief system proposes that life is a process of the "survival of the fittest." Individuals struggle for scarce resources against each other in the "competition of life," and since some are more fit for this struggle than others, some will win while others will lose. In this competition, individuals should freely compete without intervention of any kind. For the state or anyone to intervene on an individual's behalf would endanger society since this intervention would be tantamount to the disruption of a natural process.

Sumner had little use for socialists who would use government to uplift everyone because he saw them as tampering with a basic and universal process. At the same time, however, he also was opposed to government that was used by the rich to advance their own interests. Free competition for all is the key to justice. As in the biological process, society perfects itself through the process of open competition in which the best prosper while the worst sink to the bottom. Sumner criticized those economists who disliked competition because it resulted in the weak suffering. He made his point very clearly: "Let it be understood that we cannot go outside of this alternative: liberty, inequality, survival of the fittest; not liberty, equality, survival of the unfittest. The former carries society forward and favors all its best members; the latter carries society downwards and favors all its worst members. . . . The former is the law of civilization; the latter is the law of anti-civilization" (quoted in Hofstadter 1944, p. 51; Davie 1963, p. 16). Sumner emphasized the process as the basis for justice. If the result turns out to be inequality, then it is nevertheless just. "If then, there is liberty, the results can not be equal. . . . Liberty of development and equality of result are therefore diametrically opposed to each other" (Davie 1963, p. 36).

Differences between individuals that affect the distribution of rewards need not be inborn or natural as Sumner suggests. There also can be differences in the efforts people put forth, in the contributions they make to the society. People often express the belief that others should get what they deserve, meaning that they should receive a reward consistent with the efforts and contributions they are making. A person can, of course, put forth great effort without making any substantial contribution. "The investment norm rewards effort, whereas the norm of results commends effort, but rewards only success" (Hochschild 1981, p. 64). While there is this difference between effort and contribution, what these norms have in common is the broad belief that what rewards individuals get out of a society should be commensurate with what they put into it. People have to *merit* the rewards they receive. Isaac Cohen, a business owner who rose up from poverty and was interviewed by Hochschild in her study

on fairness, argues that people should only get out of the system what they put into it. "If you're healthy there's no reason why you can't work and earn." If people are unwilling to put forth effort then they don't deserve support. "You have to suffer," Cohen argues, "you have to have an *incentive* to get out of the dirt" (ibid., p. 31).

As simple as this formula sounds, there are difficulties in knowing when it is in operation. As we saw with the functionalist explanation of inequality by Davis and Moore, it is difficult to determine and measure relative contribution, as it is difficult to measure effort. Ryan (1981) contends that "when we assert that one group of persons is, on the average, four or five times more meritorious than another group, we are at the very outer margins of credibility. . . . One struggles to imagine any measure of merit, any sign of membership in a 'natural aristocracy,' that would manifest itself in nature in such a way that one sizeable group of persons would 'have' eight or ten or twenty times more of it—whatever 'it' might be—than another sizeable group has" (pp. 11–12). In the absence of such indisputable measures, one could just as easily argue that allusions to differential "effort" and "contribution" are ideologies used to justify the unequal distribution of rewards. In other words, rather than occurring *before* the distribution of rewards and serving as causes for such distributions, references to effort and contributions can and often do occur *after* the distribution of rewards has been completed. These references may or may not be accurate descriptions of the means by which individuals have been distributed along the rewards hierarchy.

Justice under the Principle of Equality

In one way or another, all of the preceding positions emphasize the significance of differences between individuals in justifying inequality. The belief is that since individuals have different endowments, levels of effort, contributions, positions, characteristics, and so on, they are entitled to different levels of rewards. Most of these conceptualizations of a just distribution focus on the fairness of the *process* by which a given distribution of rewards is reached. The principle of equality, in contrast, "assumes that people begin with equal value and can make equal claims on society" (Hochschild 1981, p. 51). More often than not, the focus is not on the fairness of the process but on the fairness of the *end result*. Defining a just distribution as one in which everyone gets the same amount or in which everyone has their needs equally satisfied are examples of conceptions of a fair distribution that emphasize end results.

Rawls's (1971) theory of just distribution incorporates a concern for both the process and the resulting distribution. It has egalitarian elements but still allows for the presence of some inequality in "all social values—liberty and opportunity, income and wealth, and the bases of self-respect" (p. 62). Rawls posits an "original position" or starting point in which individuals, who are assumed to have particular characteristics, come to a conclusion about the rules determining how resources should be distributed. In this "original" state, people are operating behind a "veil of ignorance" in which they know little about the talents or other qualities of others. They are asked, hypothetically, to make a decision about a just distribution of rewards. These people are assumed to (1) be basically rational, (2) be self-centered but roughly equal in power to others, (3) have needs similar to others, (4) be careful to avoid risks, (5) be basically unenvious, and (6) be hostile toward having their own freedom curtailed.

In the process of figuring out what the distribution should be, given their personality characteristics, Rawls says that people in this original situation will eventually create two "principles of justice": (1) "Each person is to have an equal right to the most extensive basic liberty compatible with a similar liberty for others"; (2) "Social and economic inequalities are to be arranged so that they are both: (a) reasonably expected to be to everyone's advantage; and (b) attached to offices and positions open to all" (ibid., p. 228).

The first principle is consistent with the point made by others that freedom of opportunity and competition are necessary processes in determining a just distribution. The second point suggests Rawls's "maximin" principle, that is, greater goods may go to those on top as long as those on the bottom do not suffer as a result. Inequality is justified under two conditions. First, inequalities are acceptable only as long as everyone benefits from them and they are the result of occupying positions "open to all." As long as society's poorest person benefits from the inequality, then it will be acceptable; the minimum prize will be maximized. Rawls's conclusion seems to be that people making a decision in ignorance of the characteristics of others will choose greater equality than would result from completely open conflict (Frank 1985). Second, inequalities also are justified when the rewards involved serve to motivate individuals to perform certain roles. The latter point is reminiscent of the argument made by Davis and Moore for the existence of social stratification. The conclusion that inequality is justified to a degree because it serves as an incentive also reflects the views of most Americans, as we will see shortly.

Advocates of the most extreme version of justice using the principle of equality would contend that everyone should get the same amount of income, wealth, or rewards. The assumption is that all people are created equal and are of equal worth by definition. No matter what they do or what occupations they occupy or where they come from, people are to be treated equally. There should be equality of *result*, not merely equality of *opportunity*. Equality is viewed as a source of bonding among people; it creates a sense of community and sharing. Instead of seeing inequality of rewards as a source of motivation and survival for society, egalitarians see it as a potential source of division among people, promoting envy, conflict, and lower self-esteem (Hochschild 1981).

It has been suggested that those who desire economic equality are especially concerned about those who do not have economic resources to live decently. That is, their focus is on the poor and their dismal standards of living. If equality were present, this problem would be eliminated. On the other hand, and in contrast to egalitarians, it would also be eliminated if the poor had enough to live comfortably. In other words, what may be important is that every individual should have *enough,* but not necessarily the *same* amount as everyone else (Frankfurt 1985). This situation would be considered fair by those who desire a reduction in the *extent* of economic inequality, but not necessarily its complete *elimination.* An insistence upon complete equality may blind people to their own needs, which may be more or less or different from those of others. Complete equality would lead to some having their needs left unsatisfied (Frankfurt 1985). A just or fair distribution of economic resources might be one, then, in which there is inequality but given individual tastes and needs, no one envies the resources of anyone else and there is no other distribution that would make anyone better off without hurting someone else (Varian 1978).

In this definition of a fair distribution, everyone's needs are satisfied to as great extent as possible. But because individuals may have different kinds, priorities, and numbers of needs, the actual distribution of resources may be unequal even though it would be considered fair by many (Hochschild 1981). Acceptance of this definition of a just distribution is based on the assumption that people, even though each may be different from all others, are of the same, equal worth and entitled to have their needs satisfied. One of the potential difficulties of following this approach is that it may result in extreme inequality. "According to this reasoning, some people may, for the most part, give, and others receive, but the welfare of all is promoted equally" (Hochschild 1981, p. 59). Moreover, the adequacy of this approach depends upon the extent to which "needs" can be measured and compared in an acceptable manner, and this has proven to be a very intractable problem (Hochschild 1981).

The darker consequences of an absolute equality of rewards were anticipated by numerous scholars. Perhaps the greatest concern about absolute equality is that it does not appear to acknowledge those who are unique or superior in any way. In this sense, each individual is submerged with everyone else. The sameness that

supposedly accompanies equality of reward disturbs many. Among the interviews in Hochschild's (1981) study mentioned earlier, several respondents spoke against full economic equality, saying that it would "homogenize the country" or that "there has to be a difference. . . . The sameness can kill me" (pp. 31–32). The danger seen here is that while beginning with the assumption that *every* individual is valuable and should be so rewarded, a mindless emphasis on strict equality can lead to a lack of recognition of the unique qualities of *each* individual.

Ryan (1981) takes exception to several of the arguments about the assumed negative effects of equality just noted. He says that the argument that economic equality would remove incentives to work in important areas is based on the faulty assumption that people choose an area of work simply or primarily because of the material benefits associated with it. Rather, he says, people are motivated not only by money, but by their interests and the possibilities of enjoyment and autonomy. He argues that material rewards have to be used not to entice people into performing interesting and important jobs, but into doing mindless ones in which they use little of their abilities. Moreover, not all the important positions require great effort and abilities for successful performance. Research does indicate that individuals are motivated to put forth effort in particular tasks or jobs by a wide variety of factors, including their expectations about successful completion of the task, assessments of obstacles, evaluation of alternative means of reaching favored goals, and the relative importance of various goals for the individual (Steers and Porter 1975; Miner 1980).

Ryan argues further that equality does not endanger individual freedom or uniqueness. The suggested danger to human freedom and uniqueness is really the result of extreme political inequality, the domination of the many by a few, as in a totalitarian society. Therefore, it is not the result of equality but inequality. The idea that equality would lead to a neglect of the uniqueness and varied excellence of individuals is a proposition that Ryan also sees as fallacious. Part of the reason equality has been interpreted in negative terms is that excellence in this case is seen as an *individual's attribute* to be used only by and for that person for his or her own advancement. However, we can also view excellence as a quality to be shared and something from which all can benefit, in other words, as a *social resource.* Ryan contends that many of the great achievements of excellence in various fields are benefits for the whole society rather than only for that individual. Given this interpretation of the role of excellence, it is difficult to believe it would be ignored in an egalitarian society. "Excellence and talent would not be buried and thrown away in order to keep the supply down and the price up. It would be assiduously sought . . . not for the profit of a few individuals, but for the benefit of us all" (Ryan 1981, p. 96).

There are obviously difficulties in developing an absolute definition of a just distribution of scarce resources. People often vary the criteria they use when deciding whether a distribution is fair. In some spheres of life, individuals may use one set of criteria in deciding what is a fair distribution while in another they may use a completely different set of criteria. For example, based on her research, Hochschild (1981) concludes that people usually apply egalitarian standards when assessing the fairness of the distribution of political power and the socialization of different kinds of children, but use a principle of differentiation (differences in talent, effort, etc.) when appraising the fairness of an economic distribution.

Clearly, there is no single accepted definition of a just distribution. There are a wide variety of ways to define a just distribution of scarce resources, and many are quite different from the others. Now that we have reviewed these various approaches to justice, let us see what criteria Americans use to define a just distribution.

Standards Used by Americans to Determine a Just Distribution

Most of the research on distributive justice has been carried out using an experimental design to study real or hypothetical exchanges within small groups. Only recently have issues regarding the fairness of economic inequality on the societal level been systematically and empirically addressed (Cook and Hegtvedt 1983). In other words, the emphasis has been on matters of "microjustice" rather than "macrojustice" (Brickman et al. 1981). One of the questions of interest to social scientists regarding attitudes toward the fairness of economic inequality concerns the factors that affect the criteria that are used in judging an economic distribution. When people make a decision about what is just, do they compare *what is* with *what ought to be* in some ideal sense (i.e., use *utopian* criteria), or do they compare their *actual lot* with what they believe to be the criteria *actually being used* in the market place (i.e., *existential* criteria)? That is, do they use an abstract set of principles in deciding what is just or unjust, or do they compare themselves with others and, using the principles that seem to be operating in society, make a decision about justice.

There is some theoretical justification for deducing that at the small-group level individuals are more likely to use existential rather than utopian criteria. Some personal characteristics appear to affect the distribution rules that are chosen by individuals in group situations. Individuals who see each other as being similar in attitude or who contribute highly to a task and like each other seem to prefer *equality* as a basis for a just distribution (Greenberg 1978; Cook and Hegvedt 1983). *Need* and *effort* rather than *contribution* are more likely to be used as criteria among friends than among nonacquaintances (Lamm and Kayser 1978; Lamm and Schwinger 1980).

Social conditions and settings also appear to influence which criteria are used. We saw in an earlier study that individuals use different criteria for the economic, political, and socializing spheres of life (Hochschild 1981). In the political and economic arenas, it has been suggested that the nature, stability, and history of power/dependence relationships between groups will influence the kinds of distribution rules that are used to determine a just situation (Stolte 1987). It has also been proposed, though not fully demonstrated, that a person's beliefs about the causes of economic inequality may affect his or her attitudes about its fairness (Shepelak and Alwin 1986). This is especially likely to be the case if characteristics of the *process* (e.g., effort, contribution, etc.) by which an individual receives an income are examined and used as criteria by most to reach a conclusion about fairness. Finally, the dominant ideology in a society will affect the criteria individuals choose to use.

Americans appear to give mixed messages when asked what they believe determines an individual's economic position. Data from national surveys during the mid to late 1980s indicate that they are close to being split in half on whether they agree that when a person has a high position it demonstrates that the person has "special abilities or great accomplishments," or that "what one can achieve in life depends mainly upon one's family background." At the same time, a large

majority believe that, in general, "one can live well in America" and that how far one gets in life depends "on the abilities one has and the education one acquires" (Davis and Smith 1989). The variations in the patterns of responses may be linked to variations in the wording of questions, but very likely also reflect the ambivalence of Americans about the system of inequality mentioned earlier.

The NORC survey asked respondents how important various factors were for "getting ahead in life." The response distributions were as shown in Table 12.1. The data in the table show clearly that the vast majority of Americans believe that individually achieved factors such as hard work, ambition, and having a good education are critically important if a person wants to get ahead in life. The majority also believe that "natural ability" is very important as well. Structural factors or those over which individuals have little control such as race, sex, being from a wealthy family, and region of origin are believed by most Americans to be quite unimportant in determining how

TABLE 12.1 Perceived Importance of Various Factors in "Getting Ahead in Life" (National Sample)

	Essential/ Very Important	Fairly Important	Not Very Important/ Not Important
Being from a wealthy family	20%	29%	51%
Having well-educated parents	39	41	20
Having a good education	84	15	0
Having ambition	88	11	0
Having natural ability	59	36	4
One's hard work	89	9	2
Knowing the right people	40	45	14
Having political connections	16	31	52
One's race	15	26	60
One's religion	15	14	71
One's sex	15	24	62
One's political beliefs	9	26	65
Region of country one comes from	7	15	78

Source: Davis and Smith (1989), pp. 490–493.

far a person gets in life. These and other data indicate that Americans tend to underestimate the real effects of race and sex on occupational attainment and earnings, because in an earlier chapter it was demonstrated that both race and sex have a significant impact on attainment (Shepelak and Alwin 1986).

The general pattern of these results is supported by other studies (e.g., Kluegel and Smith 1986). A majority of individuals in all social classes feel that intelligence and selfishness (personal ambition?) increase as an individual goes up the class ladder (Jackman and Senter 1983). But despite the strong belief by most Americans that education is very important in explaining attainment, research suggests that it explains well under half of the variation in occupational attainment and that its tie to occupational attainment is much weaker than would be expected in a society in which merit determines accomplishment (Krauze and Slomczynski 1985). In other words, despite some concrete evidence to the contrary, most Americans subscribe to the "dominant ideology" that: (1) opportunity for economic mobility is prevalent; (2) each individual is personally responsible for the extent of his or her own economic success; and (3) in general, therefore, the system of inequality is fair (Kluegel and Smith 1986).

Not everyone, of course, is equally likely to subscribe to the belief that individuals are primarily responsible for where they wind up. When it comes to explaining why some people are wealthy, for example, blacks, regardless of their incomes, and women are more likely than white males to cite structural reasons such as inheritance, the connection between political and economic power, and the ability of the rich to exploit the poor. They are also more likely to believe that structural factors, such as the lack of schooling provided by society and the low wages provided in some parts of the economy, are involved in explaining poverty (Kluegel and Smith 1986).

Other techniques also have been used to uncover the criteria Americans believe actually do

and should be used to determine income. When asked to judge what incomes certain kinds of hypothetical households received, respondents in an Indianapolis study, perhaps not unexpectedly, associated higher occupational status, higher education, being white, and being male in a single-person household with higher incomes, while those with larger families were believed to receive lower incomes (Shepelak and Alwin 1986). Another study presented hypothetical vignettes to a sample of 200 white adults (Jasso and Rossi 1977). The individuals in these vignettes varied in sex, marital status, number of children, educational attainment, occupation, and earnings. Six hundred different vignettes were created, and respondents were asked if the fictitious person in each of a limited number of vignettes presented to them was (1) overpaid, (2) fairly paid, or (3) underpaid. There was a nine-point rating scale ranging from "extremely underpaid" to "fairly paid" to "extremely overpaid." The results revealed some interesting patterns. Single females were more likely than married females to be seen as being overpaid. Those with higher education and occupational status (especially males) and those with a greater number of children who are married and male were more likely than opposite groups to be viewed as underpaid.

These findings indicate that people use a mixture of achievement-related and unrelated criteria to make decisions about what is fair. While occupation and education are used to make judgments, so are sex and marital status. Most Americans, including blacks and women, also apparently feel that income should be based more on skills than on level of need (Kluegel and Smith 1986). A direct implication of all these findings is that an equal distribution of income among the individuals in these vignettes would be considered unfair, although they are not in favor of the range of incomes that presently exists. When respondents were asked in the Jasso and Rossi study to attribute a fair income to each of the fictitious individuals, the responses ranged from just over $7,000 for a single female with seven years of education and a low-status job, to about

$34,500 for a college-education married couple with high-status professional jobs. This suggested fair range in earnings is much smaller than the range that actually exists in the labor market. The conclusion that most Americans believe that the range of incomes from bottom to top is too great is supported by other research as well (Davis and Smith 1989; Kluegel and Smith 1986; Alves and Rossi 1978; Rainwater 1974).

BASES FOR THE LEGITIMATION OF STRUCTURED INEQUALITY

The preceding studies indicate that most people in the United States believe that it *is* the individual more than anything else that determines upward mobility in the socioeconomic hierarchy. Most Americans subscribe to the dominant ideology mentioned earlier. Fitting this in with the earlier theories of a just distribution, most individuals use the "principle of differentiation" in defining a just distribution. It is the *process* that must be seen as being just. The evidence also suggests that criteria over which the individual presumably has great control, such as education and skills, *should* be used more than other kinds of factors to determine income. These beliefs obviously fit into the dominant American ideology that, if people invest in themselves, they can improve their economic fate in life. Yet, as mentioned earlier, the evidence suggests that there are obstacles to equal opportunity for certain categories of individuals, and that not everyone with the same kind of job and education earns the same amount of income. The question then is how do individuals come to accept a belief system even though there is evidence that contradicts it? How is an ideology internalized so that Americans come to believe that inequality is legitimate and justified? Most Americans, for example, believe that income incentives, and therefore economic inequalities between them, are needed and justified to motivate people to work harder and take on extra responsibilities at work and to accept the sacrifice to obtain extra education to become a lawyer or doctor (Davis and Smith 1989). While

Americans on occasion will state that they believe that structural factors such as inheritance patterns influence wealth attainment, for the most part they subscribe to the individualism ethos.

In this section, we will explore various mechanisms through which the system of inequality in the United States is legitimated. These mechanisms exist on the level of the *individual* in her or his everyday experiences as well as on the *institutional* level, working through the family, the education system, and other institutions. Let us begin at the level of the individual to see how people internalize the belief that inequality is fair.

Legitimation at the Level of the Individual

How do ideologies become internalized by people? This is a question addressed by Della Fave (1980), who tries to describe how individuals develop self-evaluations and judgments about the fairness of inequality. To begin with, individuals are social beings, that is, they develop only in relationship with each other. As individuals grow and develop, they come into contact with greater numbers of people who react to them in a variety of ways. Individuals learn the expectations others have of them by noticing how others behave toward them. This combination of the expectations and reactions of others toward us makes up what Mead called the "generalized other" (Della Fave 1980). It is through the relationship with the generalized other that individuals develop a definition and image of themselves. Seeing how others react to us leads to the development of a particular self-image. We can see ourselves as others see us; we can view ourselves as an object, from the outside as it were. By viewing ourselves as others see us, we come to a conclusion about our own worth and our contributions to society.

A consistent self-image over time requires the social support of others. "A person who maintains a self-definition with no social support is mad; with minimum support, a pioneer; and with broad support, a lemming. Most of us are lemmings" (Huber 1988, p. 92). Clearly, from the surveys we have discussed, since ambition and hard work are seen by a large majority as central and justifiable reasons for wealth, most of us see the wealthy as deserving of their position. A linkage has been made here between a person's position and its deserved nature. This positive assessment of the wealthy influences how we react to them and, therefore, their own self-images.

But how does the individual reach the conclusion that those who are wealthy work harder, contribute more to society, and therefore deserve more than others? Briefly, Della Fave (1980) argues that individuals reach conclusions about the reasonableness of their beliefs from what they consider to be an "objective outside observer." In other words, it is from this "observer" that individuals develop ideas about what reality is and how it operates and it is this "observer" whose judgments are internalized. It is the generalized other who fulfills the role of this observer, and it is the reactions of the generalized other to others that individuals internalize. Since a wide variety of people subscribe to the dominant ideology mentioned earlier, they react to the wealthy as being deserving. This appears to be an objective evaluation, and so they come to interpret them, others, and themselves accordingly. Those who are reacted to favorably or are treated as if they were important by almost everyone, including other important people, develop a very positive self-image while others develop self-evaluations that are not quite as positive. "It is from the generalized other that individuals form an evaluation of self and, thus, of the worth of their 'contributions.' It is upon these evaluations, in turn, that judgements of equity are made in accordance with the principle of distributive justice" (ibid., p. 961).

Those who are successful also develop feelings of self-efficacy, that is, they believe that their own actions can bring about successful rewards. This is largely because of positive reactions to their success by others, which then encourages them to do more and reinforces their high self-efficacy. Viewing their own success as being a result of their own actions, they come to define it as legitimate and deserving (Stolte 1983).

Those who possess very positive self-evaluations, in turn, come to view their own high level of rewards as being deserved relative to others, whereas those with more negative self-images see themselves as being worthy of fewer rewards. Since in a large complex society individuals have to piece together general images of what others are like and what their contributions are on the basis of the limited information they have access to, individuals make conclusions about the contributions of others based on the information that shows on the surface, namely, their wealth and income. Those with high incomes, in turn, can use their resources to "manage the impressions" that others have of them, that is, manipulate the interpretations of others in such a way that the latter develop a positive image of them (Goffman 1959). As was noted in Chapter 3, the demeanor of upper class people can be tailored in such a way as to elicit deference and respect. Moreover, their ability to maintain high positions in educational, work, and other institutions reinforces the image of their greater contributions and worthiness for higher rewards. Those with greater amounts are viewed as making greater contributions, as deserving of their economic resources, given the widespread belief that rewards should be commensurate with contributions. Essentially, the process of legitimation in this case is circular: Those with greater rewards elicit greater respect and the feeling from others that they deserve what they have, which in turn reinforces the inequality found in the hierarchy of rewards (Della Fave 1980). A skeletal interpretation of this process is presented in Figure 12.1.

According to Della Fave (1980), the entire internalization and social process just described bears directly on the extent to which the system of inequality is legitimated. The greater the degree to which the distribution of self-evaluations in society matches the distribution of rewards, the more legitimate the system of inequality will be considered and the more stable the society's structure of inequality will be. Conversely, if the two sets of distributions are not matched, then the stratification system is less likely to be defined as legitimate.

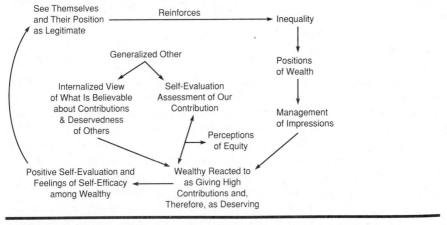

FIGURE 12.1   The Internalized Process of the Legitimation of Inequality
Source: Based on Della Fave (1980), pp. 955–968.

Several of the relationships suggested have been tested recently. Following Della Fave's theory, Shepelak (1987) tested relationships among income, self-evaluations, and the belief in individual responsibility for a person's position. Her interviews with over 300 Indianapolis residents revealed that those with higher incomes did indeed have more favorable self-evaluations than those with low incomes, and that those with better self-evaluations were more likely than others to attribute their incomes to their own effort. However, the latter explanations were not related to either family income or estimates of equity/ fairness. Family income and self-appraisals were both found to be positively related to the feeling that an individual's income was fair.

Conversely, those with low incomes were more likely to say that they were being underrewarded. In other words, contrary to Della Fave's self-evaluation theory, those with lower incomes do not feel that they deserve less than those above them. In fact, family income is more strongly linked to beliefs in the fairness of one's family income than are either self-evaluations or explanations of income level. "These findings fail to substantiate the view that disadvantaged persons believe they deserve less" (Shepelak 1987, p. 501). Rather, they provide support for those who found that income is inversely related to the

belief that the system of inequality is legitimate (Form and Rytina 1969; Robinson and Bell 1978). On the other hand, support was found for the conclusions that a person's income standing and explanation of present position do affect feelings of self-worth. Figure 12.2 shows the interrelationships found among self-evaluations, income, perceptions of fairness, and perceived causes of income.

In addition to the self-evaluation process just discussed, there are other bases of legitimacy that exist at the level of the everyday lives of individuals. Most people, perhaps especially those who have to scramble to eke out a living, are too

FIGURE 12.2   Relationships between Self-Evaluations, Income, and Fairness
Source: Based on Shepelak (1987), pp. 500–501.

wrapped up in their ordinary lives and "personal troubles" to give much thought to the broad public issues of legitimacy and stability. "What ordinary men are directly aware of and what they try to do are bounded by the private orbits in which they live; their visions and their powers are limited to the close-up scenes of job, family, neighborhood; in other milieux, they move vicariously and remain spectators" (Mills 1959, p. 3). While they may not be happy with the "way things are," they are unsure of the structural sources of this vague discontent. The result is that more often than not they go along with the way things are and do not question the culture or social structure of the society, thereby lending legitimacy to social arrangements by default.

Some research studies show that the social activities of those in the working and lower classes are usually limited to those involving friends and relatives; exposure to a wide range of types of people and geographic areas is restricted. The value and belief system that develops out of involvement in this immediate environment is basically "accommodative" in nature, helping individuals to make sense out of their everyday concrete situation. Thus, it also tends to be "parochial," that is, tailored to explain or deal with the specific and immediate context in which these individuals live (Parkin 1971). As it concerns social inequality, part of the accommodation in this value system is to accept inequality but also to try to improve one's position within it. Thus, the value system generated in the local neighborhood does not ordinarily lead to a basic questioning of the system of inequality and its bases or to development of a radical ideology. Rather, people accept it in the abstract and then try to concretely adjust to it. So, "dominant values are not so much rejected or opposed as modified by the subordinate class as a result of their social circumstances and restricted opportunities" (Parkin 1971, p. 92). Marx further suggested, it will be recalled, that close-up involvement in the monotonous routine of everyday life by members of the working class leads them to begin to believe that their situation is normal and natural,

and not to believe in or even to imagine an alternative situation.

Legitimation at the Macro/Institutional Level

Because most people are too involved in their everyday affairs, they ordinarily do not give much thought to how wider social structures and broader cultural frameworks may affect their lives. Social structures usually are accepted as givens; even those on the bottom who benefit least from the existing social arrangements seldom revolt or organize social movements to bring about change. While it is clear that self-evaluation and similar social-psychological processes are involved in legitimating social inequality, a society's culture and its social institutions are also directly implicated in the legitimation process. As in the case of self-evaluation's role, the basic question is how do institutions and cultural values operate in ways that justify and maintain the hierarchy of social inequality?

It has been noted several times that Americans have ambivalent feelings about inequality. A large part of the reason for this ambivalence lies in the frequently inconsistent values that make up U.S. culture. At the abstract level, a core value in the culture is the belief in equal opportunity or "fair play." Americans generally subscribe more to "equality of opportunity" than to "equality of results." In addition to a belief in equal opportunity, dominant value "tendencies" in U.S. society also include a belief in competition, achievement, success, work or activity, efficiency, individual personality, progress, freedom, nationalism and racism.

At the same time, the general culture incorporates values of humanitarianism and morality (Williams 1970). While they are not all consistent—for example, the belief in the sacredness of the individual versus the value of racism—most of these values help to justify social and economic inequality in U.S. society. We have seen that differential rewards are more often believed to be the result of differential effort or work by individual personalities striving to achieve success in a context of free, open competition with others. To attack capitalism or the structure of inequality that has existed for generations would be for many not only unfair, but unpatriotic. So these values, by and large, push people in the direction of supporting the existing system, while other, though apparently fewer, values such as humanitarianism and moralism imply a questioning of inequality as inequitable.

Ultimately, it must be individuals who endorse any system of inequality if it is to be considered legitimate. At the same time, however, the beliefs and values that individuals endorse derive, in large part, from the broader institutional and cultural framework in which they are embedded. Our task here is to describe how the system of inequality and the supporting values infiltrate the social institutions so that institutions foster activities and reinforce beliefs that legitimate inequality. How do institutions help to maintain the hierarchy of social inequality?

Before examining the roles of specific institutions, let us look at several ways in which dominant institutions in general influence behavior and attitudes. Institutions consist of rules and structures that circumscribe what can and cannot be done. Moreover, these features of institutions help to define what is permissible and what is not, what is a legitimate issue or problem and what is not. "In various ways, the institutional forms confine the boldness of our thinking, the adventures of our knowledge, the formation of a feminist social consciousness, the redistribution of resources to organize the unorganized, and the full completion of the enterprise of liberation" (Smith 1987, p. 218). Smith (1987) relates how her research on mothering and education, which might help parents organize their "collective interests" in the schools, was controlled by the local school system. All research in the schools has to be cleared by the school board, and because of this, it has to be organized, proposed, and conducted in a manner that is consistent with the perspective of professional educators, not parents. "Professionalism" defines what is allowable and professionalism is defined by those most es-

teemed and dominant in the profession (generally white, higher status males). This creates limits on what information can be collected and what can be done with it.

The preceding example suggests that one of the tools used by institutions to legitimate social structure, including the system of inequality, is to frame the image of that structure and the processes associated with it in a particular way with the use of certain kinds of concepts and terms. Language can importantly influence the interpretations placed upon issues like "poverty," "welfare," and "political participation." The terms used to describe what is defined as a "social problem" also can influence how people react to them. "Quiescent public acceptance of poverty as a fact of social life depends upon how it is defined, far more than upon its severity" (Edelman 1977, p. 7). Governments can affect the extent to which citizens interpret "poverty" as legitimate by using particular symbols to describe it. To indicate that some people are on "welfare" to most Americans suggests something about the character of these individuals and their responsibility for their fate. Someone who is seen as a "welfare case" by an outsider is usually thought to be a person who does not work and probably does not want to work, one who is "living off" the rest of society. The term itself evokes an image quite different from the term "poor."

When poverty is attributed glibly to "human nature" or to "economic laws" it allows people to justify denying help to the poor while at the same time permitting them to feel sorry for the poor. The result is that inequality is accepted and policies do not change (Edelman 1977). When arguments explaining the existence of inequality are couched in terms that cannot be tested empirically but yet are emotionally powerful, it is difficult to argue against such reward differences. Referring to income as "rewards" or "earnings" plants the belief that the money is "earned" and therefore deserved. Attributing the high rewards of a position to its "functional importance" to society helps to legitimize differential rewards. People have been socialized to react positively to the "needs" of "society," "the national interest," and "earnings." Terms such as these encourage the acceptance and legitimation of "material sacrifices, constricted roles, political weakness, existing power hierarchies, and unfulfilled lives" (Edelman 1977, pp. 153–4).

Institutions of all types use language and symbols to create an imagery that legitimates the existing social reality. The use of certain terms to evoke images and to thus encourage the acceptance of inequalities between individuals applies not only to economic differences between rich and poor, but between men and women and blacks and whites (see Chapter 4). Because of the symbolic power of the concepts used by institutions and because of the intrusion of major institutions into most corners of their lives, people develop certain interpretations about society and other people, including those who are meritorious and deserving and those who are not. We will discuss the images of the poor more fully in Chapter 14.

The family, education, and religion all contain elements that encourage acceptance of inequality. Let us explore some of the ways in which each of these institutions fosters legitimation of social inequality.

Family   The family is a principal instrument of socialization. It is within the domestic sphere that men and women learn much about how they should define themselves, their proper roles, and what they can expect from each other and society. Women are associated traditionally with an "expressive" role in the family; their primary responsibility is for nurturing and addressing the emotional needs of family members. In the urban setting of modern society, "the woman's fundamental status is that of her husband's wife, the mother of his children, and traditionally the person responsible for a complex of activities in connection with the management of the household, care of children, etc." (Parsons 1964, p. 95). Women can, of course, choose to pursue a career instead, but if this occurred on a large scale, it would be necessary to bring about "profound al-

terations in the structure of the family" (Parsons 1964, p. 96).

Men, on the other hand, have been expected to perform an "instrumental" role, which means that while the women's focus is on the internal life of the family, men's concerns are with adapting to the outside world, primarily in making a living to support the family. Functionalists like Parsons have viewed this role differentiation as a source of complementarity and efficiency. Women have a central role in reproduction and, since this occurs in the domestic sphere, it is more efficient, "natural," to have them be responsible for the expressive role in the family. The whole trend in social evolution, in this view, has been toward increased specialization and differentiation of function, which further legitimizes the role specialization of the two sexes.

Over generations, the continual socialization of men and women into these roles leads them eventually to be thought of as "natural." The fact that this role differentiation has generally been thought of in the past as ideal by many Americans, and that most women have been content with the role indicates how powerful this ideology has been (Bem and Bem 1970). The balance that comes from the complementarity of these roles in the traditional functionalist view has integrative consequences for the society; it keeps society functioning smoothly. Of course, the behavior of others outside the family, such as nurses at the hospital when the child is born, babysitters, teachers, and relatives, further reinforce the gender-role distinctions considered appropriate for the sexes (Bernard 1981). The personality stereotypes of the sexes are consistent with their traditional roles. Men are still thought of favorably as being basically competitive, ambitious, independent, and logical, while women are well thought of for having good manners, being gentle, warm, soft-hearted, and affectionate (Werner and La-Russa 1985).

While it may appear to be reasonable to view these personality traits and roles as merely complementary, as different but equal, the status and the power connected with each of them are quite different. As was pointed out earlier, capitalism and its values have shaped major institutions in modern society. This means that the social statuses attributed to families by individuals outside the family are based on what the occupational statuses of breadwinners are and how much income they bring home. As was noted in Chapter 10, the differences in status and power between the sexes are linked to the division of labor between them.

Education Schools also perpetuate and legitimize inequality between the sexes, races, and classes through a variety of mechanisms. In general, it has been argued that one of the principal integrative functions of education is to have individuals perceive the educational system as a microcosm of the wider society in which their attainment is dependent upon hard work and appropriate skills. The dominant ideology shapes people's view about the nature of the educational institution and achievement in it. The educational system is viewed as an institution through which individuals with varying abilities and levels of effort are channeled into appropriate levels of the occupational structure. The school appears as a forum in which students openly compete with each other and then are objectively evaluated by the experts. "The educational system fosters and reinforces the belief that economic success depends essentially on the possession of technical and cognitive skills—skills which it is organized to provide in an efficient, equitable, and unbiased manner on the basis of meritocratic principle" (Bowles and Gintis 1976, p. 103). But, Bowles and Gintis argue, the skills learned in school and IQ and test scores do not have a strong effect on an individual's economic success. Rather, according to this argument, schools are in the business of preparing students to be funneled into work roles at appropriate status levels.

At another level, various aspects of teacher-student relations encourage acceptance of an individual's traditional place in the structure of inequality. By teaching students about the nature of social reality, such as the values of the "free market," intellectuals help to support the status quo.

In Gramsci's (1971) phrase, intellectuals often have been "managers of legitimation" (also see Miliband 1977). This includes members of the "helping professions," such as social workers, psychiatrists, and teachers. While educators often have encouraged happiness through adjustment to the status quo, those involved in these professions "have reinforced inequality by equating adjustment to existing social, economic, and political institutions with psychological health" (Edelman 1977, p. 152). People who deviate from their expected roles or who criticize the social structure are defined as "deviant" and are dealt with accordingly (Mills 1959).

Some of the teacher behaviors that encourage adjustment also reinforce traditional gender roles in U.S. society. Teachers in elementary schools pay more attention to males when they fight, suggesting that boys are more prone to aggression. At the same time, they pay more attention to the needs of girls by giving them more assistance than boys, thereby inadvertently encouraging their dependence on authority figures (Serbin et al. 1973; Fagot 1977). Since men are more likely to be in positions of authority, for example, as principals in schools, children learn that it is normal for men rather than women to have power. Exposure to opposite situations appears to reduce the chances of children developing stereotypical views of gender roles (Paradiso and Wall 1986). What children read and how men and women are portrayed pictorially in textbooks also have their impact. When children act in a way that violates traditional sex-role expectations, they are ridiculed by their peers (Lamb et al. 1980).

Thorne's (1989) recent study in a California working-class elementary school further reveals the variety of ways in which traditional sex roles and inequalities are legitimated. For example, through participant observation research she found that boys and girls frequently engage in "borderwork." This refers to "forms of cross-sex interaction which are based upon and reaffirm boundaries and asymmetries between girls' and boys' groups" (p. 76). Types of borderwork include various contests inside and outside the classroom in which the sexes are pitted against each other. Another form is "chasing" in which boys and girls tease and try to elude each other on the playground. "Invasions" also occur in which members of one sex will "invade" the game being played by the other sex. These activities and what is said while each is going on reinforce and legitimize traditional ideas about what is appropriate for each sex. The dominance of boys in this informal world is demonstrated by (1) the greater playground space that they control, (2) the greater probability of invasion by boys in girls' games, and (3) the association of greater "pollution" (e.g., "cooties") with girls (Thorne 1989).

Class content is another avenue through which political and economic inequalities are legitimated. By and large, the information presented in classrooms and textbooks serves to reinforce a favorable interpretation of the United States and its history. Children have seldom been told in detail about unethical acts by national leaders or of the brutalization of such groups as Native Americans. "None of this is very surprising. . . . Throughout history all children have been socialized to accept the dominant values and institutions of their society" (Kerbo 1983, p. 388).

Teacher expectations of blacks and whites and members of higher and lower classes also have been shown to be different. The images teachers have of lower status groups influence their expectations of them. Less is expected from them, which ultimately affects how well they do in school. Their lower performance then only reinforces the initial negative image held by teachers, resulting in a "self-fulfilling prophecy." Their lower performance also appears to justify their lower attainment, further strengthening the belief that attainment is linked to merit. The lower expectations by teachers of lower status individuals influence them to place these students in lower noncollege-oriented tracks. Their placement in these tracks helps to ensure their lower educational attainment (Farley 1982).

Not only the curricula but the social organization of schools at the secondary and university levels are different for those that primarily serve students who will enter relatively low-status positions upon graduation, and those that have students who will enter elite positions. In the lesser junior colleges and lower tracks of high school, "students will be given more frequent assignments, have less choice in how to carry out those assignments, and will be subject to more detailed supervision by the teaching staff" (Hurn 1987, p. 331). This is in sharp contrast to the greater autonomy and flexibility permitted at more elite schools. The organization, rules, and curricula of each level of education are organized to prepare students for the tasks they will confront in the occupations they will likely enter. In this sense, education helps to keep the system of inequality intact by accommodating its students to the demands of the economy. Social reproduction explains more fully how the educational process works to maintain inequality from generation to generation (see Chapter 9). What is important about all these mechanisms is that their effects are largely unrecognized, while most perceive that attainment is the result of individual effort and abilities. Schools are for learning, teachers are the objective experts, and students study and take valid tests, are judged on the basis of their performance, and are placed accordingly in the hierarchy of attainment. Where students end up appears to be solely up to them. This reinforces the individualist ideology accounting for social inequality in the wider society.

Religion   The French sociologist Emile Durkheim argued that the religious institution was functional for both the individual and society. For individuals, it helps them to deal with difficult problems, provides some answers to difficult questions, and makes their lives meaningful. For society, religion is integrative because its beliefs and rituals take individuals out of their secular lives and bring them together to form a community. Religion, for Durkheim, was primarily a *social institution* rather than a *personal psychological experience*. It is out of the social gathering of individuals that feelings of a superior force or power outside individuals first arises. Thus, he argued that the worship of supernatural forces in religious rituals is really an adoration of the powers in society. "In the divine, men realize to themselves the moral authority of society, the discipline beyond themselves to which they submit, which constrains their behavior even in spite of themselves, contradicts their impulses, rewards their compliance, and so renders them dependent and grateful for it" (Sahlins 1968, pp. 96–97).

Given this description, it should come as no surprise that images of the supernatural world often mirror the social structure of society. Swanson (1974) showed concretely in his study of non-western societies that a social hierarchy on earth is reflected in a social hierarchy among the supernatural. In societies in which older people occupied positions of importance, ancestors were a subject of worship, and in societies in which there was a great deal of social inequality, religion helped to legitimate the differences between the top and the bottom. A good example of this legitimation occurs in Hinduism in which the concepts of karma, dharma, and samsara combine to explain and justify the continuous inequality generation after generation. "Karma" indicates the belief that a person's present situation is the result of his or her actions in a previous life, and "dharma" refers to the duties and norms attached to each caste. Finally, "samsara" refers to the continual birth and rebirth of life. In other words, central beliefs in Hinduism absolve society or others from responsibility for social inequality. It is the result of individual actions (Turner 1986).

Particular branches of Christianity also, of course, have legitimated people's beliefs about inequality. Protestantism, in general, which focuses on the individual relationship between each individual and God, stresses the importance of hard work and equality of opportunity in attaining success. Success is expected to be the result of self-denial and continuous effort, not the result of easy inheritance. This kind of "spirit" is what is embodied in Weber's concept of the "Protestant ethic" and is especially associated with specific forms of Protestantism. Hard work and religious beliefs were intermingled by many famous

preachers early in U.S. history. Cotton Mather, a charismatic Puritan preacher of the late seventeenth century, lectured that business and people's occupations were "callings" and not to be ignored. If individuals do not engage in their occupations, but rather remain idle (slothful), poverty will befall them. Riches are the result of industry, and poverty is the result of individual laziness. Those who are poor should expect no help from others since it is their own behavior that has resulted in their dismal situation. By engaging in business, people are doing what God intended: "Yea a *Calling* is not only our *Duty,* but also our *Safety.* Men will ordinarily fall into horrible *Snares,* and infinite *Sins,* if they have not a *Calling,* to be their preservative. . . . If the Lord Jesus Christ might find thee, in thy *Store House,* in thy *Shop,* or in thy *Ship,* or in thy *Field,* or where thy *Business* lies, who knows, what *Blessings* He might bestow upon thee?" (in Rischim 1965, pp. 24, 26). It is only a short jump from this statement to the belief that those who are successful are so because of their own efforts and are among the favored of God, while those on the bottom do not work and are sinful.

Advocates of Dutch Calvinism justified slavery by viewing blacks as sinners and slavery as a just condition for their sins and inferiority in the eyes of God. The legacy of these beliefs can be found in the contemporary dilemmas of inequality in South Africa (Turner 1986; also see Chapter 4). In the United States, a slave catechism was used in many churches during the period of slavery to justify domination by masters, to encourage work, and to attribute lack of work to personal laziness. White pastors told blacks that God created the masters over them and that the Bible tells them that they must obey their white masters (Fishel and Quarles 1967). There are also elements in Christianity that have been used to support continual subordination of women to men, including the Biblical argument about the origins of woman out of man and the injunctions to obey one's husband in marriage.

"Civil religion" also uses religion to justify the "American way of life." It is a mixture of religious and political ideology in which the U.S. social structure and culture are seen as favored by God. God and Americanism go hand in hand in this ideology. This is a nation "under God" and its institutions are sanctified by the Almighty. At civil ceremonies and during certain public occasions, such as the opening of Congress, presidential inaugurations, and the pledge of allegiance, God is mentioned and the United States is his (her) benefactor. A recent study indicated that most elementary-school children believe that the United States "has been placed on this earth for a special purpose," that it has a "chosen" status with God, and that it is successful because it is morally good (Smidt 1980). The "American way" that is so blessed incorporates the values of individualism, freedom, capitalism, and equality of opportunity which make up a core part of the ideology supporting inequality. Increasingly, many television evangelists have developed large numbers of followers, numbering over 20 million in 1980 (Hadden and Swann 1981). Preachers such as Pat Robertson and Jerry Falwell conjoin Christianity and Americanism in a manner that makes them not only mutually supportive but almost indistinguishable. In this ideology, to attack Americanism becomes tantamount to committing a serious sin. Americanism is supposed to be accepted, not criticized or undermined.

Karl Marx viewed religion under capitalism as having many of the effects on inequality just discussed. People are expected to put up with inequality; religion lulls them into a false sense of complacency. That is, it makes them *falsely conscious* of their real situation. It blinds them to the real causes of their predicament (i.e., class exploitation not personal sin). In this way, socioeconomic inequality is seen as legitimate by those who only blame themselves or look forward to another life when conditions will be better for them.

Of course Marx realized that historically, before capitalism, religion had been used to support the oppressed; even in our own time, religions have not always supported the status quo. Martin Luther King, Jr., and the Southern Leadership Christian Conference used religious ideas to try

to improve conditions of blacks in the United States, and Catholic bishops have fought on the side of the poor against many Latin American dictatorships (Light et al. 1989; Hehir 1981). Catholicism also has been a force for change in communist Eastern Europe (Parkin 1971). Despite these instances where religion has opposed inequality, historically it has been more closely associated with its legitimation and maintenance. This has been the case with each of the social institutions we have discussed. By and large, each has served to support the dominant value system as it pertains to inequality, and it is through each of them that individuals come to believe that the social inequality around them is legitimate.

SUMMARY

The principal focus of this chapter has been on examining the reactions to the fairness of social and economic inequality, the criteria that define such fairness, and to explore the factors that contribute to the legitimation and, therefore, the stability of inequality in the United States. Americans are clearly torn on the fairness issue. On the one hand, they believe that hard work, education, and similar personal investments are important for economic achievement and believe that they should be important. On the other hand, most feel that the extent of inequality is too great, but they do not think that full equality of income or wealth would be fair either. Moreover, when asked what they think determines success, they tend to overestimate the significance of some factors and underestimate the impact of others, most notably race and sex. In their assessments of criteria to be used in determining a fair income, Americans tend to use a mixture of achievement and other factors (e.g., education, marital status, sex, occupational status).

The system of inequality itself is legitimated at the individual and institutional levels. On the one hand, individuals develop interpretations of their own and others' rewards and contributions from the reactions of others to inequality. Their position in the rewards hierarchy affects their own self-evaluations and their appraisal of the fairness of their own incomes. At the same time, those with positive self-evaluations interpret their own incomes as being the result of their own efforts.

Through their social organization and norms, institutions help to encourage traditional beliefs about the causes of inequality maintaining, thereby, the structure of inequality. Generally, the values impressed upon members and clients of those institutions are those of individualism and capitalism. Through the language and symbols used and their rules of knowledge, institutions define what is "real" and proper. In the case of the family and education, institutions shape beliefs and roles for those in different positions of the system of inequality and encourage a belief in the legitimacy of their positions. Religion also has used its resources on many occasions to legitimate the socioeconomic inequality that surrounds individuals.

At one point in the chapter, we noted conditions under which such inequality might be perceived as illegitimate. Illegitimacy is one of the factors motivating attempts to change the structure of inequality. The next three chapters deal more fully with concerted attempts to bring about such change. While the last two deal with formal government policies aimed at dealing with issues of economic inequality and poverty, the next chapter deals with selected social movements that have tried to reduce social and economic inequality.

CHAPTER 13

SOCIAL INEQUALITY
AND SOCIAL MOVEMENTS

Thru this dread shape humanity betrayed,
plundered, profaned and disinherited,
cries protest to the judges of the world,
a protest that is also a prophecy.
—Edwin Markham

In societies where extensive social inequality not only exists but is perceived as being unjust, it is not unusual for people to demonstrate their feelings against it. A variety of potential devices exist for redressing or reducing such inequality. In this chapter, we will explore three social movements that were explicitly aimed at doing just that. Each of them focuses on the grievances of a different group, but all of the movements attempted to improve the life chances of the groups in question. The early labor movement of the latter part of the last and the first decades of this century in the United States, the civil rights movement of the 1960s, and the women's movement of recent decades are examples of concerted efforts to change social and economic conditions for their constituencies. Our purpose here is not to provide an exhaustive history of these movements, but rather to demonstrate systematically how each of them grew out of conditions relating to the structure of social inequality at the time, and how that structure affected the ebb and flow, goals and tactics of those movements.

THE EARLY LABOR MOVEMENT

One of the first things to understand when examining any social movement is that the wider so-cial, historical, and cultural context in which it takes place has an impact on the development, shape, and ultimate fate of the movement. Obviously, the poor conditions and deprivations experienced by industrial workers in the latter part of the nineteenth and early part of the twentieth centuries created dissatisfaction and feelings of hostility. Even though there was some improvement in wages after 1880, hours were long, wages were still low, and work conditions were dangerous. There were few if any protections against the hazards of chemicals, machinery, and inhalants from work in the mines and mills. Laborers on the railroads and in construction and logging industries also were exposed to extreme dangers. There was little concern for safety, and many of the wildcat strikes of this time were related to safety issues.

Writing of the period between 1865 and 1917, Asher (1986) observes that "industrial workers have been victimized by low wages, company stores, blacklisting, arbitrary dismissals, forced overtime, sexual exploitation, company spies, police brutality, and a host of other ills" (p. 115). Some of the dangers were inherent in the nature of the work and the technology used, and the fear of competition and concern for profit kept employers preoccupied with matters other than safety (Asher 1986). The early scientific-management movement among employers sought to organize, systematize, and thoroughly gain control of the workplace for management. In order to keep production and efficiency up early in the twentieth century, the pace of work in many plants was accelerated, stop watches were used, and work was constantly checked by inspectors. This created further alienation among workers.

Living conditions in most instances also left much to be desired. Dubofsky (1975) describes a typical immigrant residential area in Pittsburgh: "Situated in what is known as the Dump of Schoenville runs a narrow dirt road. Frequently strewn with tin cans and debris, it is bereft of trees and the glaring sun shines pitilessly down on hundreds of ragged, unkempt, and poorly fed chidren" (p. 23). The company towns and cramped urban ghettos made for dreary living conditions. In his study of "How the Other Half Lives," Riis (1890) described the conditions in which New York City workers lived. He found "an urban jungle of exploitation, family disintegration, crime, and human degradation" (quoted in Green 1980, p. 20). Even as late as the 1920s, living conditions for most workers were still poor. During these years, even though some improvements had been made, work was hard, hours were long, and the level of wages left little money for leisure and recreational activities. In 1929, 42 percent of families had incomes below $1,500, which was barely enough to keep a four-person family going (Zieger 1986).

Despite the awful circumstances of the lives of most industrial workers, however, more is needed to explain the development and continuation of the labor movement over time. Certainly, workers responded to negative changes in their workplaces and in the wider political economy. But as was discussed in Chapter 7, it takes more than deprivation to explain the development of collective action on the part of an aggrieved group. While exploitation and deprivation may have induced solidarity among workers, the strength of organized labor depends upon other conditions as well.

The growth of the labor movement was affected by a combination of external and internal factors. Externally, the strength of workers tended to be greater when there was a tight labor market; this gave them greater bargaining power. Strength also grew when economic opportunities were plentiful. The chances of a labor movement being successful also were enhanced when society allowed a variety of political and legal expressions and permitted greater access to resources (Jenkins 1983). For example, this occurred during the 1930s after FDR's election and passage of the Wagner Act which legalized the right to unionize. These events created alternate sources of power, and when the potential for political and economic power of labor were high, so was the solidarity of workers. The belief by workers that they would be spending a large part of their lives in their jobs and that they could make a political difference in society also increased their solidarity and the probability of a labor movement.

Sources of Control over Workers

Cohesiveness is a source of strength. Greater solidarity means greater organizational or collective power, and the relative strength of organization among opposing groups implicated in the situation affects the probability that a movement will develop (McAdam 1982). Employers who were more often better organized and had broader political resources on their side fought workers in many bloody battles in the latter part of the nineteenth and well into the twentieth century. Around the turn of the century, as now, it was in the economic interest of employers to minimize the solidarity among workers, thereby hindering the development of a labor movement. A variety of techniques were used to do this (Griffin et al. 1986). One of these was the use of largely unskilled immigrant laborers, many of whom, as machine tenders, replaced natives. Blacks and foreign labor also were used as strikebreakers. These moves on the part of employers created animosity against foreign laborers and weakened the cohesiveness of labor in general.

A second technique that created divisions within the ranks of labor involved the redesigning of the division of labor. For much of the nineteenth century, craftsworkers had held control over their work and occupied indispensable positions in the iron, steel, and machinery industries (Dubofsky 1975). Nevertheless, employers and their foremen controlled the workers through direct personal control, "intervening in the labor process often to exhort workers, bully and threaten them, reward good performance, hire and fire on the spot, favor loyal workers, and generally act as despots, benevolent or otherwise" (Edwards 1979, p. 19). The "scientific-management" movement further strengthened the power of supervisors over workers. It prescribed the dividing of tasks into their smallest, elemental components in order to increase efficiency and output. But in so doing, it also introduced extreme specialization and monotonous work on the shop floor. Tasks were divided up into such small parts that even completely unskilled individuals could perform them.

While not universally implemented in industry, scientific management reflected an important perennial source of labor-management conflict, that is, the issue of who controls the work process. Numerous early confrontations were over the question of who should direct the pace of work tasks (Dubofsky, 1975; Piven and Cloward 1977; Edwards 1979; Stephenson and Asher 1986). Through the use of scientific management, management was able to wrest control of production and the labor process from craftsworkers, who up until this point had been the experts on how to accomplish given work tasks. All of this expropriation of control was done under the guise of being a "scientific method" for organizing work. Scientific management removed the planning and control aspects of the work process from the worker and placed it in the hands of the manager. Workers generally fought the use of scientific management.

The techniques for controlling the work process changed as capitalism perfected its technology. Improved manufacturing techniques such as the assembly line, created technical controls. *"Technical control* involves designing machinery

and planning the flow of work to minimize the problem of transforming labor power into labor as well as to maximize the purely physically based possibilities for achieving efficiencies" (Edwards 1979, p. 112). Later, control was achieved through the widespread implementation of bureaucratic structure, which builds control into formal sets of rules, positions, and authority hierarchies. Both technical and bureaucratic methods build control into the very fiber of the organization, replacing the personal control of the manager or foreman, which was often perceived as being arbitrary. The evolution of different forms of control can be legitimately viewed as attempts by industrialists to increase efficiency, production, and profit.

But the use of foreign and black labor along with changes in the mechanisms of control were only two of the techniques used to weaken labor. Industrial management also used another technique that had the effect of minimizing solidarity among workers—"welfare capitalism." Briefly, welfare capitalism included special savings plans and bonuses, homeownership aid programs, stock-purchasing options, and group-insurance plans. Most significant among the programs offered were employee representation plans or work councils and company unions. The latter plans presumably gave workers a meaningful voice in the operation of the organization. Around World War I, the concept of "industrial democracy" had become quite popular. Clearly, these employee representation plans, while suggesting a democratic and more equal relationship between employer and employee, were aimed at reducing worker allegiance to outside unions and slowing their attempts to organize themselves (Brody 1980; Griffin et al. 1986).

There is some question as to whether the programs involved in this approach were primarily a conscious attempt by employers to reduce identification with other workers by making workers dependent on and loyal to industry, or rather an honest attempt to deal with the problems that attended changes in industrialization and to treat employees more humanely. The motivation was very likely a combination of paternalistic concern for workers, the belief that a more satisfied workforce would increase productivity and efficiency, and a desire on the part of employers to control labor. The latter function, however, appears to have been the most important (Griffin et al. 1986; Brody 1980).

A variety of conditions contributed to the demise of welfare capitalism after the late 1920s. Many of the basic concerns of workers were still not being addressed, such as, full control over the work process, protection against unemployment, higher wages, and a shorter work week. On top of these factors was the fact that welfare capitalism was expensive and only some large firms could afford the programs. Hence, it was not widespread among all industries. Finally, the Depression made it virtually impossible for firms to meet the idealized goals of welfare capitalism (Edwards 1979; Brody 1980).

Employers also fought the organized labor movement by fighting against closed or union shops, advocating open shops in their place. In the latter, employees need not be members of unions to remain employed. This push for open shops under the "American Plan" label was especially dominant during the first decade of this century. The National Association of Manufacturers launched a campaign for open shops across industries, while other business-oriented groups (e.g., National Civic Foundation) argued that if unions were to exist and be acceptable, they had to be "responsible" in nature. In response to business attacks on union shops, some trade unions began to take in more unskilled workers as members (Green 1980). The conservative trade unionism of the AFL was preferable to the more militant and revolutionary approach of the IWW (Griffin et al. 1986). The espousal of welfare capitalism and a conservative brand of labor organization helped create an appearance of employers as being reasonable and fair. But neither of these enhanced the ability of labor to organize effectively in its own interests.

Employers had, of course, other resources by which to resist encroachment by labor. Spies were employed to monitor labor activities; legal actions were encouraged against militant workers and organizations; and the power of police, state militia, and federal troops also were used to quell labor unrest. Some states had laws specifically outlawing unions that were considered to be "revolutionary" or that openly advocated the taking over of industries by workers (syndicalism). Leaders of such unions could be and were put in prison or deported (Perlman and Taft 1935; Griffin et al. 1986). The informal political alliance between business and government was reflected in the frequent use of police or military might in putting down worker protests.

In the late nineteenth century, workers often had the support of local officials, so industries had to get help from state and federal sources (Dubofsky 1975; Green 1980). In numerous strike actions between 1890 and 1920, state militia and federal troops were used against workers. The steel plant conflict at Homestead, Pennsylvania, in 1892 and the Pullman railroad boycott of 1894 are only two instances in which soldiers were used against strikers. In Lawrence, Massachusetts, in 1912, the American Woolen mill employed roughly 40,000, about half the city's population. About half of the employees were young women and most were foreign born. But when a group of young Polish women were given reduced wages for no explicit reason, a strike was organized and spread to other mills. In this case, too, police and militia were used against strikers, but after a couple of months the workers in the "Bread and Roses" strike, as it was called, won wage gains (Green 1980). In 1914, militia in Colorado waged a violent attack on coal miners, shooting strikers and burning their families out of homes. Their violence across the southern part of the state reminded some of the tactics that had been used in the earlier Indian Wars (Zieger 1986). Many other labor-employer confrontations occurred during this period. Throughout World War I up to 1920, large strikes by rail, meatpacking, and steel workers occurred. In 1919 alone, there were 3,600 strikes (Zieger 1986). But in most cases, employers emerged as the victors (Piven and Cloward 1977; Brody 1980).

In the last years of the nineteenth century and the early years of the twentieth century, workers simply did not have the political or organizational power to be consistently successful against industrial owners. "Whatever force workers mounted against their bosses, whatever their determination and their unity, they could not withstand the legal and military power of the state, and that power was regularly used against them" (Piven and Cloward 1977, p. 102). The only effective legal control on the contract imposed by the employer at the turn of the century was the condition of the labor market. As long as employers had government, the press, and the market behind them and a large number of immigrant workers available, there was little that could get employers to voluntarily improve their contracts with workers (Ginzberg and Berman 1963). All of the preceding discussion demonstrates that changing technological conditions, population composition, and the differential availability of political and economic resources to labor and management decisively affected the development of the labor movement. Access to resources had an especially significant impact on the effectiveness of countermovements and countertactics by each side in the conflict (Griffin et al. 1986).

Internal Divisions in the Labor Movement

The particular *directions* taken by the labor movement have been explained in a variety of ways, but not altogether successfully (cf., Laslett 1987). The varying images of the roles of unions, industrial changes, and social and cultural heterogeneity within the working class and disagreements on the goals of unions all helped to shape the differentiation within the movement. An early approach of the 1880s emphasized the educational function of unions. These organizations were seen as educators of immigrants, proponents of public schools, and often supporters of the socialization of private industry. Thus, in this

approach, unions were not seen as being preoccupied with wages and job conditions alone, but with broader issues. The actions and goals of several early unions (Knights of Labor, IWW, CIO) make that clear. Another approach to understanding unions saw them as organizations created to buffer the effect of the ill fit between humans who desired to be free and the controls inherent in modern mechanization. The Marxian approach viewed unions as being rooted in class struggle over control of the means of production.

A final and most influential view of labor unions in early America was to view them as tools for increasing the economic benefits of workers. Perlman (1928) argued that in surveying all the changes that have taken place in the economy and technology, workers came to the conclusion that they cannot operate independently as separate entrepreneurs. Rather, Perlman argued, they became reconciled to their positions as employees in businesses owned by others and realized there was not a great deal they could do to change the way things were. Given this situation, workers could hardly be expected to be revolutionary; they were only willing to fight for better wages and job conditions. It should be remembered that Perlman presented his theory before the Great Depression had occurred and before development of the CIO. He also does not appear to give much credit to the imagination and ambition of workers (Laslett 1987).

There is no question that some of these emphases were reflected in the internal structure of the organized labor movement of the early twentieth century. The *forms* the labor movement took in the United States were also conditioned by industrial changes. In the waning decades of the nineteenth century, the social organization of the economy was undergoing rapid change, and these changes had implications for both employer and employee. For example, the period beginning with the late 1880s was one in which economic enterprises dramatically increased in size and frequently merged with each other. In other words, it was a period in which economic power became more consolidated and concentrated (Edwards 1979). Even though in most of the nineteenth-century factories, authority was decentralized among foremen and various craftsworkers, industrialization brought in its wake a more simplified, detailed division of labor, increasing the need for less skilled laborers.

Machines often fomented dissatisfaction among skilled craftsworkers and encouraged antagonism between the unskilled industrial workers who could do simple work and operate basic machines, and those who were skilled craftsworkers before machines became dominant (Stephenson and Asher 1986). Machines rapidly took the place of workers, and control over the workplace more frequently fell into the hands of owners and their foremen. "For more and more wage earners, the power over their working lives receded far off into distant central offices and into the hands of men probably unknown to them" (Brody 1980, p. 8). These shifts in technology helped to drive wedges between unskilled and skilled workers, thereby stimulating the different directions in which the organized labor movement would go.

Along with technological changes, productivity rose rapidly, but so did the demand for labor. Immigrants flooded into the United States from a variety of countries. Consequently, the late nineteenth century was also a period in which the size of company workforces increased. The industrial working class grew significantly, but it was composed of individuals from sharply contrasting social and cultural backgrounds. The industrial working class for much of the latter half of the nineteenth century was a conglomeration of native-born craftsworkers, some farmers who had left the land to come to the cities of New York and New England, skilled immigrants from Britain and western Europe, Irish who came to the United States after the potato famine in their native land, and Chinese who became employed primarily in the railroad industry.

After 1880, immigrants from eastern and southern Europe joined the ranks of the less skilled in industry and became an increasingly large part of the industrial working class (Aronowitz 1973). As the demand for labor grew and these immigrants flooded into the country to take lower positions in the mines, mills, and factories, the labor force in the North was almost as segregated by nationality in 1900 as the Southern market was by race (Green 1980). Moreover, as the century came to an end, the proportion of women and blacks involved in industry also increased. In 1900, almost a quarter of all women were in the labor force. The point of all this is that the heterogeneous nature of the working class at this time created divisions that often hindered the solidarity of workers when conflict arose with their employers.

This heterogeneity was used by employers to minimize worker cohesion. Businesses consciously recruited large numbers of unskilled immigrants who served as an available labor supply; this was used to regulate employment and possibly even wages. The employment of ethnically diverse workers stirred antiforeign sentiments among natives which discouraged the organization of all workers. Blacks, Mexicans, and ethnic whites also were used as strikebreakers, again discouraging unification among workers.

The racial and ethnic differences within the working class meant language, skill, and religious differences as well, making control of working-class militancy easier. So these internal divisions had direct implications for both the working class and its employers. Some labor leaders had no wish at all to bring "nonwhites" into the organized labor movement, but rather were primarily interested in advancing the interests of white, skilled craftsworkers. Exclusionary practices, including explicit policies prohibiting admission of nonwhites, were not uncommon among many AFL unions (Green 1980). This was to be a bitter source of antagonism within the labor movement. On the one hand, Samuel Gompers, who founded the American Federation of Labor in 1881 was against the inclusion of nonwhite, nonskilled workers. In 1905, Gompers proclaimed to a group of union members in Minneapolis that "caucasians" were "not going to let their standard of living be destroyed by negroes, Chinamen, Japs, or any others" (quoted in Green 1980, p. 46). The miscellaneous category of "others" referred to people from what were considered at that time the less desirable regions of Europe, such as the Slavic countries and Italy. Keep in mind that ideas about the biological inferiority of different groups were still circulating at this time (see Chapter 4).

In contrast to the AFL which sought to unionize skilled white craftsworkers, other organizers felt that it was crucial to organize all industrial workers. Among those groups that supported the organization of all workers, some had socialist or communist leanings. The Knights of Labor, briefly popular in the 1880s, was among those groups that argued that all workers should be included in the organized labor movement. Rather than advocating the homogeneous composition found in the trade and crafts unions of the AFL, the Knights preferred mixed groupings of workers. The Socialist Party of America, founded in 1901 and under the leadership of the charismatic Eugene Debs, also favored an organizational umbrella that would cover the mass of workers in industry. A few years later, the IWW, and several decades later, the CIO also actively sought the membership of blacks and all industrial workers.

As their views about the compositions of labor organizations varied, so did labor leaders' views on the appropriate goals for the labor movement. The goals of the Knights of Labor were broad and involved the reorganization of the industrial order to create a more just society. Internal divisions and the increased power of employers helped to push the Knights into decline (Grob 1971; Dubofsky 1975). These "utopian" goals were eschewed by the newer AFL trade unions which sought more immediate narrow rewards for their members, such as higher wages and better working conditions. This "pure-and-simple" or "business" unionism was more consistent with native American values according to some interpreters. Lipset (1971) argues that U.S. workers have been more interested in fighting for

better wages and working conditions than for reconstructing U.S. society. A large part of the reason for this orientation, argues Lipset, is due to the openness of the class structure, and the values of materialism, equalitarianism, and individual opportunity. Individuals in this context see themselves more as *individuals* than as members of a *class* and see social change as resulting more from individual efforts than from mass organization or social structure as an agent for social change. The American values of work, social and geographic mobility, comfort, and "common sense" also lie behind the belief that individuals do and should determine their own economic fates (Dunlop 1987).

The AFL's trade unionism has aimed at working within the present economic system rather than trying to change it. The emphasis on increasing labor's power has been for the purpose of more effective collective bargaining than for political reasons. Early AFL leaders felt that government should not interfere in labor matters. It should be up to labor to chart its own course and make its own gains (Brody 1971). Gompers' "voluntarism" perspective underscored the belief that labor should not solicit aid from the government for those goals it can accomplish by itself (Green 1980). Paradoxically, this stance helped to create a bond between the AFL and establishment forces, fostering increased cooperation between the union, management, and the government (Rogin 1971; Brody 1980).

In this interpretation, because of cultural and other differences U.S. workers are not as interested as their European counterparts in a basic change *of* the economic system as much as they are in changing their individual positions *within* the system. "Within the American working class, no significant movement or section of workers defines itself as a class and sees its mission to be the same as the liberation of society from corporate capitalist social relations" (Aronowitz 1973, p. 260). "Most men and women live in a real world," writes Dobofsky (1975), "a world of simple, everyday happenings, small pleasures and recurrent sufferings, which shape their attitudes as much as abstract principles" (p. 48). The trade unions, with their narrow orientation, help to sustain the "job consciousness" of U.S. workers. Similarly, Brody (1980) also has concluded that in the waning years of the last century, the labor movement was (1) practical rather than utopian or theoretical, (2) nonrevolutionary with narrow material interests, and (3) impatient with intellectuals and academicians who had theories about the direction the labor movement should pursue.

Despite the narrow orientation of many workers, however, one should not conclude that there has been no revolutionary fervor or concerns at all within labor. "Such an approach has always been unfair, especially during the heyday of the IWW between 1905 and 1917, and in the early years of the history of the CIO. It was especially untrue during the period of the Knights of Labor . . . which . . . upheld producer's and consumer's cooperation, equal pay for women, and a 'proper share of the wealth that they (the workers) create' " (quoted in Laslett 1987, p. 362). Organized labor has not been a uniform homogeneous mass.

As suggested earlier, differences in races, cultures, goals, and organizing principles have created fissures in the "house of labor." There has been a consistent thread of concern among many workers since the last century over who controls and directs their work. Part of the battle that has been waged between labor and management has involved such issues. "In fact, American workers have waged a running battle over the ways in which their daily work and the human relations at work were organized over the last century, and in the process they have raised issues which go far beyond the confines of 'wage and job consciousness' or 'bread and butter' unionism, into which historians have long tried to compress the experiences and aspirations of American workers" (Montgomery 1983, p. 389). As the number of industrial workers has grown, employers have had to wrestle with the problem of how to control them, and the mechanisms of control have evolved as technological and organizational innovations have developed (Edwards 1979). In the

late 1920s, there was a clear division between the working and business classes (Lynd and Lynd 1929), even though most workers did not identify with the Socialist or Communist parties (Zieger 1986).

Just prior to World War I, then, organized labor contained several different types of organizations and orientations. The trade-union wing, exemplified by the AFL, was solidly on its way but did not incorporate most unskilled and semiskilled industrial workers. The Socialists had political influence on many workers even though the latter's trade-union orientation remained intact. The IWW organized those left out by the more conservative AFL affiliates, was active and militant, and was led by the imposing Big Bill Haywood (Brody 1980).

The Russian Revolution, America's involvement in World War I, and the accompanying patriotic fervor that swept the nation legitimated political and coercive attacks upon Socialist organizations and the IWW, and as a result the power of the Left in organized labor declined. "The labor hopes of the American left, hitherto bright, died in World War I and its aftermath" (Brody 1980, p. 41). In the patriotic context of the postwar period, organized labor in general was a victim of attacks from industry. The "American Plan" of business proclaimed the consistency of the "open shop" with U.S. values. In this hostile atmosphere, the AFL became more cooperative with industry and government. With the restrictive immigration laws of the 1920s reducing the inflow of unskilled labor from culturally undesirable countries, industry's source of fresh workers was weakened. By the late 1920s, labor unrest had calmed down even though the benefits of welfare capitalism did not include all industrial workers. Moreover, the cost of living was increasing, erasing many of the gains that had been made by some workers (Zieger 1986).

From the Depression to the Present

On the whole, the 1920s and the early 1930s were not kind to U.S. workers. "The symbol of the twenties is gold . . . the twenties were, indeed, golden, but only for a privileged segment of the American population. For the great mass of people . . . —workers and their families—the appropriate symbol may be nickel or copper or perhaps even tin, but certainly not gold" (Bernstein 1960, p. 47). Bernstein labels the 1920 to 1933 period as "the lean years" for the worker (ibid.). A litany of the problems for workers would include the stagnation of the union movement during the period (union membership fell from 5 million in 1920 to 3.5 million in 1929) and the absence of any effective industrywide collective-bargaining tools. Employers could hire who they wanted and workers had little recourse in the matter. Immigration slowed during the 1920s, which meant that it was no longer as easy for native workers to move up occupationally. Older workers found it more and more difficult to hold on to their jobs, as farm migrants and women increasingly entered the urban labor force. Mechanization displaced workers. Between 1920 and 1929, it is estimated that about one-third of those displaced by machines in the manufacturing, coal mining, and railways industries remained unemployed (Bernstein 1960). Moreover, the shift to more mechanized professional positions did not help many workers, who did not have the qualifications for such positions. Income inequality was also extensive in the society. The combined incomes of the top 0.1 percent of families were as great as those of the bottom 42 percent of the population. Within the working class there were also divisions in wages based on regional, ethnic, racial, skill, union membership, sex, and residential differences. Irish, Italian, Jewish, Black, and Mexican workers were generally worse off than native white workers (Bernstein 1960).

The effects of the Great Depression on employment were disastrous. In the middle of 1930, almost 4.5 million were without jobs. Shanty areas cropped up in and around cities, places of makeshift residences sometimes called "Hoover-

The Depression had a serious impact on the life chances of most working people in the United States. By 1933, an estimated 15 million people—about one-third of all workers—were unemployed.

villes." Hunger also rose dramatically. By early 1931, there were an estimated 8.3 million unemployed, but the number was to rise even further to 13.6 million by the end of that year, and to 15 million by early 1933. At that time, about one-third of all wage/salary workers were completely out of work. Many others were only working on a part-time basis (Bernstein 1960).

Needless to say, the Depression in the early 1930s changed political dynamics inside and outside the labor movement. The AFL had successfully cultivated close relationships with industrial management and government forces. It stressed union-management harmony and fought against leftist elements in the labor movement. The Depression made many workers and unions realize the need for state help and intervention. The Depression raised questions among the unemployed about the ability of the present economic and political systems to deal with catastrophic problems, especially as it became clear over the bitter years of the 1930s that it was not the lack of individual efforts but rather broader social forces that were behind much of the misery being experienced (Piven and Cloward 1977). At the same time, however, the vast majority of citizens still had faith in the U.S. system and did not see Socialism or Communism as a viable alternative. Nor did they think of themselves as a full-fledged working class fighting capitalism (Aronowitz 1973; Dubofsky 1986; Zieger 1986).

In the early part of the century, labor had received little help from the federal government, especially during the Republican administrations of the 1920s. This was a difficult time for government because in the past it had actively supported industry, even to the point of using federal troops against workers. Hoover had favored the voluntaristic and self-help approach to solving economic problems, but because of the continuing difficulties faced by labor during the Depression, there was also pressure for the federal government to step in and help solve the problems faced by average families. The massive problems caused by the Depression revealed "the primitive character of public assistance in America" (Zieger 1986).

At the same time, the recently elected Roosevelt was viewed by workers as being more sympathetic to labor's cause. In essence, government had to carry on a balancing act between business and labor during the 1930s.

The feeling on the part of many workers that they had a more sympathetic president emboldened them to drive for more gains, but especially for the right to unionize without reprisals from management. The workers were told by labor leaders that the President wanted them to join unions. Labor was on the march, and union membership grew dramatically during the late 1930s.

While workers sought government support in the early 1930s, the AFL was against governmental unemployment and welfare programs as a means to improve the conditions of workers. Rather, they tried to rely upon deliberations with employers as a means to keep earnings up to a decent level (Zieger 1986).

Given the conservative orientation of the dominant AFL, many still unorganized workers had to continue to fight for unionization and often fought against the approaches advocated by the AFL. Workers were pitted against mainstream unions which tried to appease and mollify increasingly militant workers (Piven and Cloward 1977). The Depression had helped to destroy belief in the existing relationship between labor and management and to legitimate a move for the greater structural protection afforded by unionizing (Brody 1980). During the 1930s, labor became "uncommonly militant" (Zieger 1986). In this period, hundreds of sit-down strikes occurred. In 1937 alone there were almost 500, involving approximately 400,000 workers (Piven and Cloward 1977).

Several critical events strengthened labor's hand during the 1930s, in addition to the political-administration changes that had occurred. One was the rising prospect of war in Europe. American companies that had armament contracts with European countries could not afford major labor unrest to disrupt production. A second event was the passage of the Wagner Act in

1935 which legalized the right of workers to organize and bargain collectively under the protection of the National Labor Relations Board, which could monitor business compliance with the law. This law, bitterly fought by business, resulted in a rapid upsurge in union membership. In the mid- and late 1930s, union membership tripled, reaching about 9 million in 1939 (Zieger 1986). A third event that increased the power of labor was the creation of the CIO in 1935. The Congress of Industrial Organizations unionized many of the previously unorganized mass-production industrial workers. Unlike the AFL, it aimed at being a union for all workers. Its leader, John L. Lewis, also realized that the CIO had to recruit skeptical blacks to prevent their being used as strikebreakers. In 1937, the CIO had about 4 million members. The New Deal and events during the 1930s left in their wake a triumvirate of power: big government, big business, and big labor.

During and after World War II, union membership was still high and growing, and unions had become a powerful and effective force for improving the working conditions of their members. But the ideological tide began to shift against organized labor in the late 1930s. The recession of 1938–1939, which led to a weakening of federal recovery programs, factionalism within the CIO which many suspected had communist leanings, the increasing patriotism during the early years of World War II, and the impatience of many with the increased militancy of workers immediately after the war strengthened conservative forces against unions (Zieger 1986). The increased bureaucratization and job consciousness of unions over the years and the routinization of formal contracts and the "rule of law" in industry also helped to institutionalize labor-industry conflict. Employers were more willing to buy off workers with higher wages than to relinquish control of the production process (Brody 1980; Zieger 1986). The Taft-Hartley Act of 1947 renewed many of the powers that had been lost to business in the Wagner Act. It also curbed the power of unions to strike, required an anti-Communist

pledge from workers, and redefined labor's rights in much narrower terms (Piven and Cloward 1977; Zieger 1986).

The increased conservatism and narrowness of unions meant that workers often fought against the wishes of union leadership. The interests of workers and those of the union leadership did not always coincide. This internal division within the labor movement has continued. While union membership generally grew during the 1950s and 1960s, and more public employees initiated unionization drives, differences of opinion within the labor community surfaced over Vietnam and the civil rights and women's movements of the 1960s. In the conservative 1980s and early 1990s, unions were again under attack, membership declined, and union leadership appeared weaker than in the earlier heyday of organized labor. These circumstances, coupled with revealed corruption and apparent rigidification of unions, have raised questions about whether the organized labor movement has been seriously, or perhaps even fatally, wounded (Brody 1971, 1980; Zieger 1986). Perhaps the labor movement has come full circle back to the 1920s. But as we have seen, changes in historical, economic, and political conditions can rejuvenate this ailing patient.

THE MODERN CIVIL RIGHTS MOVEMENT

Although it often discriminated against both blacks and women, the labor movement was driven by concerns over inequities in political and economic power, and historical, cultural, and social conditions shaped its development and form. In general terms, the same can be said of the civil rights movement of the mid-1950s and 1960s. While an indisputable specific date for its beginning cannot be given, there is general agreement that it began in the period between 1953 and 1955 during which the historic *Brown* v. *Board of Education* Supreme Court decision was made, and systematic bus boycotts had occurred in Baton Rouge, Louisiana, and Montgomery, Alabama. The nonviolent movement extended into the mid-1960s up to the point when other more radical, black-power elements were becoming increasingly important.

As is the case of the labor movement, there had been many instances of protest by blacks against whites before the civil rights movement. Revolts by slaves against their masters, the underground railroad, the massive growth of the NAACP membership to almost half a million during World War II, the demands that led Roosevelt to establish a Fair Employment Practices Committee, and A. Philip Randolph's political activity in Washington and before Congress in the 1940s all provide evidence of racial protest and a push for racial equality before the civil rights movement (Morris 1984). Thus, the movements of the 1950s and 1960s did not just suddenly appear out of nowhere. Public activism in movements waxes and wanes as social, economic, and political circumstances in the surrounding environment change. Consequently, what may appear to be the beginning of a social movement may only be a resurgence of activism that had been kept in "abeyance" because of lack of opportunity structures in the social context (Taylor 1989). As was found in the labor movement's history, particular historical, political, economic, and social conditions created a context in which effective mass protest could be initiated, and the civil rights movement could be nurtured. The actual battle for racial justice predates, then, the so-called modern civil rights movement.

In the late nineteenth and early twentieth centuries, blacks had few resources with which to launch a massive civil rights campaign. First of all, racist ideologies discouraged support from whites. Second, most blacks were fully but exploitively integrated into the southern economic and political structure. There were few economic opportunities open to them and Jim Crow laws kept them in their assigned place. In other words, the social context offered few political and economic opportunities or alternatives. Third, the Congress and the Supreme Court did little to alleviate the oppressive conditions under which blacks lived. While Congress stood by as blacks were disenfranchised and violently treated in the South, the Supreme Court stamped its approval of the belief in black inferiority into the Constitution.

The North and the federal government did little while black subjugation and white supremacy were being systematically institutionalized in the South. This structured inequality was especially evident in the political realm. Blacks were effectively prevented from voting through the use of various devices including poll taxes, tests of literacy and "good character," grandfather requirements, and primaries limited to whites. Laws in the South prohibited the integration of blacks and whites in schools, hospitals, motels, places of recreation, and even funeral homes and cemeteries. These "Jim Crow" laws made it legal to spend less public money on black than on white institutions (Sitkoff 1981).

The Changing Context of Racial Inequality

However, after World War I, it was clear that changing *economic* and political conditions would strengthen the power position of blacks in the United States. Among these economic changes was a decline in the centrality of agriculture in the southern economy coupled with increasing industrialization of the urban South. This agrarian decline was fostered in part by declines in immigration and agricultural exports during the war. Accompanying the decline in immigration was an increase in the demand by northern industry for laborers from the South. Both "King Cotton" and industry needed workers, but changing circumstances created a shift in demand from agriculture to industry. Before and after World War I, there was massive black migration to the North and to cities to seek employment in industries (Piven and Cloward 1977; Sitkoff 1981; McAdam 1982). Southern agriculture suffered again during the Great Depression of the early 1930s. An overproduction of cotton due to decreased demand led to a drastic decline in its price, which spelled disaster for many southern farmers. In Mississippi, at that time perhaps the greatest stronghold of white supremacy, farmers lost their land at about twice the national rate (Bloom 1987). Later, during the 1940s, as mechanization also became more and more essential in agriculture, some farmers left agriculture behind, and the average size of landholdings increased. This meant that more black as well as white farm workers were economically displaced and needed to seek employment in the industries of northern and southern cities (Piven and Cloward 1977). Southern agriculture also had to diversify its products to feed the soldiers in military camps during World War II (Bloom 1987). All of these circumstances served to shake up the foundations of the traditional economy in the South.

The changed *geographic* and economic base of blacks helped to develop the voting power of blacks and the indigenous institutional bases needed for the civil rights movement (McAdam 1982). The city provided greater opportunities for blacks to get organized, to receive more education, and to lay the basis for an expanded black middle class. The growth of these basic strengths within the black community was important in the genesis of the civil rights movement. There is good evidence that, despite the importance of external resources to the movement, its origins and development can be traced to reliance on institutions indigenous to the black community (Oberschall 1973; McAdam 1982; Morris 1984; Jenkins and Eckert 1986).

However, some have suggested that professional organizations gave impetus to the civil rights movements (McCarthy and Zald 1973, 1977). These organizations, in contrast to "mass-based" organizations, have outside leaders, have a full-time staff on salary, have significant outside benefactors, and play the role of "speaking for" aggrieved groups (Jenkins and Eckert 1986). Despite the argument that the origins of the movement can be traced to these organizations, evidence suggests otherwise. Jenkins and Eckert traced the involvement and support of indigenous and professional organizations over an approximately thirty-year period (the late 1940s to 1980). Their conclusions were clear enough:

"Professional SMOs were not the model actors at any point in the civil rights movement. Nor did they initiate the challenge, their efforts coming on the heels of indigenous actions. . . . [T]he challenge was initiated by the grassroots groups, especially the churches and student groups" (p. 819).

Black colleges, churches, and civic and fraternal institutions provided not only economic resources, but the communication network and most of the leaders needed to organize the movement. Martin Luther King, Jr., for example, was influential as a movement leader not only because of his charisma but, crucially, because of the personal and organizational backing he received. The influence of the Southern Christian Leadership Conference during most of the movement's career suggests the relevance of religious institutions. Local colleges also provided most of the students who, early in the 1960s, were involved in the civil disobedience actions that helped bring about legislative changes.

External support of protests generally comes *after* the protests themselves. These additional resources are a *product* rather than a *cause* of protest (McAdam 1979). The patronage that did come later from outsiders appears to have been given less out of feelings of conscience and injustice than out of concern to keep the movement moderate and weaken the radical element, that is, to exercise some control over the direction of the movement (Jenkins and Eckert 1986). The non-violent sit-ins of college students and others in the South in the early 1960s, for example, brought much financial and other support from outside, northern groups. The violent protests later in the 1960s in northern and western cities, on the other hand, produced a white backlash, partly because of the violence, but also because of the switch in focus of problems from the rural South to the urban ghettos of the North.

The economic and attending geographic shifts that were occurring in the South, then, provided blacks with the opportunity to "construct the occupational and institutional foundation from which to mount resistance to white oppression" (Piven and Cloward 1977, p. 205). It has been argued that the southern agricultural power structure benefited most from the traditional racist structure in the South. In this view, the southern agricultural elite, that is, large plantation owners, had the most to lose from desegregation and equality for blacks as they relied upon the cheap, accessible black labor source. On the other hand, cities and businesses stood to suffer from the racial unrest caused by segregationist laws (Bloom 1987). Business growth and investment in Little Rock, Arkansas, were seriously damaged, for example, after the school desegregation confrontations in the late 1950s. With the growth of industries, cities gradually became more influential politically than agrarian areas (Bloom 1987). Consequently, changing economic and social conditions created a split in the "Solid South" between the interests of business and agriculture.

In addition to the shrinking role of agriculture and the expanding presence of industry, the increased stridence and militancy of the reaction against black protests for equality also helped to isolate the South, especially the Deep South, from the rest of the nation. Thus, changes and reactions to them not only created deeper fissures within the South itself, but served to increasingly alienate the South from the remainder of the country. In other words, Bloom argues, the traditional social and political structure was grounded in a particular kind of economy. A weakening in the basis of that agricultural economy threatened the survival of sociopolitical arrangements that primarily benefited the rich landowner and discriminated against blacks. "Racial patterns and racial consciousness have as their foundation particular class structures, and they develop and change as these structures themselves change." At the same time, however, "class structure may set the parameters of racial action, but it cannot reduce race to class" (Bloom 1987, p. 3).

This last point is very important because, while class and economic factors were implicated in the shifting allegiances to racial inequality, *racist ideology* was still an underlying element in accounting for not only social and economic inequality in the South, but reactions to black attempts to eliminate it. Recall that in the latter part of the nineteenth and well into the twentieth centuries, there were a variety of established racial ideologies justifying unequal treatment of blacks. And beliefs about the inferiority of blacks go back even further than that to the early founding of the United States (see Chapter 4). The continued significance of racism itself was manifested in the support given by lower class as well as upper class white southerners to the discriminatory treatment of blacks. Upper class white southerners who had vested local economic interests fought the hardest against voting rights for blacks because to afford this right would have been tantamount to surrendering power to them.

But while the voting regulations effectively eliminated many lower class whites as well as blacks from voting, the former went along with their upper class brethren in supporting the laws. The southern aristocracy played upon racist images of blacks and used the image of competition between blacks and whites as a means to obtain the support of lower class whites (Piven and Cloward 1977). In addition, not only southern agricultural aristocrats, but also local town and city businessmen fought against those who pushed for integration into local restaurants, motels, and so on. In essence, both economic factors and racism played roles in the dynamics of racial inequality and reactions to it.

Other *social* and *cultural* events also gave strength to the black effort to confront racial inequality. During the 1920s, the Harlem Renaissance encouraged blacks to take pride in themselves and their cultural and literary heritage. In addition, the civil rights activists of the late 1920s and 1930s often fought alongside white radical unionists who were pushing the New Deal policies (Sitkoff 1981). Radical union leaders, it will be recalled, wanted to include not only whites and skilled workers, but blacks and unskilled industrial workers as well. Both radical unions and black organizations, however, were often labeled as being infiltrated by Communists.

This would become a familiar theme again after World War II, especially with the rise of McCarthyism.

In addition to the changes in the U.S. economy and social-cultural factors that strengthened black unity, other historical events and conditions also helped to lay the groundwork for the civil rights movement that was to come in the 1950s. *Political* circumstances were weakening the South's grip on blacks and providing the latter with resources that could be used in their battle against racism. Migration to the North meant not only a greater probability of voting but also led to blacks holding political office in several major cities (Sitkoff 1981; Bloom 1987). "Estimates of voting strength in 1948 saw blacks holding the balance of power in sixteen states with a total of 278 electoral votes, compared to 127 electoral votes controlled by the South" (Bloom 1987, p. 76). Politicians with presidential aspirations became increasingly concerned about potential black political defections and as a result often courted the black vote.

Despite this courtship, governmental policies continued to underrepresent the interests of blacks. But they also, perhaps inadvertently, strengthened the position of blacks. As we saw in the history of the early labor movement, the New Deal's policies had an impact on the fate of the labor movement. Similarly, the public works programs of the New Deal provided blacks with an alternate source of income outside the relatively narrow range of private positions open to them. Having another source of income, which meant less dependence, created a source of power with which to fight oppression (Piven and Cloward 1971, 1982; Bloom 1987). This federal source of work and the increased demand for labor in industry helped to drive wages up, wages that dominant agricultural groups were increasingly hesitant to pay (Bloom 1987). Federal loans also became available as a substitute for local ones, again making blacks less dependent upon local white funding institutions.

World War II brought further changes to the situation of blacks. Unionization of blacks was less difficult than had been the case only a decade earlier. Employment conditions had improved, especially with the wartime economy. But national unity was the preferred emphasis and most blacks did not favor protest in these circumstances (Sitkoff 1981). Despite continued demands by black groups, any serious attempts to deal with racial problems took a back seat to dealing with the Axis powers. While the war brought some positive changes, blacks were still much worse off than whites politically and economically, and discrimination was still prevalent.

After the war, several political events occurred which affected efforts for racial equality. The international situation was such that the United States became more involved with a larger number of countries, including some with non-white populations. This change coupled with the racist overtones of Nazism, against which we had fought, meant that continued racial inequality at home could prove to be an embarrassment. Harry Truman, in running for the presidency in 1948, had to present a platform that showed a strong desire for civil rights if he was to defeat opponents who also were courting the vote of those blacks who had migrated to the cities of the North. In doing so, however, he alienated democrats from the Deep South who went on to present their own State's Rights Party candidate. He also ordered the desegregation of the military. The economic and political context had shifted to the extent that Truman was advised to court blacks even at the risk of turning away southern democrats (Piven and Cloward 1977).

A final political element in the late 1940s that affected civil rights efforts came out of the developing "Cold War" with Russia. "Red-baiting" was fashionable, and civil rights groups and leaders were not immune to accusations of being Communist. White supremacists argued that Communists were behind the movement for black equality. It will be recalled that similar accusations had been made about unions and their leadership when they also pushed for greater economic and political power. McCarthyism frightened blacks, and the majority of black leaders took a gradual and calm approach. "The NAACP became less a protest organization and more an agency of litigation and lobbying after World War II" (Sitkoff 1981, p. 18).

All of the conditions discussed thus far composed the context in which the Supreme Court made its momentous *Brown* v. *Board of Education* decision in 1954. To summarize, several changes had occurred since World War I which changed the social context and the political and economic position of blacks:

1. The basis of the South's economy had shifted from agriculture to industry, weakening the economic status of the traditional southern upper class. This change led to economic and political splits within the southern upper class. The interests of industrial leaders in the maintenance of Jim Crow were simply not as strong nor as necessary as they were for the agricultural elite. The South's social and political structure was becoming increasingly out of step with other macrochanges occurring in the region and the nation.

2. The decline in agriculture and the growth of industry in the nation as a whole opened up new economic opportunities for blacks, and for those who moved to cities and to the North, new political/power bases as well. This served to build up institutions within the black community and in addition created a "cognitive liberation" for blacks, the latter referring to a new understanding of their situation and the potentiality for change (McAdam 1982). In other words, these structural changes had positive psychological effects on blacks' self-image and self-efficacy. The combination of increased internal solidarity within the black community and being tied to the white economic power structure in an exploitative relationship created a situation favorable to the mobilization of blacks (Obserschall 1973).

3. Racism continued to provide a backdrop against which economic changes and battles for equality were fought.

4. Political policies brought on by the Depression, the Nazism of World War II, and the growing black voting bloc were moving in the direction of being helpful for blacks. Moreover, in the 1950s, growing awareness of independence movements by oppressed nonwhite groups against colonial powers gave encouragement to civil rights forces in the United States. For example, in the late 1940s, India had achieved independence from England, and several African nations had achieved independence from their colonial masters in the late 1950s and early 1960s. These events suggested to the U.S government that it might make geopolitical sense for the state not to appear racist. The liberation struggles abroad also heartened many black leaders who became convinced that change was possible (Rollins 1986).

The development and character of a social movement is determined by factors outside and within it. These affect each other, and as external and internal conditions change, so does the character of the movement (McAdam 1982; Blumberg 1984). Just as economic, cultural, political, and social changes in the long run helped to shift more power into the hands of blacks, in the short run economic, cultural, political, and social devices were used to counteract the movement for equality. The events and conditions that have just been discussed interacted with institutions and individuals in the black community to make the situation ripe for the development of a civil rights movement.

As stated at the beginning of this section, the date on which the civil rights movement formally began is debatable. Some tie its start to the 1953 bus boycott in Baton Rouge, Louisiana, while others associate it with Rosa Parks's refusal to give her bus seat to a white man and the Montgomery bus boycott that followed in 1955. In any case, the mid-1950s is generally agreed to mark the start of the movement, and no single event was any more consequential than the Supreme Court's decision of 1954. To suggest the specific dynamics involved in the process, we can offer a sketchy history of the movement from that point to the mid-1960s when it began to disintegrate into various factions.

A Brief History

The *Brown* v. *Board of Education* decision was a true watershed in the effort for civil rights. It declared segregation in education to be unconstitutional. In concluding his argument, Chief Justice Earl Warren stated simply: "We conclude that in the field of public education the doctrine of 'separate but equal' has no place. Separate educational facilities are inherently unequal" (quoted in Sitkoff 1981, p. 22). This decision had a powerful effect on both blacks and southern whites. The black movement for equality was given a boost, but at the same time a white "countermovement" was established to fight these advances. While blacks were jubilant about the decision, the South's white elite were not about to accept it without a fight. Many said unequivocably that they would not comply with the law in this case. "The prospect of desegregating public schools was fundamentally appalling to the average white Southerner. The thought of young 'niggers' mixing in school with little white children jarred the sensibilities of Southern whites, whether poor farmers or highly placed government officials" (Morris 1984, p. 27). Even though the decision by the Court to segregate had been unanimous, it had not come to this decision easily. In order to get the unanimous ruling, Warren had to agree on a policy of gradual implementation of the desegregation policy. The qualification of gradualism left room for southern dissenters to fight enforcement, and it led to frustration on the part of blacks who wished speedy implementation of the law.

President Eisenhower demonstrated no strong endorsement of the decision, nor did he actively move to have it enforced. He did not really believe that one could effectively legislate on such moral-laden matters (Sitkoff 1981). Before the decision had been made, he had tried to soften Warren's position by alluding to the basic goodness of the South's people: "These are not bad people. All they are concerned about is to see that their sweet little girls are not required to sit in school alongside some big overgrown Negroes" (quoted in Bloom 1987, p. 106). Eisenhower, then, was not an active supporter of civil rights, but later black protests and militant white reactions to those actions would force him to intervene.

As mentioned, reaction from the southern white power structure to the Court's decision was immediate and strong. There was no strong push on the part of the government for swift implementation of the law; the dominance by conservative elements of the major political parties in Congress meant no rapid enforcement would be forthcoming. The FBI's J. Edgar Hoover still saw racial unrest as being Communist inspired (Bloom 1987). In the South, white churches and the press generally opposed the ruling, and local White Citizens' Councils were set up to fight desegregation (Sitkoff 1981). In 1956, the membership in these Councils approached 250,000 (Piven and Cloward 1977).

In the mid-1950s, notable bus boycotts by blacks occurred in Baton Rouge, Montgomery, and Tallahassee. Perhaps the most famous of these was initiated by Rosa Parks in Montgomery in December of 1955. Mrs. Parks, who was an active NAACP participant and had been put off the bus previously for refusing to move to the back, had gotten on a crowded bus and refused to surrender her seat to a white male adult. At the next bus stop, Mrs. Parks was taken off the bus and arrested for violating the local bus ordinance (Sitkoff 1981). News of her arrest spread, and a bus boycott was organized by a group of local black leaders. Assuming that it would be best to appoint an outsider as its leader, they appointed a hesitant young, middle-class, nonviolent, and intellectually sophisticated black minister to lead the boycott.

The Reverend Martin Luther King, Jr., was well educated, a newcomer to the area, and had attended theological school in the North. He was stunned by the blatant racism that seemed to be so out of place in a period when blacks had become more educated and urbanized (Sitkoff 1981). Given his background and training, King assumed initially that whites would respect logic and listen to reason, but he was wrong. "He now realized that the matter was one of power, not reason, that 'no one gives up his privileges without strong resistance' " (Sitkoff 1981, p. 51). Under his new organization, dubbed the Montgomery Improvement Association, King led a nonviolent boycott of the bus system. Local black churches provided sites for meetings and arranged for alternative modes of transportation. The boycott went on for over a year, and during that time white resistance had tried a range of tactics to bring it to an end. Legal tactics such as arrests and jailings for minor or fictitious infractions of local laws were used. Economic sanctions also were tried; some deeply involved in the boycott lost their jobs. Finally, violent tactics were used: many beatings occurred, four black churches and the homes of King, his associate Ralph Abernathy, and another supporter were bombed. In the last analysis, however, the nonviolent boycott prevailed and the U.S. Supreme Court declared Alabama's bus segregation laws unconstitutional.

The nonviolent, long-suffering, patient approach of the boycott contrasted in the national media with the harsh white reaction. Many outside the South were appalled at the tactics used by the white resistance. In contrast, King's "neo-Gandhian persuasion" seemed reasonable and acceptable as a means for obtaining equal rights. Above all, it was nonviolent and embraced the Christian beliefs of turning the other cheek and not condemning individual racists. It blamed the system of segregation rather than the individuals who enforced it (King 1958; Sitkoff 1981). As a result of the boycott, King and his approach to injustice gained worldwide attention. Out of the boycott, other civil rights groups were organized, most notably the Southern Christian Leadership Conference (SCLC) under King's leadership.

A familiar pattern of black/white confrontation began to develop as a result of the early boycotts. Basically, the sequence would begin with nonviolent black protests, followed by a militant white response, which in turn often led to federal intervention. It did not take long for black leaders to figure out how to get the attention of federal officials who had been unreliable and largely unresponsive in the past in enforcing rights that were theirs under the Constitution.

Another prominent illustration of black/white confrontation occurred a couple of years after Mrs. Parks's historic bus ride. In late 1957, Governor Orval Faubus of Arkansas called in national guard troops to prevent black students from entering the all-white Central High School in Little Rock. Ignoring another federal court order, troops would still not let these students in the next day. After threats of white mob violence, Eisenhower was forced to act by federalizing national guard troops and bringing in paratroopers to guarantee safe admission for the students. The troops remained for the rest of the year.

The violent repressive tactics of whites against nonviolent protestors angered many in the black community and made them not altogether happy with King's patient, nonmilitant approach. This was especially the case as hostile white resistance intensified during the late 1950s and early 1960s. However, many young college-educated blacks had had their resolve stiffened by the growing number of successes from King's approach. Beside boycotts and marches, additional nonviolent tactics were used. Among these was the sit-in, which also had been used effectively in the past in union strikes.

In the early 1960s, sit-ins were held throughout the South protesting segregation of public facilities. Similar protests were held in northern cities to demonstrate sympathetic support of the civil rights protestors. These protests involved thousands of individuals, many of them college students. One of the most famous of the sit-ins occurred in early February 1960 in Greensboro, North Carolina. Four black students sat down at a Woolworth's lunch counter and asked for coffee and donuts. When refused, they kept their seats until the store closed. The next day more students did the same thing, but white officials remained implacable, and it was only after repeated sit-ins that Greensboro allowed such service six months later. This sit-in inspired similar protests throughout the South and afforded a means by which college students could become meaningfully involved in the civil rights movement. Adults also joined in these protests. Within one-and-a-half years of the Greenboro sit-in, demonstrations had been carried out in over a hundred cities and towns in all the southern states (Blumberg 1984). Not only sit-ins at lunch counters, but "sleep-ins" in the lobbies of motels, "swim-ins" at pools, "play-ins" at recreational areas, "kneel-ins" at churches, and "read-ins" at libraries followed. Boycotts also were carried out against merchants who refused desegregation (Sitkoff 1981). Local white reactions were often swift and violent. Floggings, kickings, pistol-whippings, dog attacks, jailings, and even acid throwings were among the repressive means used against the protestors. But still the sit-ins continued.

One of the results of these demonstrations was that they showed southerners the depth of black feelings about these matters. They also brought powerfully to the attention of the nation the injustice of widespread legal segregation practices. Largely as a result of the active concern of black college youth, their impatience with years of waiting, and the seemingly futile legal maneuverings of the more conservative approaches in the civil rights movement as typified by the NAACP, other, more militant types of organizations (such as SNCC) began appearing in the early 1960s (Blumberg 1984; Sitkoff 1981).

In 1961, the Congress of Racial Equality (CORE), which had been founded in 1942 and had advocated direct nonviolent means of protest, organized a "freedom ride" from Washington, D.C., to New Orleans to see if states and municipalities were complying with the federal law against discrimination in interstate bus terminals. These rides went into the Deep South where white resistance was strongest. As in other peaceful protests, these too evoked violent white resistance. Beatings and deaths of protestors, for example, took place in several Alabama cities, including Birmingham and Montgomery. Again,

much of the violence was broadcast through the media.

It was only when waves of public sympathy came that the federal government acted to protect the protestors and enforce the law. When there was no publicity, little was done; violations of the law were left unpunished. It became clear to protestors that they apparently had to elicit a violent response to receive public attention and sympathy, and to trigger the government to act. When the white resistance reacted with legal nonviolent measures, such publicity and sympathy was not as likely, nor as a result, was governmental intervention. Barkan (1984) suggests that had whites used these means more often, the results may have been different. Examining the confrontations in Montgomery, Selma, Birmingham, Albany (Georgia), and Danville (Virginia), he concludes that in those cities where legal means such as arrests, high bails, court proceedings, and injunctions had been used, protestors were less successful (see also Sitkoff 1981).

Federal officials were always reluctant to intervene in civil rights protests. Many of the reasons were political in nature. Both major political parties were still concerned with alienating the power structure and white voters of the Deep South. As in the 1930s when the federal administration was trying to balance allegiances between labor and business, the government in the 1950s and early 1960s did not want to antagonize either blacks or whites. The result was a lot of fence-sitting, and many acts of violence against legitimate protests evoked no response from Washington (Piven and Cloward 1977; Sitkoff 1981).

One of the most brutal reactions to the nonviolent demonstrations of King and the SCLC occurred in Birmingham in the spring of 1963. Sit-ins, marches, and similar techniques had been used to protest local segregation. After these had been going on for a time, the local police commissioner, Eugene "Bull" Connor came down violently on the protestors. His violent response was seen by millions on television. Officials used dogs, high-pressure hoses, cattle prods, clubs, and even a police tank to beat down the protes-

Marches were a prominent form of nonviolent protest in the civil rights movement of the early 1960s.

tors. President Kennedy and his brother Robert, who had wanted "cooling-down" periods by blacks and a more gradual approach to desegregation, sent federal representatives to help reach a compromise between King and local officials. But the protestors would not back down. Finally, the SCLC obtained desegregation of some public facilities, a promise of nondiscriminatory hiring, and the formation of a biracial committee in Birmingham (Sitkoff 1981). The local reaction to the agreement was not completely positive. Bombings resulted, causing some blacks to again question King's nonviolent approach.

As successful protests became more frequent, more working-class blacks were drawn into the movement. Greater competition among the major black organizations (SCLC, SNCC, CORE, NAACP) occurred with each group vying for the dominant position. They sponsored massive demonstrations throughout the country. A national March on Washington was made in August 1963, sponsored by numerous civil rights, union, and church organizations and involving well over 200,000 individuals. During the summer of 1964, hundreds of individuals worked in Mississippi to increase voter registration, and three workers were brutally murdered. The government asked workers to remain calm, but this request only deepened their distrust of administration policies and motives. Riots broke out in several cities. President Kennedy began to press for a civil rights law in 1963, and shortly thereafter the Civil Rights and Voting Rights Acts were passed under President Johnson. This national legislative response to the basic problems of blacks, particularly in the South, helped to delegitimize the need for protest, especially in the eyes of northern whites.

But despite the passage of these laws, as has already been suggested, several other changes had occurred that helped alter the nature of the black movement from the nonviolent protest tactics of King to cries for "Black Power" and black "liberation." First, the slow, compromising approach of the federal government to the problems experienced by blacks on a day-to-day basis, coupled with the patient nonviolent method of King, convinced some in the civil rights movement of the need for more drastic action on their own behalf. The consistently violent reactions by whites to the nonviolent protests of blacks over the years widened the gap between factions within the civil rights movement in the early 1960s.

Second, the focus of the civil rights movement had been on the South, but the migration of many blacks into the cities of the North and West led to a shift in goal emphasis within the movement. The problems of black city dwellers became the focus: poverty, employment, housing, poor schools, and so on. The civil rights movement has been interpreted by some as largely a movement by and for middle-class individuals, while the focus of the black movement on problems of city residents appeared to demonstrate a greater concern for the black working and lower classes (Oberschall 1973; Blumberg 1984; Bloom 1987). In total, the shift in the movement was from an emphasis on integration, political and social rights, and nonviolence to one on black separatism, economic needs, and more militant tactics (Blumberg 1984; Bloom 1987; Schaefer 1988). Different segments stressed the importance of cultural and black nationalism, while others spoke of black power. Despite their dissimilarities, all of these more militant perspectives betrayed a basic distrust of white institutions, the need for blacks to develop their own institutions or identities, and the need for stronger reactions to discrimination against blacks. Stokely Carmichael's statement about the need for black power suggests the feelings that some were having: "Power is the only thing respected in this world, and we must get it at any cost" (in Sitkoff 1981, p. 214).

Serious outbreaks occurred during these "long hot summers" in many major cities including Chicago, Cleveland, Milwaukee, Dayton, San Francisco, Detroit, Newark, New Haven, Boston, Buffalo, and others. During 1967 alone, there were 150 such outbreaks (Sitkoff 1981). Certainly with this turn of events, it was clear that

by the mid-1960s, while the black push for equality was continuing, the nonviolent civil rights movement phase had passed.

THE WOMEN'S MOVEMENT

In both the civil rights and earlier labor movements, women had been victims of discrimination. Women needed their own movement to advance their interests. Like the civil rights movement, the women's movement has had an uneven history. Its unevenness is reflected in the fact that some scholars suggest that there were two or three separate such movements in history while others suggest that a single women's movement went through several phases. Freeman (1975), for example, states that "sometime during the 1920s, feminism died in the United States" (p. 448). But as is the case in the other movements, the push for political, economic, and other rights for women never completely "died." Rather, during the natural history of the women's movement, there were times when the movement was widely and publicly active, while in other times, those in the movement were retrenching and the movement was, so to speak, being held in suspension or in "abeyance." Taylor's (1989a) research on the women's movement indicates that "movements do not die, but scale down and retrench to adapt to changes in the political climate. Perhaps movements are never really born anew. Rather, they contract and hibernate, sustaining the totally dedicated and devising strategies appropriate to the external environment" (p. 772). When the external environment is inhospitable to the flowering of an overtly active movement, but internally there is a strongly committed cadre of activists, the movement can weather the difficult times until conditions prove to be more amenable to active and widespread protest. The point is that what may appear to be separate women's movements can be viewed as distinct phases of one movement. As was the case with the other movements we have surveyed, internal conditions interacted with external circumstances to determine the nature of the movement. Many of those conditions were related to structures of economic, racial, and sexual inequality in the society, as we will see.

The women's movement in the United States began in the late 1700s and early 1800s and has continued, although not always actively and publicly, to this day (Hole and Levine 1975; Chafe 1977; Snyder 1979). Throughout its history, feminism has incorporated two seemingly paradoxical general goals. One is the belief that since women are in most respects the *same* as men in their potential and abilities, they are deserving of the *same* rights as men. The other is the belief that since women are *different* from men they deserve special protections. At different times and by different groups, each of these positions has been emphasized. Women's rights are then defined according to which of these two sets of beliefs and goals is stressed (Cott 1986). For example, in the nineteenth and early twentieth centuries, women argued that they were entitled to the same options and opportunities as men, but also that such equal opportunity would allow society to benefit from the unique contributions of both sexes. Harriet Burton Laidlaw, an early suffragist, distilled both these beliefs in her statement that to the extent that women were like men they ought to have the same rights, but to the extent that they were unlike men they alone should represent themselves. This bifurcation of beliefs and goals was reflected in the specific goals set by various women's organizations throughout the movement's history. It will be recalled that interpretations of justice and fairness are often based on beliefs about the fundamental differences and similarities between individuals (see Chapter 12).

The earliest organized efforts by women involved attempts to increase their educational rights and to fight for the abolition of slavery, and it was during involvement in the abolitionist movement of the 1830s that some women became acutely aware of their own low political status. As proved to be the case with their involvement in other historical movements, women were not given significant status or voice in the abolitionist

movement. Indeed, while this movement was fighting for an end to slavery, women were being prevented from joining some abolitionist organizations and were being muzzled in their attempt to speak in public on the issues. Women had to create their own antislavery organizations because they were being excluded from many of the men's organizations (Hole and Levine 1975). It will be recalled that women had a similar experience in the early labor union movement. While demanding rights and social justice for workers, many unions were at the same time barring women from membership. In those cases where women were members, few held leadership positions.

In 1840, a world antislavery meeting was held in London. Men at the meeting, including so-called radicals, were shocked to see women present and had them put in galleries where they could not participate effectively in the meeting. Later in 1867, Sojourner Truth, a crusader for both women's and black's rights wrote of the neglect of women's rights among those who advocated such rights for blacks: "There is a great stir about colored men getting their rights, but not a word about colored women; and if colored men get their rights and not colored women theirs, you see the colored men will be masters over the women, and it will be just as bad as it was before" (quoted in Ferree and Hess 1985, p. 32). Time and again, it became clear to many women that they would have to have their own organizations and movement if their rights were ever to be granted (Hole and Levine 1975; Snyder 1979).

Two of the women who had attended the antislavery convention in London were Elizabeth Cady Stanton and Lucretia Mott. Convinced of the need for an organization exclusively for women's rights, these women organized a meeting that was held in Seneca Falls, New York, in July of 1848. About three hundred men and women attended, including Frederick Douglass and Susan B. Anthony. The attendees approved a "Declaration of Sentiments" based loosely on the wording of the Declaration of Independence. Among other things, this document argued for the basic equality of men and women and stressed that historically men had dominated over women in religious institutions, employment opportunities, and family and political life. Included among the declarations made was a demand for the right to vote. While this latter demand has been said to signal the beginning of the suffrage movement, most of the women at the Seneca Falls meeting were more concerned with issues in their immediate experience: control of property and earnings, rights over children, rights to divorce, and so forth. From 1848 to the Civil War, women's conventions were held almost every year in different cities of the East and Midwest (Hole and Levine 1975).

The Early Social Context and Directions

The social environment within which women were advocating greater freedoms and rights was not hospitable. Not only was this reflected in women's imposed marginal status in male abolitionist and labor organizations, but in the reactions within other dominant institutions. Religious institutions and the media railed against the embryonic women's movement. It was as if a natural and supernatural order were being violated by the attempts to gain women rights equal to those of men. In order to spread the word, women had to rely on some abolitionist papers and their own journals. Late in the nineteenth century, Stanton and others produced *The Woman's Bible,* a systematic critique to demonstrate that the traditional Bible was a major source of the subjugation of women.

The early formation of the movement also was affected by the forces of early industrialization. Not being allowed to learn skills, women who needed to work were relegated to either household or low-paying work (Huber 1982). Women who were from the middle or upper class, on the other hand, were not expected to work but rather to appear and act as "ladies." "The nineteenth-century concept of a lady was that of a fragile, idle, pure creature, submissive and subservient to her husband and to domestic needs.

Her worth was based on her decorative value, a quality that embraced her beauty, her character, and her temperament. She was certainly not a paid employee" (Fox and Hesse-Biber 1984, p. 19).

This class division among women had an impact on the membership and goals of the early women's organizations. It was largely middle- and upper class women who initiated the early movement and who fashioned its goals to fit their problems and desires, such as the desire for education in the professions and civil service and property and voting rights. At the same time, they pushed for lower numbers of hours for female factory workers (Huber 1982). While the latter appeared as a form of protection for women, it also was seen by many men as a way to minimize work competition from women. This suggests, as discussed earlier, the varying emphases on women as being different as well as the same as men. A desire for protection implies that women are different and more vulnerable than men, while the desire on the part of some women for equal employment opportunities implies that they are the equals of men. In sum, the religious and cultural milieu, along with the conditions of industrialization and slavery, helped to shape the form of the early women's movement as well as reactions to it. As we will see later, the 1980s did not afford the movement a hospitable environment either and for some of the same basic reasons.

After the Civil War, when the Fourteenth and Fifteenth Amendments on black rights were being debated, women were told that attempts to include women in these amendments would only diffuse the focus that was being placed on rights for blacks alone. The incorporation of women as well as men into the amendments, they were told, would only hinder their passage (Hole and Levine 1975; Snyder 1979). The thrust for a separate women's movement accelerated, and basically two strands developed. One, under Elizabeth Cady Stanton and Susan B. Anthony, formed the National Woman Suffrage Association. It emphasized a variety of rights for women and viewed the vote as a means to obtaining them. The other, exemplified by the American Woman Suffrage Association under Lucy Stone and others, focused only on the vote. Eventually, the emphasis on the vote won out in the movement and the two organizations merged into the National American Woman Suffrage Association (Hole and Levine 1975). "By the decade beginning in 1910 the demand for woman suffrage was a capacious umbrella under which a large diversity of beliefs and organizations could shelter, or . . . an expansive platform on which they could all comfortably, if temporarily, stand" (Cott 1986, p. 52). It is during this period that the term "feminism" came on to the public scene. It would have been unthinkable to use such a term during the "woman movement" of the nineteenth century. Feminism suggested a radical change in all relations with men and also attracted smaller numbers of followers than the earlier "woman movement" (Cott 1987).

Two of the most militantly active groups pushing for the enfranchisement of women were the Congressional Union and the group derived from it, the National Woman's Party (NWP). Both were at the forefront of the movement between 1910 and 1920. Their intellectual leaders, Alice Paul and Lucy Burns, were both highly educated, militant, and single-minded in their pursuit of enfranchisement. By all accounts, Paul was a highly charismatic and enthusiastic individual who was an ardent advocate of single-issue politics (Cott 1987). Apparently, she also practiced a "dictatorial" style of leadership in the National Woman's Party which drove some women from the group (Taylor 1989a). The militance of the Party was evident in mass protests, picketing and marches on Wilson's White House, hunger strikes, and even jailings (Hole and Levine 1975; Cott 1987).

The NWP was viewed as having a single objective and any diversion from its pursuit was considered harmful. The rigid adherence to this philosophy resulted in insensitivity to the unique goals and problems of subgroups within the female population. "Only women holding cultur-

ally hegemonic values and positions—that is, in the United States, women who are white, heterosexual, middle class, politically midstream—have the privilege (or deception) of seeing their condition as that of 'woman,' glossing over their other characteristics," observes Cott perceptively (1986, p. 58). For example, some blacks felt that the NWP was basically racist and did not care about the rights of blacks. Most suffragist groups of the time were imbued with the racism of the broader culture and did little to combat it. Black women's concerns were considered by Paul to be "racial" rather than "feminist" problems (Cott 1987).

In 1919, shortly before the passage of the Nineteenth Amendment enfranchising women, Walter White, leader of the NAACP, remarked about the NWP and its leadership: "If they could get the Suffrage Amendment through without enfranchising colored women, they would do it in a moment" (quoted in Cott 1987, p. 69). Just as women had been marginalized in the abolitionist movement by those fighting for black rights, the specific problems of blacks were now being put aside to focus on those of women only. In the same vein, some educated women were fighting for the same right to vote that "drunken male immigrant layabouts" possessed. This implied a kind of elitism among some segments of the suffrage movement (Ferree and Hess 1985). But it also reflected a class and race elitism present in the wider society in the early 1900s, a division whose implications for the suffrage movement were not fully understood by its leaders. Those in the movement "profoundly misread the degree to which ethnic, class, and family allegiances undermined the prospect of sex-based political behavior" (Chafe 1977, p. 118).

In April 1917 the United States entered World War I, but not all groups championed this. The Socialist Party condemned it, while the moderate suffragists in the National American Woman Suffrage Association (NAWSA) took a patriotic stance and endorsed it. The militant National Woman's Party, on the other hand, took no official stand on the war, or on socialism for that matter. The two women's organizations just mentioned were substantially different from each other. The NAWSA was as moderate and nonmilitant in its tactics as the NWP was radical. It was disgusted by the militant and unseemly activities of the NWP (Cott 1987). In a period when anti-Russian and antisocialist feelings were running strong in much of the nation, the alignment of militant feminists with socialists and pacifists alienated the nonaligned NWP from the rest of the country. Antisuffrage groups cropped up attempting to link the "dangers" of socialism, communism, and feminism.

After the enfranchisement of women was accomplished in 1920, the movement for women's rights changed drastically. One interpretation is that "the woman's movement virtually died in 1920 and, with the exception of a few organizations, feminism was to lie dormant for forty years" (Hole and Levine 1975, p. 446). Rather than completely dying, the movement became fractured internally in large part because the attainment of the franchise had meant different things to different organizations and individuals. Some had wanted it simply because all kinds of men possessed the right, while others had seen it as a means to accomplish other goals, including legislation to protect the less fortunate of society. In essence, some women saw enfranchisement as an end in itself while others viewed it as a means to reach more important goals, such as an equal rights amendment (ERA) for women.

The latter was now the goal of the National Woman's Party, while the more conservative National American Woman Suffrage Association fought against the ERA, formed the League of Women Voters, and worked for the active citizenship of women. The idea of universalistic legislation covering women's rights also was opposed by the Women's Bureau of the Department of Labor and a number of voluntary women's organizations. They feared that the legalization of such equality with men would remove the shelters women received under the protectionist legislation of the 1920s which limited women's involvement in the labor force. Part of the motivation on

the part of the government for passing protective legislation was concern over the declining fertility rate early in this century. Officials feared that too drastic a decline would have harmful effects on the size of the defense forces and on the growth of the economy. It was believed that encouraging women to remain at home might stem the tide toward a lower birth rate.

At bottom, what divided women was the question of the priority of women's maternal role compared to their employment opportunities. Protectionist legislation was interpreted by its adherents as conserving the maternal role of women (Huber 1982). Those pressing for an ERA, on the other hand, expressed an interest in the full potentiality of women, not merely their roles in the family. In a real sense, this difference of opinion on ERA resurrected the old question about the natures of men and women. Those who were in favor of the ERA were saying that women and men were basically the same, while those opposed to it and in support of protective legislation were saying that the two groups were basically different. While both groups believed that sex inequality existed, the first group saw it as unnecessary and undesirable while the second saw it as a given and, therefore, women needed protection. This division in position was duplicated in England (Cott 1986).

The movement also was splintered by the multiple ties of many women to other social movements. Once the Nineteenth Amendment had passed, many women moved on to other causes, such as, temperance, birth control, union organizing, and poverty (Ferree and Hess 1985). Black women and working women had concerns other than those held by middle- or upper class, educated women, and some eventually formed their own organizations. Given the different class, cultural, employment, racial, and other differences among women, it should be expected that there would be significant fissures within the women's movement. Another source of division among women in the 1920s was a cultural phenomenon of the time. Some women became caught up in the flapper movement of the 1920s and sought to improve their positions through the statuses attained by dress and lifestyle (Snyder 1979). With the defection of many women in different directions, some of the more militant organizations like the National Woman's Party became increasingly isolated. In sum, whatever mass base existed in the women's movement in 1920 dwindled because of (1) internal divisions, (2) the accomplishment of suffrage, that is, "goal attainment," and (3) the growing diversity in the lives of women (Taylor 1989a).

Whether or not significant divisions in a movement can be minimized or made to appear invisible or unimportant depends upon the style and message of leadership in the movement, the definition of feminism at the time, and the presence of widespread cultural and social unrest in the society. When the style of leadership is liberal and the interpretation of feminism is broad, the presence of multifaceted rebellion can forge effective though often only temporary alliances among factions. Groups can then fight for the same thing even though it is for different reasons (Cott 1986).

From Limbo to Resurgence

From 1945 to the 1960s, the women's movement was in limbo. In the immediate years after World War II, the social and cultural environment was not hospitable to protest from any minority group. We have mentioned the "anti-Red" climate and the narrow and frightening jingoism of McCarthyism in another context. At the same time, the "feminine mystique" perception of the perfect woman was dominant. This woman was expected to be married, have children, be a helpmate to her husband and his career, and to be happy in her domestic life. In other words, it was a conservative cultural period, one that sanctified the traditional male/female lifestyle. Women who protested or sought "masculine" roles were considered not only unstable and possibly neurotic, but also deviant (Rupp 1985; Taylor 1989a). Thus, even if some women wanted to protest there were few effective avenues through which to

do so, and their protests would not have had the support of the federal government. The media ridiculed feminism and reinforced traditional husband/wife roles (Taylor 1989a). It will be recalled that during this postwar expansion period, social inequality in general was an issue that was minimized.

Adding to the inhospitality of the social and cultural context, support for feminism also dwindled and extant women's groups had little mass power. The Women's Bureau of the Department of Labor had little influence and was anti-ERA anyway, and the National Woman's Party had been reduced to a relatively small number of faithful followers. None of these groups made much progress during this period, although they kept the movement for women's rights alive.

The National Woman's Party's role in this respect has been examined in detail. Most of the women still present in this organization after World War II were white, middle- or upper class, employed, well educated, unmarried, and over fifty years of age (Rupp 1985; Taylor 1989a). In other words, it was a very homogeneous group composed of women who had the time, resources, and interest to keep feminist issues alive. A variety of factors held this group together as a cohesive unit:

1. Considering their age, most had gone through similar experiences in the fight for suffrage, and this common participation was a source of identification.

2. All had identified with the "feminist" label despite hostile opposition from the traditional and dominant culture. That is, they had survived some difficult times together.

3. Most were highly, sometimes fanatically, committed to feminist activities and to the cause of the organization.

4. The members had developed deep and enduring friendship networks. They were personally committed to each other.

5. The many shared activities, living accommodations, and meetings at the Alva Belmont

House, their national headquarters in Washington, D.C., helped fuse them into a unified group (Rupp 1985).

With respect to the last factor, it should be pointed out that social arrangements in the House, with its own set of hired cooks and servants, suggest the privileges of class. Moreover, the high and almost exclusive commitment demanded of members and their need to travel to meetings in various cities made it difficult for working-class women or those with major family obligations to become involved (Rupp 1985).

In light of its persistence through the difficult climate of the postwar period, the National Woman's Party served as an "abeyance organization" for the women's movement. It provided tactics, social networks, and an identity to spur the resurgence of the movement in the 1960s. The National Organization for Women (NOW), which was founded in 1966, used many of the tactics of the NWP such as political pressure and lobbying. The NWP activists kept pressure on the government, helping to bring about President Kennedy's decision to form a Presidential Commission on the Status of Women, and to include "sex" in Title VII of the 1964 Civil Rights Act. Some NWP members also were instrumental in the founding of NOW and became openly active in the 1960s. Finally, the NWP became a source of identification for 1960s feminists who could define it as part of the history of their struggle for equal rights. As such, it helped to give the later movement a "collective identity" (Taylor 1989a).

The NWP, then, served as a link between the past and the present in the women's movement, and its internal solidarity allowed it to serve as a source for the upsurge in feminist activity in the 1960s. Taylor (1989a) has suggested that under certain circumstances, organizations can serve this abeyance function for movements. She lists five factors that affect an organization's probability of serving in this regard: (1) length of time an organization holds its members, (2) intensity of an organization's commitment to its cause, (3) exclusivity of its membership, (4) centralization of

its authority structure, and (5) uniqueness and closeness of its culture. Taylor argues that the NWP fulfilled each of these conditions. By retaining its organizational integrity, the NWP served as a lightning rod for the revitalization of the women's movement in the 1960s.

While the 1945 to 1960 period was not marked by significant advances in the women's movement, several other social, cultural, and economic changes were occurring that created the opportunity structure necessary for a later resurgence in the 1960s. External conditions provide the social context in which a movement can either prosper or whither. "Feminism does not have a story discrete from the rest of historical process" (Cott 1986, p. 60). In the period after World War II, the number of educational degrees given to women was increasing, as was women's participation in the labor force. Opportunities to work, coupled with a trend toward smaller families and a desire for more consumer goods on the part of families who could go on the installment plan, encouraged more women to enter the market. More children were moving on to attend college which further increased the need in most families for added income. The contours of the female labor force changed from one that had been primarily composed of single women in 1940 to one that consisted mainly of married women and mothers in 1950. But women also experienced significant job segregation following their removal from jobs after the war and the return of more men to the labor force (Freeman 1975; Huber 1982). Nevertheless, successful participation in traditionally male positions during the war convinced many women that they could do the same jobs as men in most cases. Moreover, their increasing participation in the labor market was at odds with the vision of the perfect family in which the wife/mother stays at home to perform domestic and wifely chores.

In other words, by the time the 1960s arrived, women were more educated, had more earnings, and many had had significant labor force experience. Women's labor force experiences brought them face to face with their limited occupational opportunities. This is important because continuous labor-force experience appears to have a positive impact on feminist attitudes (Klein 1984; Gerson 1985, 1987; Plutzer 1988). Added to this was the fact that the civil rights movement was peaking in the early 1960s and ideas about equality and personal intimacy were becoming more popular. The "sexual revolution" of the mid-1960s, which encouraged control of one's own body and tolerance of different sexual practices, also was consistent with feminist goals (Chafe 1977). All these events and conditions made the context ripe for a resurgence of the women's movement.

In 1961, after pleas from Esther Petersen of the Labor Department's Women's Bureau, President Kennedy created the President's Commission on the Status of Women, which, although of short duration, was able to thoroughly document the poor status of women relative to men in the United States. The Commission saw no reason, however, to endorse an equal rights amendment because it thought that such protection was already afforded by the Fourteenth Amendment. One of the most significant outcomes of the Commission's work was the proliferation of state-level commissions on the status of women. One consequence of these commissions was the sharing of information and the generation of a network of activists who were cognizant of the problems faced by women and were convinced of the urgency of change (Freeman 1975; Ferree and Hess 1985).

It was at a June 1966 meeting of such state commissions in Washington, D.C., that the National Organization for Women (NOW) was created, largely because of the belief that the Equal Employment Opportunity Commission, which had developed out of the Civil Rights Act of 1964 and was supposed to deal with sex discrimination, was doing little about the problems of women in the labor market. Race and sex again appeared to be working at cross-purposes. NOW's early emphasis on equal rights, which was attractive to many middle- and upper class women, turned off black women and those who

were members of unions (Giddings 1984). Conversely, when NOW leaders desired membership in the Leadership Conference on Civil Rights, they were denied with the argument that women's problems did not constitute a "civil rights" issue (Ferree and Hess 1985).

The civil rights movement and the newly resurgent women's movement of the 1960s intertwined race and sex issues in other ways as well. Experience in civil rights activities provided many women with knowledge about tactics and organizing problems and gave them a sense of their own capabilities. At the same time, however, their participation made it clear, as it had been made clear to women involved in the abolitionist movement, that they needed to develop their own organizations and movement. Women, black and white, were not accorded high status in the civil rights movement, especially in the later Black Power stage. As in society at large, women were treated largely as tools or sex objects. Stokely Carmichael's notorious statement captures one of the dominant feelings about the role of women: "The only position for women in SNCC is prone" (quoted in Freeman 1975, p. 450).

Black men in the movement often thought of white women as conquests. "Women were sexual conquests, supportive workers behind the scenes, effective organizers on a local level; only in these secondary roles were they welcome in the cause. When women questioned their limited power within the movement, and ultimately in the society, they were ridiculed, abused, and excluded" (Ferree and Hess 1985, p. 47). The perception by many young black leaders and most whites who identified with them was that it was the black male who suffered most from discrimination and poverty because his self-esteem, his "manhood" was being attacked (Ferree and Hess 1985).

Young women's experiences in the student New Left movement also left much to be desired. While the movement preached fewer restrictions on sexuality, the men generally treated the movement women as objects available for the taking. Women did not have positions of power in the

New Left. This male arrogance was in sharp contrast to the conditions in the Old Left earlier in this century. In that movement, women were accorded a more important place and the movement supported women who needed child care. It was also ideologically committed to the equality of women, something missing in the New Left (Flacks 1971; Ferree and Hess 1985).

The experiences of many younger women in both the Black Power and New Left movements helped motivate them to create a network of feminists committed to their own unique cause. Thus, another less formal branch of the women's network developed alongside the more centralized and national-level organizations of the women's movement. This strand consisted of more locally based informal groupings composed primarily of younger women. These groups arose all over, in Chicago, Toronto, Detroit, Seattle, Gainesville, and other places. They were not well organized, nor were they intended to be, and they had no central leadership. While the formal national organizations stressed legislation and lobbying as routes to "women's rights," the younger less formal and more radical strand emphasized the importance of education, "consciousness-raising," and "rapping" as means to personal power and "women's liberation."

The existence of these two major branches suggests that the organizational network of the women's movement has become extremely complex. Local groups are involved in a wide variety of issues, including family planning, health care, the organization of clerical workers, religious discrimination against women, violence against women, pornography, nuclear disarmament, Third World liberation, child care, and others (cf., Taylor 1989b). Ferree and Hess (1985) suggest that the "New Feminist Movement" of recent years has gone in four directions: career feminism, liberal feminism, socialist feminism, and radical feminism. Each of these has its own set of goal priorities and means to reach those goals. *Career feminists* focus on equality in the labor market and women being given the opportunity to demonstrate their abilities. Thus they are concerned with job segregation, union involvement of women, sexual harassment on the job, the development of female mentors for new workers, and similar issues. *Liberal feminists,* on the other hand, focus their efforts on getting appropriate political legislation passed on the national level. Both career and liberal feminists believe in working through the present system's structure. *Socialist feminists,* in contrast, believe that more than just political legislation is needed. U.S. society is basically structured to benefit those in positions of economic and political power. The focus of this strand is on policies that will directly benefit those at the bottom, that is, the poor, low-wage workers, and homemakers. Finally, *radical feminists* are concerned with transforming individual consciousness to eliminate sexism and create a social order not based on traditional or fixed ideas of sex roles and identities (Ferree and Hess 1985).

The diversity hinted at should suggest the level of richness and depth of the current women's movement. But its complexity, broadness of constituency, and decentralized organization is only one of the ways in which it differs from earlier active abolitionist and suffrage phases of the women's movement. A second difference lies in the fact that its development during the 1960s was more in tune with broader changes in the society at large, as well as more in touch with the real experiences of many women. The cultural contexts during the suffrage and abolitionist movements, it will be recalled, were much more hostile to a woman's movement for equal rights or liberation. Third, in contrast to the earlier active phases of the movement, the goals of the current phase are much more diverse. The suffrage movement concentrated on a single issue—the vote (Chafe 1977). Similarly, the abolitionist movement concentrated on a single problem—slavery. As we have seen, present-day feminist organizations are attacking a variety of separate problems. Finally, there appears to be more of a concern for the actual *transcendence* of sex roles in the contemporary phase of the movement, rather than a simple concern for equal treatment of men and women under the law.

Its diveristy, depth, structural flexibility, relatively broad base of adherents, and institutionalized organization make it likely that the present movement will remain active far longer than the earlier suffrage movement. It has "a momentum of its own, almost independent of the generating conditions that gave rise to it" (Taylor 1989b, p. 484). At the same time, the political, economic, and social conditions of the 1980s generated a strong antifeminist countermovement. By the end of the 1970s, many average citizens had been told by the media that women had reached their goals. In 1980, Republicans dropped advocacy of the ERA from their platform after forty years of supporting it. The New Right began to flower in the late 1970s and has consistently attacked the feminist agenda. This movement is composed of professionals, ministers, and politicians who subscribe to a combination of fundamentalist religious dogma and conservative politics antagonistic to feminism. It has appealed to traditional American labels as a way of discrediting the women's movement. "Family," "pro-life," and "Moral Majority" are only some of the buzzwords used to strengthen the countermovement (Taylor 1989b). The recent AIDS epidemic has probably also reinforced those antifeminists who link together sin, homosexuality, free sex, and feminism. While the efforts of countermovement organizations have whittled away at changes advocated and instituted at the urging of those in the women's movement, their efforts also have strengthened the resolve of many radical feminists (Taylor 1989b).

At this point in time, the vast majority of Americans appear to support many of the specific ideas associated with the equality of men and women, even though for most women's rights is an issue of only moderate importance. For example, most do not believe that men are better suited than women for politics or running the country, nor do they agree that a women's place is neces-

sarily in the home or that a woman should not go out and earn money if she has a husband who can do so (Davis and Smith, 1989). At the same time, however, race and class divisions reveal differences in opinions about feminism. Black males tend to be more traditional than white males in their ideas about sex roles, especially when it comes to believing that women's place is in the home and the belief that women are not emotionally equipped for active political life. On the other hand, there appear to be few differences among black and white women in their support of feminism. Finally, among black males and females, the middle class is more traditional than the working class (Ransford and Miller 1983).

While blacks and working-class women have been brought in and attempts have been made to integrate issues of concern to them, the movement has traditionally been a white middle-class one and complete integration of these groups has not yet occurred (Ferree and Hess 1985; Taylor 1989b). The diversity within the movement with respect to race, class, specific goals, and assumptions about the nature of men and women has provided a source of strength. But under the pressures of a countermovement against feminism, these divisions could widen and splinter the movement. What can be a source of strength can also be a source of damaging division. At this point, the future is still open.

INEQUALITY, CONTEXT, AND SOCIAL MOVEMENTS: A SYNTHESIS

In this brief section, and instead of a summary, we will use the preceding discussions on the labor, civil rights, and women's movements to distill some more general observations about the implications of social inequality for social movements. The focus here will be on the effects of external economic, political, cultural, and social environmental factors on the development and internal structure of social movements. Because the principle concern of this book is social inequality, particular attention will be paid to the interactions among race, class, and sex outside and inside these social movements.

It is a given that in each case, the social movements centered around deep and systematic *grievances* on the part of labor, women, or blacks. It would seem that there would be little reason for a movement to spring up or for one to develop were it not for the presence of some perceived injustice or serious problem. Movements do seem to develop when there is a widespread sensitivity to or awareness of injustice (Chafe 1977; Taylor 1989b). Each of the movements, but especially those in the 1960s, can be viewed as movements aimed at inequality (Gans 1974). But as has been noted before, such grievance is not sufficient for either the development or continuance of a social movement.

Both the surrounding *structure of opportunities* and *cultural context* affect the probability of a movement developing and flowering over time. Both affect the amount of power that aggrieved groups can develop. With respect to the structure of opportunities, it is not enough to say that social unrest of upheaval generates social movements. World wars, for example, certainly periods of drastic change in society, often have had a muffling effect on movements, as we have seen. It is the potential economic and political opportunities created by such events, however, rather than the events themselves, that are related to the appearance of social movements. The same can be said of industrialization, which created new opportunities for many individuals. For example, in the early labor movement it is clear that a tighter labor market created more favorable opportunities for labor, providing it with more bargaining power than it might have had otherwise. Economic expansion and the increased movement of women into the labor force provided them with new opportunities, greater awareness of occupational discrimination, and helped to restructure their images of what was possible for them. It also gave them a greater potential for economic independence. Each of these was important in generating the recent women's movement. In the case of the civil rights movement, massive indus-

trialization created new occupational opportunities for freed blacks, allowing them to build up a more independent and resource-laden set of social institutions that could serve as a basis for a social movement.

Political opportunities also play a role in creating an environment conducive to social movements. Certainly, at the most fundamental level, a formally democratic political structure is supposed to tolerate dissent, freedom to organize, and peaceful protest. In addition, any political situation favorable to the aggrieved creates another political opportunity. For example, the perception on the part of many of those in the labor movement that President Roosevelt was sympathetic with their cause provided them with a resource that strengthened their cause. The Wagner Act, the Nineteenth Amendment, and the Civil Rights Act of 1964 all provided political avenues that could be used by aggrieved groups to organize and protest.

Moreover, the political vulnerability of those in power also provided those who perceived themselves as victims (i.e., workers, blacks, women) with a political trump card to use in organizing. It has been pointed out in the case of each movement, for example, that presidents often acted in support of a minority's cause despite occasional personal feelings to the contrary because of fear of alienating a potentially powerful voting bloc. Roosevelt had to weigh the relative benefits of supporting business against unions and workers. Truman and Eisenhower had to worry about supporting southern politicians against a growing black voting bloc. Kennedy had to deal with pressure from women's groups and, consequently, created a Presidential Commission to examine discrimination against women.

Finally, social movements themselves often offer opportunities to be used in the genesis of new movements. Many of the younger women active in the current women's movement got much of their tactical and organizational training by working in the civil rights movement, and women active in the suffrage movement were also frequently active in the union movement. In sum, the existence of both economic and political structural opportunities creates a social context in which social movements can grow.

The cultural context also affects the life and structure of a social movement. We have seen how a variety of societal values and ideologies have been reflected in the character of labor, women's, and civil rights movements. Individualism and antisocialism undergirded several of the goals of the mainstream strand of the early labor movement. The AFL's business unionism, with its emphasis on the accomplishment of narrow, material, economic goals for union members as opposed to goals emphasizing the restructuring of capitalism, is an example of these values at work. A fundamental belief in capitalism on the part of most workers affected what they believed the labor movement should be all about. At the same time, however, the important strain of socialist and communist thinking among a minority of workers helped to diversify the internal structure of the labor movement. The cultural heterogeneity of immigrants who entered the labor force and the anticommunist feelings following World War I and the Russian Revolution also were factors determining the future direction of the labor movement. These values, along with racism, also affected the composition of the women's suffrage movement, as did the "flapper" values of the 1920s.

Racist, sexist, and class values and their intersection deeply influenced membership in each movement, creating internal divisions and pressures toward homogeneous organizations. In the early labor movement, both blacks and women were frequently not wanted by unions. When women were permitted into unions, they seldom were permitted to occupy positions of power. Unskilled immigrants also were not invited to join the craft unions of more skilled workers. Women often were seen as potential competitors in the labor force by men. Blacks were used as strikebreakers by employers in factories made up of white workers. In the civil rights movement, middle-class blacks dominated, leaving many immediate working-class concerns for the later de-

velopment of Black Power in the cities. Women often were used as tools in civil rights and Black Power organizations. Earlier, they had been shunned by male abolitionist organizations. Whites as well were discouraged from being part of the Black Power movement of the mid-1960s. With respect to the women's movement, early suffrage organizations often had little use for immigrant or working-class women. Their composition and goals also reflected the racism of the time. Many black women found themselves in an uncomfortable position in the 1960s feminist movement primarily made up of college-educated, white, middle-class women. Working-class women also did not make up a large part of that movement.

What all this indicates is that prevailing social norms with respect to race, sex, and class impress themselves on the internal dynamics and structure of social movements at the same time that they are related to the structural opportunities afforded each of these groups. The diversity of a movement's membership affects not only its stability but the diversity and depth of the goals it seeks and the tactics it uses. As we have seen in the histories of each of the three movements covered, there often has been a tendency to develop homogeneous organizations within the movement by barring individuals with undesirable racial, sexual, or class characteristics.

In some cases, the structure of opportunities and the prevailing cultural context are both supportive of minority protests. Such was the case in the 1960s with the women's movements, as we have noted. But in other cases, while the structure may provide an amenable setting, the trend in cultural values is against the minority and its protest. Many of the feelings and dominant ideologies after each war, for example, worked against a movement opening up and expanding. In these instances, a movement is often held in "abeyance," squelched, or denied birth. Clearly, the interaction of the structure and culture in a society affect the favorableness of the environment for given social movements. In a culturally hostile setting, countermovements are especially important. In the conservative 1980s and early 1990s, for example, countermovements influenced by fundamentalist religious beliefs and political conservatism offer a serious threat to "liberating" movements such as feminism. The survival of a movement depends upon both its structural strength relative to opposing groups and the cultural values dominant at the time.

In addition to structural opportunities and cultural milieu, the *resources* available to a group affect the development of a movement. One of the most influential recent theories of social movements, resource mobilization, proposes that access to resources is the most critical factor in the development of movements (Jenkins and Perrow 1977; Jenkins 1983). Resources are of all types and include leadership, organization, money, skills, communication networks, space, and time. Of course, whether an aggrieved group can obtain such resources also depends upon the structure of opportunities and cultural milieu just mentioned. The early civil rights movements could rely largely upon an indigenous set of reli-

gious and educational institutions for many of the resources it needed to develop. Later, as the movement gained strength, the nonviolent nature of the protests, which was consistent with prevailing values, also attracted resources from outside groups. The early suffragists depended upon resources from more wealthy donors and supporters among the middle and upper classes of women. In the case of the labor, women's, and civil rights movements, effective leadership was also a valuable resource that helped organize and strengthen each movement.

Finally, the presence of opportunities, resources, and a favorable cultural milieu foster the development of power and a sense of a *cognitive liberation* in which groups of aggrieved individuals redefine their situation and their potential for successful solutions (McAdam 1982). On the other hand, when groups have few opportunities, no resources, and the culture is adverse, the chances of a new revolutionary consciousness and a successful social movement are slim indeed.

CHAPTER 14

INCOME-MAINTENANCE PROGRAMS: FOUNDATIONS AND CHARACTERISTICS

The war on poverty has been won, except for perhaps a few mopping up operations.
—Martin Anderson

In large measure, our assessments of the moment are very much a function of what we believe and what we wish to see happen.
—Leonard Reissman

The last chapter concerned social movements on the part of groups who are in a disadvantaged position in the system of economic and political inequality. Those movements were sometimes informal and sporadic and sometimes formal and continuous attempts to rectify the poor situations experienced by the groups in question. This chapter deals with formal policy attempts by the government to address the problem of poverty. The statistics on poverty, its definition, and the characteristics of income-maintenance programs are riddled with hidden assumptions and social values that have affected approaches to understanding and grappling with poverty. We begin with the thorny issue of defining "poverty," then proceed with an analysis of the social values and orientations and myths that have affected the approach to poverty in the United States. From there we review the statistics on the extent of poverty among various groups and survey some of the major programs at the heart of the U.S. income-maintenance system.

THE CONUNDRUM OF DEFINING POVERTY

Defining poverty is basically a political act and how it is defined depends in large part upon one's values. "The concept of poverty, like those of unemployment, disability, and well-being, is elastic, multidimensional, nonobjective, and culturally determined" (Haveman 1987, p. 56). The definition one chooses powerfully and directly affects the rate of poverty and, ultimately, the kinds of policies prescribed to confront the problem. For a variety of reasons, as will become apparent, no one definition or set of programs has proven to be completely acceptable. A large portion of the reason for this is that the values that underlie these definitions frequently are in conflict (Ellwood 1988).

There have been a wide variety of attempts to define poverty. Some of these stress the *broad* nature of the conditions of poverty, while others focus only on the economic, and more *narrowly*, the income level of the individuals involved. Poverty can be defined in terms of income before *any* aid from the government (*pretransfer* poverty) or after cash or other transfers of various kinds are taken into account (*posttransfer* poverty). Moreover, poverty can be defined in terms of an *absolute* level or in terms of the position of a group *relative* to others. In sum, poverty can be defined differently along several dimensions: broad/narrow, pretransfer/posttransfer, and absolute/relative. We will look at each of these conceptions before assessing the extent of poverty in the United States.

Broad and Narrow Definitions of Poverty

Several persons have suggested that poverty is a multidimensional phenomenon and should be defined in broad terms. Consequently, from this point of view, simple economic definitions are inadequate because they do not capture all of what it means to be poor. Low income and minimal consumption level are important aspects of being poor, but poverty also has other class, status, and party implications. According to some, assets, basic services, self-respect, educational opportunities, and political participation must all be considered if one is to have a well-rounded conception of poverty (Miller and Roby 1970; Valentine 1968). Valentine has argued that "the primary meaning of poverty is a condition of being in want of something that is needed, desired, or generally recognized as having value" (1968, p. 12).

"A wide variety of locational, family-based, or job attributes directly determine economic well-being—children; neighborhood and environmental quality; and the danger, exposure, difficulty, and conditions of jobs come immediately to mind. A full assessment of these factors . . . is essential if true poverty or inequality is to be assessed accurately" (Haveman 1987, p. 78). By this definition, a variety of resources would have to be incorporated in the definition of poverty.

Unfortunately, broad concepts of poverty have been difficult to measure because of the multiple dimensions in them and because there are disagreements about how best to measure

each of them. Concepts such as "alienation," "instability," and "self-respect" have been measured in a number of ways, not all equally reliable and valid. A reasonable attempt to develop an adequate measure of poverty including all these dimensions into some kind of index of poverty has not yet been carried out (Plotnick and Skidmore 1975, p. 41).

Consequently, the measures used have virtually always been narrowly economic in nature. Attempts were made as far back as the turn of the century to assess the minimum level of income needed for a family to "subsist," and, at a higher level, to live "decently" (Rainwater 1974, Ch. 3). Despite the relatively long history of concern with adequate levels of income and economic resources, there is still no consensus on what measure of income should be used or what level ought to be used to define poverty. And, of course, conclusions about the extent of poverty are determined in large part by the measures and levels we accept. This means that defining poverty is a political act, with those wishing to downplay the amount of poverty defining it one way and others defining it in another.

A number of problems even face investigators who wish to use only income as the measure of poverty. Should they use gross or disposable cash income? What about in-kind transfers, such as food stamps, which can stand as a proxy for cash, or services from the government and other sources? Moreover, it must be remembered that current income is not necessarily the same as one's assets having a cash value. Specifically, current income does not always accurately indicate what one's *future* income will be, especially if one is early in a career. Nor does it reflect *past* income and expenditures adequately. In sum, the present income level of a family or individual may not be an accurate indicator of real economic status. "A family's yearly income may be unusually high or low relative to its normal level, depending upon factors such as spells of unemployment, labor force participation choices of family members, windfall gains or losses, and illness. Income variations due to such causes are particularly important among low-income groups" (Plotnick and Skidmore, p. 35; see also Miller and Roby 1970; Mirer 1974).

Absolute and Relative Definitions of Poverty

The absolute approach to defining poverty is characterized by determining a specific level of income that serves as a threshold separating the poor from the nonpoor. A poverty income "line" is determined and anyone falling below that line is considered poor. One of the difficulties with the absolute approach is that a decision has to be made about where that threshold should be, and that in turn depends upon one's values. Generally, when individuals have been asked what minimum amount would be needed to keep a family going, they suggest a minimum that is higher than that established by the government.

To establish a minimum level of required income, a list of basic needs is usually composed (e.g., food, fuel, shelter, clothing, transportation) and then it is asked how much would it cost to satisfy minimum needs in each of these areas. On this basis, a budget is developed that constitutes the basic income threshold separating the poor from the nonpoor. One of the problems with determining the absolute minimum necessary to live above the poverty level is that what is defined as a "necessity" varies from time to time and group to group (Schiller 1989). What may be one person's luxury is another person's necessity. Clearly, values and judgments are involved even in the case of establishing an absolute minimum threshold.

One of the consequences of using an absolute measure of poverty is that nothing is being said about the distribution or range of income in the society. A threshold can be set without concern for the extent of income inequality. When using this measure, "poverty" and "inequality" are really different issues. Under certain conditions, for example, absolute poverty might disappear but extensive income inequality remains (Morris and Williamson 1986).

In contrast, *relative* measures of poverty are tied to how the rest of the society, that is, the non-

poor, are doing in terms of income. The assumption is that poverty is relative to the social and economic context in which people live. People compare themselves with others to assess how well they are doing, that is, their conclusions about the rank of their economic position are relative to that of others. For example, an individual who may be nonpoor by absolute standards may be considered poor in comparison to others in the society. Thus, a relative definition of poverty is linked to the broader system of income inequality in society. Poverty and inequality are not considered to be discrete problems, and relative poverty can only disappear if income inequality is reduced or eliminated.

In relative measures of poverty, as the median or mean income of the population changes, so does the level defining poverty. A frequently used form of the relative measure is to define the poor as those who have only a given percentage, usually around 50 percent, of the household median income in the country. If poverty is defined in relation to the median, the decline of poverty is dependent on what happens in the overall distribution of income, that is, to income inequality. The 50 percent level is frequently picked because in 1967 it defined the same families as poor that were defined as poor by the official standard of the government. However, in recent times the rises in the median income have outstripped the poverty threshold set by the government, meaning that a measure that defines poverty as 50 percent of the median income is significantly higher than the official poverty threshold. In 1965, the official poverty threshold was 46 percent of the median income for a four-person family, whereas in 1986, it had dropped to 32 percent (Sawhill 1988). In other words, if the relative measure were used officially, many more would be defined as poor.

Pretransfer and Posttransfer Definitions

Once a decision has been made about the relative/absolute issue, it still has to be determined if the level of income for a family or individual is to incorporate *all* sources of income, or include only income from private sources. Using a *pretransfer* measure for determining income levels means that only income obtained from private sources such as earnings, private pensions or gifts, and alimony or child support are included. That is, a pretransfer poverty measure of this kind includes only those individuals and families whose incomes do not reach a given threshold before government economic aid is considered. A *posttransfer* measure of poverty, in contrast, includes income from any source, private or public, in determining an individual's poverty status. So if we wanted to get some idea as to how effective the government's cash-assistance programs are in reducing the poverty rate, we would compare the rate of poverty under the pretransfer measure with the rate under the posttransfer measure.

When it comes to incorporating the effect of government transfers on a family's income, some have argued that all government transfers should be considered, that is, not just cash assistance but the economic value of food stamps, housing, and educational and medical assistance, and then subtracting the taxes paid to arrive at a net income level for the family. One would also attempt to take into account a certain degree of underreporting of income that occurs (Danziger and Plotnick 1977; *Focus* Winter 1984). This *adjusted-income* measure, which incorporates the value of numerous benefits received, is argued by many to give a more complete and accurate reading of a family's actual economic situation. A measure using only money income "ignores or understates many resources available to the aged. Net worth, eligibility for in-kind transfers, the amount of leisure time taken, and living arrangements are among the determinants of consumption, possibilities inadequately captured in money income" (Moon and Smolensky 1977, p. 47). It is suggested that if the value of food stamps and the like were incorporated into the family's income, many fewer families would be considered poor (Haveman 1987; Danziger and Gottschalk 1983; Smeeding 1982).

On the other hand, several other decisions would have to be made if it was decided to include the value of such nonincome or in-kind government transfers in the determination of family income. First, one would have to decide which in-kind benefits should be included. Do we include private as well as public in-kind transfers, that is, exchanges, gifts, and services from private individuals in addition to such governmental transfers? (Haveman 1987). Should only those transfers that are aimed primarily at the poor, such as food stamps and Medicaid, be included, or should *all* noncash transfers, such as Medicare, educational benefits, housing, government loans at low interest rates, depreciation allowances, and so on, be included? While in-kind benefits from "welfare" programs go disproportionately to the poor, when all government in-kind transfers are considered, the value of the amount received goes up with increasing income (Haverman 1987). In other words, the nonpoor benefit more from government policies than the poor. The nonpoor receive at least 50 percent of all government in-kind benefits, and over 25 percent of those who are poor receive no in-kind transfers from the government (Rodgers 1982). What this means is that if all governmental benefits were included, even the incomes of the nonpoor would be inflated.

Second, one also has to develop a method by which the "value" of an in-kind transfer is determined. One method might be to find out how much an individual would have to pay for it on the open market were it to be purchased (i.e., "market value"), while another would be to determine the value of the transfer to the given recipient by finding out how much the person would be willing to pay for it (i.e., "recipient value"). A third method of determining value would be to determine how much a person or family actually spent on the given good before such goods were given by the government (i.e., "poverty-budget-share value") (*Focus* Winter 1984). Once the value of an in-kind benefit has been determined, however, one still has to consider whether or not the recipient's economic level has been raised because of it (see Chapter 2). "A $5,000 Medicaid payment to cover the costs of surgery, for example, merely increases the family's resources by the same amount as the family's needs were increased by the costs of surgery: the net effect on a family's ability to meet its basic needs is virtually unchanged" (Duncan 1984, p. 36). A family's standard of living is not increased because its members have some of their medical expenses paid for by the government. In this light, if we define poverty in terms of the family's ability to meet basic needs, then the addition of certain in-kind benefits may not actually improve its economic situation.

All of the distinctions and definitions of poverty that we have discussed tell us something about poverty. The absolute measure focuses our attention on the fact that a certain minimum level of income is needed for subsistence. The relative measures bring out the fact that people's conceptions of their economic situation are affected by how others in the society are doing. Finally, the adjusted-income definition attempts to delineate a more accurate picture of the economic condition of the individuals involved.

The Official Measure of Poverty

The official government definition of poverty is based on a formulation developed by the Social Security Administration in 1965, which was then formally adopted by the government in 1969. In this definition, total family income refers to post-transfer *cash* income *before taxes*. It does not include capital gains or losses. The poverty threshold was determined by using the Department of Agriculture's 1961 Economy Food Plan, which reflects the different consumption needs of families of different sizes and composition, with heads of different sex and age, and place of residence. This food plan, in turn, had been developed using the Department of Agriculture's 1955 survey of food consumption, which revealed that families of three or more persons spent about one-third of their incomes on food. A family was then defined as poor if it spent more than one-

third of its income while following the economy food plan. The poverty level, consequently, was set as being equal to three times the cost of the food plan. In the early sixties, for example, it was estimated that the minimal diet would cost $1,000. Thus, the poverty level was set at $3,000 in 1964. In 1989, the average poverty threshold for a family of four was $12,675. Every year, the level is adjusted according to changes in the Consumer Price Index. Adjustments are also made for differences in the size, composition, and residences of families. The poverty thresholds for farm families are slightly lower than those for nonfarm families to allow for in-kind income, primarily in the form of food grown on the farm. In the table that appears later in the chapter, this conception of poverty is referred to as the "official definition" of poverty.

Problems with the Official Measure   One of the major sources of debate about the official poverty measure is that it does not include the noncash transfers to the poor just discussed even though expenditures on programs like food stamps, Medicaid, subsidized housing, and school lunches more than doubled in the period from 1970 to 1986 (Sawhill 1988). There is also related debate, of course, on which noncash transfers to include, with expenditures on medical care being the most controversial. "To include actual medical benefits received would imply that people who have poorer health are better off, other things being equal" (Sawhill 1988, p. 1078). In addition to the issue of what should be included, there are other problems surrounding the official measure.

First, there are problems with the measure of income used. There appears to be little question that individuals' net or disposable incomes are a better measure of the economic resources available to them than their incomes before taxes (Sawhill 1988). Yet the Bureau of the Census continues to use pretax income in its official measure of poverty. If taxes are not considered, the official measure is *too broad* a definition, and if corporate profits, capital gains or losses, non-money income (such as rent and do-it-yourself production), and employer and government non-income benefits of various kinds are not incorporated, it is *too narrow* a definition (Plotnick and Skidmore 1975; Danziger and Plotnick 1977). In addition to not including the goods and services a family receives from others, it does not include the value of the services a family provides for itself, such as child care and housework (Duncan 1984).

Second, its use of current instead of permanent income creates difficulties in assessing the "true levels of well-being" of families at the proposed poverty level (Plotnick and Skidmore 1975, p. 35). Assessing a family's economic status by using its income at one point does not allow us to distinguish those who have consistent levels of income from those whose incomes have fluctuated from year to year. Moreover, by using the one-year snapshot as the unit for determining how many are and who is poor, the official measure does not permit distinctions to be made between those who are poor only for a short time from those who are more "persistently poor." This distinction is important because these groups have different characteristics, which means that the programs that may prove effective in reducing their poverty would probably differ. Those who are only poor for a brief period are not significantly different in their characteristics from the rest of the population, while those who are poor for long periods are different from the majority in major ways. They tend to be "heavily concentrated" among black and female-headed households. Those from rural areas and the South are also disproportionately represented among the "persistently poor" (Duncan 1984).

Third, the use of the 33 percent formula to arrive at the poverty threshold assumes that the Department of Agriculture's costing method and food plan apply to all families of a given type. This may not be the case at all. Given the differences in sizes and age distributions of families and, therefore, varying demands or needs among them, it is unrealistic to assume that one-third of the budgets of all these families is spent on food. In addition, while the one-third formula was orig-

inally based on *posttax* income, the Social Security Administration (SSA) applied it to income *before taxes*. Perhaps most importantly, the official formula was based on an emergency, temporary budget, not on food budgets actually observed among families under ordinary circumstances (Duncan 1984; Haveman 1987). "The official thresholds . . . simply reflect one rather stringent view of how much income is needed by different families to reach a minimum 'level of decency' relative to average American standards" (Plotnick and Skidmore 1975, p. 37).

Fourth, establishing a given threshold tells us nothing about how far below that threshold given percentages of the poor really are. Certainly, knowing how impoverished the poor are is an important dimension of their predicament. Finally, many have argued that poverty ought to be defined in terms of changes in the standard of living, so that as the standards go up, the level that is designated as the poverty threshold also goes up. While the official poverty rate fluctuates with the Consumer Price Index, it does not take into account rises in income standards (Haveman 1987). It ignores the fact that these same individuals compare their incomes to those around them. Poverty in this sense is a relative matter, not an absolute one.

LEVELS AND TRENDS IN POVERTY

As the discussion thus far should make evident, what conclusions are drawn about the extent of and trends in poverty depends on the definition adopted. Since giving only information on the extent of official poverty would present a misleading picture of the amount of poverty, three definitions are used in discussing poverty after 1958: the official measure, a relative measure, and the adjusted-income measure.

Poverty Before 1959

Before poverty in the contemporary United States is discussed, some note should be made of poverty as it existed earlier in the country. Even though the concern for the poor was increasing during the latter half of the nineteenth century, there was little information about the actual extent of poverty at the time. Jacob Riis estimated that between 20 and 30 percent of the population of New York lived in poverty near the end of the nineteenth century; Spahr also suggested that the number of poor was quite large (Bremner 1956). Using a minimum decency standard, Hartley (1969) estimated that the proportion of the population in poverty was about 45 percent in 1870 and 35 percent in 1910, indicating a general decrease in the intervening decades. Using another minimum-decency standard, Ornati (1966) put the proportion of the population in poverty in the mid-1930s at around 45 percent. With the exception of 1944, poverty in the 1940s appears to have been near the 30 percent mark, and in the early 1950s it was between 22 and 29 percent of the population (Hartley 1969; Ornati 1966; Weinstein and Smolensky 1978).

Among those who were poor in the latter part of the 1800s, blacks and immigrants were overrepresented. Moreover, a significant percentage, more so than today, of those who were fully employed were among the poor. The terrible conditions under which employed workers labored around the turn of the century were outlined in the Pittsburgh survey carried out in 1907 and 1908. Briefly, the findings showed a great deal of overwork, ranging up to a twelve-hour day, seven days a week in some firms; wages "so low as to be inadequate to the maintenance of a normal American standard of living," and even lower wages for women; absentee capitalism with effects similar to those of absentee landlordism; destruction of the family under extraordinary work demands on men, women, and children; and a high incidence of contagious disease and industrial accidents (Devine 1908–1909). Programs developed since that time have helped to reduce the amount of needless suffering and *absolute* poverty in the U.S. population.

Poverty from 1959 to the Present

Only a brief discussion was devoted to assessing the extent of poverty before 1959 because data were not as thoroughly and systematically collected nor were the measures as carefully developed prior to that date. Poverty data based on the official government definition were first collected for 1959. Using that measure, the poverty rate fell significantly from 22 to 12 percent between 1959 and 1969. During that decade, the number of people who were poor dropped from 39.9 million to 24.1 million. Between 1970 and 1977, the number of poor people vacillated between 23 and just over 26 million. The poverty rate for those years varied between 11.1 and 12.6 percent. However, from 1978 to 1983, the poverty population increased by 44 percent, going from 24.5 to 35.3 million. Correspondingly, the poverty rate jumped from 11.4 to 15.2 percent. Since then the poverty rate has dropped. In 1989, it was 12.8 percent, and the number of poor persons totaled 31.5 million. This rate, however, is still above what it was a decade after the War on Poverty in the mid-1960s. At the same time, it is significantly lower than the 22.4 percent poverty rate of 1959 (U.S. Bureau of the Census, February 1989).

The relative stagnation in the decline in the official poverty rate during the 1970s appears to have been due to a variety of factors. There had been a rise in the proportion of families headed by females, and a greater percentage of these family types were poor. Second, the 1970s witnessed high inflation and recession. These conditions have more negative consequences for those in lower income than high-income groups. Higher unemployment in the latter part of the 1970s and early 1980s also had negative effects on the incomes of workers. Third, there has been a growing inequality in earnings in the last few decades. This inequality helped increase the poverty rate for those below the median (Sawhill 1988).

In comparing blacks and whites, the poverty rate for both groups is about 60 percent of what it was in 1959. At the same time, however, the poverty rate for blacks is over three times the 1989 rate of whites (30.7 versus 10.0 percent, respectively). Still, whites make up the majority of the poor population. Since 1959, generally about two-thirds of the poverty population has been white.

The poverty rates of families with female heads also has decreased by about one-third since 1959. In 1959, over 49 percent of such families were poor, compared to a still significant 32.2 percent in 1989. The percentage of the poor who live in families with female heads also increased dramatically in the 1959 to 1989 period. In 1959, just over 20 percent of the poor lived in such families, compared to over 50 percent in 1989. Female-headed families made up almost 52 percent of all poor families in 1989. It is these kinds of figures that suggest to many the "feminization" of poverty. This trend is especially visible among blacks. In 1959, just over 26 percent of the black poor who lived in families resided in female-headed families. In 1989, the figure was almost 73 percent.

With respect to age trends, declines in poverty rates have been especially noticeable among older Americans. The 1989 poverty rate for those sixty-five years of age or over was 11.4 percent compared to 35.2 in 1959. This decline occurred for both blacks and whites, although the rate for older whites has decreased farther. Currently, roughly half of the nation's poor are either under eighteen or over sixty-five years of age (U.S. Bureau of the Census, September 1990).

Trends under Different Definitions of Poverty We noted earlier in this chapter that the definition of poverty one chooses has a significant impact upon one's perception of the extent of poverty. This becomes clear when we examine different measures of poverty and the varying poverty rates associated with them. *Pretransfer poverty measures,* it will be recalled, do not take into account any program interventions on the part of the government. In other words, they show what the individual's income would be from private sources, primarily earnings. If one wants to find out how fluctuations in the operation of the economy alone affect the poverty rate, a pretransfer measure is what should be used.

Overall, pretransfer measures of poverty

show little progress in poverty-rate reduction in the last decade or two. In 1965, the pretransfer poverty rate was over 21 percent. Almost ten years later, in 1974, it was just over 20 percent, and in 1982 it was 24 percent (*Focus* Winter 1984). Congressional figures vary slightly from these but show that since 1980 the pretransfer rate has been between 21 and 23 percent (U.S. Congress 1988). Since about the time of the launching of the War on Poverty in the mid-1960s, the amount of pretransfer has remained remarkably stable. More recent evidence also suggests little change in poverty rates when relative measures are used (Sawhill 1988). These conclusions call into question the ability of the present economy to bring about significant reductions in the proportion of people who are poor.

The lack of noticeable reduction in pretransfer poverty in the last decade suggests that we should be wary of "any belief that economic growth, by itself, will cause poverty to wither away fairly quickly" (Plotnick and Skidmore 1975, p. 116). What does seem to have an effect on the level of poverty is the unemployment rate. When full-employment conditions prevail and the labor market is tight, poverty declines. In this light, one should keep in mind that the poor in the labor market tend to be among the most unskilled and least educated and are members of the secondary labor market. Consequently, they are the most likely to be affected by changes in the employment conditions in the economy since they are among the first to be laid off and the least likely to find other jobs. The effect of fluctuations in employment conditions on these persons is even more magnified because earnings make up a greater proportion of their total incomes than is the case among the nonpoor. Hence, their economic situation is highly sensitive to shifts in the market (Plotnick and Skidmore 1975, pp. 117–119). As might be expected, these shifts affect those who are ordinarily actively involved in the labor force, in other words, the nonaged, rather than those who have retired.

When the economic value of various kinds of

in-kind government transfers is added to income, as in an *adjusted-income poverty measure,* the percentage of those who are still poor using the government's threshold goes down, as would be expected. Table 14.1 presents the national poverty rates for 1980 to 1987 under different measures of poverty. The table reveals distinct differences in the rates depending upon the measure used. For example, while in 1987, 13.5 percent of the population was poor under the official measure, only 12.0 percent fall below the government's income threshold for poverty when the market value of food and housing is added to the incomes of individuals. When the market value of medical benefits is added to food and housing, the poverty rate falls to 8.5 percent. Since, generally, the market value for these in-kind benefits is higher than their assessed value to recipients, the poverty rates under the recipient-value method are slightly higher than those found when the market value of these benefits is used.

While the data in Table 14.1 do not suggest any clear linear decline in the poverty rate for 1980 to 1987 under any of the measures used, data going back to the 1959 to 1965 period do indicate a decline since then when in-kind benefits are included in the measure of poverty (Danziger, Haveman, and Plotnick 1986). The elderly

appear to benefit most from the inclusion of these in-kind benefits. But the reader should keep in mind the reservations and issues surrounding the use of such a poverty measure. It is clear that the conclusions one draws about trends in poverty depend not only on the measure used but on the length of the time period selected.

PERCEPTIONS OF THE POOR

The preceding data indicate that poverty in the United States continues. What one suggests as a means to reduce or eliminate poverty is heavily conditioned not only by the manner in which one defines the extent of poverty but by the images one holds concerning the causes of poverty and the characteristics of the poor. As Reissman neatly puts it: "In large measure, our assessments of the moment are very much a function of what we believe and what we wish to see happen" (1973, p. 7). The policies, programs, and organizations that have been created in the last 150 years to deal with the "problem" of poverty are based on distinct kinds of values, which, in turn, flow from the historical events and institutional arrangements that have characterized the United States. Consequently, if we are to understand U.S. policy reactions to poverty, we must first un-

TABLE 14.1 U.S. Poverty Rates under Different Measures of Poverty: 1980–1987

	1980	1982	1983	1984	1985	1986	1987
Official definition	13.0%	15.0%	15.3%	14.4%	14.0%	13.6%	13.5%
Market-value approach							
Including food and housing	11.1	13.4	13.9	12.9	12.5	12.1	12.0
Including food, housing, medical benefits; excluding institutional expenditures	8.1	10.3	10.6	9.8	9.3	8.8	8.5
Recipient and/or cash-equivalent approach							
Including food and housing	11.4	13.7	14.1	13.2	12.8	12.5	12.4
Including food, housing, medical benefits; excluding institutional expenditures	10.6	12.8	13.3	12.4	12.0	11.1	11.0

Source: U.S. Bureau of the Census, *Statistical Abstract of the United States: 1989* (109th edition). Washington, D.C.: U.S. Government Printing Office, 1989. Table 742, p. 457.

derstand the cultural and historical bases for them.

Most of the images of the poor and the causes of poverty that have dominated U.S. history have focused in one way or another on alleged weaknesses among the poor themselves. In seventeenth-century England, the poor were thought to be "eternally damned" and were not considered a part of the society (Coser 1965). "Rogues, beggars, vagabonds . . . commonly are of no civil society or corporation, nor of any particular Church: and are as rotten legges, and armes, that droppe from the body . . . (Hill 1964, pp. 227–228). This focus on the individual's characteristics as the basic cause of poverty emerged in fourteenth-century Europe with the rise of industrialism, the new freed wage-laborer, and the growth of international commerce. The massive economic changes occurring on the continent during this period, in addition to famines, widespread diseases, and war, generated a large number of paupers and beggars. Something had to be done to deal with these individuals. At the same time, the process of industrialization required the ready availability of workers.

As the dominant source of relief and welfare moved progressively out of the hands of the Church and private charity and into the hands of public institutions and officials, a clear distinction between the "deserving" and "undeserving" poor developed in the latter part of the fifteenth century. Women who were pregnant, individuals who were seriously ill, and the elderly were among those who were considered worthy of help. Individuals who could, but did not work, were considered undeserving of assistance. The principle of "less eligibility" was used, that is, the idea that any relief given not be great enough to discourage work. The amount of relief was not expected to be higher than the wages of the lowest ranked worker in the community (Dolgoff and Feldstein 1984).

The Elizabethan Poor Law of 1601 distinguished among the "able-bodied poor," the "impotent poor," and "dependent children." The former were required to work; refusal to do so would

mean punishment, and nonpoor citizens were forbidden to aid them. Those classified as being "impotent," such as the handicapped, deaf, blind, elderly, and mothers with small children, were given either "in-door relief," that is, placed in an institution or almshouse, or given "outdoor relief," that is, allowed to stay in their own homes but given relief such as food, clothing, or other needed goods. "Dependent children" who could not be supported by their families were farmed out as apprentices, taught trades, and were expected to serve in this capacity until early adulthood (Zastrow 1982). To be eligible for aid, the poor person was expected to have been a stable member of the community and without family support.

The distinction between the deserving and undeserving poor found in the Elizabethan Poor Law became deeply ingrained in the approaches taken to the poor and welfare in Britain and the United States and have remained so to this day. In early America, poverty was becoming a serious problem. Before the Civil War, upheavals in the economy, sickness, immigration, and demographic changes generated large numbers of poor individuals. Specifically, the decline of home manufacture of goods, unemployment, the rise of low-wage labor, the seasonality of much work, and crop failures were among the economic changes responsible for poverty. Growing population pressure on the land, the changing age structure of the population, and increasing immigration also led to increased poverty levels (Katz 1986).

Reaction to the poverty problem was heavily influenced by the English reaction. Relief was considered a public responsibility, it was to be locally administered and controlled; it was not to be given to those who had families who could support them, and those who could work were expected to do so (Katz 1986). Even then, however, many believed that any relief would discourage the motivation to work and weaken character. Efforts were placed then, as now, on seeking out and eliminating the "able-bodied" from the relief rolls. The Quincy Report, a 1821 Massachusetts study of poverty and welfare, made the by-now familiar distinction between the impotent poor and the able poor. "Poorhouses" were created to take care of the poor, but principally to rehabilitate the able poor and train children under severe, disciplinary conditions. The poorhouses had several goals (Katz 1986). First, they aimed to reduce the expense of welfare through cheaper care and by deterring many who would otherwise seek welfare aid. The requirement of work and the ban on alcohol use in the poorhouse, it was assumed, would stop the lazy and the drunkards from applying for poorhouse help. Second, it was hoped that work and discipline would work wonders on those exposed to them. The education of children would also help prepare them for nonpoor adulthoods. Thus, the goal was to transform the character and behavior of those in the poorhouse.

The poorhouses did not work out very well. The conflict in goals that plagues many current welfare programs was already present in the early poorhouse program. A concern for order, cost, routine, and custody overcame the initial goal of reforming the individuals in them. Many became rundown and the care given became less than adequate. Officers of the poorhouses were often found to be guilty of graft. Inmates had greater and greater control over their behavior in the poorhouse; discipline was not enforced nor was useful work found for most inmates (Katz 1986).

Cultural Values and the Poor

Historically, perceptions of the poor have been conditioned by the cultural context. A number of U.S. values that have had a significant impact on our views of the poor. Among the most central of these are (1) individualism/autonomy, and (2) the belief in work, intertwined with its *moral* character. The roots of these values go back several centuries and originated in intellectual and religious events in Europe.

Individualism/Autonomy One of the most important of these values is *individualism* or the belief in *autonomy* (Dolgoff and Feldstein 1984;

Ellwood 1988; Tropman 1989). The image of the quintessential pioneer as someone who was an island unto himself or herself, a singular and stalwart rock against the rigors of frontier life, has captivated the idea of what true Americans should be like. Despite the fact that most early Americans traveled and lived in groups, the idea of the rugged individual has had great appeal (Boorstin 1967). Basic to this ideal image of the heroic American are several components:

1. This person is physically and psychologically independent; the person needs no help from others.
2. Individual achievement is sought despite difficult obstacles.
3. Achievement under even difficult circumstances means that anyone can succeed if they try hard enough.
4. Those who don't make it either lack the ability or are lazy and therefore immoral. In any case, they don't have what it takes to succeed.
5. The possibility of material gain is needed to motivate people (Dolgoff and Feldstein 1984).

These components suggest the scenario that being poor or rich is largely a result of "contest mobility" in which the best win and the worst fail. Clearly in this view, individuals who are poor either do not have the personal qualities necessary to succeed or do not put forth enough effort. Moreover, being poor and on "welfare" indicates dependency and, therefore, flies in the face of the ideal autonomous person.

The Enlightenment of the eighteenth century and Adam Smith's economic theories also provided intellectual support to the centrality of the autonomous individual. It was believed that intelligent individuals, equipped with modern knowledge, could do almost anything for themselves as well as society. Smith's economic theories stressed a laissez-faire approach to economic affairs. Free individuals, unencumbered by governmental and other regulations, seeking their own goals would create the most efficient and productive society. Governmental interference in the form of any aid was believed to violate the intricate processes of freely working, "natural systems." "The 'inefficient poor' like inefficient businesses, were to die off through natural selection" (Tropman 1989, p. 137).

Thomas Malthus, the principal architect of early population theory, also did not favor outside relief for the destitute because "natural positive checks" (poverty, pestilence, hunger, etc.) were thought necessary to encourage the growth of self-restraint and self-reliance, especially in childbearing. One of the myths that was derived from this belief, of which we will speak later, was that the poor have more children to obtain more welfare (Bell 1987).

The Moral Character of Work   "God helps those who help themselves" goes the old saying. The belief that individuals are responsible for their own destinies can be traced back to religious doctrines that meshed with a society having a large frontier to be explored, conquered, and populated by a motley collection of individuals who had emigrated from Europe largely in the nineteenth century. One of these religious strands was Calvinism, which Miller (1977) has called "the most individualistic development out of the most individualistic wing of the most individualistic part of the Judeo-Christian heritage" (p. 3). Calvinism is a puritanical, grim religion that stresses the importance of the individual and his or her own work as an indication of whether he or she is among the "elected."

The Calvinism of England, in particular, emphasized the importance of individual responsibility, discipline, and an ascetic lifestyle. Under this doctrine, work is considered crucial to a meaningful life. Idleness is not only a sin but a "social evil" as well. People who become poor do so because they lack character. Since they are not successful, it is a sign that they are not among God's elect. Calvin even was against free almsgiving to those he considered idle and lazy (Dolgoff and Feldstein 1984).

The Puritan minister Cotton Mather (1663 to 1728) confirmed the religious importance of work in his exhortations about the importance of having "a calling." Every man should have an occupation through which he contributes to society, argued Mather, otherwise he cannot expect anything from society. "How can a man Reasonably look for the *Help of other men,* if he be not in some *Calling* Helpful to *other men?*" wrote the minister. When men do not put forth their efforts, what happens? "By *Slothfulness* men bring upon themselves . . . Poverty . . . Misery . . . all sorts of Confusion. . . . On the other Side . . . a *Diligent* man is very rarely an *Indigent* man" (Rischin 1965, pp. 24–28; emphases in original). It would be easy to see why those in positions of wealth and power might subscribe to these views, since they not only justify the wealth of those at the top but locate the source of poverty in a lack of effort by the poor individual.

While the explicitly religious character of many of these pronouncements has become less evident, the hold of the essential ideas continues strong. Individual work still dominates much of our thinking about what it takes to succeed, and the dominant American belief system continues to place the "individual" on a pedestal (see Williams 1970; Miller 1977; Reissman 1973). To place the reason for economic success or failure on the individual is (1) to exonerate society and others from playing a role in the creation of poverty, and just as important, (2) to isolate the poor from the rest of society and to foster a "them versus us" imagery of the population. The further perception, though inaccurate, of most of the poor as black intensifies the belief that the poor are qualitatively different in character from the rest of the population.

Moreover, the work ethic, referring to work in the *marketplace* (not housework, for example), dominates much of the rationale in current welfare policies. The thrust is on getting able-bodied people to work outside the home so that they will not take advantage of welfare benefits. Only the deserving poor should receive help. The notion that those without jobs, especially during times of relative prosperity, are to blame for their own economic troubles goes back deep in our history. As Bremner (1956) notes in his analysis of reactions to poverty during the nineteenth century "In normal times Americans were accustomed to think of unemployment as exclusively the problem of the inefficient and indolent. Conservatives stuck to this view even in depression years." Bremner continues by characterizing the nineteenth-century view of poverty in the following manner: "Poverty is unnecessary . . . but the varying ability and virtue of men make its presence inevitable . . . where it exists, poverty is usually a temporary problem and, both in its cause and cure, it is always an individual matter." It was also believed that the presence and fear of poverty served as incentives to work and to use one's abilities to the fullest (Bremner 1956, pp. 16–17).

The beliefs in individualism, work and its moral character influence present-day images of the poor and welfare. This is not to say that other values are not also implicated in current images. A sense of community and compassion (humanitarianism), the beliefs in achievement and success as upward mobility, and the belief that the family is supposed to play a crucial role in maintaining its members are all additional values that have helped to shape our perceptions of the poor and what is to be done with them. The focus here has been on individualism and the work ethic because, more often than not, these values have been most salient in those perceptions and have informed those responsible for crafting welfare policies. These values also lead to an underemphasis on capitalism and an overemphasis on individual flaws as sources of poverty.

Myths about the Poor

Values and beliefs often distort social reality by suggesting that most of the poor have characteristics that they, in fact, do not possess. While blacks are often believed to make up the bulk of those who are poor and on welfare, in fact whites comprised over two-thirds of the poor in 1989 (U.S. Bureau of the Census, September 1990).

Given their beliefs about ~~~~~ about those on welfare, s~ the majority of those receivin~ bodied, middle-aged men who are ~ work. In fact, about 40 percent of the poor ~ below eighteen years of age, and another 11 percent are individuals over sixty-five years old (U.S. Bureau of the Census, September 1990). Of the remainder, there are also those nonaged who are disabled in some way and families in which no husband is present. Thus, the majority are not able-bodied, middle-aged men. But women who receive aid are now considered part of the "able-bodied poor." They are viewed as the new paupers of poverty. That is, they are considered a danger to society if they do not work and also are considered to be perfectly capable of working.

There are other misconceptions about the poor that reinforce the belief that they are undeserving. One is that they have a significantly greater number of children than the nonpoor. This is plainly not the case. There is only a slight difference in the average size of poor and nonpoor families. In 1989, the average size of U.S. families in general was 3.17 while that of poor families was 3.55, less than half a person larger. Nor is there any good evidence that poor mothers have children, including illegitimate ones, to increase their benefits. A majority of Americans apparently believe that the presence of welfare encourages young women to have children and discourages those who get pregnant from marrying the fathers (Davis and Smith 1989). The assumption that people have children to get more support from the government simply does not hold up when the evidence is examined (Morris and Williamson 1986).

First, in general, benefits from Aid to Families with Dependent Children (AFDC) tend to be quite low. In 1985, for example, the maximum monthly levels of AFDC benefits for a woman with two children ranged from $96 in Mississippi to $555 in California. Second, over four-fifths of unmarried mothers on AFDC in recent years have had only one child (Bell 1987). Moreover,

dence indicates that illegitimacy rates tend to be *lower* in states with higher welfare benefits (Ellwood and Bane 1984). Finally, given the small size of the extra amount recipients receive each month for each additional child makes it highly unlikely that economic motivation is the reason for their having children.

When one considers that it has been estimated that it cost over $50,000 in 1980, and several times that in the early 1990s, to raise one child through her or his teenage years, receiving under $100 per month for each child hardly makes it economically worthwhile to have large numbers of children (Zastrow 1982). As an example, in Ohio having a second child adds $79 per month to a family's ADC check, and having a third adds only $58 per month to it (Brett 1989). The level of these benefits is not going to make anyone rich. In European countries, in fact, which generally have much higher benefits for children than the United States, there have been concerns over the *declining* birth rates in recent

years (Bell 1987). This again suggests that benefit levels are not a major cause of birth rates.

Clearly, the image of those *on welfare* is much more negative than the view most people have of the poor. Those on welfare are often thought to be guilty of fraud and cheating. But, in fact, only an extremely small percentage cheat and then, in almost all cases, only a small amount of money is involved. More prevalent and more serious than cheating by recipients are the honest mistakes and errors made by public officials when determining eligibility for and level of public aid (Zastrow 1982; Bell 1987). In addition, recent exposures of pervasive fraud by building contractors and others who profit from the government's housing program, as well as overcharging and similar behaviors by health-care providers, strongly suggest that if fraud is a problem in income-maintenance programs, the recipients are not its primary source.

When people become knowledgeable about who actually receives welfare, they are likely to

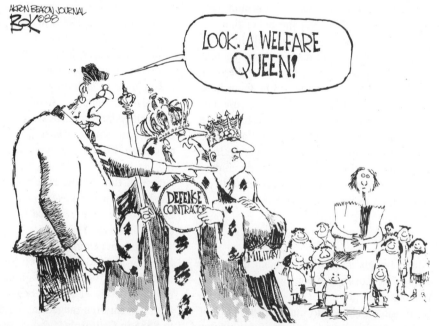

Our images of the poor and those on welfare often are distorted by stereotypes. Many of those who are not poor but who receive a great deal of help from the government are not seen in this same negative light.

change their minds about the "worthiness" of the recipients. An eight-state study by the University of Southern California revealed that the vast majority of those who were antiwelfare for the chronically unemployed had a change of heart when told that most recipients are blind, disabled, mothers with small children, or otherwise unable to meet employment requirements. When informed of these characteristics, over 75 percent of those who originally had opposed welfare changed their minds (Jaffe 1977, p. 6).

In the past, certain kinds of individuals have been more likely than others to oppose welfare. Feagin (1972) found that the higher the income of the respondent, the more antiwelfare the person was; the lower the education, the more prowelfare, although those with seven to twelve years of education were the most antiwelfare, with the college educated not far behind (Feagin 1972; Rytina et al. 1970). Similarly, Ransford (1972) found that blue-collar workers were more antagonistic than white-collar workers toward protests by blacks even when educational level was taken into account. He suggests that one reason for this may be the belief by white blue-collar workers that since the United States is the land of opportunity, and they had to work hard to get where they are, blacks should not receive special favors (such as welfare). And to find that many of them believe that the government will aid blacks more than whites makes the situation even worse. A large majority of the white working class felt that "there's more concern today for the 'welfare bum' who doesn't want to work than for the hard working person struggling to make a living" (Ransford 1972, p. 338). Blue-collar workers who felt powerless were especially likely to feel antagonistic about blacks. Ransford concludes that many of the reactions of blue-collarites are founded in real strains that they face rather than in personal injustices.

All of the evidence we have discussed and other findings suggest that the view of the poor as "undeserving" and disreputable" with "flawed character" is still with us. In addition to blaming the poor for their own conditions, people often view the poor as being content with their conditions "The image is that of the 'noble savage'—uninhibited, enjoying nature, unfettered by the responsibilities of middle-class life" (Reissman 1965, p. 40). The condition of poverty has even been considered good fortune in disguise, since those who are in that state luckily have to work hard to succeed and are not exposed to the temptations of wealth. Because they have to earn their living the hard way, they become "athletes trained for the contest, with sinews braced, indomitable wills, resolved to do or die" (Carnegie 1901). It is unlikely that many today would look on poverty as a blessing, and needless to say, this romantic view is largely inaccurate; few of the poor ever move up to the top rungs of the occupational ladder in their lifetimes, as we noted in Chapter 11.

The Poor and Incentive to Work Perhaps the most consequential perception of the poor involves their attachment to work and the work ethic. As mentioned earlier, the value of work is deeply ingrained in U.S. culture, as is the belief that most people can succeed if they try hard enough. These beliefs force us to raise some important questions about the poor. First, are people poor primarily because they do not work? Second, do the poor believe in the work ethic or do they prefer not to work? With respect to the first question, census data indicate that a significant proportion of the poor work, many of them full time. About 41 percent of *individuals* who were poor and over fifteen years of age worked at least some time during 1989. About one-quarter of these worked full time for 50 to 52 weeks (U.S. Bureau of the Census, September 1990). Over 40 percent of poor female heads also work. In other words, almost a quarter of poor individuals fifteen years of age and over worked full time during 1989, but they were still poor. Low earnings/wages along with subemployment are principal reasons for the poverty of many families (Danziger and Gottschalk 1986; Schiller 1989). "It's an interesting phenomenon," says Patrick McGrath, director of a county Department of Human Services in Ohio; "A lot of our people do work and are still eligible for assistance. It's a myth that our people are lazy and don't work" (Brett 1989). Of those poor who did not work at all in the United States in 1989, well over half were either ill, disabled, retired, or going to school. An additional 32 percent were not working because they were keeping house.

Among poor *family* householders, almost 49 percent worked some time during 1989, and 16 percent worked full time, year-round (U.S. Bureau of the Census, September 1990). Earnings from work is a major source of income for male-headed poor families. Over 80 percent of these families get some income from earnings, and in this case, almost 63 percent of their incomes comes from earnings. The pattern of sources of income is much different among poor female-headed families. In those, just under half receive income from earnings and only about one-fourth of their incomes as a whole comes from earnings. The result is that welfare sources of income are much more significant for female-headed households (U.S. Congress 1988).

What these data indicate is that many poor individuals work, but despite their efforts they remain poor. Because of the importance of earnings as a source of income for most families, it is important that programs like AFDC, for example, be designed with work incentives in mind. Both the poor and the nonpoor respond to such incentives (Danziger et al. 1986). Most Americans want to work. When asked if they would continue to work even if they had enough money to live on comfortably for the rest of their lives, a vast majority of Americans say they would continue to work (Davis and Smith 1989). Given that work is a hub around which many Americans' most cherished values revolve, these findings should not be surprising. Work is a major source of self-esteem and identity. Walinsky (1965) suggested that "work has been the organizing principle of American society in more than an economic sense; it has in large part displaced and substituted for ancestry, social class, tradition, and family as bench-marks for men's knowledge of self and their relations to others" (p. 162). As a result,

those few who are able-bodied but do not work frequently suffer in more ways than one from their lack of employment (Weiss and Riesman 1966; James 1972).

A large number of studies have found that there is virtually no difference between the poor and nonpoor in their desire to work (Goodwin 1971, 1983; Kaplan and Tausky 1972, 1974; Smith 1974; Davidson and Gaitz 1974; Morris and Williamson 1986). A study of over 1,400 participants in the Work Incentive Program (WIN) and more than 1,000 whites and blacks who were not poor "clearly indicate that people on welfare who are in the WIN program have the same dedication to the work ethic as persons from families whose members work regularly" (Goodwin 1971, pp. 2–3). Moreover, these WIN participants show a similar interest in working even when they do not economically need to do so. In sum, the findings indicate that their attitudes about work are virtually the same as those of the employed (Goodwin 1971, p. 3). But when they cannot earn enough money to support their families, WIN participants are more likely to be accepting of welfare than nonpoor individuals.

A study of the federally identified "hard-core unemployed" in New England revealed that a large majority (over 75 percent) gave wanting "to make a living and support my family" as a reason for wanting a job. A similar proportion said that they would work even if they did not need the money. One simple reason is that it is boring not to work. As one respondent put it: "Sure I'd work. It's too boring doin' nothing. I've been out of work before and you get tired of doin' nothin'. Even if I was retired, I'd work at something" (Kaplan and Tausky 1974, p. 193). Another respondent to a study on the chronically unemployed expressed a similar view about work and welfare: "It's a feeling of independence. If I'm on welfare my kids won't want to work. There's too many people on welfare. You go up there [to the welfare office] and can't even get in the door. Healthy people who are able to work should (Kaplan and Tausky 1972, p. 475). For these reasons and other more important ones, many who are poor do not participate in any welfare programs at all. Statistics suggest that less than 50 percent of those who are eligible for food stamps actually participate in the program, and only about half of the elderly who are eligible participate in the Supplemental Security Income (SSI) program designed for them (Duncan 1984; see also Rodgers 1982; Morris and Williamson 1986). These results contradict the prevalent stereotype that the poor do not want to work, though they do not mean that the poor are psychologically committed to the kinds of menial jobs they are likely to get.

POVERTY PROGRAMS

Concerted policy efforts to reduce the amount of inequality in the United States also have centered on the individual and have focused publicly only on the reduction of poverty. Thus, the programs we will discuss concern income *maintenance* rather than income *redistribution*. In other words, instead of the analytic spotlight being turned on the system of inequality as a whole, only the lowest economic segment of the population has been singled out and examined *independently* from the rest of the population. Focusing on income difficulties in this fashion diverts attention away from the broader and deeper problem of inequality. As Miller and Roby (1970) aptly put it, poverty, especially the official definition of it, is a convenient and politically acceptable way of dealing with the more disturbing idea of inequality.

Historically, there have been different kinds of attempts to address the problem of poverty. Some of the earliest were private and local in nature, while many of the contemporary programs involve different levels of governmental participation. The extent to which government should be directly involved in solving this problem has been a source of controversy. It has been argued by some that governmental programs have significantly reduced poverty while others have suggested that they have either encouraged dependency, thereby exacerbating the problem, or have had little effect. Governmental involvement

in the poverty issue, however, has not always been as extensive as it is today.

Changes in historical conditions, the conflicts in people's values and feelings about the poor, and the controversy over government involvement in the poverty issue have led to the development of several conflicting perspectives on social welfare. The most stringent, the *residual* or conservative view, holds that social welfare aid should only be given to the poor when their families and their involvement in the private economy have not been able to lift them out of poverty. In this sense, welfare is only to provide a "residual" function, coming in only after other more traditional, nongovernmental sources of help have been exhausted. As this function implies, social welfare expenditures and programs are expected to be kept to a minimum and only those who demonstrate indisputably that they are in need are considered eligible for welfare help. Even then, benefits will be low and short term so as to provide a work incentive. Poverty is viewed as being caused primarily by individual defects and character flaws, rather than by wider social or cultural conditions. The result is that there is a social stigma for those seeking welfare under these circumstances. This also helps keep aid to the desired minimum. Up until the New Deal, this approach to welfare dominated the U.S. welfare system (Zastrow 1982; Bell 1987).

The second view of social welfare, the *institutional* or liberal perspective, has basically the opposite characteristics from the residual approach. Specifically, it assumes that social welfare programs are an integral part of the institutional structure of modern society, that like other institutions they play a vital role in dealing with many of the problems generated by society's social structure and events, such as aging, which are largely inevitable. Since these problems are largely beyond their control, people should be able to expect help without stigmas being attached to such aid. Beginning with the New Deal in the 1930s, an institutional element was formally introduced on a broad scale into the general income-maintenance system of the United States.

The result is that the present system is largely a mixture of both approaches.

A third view of social welfare programs interprets them differently than either conservatives or liberals. Instead of being considered either an unnecessary burden on government or as an integral and humane part of it, this more radical perspective views social welfare programs as a means of controlling the working class and the poor. Social welfare programs expand when there is rising unrest among these groups and contract when these groups are calm (Piven and Cloward 1971). This pacifying function of welfare is closely related to the uneven operation of the capitalist economy. Oversupplies of labor lead to increases in government-sponsored programs. At the same time, however, the work requirements and benefit levels of welfare programs are stringent enough to ensure the availability of a cheap labor force to employers.

The War on Poverty

In the nineteenth century, the care of the poor was left largely in the hands of private charity and philanthropy, and it was not until individual states got involved in welfare legislation of various sorts that the federal government became involved (Bremner 1956). Early in the twentieth century, there was a growing conviction that perhaps not all of the poor were in their condition because of their own fault. It was in this setting and in the aftereffects of the Great Depression that the federal government became significantly involved in the development of programs to help the needy.

The Social Security Act of 1935 was the first major permanent attempt to help wipe out poverty. It created five new and permanent income-support programs. Of the five, two were social insurance programs and the other three were welfare programs. The Old Age and Unemployment Insurance programs were controlled and financed by the federal government, and the three welfare programs (Aid to the Blind, Aid to the Aged, and Aid to Dependent Children) were funded by both state and federal monies but administered on the state and local levels.

For the next several decades after the Act's original passage, the programs created in 1935 were expanded and tinkered with. It had not been anticipated that these programs would grow at a rapid rate. None of its creators, for example, thought that ADC would develop into a major and controversial program as it did during the 1960s and later (Garfinkel 1978, p. 32).

The War on Poverty and the 1960s   A number of events helped to form the context in which the War on Poverty was begun by the Johnson administration in 1964. First, because of the publication of several studies, there was an increased awareness of poverty's presence, particularly in certain pockets of the country. Second, the civil rights movement raised the consciousness of many about the extent of injustice to the poor, especially blacks. Third, there was the real possibility of growing discontent over inequality developing into violence. This became even truer in the mid- and late 1960s when "certain economic and political events coalesced to create a crisis of ideological legitimacy. Several strata were simultaneously exposed to conditions which made people question the traditional belief that individuals are responsible for their economic situation or their social malaise" (Huber and Form 1973, p. 7). Fourth, there was sympathy in Congress for the legislative proposals of a president who had just been assassinated, many of which aimed at the expansion of welfare programs. And finally, the belief in the viability of social planning was promoted by social scientists whose public esteem was at its peak (Haveman 1977; Garfinkel 1978).

In this setting, in March 1964, President Johnson declared a "national war on poverty," with an objective of "total victory." Like others before him, Johnson said he would focus on the *causes* of poverty rather than its *symptoms.* Nevertheless, those roots, as before, were thought to lie in the lack of competencies in the poor population—they had "low labor market productivity." The poor were thought to be poor "because they did not work enough, or because they did not work hard enough, or because their meager skills and qualifications were insufficient to raise them out of poverty even if they did work hard" (Haveman 1977, p. 5). Reflecting this perspective, the Economic Opportunity Act of 1964 created a battery of education/training and employment programs, such as Head Start, Upward Bound, Volunteers in Service to America, the Neighborhood Youth Corps, and the Work Experience Program for mothers under AFDC. By the early seventies, a number of these programs had been grouped under the Comprehensive Employment and Training Act (CETA).

In addition to these programs, social security benefits were raised or expanded five times during the 1964 to 1974 decade. Such benefits became more capable of replacing the earnings lost by retirement, and in some cases the benefits were even greater than the earnings (Lynn 1977, pp. 68–69). Under Johnson, Congress also passed legislation creating the Food Stamp Program, Medicare and Medicaid, the Elementary and Secondary Education Act, and the Higher Education Act.

The expenditures on the resulting programs grew rapidly since their creation, so that in fiscal year 1977 well over $4 billion was spent on food stamps and over $21 billion and $17 billion on Medicare and Medicaid, respectively (Garfinkel 1978, pp. 37–38). Workmen's Compensation, Unemployment Insurance, and veterans' benefits grew, as did education grants and work-study, day-care, and housing programs. Altogether, benefits aimed at the poor rose from $31 billion to $143 billion during the 1965 to 1976 decade. Total federal expenditures for all income-support programs for 1977, some of whose benefits went to the nonpoor, were estimated at about $186 billion (Garfinkel 1978, p. 51; Plotnick 1977). But as we have seen, however it is measured, poverty has not disappeared, and not all of the costs of programs go into direct aid for the poor.

As the 1960s wore on, changes in addition to the increased costs occurred in these programs. In the food aid program, authorization since 1967 allowing free stamps to families with very low monthly incomes, requirements not permitting a family to spend more than about one-third of its income on food stamps, and allowances for changes in the cost of living were among the changes. But a work requirement was attached to the food stamp program and became mandatory in 1973. Nutrition plans for school children and the elderly were also enacted in the late 1960s.

Perhaps the most controversial of the greatly expanded programs is Aid to Families with Dependent Children. The program grew increasingly to include a greater proportion of black and urban recipients. By the early 1960s, the program involved dependent children whose parents were neither blind, old, disabled, or otherwise seemingly incapable of work. The program also increasingly involved fathers who had left their wives or who were not married to the mothers of the children. These conditions ran against the grain of many who felt that they were unworthy charity cases. As Lynn (1977) put it: "No aspect of our national ideology was consistent with a continuation of this situation" (p. 74). Attempts were made in the late 1960s to promote work among these individuals, including WIN, but for a variety of reasons they were not very effective; few participated, the training did not lead to stable employment, and the provisions for day care of the children were clearly inadequate (ibid., pp. 74–75).

A Profile of Some Current Major Programs

Current U.S. income-maintenance programs can be divided into two general parts: social insurance and public assistance. Both parts include cash and in-kind benefits. Social insurance is aimed at replacing income lost because of death, unemployment, disability, or retirement. Most of the social insurance programs were developed under the Social Security Act of 1935; they include old-age insurance, survivors' insurance, disability insurance, unemployment insurance, and in many cases, worker's compensation. Medicare is also a social insurance program. These programs are financed by the insured through payroll taxes, by the employer, and by the government. Eligibility for participation depends upon the extent of a person's prior work history.

As long as individuals satisfy certain basic requirements, they are automatically eligible for these programs. There is little stigma attached to participation in these programs because individuals are thought of as deserving of such benefits. These programs are most illustrative of the "institutional" perspective on welfare.

Public-assistance programs, which have been more "residual" in the assumptions built into them, are "means-tested" programs that aim at temporarily assisting poor individuals and families. These make up what most people think of as "welfare." The major programs included in the public-assistance category are Aid to Families with Dependent Children (AFDC), Supplemental Security Income (SSI), Food Stamps, and Medicaid. In addition, local general assistance and housing also are included under this category. Public-assistance programs are financed by general revenues, and instead of individuals being automatic participants upon the satisfaction of basic requirements, persons wishing to receive "welfare" (i.e., public assistance) must prove that

their income is low enough to justify their receiving aid (Lynn 1977; Sawhill 1988). Thus, there tends to be more of a stigma attached to applying for and receiving welfare than is the case, for example, when one receives social security income in the mail. However, the stigma appears to be largely attached to recipients by others rather than one held by the recipients themselves (Morris and Williamson 1986).

Table 14.2 indicates number of recipients, federal amount, and source of sponsorship for the major social insurance and public-assistance programs in 1991. According to the federal government, "social welfare" programs and expenditures include all the programs included under social security, unemployment insurance, worker's compensation, public-assistance programs (e.g., food stamps, AFDC), veteran's programs, education, housing, and a variety of other programs aimed at aiding specific groups such as children and the vocationally disabled. The total governmental expenditures for all these public programs was $770.5 billion in 1986. In 1970, by comparison,

TABLE 14.2 Number of Beneficiaries, Amount of Federal Payments, and Sponsorship of Major Social Insurance and Public Assistance Programs: 1991

Program	No. Receiving Benefits (in millions)	Federal Payments (in millions)	Sponsorship
Social insurance			
Social Security (Retirement)	28,508	$181,633	Federal
Social Security (Disability)	4,189	25,700	Federal
Social Security (Survivors)	7,231	53,528	Federal
Medicare			
Hospital insurance (part A)	33,813	67,692	Federal
Supplementary ins. (part B)	32,732	46,638	Federal
Public assistance			
AFDC	11,195*	11,460	Federal/state/local
SSI	4,282	13,213	Federal/state
Food Stamps	18,800*	14,134	Federal
Medicaid	26,579	45,015	Federal/state/local

Source: Catalog of Federal Domestic Assistance 1990 and *Update Catalog of Federal Domestic Assistance 1990,* Superintendent of Documents, U.S. Government Printing Office, Washington, D.C. 20402.

*per month

these expenditures totaled $145.9 billion. Despite the size of these expenditures, they equaled only 18.4 percent of the total GNP for the United States (U.S. Bureau of the Census, *Statistical Abstract 1989*).

Let's take a closer look at some of the major social insurance and public assistance programs.

Social Insurance under the Social Security Act Social insurance benefits take up about one-half of all expenditures of income-maintenance programs. The cash-benefit component of the insurance programs provides monthly cash benefits to retired or disabled workers and their dependents as well as to survivors of insured workers. To receive full retirement benefits at age sixty-five, the person must have worked for a specified period of time and paid social security taxes out of his or her paycheck. The level of benefits received depends upon the presence of a spouse and young or disabled children. If a recipient continues to work after retiring, the amount of the benefits received is reduced accordingly once the earnings reaches a particular point. In 1990, benefits were reduced $1.00 for every $3.00 earned over $9,360 for persons sixty-five or older. In 1991, almost 29 million received retirement benefits totaling about $182 billion (*Catalog* 1990).

One of the problems with social security has been the difficulty of establishing a minimum payment that would be adequate for those who have no other source of income, but at the same time keeping the cost down so that those who have plenty to retire on do not have to pay higher and higher taxes on the program. Supplemental Security Income (SSI), which we will discuss shortly, was aimed at helping those who need more income beyond what they receive from social security. Another problem is that under its present financing scheme, the social security tax is very *regressive* in nature. This means that (1) individuals with widely varying incomes pay the same percentage of their incomes in social security taxes (e.g., 6%), and that (2) if one's income goes beyond the income ceiling for social security taxing (e.g., $53,400), then the amount paid by

that person and by someone with an income of $53,400 is the same. A progressive tax would be one in which the percentage of a person's contribution rises with his or her income (Dolgoff and Feldstein 1984). At the same time, however, there are *progressive* features to social security largely because there are minimum and maximum limits placed on the size of the benefits. This means that low-wage earners cannot receive less than a certain amount in retirement (Schiller 1989)

Survivors' and disability insurance are also a part of social security. Under the first, a worker's surviving dependents receive cash benefits. These survivors can include children under eighteen, spouses who have a child in their care who is under sixteen years of age, dependent parents of the deceased, and disabled unmarried children of any age. As in the case of retirement insurance, the survivors' plan is also subject to an earnings test. Disability insurance provides protection against the loss of family income resulting from a "breadwinner" being disabled. An individual is considered "disabled" if he or she is incapable, because of severe mental and/or physical impairments, of working for at least a year or is expected to die as a result of those impairments. Medical evidence must be provided to prove disability. Generally, disability benefits begin only after the person has had the disability a full five months. Statistics for survivors' and disability insurance are given in Table 14.2.

In 1965, Medicare was added to the social security package. Its purpose is to provide hospital and medical insurance to people sixty-five or older and those who are disabled but covered by social security. The hospital component (Part A) helps to pay for in-patient care and some follow-up care, while the voluntary medical insurance component (Part B) takes care of many of the expenses derived from doctor's care and related medical services. Part B is optional and paid for by a combination of individual premium payments and general revenues. Payment under Medicare is made directly to the care provider. At the present time, Medicare does not pay for all medical services. For example, it does not cover custodial or routine dental care, nor does it pay for long-term nursing home care. The latter has been an issue of increasing concern, especially as the number of elderly increases.

In recent years, as we have noted elsewhere, medical costs have skyrocketed, with the result being that greater strain has been placed upon the federal budget with respect to payments for health care. For example, in 1970 the total federal benefits for Medicare were $7 billion, in 1980 almost $36 billion, and in 1991 the costs of benefits were expected to be over $114 billion (U.S. Bureau of the Census, *Statistical Abstract 1990; Catalog 1990*). In response to these dramatic increases, a variety of techniques has been used since the early 1970s in an attempt to control such costs. These include the establishment of professional standards review organizations (PSROs), which are groups made up of local doctors who are supposed to check on Medicare and Medicaid services with an eye toward minimizing waste and fraud. Prepayment schemes, establishing relatively fixed "usual" payments for given kinds of medical services, and increasing the monthly premium payments for those participating in Part B of Medicare are some of the other means that have been used to reduce government costs for medical care (Levitan 1985).

Public-Assistance Programs   The programs that we have been discussing are largely based on the assumption that their beneficiaries have contributed both to the financial support of those programs and to the society through their years of employment. Thus, the benefits are interpreted more as a *right* than as a handout; that is, they are deserved. The most socially controversial programs designed to maintain the economic status of families and individuals are those that fall under the "public-assistance" category. It is with these programs that questions about fraud, laziness, and deservedness arise most often. Groups that traditionally have been the most vulnerable to poverty conditions are most likely to receive

"welfare." These include women, children, blacks and Hispanics, and individuals living in the South and in central cities. In 1986, for example, 22 percent of females, 51 percent of blacks, 30 percent of children under sixteen, 22 percent of southerners, and 27 percent of people living in the central cities received public-assistance benefits (O'Hare 1987).

Under the public-assistance umbrella are the AFDC, Food Stamps, Medicaid, and SSI programs. All of them are *means-tested;* that is, individuals are required to prove that their level of need is such that they require help. Most of them involve at least two levels of government in their administration or funding. The form of benefit also varies. The benefits from the AFDC and SSI programs come in the form of cash assistance while those from Food Stamps and Medicaid come in the form of in-kind benefits; that is, checks are not sent to the beneficiaries. Rather it is goods or services that are provided to them. Let us look briefly at each of these major programs.

Aid to Families with Dependent Children (AFDC) is the most expensive of the cash public-assistance programs. Its professed purpose is to provide financial support for "needy families with dependent children deprived of parental support or care, and for families with children needing emergency welfare assistance" *(Catalog* 1989, p. 344). It is a combined federal/state program, with the state determining the definition of "need" and the level of payment. The latter, of course, varies from state to state. States often have their own rules about what constitutes a "suitable home." In all states, the eligible families are those in which there is only one parent and children under eighteen. But in about half of the states, there is also coverage for two-parent families in which the father is unemployed (AFDC-UP) (O'Hare 1987). In 1988, the Congress required that all states institute AFDC-UP programs (Schiller 1989). In 1988, the *total* federal and state payments to AFDC were almost $17 billion and during any given month there were about 11 million recipients of aid. The average monthly benefit to AFDC families in 1988 was $379 (U.S. Bureau of the Census, *Statistical Abstract 1990).*

In addition to being the most expensive, AFDC is also the most controversial of the welfare programs. It is the one that most often conjures up images of large families with able-bodied parents living off "welfare." Originally, the ADC (Aid to Dependent Children) program, established under the Social Security of 1935, was created to provide cash to assist the support of children who had been left without a parent because of disability, death, or continued absence. This program, in turn, had been influenced by the mothers' pension programs passed by many states in the early 1900s. Under the ADC program, most of the recipients consisted of widows and their children. While generally thought to be deserving, it was still considered crucial to check up on the family to make sure that the widow especially was found to be deserving of help.

The changing racial and marital-status composition (e.g., unwed mothers) of the beneficiary group has tended to increase dissatisfaction with the program on the part of taxpayers (Morris and Williamson 1986). In the 1980s, just over half of those on AFDC were nonwhite. Approximately three-quarters of the mothers in AFDC families were nineteen to twenty-nine years of age. The average AFDC family contained only two children under eighteen, that is, about the same as the average U.S. family. But they were more likely to be very young children. On average then, these are not large families. Nor are they getting rich off welfare. In 1983, only about one-fifth of the families on AFDC had any assets, and in that case their total assets averaged only $876 compared to average assets near $30,000 for all households. Nor did they drive fancy cars. Only 7 percent of these families owned any car at all (O'Hare 1987).

To receive AFDC benefits, individuals must satisfy state eligibility requirements. As mentioned, these vary between states. In all states, recipients must register for employment and training (Dolgoff and Feldstein 1984). Recipients must also pass income and assets tests to prove their suitability for the program. In determining eligibility, states establish a "standard of need" and then anyone with an income under 150 percent of that standard is eligible for aid under federal guidelines. In many states, the standard of need was set below the official poverty level, making even many of those who are poor ineligible for aid (Levitan 1985). Benefit levels also differ among states. In early 1988, the average monthly AFDC benefit for a three-person family was $114 in Alabama, while in Alaska it was $567. On the whole, the combined value of AFDC and food stamps for the average recipient family is only about 74 percent of the official poverty threshold. In Alabama and Mississippi, it is only 46 percent of that threshold (O'Hare 1987).

Aside from questions about the adequacy of the level of benefit in many states, AFDC has been heavily criticized for other reasons. Perhaps most seriously, because of the absence of AFDC-UP programs in many states, it has been accused of encouraging the breakup of families and not serving different types of families that are in equal need of help. In addition, because of its benefit structure, many argue that work disincentives are built into the program. We will discuss these and other criticisms of the current system at the beginning of the next chapter.

Supplemental Security Income (SSI) is another cash-benefit welfare program aimed at people who are in financial need, and who are either sixty-five or older, blind, or disabled. Implemented in 1974, it replaced federally reimbursed programs being run by the state to help the elderly, blind, and disabled. It is a federal means-tested program, and to be eligible individuals have to satisfy basic income and assets limitations. Specifically, in 1990 the first $20 per month a person received from social security, and the first $65 he or she received from earnings were not counted. If after that the individual's 1990 monthly income fell below $386 and his or her resources were below $2,000 in value, then the person would qualify for SSI. The value of a person's home, automobile, property needed for self-support, life insurance policies, and household goods are not included in resource valuation. There is no work requirement attached to eligibility. In 1990, an average of 4 million persons were SSI recipients, and benefits exceeded $13 billion.

The two programs just examined, AFDC and SSI, are cash-assistance programs. In addition to these types of programs, welfare also includes a variety of in-kind programs. Included are several food programs aimed at helping the needy. Among these are the Supplemental Food Program for Women, Infants, and Children (WIC), School Lunch and Breakfast Programs, and Food Stamps. The first of these programs had 4.1 million participants each month in 1989 at a cost of almost $2 billion. The lunch program served 4 billion lunches at a cost of $4 billion, while the breakfast program served 657 million breakfasts and cost $513 million *(Catalog* 1990). In 1991 each of these programs increased $75 to $500 million. The Food Stamps program is much larger and, consequently, it is one of the major in-kind public-assistance programs offered by the federal government. Although such a program operated during the period from 1939 to 1943, it was not reinstituted again until the early 1960s. The motivations for restoring the program varied among interest groups. Some were concerned about rumors of rising hunger in the country, while others felt that an in-kind benefit or direct food distribution would be wiser and more prudent than an increased cash benefit to the poor, and at the same time it would keep the demand for agricultural products high (Levitan 1985).

While some experts would have preferred increases in cash benefits to a food stamp program, the program has grown significantly since its reintroduction in the 1960s. In 1991, over $14 billion was spent on the program, and during any given month there were almost 19 million recipients. In 1987, the most a four-person family without income could receive in food stamps was $271, and the average amount received was only

about $180 per month. This boils down to about 50 cents for each meal for each person (Schiller 1989). While the value of food stamps is raised each year to keep up with rising food prices, the average benefit requires a family to exercise great care if anything close to a nutritionally adequate diet is to be kept. Obviously, to eat nutritiously with this level of benefit requires not only planning skills and discipline, but access to low-cost stores and places to store food adequately. Unfortunately, the latter two are not as likely to be available to the poor as to others (Levitan 1985).

Only individuals who satisfy certain economic requirements are eligible. Under the current program, single persons and those living in households meeting nationwide standards for income and assets may receive stamps which can be redeemed at most retail stores. Before changes were made in the late 1970s, individuals were required to purchase the stamps with their own cash. Now they receive them without needing to purchase them. The stamps are to be used for providing a nutritionally adequate diet and cannot be used for certain purchases such as tobacco, alcohol, and some other nonfood items. For a person under sixty years old to be eligible to participate in the program, a household's disposable assets must be below $2,000 in value. Their gross income must be below 130 percent of the official poverty threshold, and their net income below 100 percent of that line (U.S. Bureau of the Census, *Statistical Abstract 1989).* How much an individual or family receives depends on the size of the family as well as the level of income and resources. To make sure that only those who are not able to support themselves are eligible to receive food stamps, it is also required that able-bodied persons between the ages of eighteen and sixty register for employment and accept any appropriate work at the going wage rate in the area, even if that rate is below the minimum wage (Levitan 1985).

Despite the large numbers of individuals receiving food stamps, the number of food-stamp recipients has declined by about 3 million since 1980. Part of this has been a decline in the percentage of the poor who have children under six years old who receive stamps. However, the major reason for this involves attempts to reduce welfare costs and focus those programs only on those considered "truly needy." In the early 1980s, the Reagan administration made it more difficult to receive such aid by lowering the income limits that make an individual eligible, excluding striking workers, making reporting requirements more stringent, complicating the processing procedures which delayed notification about eligibility, and reducing the benefits (Bell 1987).

Almost all of those who receive food stamps are among the poor. According to government sources, in the 1980s about two-thirds of the households that received stamps were headed by women, and about half of those who benefited were children. In 1984, the average gross income for recipient households was $4,152 (Levitan 1985). The dominant profile of the food-stamp recipient as poor was valid even before the government tightened restrictions in 1977 and the early 1980s (Rodgers 1982).

Food stamps have obviously been an important potential source of nutrition for many poor families. But there is no guarantee that families will use the stamps to purchase the most nutritious foods. Nor is there any rigorous monitoring to make sure that unscrupulous storeowners do not take advantage of food-stamp recipients. So that while the stamps may enable families to eat more, it does not necessarily mean that they will eat better (Morris and Williamson 1986). The program also has been criticized for fostering a stigma among those who use them, causing them to "parade dependency in stores and wherever a purchase is made" (Dolgoff and Feldstein 1984, p. 199). Moreover, eligible persons in rural areas often have a difficult time traveling to the agency where they need to apply, and some get so frustrated with the complications and demands of the application procedure that they give up applying for the program (Rodgers 1982). Only about half of those eligible for stamps currently receive them (Morris and Williamson 1986).

Medicaid is another in-kind program aimed at providing financial assistance to states to pay for the medical care of those on public assistance, children, pregnant women, and the elderly who meet basic economic requirements. It is different from Medicare in a number of ways. First, it is a selective program whereas Medicare is a universal program. This means that applicants have to satisfy certain economic requirements before they can receive the service; that is, the program is means-tested. In contrast, everyone in a particular age category is qualified to receive basic Medicare benefits, regardless of income. Second, Medicaid is a state-administered program whereas Medicare is nationally administered. Finally, at least on paper, Medicaid covers all kinds of services whereas Medicare is more restrictive in coverage (Dolgoff and Feldstein 1984). The primary recipients are individuals on AFDC and SSI. Those receiving Medicare also can apply for Medicaid. Established in 1965 along with Medicare, the Medicaid program includes matching grants made by the federal government to individual states so that they can pay providers to give needed medical service to those receiving cash assistance. To receive these grants, states must offer certain medical services including in- and out-patient hospital services, rural health clinic service, laboratory and x-ray services, skilled nursing home facilities, and others. Sometimes individuals have medical expenses of a magnitude that lowers their income drastically, resulting in their being considered "medically needy." Those who are "medically needy" but who have incomes above the limit qualifying them for cash assistance also may receive medical assistance if the state wishes to provide such help. In 1989, thirty-one states provided this service. Eligibility requirements for Medicaid vary between states. Each state establishes its own programs and rules within broad federal guidelines and can set benefit levels above the minimum required by federal law.

In 1991, federal expenditures for Medicaid services were estimated to be over $45 billion. In considering the size of this cost, one must realize that state costs are not included in this figure. Generally, the state contributions have been $1 to 3 billion below those by the federal government, making the total expenditures by state and federal levels almost $90 billion per year. In 1991, there were over 26 million recipients of Medicaid services (*Catalog* 1990). Almost all of the Medicaid recipients are also on AFDC, or are disabled, over sixty-five, or blind (U.S. Bureau of the Census, *Statistical Abstract 1990*).

There seems to be fairly widespread agreement that programs like Medicare and Medicaid have made it possible for more people to get needed medical care. More people have used more health services than before the inception of these programs (Rodgers 1986; Morris and Williamson 1986). Despite these salutary trends, however, problems still remain. Over half of the poor still do not receive Medicaid, in large part because they do not qualify for either AFDC or SSI programs. In addition, variations between states in their coverage rules and the optional facilities/services available create inequalities among individuals who are equally in need of medical care. Finally, the availability of Medicaid has not erased the differences in the care of the poor and nonpoor discussed earlier in the text. Many physicians still hesitate to take Medicaid patients (Morris and Williamson 1986).

In this section, we have discussed several of the major programs aimed at alleviating the problems associated with low income. Most people do not participate in a large number of these programs at the same time. In 1985, for example, only 5 percent of poverty households received cash as well as in-kind benefits from four noncash programs. On the other hand, as just suggested, participation in one program such as AFDC increases the probability that assistance will be obtained from others such as Food Stamps and Medicaid. In 1985, about 80 percent of AFDC recipients also received food stamps and 95 percent received Medicaid services (O'Hare 1987).

Before we leave this discussion of income-maintenance programs, it should be pointed out that there are additional programs that have not been mentioned and that make the government's involvement in poverty even more complicated.

These include unemployment insurance, workers' compensation, housing and energy assistance, locally administered general cash assistance, and employment and training programs. The latter especially have taken various forms, and criticisms of them maintain that they have included too heavy an emphasis on public-service jobs, too little focus on the poor alone, and that they have had, at best, only a modest effect on reducing poverty (Schiller 1989). A full evaluation of the effect of employment and training programs on reducing long-term poverty still needs to be done. "Despite nearly twenty years of continuous federal involvement, we still have to do a good deal of guesswork about what will work and for whom" (Bassi and Ashenfelter 1986, p. 150).

SUMMARY AND CONCLUSIONS

This chapter has discussed in detail the various definitions of poverty, people's view of the poor, and the consequent policies that have been developed to address the problem of poverty. There is no question that the measurement of poverty is laden with political implications. The official governmental measure focuses on cash income from all sources and then sets a poverty threshold based on conclusions made from a federal study done three decades ago. However, once that threshold is set, anyone falling below it is considered poor. Consequently, depending upon what is included under the category of economic resources, poverty rates may be higher or lower. Obviously, any political administration would prefer to see lower poverty rates, ostensibly occurring as a result of its policies. In any case, the controversies surrounding the definition and measurement of poverty alone make the topic a political "hot potato."

Adding to the controversy are people's images of the poor, especially those on public assistance (welfare). The traditional values of individualism, independence, hard work, material success, and others encourage a negative attitude toward those who are not economically successful. At the same time, humanitarian and community values encourage people to take care of those who are less fortunate than themselves. Believing that virtually all people can make it if they try hard, but at the same time knowing from historical events like the Depression, plant closings, and market declines, that not everything about their economic fates is in their hands to control has resulted in a somewhat bifurcated approach to income-maintenance programs for the needy. There are elements of both a residual and institutional approach in this system.

In one category, social insurance programs such as Social Security retirement, disability, and Medicare insurance provide universal coverage with a minimum of stigma to a wide variety of individuals who fall into a particular demographic category. There is no means-testing or demeaning administrative process suggesting that these recipients are receiving "welfare." They are considered individuals who have contributed to both these programs and society and are, therefore, deserving of such aid. In the other category of public assistance are those who are poor but not elderly and/or disabled. Individuals with these characteristics, often women who head their own households, children, and members of minorities, must provide proof that they are indigent. They must prove that they are deserving of benefits from Food Stamps, Medicaid, and AFDC programs.

A survey of these programs suggests the patchwork nature of the income maintenance system in the United States. Each of these programs has its own strengths and weaknesses, and some of these have been discussed. In the next chapter, an overview of the deficiencies of and alternatives to the programs are summarized.

CHAPTER 15

AN ASSESSMENT OF AND ALTERNATIVES TO CURRENT INCOME-MAINTENANCE PROGRAMS

One change always leaves the way open for the establishment of others.
—Niccolo Machiavelli

One of the greatest pains to human nature is the pain of a new idea.
—Walter Bagehot

This final chapter evaluates current strategies to alleviate poverty and presents some alternatives to the present array of programs. In recent years, welfare and poverty have become politically explosive issues, especially in light of budget deficits and a wave of popular conservative thought. Many of the controversial criticisms that had earlier been made of Great Society programs have been resurrected. The key question to ask for our purposes, of course, is how effective all of these programs have been in reducing poverty and inequality. Other sensitive issues involve welfare's relationship to single-parent families, illegitimacy, and work incentive. Given the fact that the traditional U.S. value system has stressed the importance of both work and family, it is perhaps not surprising that questions about welfare's impact on work and family structure would be two of the most hotly contested debates regarding the consequences of welfare programs. Other deficiencies in these programs have elicited less heated public responses. These involve their equity in the treatment of the poor, the level of adequacy in benefits, and conflicts among the goals of these programs. Social insurance programs, as

we have intimated elsewhere, are less controversial than public-assistance or "welfare" programs, and virtually all of the issues just mentioned have concerned welfare rather than social insurance programs.

AN EVALUATION OF PRESENT WELFARE PROGRAMS

In this assessment of current programs, we will first survey the less controversial criticisms and then move to a discussion of welfare's effectiveness in reducing poverty, and its effect on family composition and work incentive.

Equity

Inequity is one of the criticisms most often made of the welfare system. Income-maintenance programs certainly affect different groups differently. Schiller observes that while over 32 million people were considered poor by government standards in 1987, only about half of them obtained cash assistance. Moreover, less than half of the 24 million poor individuals living in families with children got any AFDC assistance (Schiller 1989).

Certain groups are also more likely to benefit from government maintenance programs. Those over sixty-five are more likely to be lifted out of poverty by these programs than other groups (Danziger et al. 1986). Male-headed families that are just as poor as female-headed families are often left out of the benefit picture. The presence of an adult male in the family is frequently taken as proof that the family can fend for itself. Historically, AFDC has been meant primarily for families without a father (Schiller 1989). Up to 1988, a number of states still did not have AFDC coverage for unemployed fathers. The hidden assumption is that such a person could and should be working and supporting his family.

At the same time, however, poor female heads of families are at a unique disadvantage for several reasons. The difficulties faced by women in these circumstances are not generally taken into account by programs, resulting in inequitable treatment. First, when a family splits up, women usually end up raising any children, and the economic costs of raising children have increased while the average benefit levels have decreased. Second, women who work are more likely than men to be poor at every level of labor-market involvement. A large part of the reason relates to the obstacles encountered by women in the market, which were discussed earlier. Moreover, the job training provided by these programs often emphasizes "female" jobs that pay low wages, thereby only reinforcing the occupational segregation already present in the marketplace. These problems are not considered when program rules require that eligible recipients either work or search for employment. Third, programs do not provide adequate child care for women with children. Each of these problems place women in a more vulnerable position and make it less likely that they can escape poverty (Pearce 1984). If a definition of equity is that equal cases should be treated equally, and unequal cases unequally, then clearly there is inequitable treatment here.

The main point of these examples is that since welfare programs cover only certain categories of individuals, there are bound to be inequities. Some of the poor will be covered while others who do not fit the category (e.g., age, sex, place of residence, etc.) but are equally poor will not be accorded benefits. Two-parent families, single individuals, and couples without children who are not of retirement age are among those slighted by current categorical programs, even though some may be just as poor as female-headed families or elderly individuals (Bell 1987).

There are also geographical inequities in benefits. Some states have much higher benefit levels than others, and since states are given a certain amount of flexibility within federal guidelines, some states offer more services and benefits than others. For example, in 1988, the average monthly AFDC benefit to a family in Alabama was $114, but it was $567 in Alaska. In general, the value of AFDC benefits plus food stamps totals about 74 percent of the official poverty level. But in Alabama and Mississippi, the combined value of these benefits equals less than half of the income that would put the family at the poverty threshold (O'Hare 1987). Since a disproportionate number of poor black women have been living in the South, which generally has lower benefits, it means that this group has suffered inordinately because of geographical inequities (Pearce 1984).

An interesting side issue to these variations in benefit levels is that the states with below-average benefits had a greater influx of migrants than the states with higher benefits. States in the South have had lower benefits than those in the Midwest and Northeast, and the migration patterns just cited indicate that it is the possibility of finding a job rather than seeking higher welfare benefits that attracts many of the poor to the South (ibid.). With respect to Medicaid, states can receive federal funding if they provide about half of the required services listed by the Health Care Financing Administration for the "medically needy" (*Catalog* 1989). This inevitably means than some states are potentially better than others in providing quality facilities and services to Medicaid patients. How local governments interpret eligibility for services is also an important source of variation between states. When considering a potential welfare recipient, for example, each may define a "suitable home" for aid differently.

Adequacy

None of the public-assistance programs has a standard benefit level that will enable a recipient to live comfortably. When one considers the stringency of the requirements for most of these programs, it is obvious that the vast majority of those receiving aid are quite poor. Many of those who are eligible have incomes that fall well below the poverty threshold. For example, female-headed households with children under eighteen years of age are eligible for AFDC cash assistance. Yet in 1987, the average incomes of these families was about $5,000 *below* the poverty line established by the government (U.S. Bureau of the Census, February 1989). Even when these families receive aid, it is often not enough to bring them up to the poverty level. In 1987, the typical family on AFDC received less than 50 percent of what it needed according to government standards (Schiller 1989). The information cited earlier on Food Stamps indicates that benefits allow well under $1.00 to be spent per person per meal, confirming the low level of benefits. Even in the late 1960s and early 1970s, when the real value of benefits had not yet eroded to the extent that it has today, those who were poor but did work often did not receive enough benefits to raise them above the poverty line (Plotnick and Skidmore 1975). Since the 1970s, the value of public-assistance benefits in real terms has not even kept pace with inflation. Between 1965 and 1978, the size of the benefits from government transfers was growing at a faster rate than real income in the society, but after 1978, this growth stopped (Greenstein 1985; Danziger and Gottschalk 1985; Danziger et al. 1986).

The Reagan Influence This trend was exacerbated by federal cutbacks in the early 1980s.

These revisions in the welfare system were based on several assumptions and goals.

First, there was the belief on the part of some conservative thinkers that poverty was not as bad a problem as it seemed to be. Martin Anderson, an advisor to Nixon and Reagan, wrote in 1975 that "the war on poverty has been won, except for perhaps a few mopping up operations" (1975, p. 37). Anderson's conclusion is that the number of poor has been drastically reduced and only a small number of the poor still are without any help. But an unfortunate side effect of welfare, according to him, is that it has made people dependent on the government, and the task should be to get them off welfare. Work disincentives should be removed from programs and individuals who are able should be required to work. This would reduce the number of dependent poor even further, and for those who cannot work through no fault of their own (e.g., old, disabled, sick), a "safety net" could be designed to catch the truly needy.

Long before becoming president, Governor Reagan of California took a similar approach to welfare, creating a task force to "purify" the welfare system by ridding it of everyone except those who were "strictly entitled" (Berkowitz 1984). The tightening of requirements and cutting back on benefits were carried out in President Reagan's first budget, the Omnibus Budget Reconciliation Act (OBRA) of 1981. Expenditures for means-tested programs for the poor fell from 21.5 percent of the 1980 budget to 16.8 percent of the 1983 budget. Estimates by the Congressional Budget Office were that households with incomes under $10,000 lost about $20 billion between 1982 and 1985 because of the spending cuts (Levitan 1985).

A second belief of the Reagan administration was that waste and fraud were prevalent in the welfare system and there was a need to eliminate it in part by making sure that only the "truly needy" were eligible for benefits. The eligibility and benefit changes were in part a result of this belief, although the importance of this motivation is open to question (Piven and Cloward 1982). Some people have gotten rich off welfare programs and it has not been the poor. Rather doctors, clinics, nursing homes, building and defense contractors, and business entrepreneurs are often the guilty culprits. "In other words, the serious profiteering in government social welfare does not result from the growth of the public bureaucracy; it results from the vigor with which private economic interests exploit bureaucratic programs" (Piven and Cloward 1982, p. 5).

Third, there was a conviction that welfare breeds dependency and encourages the break-up of families, that is, a belief that poverty programs, especially those from the Great Society's War on Poverty, make the poverty problem worse. "In 1964, the famous War on Poverty was declared and a funny thing happened," Reagan said in 1986. "Poverty as measured by dependency stopped shrinking and then actually began to grow worse. I guess you could say poverty won the war" (quoted in Kosterlitz 1986, p. 2926). The issues of work disincentive and family-composition effects are major topics of the debate on current welfare policy, and we will address them more fully later.

Fourth, the conservative administration had faith in the power of voluntarism as a solution to poverty, a belief that goes back to the fourteenth century. This approach emphasizes the critical roles of private individuals, voluntary agencies, and religious organizations in providing many of the services and goods (e.g., food, jobs, shelters) required by the truly needy (Burghardt and Fabricant 1987). This, of course, reflected a broader desire of the administration to reduce the federal government's involvement in many social problems and a belief that the private sector could accomplish most tasks more efficiently than government. Historically, however, voluntarism has never been able to effectively handle the miseries associated with widespread poverty (Katz 1986). As we have seen, in the early 1980s official poverty increased, as did homelessness and hunger. Closely related to this attempt to divest the federal government of its role in welfare, has been the effort to decentralize the programs or shift more responsibility onto local and state governments.

Fifth and finally, the Reagan administration was interested in controlling and reducing the budget, and given the convictions just mentioned, welfare programs were politically vulnerable. The oil shortages, inflation, and rising unemployment of the 1970s created frustration among many Americans and made them open to a "war on welfare" (Katz 1986). Despite the economic causes for fiscal crises just mentioned, the poor and the administration of welfare programs provided easy targets for many irate citizens. The dissatisfaction about welfare held by many individuals is based on the belief, discussed earlier, that most of those on welfare are lazy and could be working, but instead are getting a free handout. The evidence we have presented demonstrates that this is not valid. The vast majority of the poor are either sick, disabled, blind, old, children, or women trying to support a family. Recent exposure of large-scale fraud in the administrating and contracting processes in these programs also has triggered public anger.

While the preceding attitudes and assumptions permeated the Reagan administration's beliefs about welfare, others have argued that the cuts were really deliberately directed against the poor and unemployed. Piven and Cloward (1987) contend that one major function of welfare is protection from market exploitation. That is, if potential workers have an alternate source of income they do not have to work for any meager wage offered them. They argue, however, that employers have a vested interest in having a surplus army of laborers available to work at low wages. This increases their profits, and, Piven and Cloward suggest, employers are the group the administration was most interested in pleasing. They suggest that the tax revisions, recent investment and depreciation allowances for corporations, and the cutbacks in welfare are all aimed at aiding business at the expense of others.

Historically, welfare programs have been administratively supported when the poor and other disadvantaged have clamored for help. Once stability has been restored, programs have been cut back. Employers have resisted expanded welfare programs. "They exerted themselves to lower benefits, to tighten eligibility criteria so fewer people would receive benefits, and to attach such punitive conditions to the receipt of aid that few people would willingly apply for it. Such measures were intended, of course, to restore the compulsion to sell labor on whatever terms the market offered" (Piven and Cloward 1987, p. 11; see also 1971, 1977, 1982). Historically, one of the functions of welfare has been to regulate the labor market (Katz 1986). Piven and Cloward believe that Reagan's attempt to remove government from the lives of the welfare poor with arguments about laissez-faire and the necessary separation of politics and economy will not be successful as an ideological position in the long run because the poor are too aware of the past interconnection of these institutions and are thus less likely to subscribe to the laissez-faire doctrine (1982).

Given the beliefs and emphases just indicated about the recent administration, cutbacks in welfare were inevitable. Moreover, when one adds to this the fact that by some standards the government's absolute measure of the poverty level is too low and has fallen even further behind the median income in the United States, the inadequacy of benefit levels is made even more obvious.

Conflicts in Goals

Another basic problem with current income-maintenance approaches is that the proposed goals of these programs conflict with each other (Schiller 1989). Obviously, any government wants to hold down costs, to be viewed as efficient, to balance its budget, if only for political reasons. One of the ostensible goals of income-maintenance programs is to reduce the necessary cost as much as possible. A second goal is to provide a minimum income provision to those who are in need and worthy. A third goal, consistent with the work ethic, is to encourage individuals to work rather than to be on welfare. Unfortunately, these goals are generally incompatible, that is, not all of them can be accomplished to the

maximum because one's advance is at the expense of the others.

For example, let's say that we are "liberal" and out of humanitarian feelings desire to raise the poverty threshold or in some other way try to ensure that no one falls below a certain minimum. From the statistics given, we are aware of the low benefits associated with welfare programs. After all, recent evidence also has indicated that if we examine the average benefits for each of the many income-maintenance programs, only three (two under Social Security and Iowa's temporary total disability benefit) would put the recipient above the poverty line (Bell 1987). So we are feeling generous and decide to raise the minimum income floor. One of the decisions we have to make, of course, is how far up we want to put it. If we put it too high perhaps we would end up encouraging dependency on welfare because we would be making it too comfortable. In addition, the cost to the taxpayer may be prohibitive. Consequently, the desire to raise the minimum conflicts with work incentives and cost goals.

If, on the other hand, we wish to minimize costs, it means lowering benefits or reducing other related services. If we lower the benefits too far, they may then be inadequate to sustain a minimal standard of living. In trying to reduce costs, we might lower the benefit-reduction rate for earnings obtained by recipients, that is, we may want to either tax those earnings more or reduce their benefits in a way commensurate with their additional income from earnings. For example, we might want to reduce their benefits 67 cents for every dollar earned, or perhaps 100 percent—a dollar reduction for every dollar earned beyond some small amount, such as $30 a month. But in trying to reduce costs by increasing benefit reductions as individuals earn more money, we may inadvertently lower the incentive to work.

Theoretically, by raising the tax on working for welfare recipients, one would discourage them from working, while lowering the cost of working to the recipient would increase the motivation to work (*Focus* 1985). Often those on cash-assistance programs have been caught in this dilemma, the "notch" as it is sometimes called. Specifically, they may be able to get a job or a raise in pay, but in doing so they may become ineligible for given kinds of aid such as Food Stamps or even Medicaid. If the value of the aid to them is greater than the increase in salary, should they take the raise or not? Whatever answer is given, it would not be acceptable to everyone. So in trying to lower costs, we may frustrate our ability to reach the goals of having an adequate benefit and a program that encourages rather than discourages work.

Finally, suppose we wish to increase the work incentive of those on welfare. We might do this by lowering the rate at which earnings are taxed and not lowering any benefits. This might help to increase the income levels of recipients, but it also would increase the costs of the program. But perhaps we do not have to be concerned about encouraging the work incentive for all of the poor, certainly not the elderly, disabled, children, or blind. Thus, for some groups we might want to emphasize maximizing the minimum income and downplay work incentives since they do not apply to some individuals. But for other groups, such as the nonaged healthy poor, we might want to encourage work incentives. But in doing that we may raise the short-term costs of the program. In any case, for any given program the three goals of low cost, adequacy, and work incentive have been found to be incompatible.

Work Incentive, Family Structure, and Welfare Effectiveness

In *Losing Ground,* Murray (1984) presents a conservative critique of the effectiveness of welfare programs. Because of the widespread publicity his work has received, we will examine his ideas in detail. Murray argues that welfare programs have (1) helped to increase pretransfer or what he calls "latent" poverty, (2) created work disincentives and encouraged individuals to drop out of the labor force, and (3) undermined traditional family structure by fostering the disintegration of married arrangements and the growth of female-headed households and illegitimacy. In effect, he says that welfare programs changed the "rules of the game" under which ordinary individuals operate. Acting rationally, people respond to the "carrots and sticks" they find around them. Welfare afforded them the opportunity to survive without working, with minimal pain. These programs made "it profitable for the poor to behave in the short term in ways that were destructive in the long term" (Murray 1984, p. 9). "As people became less inclined to take low-paying jobs, hold onto them, and use them to get out of poverty, they became dependent on government assistance." In effect, welfare programs made the situation for the poor worse by "emasculating the work ethic and creating 'work disincentives' " (Murray, 1982, p. 11).

Murray goes on to say that welfare benefits also have had a destructive impact on the family by encouraging the break-up of two-parent families and promoting the growth of female-headed families and illegitimacy. He presents a hypothetical vignette in which the only rational behavior for the persons in the fable is not to get married and work regularly for fear of losing welfare benefits. According to Murray, the best scenario for a young man and woman who wished to be together in 1970 under the Great Society programs was to live together unmarried, have their children, and for "Harold" to work occasionally as money was needed.

What are we to make of Murray's arguments? Does welfare break up families? Do such programs discourage work efforts? Have income-maintenance programs reduced or exacerbated the poverty problem? Let us take up each of these questions in turn. Not too long ago, President Reagan made the observation that "there is no question that many well-intentioned Great Society-type programs contributed to family break-ups, welfare dependency, and a large increase in out-of-wedlock births" (Moynihan 1986, p. 69). Despite the matter-of-factness of this statement, most of the evidence does not support it. There does not appear to be any firm evidence to support the claim that welfare benefits encourage families to have illegitimate children. Most studies find no relationship between benefits and out-of-wedlock births (Winegarden 1974; Fechter and Greenfield, 1973; Ellwood and Bane 1984).

The most thorough statistical study of the relationship between welfare benefits, family dissolution and illegitimacy was conducted by Ellwood and Bane (1984). They found no evidence of welfare benefits having an impact on the fertility rates of unmarried women. They also found little support for the belief that welfare promotes divorce or separation of in-tact families. In his hypothetical example of what a father would do in deciding whether to marry or not, Murray (1982) uses Pennsylvania data, a state in which benefits have increased twice as fast as the rest of the nation. In other words, it is a state with higher-than-average benefits. In most states, it was *not* more profitable to go on welfare than to be employed in 1970 (Greenstein 1985). Were data taken from a state with average or below-average benefits, the rational decision "Harold" might make about marriage would probably be different. It should be pointed out, however, that there was evidence in the Ellwood and Bane study that young single mothers were more likely to set up independent households in states with high benefits, instead of living with parents or relatives. But it should also be mentioned that in most states, pregnant single women do not qualify for benefits *unless* they live independently. Those single mothers in states with lower benefits were more inclined to live with their parents.

Murray specifically links high benefit levels with high rates of female-headed households. Given this position, we would expect those states with higher benefits to have higher rates of such households, but this is not the case. Increases in female-headed households have occurred everywhere (Greenstein 1985). States with high levels of benefits have about the same proportion of female-headed households as those with low benefit levels. "In 1980, monthly AFDC payments for a family of four were lowest in Mississippi ($160) and highest in New York and California (above $500), but the percentage of households headed

by women in these states were almost identical in 1980" (O'Hare 1987, p. 10).

In sum, there does not appear to be a close relationship between family composition and benefit levels; they do not seem to change together. Welfare is not the most important cause of the increase in female-headed families (Sawhill 1988). In recent years, benefits have been cut, yet changes in family structure have continued to occur. Moreover, the growth of female-headed households has been higher than the growth in the number of families on welfare (Ellwood and Summers 1986; Schiller 1989). Between 1975 and 1985, the number of single-parent families went up 42 percent, but the number of families on AFDC stayed about the same. If welfare caused families to break up, one would think that the number of AFDC families would have gone up as the number of single-parent families increased. But it didn't. Moreover, while welfare benefits have declined in real value, the number of female-headed families has accelerated in recent years. If high welfare benefits increase the dissolution of families, why did the numbers of these single-parent families continue to grow in the face of the declining value of benefits (O'Hare 1987)?

Benefit levels are not a major factor in the break-up of families or illegitimacy rates (Danziger et al. 1986; Ellwood and Summers 1986; Wilson 1987). Instead, the reasons for the basic changes in family composition we are discussing may be tied to broader events in the economy. Specifically, it has been suggested that the factor most responsible for the increase in family dissolution (separation, divorce) among whites is the greater availability of employment opportunities for women, which can make them economically independent and allow them to escape oppressive marriages. Among young black women, on the other hand, the reluctance to marry initially or remarry later is tied to the problems of employment encountered by black men (Wilson 1987; Wilson and Neckerman 1986; Ellwood and Summers 1986).

The problem of black joblessness, Wilson

(1987) argues, has little to do with welfare. Rather it is deeply related to macroeconomic changes: (1) the shift from the production of goods to services, (2) the movement of jobs out of the central city to other regions in the country, (3) the decline in demand for particular kinds of unskilled labor, (4) a growing "mismatch" between the work skills of blacks and the types of job opportunities available because of the decline of entry-level positions in the central city, and (5) the inadequacy of ghetto schools in preparing their students for economic opportunities. It also has been suggested that changing attitudes about families, divorce, and welfare during the latter years of the 1960s may help account for the growth of single-parent households (Ellwood and Summers 1986; Sawhill 1988).

Work Disincentives, Employment, and the Effectiveness of Transfers

Murray (1984) intimates that in a general and perverse way, welfare alters the attitudes and behavior of rational individuals. Among Murray's arguments is the suggestion that welfare causes work disincentives, that is, encourages individuals not to work. In doing so, it pushes unemployment up thereby increasing pretransfer poverty rates. If this is the case, then welfare programs may be more of a cause than a consequence of poverty (Murray 1984). He points out that, during the 1950s and early 1960s, official poverty was declining at a time when income-maintenance programs were growing at only a low rate, but that during the heyday of the Great Society programs in the late 1960s, not only were benefits increasing but pretransfer poverty was increasing at the same time. He says specifically that the pretransfer poverty rate increased between 1968 and 1980 and that black employment decreased during roughly the same period, indicating that increases in welfare programs led to less black employment which in turn led to higher pretransfer poverty rates.

Other evidence suggests that pretransfer poverty was decreasing when benefits were rising between 1965 and 1968, but it also increased for a few years after that up to the early 1970s, when benefits also were rising. Thus, during a period in which benefits were rising, the pretransfer poverty decreased and then increased. Moreover, the real value of cash benefits was about the same in 1977 as it was in 1983, yet pretransfer poverty rates increased significantly.

These data suggest that increases in benefits are not a major cause of pretransfer poverty. Instead pretransfer poverty is sensitive to changes in the economy and unemployment rates. In 1965–1969, unemployment was relatively low and pretransfer poverty dropped. After that, unemployment rose as did pretransfer poverty. When the growth of transfers stalled and unemployment continued to rise, the official poverty rate also began to rise (Danziger and Gottschalk 1985). Data presented in the last chapter indicate that the addition of welfare benefits reduces the official poverty rate (see also Levitan 1985; Sawhill 1988; Schiller 1989). However, not everyone is equally likely to be lifted out of poverty by government programs. Primarily because of social security and related insurance benefits, persons over sixty-five are most likely to be pushed above the poverty threshold. In terms of their relative effectiveness in removing individuals from poverty, cash social insurance was best, followed by in-kind transfers and cash public assistance, respectively (Danziger et al. 1986).

While social insurance and public-assistance programs alleviate poverty, they deal with the symptoms rather than the causes of pretransfer poverty. They help people who are poor, but do not address in any deep or systematic way the root causes of poverty. It is higher productivity and economic growth that lead to more jobs and economic opportunities and, consequently, lower pretransfer poverty rates (Danziger et al. 1986; Ellwood and Summers 1986). It is widely accepted that exogenous economic and employment conditions are a principal if not *the* principal cause of the poverty rate (Danziger and Gottschalk 1985; Greenstein 1985; Danziger et al. 1986; Rodgers Jr. 1986; Ellwood and Summers 1986; Kosterlitz 1986; Wilson 1987; Sawhill 1988).

If welfare affects employment negatively as proposed by Murray, then we would expect that welfare is reducing the available labor supply. But exhaustive reviews of the literature on this subject indicate that welfare's effect on labor supply is modest (Danziger et al. 1981). Danziger and his colleagues estimate that the presence of income transfers reduces the hours a recipient would have worked by under 5 percent, and most of this reduction is due to social insurance rather than public-assistance benefits. Thus, the impact of welfare on labor supply and hours worked does not appear to be very great (Danziger et al. 1986). The modest negative effect of welfare on the labor supply appears to exist for two reasons: (1) the presence of cash transfers gives individuals income, reducing the degree of need for income from earnings; and (2) the tax or benefit-reduction rate that goes into effect when one works reduces one's net wages thereby lowering incentive to work (Sawhill 1988).

Looking more closely at the relationship between welfare, employment, and poverty, we must ask whether fluctuations in the poverty rate are due more to changes in welfare benefits or employment/economic conditions. During the 1950s and early 1960s, the economy was strong and transfers did increase but only slightly. Posttransfer poverty rates declined in this context (Danziger and Gottschalk 1985). At the same time, during the 1950s, before the War on Poverty, unemployment among black youth increased. In other words, *at a time when programs were not growing rapidly, employment in this group was declining,* which is the opposite of what one would expect if the growth of benefits were positively related to unemployment. The employment of black teenagers declined in the 1960s, especially in the South, because of technological advancements in agriculture and the elimination of many low-wage jobs that they had held. Up North, on the other hand, where welfare benefits were *better,* the employment of blacks did *not* drop (Greenstein 1985). In the period be-

tween 1960 and 1968 *when benefits were rising, unemployment was falling* rather than rising (Danziger and Gottschalk 1985).

During the very late 1960s and 1970s, the economy weakened, inflation increased, and unemployment rose. In addition, the real value of benefits began to decline in the early 1970s. Under the conditions of a weakened economy and the declining real value of benefits, those who were protected by social insurance saw their poverty rates decline while the rates of others increased (Danziger and Gottschalk 1985). By 1980, the combined real value of AFDC and Food Stamps had declined 16 percent from its 1972 value, and by 1984 their value was only 4 percent above what it had been in 1960, and 22 percent below what it had reached in 1972 (Danziger and Gottschalk 1985). In the mid-1970s, low-income individuals also were given an incentive to work in the form of the Earned Income Tax Credit (EITC). This allowed low-income workers to claim a tax credit of 10 percent of their earned income up to $5,000, giving them a maximum benefit of $500 (Levitan 1985).

One would think that if Murray is correct about the relationship between welfare benefits and employment, that with the combined work incentive of the EITC and the decreased value of benefits since the early 1970s, unemployment would be down and employment would be up. Instead unemployment rose during the 1970s (Greenstein 1985; Wilson 1987). This suggests strongly that broader economic conditions are more closely related to employment rates than are welfare benefits. While high benefit levels combined with high benefit-reduction rates if one works may have some disincentive effects, these effects appear to be small. For example, when the tax or reduction rates on benefits were increased to 100 percent under the Omnibus Budget Reconciliation Act of 1981, women who were welfare recipients and working continued to work, and those who did not work did not reduce the rate at which they entered the labor market. Working women kept working either to perfect their skills or to demonstrate to other employers that they were employable (Danziger and Gottschalk 1985; Rodgers 1986).

In sum, what this tangle of evidence seems to indicate is that economic conditions are closely related to employment, which in turn significantly affects the pretransfer poverty rate. Welfare and social insurance benefits reduce the poverty levels created by these economic conditions, and the reductions are reflected in lower posttransfer poverty rates. Cutbacks in welfare and social insurance programs increase rather than decrease poverty, and in recent years reductions in the real value of benefits have led to higher official poverty rates. While high benefit levels may have small disincentive effects, it is economic conditions that are most directly and powerfully related to employment rates.

SUGGESTED ALTERNATIVES TO THE PRESENT SYSTEM

We have reached the conclusion that income-maintenance programs have helped to reduce poverty. Poverty is still with us but "the failure to conquer poverty cannot be attributed to the failure of anti-poverty programs themselves" (Sawhill 1988, p. 1113). Cash-transfer programs such as Social Security and AFDC have helped to stabilize conditions for individuals and society when economic circumstances are difficult. In spite of their documented deficiencies, Food Stamps and the school lunch program create opportunities for better nutrition and health for millions of children and adults, and AFDC has helped to send generations of poor children to school on a regular basis (Bell 1987). Despite these effects, however, continued disagreement about the system's effectiveness and the other weaknesses we have discussed have led to suggestions for alternative income-maintenance programs.

The shortcomings of current programs indicate that some changes are in order not only in the programs themselves but, more fundamentally, in our orientations toward poverty and its causes. Few people today define economic in-

equality as a major social problem, and too many are still worried that in helping the poor we are really helping the undeserving. Moreover, inequality and poverty have been interpreted as separate issues, whereas in fact the two are inextricably intertwined. In recent years, both income inequality and poverty rates have increased. Poverty is basically a problem stemming from economic and inequality processes in U.S. society.

How can we explain the reluctance to view poverty in terms of economic inequality? Why isn't inequality defined as a major problem by most of the public? We discussed the ideologies and conditions that help to legitimate present arrangements in an earlier chapter, and in the previous chapter we reviewed the traditional value assumptions built into the U.S. approach to income-maintenance programs. We also raised questions about the consequences such assumptions, and the programs that are derived from them, have for recipients of benefits and for the reduction of poverty.

Public policies regarding poverty are based on the interpretations and beliefs about the poor held by those who make the policies. These interpretations and beliefs tend to reflect the interests of policymakers rather than the poor themselves (Edelman 1977). It should not be surprising that different views about the causes of poverty and the characteristics of the poor can be found among groups occupying different positions in the system of social inequality. Martin Anderson, for example, a poverty advisor to both Nixon and Reagan, argued against a guaranteed minimum income for all as a way of dealing with the poverty problem. He did so in part because he associated that position with liberal, intellectual elites who naively assumed that people like to work. It is certainly the case that alternative proposals offered reflect the different positions of individuals along political and economic continua.

The social services and programs that arise from policies do not, consequently, originate with the poor, and in any case rarely call for fundamental changes in the economic and/or political conditions in the society. Rather, the emphasis is on working within present economic and political arrangements, thereby maintaining the status quo. Although some Americans feel that economic inequality has grown too much, traditionally they have not defined inequality as a major problem (Morris and Williamson 1986). The continued persistence of poverty has suggested to some that the poor may serve basic functions for the society and particular nonpoor groups within it. A number of years ago, Herbert Gans (1972) suggested these functions of poverty:

1. It ensures a low-wage labor force to perform the necessary menial tasks in the economy. These tasks are "necessary" because certain industries rely on the existence of such a labor pool.

2. By working for low wages and giving a higher percentage of their incomes in taxes, the poor are in effect subsidizing the private economy and many of the governmental programs that benefit the rich.

3. The existence of poverty means that a battery of professional "help" occupations can be sustained in the economy. Poverty creates jobs for some while at the same time many of the poor cannot find jobs. It has been suggested that any radical reform in the welfare system would cause severe dislocation in the labor force caused by the shifting and displacement of employees in the social-service sector (Solomon 1987).

4. Even though they often work harder and cheat less than others, by being defined as "deviant" or "lazy," the poor legitimate and clarify the norms of the dominant society. Lacking power and being internally divided, the poor are unable to correct the stereotypes that plague them.

5. The poor, having no political power, "can be made to absorb the economic and political costs of change and growth in American society." When "progress" occurs in the society, the poor are the ones who suffer most.

By indicating these and other basic functions performed by the poor in U.S. society, Gans implies that poor people are not an *isolated* group who are poor because of their lack of integration

into the mainstream of society, but rather are an *integral* part of the society. Alternative poverty programs that have been suggested vary in the extent to which their recommendations focus on the uniqueness and isolated nature of the poor, or on the nature of their integration into society. Some recommendations have emphasized the similarities of problems among the poor and prescribe a more simplified, universalistic program to cover most or all of the poor. Others note the heterogeneity among the poor population, the differences in their problems, and the differences in their degrees and types integration into the economy. These policy analysts then usually recommend different programs for different categories of the poor. Let us look briefly at a couple of the programs that have been proposed as alternatives to the present income-maintenance or welfare system.

Reform Alternatives

Many scholars have offered proposals to reform the income-maintenance system, especially its public-assistance component. Most of these emphasize the importance of economic growth and the promotion of recipient self-sufficiency through the availability of stable, meaningful jobs (Danziger et al. 1986; Wilson and Neckerman 1986; Ellwood and Summers 1986; Morris and Williamson 1986; Solomon 1987; Sawhill 1988; Ellwood 1988). Most agree that current public-assistance programs sometimes encourage dependency and do little to provide a long-term solution even though they provide short-term help with the problems associated with poverty. Thus, some explicitly label their proposals "nonwelfare" programs because they attempt to remove many of the stigmatizing, dependency, disincentive features often associated with public assistance. For those who can work, it is crucial that self-sufficiency be promoted and work incentive maximized (e.g., Levitan 1985; Danziger and Gottschalk 1985; Morris and Williamson 1986; Schiller 1989). Most scholars recognize that there are different kinds of poor people and that diverse strategies and programs will be needed to address the unique problems of each group. Most recognize, for example, that some poor can work while others cannot.

While acknowledging these internal differences among the poor, there is also the realization that present administrative complexities, duplications, and waste must be significantly reduced. The hope is that greater efficiency and specific program categories can go together harmoniously. Another feature that many reform proposals have in common is a suggestion for a more meaningful child-support/allowance program. These vary in form from the more traditional recommendation of increasing benefits according to the number of children, to implementing more child-care facilities and support, to providing an across-the-board children's allowance as applied in some European countries. While a more aggressive redistribution of wealth and income is recommended by a few, those same individuals recognize the reluctance with which most Americans would accept such a proposal.

In some ways, these proposals have elements in common with welfare programs found in many European countries. First, those programs are generally characterized by universal rather than means-tested criteria; in other words, programs often apply to everyone regardless of family status or income. Second, European programs also usually contain some kind of child-allowance benefit. Third, two-parent as well as one-parent families are under the umbrella of assistance. Cash assistance goes to all the poor, regardless of the nature of their families (Rodgers 1986).

In contrast to European programs, the United States has not had a single, basic cash program for all poor families. Rather, in the public-assistance sphere, the emphasis for help has been on single-parent, primarily female-headed, families. Moreover, we have had no legislated set of maternity benefits, nor universal child-care assistance program. Nor do we have a national program of health care (Rodgers 1986). But, as mentioned throughout this chapter, proposals have been made to change the welfare and/or entire in-come-maintenance system. Following are specific reform programs suggested by Martha Ozawa and David Ellwood.

Ozawa's Layered Income-Maintenance System   In 1982, Martha Ozawa recommended drastic changes in the U.S. approach to helping those with low incomes. Ozawa is an expert on social security, and one of the things that is interesting about her proposal is that she intends her program for all citizens, regardless of age. In other words, it incorporates both social insurance and public-assistance aspects. Her critique of the present income maintenance is by now familiar: It is out of control, contains contradictory values and vertical and horizontal inequities, weakens work incentives, and perpetuates the stigma of needing economic help. What she tries to do is develop a more simplified, unified, equitable, and adequate plan than presently exists.

Several principles guide the development of her proposal. First, Ozawa believes that children should be treated separately. That is, their fates and support should not be dependent on how many parents they happen to have or who their parents happen to be. This suggests her second principle, that the individual rather than the family or social group should be the unit of allocation. Third, there should be a hierarchical ordering of income provision, with each "lower" level being greater in amount than the next highest one. The meaning of this principle will become apparent when we examine her program. Finally, the program should be guided by the "principle of less eligibility." This means that wages must always be higher than welfare, making work more attractive by promoting the incentive to work.

There are two basic parts to her plan, one to provide income to adults and the other to provide for children. This is consistent with the first principle just mentioned. The adult component has three layers to it. Welfare is only a last resort after the other two layers of support have been by-passed. The first concern is to try to make sure that those who are not elderly or disabled and are employable can earn a decent wage when they work. This is in tune with the fourth principle, making work attractive. Therefore, the first layer of support concerns a minimum-wage standard. Ozawa recommends that the national minimum wage be raised to 200 percent of the poverty-line income for a one-person family. One might ask what would be done with families who have one or more children. What should be kept in mind at this point is that Ozawa has separated out children for distinct consideration in a children's allowance program that will be commented upon shortly.

The second layer of adult income support is basically a social-insurance layer. The social security system itself would involve two tiers, that is, it would be a "double-decker" system. It includes all the traditional insurance programs (old-age retirement, survivors, disability, unemployment insurance, workers' compensation). The first tier would be an amount fixed at the poverty line for one person for those over sixty-five years of age. At the time Ozawa made her proposal, the monthly amount required was very similar to the average monthly retirement or disability benefits going to someone under Social Security (about $300). So this amount is like a basic floor for the retired, disabled, and surviving spouses of workers. Benefits for other dependents would be eliminated. The second tier of social insurance would be an additional annuity on top of the poverty-line minimum. Its size would vary with the individual covered and depend on her or his past *contributions* to the program, not earnings. Surviving nonelderly spouses would receive a certain percentage of the average monthly earnings of the worker. However, that benefit would run out after a fixed time period (about three years). This would give the surviving spouse time to adjust and seek employment. Ozawa argues that the first tier addresses the goal of adequacy for any program, while the second tier deals with the goal of equity or fairness in benefit level.

Under present Social Security rules, there is an earnings test. Individuals' benefits can be reduced if they earn too much in wages or salary during the month. Ozawa would eliminate the earnings test. Her assumption is that work should be encouraged if an individual is capable and willing to do it. However, she does leave open the possibility that social insurance income might be taxable. Neither should the earnings of a *non*-elderly spouse be subject to an earnings test, but to an ordinary income tax. Ozawa also recommends that there be no minimum employment time required to participate in the social security insurance program on either tier. In other words, one would not have to have worked a prescribed number of quarters to be eligible for benefits. Removing this requirement would make the SSI (Supplemental Security Income) program duplicative, and it could be abolished.

The third layer of income support for adults would consist of a cash-assistance program much smaller than present public-assistance programs. It would provide for those not covered in either of the two lower layers. In most cases, these recipients would be nonelderly, nondisabled persons who cannot earn enough income to live on. This would include many single parents, primarily females. The level of assistance would be equivalent to one-half of the poverty-line income for one person. Any earned income would be taxed at a 50 percent rate, and any nonearned income (rent, interest, etc.) would be taxed at 100 percent. An assets test also might be present.

The separate children's allowance program would be universal, applying to all children younger than eighteen regardless of family income. Evidence indicates that women would not have more children just to receive the additional allowance. The amount of the benefit would be the amount required to support a dependent at the poverty level. This allowance would be taxable and current tax exemptions for children would be eliminated. A progressive income tax system would help bear the cost of this program.

In sum, Ozawa's suggested program streamlines many of the current programs. It also acknowledges the need to support children wherever or whoever they are. It attempts to build in work incentives and minimize the "welfare" component of income assistance. But greater attention would have to be given to generating economic conditions that would allow for meaningful employment for all those who needed it.

Ellwood's Categorical Approach to Reform

David Ellwood's suggestions to reform begin with the premise that there are different kinds of poor groups who are poor for different kinds of reasons (1988). His program is aimed only at families with children, which in many ways make up the most vulnerable component of the poverty population. Generally, they do not have the benefits of social security and are those who, if they need temporary help, have to go to public assistance. Briefly, Ellwood divides poor families into three basic groups: (1) two-parent families or the working poor, (2) single-parent families, or in his emphasis, female-headed families, and (3) ghetto or urban minority poor. In each case, he stresses the importance of looking for the causes of poverty because an understanding of causes is basic for an enlightened approach to poverty. He does not believe that the present welfare system does this and, therefore, he stresses nonwelfare programs. "Welfare does not try to decide why people are poor; it only guarantees some minimal support. But adopting a policy that recognizes no causes leads to no solutions" (Ellwood 1988, p. 87).

Forty-four percent of the poor two-parent families have a parent who works full time. Especially for them low wages are a major cause of poverty. Even when working full time, their wages are not enough to bring them up to the poverty level. About one-third of these families contain parents who are unemployed, while the remaining quarter of two-parent poor families are retired.

It is the two-parent family that is most helped by the "trickle-down" effect of economic fluctuations. When the economy is booming, these families do better; but when there are economic downturns, their incomes suffer accordingly. For this group, Ellwood recommends (1) a program that would ensure coverage of basic medical needs; (2) making work attractive either through spurring economic growth/production or through raising the minimum wage or the earned income tax credit; (3) providing "transitional" help for those who are in temporary need of help, such as, training, job-search assistance, support for short-term disabled and unemployed; and (4) developing a *small* jobs programs for those who simply cannot find employment.

With respect to the first recommendation, medical insurance coverage would require either expansion of the present Medicaid system, have to be provided by employers, or be offered for purchase as a residual medical insurance policy by the government. To make work more attractive, Ellwood prefers use of the earned income tax credit rather than raising the minimum wage. Doing the latter is less efficient because many of those who do earn a minimum wage are not poor. The result is that the change would not focus on those who need help the most. In giving temporary help to those who need it to be launched into self-sufficiency, Ellwood also suggests that some kind of child-care program would be helpful. On the last point, he insists that a small jobs program must be used only as a "last resort."

Single-parent families make up the second type of poor families requiring help. Ellwood focuses primarily on female-headed families in this case. Like the two-parent families, the causes of poverty lie partially in employment problems. But what makes the causes of their poverty distinctive from the first group is that (1) their poverty is often linked to the fact that the single parent is performing dual roles as nurturant and provider, and (2) the present welfare system encourages dependency by, in essence, requesting female heads to either work *or* be on welfare. If they work full time, they may neglect their children; but if they go on welfare, they become dependent. Neither of these is an attractive choice.

As in two-parent families, there are different kinds of female heads. There are those who are healthy and who work full time, work part-time, or who do not work at all. In addition, there are those who are sick or disabled. According to

Ellwood, about 40 percent of single parents work full time. But they work full time because they make well above the minimum wage and have only modest child-care costs. This is not surprising. Those who do not work tend to be those who have more family responsibilities and have little education. Thus, because of both of these conditions it would not be expected that they could command full-time, high-salary positions in the labor force. Those who work part time generally fall in between the other two groups in terms of characteristics.

Ellwood argues that single parents cannot be expected to do nurturing *and* work full-time. At the present time, however, only a small proportion of single mothers get any payments in child support. The present child-support program is a disaster. Currently, only one-half of single parents have been labeled as eligible for such support, and among those only one-third have ever received any money. According to Ellwood's proposal, the other parent (usually the father) should be required to provide support. He suggests that perhaps 25 percent of the absent parent's income could be used for support of two children. Instead of trying to hunt down the father or force payment, Ellwood recommends that such payments be deducted from earnings checks by employers in the same way as Social Security money is currently collected. If the amount collected was not enough for child support because of the father's low wages, the federal government could make up the difference. Ellwood views this as a kind of unemployment insurance for children. This support money could provide the female head with a basis on which to build for her future independence. To this proposal for child support, Ellwood would add the medical, work, transitional, and job features mentioned in the two-parent program.

The third and final poor family group covered by Ellwood's plan is the ghetto poor. As pointed out by him, it is this group that fixes in the imagination of most people when they think about welfare recipients. This is the group known as the "underclass," a group discussed earlier in the book. The list of their problems is long and serious: Families are frequently broken; economic resources are low; individuals are concentrated and isolated from other groups; education is poor; economic opportunities are few and disappearing; deviance is prevalent; welfare is a source of dependency; and discrimination makes life even more difficult. In the face of these monumental difficulties, Ellwood considers Charles Murray's suggestion to "cut off the lifeline" ridiculous.

As he does for the other groups, Ellwood recommends medical, work, transitional, and jobs components. But given the qualitative differences in the problems faced by the ghetto poor, he also argues for improved education. This could come in the form of better preschool programs, a school/job co-op program, employment training programs, or even extending the length of the school year. Given the flight of industry, manufacturing, and the middle class from the central city, Ellwood proposes an experimental jobs program for the ghetto in an attempt to generate jobs. Finally, he advocates attempts to empower these residents who often feel powerless, to find ways to teach and promote the value of personal responsibility, and to speed integration with other groups in society. Each of the latter would be attempts to deal with some of the unique causes of poverty in the ghetto.

Wilson (1987) also makes some policy recommendations for the ghetto poor. He argues that, too often, present policies that stress equality of opportunity result in middle class blacks benefiting rather than those in the lower class. Too often lower class blacks are not the most qualified for the job opportunities presented; thus those who are "truly disadvantaged" are not helped. Moreover, the benefits that do go to the middle class do not trickle down. More often than not benefits wind up leaving the central city. Wilson argues that instead of having a program for minorities that emphasizes "equality of opportunity" or "affirmative action," the program ought to stress "equality of life chances." This would ensure that benefits would be targeted on *poor* minority members. He argues that both blacks and whites would benefit from such a plan. He believes that an approach that applies to all kinds of poor people is important because to focus on only one group of the poor, that is, those in the ghetto, would mean that many nonpoor would not support it. "I am convinced that, in the last few years of the twentieth century, the problems of the truly disadvantaged in the United States will have to be attacked primarily through universal programs that enjoy the support and commitment of a broad constituency" (Wilson 1987, p. 120).

Wilson contends that problems in the economy lie at the root of poverty in the ghetto. Therefore, meaningful programs have to include attempts to spur economic growth, employment, job stability, and the integration of education and employment training. In deciding on specific strategies, the aim should be economic growth with full employment and, therefore, a tight labor market. This benefits everyone. To aid full-time employment, a child-care plan is also needed, and more specific attention has to be paid to the problems of two-parent families, state inequities, and work disincentives. Child allowances and a national minimum AFDC benefit might be ways to deal with some of these problems according to Wilson. In any case, the "hidden agenda" for liberals is to develop programs that will help the truly disadvantaged but at the same time not alienate those in the mainstream.

SUMMARY AND CONCLUSION

This final chapter has covered many of the weaknesses associated with the present income-maintenance system. Problems of inequity, inadequacy, and goal conflict have permeated the network of programs for the poor. In addition, questions about how they affect work incentive, family composition, and effectiveness have also arisen, generating heated debate. By and large, it does not appear that the present system has had major effects on either work incentive or family composition. Rather, broader economic conditions are related to both employment possibilities

and the rise of single-parent families, especially among blacks. The present programs, despite their deficiencies, have reduced poverty.

A variety of alternative proposals also were summarized. Suggestions by Ozawa, Ellwood, and Wilson each attempt to grapple with the issues of adequacy, employment, work incentives, and so on. Each of them suggests reforms that work within the confines of a capitalist economy. Yet we still do not know enough about how to generate stable, long-term, full employment in the private economy, nor, as witnessed by the arguments about welfare effects, do we agree on much concerning the underlying specific causes of poverty. Many have suggested economic growth and full employment as the key to the puzzle of poverty. This would mean greater self-sufficiency for everyone. But this leaves some pessimistic: "Put another way, if the problem of poverty is defined such that the only way to solve it is through greatly increased self-sufficiency, we believe that there is no realistic solution to poverty in the United States" (Morris and Williamson 1986, p. 172). As difficult as poverty may be to understand, we still have not confronted the issue of economic inequality. If it continues to grow as it has in recent years, we may be forced to address this topic. The real question is whether poverty, let alone inequality, can be eliminated within a democratic capitalist society. This brings us back to some of the core questions with which we began this book.

If poverty is generated not merely by differences among individuals, but by conditions that are part of a capitalist economy, such as unemployment and the pressure for profit and lower wages, then a permanent solution, as Morris and Williamson suggest, is very unlikely unless fundamental changes in the political economy occur. Are inequality and poverty inevitable? Given the present social structure, the answer is probably "yes." Are inequality and poverty desirable? It depends. While it is a serious problem for those who must suffer with it, poverty appears to be functional for others. It helps maintain the attractiveness of low wages and menial jobs, especially when coupled with low benefits from programs. At the same time, it provides employment for many middle-class professionals (Gans 1972). As to the immediate future of inequality and poverty, the fact that income inequality has increased in recent years, despite the presence of income-maintenance programs, suggests that either (1) we don't really consider inequality to be a major problem, (2) we don't really know what causes it to fluctuate, and/or (3) some find inequality beneficial. None of these possibilities bodes well for the systematic reduction of inequality.

REFERENCES

Aberle, D. F., A. K. Cohen, A. D. Davis, M. J. Levy, and F. X. Sutton, 1950. "The Functional Prerequisites of a Society." *Ethics* 60:100–11.

Abrahamson, Mark. 1973. "Functionalism and the Functional Theory of Stratification: An Empirical Assessment." *American Journal of Sociology* 78:1236–46.

Acker, Joan. 1973. "Women and Social Stratification: A Case of Intellectual Sexism." *American Journal of Sociology* 78:936–45.

Acker, Joan R. 1980. "Women and Stratification: A Review of Recent Literature." *Contemporary Sociology* 9:25.

Acker, Joan 1988. "Class, Gender, and the Relations of Distribution." *Signs: Journal of Women in Culture and Society* 13:473–97.

Ad Hoc Task Force on the Homeless and Housing. January 21, 1988. *Effect of Our Nation's Housing Policy on Homelessness*. Serial No. AH 100-3. Washington, D.C.: U.S. Government Printing Office.

Adams, Bert N. 1975. *The Family: A Sociological Interpretation*. Skokie, IL: Rand McNally.

Adams, Charles Francis, ed. 1969. *The Works of John Adams*, vol. IX. Freeport, NY: Books for Libraries Press.

Agnello, T. J. 1973. "Aging and the Sense of Political Powerlessness." *Public Opinion Quarterly* 37:251–259.

Alba, Richard D., and Gwen Moore. 1982. "Ethnicity in the American Elite." *American Sociological Review* 47:373–83.

Aldrich, Howard, and Jane Weiss. 1981. "Differentiation Within the United States Capitalist Class: Workforce Size and Income Differences." *American Sociological Review* 46:279–90.

Alexander, Herbert E. 1976a. *Campaign Money*. New York: The Free Press.

Alexander, Herbert E. 1976b. *Financing the 1972 Election*. Lexington, MA: D.C. Heath.

Alexander, Herbert E. 1983. *Financing the 1980 Election*. Lexington, MA: Lexington Books.

Alexander, Karl L., and Bruce K. Eckland. 1974. "Sex Differences in the Educational Attainment Process." *American Sociological Review* 39:668–82.

Alexander, Karl L., Bruce K. Eckland, and Larry J. Griffin. 1975. "The Wisconsin Model of Socioeconomic Achievement: A Replication." *American Journal of Sociology* 81:324–42.

Alexander, Karl L., Martha Cook, and Edward L. McDill. 1978. "Curriculum Tracking and Educational Stratification: Some Further Evidence." *American Sociological Review* 43:47–66.

Allen, Emilie Andersen, and Darrell J. Steffensmeier. 1989. "Youth, Underemployment, and Property Crime: Differential Effects of Job Availability and Job Quality on Juvenile and Young Adult Arrest Rates." *American Sociological Review* 54:107–123.

Allen, Michael Patrick. 1987. *The Founding Fortunes: A New Anatomy of the Super-Rich Families in America*. New York: Truman Talley Books.

Allen, Robert L. 1969. *Black Awakening in Capitalist America*. Garden City, NY: Anchor.

Allen, Walter R., and Reynolds Farley. 1986. "The Shifting Social and Economic Tides of Black America, 1950–1980." Pp. 277–306 in *Annual Review of Sociology,* edited by R. H. Turner and J. F. Short, Jr. Palo Alto, CA: Annual Reviews.

Almond, Gabriel A., and Sidney Verba. 1963. *The Civic Culture: Political Attitudes and Democracy in Five Nations*. Princeton, NJ: Princeton University Press.

Almquist, Elizabeth McTaggart. 1984. "Race and Ethnicity in the Lives of Minority Women." Pp. 423–453 in *Women: A Feminist Perspective,* edited by J. Freeman. Palo Alto, CA: Mayfield.

Alves, W. M., and P. H. Rossi. 1978. "Who Should Get What? Fairness Judgments of the Distribution of Earnings." *American Journal of Sociology* 84:541–65.

Alwin, Duane F. 1974. "College Effects on Educational and Occupational Attainments." *American Sociological Review* 39:210–23.

Anderson, Charles, H. 1974. *The Political Economy of Social Class*. Englewood Cliffs, NJ: Prentice-Hall.

Anderson, Martin. 1975. *Welfare*. Palo Alto, CA: Hoover Institute.

Andrews, Frank M., and Stephen B. Withey. 1976. *Social Indicators of Well-Being*. New York: Plenum.

Angell, Robert. 1962. "Preferences for Moral Norms in Three Problem Areas." *American Journal of Sociology* 67:650–60.

Angle, John. 1986. "The Surplus Theory of Social Stratification and the Size Distribution of Personal Wealth." *Social Forces* 65:293–326.

Ansberry, Clare. November 29, 1988. "Dumping the Poor: Despite Federal Law, Hospitals Still Reject Sick Who Can't Pay." *The Wall Street Journal,* pp. A1, A4.

Anson, Ofra, and Jon Anson. 1987. "Women's Health and Labour Force Status: An Enquiry Using a Multi-Point Measure of Labor Force Participation." *Social Science & Medicine* 25:57–63.

Appalachian Regional Commission. 1985. *Appalachia: Twenty Years of Progress.* Washington, DC: Author.

Archer, M. S., and S. Giner. 1971. "Social Stratification in Europe." In *Contemporary Europe: Class, Status and Power,* edited by M. S. Archer and S. Giner. New York: St. Martin's Press.

Argyle, Michael, Mansur Lalljee, and Mark Cook. 1968. "The Effects of Visibility on Interaction in a Dyad." *Human Relations* 21:3–17.

Aristotle, "Justice." pp. 16–27 in *Justice: Selected Readings,* edited by J. Feinberg and H. Gross. Encino, CA: Dickenson Publishing.

Aronowitz, Stanley. 1973. *False Promises: The Shaping of American Working Class Consciousness.* New York: McGraw-Hill.

Asher, Robert. 1986. "Industrial Safety and Labor Relations in the United States, 1865–1917." Pp. 115–130 in *Life and Labor: Dimensions of American Working-Class History,* edited by C. Stephenson and R. Asher. Albany, NY: State University of New York Press.

Askenasy, Alexander. 1974. *Attitudes Toward Mental Patients.* The Hague: Mouton.

Atkinson, A. B. 1975. *The Economics of Inequality.* London: Oxford University Press.

Austin, Roy L., and Steven Stack. 1988. "Race, Class, and Opportunity: Changing Realities and Perceptions." *The Sociological Quarterly* 29:357–69.

Bachrach, Peter, and Morton S. Baratz. 1962. Two Faces of Power. *American Political Science Review* 56:947–952.

Baltzell, E. Digby. 1958. *Philadelphia Gentleman: The Making of a National Upper Class.* Glencoe, IL: The Free Press.

Bane, Mary Jo. 1985. "Household Composition and Poverty: Which Comes First?" Albany, NY: New York State Department of Social Services.

Baran, Paul, and Paul Sweezy. 1966. *Monopoly Capital.* New York: Monthly Review Press.

Baratz, Steven S., and Joan C. Baratz. 1970. "Early Childhood Intervention: The Social Science Base of Institutional Racism." *Harvard Educational Review* 40:29–50.

Barber, Bernard. 1957. *Social Stratification.* New York: Harcourt Brace Jovanovich.

Barlow, Hugh D. 1987. *Introduction to Criminology.* Boston: Little, Brown.

Baron, James N., and William T. Bielby. 1984. "The Organization of Work in a Segmented Economy." *American Sociological Review* 49:454–73.

Barrera, Mario. 1979. *Race and Class in the Southwest: A Theory of Racial Inequality.* Notre Dame, IN: University of Notre Dame Press.

Barringer, Felicity. January 11, 1990. "The Dress for Success: A Second Time Around." *The New York Times,* p. A18.

Barth, Ernest A. T., and Donald L. Noel. 1972. "Conceptual Frameworks for the Analysis of Race Relations: An Evaluation." *Social Forces* 50:333–48.

Bashshur, R. L., and C. A. Metzner. 1970. "Vulnerability to Risk and Awareness of Dual Choice of Health Insurance Plan." *Health Services Research* 5:106–13.

Bassett, Mary T., and Nancy Krieger. 1986. "Social Class and Black-White Differences in Breast Cancer Survival." *American Journal of Public Health* 76:1400–3.

Bassi, Laurie J., and Orley Ashenfelter. 1986. "The Effect of Direct Job Creation and Training Programs on Low-Skilled Workers." Pp. 133–51 in *Fighting Poverty: What Works and What Doesn't,* edited by S. H. Danziger and D. H. Weinberg. Cambridge, MA: Harvard University Press, 1986.

Batteau, Allen. 1984. "The Sacrifice of Nature: A Study in the Social Production of Consciousness." Pp. 94–106 in *Cultural Adaptation to Mountain Environments,* edited by P. D. Beaver and B. L. Purrington. Athens, GA: The University of Georgia Press.

Beaver, Patricia D. 1984. "Appalachian Cultural Adaptations: An Overview." Pp. 73–93 in *Cultural Adaptation to Mountain Environments,* edited by P.

D. Beaver and B. L. Purrington, Athens, GA: The University of Georgia Press.

Beck, E. M., Patrick M. Horan, and Charles M. Tolbert, II. 1980. "Industrial Segmentation and Labor Market Discrimination." *Social Problems* 28:113–30.

Becker, Gary S. 1971. *The Economics of Discrimination.* Chicago: University of Chicago Press.

Becker, Howard S. 1963. *Outsiders.* New York: The Free Press.

Bedau, H. A. 1964. "Death Sentences in New Jersey." *Rutgers Law Review* 19:1–55.

Beeghley, Leonard. 1983. *Living Poorly in America.* New York: Praeger.

Bell, Wendell. 1957. "Anomie, Social Isolation, and the Class Structure." *Sociometry* 20:105–16.

Bell, Winifred. 1987. *Contemporary Social Welfare.* New York: Macmillan.

Beller, Andrea H. 1984. "Trends in Occupational Segregation by Sex and Race, 1960–1981." Pp. 11–26 in *Sex Segregation in the Workplace: Trends, Explanations, Remedies,* edited by B. F. Reskin. Washington, D.C.: National Academy Press.

Bem, Sandra L., and Daryl J. Bem. 1970. "Case Study of a Nonconscious Ideology: Training the Woman to Know Her Place." Pp. 89–99 in *Beliefs, Attitudes and Human Affairs,* edited by D. J. Bem. Belmont, CA: Brooks/Cole.

Benokraitis, Nijole V., and Joe R. Feagin. 1986. *Modern Sexism.* Englewood Cliffs, NJ: Prentice-Hall.

Bensman, Joseph. 1972. "Status Communities in an Urban Society: The Musical Community." Pp. 113–130 in *Status Communities in Modern Society,* edited by H. R. Stub. Hinsdale, IL: Dryden.

Benson, Michael L., and Esteban Walker. 1988. "Sentencing the White-Collar Offender." *American Sociological Review* 53:294–302.

Benston, Margaret. 1969. "The Political Economy of Women's Liberation." *Monthly Review* 21:15–6.

Bergel, Egon Ernest. 1962. *Social Stratification.* New York: McGraw-Hill.

Berger, J., M. H. Fisek, R. Z. Norman, and M. Zelditch, Jr. 1977. *Status Characteristics and Social Interaction: An Expectation States Approach.* New York: Elsevier.

Berger, J., P. Cohen, and M. Zelditch, Jr. 1972. "Status Characteristics and Social Interaction." *American Sociological Review* 37:241–55.

Bergmann, Barbara R. 1974. "Occupational Segrega-

tion, Wages and Profits When Employers Discriminate by Race or Sex." *Eastern Economic Journal* 1:103–10.

Berk, Richard A., Kenneth J. Lenihan, and Peter H. Rossi. 1980. "Crime and Poverty: Some Experimental Evidence from Ex-Offenders." *American Sociological Review* 45:766–86.

Berki, S. E. 1980. "HMO Enrollment: Who Joins What and Why, A Review of the Literature." *Milbank Memorial Fund Quarterly/Health and Society* 58:588–632.

Berki, S. E., M. Ashcraft, R. Penchansky, and R. Fortus. 1977. "Enrollment Choice in a Multi-HMO Setting: The Roles of Health Risk, Financial Vulnerability, and Access to Care." *Medical Care* 15:95–114.

Berki, S. E., R. Penchansky, R. Fortus, and M. Ashcraft. 1978. "Enrollment Choices in Different Types of HMOs: A Multivariate Analysis." *Medical Care* 16:682–97.

Berkowitz, Edward D. 1984. "Changing the Meaning of Welfare Reform." Pp. 23–42 in *Maintaining the Safety Net: Income Redistribution Programs in the Reagan Administration,* edited by J. C. Weicher. Washington, D.C.: American Enterprise Institute for Public Policy Research.

Berle, Adolf. 1959. *Power without Property.* New York: Harcourt Brace Jovanovich.

Bernard, Jessie. 1972. *The Sex Game.* New York: Atheneum.

Bernard, Jessie. 1981. *The Female World.* New York: The Free Press.

Bernstein, Irving. 1960. *The Lean Years: A History of the American Worker 1920-1933.* Boston: Houghton Mifflin.

Berreman, Gerald D. 1960. "Caste in India and the United States." *American Journal of Sociology* 66 120–127.

Berreman, Gerald D. 1972. "Race, Caste, and Other Invidious Distinctions in Social Stratification." *Race* 13:385–414. Reprinted on Pp. 21–39 in *Majority & Minority: The Dynamics of Race and Ethnicity in American Life,* edited by N. R. Yetman. Boston: Allyn & Bacon, 1985.

Bersani, Carl A., and Huey-Tsyh Chen. 1988. "Sociological Perspectives in Family Violence." Pp. 57–86 in *Handbook of Family Violence,* edited by V. B. Van Hasselt, R. L. Morrison, A. S. Bellack, and M. Hersen. New York: Plenum.

Bertoli, Fernando, Clyda S. Rent, and George S. Rent. 1984. "Infant Mortality by Socioeconomic Status for Blacks, Indians, and Whites: A Longitudinal Analysis of North Carolina, 1968–1977." *Sociology and Social Research* 68:364–77.

Beverly, Creigs C., and Howard J. Stanback. 1986. "The Black Underclass: Theory and Reality." *Black Scholar* 17:24–32.

Bibb, Robert, and William H. Form. 1977. "The Effects of Industrial, Occupational, and Sex Stratification on Wages in Blue-Collar Markets." *Social Forces* 55:974–96.

Bielby, Denise D., and William T. Bielby. 1988. "She Works Hard for the Money: Household Responsibilities and the Allocation of Work Effort." *American Journal of Sociology* 93:1031–59.

Bielby, William T. 1981. "Models of Status Attainment." Pp. 3–26 in *Research in Social Stratification and Mobility,* edited by D. J. Treiman and R. V. Robinson. Greenwich, CT: JAI Press.

Bielby, William T., and James N. Baron. 1984. "A Woman's Place is with Other Women: Sex Segregation within Organizations." Pp. 27–55 in *Sex Segregation in the Workplace,* edited by B. F. Reskin. Washington D.C.: National Academy Press.

Bielby, William T., and James N. Baron. 1986. "Men and Women at Work: Sex Segregation and Statistical Discrimination." *American Journal of Sociology* 91:759–99.

Biller, Henry B., and Richard S. Solomon. 1986. *Child Maltreatment and Paternal Deprivation.* Lexington, MA: Lexington Books.

Billings, Dwight. 1974. "Culture and Poverty in Appalachia: A Theoretical Discussion and Empirical Analysis." *Social Forces* 53:315–324.

Bingham, Richard D., Roy E. Green, and Sammis B. White, eds. 1987. *The Homeless in Contemporary Society.* Newbury Park, CA: Sage.

Black, Donald J. 1970. "Production of Crime Rates." *American Sociological Review* 35:733–48.

Blackwell, James E. 1985. *The Black Community: Diversity and Unity.* New York: Harper & Row.

Blackwood, Evelyn. 1984. "Sexuality and Gender in Certain Native American Tribes: The Case of Cross-Gender Females." *Signs: Journal of Women in Culture and Society* 10:27–42.

Blau, Francine D. 1978. "The Data on Women Workers, Past, Present, and Future." Pp. 29–62 in *Women Working,* edited by A. H. Stromberg and S. Harkess, Palo Alto, CA: Mayfield.

Blau, Francine D. 1984. "Occupational Segregation and Labor Market Discrimination." Pp. 117–43 in *Sex Segregation in the Workplace,* edited by B. F. Reskin. Washington, D.C.: National Academy Press.

Blau, Francine D., and Carol L. Jusenius. 1976. "Economists' Approaches to Sex Segregation in the Labor Market: An Appraisal." *Signs: Journal of Women in Culture and Society* 1:181–99.

Blau, Francine D., and Lawrence M. Kahn. 1981. "Race and Sex Differences in Quits by Young Workers." *Industrial and Labor Relations Review* 34: 563–77.

Blau, Francine D., and Marianne A. Ferber. 1986. *The Economics of Women, Men, and Work.* Englewood Cliffs, NJ: Prentice-Hall.

Blau, Judith R., and Peter M. Blau. 1982. "The Cost of Inequality: Metropolitan Structure and Violent Crime." *American Sociological Review* 47: 114–29.

Blau, Peter M. 1964. *Exchange and Power in Social Life.* New York: John Wiley & Sons.

Blau, Peter M., and Otis Dudley Duncan. 1967. *The American Occupational Structure.* New York: John Wiley & Sons.

Blauner, Robert. 1964. *Alienation and Freedom: The Factory Worker and His Industry.* Chicago: University of Chicago.

Blauner, Robert. 1972. *Racial Oppression in America.* New York: Harper & Row.

Blendon, Robert J., Linda H. Aiken, Howard E. Freeman, and Christopher R. Corey. 1989. "Access to Medical Care for Black and White Americans: A Matter of Continuing Concern." *Journal of the American Medical Association* 261:278–281.

Blishen, Bernard R. 1958. "The Construction and Use of an Occupational Class Scale." *Canadian Journal of Economic and Political Science* 24:519–538.

Block, Fred. 1977. "The Ruling Class Does Not Rule: Notes on the Marxist Theory of the State." *Socialist Revolution* 7:6–28.

Block, N. J., and Gerald Dworkin, eds. 1976. *The IQ Controversy.* New York: Pantheon Books.

Bloom, Allan, trans. 1968. *The Republic of Plato.* New York: Basic Books.

Bloom, Jack M. 1987. *Class, Race & the Civil Rights*

Movement. Bloomington, IN: Indiana University Press.

Bluestone, Barry. 1977. "The Characteristics of Marginal Industries." Pp. 97–102 in *Problems in Political Economy: An Urban Perspective,* edited by D. M. Gordon. Lexington, MA: D. C. Heath.

Blumberg, Paul. 1980. *Inequality in an Age of Decline.* New York: Oxford University Press.

Blumberg, Rae Lesser. 1978. *Stratification: Socioeconomic and Sexual Inequality.* Dubuque, IA: William C. Brown.

Blumberg, Rae Lesser. 1984. "A General Theory of Gender Stratification." Pp. 23–101 in *Sociological Theory,* edited by R. Collins. San Francisco, CA: Jossey-Bass.

Blumberg, Rhoda Lois. 1984. *Civil Rights: The 1960s Freedom Struggle.* Boston: Twayne.

Blumenthal, Monica D., Robert L. Kahn, Frank M. Andrews, and Kendra B. Head. 1972. *Justifying Violence: Attitudes of American Men.* Ann Arbor, MI: Survey Research Center, Institute for Social Research, University of Michigan.

Bogue, Donald J. 1963. *Skid Row in American Cities.* Chicago: Community and Family Study Center, University of Chicago.

Bollen, Kenneth A. 1983. "World System Position, Dependency and Democracy." *American Sociological Review* 48:468–479.

Bonacich, Edna. 1976. "Advanced Capitalism and Black/White Relations in the United States: A Split Labor Market Interpretation." *American Sociological Review* 41:34–51.

Bonacich, Edna. 1980. "Class Approaches to Ethnicity and Race." *Insurgent Sociologist* 10(2).

Bonacich, Edna. 1985. "Class Approaches to Ethnicity and Race." Pp. 62–77 in *Majority and Minority: The Dynamics of Race and Ethnicity in American Life,* edited by N. R. Yetman. Boston: Allyn & Bacon.

Boocock, Sarane Spence. 1978. "The Social Organization of the Classroom." Pp. 1–28 in *Annual Review of Sociology,* edited by R. H. Turner, J. Coleman, and R. C. Fox. Palo Alto, CA: Annual Reviews.

Boorstin, Daniel J. 1967. *The Americans.* New York: Vintage.

Bord, R. 1971. "Rejection of the Mentally Ill: Continuities and Further Developments." *Social Problems* 18:496–509.

Bornschier, Volker, and Thanh-Huyen Ballmer-Cao. 1979. "Income Inequality: A Cross-national Study of the Relationship Between MNC-Penetration, Dimensions of the Power Structure and Income Distribution." *American Sociological Review* 44:487–506.

Boskin, Michael J. 1987. *Reagan and the Economy.* San Francisco: ICS Press.

Bottomore, Tom B. 1964. *Elites and Society.* Baltimore: Penguin.

Bottomore, Tom B. 1966. *Classes in Modern Society.* New York: Pantheon.

Bottomore, Tom B., and Maximilien Rubel, eds. 1956. *Karl Marx: Selected Writings in Sociology and Social Philosophy.* New York: McGraw-Hill.

Bourdieu, Pierre. 1977a. "Cultural Reproduction and Social Reproduction." In *Power and Ideology in Education,* edited by J. Karabel and A. H. Halsey, New York: Oxford University Press.

Bourdieu, Pierre. 1977b. *Outline of a Theory of Practice.* Cambridge: Cambridge University Press.

Bowles, Samuel, and Herbert Gintis. 1976. *Schooling in Capitalist America.* New York: Basic Books.

Box, Steven. 1983. *Power, Crime, and Mystification.* London: Tavistock.

Braithwaite, John. 1981. "The Myth of Social Class and Criminality Reconsidered." *American Sociological Review* 46:36–57.

Braverman, Harry. 1974. *Labor and Monopoly Capital.* New York: Monthly Review Press.

Bremner, Robert H. 1956. *From the Depths: The Discovery of Poverty in the United States.* New York: New York University Press.

Brenner, M. Harvey. 1977. "Personal Stability and Economic Security." *Social Policy* 8:2–4.

Brenner, R. 1977. "The Origins of Capitalist Development: A Critique of Neo-Smithian Marxism." *New Left Review* 104:25–92.

Brett, Regina. February 5, 1989. "Myths Disguise Extent, Severity of Problem." *Akron Beacon Journal,* p. A7.

Brewer, Rose M. 1988. "Black Women in Poverty: Some Comments on Female-Headed Families." *Signs: Journal of Women in Culture and Society* 13:331–39.

Brickman, P., R. Folger, E. Goode, and Y. Schul. 1981. "Microjustice and Macrojustice." Pp. 173–202 in *The Justice Motive in Social Behavior,* edited by M. J. Lerner and C. S. Lerner. New York: Plenum.

Britt, David W., and Omer Galle. "Structural Antecedents of the Shape of Strikes: A Comparative Analysis." *American Sociological Review* 39:642–51.

Brody, David, ed. 1971. *The American Labor Movement.* New York: Harper & Row.

Brody, David. 1980. *Workers in Industrial America: Essays on the Twentieth Century Struggle.* New York: Oxford University Press.

Brooks, John. 1979. *Showing Off in America.* Boston: Little, Brown.

Brophy, Jere E. 1983. "Research on the Self-Fulfilling Prophecy and Teacher Expectations." *Journal of Educational Psychology* 75:631–61.

Brown, Diane Robinson, and Lawrence E. Gary. 1988. "Unemployment and Psychological Distress Among Black American Women." *Sociological Focus* 21:209–21.

Brown, James S., and Harry K. Schwarzweller. 1970. "The Appalachian Family." Pp. 85–97 in *Change in Rural Appalachia: Implications for Action Programs,* edited by J. D. Photiadis and H. K. Schwarzweller. Philadelphia: University of Pennsylvania Press.

Brown, Judith K. 1975. "Iroquois Women: An Ethnohistoric Note." In *Toward an Anthropology of Women,* edited by R. R. Reiter. New York: Monthly Review Press.

Brownmiller, Susan. 1976. *Against Our Will: Men, Women and Rape.* New York: Penguin.

Buchanan, J. L., and S. Cretin. 1986. "Risk Selection of Families Electing HMO Membership." *Medical Care* 24:39–51.

Buckley, Walter. 1958. "Social Stratification and the Functional Theory of Social Differentiation." *American Sociological Review* 23:369–75.

Burghardt, Steve, and Michael Fabricant. 1987. *Working Under the Safety Net: Policy and Practice with the New American Poor.* Newbury Park, CA: Sage.

Burke, Peter, and Austin Turk. 1975. "Factors Affecting Postarrest Dispositions: A Model for Analysis." *Social Problems* 22:313–32.

Burnham, Linda. 1985. "Has Poverty Been Feminized in Black America?" *Black Scholar* 16:14–16.

Burris, Val. 1988. "New Directions in Class Analysis." *Critical Sociology* 15:57–66.

Cain, Glen G. 1976. "The Challenge of Segmented Labor Market Theories to Orthodox Theory." *Journal of Economic Literature* Dec.: 1215–57.

Campaign Financing Monitoring Project, Common Cause, 1974. *1972 Federal Campaign Finances Interest Groups and Political Parties.* Washington, D.C.: Common Cause.

Cannon, Lynn Weber. 1984. "The Trends in Class Identification Among Black Americans from 1952 to 1978." *Social Science Quarterly* 65:112–26.

Cantor, David, and Kenneth C. Land. 1985. "Unemployment and Crime Rates in the Post-World War II United States: A Theoretical and Empirical Analysis." *American Sociological Review* 50: 317–32.

Caplan, Pat, ed. 1987. *The Cultural Construction of Sexuality.* London: Tavistock.

Caplovitz, David. 1963. *The Poor Pay More: Consumer Practices of Low Income Families.* New York: The Free Press.

Carawan, Guy, and Candie Carawan. 1975. *Voices from the Mountains.* New York: Knopf.

Carliner, Michael S. 1987. "Homelessness: A Housing Problem?" Pp. 119–128 in *The Homeless in Contemporary Society,* edited by R. D. Bingham, R. E. Green, and S. B. White, Newbury Park, CA: Sage.

Carlson, Lewis H., and George A. Colburn. 1972. *In Their Place: White America Defines Her Minorities 1850-1950.* New York: John Wiley & Sons.

Carmichael, Stokely, and Charles V. Hamilton. 1967. *Black Power.* New York: Vintage.

Carnegie, Andrew. 1901. *Gospel of Wealth and Other Essays.* Cambridge, MA: Belknap Press of Harvard University Press, 1962.

Casanave, N. A., and M. A. Straus. 1979. "Race, Class, Network Embeddedness and Family Violence: A Search for Potent Support Systems." *Journal of Comparative Family Studies* 10: 281–99.

Catalano, Ralph, and David Dooley. 1983. "Health Effects of Economic Instability: A Test of Economic Stress Hypothesis." *Journal of Health and Social Behavior* 24:46–60.

Catalano, Ralph, and C. David Dooley. 1977. "Economic Predictors of Depressed Mood and Stressful Life Events in a Metropolitan Community." *Journal of Health and Social Behavior* 18:292–307.

Catalog of Federal Domestic Assistance. 1989. Washington, D.C.: U.S. Government Printing Office.

Catalog of Federal Domestic Assistance. 1990. Washington, D.C.: U.S. Government Printing Office.

Caudill, Harry M. 1962. *Night Comes to the Cumberlands: A Biography of a Depressed Area.* Boston: Little, Brown.

Cauthen, Kenneth. 1987. *The Passion for Equality.* Totowa, NJ: Rowman & Littlefield.

Chafe, William H. 1977. *Women and Equality: Changing Patterns in American Culture.* New York: Oxford University Press.

Chafetz, Janet Saltzman. 1984. *Sex and Advantage: A Comparative, Macro-Structural Theory of Sex Stratification.* Totowa, NJ: Rowman & Allanheld.

Chafetz, Janet Saltzman. 1988. *Feminist Sociology: An Overview of Contemporary Theories.* Itasca, IL: F. E. Peacock.

Chagnon, Napoleon A. 1977. *Yanomamo: The Fierce People.* New York: Holt, Rinehart and Winston.

Chakravarti, Anand. 1983. "Some Aspects of Inequality in Rural India: A Sociological Perspective." Pp. 129–81 in *Equality and Inequality: Theory and Practice,* edited by A. Beteille. Delhi: Oxford University Press.

Chambliss, William J. 1969. *Crime and the Legal Process.* New York: McGraw-Hill.

Charles, Enid. 1948. *The Changing Size of the Family in Canada, Census Monograph No. 1.* Ottawa, Canada: Bureau of Statistics, Cloutier.

Chase, Ivan D. 1975. "A Comparison of Men's and Women's Intergenerational Mobility in the United States." *American Sociological Review* 40: 483–505.

Chase-Dunn, Christopher. 1975. "The Effects of International Economic Dependence on Development and Inequality: A Cross-National Study." *American Sociological Review* 40:720–738.

Cherlin, Andrew, and Pamela Barnhouse Walters. 1981. "Trends in United States Men's and Women's Sex-Role Attitudes: 1972–1978." *American Sociological Review* 46:453–60.

Chinoy, Ely. 1955. "Social Mobility Trends in the United States." *American Sociological Review* 20:180–86.

Chiricos, T. G., and G. P. Waldo. 1975. "Socioeconomic Status and Criminal Sentencing: An Empirical Assessment of a Conflict Proposition." *American Sociological Review* 40:753–72.

Chiricos, T. G., P. D. Jackson, and G. P. Waldo. 1972. "Inequality in the Imposition of a Criminal Label." *Social Problems* 19:553–72.

Chiricos, Theodore G. 1987. "Rates of Crime and Unemployment: An Analysis of Aggregate Research Evidence." *Social Problems* 34:187–212.

Chirot, Daniel, and Thomas D. Hall. 1982. "World-System Theory." Pp. 81–106 in *Annual Review of Sociology* vol. 8, edited by R. H. Turner and J. F. Short, Jr. Palo Alto, CA: Annual Reviews.

Clark, John P., and Eugene P. Wenninger. 1962. "Socioeconomic Class and Area as Correlates of Illegal Behavior Among Juveniles." *American Sociological Review* 27:826–34.

Clark, Ramsey. 1970. *Crime in America.* New York: Simon & Schuster.

Clark, Terry N. 1968. *Community Structure and Decision Making: Comparative Analysis.* Corte Madera, CA: Chandler & Sharp.

Clarke, Stevens H., and Gary G. Koch. 1976. "The Influence of Income and Other Factors on Whether Criminal Defendants Go to Prison." *Law and Society Review* 11:57–92.

Clawson, Dan, Alan Neustadtl, and James Bearden. 1986. "The Logic of Business Unity: Corporate Contributions to the 1980 Congressional Elections." *American Sociological Review* 51: 797–811.

Cleary, Paul D., and David Mechanic. 1983. "Sex Differences in Psychological Distress Among Married People." *Journal of Health and Social Behavior* 24:111–21.

Cockerham, William C., Gerhard Kunz, Guenther Leuschen, and Joe L. Spaeth. 1986. "Symptoms, Social Stratification and Self-Responsibility for Health in the United States and West Germany." *Social Science & Medicine* 22:1263–71.

Cockerham, William C., Guenther Leuschen, Gerhard Kunz, and Joe L. Spaeth. 1986. "Social Stratification and Self-Management of Health." *Journal of Health and Social Behavior* 27:1–14.

Cohen, Albert K., and Harold M. Hodges, Jr. 1963. "Characteristics of the Lower-Blue-Collar Classes." *Social Problems* 10:303–34.

Coleman, James S. 1982. *The Asymmetric Society.* Syracuse, NY: Syracuse University Press.

Coleman, Richard P., and Lee Rainwater. 1978. *Social Standing in America.* New York: Basic Books.

Coles, Robert, and Jon Erikson. 1971. *The Middle Americans.* Boston: Little, Brown.

Collier, Jane Fishburne, and Sylvai Junko Yanagisako, eds. 1987. *Gender and Kinship: Essays Toward a Unified Analysis.* Stanford, CA: Stanford University Press.

Collins, Randall. 1971. "Functional and Conflict Theories of Educational Stratification." *American Sociological Review* 36:1002–19.

Collins, Randall. 1975. *Conflict Sociology: Toward an Explanatory Science.* New York: Academic Press.

Collins, Randall, ed. 1984. *Sociological Theory 1984.* San Francisco: Jossey-Bass.

Collins, Randall. 1986. *Weberian Sociological Theory.* Cambridge and New York: Cambridge University Press.

Collins, Randall. 1988. *Theoretical Sociology.* New York: Harcourt Brace Jovanovich.

Collins, Sharon. 1983. "The Making of the Black Middle Class." *Social Problems* 30:369–81.

Congressional Quarterly. May 1968. *Legislators and the Lobbyists.* ed. 2. Washington, D.C. Congressional Quarterly Service.

Congressional Quarterly. November 12, 1988. "Record Number of Women, Blacks in Congress." 46:3293–5.

Connolly, William E. 1969. *The Bias of Pluralism.* New York: Lieber-Atherton.

Cook, Alice H. 1987. "International Comparisons: Problems and Research in the Industrialized World." Pp. 332–373 in *Working Women: Past, Present, Future,* edited by K. S. Koziara, M. H. Moskow, and L. D. Tanner. Washington, D.C.: Bureau of National Affairs.

Cook, Karen, and Karen Hegtvedt. 1983. "Distributive Justice, Equity, and Commitment in Exchange Networks." Pp. 217–41 in *Annual Review of Sociology,* vol. 9, edited by A. Inkeles, J. Coleman, and N. Smelser, Palo Alto, CA: Annual Reviews.

Cookson, Jr., Peter W., and Caroline Hodges Persell. 1985. *Preparing for Power: America's Elite Boarding Schools.* New York: Basic Books.

Coontz, Stephanie, and Peta Henderson, eds. 1986. *Women's Work, Men's Property: The Origins of Gender and Class.* London: Verso.

Corcoran, Mary, and Greg J. Duncan. 1979. "Work History, Labor Force Attachment, and Earnings Differences Between the Races and Sexes." *Journal of Human Resources* 14:3–20.

Coreil, Jeannine, and Patricia A. Marshall. 1982. "Locus of Illness Control: A Cross Cultural Study." *Human Organizations* 41:131–38.

Coser, Lewis. 1965. "The Sociology of Poverty." *Social Problems* 13:140–8.

Coser, Lewis A. 1967. *Continuities in the Study of Social Conflict.* New York: The Free Press.

Coser, Lewis A. 1971. *Masters of Sociological Thought.* New York: Harcourt Brace Jovanovich.

Coser, Lewis A. 1975. "Presidential Address: Two Methods in Search of a Substance." *American Sociological Review* 40:691–700.

Cott, Nancy F. 1986. "Feminist Theory and Feminist Movements: The Past Before Us." Pp. 49–62 in *What is Feminism?,* edited by J. Mitchell and A. Oakley. New York: Pantheon.

Cott, Nancy F. 1987. *The Grounding of Modern Feminism.* New Haven, CT: Yale University Press.

Counts, George S. 1925. "The Social Status of Occupations: A Problem in Vocational Guidance." *School Review* 33:16–27.

Coverdill, James E. 1988. "The Dual Economy and Size Differences in Earnings." *Social Forces* 66:970–93.

Cox, Oliver C. 1942. "The Modern Caste School of Race Relations." *Social Forces* 21:218–26.

Cox, Oliver C. 1945. "Race and Caste: A Distinction." *American Journal of Sociology* 50:360–8.

Cox, Oliver C. 1948. *Caste, Class and Race.* New York: Monthly Review Press.

Cox, Oliver C. 1959. *The Foundations of Capitalism.* New York: Philosophical Library.

Cox, Oliver C. 1964. *Capitalism as a System.* New York: Monthly Review Press.

Cox, Oliver C. 1976. *Race Relations: Elements and Social Dynamics.* Detroit: Wayne State University Press.

Cramer, James C. 1980. "Fertility and Female Employment: Problems of Causal Direction." *American Sociological Review* 45:167–90.

Crompton, Rosemary, and Gareth Jones. 1984. *White Collar Proletariat: Deskilling and Gender in Clerical Work.* Philadelphia: Temple University Press.

Crowder, N. David. 1974. "A Critique of Duncan's Stratification Research." *Sociology* 8:19–45.

Crozier, Michel. 1971. *The World of the Office Worker.* Chicago: University of Chicago Press.

Crozier, Michel. 1973. "The Problem of Power." *Social Research* 40:211–28.

Cuber, John F., and William F. Kenkel. 1954. *Social Stratification in the United States.* New York: Appleton-Century-Crofts.

Cukor, E., and G. Kertesi. 1985. "Differences in Pay and Modes of Earning." Pp. 70–120 in *Labour Market and Second Economy in Hungary,* edited by P. Galasi and G. Sziraczki. Frankfurt: Campus Verlag.

Cunningham, Frank. 1975–1976. "Pluralism and Class Struggle." *Science and Society* 39:385–416.

Curran, Debra A. 1983. "Judicial Discretion and Defendant's Sex." *Criminology* 21:41–58.

Currie, Elliott, and Jerome H. Skolnick. 1988. *Ameri-*

ca's Problems: Social Issues and Public Policy. Glenview, IL: Scott, Foresman.

d'Houtaud A., and Mark G. Field. 1984. "The Image of Health: Variations in Perception by Social Class in a French Population." *Sociology of Health and Illness* 6:30–59.

Dahl, Robert A. 1982. *Dilemmas of Pluralist Democracy.* New Haven, CT: Yale University Press.

Dahrendorf, Ralf. 1958a. "Out of Utopia: Toward a Reorientation of Sociological Analysis." *American Journal of Sociology* 64:115–27.

Dahrendorf, Ralf. 1958b. "Toward a Theory of Social Conflict." *Journal of Conflict Resolution.* 2:170–83.

Dahrendorf, Ralf. 1959. *Class and Class Conflict in Industrial Society.* Stanford, CA: Stanford University Press.

Dahrendorf, Ralf. 1970. "On the Origin of Inequality Among Men." Pp. 3–30 in *The Logic of Social Hierarchies,* edited by E. O. Laumann, P. M. Siegel, and R. W. Hodge, Chicago: Markham.

Danigelis, Nicholas L. 1978. "Black Political Participation in the United States." *American Sociological Review* 43:756–71.

Danziger, Sheldon, and Peter Gottschalk. 1983. "The Measurement of Poverty: Implications for Antipoverty Policy." *American Behavioral Scientist* 26:739–56.

Danziger, Sheldon, and Peter Gottschalk. 1985. "The Poverty of Losing Ground." *Challenge* May-June:32–38.

Danziger, Sheldon, and Peter Gottschalk. 1986. "Work, Poverty, and the Working Poor: A Multifaceted Problem." *Monthly Labor Review* 109:17–21.

Danziger, Sheldon, and Robert Plotnick. November 1977. "Poverty Today: Does It Persist or Has it Been Eliminated?" Paper prepared for the Center for the Study of Democratic Institutions, Santa Barbara, California.

Danziger, Sheldon, and David Wheeler. 1975. "The Economics of Crime: Punishment or Income Distribution." *Review of Social Economy* 33:113–31.

Danziger, Sheldon H., Robert H. Haveman, and Robert D. Plotnick. 1986. "Antipoverty Policy: Effects on the Poor and the Nonpoor." Pp. 50–77 in *Fighting Poverty: What Works and What Doesn't,* edited by S. H. Danziger and D. H. Weinberg. Cambridge, MA: Harvard University Press.

Darling, Sharon. 1984. "Illiteracy: An Everyday Problem for Millions." *Appalachia* 18:22–23.

Daro, Deborah. 1988. *Confronting Child Abuse: Research for Effective Program Design.* New York: The Free Press.

Das, Man Singh, and F. Gene Acuff. 1970. "The Caste Controversy in Comparative Perspective: India and the United States." *International Journal of Comparative Sociology* 11:48–54.

Davidson, Chandler, and Charles M. Gaitz. 1974. "Are the Poor Different? A Comparison of Work Behavior and Attitude Among the Urban Poor and Nonpoor." *Social Problems* 22:229–45.

Davie, Maurice R. 1963. *William Graham Sumner.* New York: Thomas Y. Crowell.

Davies, James C. 1969. "The J-Curve of Rising and Declining Satisfactions as a Cause of Some Great Revolutions and a Contained Rebellion." In *Violence in America: Historical and Comparative Perspectives,* edited by H. D. Graham and T. R. Gurr. Washington, D.C.: National Commission on the Causes and Prevention of Violence.

Davies, James C. 1971. "Introduction." Pp. 3–9 in *When Men Revolt and Why,* edited by J. C. Davies. New York: The Free Press.

Davis, Allison, Burleigh B. Gardner, and Mary R. Gardner. 1941. *Deep South.* Chicago: University of Chicago Press.

Davis, Angela. 1981. *Women, Race and Class.* New York: Random House.

Davis, James Allan, and Tom W. Smith. 1989. *General Society Surveys, 1972–1989.* Principal Investigator, James A. Davis; Director and Co-Principal Investigator, Tom W. Smith. NORC ed. Chicago: National Opinion Research Center, producer; Storrs, CT: The Roper Center for Public Opinion Research, University of Connecticut, distributor.

Davis, John A. 1974. "Justification for No Obligation: View of Black Males Toward Crime and the Criminal Law." *Issues in Criminology* 9:69–87.

Davis, Kingsley, and Wilbert E. Moore. 1945. "Some Principles of Stratification." *American Sociological Review* 10:242–9.

Davis, Kingsley. 1948-1949. *Human Society.* New York: Macmillan.

Davis, Kingsley. 1953. "Reply to Tumin." *American Sociological Review* 18:394–7.

Daymont, Thomas N. 1977. "Black-White Differences in Labor Market Allocation Processes in the Late

1960's." Madison, WI: Center for Demography nd Ecology Working Paper No. 77-21, University of Wisconsin.

de Tocqueville, Alexis. 1969. Quoted in *Democracy in America,* edited by J. P. Mayer. New York: Doubleday.

Della Fave, Richard. 1980. "The Meek Shall Not Inherit the Earth: Self-Evaluation and the Legitimacy of Stratification." *American Sociological Review* 45:955-71.

Democratic Staff of the Joint Committee. 1986. *The Concentration of Wealth in the United States: Trends in the Distribution of Wealth Among American Families.* Washington, D.C.: Joint Economic Committee, U.S. Congress.

Devine, Edward T. 1908-1909. "The Pittsburgh Survey." *Charities and the Commons* 21:1035-36.

Devine, Joel A., Joseph F. Sheley, and M. Dwayne Smith. 1988. "Macroeconomic and Social-Control Policy Influences on Crime Rate Changes, 1948-1985." *American Sociological Review* 53:407-20.

"Did Milken Get Off Too Lightly?" May 7, 1990. *U.S. News and World Report,* pp. 22-24.

DiMaggio, Paul, and John Mohr. 1985. "Cultural Capital, Educational Attainment, and Marital Selection." *American Sociological Review* 90: 1231-57.

Dionne, Jr., E. J. April 18, 1989. "Poor Paying More for Their Shelter." *The New York Times,* p. A18.

DiPrete, Thomas A., and Whitman T. Soule. 1988. "Gender and Promotion in Segmented Job Ladder Systems." *American Sociological Review* 53: 26-40.

Dobash, R. E., and R. P. Dobash. 1979. *Violence Against Wives: A Case Against Patriarchy.* New York: The Free Press.

Doeringer, Peter B., and Michael J. Piore. 1971. *Internal Labor Markets and Manpower Analysis.* Lexington, MA: D. C. Heath.

Dohrenwend, Bruce P. 1975. "Sociocultural and Social-Psychological Factors in the Genesis of Mental Disorders." *Journal of Health and Social Behavior* 16:365-92.

Dohrenwend, Bruce P., and Barbara Snell Dohrenwend. 1969. *Social Status and Psychological Disorder: A Causal Inquiry.* New York: John Wiley & Sons.

Dolbeare, Kenneth M., and Murray J. Edelman. 1971. *American Politics.* Lexington, MA: D.C. Heath.

Dolgoff, Ralph, and Donald Feldstein. 1984. *Understanding Social Welfare.* New York: Longman.

Dollard, John. 1957. *Caste and Class in a Southern Town.* Garden City, NY: Doubleday.

Domhoff, G. William. 1967. *Who Rules America?* Englewood Cliffs, N.J.: Prentice-Hall.

Domhoff, G. William. 1971. *The Higher Circles.* New York: Vintage Books.

Domhoff, G. William, 1979. *The Powers That Be: Processes of Ruling Class Domination in America.* New York: Vintage Books.

Domhoff, G. William. 1983. *Who Rules America Now?: A View for the '80s.* New York: Simon & Schuster.

Dublin, Thomas. 1979. *Women at Work.* New York: Columbia University Press.

Dubofsky, Melvyn. 1975. *Industrialism and the American Workers, 1865-1920.* Arlington Heights, IL: AHM Publishing.

Duke, James T. 1976. *Conflict and Power in Social Life.* Provo, UT: Brigham Young University Press.

Dumont, Louis and D. Pocock, eds. 1961. *Contributions to Indian Sociology,* vol. 5. The Hague: Mouton.

Dumont, Louis. 1970. *Homo Hierarchicus,* trans. M. Sainsbury, Chicago: University of Chicago Press.

Duncan, Greg J. 1984. *Years of Poverty, Years of Plenty: The Changing Economic Fortunes of American Workers and Families.* Ann Arbor, MI: Institute for Social Research, University of Michigan.

Duncan, Otis Dudley. 1961. "A Socioeconomic Index for All Occupations." Chapter 6 in *Occupations and Social Status,* edited by Albert J. Reiss, Jr. New York: The Free Press.

Duncan, Otis Dudley. 1966. "Methodological Issues in the Analysis of Social Mobility." Pp. 51-97 in *Social Structure and Mobility in Economic Development,* edited by N. J. Smelser and S. M. Lipset. Chicago: Aldine.

Duncan, Otis Dudley. 1968. "Social Stratification and Mobility: Problems in the Measurement of Trend." Chapter 13 in *Indicators of Social Change,* edited by E. B. Sheldon and W. E. Moore. New York: Russell Sage Foundation.

Dunlap, David W. January 22, 1990. "Census Surveys Show Where Homeless Stay." *New York Times,* p. A16.

Dunlop, John T. 1987. "The Development of Labor Organization: A Theoretical Framework." Pp. 12–22 in *Theories of the Labor Movement,* edited by S. Larson and B. Nissen. Detroit: Wayne State University Press.

Durant, Jr., Thomas J., and Joyce S. Louden. 1986. "The Black Middle Class in America: Historical and Contemporary Perspectives." *Phylon* 47: 253–63.

Durkheim, Emile. 1933. *The Division of Labor in Society.* New York: The Free Press.

Dutton, Diana B. 1978. "Explaining the Low Use of Health Services by the Poor: Costs, Attitudes or Delivery Systems?" *American Sociological Review* 43:348–68.

Dye, Thomas R. 1986. *Who's Running America? The Conservative Years.* Englewood Cliffs, NJ: Prentice-Hall.

Eakins, Barbara W.., and R. Gene Eakins. 1978. *Sex Differences in Human Communication.* Boston: Houghton Mifflin.

Edelhertz, Herbert. 1970. *The Nature, Impact and Prosecution of White-Collar Crime.* Washington, D.C.: National Institute of Law Enforcement Assistance Administration, U.S. Department of Justice.

Edelman, Murray, 1977. *Political Language: Words that Succeed and Policies that Fail.* New York: Academic Press.

Edsall, Thomas Byrne. 1984. *The New Politics of Inequality.* New York: W. W. Norton.

Edwards, Alba M. 1943. *Comparative Occupations Statistics for the United States.* Washington, D.C.: U.S. Government Printing Office.

Edwards, Richard. 1979. *Contested Terrain: The Transformation of the Workplace in the Twentieth Century.* New York: Basic Books.

Ehrenreich, Barbara, and Deirdre English. 1981. "The Sexual Politics of Sickness." Pp. 327–350 in *The Sociology of Health and Illness: Critical Perspectives.* New York: St. Martin's Press.

Ehrenreich, Barbara. September 7, 1986. "Heading for a Two-Tier Society." *Akron Beacon Journal,* p. F1.

Ehrlich, Isaac. 1973. "Participation in Illegitimate Activities: A Theoretical and Empirical Investigation." *Journal of Political Economy* 81:521–65.

Eisenstein, Zillah. 1977/1990. "Constructing a Theory of Capitalist Patriarchy and Socialist Feminism." *Insurgent Sociologist* 7(1977):3–17. Reprinted on pp. 114–45 in *Women, Class, and the Feminist Imagination: A Socialist-Feminist Reader,* edited by K. V. Hansen and I. J. Philipson. Philadelphia: Temple University Press.

Eisenstein, Zillah. 1981. *The Radical Future of Liberal Feminism.* New York: Longman.

Eisler, Benita, ed. 1977. *The Lowell Offering.* Philadelphia: J. B. Lippincott.

Eismeier, Theodore J., and Philip H. Pollock III. 1986. "Strategy and Choice in Congressional Elections: The Role of Political Action Committees." *American Journal of Political Science* 30:197–213.

Elder, Glen H., and Jeffrey K. Liker. 1982. "Hard Times in Women's Lives: Historical Influences across Forty Years." *American Journal of Sociology* 88:241–69.

Elkins, Stanley. 1959. *Slavery: A Problem in American Institutional and Intellectual Life.* Chicago: University of Chicago Press.

Eller, Ronald D. 1982. *Miners, Millhands, and Mountaineers: Industrialization of the Appalachian South, 1880-1930.* Knoxville, TN: University of Tennessee Press.

Ellwood, David T. 1988. *Poor Support: Poverty in the American Family.* New York: Basic Books.

Ellwood, David T., and Lawrence H. Summers. 1986. "Poverty in America: Is Welfare the Answer or the Problem?" Pp. 78–105 in *Fighting Poverty: What Works and What Doesn't,* edited by S. H. Danziger and D. H. Weinberg. Cambridge, MA: Harvard University Press.

Ellwood, David T., and Mary Jo Bane. 1974. "The Impact of AFDC on Family Structure and Living Arrangements." Working paper prepared for the U.S. Department of Health and Human Services under grant no. 92A-82.

Emerson, Richard M. 1962. "Power-dependence Relations." *American Sociological Review* 27:31–41.

Engels, Frederick. 1973. "The Origin of the Family, Private Property and the State." Pp. 204–334 in *Karl Marx and Frederick Engels: Selected Works.* Moscow: Progress Publishers.

England, Paula, and Dana Dunn. 1985. "Why Men Dominate." *The Women's Review of Books* 2:14–15.

England, Paula, and George Farkas. 1986. *Households, Employment, and Gender: A Social, Eco-*

nomic and Demographic View. New York: Aldine.

England, Paula, George Farkas, Barbara Kilbourne, and Thomas Dou. 1988. "Explaining Occupational Sex Segregation and Wages: Findings from a Model with Fixed Effects." *American Sociological Review* 53: 544–558.

England, Paula. 1984. "Socioeconomic Explanations of Job Segregation." Pp. 28–46 in *Comparable Worth and Wage Discrimination,* edited by H. Remick. Philadelphia: Temple University Press.

Erikson, Kai T. 1976. *Everything in its Path.* New York: Simon & Schuster.

Erikson, Robert, John H. Goldthorpe, and Lucienne Portocarero. 1983. "Intergenerational Class Mobility and the Convergence Thesis: England, France, and Sweden." *British Journal of Sociology* 34: 303–43.

Erlanger, Howard S. 1974. "Social Class and Corporal Punishment in Childrearing: A Reassessment." *American Sociological Review* 39:68–85.

Fagot, Beverly I. 1977. "Consequences of Moderate Cross-Gender Behavior in Preschool Children." *Child Development* 48:902–7.

Faller, Kathleen Coulborn, and Marjorie Ziefert. 1981. "Causes of Child Abuse and Neglect." Pp. 32–51 in *Social Work with Abused and Neglected Children,* edited by K. C. Faller. New York: The Free Press.

Fallers, Lloyd A. 1966. "Review Symposium." *American Sociological Review* 31: 718–9.

Fanon, Frantz. 1963. *The Wretched of the Earth.* New York: Grove Press.

Farganis, Sondra. 1986. "Social Theory and Feminist Theory: The Need for Dialogue." *Sociological Inquiry* 56:50–68.

Faris, R. E. L., and H. W. Dunham. 1939. *Mental Disorders in Urban Areas: An Ecological Study of Schizophrenia and Other Psychoses.* Chicago: University of Chicago.

Farley, John E. 1988. *Majority-Minority Relations.* Englewood Cliffs, NJ: Prentice-Hall.

Farrell, Ronald A. 1971. "Class Linkages of Legal Treatment of Homosexuals." *Criminology* 9: 49–68.

Fatsis, Stefan. November 22, 1990. "Milken Gets 10 Years in Wall Street Scandal." *Akron Beacon Journal,* pp. A1 and A13.

Feagin, Joe R. November 1972. "Poverty: We Still Believe that God Helps Those Who Help Themselves." *Psychology Today* 101.

Featherman David L., and Robert M. Hauser. 1978. *Opportunity and Change.* New York: Academic Press.

Featherman, David L. 1977. "Has Opportunity Declined in America?" Institute for Research on Poverty Discussion Paper No. 437-77. Madison, WI: University of Wisconsin.

Featherman, David L., and Robert M. Hauser. 1976. "Sexual Inequalities and Socioeconomic Achievement in the U.S., 1962–1973." *American Sociological Review* 41:462–83.

Featherman, David L., F. Lancaster Jones, and Robert M. Hauser. 1975. "Assumptions of Social Mobility Research in the U.S.: The Case of Occupational Status." *Social Science Research* 4:329–60.

Fechter, A., and S. Greenfield, 1973. "Welfare and Illegitimacy: An Economic Model and Some Preliminary Results." Working Paper No. 963–37, Urban Institute, Washington, D.C.

Feldstein, Stanley, ed. 1972. *The Poisoned Tongue: A Documentary History of American Racism and Prejudice.* New York: William Morrow.

Felmlee, Diane H. 1982. "Women's Job Mobility Processes Within and Between Employers." *American Sociological Review* 43:142–51.

Fenton, Steve. 1984. *Durkheim and Modern Sociology.* Cambridge: Cambridge University Press.

Ferree, Myra Marx, and Beth B. Hess. 1985. *Controversy and Coalition: The New Feminist Movement.* Boston: Twayne.

Fiala, Robert and Gary LaFree. 1988. "Cross-National Determinants of Child Homicide." *American Sociological Review* 53:432–45.

Fickett, Joan G. 1975. "Merican: An Inner City Dialect-Aspects of Morphemics, Syntax, and Semology." Studies in Linguistics-Occasional Papers 13.

Fiore, Michael C., Thomas E. Novotny, John P. Pierce, Evridiki J. Hatziandreu, Kantilal M. Patel, and Ronald M. Davis. 1989. "Trends in Cigarette Smoking in the United States." *Journal of the American Medical Association* 261:49–55.

Firestone, Shulamith. 1970. *The Dialectic of Sex: The Case for Feminist Revolution.* New York: William Morrow.

Fishel, Jr., Leslie, and Benjamin Quarles. 1967. *The Negro American: A Documentary History.* Glenview, IL: Scott, Foresman.

Flacks, Richard. 1971. *Youth and Social Change.* Chicago: Markham.

Flanagan, Timothy J. and Katherine M. Jamieson, eds. 1988. *Sourcebook of Criminal Justice Statistics— 1987.* U.S. Department of Justice, Bureau of Justice Statistics. Washington, D.C.: U.S. Government Printing Office.

Flanagan, Timothy J., and Kathleen Maguire, eds. 1990. *Sourcebook of Criminal Justice Statistics— 1989.* U.S. Department of Justice Bureau of Justice Statistics. Washington, D.C.: U.S. Government Printing Office.

Focus. Spring 1985. "Measuring the Effects of the Reagan Welfare Changes on the Work Effort and Well-Being of Single Parents," pp. 1–8.

Focus. Winter 1984. "Poverty in the United States: Where Do We Stand Now?" Madison, WI: Institute for Research on Poverty, University of Wisconsin.

Foner, Philip S. 1979. *Women and the American Labor Movement,* vol. 1. New York: The Free Press.

Form, M. H., and G. P. Stone. 1957. "Urbanism, Anonymity, and Status Symbolism." *American Journal of Sociology* 62:504–514.

Form, William, and Joan Rytina. 1969. "Ideological Beliefs on the Distribution of Power in the United States." *American Sociological Review* 34:19–31.

Form, William H., and Joan Huber. 1971. "Income, Race, and the Ideology of Political Efficacy." *Journal of Politics* 33:659–688.

Form, William. 1983. "Sociological Research and the American Working Class." *The Sociological Quarterly* 24:163–184.

Fossett, Mark A., Omer R. Galle, and William R. Kelly. 1986. "Racial Occupational Inequality, 1940–1980: National and Regional Trends." *American Sociological Review* 51:421–9.

Foster, George M. 1973. *Traditional Societies in Technological Change,* 2nd ed. New York: Harper & Row.

Fosu, Augustin Kwasi. 1988. "Trends in Relative Earnings Gains by Black Women: Implications for the Future." *The Review of Black Political Economy* 17:31–45.

"The 400 Richest People in America: The Forbes Four Hundred." 1987. *Forbes* 140:106–240.

Fox, Mary Frank, and Sharlene Hesse-Biber. 1984. *Women At Work.* Palo Alto, CA: Mayfield.

Frank, Andre Gunder. 1969. *Latin America: Under-development or Revolution.* New York: Monthly Review Press.

Frank, Robert H. 1985. *Choosing the Right Pond.* New York: Oxford University Press.

Frankfurt, Harry. 1987. "Equality as a Moral Ideal." *Ethics* 98:21–43.

Franklin, John Hope. 1980. *From Slavery to Freedom: A History of Negro Americans.* New York: Knopf.

Frazier, E. Franklin. 1937. "Negro Harlem: An Ecological Study." *American Journal of Sociology* 43:72–88.

Frazier, E. Franklin. 1957. *Race and Culture Contacts in the Modern World.* Westport, CT: Greenwood Press.

Fredrickson, George M. 1971. *The Black Image in the White Mind: The Debate on Afro-American Character and Destiny, 1817–1914.* New York: Harper & Row.

Fredrickson, George M. 1981. *White Supremacy: A Comparative Study in American and South African History.* New York: Oxford University Press.

Freeborn, D., and C. Pope. 1982. "Health Status, Utilization, and Satisfaction Among Enrollees in Three Types of Private Health Insurance Plans." *The Group Health Journal* 3:4–11.

Freeman, Jo, ed. 1975. *Women: A Feminist Perspective.* Palo Alto, CA: Mayfield.

Freeman, Jo. 1975. "The Women's Liberation Movement: Its Origins, Structures, Impact, and Ideas." Pp. 448–60 in *Women: A Feminist Perspective,* edited by J. Freeman, Palo Alto, CA: Mayfield.

Freeman, Richard B. 1989. "The Relation of Criminal Activity to Black Youth Employment." *Review of Black Political Economy* 16:99–107.

Freire, Paulo. 1986. *Pedagogy of the Oppressed.* New York: Continuum.

Freitag, Peter J. 1975. "The Cabinet and Big Business: A Study of Interlocks." *Social Problems* 23: 137–52.

Friedmann, Wolfgang. 1959. *Law in a Changing Society.* Berkeley, CA: University of California Press.

Fuchs, Victor R. 1983. *Who Shall Live?* New York: Basic Books.

Fusfeld, Daniel R. 1972. "The Rise of the Corporate State in America." *Journal of Economic Issues* 6:1–22.

Fussell, Paul. 1983. *Class.* New York: Summit Books.

Galbraith, John Kenneth. 1952. *American Capitalism: The Concept of Countervailing Power.* Boston: Houghton Mifflin.

Galle, Omer R., Candace Hinson Wiswell, and Jeffrey A. Burr. 1985. "Racial Mix and Industrial Productivity." *American Sociological Review* 50: 20–33.

Gallup, Jr., George. 1985. "Mood of the Nation." *The Gallup Report* 243:22–4.

Gallup, George, Jr. 1986. *The Gallup Poll: Public Opinion 1985.* Wilmington, DE: Scholarly Resources.

Gallup, George, Jr. 1988. *The Gallup Poll: Public Opinion 1987.* Wilmington, DE: Scholarly Resources, Inc.

Gallup, Jr., George. 1989. *The Gallup Poll: Public Opinion 1988.* Wilmington, DE: Scholarly Resources.

The Gallup Report. January/February 1987. Report No. 256-57, p. 14.

Gans, Herbert J. 1968. *More Equality.* New York: Vintage Books.

Gans, Herbert J. 1972. "Positive Functions of Poverty." *American Journal of Sociology* 78:275–89.

Gans, Herbert J., ed. 1974. "The Equality Revolution." Pp. 7–35 in *More Equality,* edited by H. J. Gans. New York: Vintage.

Garbarino, Merwyn S. 1976. *American Indian Heritage.* Boston: Little, Brown.

Garfinkel, Irwin. 1978. "Income Support Policy: Where We've Come From and Where We Should be Going." Institute for Research on Poverty Discussion Paper No. 490-78. Madison, WI: University of Wisconsin.

Garfinkel, S. A., W. E. Schlenger, K.R. McLeroy, F. A. Bryan, Jr., B. J. G. York, G. H. Dunteman, and A. S. Friedlob. 1986. "Choice of Payment Plan in the Medicare Capitation Demonstration." *Medical Care* 24:628–40.

Garrett, Marcia, and James F. Short, Jr. 1975. "Social Class and Delinquency: Predictions and Outcomes of Police-Juvenile Encounters." *Social Problems* 22: 368–83.

Garson, Barbara. 1988. *The Electronic Sweatshop.* New York: Simon & Schuster.

Gaventa, John. 1980. *Power and Powerlessness: Quiescence and Rebellion in an Appalachian Valley.* Urbana, IL: University of Illinois Press.

Gaventa, John. 1984. "Land Ownership, Power, and Powerlessness in the Appalachian Highlands." Pp. 142–155 in *Cultural Adaptation to Mountain Environments,* edited by P. D Beaver and B. L. Purrington. Athens, GA: University of Georgia Press.

Geis, Gilbert. 1965. "Statistics Concerning Race and Crime." *Crime & Delinquency* 11:142–50.

Geis, Gilbert. 1967. "The Heavy Electrical Equipment Antitrust Cases of 1961." Pp. 139–50 in *Criminal Behavior Systems,* edited by M. Clinard and R. Quinney. New York: Holt, Rinehart & Winston.

Geis, Gilbert. 1974. "Upperworld Crime." Pp. 114–37 in *Crime Perspectives on Criminal Behavior,* edited by A. S. Blumberg. New York: Knopf.

Gelles, Richard J. 1975. "The Social Construction of Child Abuse." *American Journal of Orthopsychiatry* 45:363–71.

Gelles, Richard J. and Claire Pedrick Cornell. 1985. *Intimate Violence in Families.* Beverly Hills, CA: Sage.

Gerson, Kathleen. 1985. *Hard Choices: How Women Decide About Work, Career, and Motherhood.* Berkeley: University of California Press.

Gerson, Kathleen. 1987. "Emerging Social Divisions Among Women: Implications for Welfare State Politics." *Politics and Society* 15:213–21.

Gerth, Hans H., and C. Wright Mills, eds. 1962. *From Max Weber: Essays in Sociology.* New York: Oxford University Press.

Ghali, Moheb, and Meda Chesney-Lind. 1986. "Gender Bias and the Criminal Justice System: An Empirical Investigation." *Sociology and Social Research* 70:164–71.

Giddens, Anthony. 1973. *The Class Structure of the Advanced Societies.* New York: Harper & Row.

Giddens, Anthony. 1978. *Emile Durkheim.* New York: Penguin Books.

Giddens, Anthony. 1982. *Sociology: A Brief But Critical Introduction.* New York: Harcourt Brace Jovanovich.

Giddings, Paula. 1984. *When and Where I Enter: The Impact of Black Women on Race and Sex in America.* New York: Bantam.

Gil, D. G. 1971. "Violence Against Children." *Journal of Marriage and the Family* 33:637–48.

Gil, D. G. 1975. "Unraveling Child Abuse." *American Journal of Orthopsychiatry* 45:346–56.

Gilbert, Dennis, and Joseph A. Kahl. 1987. *The American Class Structure.* Chicago: Dorsey.

Gillespie, Robert. 1978. "Economic Factors in Crime and Delinquency: A Critical Review of the Empirical Evidence." *Hearings, Subcommittee on Crime of the Committee of the Judiciary House of Repre-*

sentatives 95th Congress, Serial 47, pp. 601–25. Washington, D.C.: U.S. Government Printing Office.

Gilliam, Jr., Franklin D. 1986. "Black America: Divided by Class." *Public Opinion* 9:53–60.

Gillison, Gilliam. 1980. "Images of Nature in Gimi Thought." Pp. 143–73 in *Nature, Culture and Gender,* edited by C. MacCormack and M. Strathem. Cambridge: Cambridge University Press.

Ginsberg, Eli, and Hyman Berman. 1963. *The American Worker in the Twentieth Century.* New York: The Free Press.

Giovannoni, Jeanne M., and Andrew Billingsley. 1970. "Child Neglect Among the Poor: A Study of Parental Adequacy in Three Ethnic Groups." *Child Welfare* 49:196–204.

Giroux, Henry A. 1983. *Theory & Resistance in Education: A Pedagogy for the Opposition.* South Hadley, MA: Bergin & Garvey.

Glasgow, Douglas G. 1980. *The Black Underclass.* San Francisco: Jossey-Bass.

Glasgow, Douglas G. 1987. "The Black Underclass in Perspective." Pp. 129–144 in *The State of Black America 1987.* New York: National Urban League.

Glenn, Evelyn Nakano, and Roslyn L. Feldberg. 1977. "Degraded and Deskilled: The Proletarianization of Clerical Work." *Social Problems* 25:52–64.

Goffman, Erving. 1959. *The Presentation of Self in Everyday Life.* Garden City, NY: Doubleday.

Goffman, Erving. 1967. *Interaction Ritual.* Garden City, NY: Anchor Books, Doubleday.

Gold, David A., Clarence Y. H. Lo, and Erik Olin Wright. 1975. "Recent Developments in the Marxist Theories of the Capitalist State." *Monthly Review* 27(Oct.):29–43 and 27(Nov.):36–51.

Gold, M. 1966. "Undetected Delinquent Behavior." *Journal of Research on Crime & Delinquency* 3:27–46.

Goldberg, Steven. 1973. *The Inevitability of Patriarchy.* New York: Morrow.

Goldhamer, Herbert. 1968. "Social Mobility." *International Encyclopedia of the Social Sciences* 14:429–38.

Goldman, Robert, and Ann Tickameyer. 1984. "Status Attainment and the Commodity Form: Stratification in Historical Perspective." *American Sociological Review* 49:196–209.

Goldthorpe, John H. 1964. "Social Stratification in Industrial Society." Pp. 97–122 in *Development of Industrial Society,* edited by P. Halmos under the auspices of *The Sociological Review,* Monograph No. 8. Reprinted on pp. 452–65 in *Structured Social Inequality,* edited by C. S. Heller. New York: Macmillan, 1969.

Goldthorpe, John H. 1985, "On Economic Development and Social Mobility." *British Journal of Sociology* 36:549–73.

Good, David H., and Maureen A. Pirog-Good. 1987. "A Simultaneous Probit Model of Crime and Employment for Black and White Teenage Males." *Review of Black Political Economy* 16:109–27.

Goode, William J. 1971. "Force and Violence in the Family." *Journal of Marriage and the Family* 33:624–636.

Goodwin, Leonard. 1971. *A Study of the Work Orientations of Welfare Recipients Participating in the Work Incentive Program.* Washington, D.C.: The Brookings Institution.

Goodwin, Leonard. 1983. *Causes and Cures of Welfare: New Evidence on the Social Psychology of the Poor.* Lexington, MA: Lexington Books.

Gordon, David M. 1972. *Theories of Poverty and Underemployment.* Lexington, MA: D. C. Heath.

Gordon, David M. 1973. "Class and the Economics of Crime." Warner Modular Publication Reprint No. 350. Andover, MA: Warner Modular Publications.

Gordon, Milton M. 1949. "Social Class in American Sociology." *American Journal of Sociology* 55:262–68.

Gordon, Milton M. 1963. *Social Class in American Sociology.* New York: McGraw-Hill.

Gossett, Thomas F. 1963. *Race: The History of an Idea in America.* Dallas, TX: Southern Methodist University Press.

Gove, W. R. and M. R. Geerken, 1977. "The Effect of Children and Employment on the Mental Health of Married Men and Women." *Social Forces* 56:66–76.

Grabb, Edward G. 1984. *Social Inequality: Classical and Contemporary Theorists.* Toronto: Holt, Rinehart and Winston of Canada.

Gramlich, Edward M. 1986. "The Main Themes." Pp. 341–47 in *Fighting Poverty: What Works and What Doesn't,* edited by S. H. Danziger and D. H. Weinberg. Cambridge, MA: Harvard University Press.

Gramsci, Antonio. 1971. *Selections from the Prison Notebooks.* London: Lawrence and Wishart.

Grandjean, Burke D. 1975. "An Economic Analysis of

the Davis-Moore Theory of Stratification." *Social Forces* 53:543–52.

Green, Edward. 1970. "Race, Social Status, and Criminal Arrest." *American Sociological Review* 35:476–90.

Green, James R. 1980. *The World of the Worker: Labor in Twentieth-Century America.* New York: Hill and Wang.

Greenberg J. 1978. "Allocator-recipient Similarity and the Equitable Division of Rewards." *Social Psychology* 41:337–41.

Greenley, James R., and David Mechanic. 1974. "Patterns of Seeking Care for Psychological Problems." Research and Analytic Report No. 16-74. Madison, WI: Center for Medical Sociology and Health Services Research, University of Wisconsin.

Greenlick, M. R. 1984. "An Investigation of Selection Bias in an HMO Enrollment Experiment." *The Group Health Journal* 5:22–30.

Greenstein, Robert. 1985. "Losing Faith in 'Losing Ground.'" *The New Republic* March 25:12–17.

Grenzke, Janet M. 1989. "PACs and the Congressional Supermarket: The Currency Is Complex." *American Journal of Political Science* 33:1–24.

Griffin, Larry J., Michael E. Wallace, and Beth A. Rubin. 1986. "Capitalist Resistance to the Organization of Labor Before the New Deal: Why? How? Success?" *American Sociological Review* 51:147–67.

Grob, Gerald N. 1971. "Knights of Labor versus American Federation of Labor." Pp. 30–43 in *The American Labor Movement,* edited by D. Brody. New York: Harper & Row.

Gross, Jane. March 27, 1989. "What Medical Care the Poor Can Have: Lists are Drawn Up." *The New York Times,* pp. A1, A12.

Grusky, David B., and Robert M. Hauser. 1984. "Comparative Social Mobility Revisited: Models of Convergence and Divergence in 16 Countries." *American Sociological Review* 49:19–38.

Gurin, Gerald, J. Veroff, and S. Feld. 1960. *Americans View their Mental Health.* New York: Basic Books.

Gurney, Joan Neff, and Kathleen J. Tierney. 1982. "Relative Deprivation and Social Movements: A Critical Look at Twenty Years of Theory and Research." *Sociological Quarterly* 23:33–47.

Gusfield Joseph R. 1962. "Mass Society and Extremist Politics." *American Sociological Review* 27:19–30.

Hacker, Helen. 1951. "Women as a Minority Group." *Social Forces* 30:60–69.

Hadden, Jeffrey K., and Charles E. Swann. 1981. *Prime Time Preachers: The Rising Power of Televangelism.* Reading, MA: Addison-Wesley.

Hagan, John, and Celesta Albonetti. 1982. "Race, Class, and the Perception of Criminal Injustice in America." *American Journal of Sociology* 88:329–55.

Hagan, John, and Alberto Palloni. 1986. " 'Club Fed' and the Sentencing of White-Collar Offenders Before and After Watergate." *Criminology* 24:603–22.

Hagan, John, A. R. Gillis, and John Simpson. 1985. "The Class Structure of Gender and Delinquency: Toward a Power-Control Theory of Common Delinquent Behavior." *American Journal of Sociology* 90:1151–78.

Hagan, John, John Simpson, and A. R. Gillis. 1987. "Class in the Household: A Power-Control Theory of Gender and Delinquency." *American Journal of Sociology* 92:788–816.

Hagen, Everett E. 1962. *On the Theory of Social Change.* Homewood, IL: Dorsey.

Hall, Edwin L., and Albert A. Simkus. 1975. "Inequality in the Types of Sentences Received by Native Americans and Whites." *Criminology* 13:199–222.

Haller, Archibald O., and Alejandro Portes. 1973. "Status Attainment Processes." *Sociology of Education* 46:51–91.

Hamilton, Richard F. 1966. "The Marginal Middle Class: A Reconsideration." *American Sociological Review* 31:192–193.

Hampton, Robert L. 1987. *Violence in the Black Family: Correlates and Consequences.* Lexington, MA: Lexington Books.

Haney, C. Allen, Kent S. Miller, and Robert Michielutte. 1969. "The Interaction of Petitioner and Deviant Social Characteristics in the Adjudication of Incompetency." *Sociometry* 32:182–93.

Hannum, Alberta Pierson. 1969. *Look Back with Love: A Recollection of the Blue Ridge.* New York: Vanguard.

Hansen, Karen V., and Ilene J. Philipson, eds. 1990. *Women, Class, and Feminist Imagination: A Socialist-Feminist Reader.* Philadelphia: Temple University Press.

"The Hard Choices Facing Low-Income American Families." June 1987. *Consumer Reports,* pp. 375–378.

Haring, Marilyn H., William A. Stock, and Morris A. Okun. 1984. "A Research Synthesis of Gender and Social Class as Correlates of Subjective Well-Being." *Human Relations* 37:645–57.

Harkey, John, David L. Miles, and William A. Rushing. 1976. "The Relation Between Social Class and Functional Status: A New Look at the Drift Hypothesis." *Journal of Health and Social Behavior* 17:194–204.

Harris Survey. August 21, 1967, *Newseek,* p. 19.

Harris, Olivia. 1980. "The Power of Signs: Gender, Culture and the Wild in the Bolivian Andes." Pp. 70–94 in *Nature, Culture and Gender,* edited by C. MacCormack and M. Strathem. Cambridge: Cambridge University Press.

Harrison, Bennett, Chris Tily, and Barry Bluestone. 1986. "Rising Inequality." In *The Changing American Economy,* edited by David Obey and Paul Sarbanes. New York: Blackwell.

Hart, C. W. M., and Arnold R. Pilling. 1966. *The Tiwi of North Australia.* New York: Holt, Rinehart & Winston.

Hartley, W. B. 1969. *Estimation of the Incidence of Poverty in the United States, 1870-1914.* Ph.D. dissertation, University of Wisconsin, Madison.

Hartmann, Heidi, I. 1976/1990. "Capitalism, Patriarchy, and Job Segregation by Sex." *Signs: A Journal of Women in Culture and Society* 1:137–169. Reprinted in *Women, Class, and the Feminist Imagination: A Socialist-Feminist Reader,* edited by K. V. Hansen and I. J. Philipson. Philadelphia: Temple University Press.

Hartmann, Heidi. 1981. "The Unhappy Marriage of Marxism and Feminism." Pp. 15–29 in *Women and Revolution,* edited by L. Sargent. Boston: South End Press.

Hartmann, Heidi I. 1987. "Internal Labor Markets and Gender: A Case Study of Promotion." Pp. 59–92 in *Gender in the Workplace,* edited by C. Brown and J. A. Pechman. Washington, D.C.: Brookings Institution.

Harvey, D. G., and G. T. Slatin. 1975. "The Relationship as Hypothesis." *Social Forces* 54:140–59.

Haug, Marie. 1972. "Social-Class Measurement: A Methodological Critique," Pp. 429–451 in *Issues in Social Inequality,* edited by Gerald W. Thielbar and Saul D. Feldman. Boston: Little, Brown.

Hauser, Robert M., and David B. Grusky. 1988. "Cross-National Variation in Occupational Distribution, Relative Mobility Chances, and Intergenerational Shifts in Occupational Distribu-

tions." *American Sociological Review* 53:723–41.

Haveman, Robert H. 1977. "Poverty Income Distribution and Social Policy: The Last Decade and the Next." *Public Policy* 25:3–24.

Haveman, Robert H. 1987. *Poverty Policy and Poverty Research: The Great Society and the Social Sciences.* Madison, WI: University of Wisconsin Press.

Hawley, Amos. 1963. "Community Power and Urban Renewal Success." *American Journal of Sociology* 68:422–431.

Hazelrigg, Lawrence E. 1972. "Class, Property, and Authority: Dahrendorf's Critique of Marx's Theory of Class." *Social Forces* 50:473–87.

Hazelrigg, Lawrence E. 1974. "Cross-National Comparisons of Father-to-Son Occupational Mobility." Pp. 469–93 in *Social Stratification: A Reader,* edited by J. Lopreato and L. S. Lewis. New York: Harper & Row.

Hazelrigg, Lawrence E., and Maurice A. Garnier. 1976. "Occupational Mobility in Industrial Societies: A Comparative Analysis of Differential Access to Occupational Ranks in Seventeen Countries." *American Sociologic Review* 41:498–511.

Hehir, J. Bryan 1981. "The Bishops Speak on El Salvador." *Commonweal* April 10:199,223.

Heller, Celia S., ed. 1969. *Structured Social Inequality.* New York: Macmillan.

Henderson, A. M., and Talcott Parsons, trans. 1947. *Max Weber: The Theory of Social and Economic Organization.* New York: The Free Press.

Henley, Nancy, and Jo Freeman. 1984. "The Sexual Politics of Interpersonal Behavior." Pp. 465–77 in *Women: A Feminist Perspective,* edited by J. Freeman. Palo Alto, CA: Mayfield.

Hertzler, J. O. 1952. "Some Tendencies Toward a Closed Class System in the United States." *Social Forces* 30:313–23.

Hess, Robert D., and Judith V. Torney. 1968. *The Development of the Political Attitudes in Children.* New York: Anchor Books.

Hevesi, Dennis. February 15, 1989. "Polls Show Discontent with Health Care." *The New York Times,* p. A16.

Hibbard, Judith H., and Clyde R. Pope. 1987. "Employment Characteristics and Health Status Among Men and Women." *Women & Health* 12:85–102.

Higley, John, and Given Moore. 1981. "Elite Integration in the United States and Australia." *American Political Science Review* 75:581–97.

Hill, Christopher. 1964. *Puritanism and Revolution.* New York: Schocken Books.

Hindelang, Michael J., Travis Hirschi, and Joseph G. Weis. 1979. "Correlates of Delinquency: The Illusion of Discrepancy between Self-Report and Official Measures." *American Sociological Review* 44:995–1014.

Hinkle, Jr., Roscoe C., and Gisela J. Hinkle. 1965. *The Development of Modern Sociology.* New York: Random House.

Hirschman, Charles, and Ellen Kraly. 1988. "Immigrants, Minorities, and Earnings in the United States in 1950." *Ethnic and Racial Studies* 11:332–65.

Hirschman, Charles, and Morrison G. Wong. 1984. "Socioeconomic Gains of Asian Americans, Blacks, and Hispanics: 1960–1976." *American Journal of Sociology* 90:584–606.

Hoch, Charles. 1987. "A Brief History of the Homeless Problem in the United States." Pp. 16–32 in *The Homeless in Contemporary Society,* edited by R. D. Bingham, R. E. Green, and S. B. White. Newbury Park, CA: Sage.

Hochschild, Jennifer. 1981. *What's Fair: American Beliefs about Distributive Justice.* Cambridge, MA: Harvard University Press.

Hodge, Robert W., and Donald J. Treiman. 1968. "Class Identification in the United States." *American Journal of Sociology* 73:535–542.

Hodge, Robert W., and Paul M. Siegel. 1968. "The Measurement of Social Class." Pp. 316–326 in *International Encyclopedia of the Social Sciences* 15:316–325.

Hodge, Robert W., Paul Siegel, and Peter H. Rossi. 1964. "Occupational Prestige in the United States, 1925–1963." *American Journal of Sociology* 70:286–302.

Hodson, Randy, and Robert L. Kaufman. 1982. "Economic Dualism: A Critical Review." *American Sociological Review* 47:727–39.

Hodson, Randy. 1984. "Companies, Industries, and the Measurement of Economic Segmentation." *American Sociological Review* 49:335–48.

Hofstadter, Richard. 1944. *Social Darwinism in American Thought.* Boston: Beacon Press.

Hole, Judith, and Ellen Levine. 1975. "The First Feminists." Pp. 436–47 in *Women: A Feminist Perspective,* edited by J. Freeman. Palo Alto, CA: Mayfield.

Hollingshead, August B., and Fredrick Redlich. 1958. *Social Class and Mental Illness.* New York: John Wiley & Sons.

Hollingsworth, J. Rogers. 1981. "Inequality in Levels of Health in England and Wales. 1891–1971." *Journal of Health and Social Behavior* 22:268–83.

Hooks, Bell. 1981. *Ain't I a Woman: Black Women and Feminism.* Boston: South End Press.

Hope, Keith. 1982. "Vertical and Nonvertical Class Mobility in Three Countries." *American Sociological Review* 47:99–113.

Hope, Marjorie, and James Young. 1986. *The Faces of Homelessness.* Lexington, MA; Lexington Books.

Horan, Patrick M. 1978. "Is Status Attainment Research Atheoretical?" *American Sociological Review* 43:534–41.

Horrigan, M. W., and S. E. Haugen. 1988. "The Declining Middle-Class Thesis: A Sensitivity Analysis." *Monthly Labor Review* 111:3–13.

Hotaling, G. T., and D. B. Sugerman. 1984. "An Identification of Risk Factors." In *Domestic Violence Surveillance System Feasibility Study, Phase I Report.* Rockville, MD: Westat.

Hout, Michael. 1984. "Occupational Mobility of Black Men: 1962 to 1973." *American Sociological Review* 49:308–22.

Hout, Michael. 1986. "Opportunity and the Minority Middle Class: A Comparison of Blacks in the United States and Catholics in Northern Ireland." *American Sociological Review* 51:214–23.

Hout, Michael. 1988. "More Universalism, Less Structural Mobility: The American Occupational Structure in the 1980s." *American Journal of Sociology* 93:1358–1400.

Howell, Joseph T. 1973. *Hard Living on Clay Street.* Garden City, NY: Anchor Books.

Huaco, George A. 1963. "A Logical Analysis of the Davis-Moore Theory of Stratification." *American Sociological Review* 28:801–4.

Huber, Joan, and William H. Form. 1973. *Income and Ideology: An Analysis of the American Political Formula.* New York: The Free Press.

Huber, Joan. 1982. "Toward a Sociotechnological Theory of the Women's Movement." Pp. 24–38 in *Women and Work: Problems and Perspectives,* edited by R. Kahn-Hut, A. K. Daniels, and R. Colvard. New York: Oxford University Press.

Huber, Joan. 1988. "From Sugar and Spice to Professor." Pp. 92–101 in *Down to Earth Sociology: Introductory Readings,* edited by J. M. Henslin. New York: The Free Press.

Huber, Joan. 1989. "A Theory of Gender Stratification." Pp. 110–119 in *Feminist Frontiers II: Rethinking Sex, Gender, and Society,* edited by L. Richardson and V. Taylor. New York: Random House.

Humphrey, Ronald, and Howard Schuman. 1984. "The Portrayal of Blacks in Magazine Advertisements: 1950–1982." *Public Opinion Quarterly* 48: 551–63.

Hunter, Herbert M., and Sameer Y. Abraham, eds. 1987. *Race, Class, and the World System: The Sociology of Oliver C. Cox.* New York: Monthly Review Press.

Hurn, Christopher. 1987. "Theories of Schooling and Society: The Functional and Radical Paradigms." Pp. 322–333 in *Introducing Sociology,* edited by R. T. Schaefer and R. P. Lamm. New York: McGraw-Hill.

Inkeles, Alex, and David H. Smith. 1974. *Becoming Modern: Individual Change in Six Developing Countries.* Cambridge, MA: Harvard University Press.

Irwin, John. 1985. *The Jail: Managing the Underclass in American Society.* Berkeley, CA: University of California Press.

Jackman, Mary R., and Mary Scheuer Senter. 1983. "Different, Therefore Unequal: Beliefs about Trait Differences Between Groups of Unequal Status," Pp. 309–335 in *Research in Social Stratification and Mobility: A Research Annual,* edited by D. J. Treiman and R. V. Robinson. Greenwich, CT: JAI Press.

Jackman, Mary R., and Robert W. Jackman. 1983. *Class Awareness in the United States.* Berkeley, CA: University of California Press.

Jackman, Robert W. 1975. *Politics and Social Equality: A Comparative Analysis.* New York: John Wiley & Sons.

Jackson, Elton F., and Harry J. Crockett, Jr. 1964. "Occupational Mobility in the United States: A Point Estimate and Trend Comparison." *American Sociological Review* 29:5–15.

Jacobs, Jerry A. 1989. "Long-Term Trends in Occupational Segregation by Sex." *American Journal of Sociology* 95:160–73.

Jaffe, Natalie. Spring 1977. *Attitudes Toward Public Welfare Programs and Recipients in the United States: A Review of Public Opinion Surveys, 1935–1976.* Welfare Policy Project, The Institute of Policy Sciences and Public Affairs of Duke University. Durham, NC: The Ford Foundation.

James, Dorothy Buckton. 1972. *Poverty, Politics, and Change.* Englewood Cliffs, NJ: Prentice-Hall.

Jasso, Guillermina, and Peter Rossi. 1977. "Distributive Justice and Earned Income." *American Sociological Review* 42:639–51.

Jencks, Christopher, Marshall Smith, Henry Acland, Mary Jo Bane, David Cohen, Herbert Gintis, Barbara Heyns, and Stephen Michelson. 1972. *Inequality: A Reassessment of the Effect of Family and Schooling in America.* New York: Colophon Books.

Jenkins, J. Craig. 1983. "Resource Mobilization Theory and the Study of Social Movements." Pp. 527–53 in *Annual Review of Sociology,* edited by R. H. Turner and J. F. Short, Jr. Palo Alto, CA: Annual Reviews.

Jenkins, J. Craig, and Craig M. Eckert. 1986. "Channeling Black Insurgency: Elite Patronage and Professional Social Movement Organizations in the Development of the Black Movement." *American Sociological Review* 51:812–29.

Jenkins, J. Craig, and Charles Perrow. 1977. "Insurgency of the Powerless: Farm Worker Movements (1946–1972)." *American Sociological Review* 42:249–68.

Johnson, Harry A., ed. 1976. *Ethnic American Minorities.* New York: R. R. Bowker.

Joint Center for Political Studies. 1989. *Black Elected Officials: A National Roster.* Washington, D.C.: Joint Center for Political Studies Press.

Jones, F. Lancaster. 1969. "Social Mobility and Industrial Society: Theses Re-examined." *Sociological Quarterly* 10:292–305.

Jones, Jr., Woodrow, and K. Robert Keiser. 1987. "Issue Visibility and the Effects of PAC Money." *Social Science Quarterly* 68:170–76.

Juba, D. A., J. R. Lave, and J. Shaddy. 1980. "An Analysis of the Choice of Health Benefits Plans." *Inquiry* 17:62–71.

Judis, John B. January 21, 1990. "Pulling U.S. Strings: Japanese Money Buys Influence." *Akron Beacon Journal,* pp. E1, E4.

Judson, C. J., J. J. Pandell, J. B. Owens, J. L. McIntosh, and D. L. Matchullat. 1969. "A Study of the

California Penalty Jury in First Degree Murder Cases." *Stanford Law Review* 21:1297–1431.

Kadushin, Charles. 1969. *Why People Go to Psychiatrists.* New York: Lieber-Atherton.

Kaelble, Harmut, 1981. *Historical Research on Social Mobility: Western Europe and the USA in the Nineteenth and Twentieth Centuries.* New York: Columbia University Press.

Kahl, Joseph A. 1957. *The American Class Structure.* New York: Holt, Rinehart & Winston.

Kaiser, S. 1985. *The Social Psychology of Clothing and Personal Adornment.* New York: Macmillan.

Kalleberg, Arne L., and Larry Griffin. 1980. "Class, Occupation, and Inequality in Job Rewards." *American Journal of Sociology* 85:731–68.

Kamerman, Sheila B. 1980. *Parenting in an Unresponsive Society: Managing Work and Family Life.* New York: The Free Press.

Kandal, Terry R. 1988. *The Woman Question in Classical Sociological Theory.* Miami: Florida International University Press.

Kane, Joseph Nathan. 1974. *Facts About the Presidents,* ed. 3. New York: H. W. Wilson.

Kanter, Rosabeth Moss. 1977a. *Men and Women of the Corporation.* New York: Basic Books.

Kanter, Rosabeth Moss. 1977b. "Some Effects of Proportions on Group Life: Skewed Sex Ratios and Responses to Token Women." *American Journal of Sociology* 82:965–90.

Kaplan, H. Roy, and Curt Tausky. 1972. "Work and the Welfare Cadillac: The Function of and Commitment to Work Among the Hardcore Unemployed." *Social Problems* 19:469–83.

Kaplan, H. Roy, and Curt Tausky. 1974. "The Meaning of Work Among the Hard-Core Unemployed." *Pacific Sociological Review* 17:185–98.

Kasarda, John D. 1989. "Urban Industrial Transition and the Underclass." *Annals of the American Academy of Political and Social Science* 501: 26–47.

Katz, Michael B. 1986. *In the Shadow of the Poorhouse: A Social History of Welfare in America.* New York: Basic Books.

Kaufman, Bruce E. 1982. "The Determinants of Strikes in the United States, 1900–1977." *Industrial and Labor Relations Review* 35: 473–90.

Kaufman, Robert L., and Thomas N. Daymont. 1981. "Racial Discrimination and the Social Organization of Industries." *Social Science Research* 10:225–55.

Keller, Suzanne, 1969. "Beyond the Ruling Class-Strategic Elites." Pp. 520–524 in *Structured Social Inequality,* edited by C. S. Heller., New York: Macmillan.

Keller, Suzanne, 1987. "Social Differentiation and Social Stratification: The Special Case of Gender." Pp. 329–49 in *Structured Social Inequality,* edited by Celia S. Heller. New York: Macmillan.

Kemper, Theodore D. 1976. "Marxist and Functionalist Theories in the Study of Stratification: Common Elements that Lead to a Test." *Social Forces* 54:559–78.

Kenkel, William F. 1952. *An Experimental Analysis of Social Stratification in Columbus, Ohio.* Unpublished Ph.D. dissertation, Ohio State University, Columbus.

Kephart, William M. 1950. "Status After Death." *American Sociological Review* 15:635–643.

Kephart, William M. 1982. *Extraordinary Groups,* 2nd ed. New York: St. Martin's Press.

Kerbo, Harold R. 1983. *Social Stratification and Inequality: Class Conflict in the United States.* New York: McGraw-Hill.

Kerbo, Harold R., and L. Richard Della Fave. 1979. "The Empirical Side of the Power Elite Debate: An Assessment and Critique of Recent Research." *The Sociological Quarterly* 20:5–22.

Kerckhoff, Alan C., Richard T. Campbell, and Idee Winfield-Laird. 1985. "Social Mobility in Great Britain and the United States." *American Journal of Sociology* 91:281–301.

Kershaw, Terry. 1987. "The Emerging Paradigm in Black Studies." Paper presented at the National Council of Black Studies, April 5, Philadelphia.

Kessler Ronald C. 1982. "A Disaggregation of the Relationship Between Socioeconomic Status and Psychological Distress." *American Sociological Review* 47: 752–64.

Kessler, Ronald C., and Paul D. Cleary. 1980. "Social Class and Psychological Distress." *American Sociological Review* 45:463–78.

Kessler, Ronald C., and Jane D. McLeod. 1984. "Sex Differences in Vulnerability to Undesirable Life Events." *American Sociological Review* 49: 620–31.

Kessler, Ronald C., and James A. McRae, Jr 1981. "Trends in the Relationship Between Sex and Psychological Distress: 1957–1976." *American Sociological Review* 46:443–52.

Kessler, Ronald C., and James A. McRae, Jr. 1983.

"Trends in the Relationship Between Sex and Attempted Suicide." *Journal of Health and Social Behavior* 24:98–110.

Kessler-Harris, Alice. 1989. "Women, Work, and the Social Order." Pp. 191–203 in *Feminist Frontiers II: Rethinking Sex, Gender, and Society,* edited by L. Richardson and V. Taylor. New York: Random House.

Killian, Lewis M. 1984. "Organization, Rationality and Spontaneity in the Civil Rights Movement." *American Sociological Review* 49:770–83.

Killian, Lewis, and Charles Grigg. 1962. "Urbanism, Race, and Anomie." *American Journal of Sociology* 68:661–5.

King, Deborah K. 1988. "Multiple Jeopardy, Multiple Consciousness: The Context of a Black Feminist Ideology." *Signs* 14:42–72.

King, Martin Luther. 1958. *Stride Toward Freedom.* New York: Harper & Row.

Kleck, Gary. 1981. "Racial Discrimination in Criminal Sentencing: A Critical Evaluation of the Evidence with Additional Evidence on the Death Penalty." *American Sociological Review* 46:783–805.

Kleck, Gary. 1982. "On the Use of Self-Report Data to Determine the Class Distribution of Criminal and Delinquent Behavior." *American Sociological Review* 47:427–33.

Klein, Ethel. 1984. *Gender Politics.* Cambridge, MA: Harvard University Press.

Klerman, Gerald L., and Myrna M. Weissman. 1989. "Increasing Rates of Depression." *Journal of the American Medical Association* 261:2229–35.

Kluegel, James R., and Eliot R. Smith. 1986. *Beliefs About Inequality: Americans' Views of What Is and What Ought to Be.* New York: Aldine de Gruyter.

Knottnerus, J. David. 1987. "Status Attainment Research and Its Image of Society." *American Sociological Review* 52:113–21.

Koch, Donald W. 1969. "Income Distribution and Political Structure in Seventeenth Century Salem, Massachusetts." *Essex Institute Historical Collections* 105:54–63.

Kohn, Melvin L. 1969. *Class and Conformity.* Homewood, IL: Dorsey.

Kohn, Melvin L., and Carmi Schooler. 1982. "Job Conditions and Personality: A Longitudinal Assessment of Their Reciprocal Effects." *American Journal of Sociology* 87:1257–86.

Kohn, Melvin. 1976a. "The Interaction of Social Class and Other Factors in the Etiology of Schizophrenia." *American Journal of Psychiatry* 133:177–80.

Kohn, Melvin. 1976b. "Occupational Structure and Alienation." *American Journal of Sociology* 82:111–30.

Kolenda, Pauline. 1978. *Caste in Contemporary India.* Prospect Heights, IL: Waveland Press.

Kollock, Peter, Philip Blumstein, and Pepper Schwartz. 1985. "Sex and Power in Interaction: Conversational Privileges and Duties." *American Sociological Review* 50:34–46.

Korpi, Walter. 1974. "Conflict, Power, and Relative Deprivation." *American Political Science Review* 68:1569–1578.

Kosterlitz, Julie. December 6, 1986. "Reexamining Welfare." *National Journal,* pp. 2926–31.

Kosters, Marvin H. and Murray N. Ross. 1988. "A Shrinking Middle Class?" *The Public Interest* 90:3–27.

Kramer, Ronald C. 1984. "Corporate Criminality: The Development of an Idea." In *Corporations as Criminals,* edited by E. Hoshstedler. Beverly Hills, CA: Sage.

Krauze, Tadeusz, and Kazimierz M. Slomczynski. 1985. "How Far to Meritocracy? Empirical Tests of a Controversial Thesis." *Social Forces* 63:623–42.

Krisberg, Barry, Ira Schwartz, Gideon Fishman, Zvi Eisikovits, Edna Guttman, and Karen Joe. 1987. "The Incarceration of Minority Youth." *Crime & Delinquency* 33:173–205.

Kruttschnitt, Candace, and Donald E. Green. 1984. "The Sex-Sanctioning Issue: Is it History?" *American Sociological Review* 49:541–51.

Kumar, Awadhesh. 1982. "The Conditions of Social Mobility in Caste-System." *Indian Journal of Social Research* 23:120–25.

Kurian, George Thomas. 1984. *The New Book of World Rankings.* New York: Facts on File.

Kurz, Karin and Walter Muller. 1987. "Class Mobility in the Industrial World." Pp. 417–42 in *Annual Review of Sociology,* vol. 13, edited by W. R. Scott and J. F. Short, Jr. Palo Alto, CA: Annual Reviews.

Kuznets, Simon. 1963. "Quantitative Aspects of the Economic Growth of Nations, VIII: The Distribution of Income by Size." *Economic Development and Cultural Change* 11:1–80.

LaFree, Gary D. 1980. "The Effect of Sexual Stratification by Race on Official Reactions to Rape."

American Sociological Review 45:842–54.

Lamm, H., and E. Kayser. 1978. "The Allocation of Monetary Gain and Loss Following Dyadic Performance: The Weight Given to Effort and Ability Under Conditions of Low and High Intra-dyadic Attraction." *European Journal of Social Psychology* 8:275–78.

Lamm, H., and T. Schwinger. 1980. "Norms Concerning Distributive Justice: Are Needs Taken into Consideration in Allocation Decisions?" *Social Psychology Quarterly* 43:425–29.

Lannoy, Richard. 1975. *The Speaking Tree: A Study of Indian Culture and Society.* New York: Oxford University Press.

Lapham, Lewis H. 1988. *Money and Class in America.* New York: Weidenfeld & Nicolson.

Lapidus, Gail W. 1976. "Occupational Segregation and Public Policy: A Comparative Analysis of American and Soviet Patterns." In *Women and the Workplace,* edited by M. Blaxall and B. Reagan. Chicago: University of Chicago Press.

Laslett, John H. M. 1987. "The American Tradition of Labor Theory and Its Relevance to the Contemporary Working Class. Pp. 359–78 in *Theories of the Labor Movement,* edited by S. Larson and B. Nissen. Detroit: Wayne State University Press.

Lawrence, Robert Z. 1984. "Sectoral Shifts and the Size of the Middle Class." *The Brookings Review.* pp. 3–11.

Leacock, Eleanor. 1986. "Women, Power and Authority." Pp. 107–35 in *Visibility and Power: Essays on Women in Society and Development,* edited by L. Dube, E. Leacock, and S. Ardener. Delhi: Oxford University Press.

Leavitt, Gregory C. 1986. "Ideology and the Materialist Model of General Evolution: A Cross-Cultural Test of Subsystem Relationships." *Social Forces* 65:525–53.

Leavy, Marvin D. 1974. "Comment on Abrahamson's 'Functionalism and the Functional Theory of Stratification: An Empirical Assessment.' " *American Journal of Sociology* 80:724–7.

Lee, Rance P. L. 1976. "The Causal Priority Between Socioeconomic Status and Psychiatric Disorder: A Prospective Study." *The International Journal of Social Psychiatry* 22:1–8.

Leftwich, Richard H. 1977. "Personal Income and Marginal Productivity." Pp. 76–81 in *Problems in Political Economy: An Urban Perspective,* edited by D. M. Gordon. Lexington, MA: D.C. Heath.

Lemann, Nicholas. July 1986. "The Origins of the Un-

derclass," *The Atlantic Monthly,* pp. 54–68.

Lemon, James T., and Gary B. Nash. 1968. "The Distribution of Wealth in the Eighteenth Century America: A Century of Change in Chester County, Pennsylvania, 1693–1802." *Journal of Social History* 2:1–24.

Lengermann, Patricia Madoo, and Jill Niebrugge-Brantley. 1988. "Contemporary Feminist Theory." Pp. 282–325 in *Contemporary Sociological Theory,* by George Ritzer. New York: Knopf.

Lenski, Gerhard E. 1966. *Power and Privilege.* New York: McGraw-Hill.

Lenski, Gerhard. 1988. "Rethinking Macrosociological Theory." *American Sociological Review* 53:163–71.

Lenski, Gerhard, and Jean Lenski. 1982. *Human Societies: An Introduction to Macrosociology.* New York: McGraw-Hill.

Levine, Steven B. 1980. "The Rise of American Boarding Schools and the Development of a National Upper Class." *Social Problems* 28:63–94.

Levinger, George. 1966. "Marital Dissatisfaction among Divorce Applicants." *American Journal of Orthopsychiatry* 36:803–7.

Levinson, David. 1988. "Family Violence in Cross-Cultural Perspective." Pp. 435–55 in *Handbook of Family Violence,* edited by V. B. Van Hasselt, R. L. Morrison, A. S. Bellack, and M. Hersen. New York: Plenum Press.

Levitan, Sar A. 1985. *Programs in Aid of the Poor.* Baltimore: Johns Hopkins University Press.

Lewis, Helen, and Edward Knipe. 1978. "The Colonialism Model: The Appalachian Case." Pp. 9–31 in *Colonialism in Modern America,* edited by H. Lewis, L. Johnson, and D. Askins. Boone, NC: Appalachian Consortium Press.

Lewis, Helen. 1974. "Fatalism or the Coal Industry." P. 222 in *Appalachia: Its People, Heritage, and Problems,* edited by Frank S. Riddel. Dubuque, IA; Kendall/Hunt.

Lichter, Daniel T. 1988. "Racial Differences in Underemployment in American Cities." *American Journal of Sociology* 93:771–92.

Lieberson, Stanley, and Donna K. Carter. 1979. "Making It in America: Differences Between Eminent Blacks and White Ethnic Groups." *American Sociological Review* 44:347–66.

Liebow, Elliot. 1967. *Tally's Corner.* Boston: Little, Brown.

Light, Donald, Susanne Keller, and Craig Calhoun. 1989. *Sociology.* New York: Knopf.

Lindblom, Charles E. 1977. *Politics and Markets.* New York: Basic Books.

Lindert, Peter, and Jeffrey G. Williamson. 1976. "Three Centuries of American Inequality." Institute for Research on Poverty Discussion Paper No. 333-76. Madison, Wisconsin: University of Wisconsin-Madison.

Link, Bruce G., Bruce P. Dohrenwend, and Andrew E. Skodol. 1986. "Socio-Economic Status and Schizophrenia: Noisome Occupational Characteristics as a Risk Factor." *American Sociological Review* 242-58.

Link, Bruce. 1983. "Reward System of Psychotherapy: Implications for Inequities in Service Delivery." *Journal of Health and Social Behavior* 24:61-9.

Linton, R. 1936. *The Study of Man.* New York: Appleton-Century-Crofts.

Lipset, Seymour Martin. 1971. "Trade Unionism and the American Social Order." Pp. 7-29 in *The American Labor Movement,* edited by D. Brody. New York: Harper & Row.

Lipset, Seymour Martin, and Reinhard Bendix. 1959. *Social Mobility in Industrial Society.* Berkeley, CA: University of California Press.

Lipset, Seymour Martin, and Hans L. Zetterberg. 1959. "Social Mobility in Industrial Societies." Pp. 11-75 in *Social Mobility in Industrial Society,* edited by S. M. Lipset and R. Bendix. Berkeley, CA: University of California Press.

Lloyd, C. B., and B. T. Niemi. 1979. *The Economics of Sex Differentials.* New York: Columbia University Press.

Loftin, Colin, and Robert H. Hill. 1974. "Regional Subculture and Homicide: An Examination of the Gastil-Hackney Thesis." *American Sociological Review* 39:714-24.

Lopreato, Joseph. 1965. *Vilfredo Pareto: Selections from his Treatise.* New York: Thomas Y. Crowell.

Lopreato, Joseph, and Lawrence E. Hazelrigg. 1972. *Class, Conflict, and Mobility.* Corte Madera, CA: Chandler & Sharp.

Lopreato, Joseph, and Lionel S. Lewis. 1963. "An Analysis of Variables in the Functional Theory of Stratification." *Sociological Quarterly* 4:301-10.

Lopreato, Joseph, and Lionel S. Lewis (eds.). 1974. *Social Stratification: A Reader.* New York: Harper & Row.

Lorence, Jon. 1987. "A Test of 'Gender' and 'Job' Models of Sex Differences in Job Involvement." *Social Forces* 66:121-42.

Loring, Marti, and Brian Powell. 1988. "Gender, Race, and DSM-III: A Study of the Objectivity of Psychiatric Behavior." *Journal of Health and Social Behavior.* 29:1-22.

Lorion, Raymond P. 1977. "Mental Health and the Disadvantaged." *Social Policy* 8:2-4.

Lowe, Marian and Ruth Hubbard, eds. 1983. *Women's Nature: Rationalizations of Inequality.* New York: Pergamon.

Luft, H. S. 1983. "Health Maintenance Organizations." Pp. 318-51 in *Handbook of Health, Health Care, and the Health Professions,* edited by D. Mechanic. New York: The Free Press.

Lurie, Alison. 1987. "Fashion and Status." Pp. 124-30 in *The Social World,* 3rd ed., edited by Ian Robertson. New York: Worth Publishers.

Lurie, Nancy Oestreich. 1982. "The American Indian: Historical Background." Pp. 131-44 in *Majority & Minority: The Dynamics of Race and Ethnicity in American Life,* 3rd ed., edited by N. R. Yetman and C. H. Steele. Boston: Allyn & Bacon.

Lynd, Robert S., and Helen M. Lynd. 1929. *Middletown: A Study in American Culture.* New York: Harcourt Brace.

Lynn, Laurence E., Jr. 1977. "A Decade of Policy Developments in the Income-Maintenance System." Pp. 55-117 in *A Decade of Federal Antipoverty Programs,* edited by R. H. Haveman. New York: Academic Press.

Lystad, M. H. 1972. "Social Alienation: A Review of Current Literature." *Sociological Quarterly* 13:90-113.

Lystad, M. H. 1975. "Violence at Home: A Review of the Literature." *American Journal of Orthopsychiatry* 45:328-45.

MacCormack, Carol, and Marilyn Strathern, eds. 1980. *Nature, Culture and Gender.* Cambridge: Cambridge University Press.

MacCormack, Carol P. 1980. "Nature, Culture and Gender: A Critique." Pp. 1-24 in *Nature, Culture and Gender,* edited by C. MacCormack and M. Strathern. Cambridge: Cambridge University Press.

MacLeod, Jay. 1987. *Ain't No Makin' It: Leveled Aspirations in a Low-Income Neighborhood.* Boulder, CO: Westview.

Main, Jackson T. 1976. "The Distribution of Property in Colonial Connecticut." Pp. 54-104 in *The Human Dimensions of Nation Making,* edited by Martin James Kirby. Madison, Wisconsin: The State Historical Society.

Manderscheid, Ronald W., and Sally A. Barrett, eds.

1987. *Mental Health, United States, 1987.* Washington, D.C.: U.S. Government Printing Office.

Manley, John F. 1983. "Neo-Pluralism: A Class Analysis of Pluralism I and Pluralism II." *American Political Science Review* 77:368–83.

Marden, Charles F., and Gladys Meyer. 1973. *Minorities in American Society.* New York: D. Van Nostrand.

Mare, Robert D. 1982. "Socioeconomic Effects on Child Mortality in the United States." *American Journal of Public Health* 72:539–47.

Mare, Robert D., and Meei-Shenn Tzeng. 1989. "Fathers' Ages and the Social Stratification of Sons." *American Journal of Sociology* 95:108–31.

Marger, Martin N. 1985. *Race and Ethnic Relations: American and Global Perspectives.* Belmont, CA: Wadsworth.

Margolin, Gayla, Linda Gorin Sibner, and Lisa Gleberman. 1988. "Wife Battering." Pp. 89–117 in *Handbook of Family Violence,* edited by V. B. Van Hasselt, R. L. Morrison, A. S. Bellack, and M. Hersen. New York: Plenum Press.

Markham, William T., and Joseph H. Pleck. 1986. "Sex and Willingness to Move for Occupational Advancement: Some National Results." *The Sociological Quarterly* 27:121–43.

Markham, William T., Patrick O. Macken, Charles M. Bonjean, and Judy Corder. 1983. "A Note on Sex, Geographic Mobility, and Career Advancement." *Social Forces* 61:1138–46.

Marshall, Ray, and Beth Paulin. 1987. "Employment and Earnings of Women: Historical Perspective." Pp. 1–36 in *Working Women: Past, Present, Future,* edited by K. S. Koziara, M. H. Moskow, and L. D. Tanner. Washington, D.C.: Bureau of National Affairs.

Martin, Roderick. 1971. "The Concept of Power: A Critical Defense." *British Journal of Sociology* 22:240–257.

Martyna, W. 1978. "What Does 'he' Mean? Use of the Generic Masculine." *Journal of Communication* 28:131–38.

Marx, Karl. 1967. *Capital,* vol. 1. New York: International Publishers.

Marx, Karl, and Federick Engels. 1969. *Selected Works,* vols. 1 and 2. Moscow: Progress Publishers.

Matras, Judah. 1975. *Social Inequality, Stratification, and Mobility.* Englewood Cliffs, NJ: Prentice-Hall.

Matras, Judah. 1980. "Comparative Social Mobility."

Pp. 401–31 in *Annual Review of Sociology,* vol. 6, edited by A. Inkeles, N. J. Smelser, and R. H. Turner. Palo Alto, CA: Annual Reviews.

Matthaei, Julie A. 1982. *An Economic History of Women in America.* New York: Schocken Books.

Matthews, Donald R. 1954. "United States Senators and the Class Structure." *Public Opinion Quarterly* 18:5–22. Reprinted on pp. 331–342 in *Social Stratification: A Reader,* edited by J. Lopreato and L. S. Lewis. New York: Harper & Row.

Mayer, Kurt B. 1972. "The Changing Shape of the American Class Structure." Pp. 62–69 in *Status Communities in Modern Society,* edited by Holger R. Stub. Hinsdale, IL: Dryden.

Mayer, Kurt B., and Walter Buckley. 1970. *Class & Society.* New York: Random House.

McAdam, Doug. 1982. *Political Process and the Development of Black Insurgency, 1930–1970.* Chicago: University of Chicago Press.

McAdam, Doug. 1983. "Tactical Innovation and the Pace of Insurgency." *American Sociological Review* 48:735–54.

McCarthy, John D., and Mayer N. Zald. 1973. *The Trend of Social Movements in America: Professionalization and Resource Mobilization.* Morristown, NJ: General Learning Press.

McCarthy, John D. and Mayer N. Zald. 1977. "Resource Mobilization and Social Movements: A Partial Theory." *American Journal of Sociology* 82:1212–14.

McClelland, David C. 1961. *The Achieving Society.* New York: The Free Press.

McClendon, McKee J. 1976. "The Occupational Status Attainment Processes of Males and Females." *American Sociological Review* 41:52–64.

McFarland, Andrew S. 1987. "Interest Groups and Theories of Power in America." *British Journal of Political Science* 17:129–47.

McFate, Katherine. 1985. "Defining the Underclass: A Contemporary Sociological Dilemma." *The Sociological Quarterly* 26:35–38.

McRoberts, Hugh A., and Kevin Selbee. 1981. "Trends in Occupational Mobility in Canada and the United States: A Comparison." *American Sociological Review* 46:406–21.

Mead, Margaret. 1963. *Sex and Temperament in Three Primitive Societies.* New York: William Morrow.

Meiksins, Peter F. 1988. "A Critique of Wright's Theory of Contradictory Class Locations," *Critical Sociology* 15:73–82.

Meisel, James H., ed. 1965. *Pareto & Mosca.* Englewood Cliffs, NJ: Prentice-Hall.

Memmi, Albert. 1965. *The Colonizer and the Colonized.* New York: Orion.

Merton, Robert K. 1957. *Social Theory and Social Structure.* Glencoe, IL: The Free Press.

Messner, Steven F. 1980. "Income Inequality and Murder Rates: Some Cross-National Findings." *Comparative Social Research* 3:185–98.

Messner, Steven F. 1989. "Economic Discrimination and Societal Homicide Rates: Further Evidence on the Cost of Inequality." *American Sociological Review* 54:597–611.

Meyers, Marcia Clark. 1979. "Presbyterian Home Missions in Appalachia, A Feminine Enterprise." M. Div. Thesis, Princeton Theological Seminary.

Michalowski, Raymond J. 1985. *Order, Law, and Crime.* New York: Random House.

Michels, Robert. 1915/1949. *Political Parties.* Glencoe, IL: The Free Press.

Milbrath, Lester. 1965. *Political Participation.* Skokie, IL: Rand McNally.

Miliband, Ralph. 1977. *Marxism and Politics.* New York: Oxford University Press.

Miller, S. M. 1956. "The Concept and Measurement of Mobility." *Transactions of the Third World Congress of Sociology* 3:144–54. Reprinted on pp. 21–31 in *Social Mobility,* edited by A. P. M. Coxon and C. L. Jones. Baltimore: Penguin Books.

Miller, S. M. 1963. *Max Weber: Selections from His Work.* New York: Thomas Y. Crowell.

Miller, S. M. 1975. "Comparative Social Mobility." Reprinted in part on pp. 79–112 in *Social Mobility,* edited by A. P. M. Coxon and C. L. Jones. Baltimore: Penguin Books.

Miller, S. M., and Pamela Roby. 1970. *The Future of Inequality.* New York: Basic Books.

Miller, William Lee. 1977. *Welfare and Values in America: A Review of Attitudes Toward Welfare and Welfare Policies in Light of American History and Culture.* Durham, NC: Welfare Policy Project, Institute of Policy Sciences and Public Affairs of Duke University, The Ford Foundation.

Mills, C. Wright. 1951. *White Collar.* New York: Oxford University Press.

Mills, C. Wright. 1956. *The Power Elite.* New York: Oxford University Press.

Mills, C. Wright. 1959. *The Sociological Imagination.* New York: Oxford University Press.

Mills, C. Wright. 1962. *The Marxists.* New York: Dell.

Milner, Jr., Murray. 1987. "Theories of Inequality: An Overview and a Strategy for Synthesis." *Social Forces* 65:1053–84.

Mincer, Jacob, and Solomon Polachek. 1974. "Family Investments in Human Capital: Earnings of Women." *Journal of Political Economy* 82:76–110.

Miner, John B. 1980. *Theories of Organizational Behavior.* Hinsdale, IL: The Dryden Press.

Mintz, Beth. 1975. "The President's Cabinet, 1897–1972: A Contribution to the Power Structure Debate." *Insurgent Sociologist* 5:131–48.

Mirer, Thad W. 1974. "Aspects of the Variability of Family Income." In *Five Thousand American Families: Patterns of Economic Progress,* vol. 2, edited by J. N. Morgan, et al. Ann Arbor, MI: Institute for Social Research.

Mirowsky, John, and Catherine E. Ross. 1983. "Paranoia and the Structure of Powerlessness." *American Sociological Review* 48:228–39.

Mirowsky, John, and Catherine E. Ross. 1986. "Social Patterns of Distress." Pp. 23–45 in *Annual Review of Sociology,* vol. 12, edited by R. H. Turner and J. F. Short, Jr. Palo Alto, CA: Annual Reviews.

Mitzman, Arthur. 1971. *The Iron Cage: An Historical Interpretation of Max Weber.* New York: Grosset & Dunlap.

Mizruchi, Ephraim. 1964. *Success and Opportunity.* New York: The Free Press.

Montgomery, David. 1983. "The Past and Future of Workers' Control." Pp. 389–405 in *Workers' Struggles, Past and Present: A 'Radical America' Reader,* edited by James Green. Philadelphia: Temple University Press.

Moon, Marilyn, and Eugene Smolensky. 1977. "Income, Economic Status, and Policy Toward the Aged." In *Income Support for the Aged.* Cambridge, MA: Ballinger.

Moore, Gwen. 1979. "The Structure of a National Elite Network." *American Sociological Review* 44:673–92.

Moore, Wilbert E. 1970. "But Some are More Equal than Others." Pp. 143–8 in *The Logic of Social Hierarchies,* edited by E. O. Laumann, P. M. Siegel, and R. W. Hodge. Skokie, IL: Markham.

Morris, Aldon D. 1984. *The Origins of the Civil Rights Movement: Black Communities Organizing for Change.* New York: The Free Press.

Morris, Michael, and John B. Williamson. 1986. *Poverty and Public Policy: An Analysis of Federal Intervention Efforts.* New York: Greenwood Press.

Mosca, Gaetano. 1939. *The Ruling Class.* New York: McGraw-Hill.

Moss, Philip I. 1988. "Employment Gains by Minorities, Women in Large City Government, 1976–83." *Monthly Labor Review* 111:18–24.

Moynihan, Daniel Patrick. 1986. *Family and Nation.* New York: Harcourt Brace Jovanovich.

Mikhopadhyay, Carol C., and Patricia Higgins. 1988. "Anthropological Studies of Women's Status Revisited: 1977–1987." Pp. 461–95 in *Annual Review of Anthropology,* vol. 17, edited by B. J. Siegel, A. R. Beals, and S. A. Tyler. Palo Alto, CA: Annual Reviews.

Muller, Edward. 1988. "Democracy, Economic Development, and Income Inequality." *American Sociological Review* 53:50–68.

Mullins, Elizabeth I., and Paul Sites. 1984. "The Origins of Contemporary Eminent Black Americans: A Three-Generation Analysis of Social Origins." *American Sociological Review* 49:672–85.

Mundinger, Mary O'Neil. 1985. "Health Service Funding Cuts and the Declining Health of the Poor." *The New England Journal of Medicine* 313:44–47.

Murray, Charles A. Summer. 1982. "The Two Wars Against Poverty: Economic Growth and the Great Society." *The Public Interest,* pp. 3–16.

Murray, Charles. 1984. *Losing Ground: American Social Policy 1950–1980.* New York: Basic Books.

Murray, Charles. 1985. "Have the Poor Been 'Losing Ground'?" *Political Science Quarterly* 100: 427–445.

Murray, Charles. Summer 1986. "No, Welfare Isn't Really the Problem." *The Public Interest,* pp. 3–11.

Myrdal, Gunnar. 1944. *An American Dilemma: The Negro Problem and Modern Democracy.* New York: Harper and Brothers.

Nagel, S. S. 1969. *The Legal Process from a Behavioral Perspective.* Homewood, IL: Dorsey Press.

Nagel, S. S., and L. J. Weitzman. 1971. "Women as Litigants." *Hastings Law Journal* 23:171–198.

National Center for Health Statistics. 1988. *Vital Statistics of the United States, 1986,* Vol. II, Mortality, Part B. DHHS Pub. No. (PHS) 88-1114. Public Health Service. Washington, D.C.: U.S. Government Printing Office.

Neal, Arthur G., and H. Theodore Groat. 1974. "Social Class Correlates of Stability and Change in Levels of Alienation: A Longitudinal Study." *Sociological Quarterly* 15:548–58.

Newman, Donald J. 1958. "White-Collar Crime: An Overview and Analysis." *Law and Contemporary Problems* 23:735–53.

Newman, Katherine S. 1989. *Falling from Grace.* New York: Vintage.

Nicholson, Linda J. 1984. "Making Our Marx." *The Women's Review of Books* 1:8–9.

Nilson, Linda Burzotta. 1974. "The Occupational and Sex Related Components of Social Standing." Ph.D. Dissertation, Madison, WI: University of Wisconsin.

Nisbet, Robert A. 1966. *The Sociological Tradition.* New York: Basic Books.

Nisbet, Robert A. 1972. "The Triumph of Status: Tocqueville," Pp. 35–44 in *Status Communities in Modern Society,* edited by Holger R. Stub. Hinsdale, IL: Dryden.

Noel, Donald L. 1968. "A Theory of the Origin of Ethnic Stratification." *Social Problems* 16: 157–72. Reprinted on pp. 109–20 in *Majority and Minority: The Dynamics of Race and Ethnicity in American Life,* edited by N. R. Yetman. Boston: Allyn & Bacon, 1985.

Northrup, Herbert R. 1985. "The Coal Mines." Pp. 159–171 in *Blacks in Appalachia,* edited by W. H. Turner and E. J. Cabbell. Lexington, KY: University Press of Kentucky.

Nozick, Robert. 1977. "Distributive Justice." Pp. 120–28 in *Justice: Selected Readings,* edited by J. Feinberg and H. Gross. Encino, CA: Dickenson Publishing.

Nye, F. I. 1958. *Family Relationships and Delinquent Behavior.* New York: John Wiley & Sons.

O'Connor, James. 1973. *The Fiscal Crisis of the State.* New York: St. Martin's Press.

O'Hare, William P. 1987. *America's Welfare Population: Who Gets What?* Publication No. 13. Washington, D.C.: Population Reference Bureau.

O'Sullivan, Katherine, and William J. Wilson. 1988. "Race and Ethnicity." Pp. 223–242 in *Handbook of Sociology,* edited by N. J. Smelser. Newbury Park, CA: Sage.

Oberschall, Anthony. 1973. *Social Conflict and Social Movements.* Englewood Cliffs, NJ: Prentice-Hall.

Offe, Claus. 1973. "Class Rule and the Political System: On the Selectiveness of Political Institutions." Mimeographed paper. A Translation of Chapter 3 of *Strukturprobleme des Kapitaliistischen Staates.* Frankfurt: Suhrkamp.

Offe, Claus. 1975. "The Theory of the Capitalist State and the Problem of Policy Formation." In *Stress and Contradiction in Modern Capitalism,* edited by L. Lindberg et al. Lexington, MA: D. C. Heath.

Okun, Arthur. 1975. *Equality and Efficiency: The Big Tradeoff.* Washington, D.C.: Brookings Institution.

Ollman, Bertell. 1968. "Marx's Use of Class." *American Journal of Sociology* 73:573–80.

Ollman, Bertell. 1987. "How to Study Class Consciousness and Why We Should." *The Insurgent Sociologist* 14:57–96.

Olsen, Marvin E. 1970a. *Power of Societies.* New York: Macmillan.

Olsen, Marvin E. 1970b. "Social and Political Participation of Blacks." *American Sociological Review* 35:682–697.

Omi, Michael, and Howard Winant. 1986. *Racial Formation in the United States: From the 1960s to the 1980s.* New York: Routledge, Kegan and Paul.

Ornati, Oscar. 1966. *Poverty Amid Affluence.* New York: The Twentieth Century Fund.

Ortner, Sherry B. 1974. "Is Female to Male as Nature is to Culture?" Pp. 67–87 in *Woman, Culture & Society,* edited by M. Z. Rosaldo and L. Lamphere. Stanford, CA: Stanford University Press.

Ortner, Sherry B., and Harriet Whitehead, eds. 1981. *Sexual Meanings: The Cultural Construction of Gender and Sexuality.* Cambridge: Cambridge University Press.

Ossowski, Stanislaw. 1963. *Class Structure in the Social Consciousness.* New York: Free Press.

Osterman, Paul. 1975. "An Empirical Study of Labor Market Segmentation." *Industrial and Labor Relations Review* 28:508–23.

Osterman, Paul. 1982. "Affirmative Action and Opportunity: A Study of Female Quit Rates." *Review of Economics and Statistics* 64:604–12.

Ostrander, Susan. 1984. *Women of the Upper Class.* Philadelphia: Temple University Press.

Otto, Luther B. 1975. "Class and Status in Family Research." *Journal of Marriage and the Family* 37:315–32.

Otto, Luther B., and David L. Featherman. 1975. "Social Structural and Psychological Antecedents of Self-Estrangement and Powerlessness." *American*

Sociological Review 40:701–19.

Ozawa, Martha N. 1982. *Income Maintenance and Work Incentives: Toward a Synthesis.* New York: Praeger.

Page, Charles H. 1969. *Class and American Sociology: From Ward to Ross.* New York: Schocken Books.

Paradiso, Louis V., and Shauvan M. Wall. 1986. "Children's Perceptions of Male and Female Principals and Teachers." *Sex Roles* 14:1–7.

Parcel, Toby L., and Charles W. Mueller. 1983. *Ascriptions and Labor Markets: Race and Sex Differences in Earnings.* New York: Academic Press.

Parenti, Michael. 1970. "Power and Pluralism: A View from the Bottom." *The Journal of Politics* 32:501–530.

Pareto, Vilfredo (Andrew Longiorno and A. Livingston, trans.). 1935. *The Mind and Society: A Treatise on General Sociology,* vols. 3 and 4. New York: Dover Publications.

Pareto, Vilfredo (Ann S. Schwier, trans.). 1971. *Manual of Political Economy.* Fairfield, NJ: Augustus M. Kelley.

Parkin, Frank. 1971. *Class Inequality and Political Order.* New York: Praeger.

Parkin, Frank. 1979. *Marxism and Class Theory: A Bourgeois Critique.* London: Tavistock.

Parlee, Mary Brown. 1979. "Conversational Politics." *Psychology Today* 12:48–91.

Parsons, Talcott. 1964. "A Revised Analytical Approach to the Theory of Social Stratification." Reprinted on pp. 386–439 in *Essays in Sociological Theory,* rev. ed., by T. Parsons. New York: The Free Press, 1964.

Parsons, Talcott. 1964. *Essays in Sociological Theory,* rev. ed. New York: The Free Press.

Parsons, Talcott. 1968. "The Distribution of Power in American Society." Reprinted in *C. Wright Mills and the Power Elite,* edited by G. W. Domhoff and H. B. Ballard. Boston: Beacon Press.

Parsons, Talcott, and Robert F. Bales. 1955. *Family, Socialization and Interaction Process.* New York: The Free Press.

Paternoster, Raymond. 1984. "Prosecutorial Discretion in Requesting the Death Penalty: A Case of Victim-Based Racial Discrimination." *Law & Society Review* 18:437–78.

Pearce, Diana M. 1984. "Farewell to Alms: Women's

Fare Under Welfare." Pp. 502–515 in *Women: A Feminist Perspective*, edited by J. Freeman. Palo Alto, CA: Mayfield.

Pearlin, L. I., E. G. Menaghan, M. A. Lieberman, and J. T. Mullan. 1981. "The Stress Process." *Journal of Health and Social Behavior* 22:337–56.

Pearlin, Leonard I. 1975. "Status Inequality and Stress in Marriage." *American Sociological Review* 40:344–57.

Pease, John, William H. Form, and Joan Huber Rytina. 1970. "Ideological Currents in American Stratification Literature." *The American Sociologist* 5:127–37.

Perlman, Selig. 1923. *A History of Trade Unionism in the United States.* New York: Macmillan.

Perlman Selig. 1928. *A Theory of the Labor Movement.* New York: Macmillan.

Peroff, Kathleen. 1987. "Who Are the Homeless and How Many Are There?" Pp. 33–45 in *The Homeless in Contemporary Society,* edited by R. D. Bingham, R. E. Green, and S. B. White. Newbury Park, CA: Sage.

Perrone, Luca. 1983. "Positional Power and Propensity to Strike." *Politics and Society* 12:231–61.

Pessen, Edward. 1973. *Riches, Class and Power Before the Civil War.* Lexington MA: D. C. Heath.

Pettigrew, Thomas F. 1985. "New Black-White Patterns: How Best to Conceptualize Them?" Pp. 329–46 in *Annual Review of Sociology,* edited by R. H. Turner and J. F. Short, Jr. Palo Alto, CA: Annual Reviews.

Phelps, Linda. 1981. "Patriarchy and Capitalism." Pp. 161–73 in *Building Feminist Theory: Essays from Quest.* New York: Longman.

Philipson, Ilene J., and Karen V. Hansen. 1990. "Women, Class, and the Feminist Imagination: An Introduction." Pp. 3–40 in *Women, Class, and the Feminist Imagination: A Socialist-Feminist Reader,* edited by K. V. Hansen and I. J. Philipson. Philadelphia: Temple University Press.

Physician Task Force on Hunger in America. 1985. *Hunger in America: The Growing Epidemic.* Middletown, CT: Wesleyan University Press.

Piliavin, Irving, and Scott Briar. 1964. "Police Encounters with Juveniles." *American Journal of Sociology* 70:206–14.

Piori, Michael J. 1977. "The Dual Labor Market: Theory and Implications." Pp. 93–7 in *Problems in Political Economy: An Urban Perspective,* edited by D. M. Gordon. Lexington, MA: D. C. Heath.

Piven, Frances Fox, and Richard A. Cloward. 1971. *Regulating the Poor: The Functions of Public Welfare.* New York: Random House.

Piven, Frances Fox, and Richard A. Cloward. 1977. *Poor People's Movements: Why They Succeed, How They Fail.* New York: Pantheon.

Piven, Frances Fox, and Richard A. Cloward. 1982. *The New Class War.* New York: Pantheon.

Piven, Frances Fox, and Richard A. Cloward. 1987. "The Historical Sources of the Contemporary Relief Debate." Pp. 3–43 in *The Mean Season: The Attack on the Welfare State,* edited by F. Block, R. A. Cloward, B. Ehrenreich, and F. F. Piven. New York: Pantheon.

Plotnick, Robert D., and Felicity Skidmore. 1975. *Progress Against Poverty: A Review of the 1964–1974 Decade.* New York: Academic Press.

Plotnick, Robert. 1977. "Welfare Expenditures and the Poor: The 1965–1976 Experience and Future Expectations." Institute for Research on Poverty Discussion Paper No. 443-77. Madison, WI: University of Wisconsin.

Plutzer, Eric. 1988. "Work Life, Family Life, and Women's Support of Feminism." *American Sociological Review* 53:640–49.

Pomer, Marshall I. 1986. "Labor Market Structure, Intragenerational Mobility, and Discrimination: Black Male Advancement Out of Low-Paying Occupations, 1962–1973." *American Sociological Review* 51:650–59.

Porter, James N. 1974. "Race, Socialization, and Mobility in Educational and Early Occupational Attainment." *American Sociological Review* 39:303–16.

Porter, John. 1967. "The Future of Upward Mobility." Lecture, Ohio Valley Sociological Association Meeting, April.

Portes, Alejandro, Kenneth L. Wilson. 1976. "Black-White Differences in Educational Attainment." *American Sociological Review* 41:414–31.

Poulantzas, Nico. 1973. *Political Power and Social Classes.* London: New Left Books.

Poulantzas, Nicos. 1974. *Classes in Contemporary Capitalism.* London: New Left Books.

Powell, G. Bingham, Jr. 1986. "American Voter Turnout in Comparative Perspective." *American Political Science Review* 80:17–43.

Powers, Charles H. 1987. *Vilfredo Pareto.* Beverly Hills, CA: Sage.

Praeger, Jeffrey. 1987. "The Meaning of Difference: A Response to Michael Banton." *Ethnic and Racial Studies* 10:469–472.

Presthus, Robert. 1962. *The Organizational Society.* New York: Vintage Books.

Prewitt, Kenneth, and Alan Stone. 1973. *The Ruling Elites.* New York: Harper & Row.

Quinney, Richard. 1970. *The Social Reality of Crime.* Boston: Little, Brown.

Quinney, Richard. 1974. *Criminology: Analysis and Critique of Crime in the United States.* Boston: Little, Brown.

Radelet, Michael L. 1981. "Racial Characteristics and the Imposition of the Death Penalty." *American Sociological Review* 46:918–27.

Radzinowicz, L. 1971. "Economic Conditions and Crime." In *The Criminal in Society,* edited by L. Radzinowicz and M. Wolfgang. New York: Basic Books.

Rainwater, Lee. 1974. *What Money Buys.* New York: Basic Books.

Ramsøy, Natalie Rogoff. 1966. "Changes in Rates and Forms of Mobility." Pp. 213–34 in *Social Structure and Mobility in Economic Development,* edited by N. J. Smelser and S. M. Lipset. Chicago: Aldine.

Ransford, H. Edward, and Jon Miller. 1983. "Race, Sex and Feminist Outlooks." *American Sociological Review* 48:46–59.

Rawls, John. 1971. *A Theory of Justice.* Cambridge, MA: Harvard University Press.

Record, Wilson. 1987. "White Sociologists and Black Studies." Paper presented at the Annual Meeting of the American Sociological Association, New Orleans.

Redburn, F. Stevens, and Terry F. Buss. 1986. *Responding to America's Homeless: Public Policy Alternatives.* New York: Praeger.

Redmond, Sonjia Parker. 1988. "An Analysis of the General Well-Being of Blacks and Whites: Results of a National Study." *Journal of Sociology and Social Welfare* 15:57–71.

Reich, Michael, David M. Gordon, and Richard C. Edwards. 1977. "A Theory of Labor Market Segmentation." Pp. 108–13 in *Problems in Political Economy: An Urban Perspective,* edited by D. M. Gordon. Lexington, MA: D. C. Heath.

Reich, Michael. 1977. "The Economics of Racism." Pp. 183–8 in *Problems in Political Economy: An Urban Perspective,* edited by D. M. Gordon. Lexington, MA: D. C. Heath.

Reid, Pamela Trotman. 1984. "Feminism Versus Minority Group Identity: Not for Black Woman Only." *Sex Roles* 10:247–55.

Reid, Sue Titus. 1988. *Crime and Criminology.* New York: Holt, Rinehart & Winston.

Reiss, Albert J., Jr., ed. 1961. *Occupations and Social Status.* New York: The Free Press.

Reissman, Leonard. 1959. *Class in American Society.* Glencoe, IL: The Free Press.

Reissman, Leonard. 1973. *Inequality in American Society.* Glenview IL: Scott, Foresman.

Reskin, Barbara F. 1984. "Introduction." Pp. 1–7 in *Sex Segregation in the Workplace: Trends, Explanations, Remedies,* edited by B. F. Reskin. Washington, D.C.: National Academy Press.

Reskin, Barbara F. 1988. "Occupational Resegregation." Pp. 258–63 in *The American Woman 1988–89: A Status Report,* edited by Sara E. Rix. New York: W.W. Norton.

Richards, Robert K. 1986. "The Declining Status of Women . . . Revisited." *Sociological Focus* 19:315–32.

Richardson, Laurel. 1987. *The Dynamics of Sex and Gender: A Sociological Perspective.* New York: Harper & Row.

Ricklefs, Roger. December 6, 1988. "Health Insurance Becomes a Big Pain for Small Firms." *The Wall Street Journal,* p. B1.

Riesman, David, with Reuel Denney and Nathan Glazer. 1950. *The Lonely Crowd.* New Haven, CT: Yale University Press.

Riessman, Frank. 1965. "The Strengths of the Poor." Pp. 40–7 in *New Perspectives on Poverty,* edited by A. B. Shostak and W. Gomberg. Englewood Cliffs, NJ: Prentice-Hall.

Riis, Jacob. 1890. *How the Other Half Lives.* Williamstown, MA: Corner House, 1972.

Rischin, Moses, ed. 1965. *The American Gospel of Success.* New York: Quadrangle/The New York Times Books.

Ritzer, George. 1988. *Contemporary Sociological Theory.* New York: Knopf.

Rix, Sara E., ed. 1988. *The American Woman 1988–89: A Status Report.* New York: W.W. Norton.

Roach, Jack L.,. Llewelyn Gross, and Orville Gurrs-lin. 1969. *Social Stratification in the United States.* Englewood Cliffs, NJ: Prentice-Hall.

Robinson, Robert V., and Jonathan Kelley. 1979. "Class as Conceived by Marx and Dahrendorf: Effects on Income Inequality, Class Consciousness, and Class Conflict in the United States and Great Britain." *American Sociological Review* 44:38-58.

Robinson, Robert, and Wendell Bell. 1978. "Equality, Success and Social Justice in England and the United States." *American Sociological Review* 43:125-43.

Rodgers, Harrell R., Jr., 1986. *Poor Women, Poor Families: The Economic Plight of America's Female-Headed Households.* Armonk, NY: M. E. Sharpe.

Rodgers, Harrell R., Jr. 1982. *The Cost of Human Neglect: America's Welfare Failure.* Armonk, NY: M. E. Sharpe.

Rogin, Michael. 1971. "Voluntarism: The Political Functions of an Anti-Political Doctrine." Pp. 100-118 in *The American Labor Movement,* edited by D. Brody. New York: Harper & Row.

Rollins, Judith. 1986. "Part of a Whole: The Interdependence of the Civil Rights Movement and Other Social Movements." *Phylon* 47:61-70.

Roos, Patricia A. 1985. *Gender & Work: A Comparative Analysis of Industrial Societies.* Albany: State University of New York Press.

Roos, Patricia A., and Barbara F. Reskin. 1984. "Institutional Factors Contributing to Sex Segregation in the Workplace." Pp. 235-60 in *Sex Segregation in the Workplace: Trends, Explanations, Remedies.* Washington, D.C.: National Academy Press.

Roosevelt, Franklin Delano. 1966. "Second Inaugural Address." In *Poverty in the Affluent Society,* edited by H. H. Meissner. New York: Harper & Row.

Ropers, Richard H. 1988. *The Invisible Homeless: A New Urban Ecology.* New York: Insight Books.

Rose, Arnold M. 1968. *The Power Structure.* New York: Oxford University Press.

Rosenau, James A. 1974. *Citizenship Between Elections.* New York: The Free Press.

Rosencranz, Mary Lou. 1962. "Clothing Symbolism." *Journalism of Home Economics* 54:18-22.

Rosenfeld, Rachel A. 1978. "Women's Intergenerational Occupational Mobility." *American Sociological Review* 43:36-46.

Rosenfield, Sarah. 1989. "The Effects of Women's Employment: Personal Control and Sex Differences in Mental Health." *Journal of Health and Social Behavior* 30:77-91.

Rosenthal, Robert, and Lenore Jacobson. 1968. *Pygmalion in the Classroom: Teacher Expectation and Pupils' Intellectual Development.* New York: Holt, Rinehart & Winston.

Ross, Irwin. 1980. "How Lawless are Big Companies." *Fortune* 102:57.

Rossi, Alice S. 1988. "Growing Up and Older in Sociology 1940-1990." Pp. 43-64 in *Sociological Lives,* edited by M. W. Riley. Newbury Park, CA: Sage.

Rossi, Peter H., and James D. Wright. 1989. "The Urban Homeless: A Portrait of Urban Dislocation." *Annals of the American Academy of Political and Social Sciences* 501:132-42.

Rossides, Daniel W. 1986. *The American Class System: An Introduction to Social Stratification.* Boston: Houghton Mifflin.

Rostow, W. W. 1960. *The Stages of Economic Growth.* Cambridge: Cambridge University Press.

Roth, Guenther, and Claus Wittich, eds. 1968. *Max Weber: Economy and Society.* 3 vols. New York: Bedminster Press.

Rothman, Barbara Katz. 1984. "Women, Health, and Medicine." Pp. 70-80 in *Women: A Feminist Perspective,* edited by J. Freeman. Palo Alto, CA: Mayfield.

Rothman, Robert A. 1978. *Inequality and Stratification in the United States.* Englewood Cliffs, NJ: Prentice-Hall.

Rubin, Beth A. 1986. "Class Struggle American Style: Unions, Strikes and Wages." *American Sociological Review* 51:618-31.

Rubin, Lillian Breslow. 1976. *Worlds of Pain: Life in the Working-Class Family.* New York: Basic Books.

Rubinson, Richard, and Dan Quinlan. 1977. "Democracy and Social Inequality: A Reanalysis." *American Sociological Review* 42:611-623.

Rubinson, Richard. 1976. "The World Economy and the Distribution of Income within States: A Cross-National Study." *American Sociological Review* 41:638-659.

Rupp, Leila J. 1985. "The Women's Community in the National Women's Party, 1945 to the 1960's." *Signs: Journal of Women in Culture and Society* 10:715-40.

Rushing, William A. 1971. "Individual Resources, Societal Reaction, and Hospital Commitment." *American Journal of Sociology* 77:511–26.

Rushing, William A. 1978. "Status Resources, Societal Reactions, and Type of Mental Hospital Admission." *American Sociological Review* 43:521–33.

Ryan, William. 1981. *Equality.* New York: Random House.

Rytina, Joan H., William H. Form, and John Pease. 1975. "Income and Stratification Ideology: Beliefs about the American Opportunity Structure." *American Journal of Sociology* 75:703–16.

Sabato, Larry J. 1984. *PAC Power: Inside the World of Political Action Committees.* New York: W. W. Norton.

Sacks, Karen. 1975. "Engels Revisited: Women, the Organization of Production, and Private Property." Pp. 211–234 in *Toward an Anthropology of Women,* edited by R. R. Reiter. New York: Monthly Review Press.

Sahlins, Marshall D. 1968. *Tribesmen.* Englewood Cliffs, NJ: Prentice-Hall.

Saltiel, John. 1985. "A Note on Models and Definers as Sources of Influence in the Status Attainment Process: Male-Female Differences." *Social Forces* 64:1069–75.

Sampson, Robert J. 1986. "Effects of Socioeconomic Context on Official Reaction to Juvenile Delinquency." *American Sociological Review* 51: 876–85.

San Marco, Louise R. 1979. *Differential Sentencing Patterns among Criminal Homicide Offenders in Harris County, Texas.* Ph.D. Dissertation, Sam Houston State University.

Sanday, Peggy Reeves. 1981. *Female Power and Male Dominance: On the Origins of Sexual Inequality.* Cambridge: Cambridge University Press.

Sanderson, Stephen K. 1988. *Macrosociology: An Introduction to Human Societies.* New York: Harper & Row.

Sandler, Bernice R. 1986. "The Campus Climate Revisited: Chilly for Women Faculty, Administrators, and Graduate Students." Washington, D.C.: Association of American Colleges.

Sawhill, Isabel V. 1988. "Poverty in the U.S.: Why Is It So Persistent?" *Journal of Economic Literature* 26:1073–1119.

Schaefer, Richard T. 1987. "Racial Prejudice in a Capitalist State: What Has Happened to the American Creed?" Pp. 162–168 in *Introducing Sociology: A Collection of Readings,* edited by R. T. Schaefer and R. P. Lamm. New York: McGraw-Hill.

Schaefer, Richard T. 1988. *Racial and Ethnic groups.* Glenview, IL: Scott, Foresman.

Schiller, Bradley R. 1989. *The Economics of Poverty and Discrimination.* Englewood Cliffs, NJ: Prentice-Hall.

Schlegel, Alice, ed. 1977. *Sexual Stratification: A Cross-Cultural View.* New York: Columbia University Press.

Schuman, Howard, Charlotte Steeh, and Lawrence Bobo. 1985. *Racial Attitudes in America: Trends and Interpretations.* Cambridge, MA: Harvard University Press.

Schur, Edwin M. 1984. *Labeling Women Deviant: Gender, Stigma, and Social Control.* New York: Random House.

Schuttinga, J. A., M. Falik, and B. Steinwald. 1985. "Health Plan Selection in the Federal Employees Health Benefits Program." *Journal of Health Politics, Policy and Law* 10:119–39.

Schwartz, Michael, ed. 1987. *The Structure of Power in America.* New York: Holmes & Meier.

Schwartz, William B., Joseph P. Newhouse, and Albert P. Williams. 1985. "Is the Teaching Hospital an Endangered Species?" *The New England Journal of Medicine* 313:157–62.

Scitovsky, A. A., N. McCall, and L. Benham. 1978. "Factors Affecting the Choice Between Two Prepaid Plans." *Medical Care* 16:660–81.

Scully, Diana, and Pauline Bart. 1981. "A Funny Thing Happened on the Way to the Orifice: Women in Gynecology Textbooks." Pp. 350–355 in *The Sociology of Health and Illness: Critical Perspectives,* edited by P. Conrad and R. Kern. New York: St. Martin's Press.

Secombe, Wally. 1973. "The Housewife and Her Labour Under Capitalism." *New Left Review* 83:19.

Segre, S. 1975. "Family Stability, Social Classes, and Values in Traditional and Industrial Societies." *Journal of Marriage and the Family* 37:431–6.

Seider, Maynard S. 1974. "American Big Business Ideology: A Content Analysis of Executive Speeches." *American Sociological Review* 39: 802–815.

Seidman, Ann. 1978. *Working Women: A Study of Women in Paid Jobs.* Boulder, CO: Westview Press.

Sell, Ralph R., and Michael P. Johnson. 1977. "Income and Occupational Differences between Men and Women in the United States." *Sociology and Social Research* 62:1–20.

Sennett, Richard, and Jonathan Cobb. 1973. *The Hidden Injuries of Class.* New York: Vintage.

Serbin, Lisa A., K. Daniel O'Leary, Ronald N. Kent, and Illene J. Tonick. 1973. "A Comparison of Teacher Response to the Preacademic and Problems Behaviors of Boys and Girls." *Child Development* 44:796–804.

Sewell, William H., and Robert M. Hauser. 1976. "Recent Developments in the Wisconsin Study of Social and Psychological Factors in Socioeconomic Achievement." Center for Demography Working Paper No. 76-11. Madison, WI: University of Wisconsin.

Sewell, William H., and Vimal Shah. 1967. "Socioeconomic Status, Intelligence, and the Attainment of Higher Education." *Sociology of Education* 40:1–23.

Sewell, William H., Archibald O. Haller, and George W. Ohlendorf. 1970. "The Educational and Early Occupational Status Attainment Process: Replication and Revision." *American Sociologic Review* 35:1014–27.

Shank, Susan E. 1988. "Women and the Labor Market: The Link Grows Stronger." *Monthly Labor Review* 111:3–8.

Shapiro, Henry D. 1978. *Appalachia on Our Mind.* Chapel Hill, NC: University of North Carolina Press.

Shepard, Jon M., and Thomas R. Panko. 1974. "Alienation and Social Referents." *Sociology and Social Research* 59:55–60.

Shepelak, Norma J. 1987. "The Role of Self-Explanations and Self-Evaluations in Legitimating Inequality." *American Sociological Review* 52:495–503.

Shepelak, Norma J., and Duane Alwin. 1986. Beliefs about Inequality and Perceptions of Distributive Justice." *American Sociological Review* 51:30–46.

Sherman, Howard J., and James L. Wood. 1989. *Sociology: Traditional and Radical Perspectives.* New York: Harper & Row.

Shils, Edward A. 1970. "Deference," Pp. 420–428 in *The Logic of Social Hierarchies,* edited by Edward O. Laumann, Paul M. Siegel, and Robert W. Hodge. Chicago: Markham.

Shortell, Stephen M. 1984. "Factors Associated with the Use of Health Services." Pp. 49–88 in *Intro-duction to Health Services,* edited by S. J. Williams and P. R. Torrens. New York: John Wiley & Sons.

Simkus, Albert A. 1981. "Comparative Stratification and Mobility." *International Journal of Comparative Sociology* 22:213–36.

Simon, R. J., and Navin Sharma. 1979. *The Female Defendant in Washington, D.C.: 1974 and 1975.* Washington, D.C.: INSLAW.

Simpson, George Eaton, and J. Milton Yinger. 1965. *Racial and Cultural Minorities.* New York: Harper & Row.

Simpson, Miles E. 1970. "Social Mobility, Normlessness, and Powerlessness in Two Cultural Contexts." *American Sociological Review* 35:1002–13.

Simpson, Richard L. 1956. "A Modification of the Functional Theory of Social Stratification." *Social Forces* 35:132–7.

Sitkoff, Harvard. 1981. *The Struggle for Black Equality, 1954-1980.* New York: Hill and Wang.

Sivaramayya, B. 1983. "Equality and Inequality: The Legal Framework." Pp. 28–70 in *Equality and Inequality: Theory and Practice,* edited by A. Beteille. Delhi: Oxford University Press.

Skeels, Jack W. 1982. "The Economic and Organizational Basis of Early United States Strikes, 1900-1948." *Industrial and Labor Relations Review* 35:491–503.

Skocpol, Theda. 1988. "An 'Uppity Generation' and the Revitalization of Macroscopic Sociology." Pp. 145–159 in *Sociological Lives,* edited by M. W. Riley. Newbury Park, CA: Sage.

Slesinger, Doris P., Richard C. Tessler, and David Mechanic. 1975. *The Effects of Social Class on the Utilization of Preventive Medical Services in Contrasting Health Care Programs.* Research and Analytic Report No. 1. Madison, WI: Center for Medical Sociology and Health Services Research, University of Wisconsin.

Smeeding, Timothy. 1982. "The Antipoverty Effects of In-Kind Transfers." *Policy Studies Journal* 10:491–521.

Smidt, Corwin. 1980. "Civil Religious Orientations Among Elementary School Children." *Sociological Analysis* 41:24–40.

Smith, Dorothy E. 1987. *The Everyday World as Problematic: A Feminist Sociology.* Boston: Northeastern University Press.

Smith, James D. 1987. "Recent Trends in the Distribution of Wealth in the U.S.: Data, Research Problems, and Prospects." Pp. 72–89 in *International Comparisons of the Distribution of Household Wealth,* edited by Edward D. Wolff. Oxford: Clarendon Press.

Smith, Kevin B., and Robert A. Bylund. 1983. "Cognitive Maps of Class, Racial, and Appalachian Inequalities Among Rural Appalachians." *Rural Sociology* 48:253–270.

Smith, Mapheus. 1943. "An Empirical Scale of Prestige Status of Occupations." *American Sociological Review* 8:185–192.

Smith, Stanley H. 1972. "The Institutional Setting of the Sociological Contributions of Black Sociologists: A Case Study." Paper presented at the Conference of Black Sociologists: Historical Contemporary Perspectives, Chicago.

Smith, Vernon K. 1974. *Welfare Work Incentives: The Earnings Exemption and Its Impact Upon AFDC Employment, Earnings, and Program Costs.* Lansing, MI: Michigan Department of Social Services.

"Sniping at the Milken Deal." 1990. *Newsweek,* May 7, p. 48.

Snipp, C. Matthew, 1985. "Occupational Mobility and Social Class: Insights from Men's Career Mobility." *American Sociological Review* 50:475–93.

Snyder, David, and Charles Tilly. 1972. "Hardship and Collective Violence in France, 1830–1960." *American Sociological Review* 37:520–32.

Snyder, David and Charles Tilly. 1974. "On Debating and Falsifying Theories of Collective Violence." *American Sociological Review* 39:610–13.

Snyder, David. 1975. "Institutional Setting and Industrial Conflict: Comparative Analyses of France, Italy, and the United States." *American Sociological Review* 40:259–78.

Snyder, Eloise C., ed. 1979. *The Study of Women: Enlarging Perspectives of Social Reality.* New York: Harper & Row.

Sobel, Michael E. 1983. "Lifestyle Differentiation and Stratification in Contemporary U.S. Society." Pp. 115–44 in *Research in Social Stratification and Mobility,* vol. 2, edited by Donald W. Treiman and Robert V. Robinson. Greenwich, CT: JAI Press, 1983.

Sobel, Michael E. 1983. "Structural Mobility, Circulation Mobility and the Analysis of Occupational Mobility: A Conceptual Mismatch." *American So-*

ciological Review 48:721–7.

Society for Hospital Social Work Directors. March–April 1989. "1988 Hospital Closings Continue at Record Pace." *Social Work Administration* 15:21–2.

Sokoloff, Natalie, J. 1988. "Evaluating Gains and Losses by Black and White Women and Men in the Professions, 1960–1980." *Social Problems* 35:36–49.

Solomon, Barbara Bryant. 1987. "Social Welfare Reform." Pp. 113–27 in *The State of Black America 1987.* Washington, D.C.: National Urban League.

Solomon, Susan Gross, ed. 1982. *Pluralism in the Soviet Union.* New York: St. Martin's Press.

Soltow, Lee. 1975. *Men and Wealth in the United States.* New Haven, CT: Yale University Press.

Sontag, Susan. 1973. "The Third World of Women." *Partisan Review* 60:201–3.

Sorensen, Annemette, and Sara McLanahan. 1987. "Married Women's Economic Dependency, 1940–1980." *American Journal of Sociology* 93:659–87.

Sorokin, Pitirim. 1959. *Social and Cultural Mobility.* New York: The Free Press. With the exception of the last chapter, originally published as *Social Mobility.* New York: Harper & Row, 1927.

Spaeth, Joe L. 1967a. "Cognitive Complexity: A Dimension Underlying the Socioeconomic Achievement Process." In *Schooling and Achievement in American Society,* edited by W. H. Sewell, R. M. Hauser, and D. L. Featherman. New York: Academic Press.

Spaeth, Joe L. 1976b. "Characteristics of the Work Setting and the Job as Determinants of Income." In *Schooling and Achievement in American Society,* edited by W. H. Sewell, R. M. Hauser, and D. L. Featherman. New York: Academic Press.

Spector, Malcolm, and John I. Kitsuse. 1977. *Constructing Social Problems.* Menlo Park, CA: Cummings Publishing.

Spilerman, Seymour. 1978. "Careers, Labor Market Structure, and Socioeconomic Achievement." *American Journal of Sociology* 83:551–93.

Srole, Leo, Thomas S. Langner, Stanley T. Michael, Marvin K. Opler, and Thomas A. C. Rennie. 1962. *Mental Illness in the Metropolis.* New York: McGraw-Hill. Reprinted in part on pp. 404–412 in *Social Stratification in the United*

States, by J. L. Roach, L. Gross, and O. Gursslin. Englewood Cliffs, NJ: Prentice-Hall.

Srole, Leo. 1956. "Social Integration and Certain Corrolaries: An Exploratory Study." *American Sociological Review* 21:709–16.

Stacey, Judith, and Barrie Thorne. 1985. "The Missing Feminist Revolution in Sociology." *Social Problems* 32:301–14.

Stack, Steven, and Delores Zimmerman. 1982. "The Effect of World Economy on Income Inequality: A Reassessment." *The Sociological Quarterly* 23:345–358.

Staples, Clifford L., Michael L. Schwalbe, and Viktor Gecas. 1984. "Social Class, Occupational Conditions, and Efficacy-Based Self-Esteem." *Sociological Perspectives* 27:85–109.

Stark, Evan, and Anne Flitcraft. 1988. "Violence Among Intimates: An Epidemiological Review." Pp. 293–317 in *Handbook of Family Violence,* edited by V. B. Van Hasselt, R. L. Morrison, A. S. Bellack, and M. Hersen. New York: Plenum Press.

Stark, Louisa. 1987. "A Century of Alcohol and Homelessness: Demographics and Stereotypes." *Alcohol Health & Research World* 2:8–13.

Starr, Jr., Raymond H. 1988. "Physical Abuse of Children." Pp. 119–55 in *Handbook of Family Violence,* edited by V. B. Van Hasselt, R. L. Morrison, A. S. Bellack, and M. Hersen. New York: Plenum Press.

Steers, Richard M., and Lyman W. Porter. 1975. *Motivation and Work Behavior.* New York: McGraw-Hill.

Stefl, Mary E. 1987. "The New Homeless: A National Perspective." Pp. 46–63 in *The Homeless in Contemporary Society,* edited by R. D. Bingham, R. E. Green and S. B. White. Newbury Park, CA: Sage.

Steil, Janice M. 1984. "Marital Relationships and Mental Health: The Psychic Costs of Inequality." Pp. 113–123 in *Women: A Feminist Perspective,* edited by J. Freeman. Palo Alto, CA: Mayfield.

Steinitz, Victoria, and Ellen R. Solomon. 1986. *Starting Out: Class and Community in the Lives of Working-Class Youth.* Philadelphia: Temple University Press.

Stephenson, Charles, and Robert Asher, eds. 1986. *Life and Labor: Dimensions of American Working-Class History.* Albany, NY: State University of New York Press.

Stern, Maxine Springer. 1977. "Social Class and Psychiatric Treatment of Adults in the Mental Health Center." *Journal of Health and Social Behavior* 18:317–25.

Stern, Philip M. 1988. *The Best Congress Money Can Buy.* New York: Pantheon.

Stevens, Gillian, and Monica Boyd. 1980. "The Importance of Mother Labor Force Participation and Intergenerational Mobility of Women." *Social Forces* 59:186–192.

Stevenson, Mary Huff. 1978. "Wage Differences Between Men and Women: Economic Theories." Pp. 89–107 in *Working Women,* edited by Ann H. Stromberg and Shirley Harkess. Palo Alto, CA: Mayfield.

Stockwell, Edward G., David A. Swanson, and Jerry W. Wicks. 1987. "Trends in the Relationship Between Infant Mortality and Socioeconomic Status." *Sociological Focus* 20:319–27.

Stoll, Clarice Stasz. 1974. *Female and Male.* Dubuque, IA: William C. Brown.

Stolte, John F. 1983. "The Legitimation of Structural Inequality: Reformulation and Test of the Self-Evaluation Argument." *American Sociological Review* 48:331–42.

Stolte, John F. 1987. "The Formation of Justice Norms." *American Sociological Review* 52:774–84.

Stone, Gregory P. 1972. "Appearance and the Self." Pp. 86–118 in *Human Behavior and Social Processes,* edited by Arnold M. Rose. Boston: Houghton Mifflin.

Strathem, Marilyn. 1980. "No Nature, No Culture: The Hagen Case." Pp. 174–222 in *Nature, Culture and Gender,* edited by C. MacCormack and M. Strathem. Cambridge: Cambridge University Press.

Strauss, Anselm L. 1971. *The Contexts of Social Mobility.* Chicago: Aldine.

Strober, Myra, and Carolyn L. Arnold. 1987. "The Dynamics of Occupational Segregation Among Bank Tellers." In *Gender in the Workplace,* edited by C. Brown and J. Pechman. Washington, D.C.: The Brookings Institution.

Sturm, James L. 1977. *Investing in the United States, 1798-1893.* New York: Arno Press.

Stub, Holger R. 1972. "The Concept of Status Community." Pp. 92–107 in *Status Communities in*

Modern Society, edited by Holger R. Stub. Hinsdale, IL: Dryden.

"Study Shows Shift to Lower-Pay Jobs." September 2, 1988. *Akron Beacon Journal.*

Sullivan, Gerard. 1983. "Uneven Development and National Income Inequality in Third World Countries: A Cross-National Study of the Effects of External Economic Dependency." *Sociological Perspectives* 26:201–231.

Susser, Merwyn, Kim Hopper, and Judith Richman. 1983. "Society, Culture, and Health." Pp. 23–49 in *Handbook of Health, Health Care, and the Health Professions,* edited by D. Mechanic. New York: The Free Press.

Sutherland, Edwin H. 1949. *White Collar Crime.* New York: Dryden Press.

Swafford, M. 1978. "Sex Differences in Soviet Earnings." *American Sociological Review* 43:657–73.

Swanson, Guy E. 1974. *The Birth of the Gods.* Ann Arbor, MI: University of Michigan.

Swinton, David. 1987. "Economic Status of Blacks 1986." Pp. 49–73 in *The State of Black America 1987.* New York. National Urban League.

Szafran, Robert F. 1982. "What Kinds of Firms Hire and Promote Women and Blacks? A Review of the Literature." *The Sociological Quarterly* 23: 171–90.

Szymanski, Albert. 1976. "Racial Discrimination and White Gain." *American Sociological Review* 41:403–14.

Szymanski, Albert. 1978. *The Capitalist State and the Politics of Class.* Cambridge, MA: Winthrop.

Tabb, William K. 1970. "Black Americans: Internal Colony or Marginal Working Class." Paper presented at the Seventh World Congress of Sociology of the International Sociological Association, September 4–11, 1970, Varna, Bulgaria.

Taussig, Michael K., and Sheldon Danziger. 1976. *Conference on the Trend of Income Inequality in the U.S.* Institute for Research on Poverty Special Report No. 11. Madison, WI: University of Wisconsin.

Taylor, Verta. 1989a. "Social Movement Continuity: The Women's Movement in Abeyance." *American Sociological Review* 54:761–75.

Taylor, Verta. 1989b. "The Future of Feminism: A Social Movement Analysis." Pp. 473–90 in *Feminist Frontiers II: Rethinking Sex, Gender, and Society,* edited by L. Richardson and V. Taylor. New York:

Random House.

Teachman, Jay D., Karen A. Polonko, and John Scanzoni. 1987. "Demography of the Family." Pp. 3–36 in *Handbook of Marriage and the Family,* edited by Marvin B. Sussman and Suzanne K. Steinmetz. New York: Plenum Press.

Tessler, R., and D. Mechanic. 1975. "Factors Affecting the Choice Between Prepaid Group Practice and Alternative Insurance Programs." *Milbank Memorial Fund Quarterly/Health and Society* 53:149–72.

Thio, Alex. 1989. *Sociology: An Introduction.* New York: Harper & Row.

Thoits, Peggy A. 1983. "Multiple Identities and Psychological Well-Being: A Reformulation and Test of the Social Isolation Hypothesis." *American Sociological Review* 48:174–87.

Thomas, Melvin E. and Michael Hughes. 1986. "The Continuing Significance of Race: A Study of Race, Class, and Quality of Life in America, 1972–1985." *American Sociological Review* 51:830–41.

Thompson, James D. 1967. *Organizations in Action.* New York: McGraw-Hill.

Thornberry, T. P. 1973. "Race, Socioeconomic Status and Sentencing in the Juvenile Justice System." *Journal of Criminal Law and Criminology* 64:90–98.

Thornberry, Terence P., and Margaret Farnworth. 1982. "Social Correlates of Criminal Involvement: Further Evidence on the Relationship Between Social Status and Criminal Behavior." *American Sociological Review* 47:505–18.

Thornberry, Terrence P., and R. L. Christenson. 1984. "Unemployment and Criminal Involvement: An Investigation of Reciprocal Causal Structures." *American Sociological Review* 49:398–411.

Thorne, Barrie. 1989. "Girls and Boys Together . . . But Mostly Apart: Gender Arrangements in Elementary Schools." Pp. 73–84 in *Feminist Frontiers II: Rethinking Sex, Gender, and Society,* edited by L. Richardson and V. Taylor. New York: Random House.

Thornton, Arland, and Deborah Freedman. 1979. "Changes in the Sex Role Attitudes of Women, 1962–1977: Evidence from a Panel Study." *American Sociological Review* 44:831–42.

Thurow, Lester C. 1969. *Poverty and Discrimination.* Washington, D.C.: The Brookings Institution.

Thurow, Lester C. 1975. *Generating Inequality.* New York: Basic Books.

Thurow, Lester C. February 5, 1984. "The Disappearance of the Middle Class," *The New York Times,* p. F3.

Thurow, Lester. 1985. "Medicine Versus Economics." *The New England Journal of Medicine* 313:611-614.

Tienda, Marta, and Ding-Tzann Lii. 1987. "Minority Concentration and Earnings Inequality: Blacks, Hispanics, and Asians Compared." *American Journal of Sociology* 93:141-65.

Tiffany, Lawrence, Yakov Avichai, and Geoffrey Peters. 1975. "A Statistical Analysis of Sentencing in Federal Courts." *Journal of Legal Studies* 4:369.

Tittle, Charles R., and Wayne J. Villemez. 1977. "Social Class and Criminality." *Social Forces* 56:474-502.

Tittle, Charles R., Wayne J. Villemez, and Douglas A. Smith. 1978. "The Myth of Social Class and Criminality: An Empirical Assessment of the Empirical Evidence." *American Sociological Review* 43:643-56.

Tolbert, Charles M. II. 1982. Industrial Segmentation and Men's Career Mobility." *American Sociological Review* 47:457-77.

Tracy, Joseph S. 1986. "An Investigation into the Determinants of U.S. Strike Activity." *American Economic Review* 76:423-36.

Treas, Judith. 1983. "Trickle Down or Transfers? Postwar Determinants of Family Income Inequality." *American Sociological Review* 48:546-59.

Treiman, D. J., and H. I. Hartmann, eds. 1981. *Women, Work, and Wages: Equal Pay for Jobs of Equal Value.* Washington, D.C.: National Academy Press.

Treiman, D. J., and P. A. Roos. 1983. "Sex and Earnings in Industrial Society: A Nine-Nation Comparison." *American Journal of Sociology* 89:612-50.

Treiman, Donald, and Kermit Terrell. 1975. "Sex and the Process of Status Attainment: A Comparison of Working Women and Men." *American Sociological Review* 40:174-200.

Treiman, Donald J., Heidi I. Hartmann and Patricia A. Roos. 1984. "Assessing Pay Discrimination Using National Data." Pp. 137-154 in *Comparable Worth and Wage Discrimination,* edited by H. Remick, Philadelphia: Temple University Press.

Tropman, John E. 1989. *American Values & Social Welfare: Cultural Contradictions in the Welfare State.* Englewood Cliffs NJ: Prentice-Hall.

Truman, David. 1959. "The American System in Crisis." *Political Science Quarterly* 74:481-497.

Tuch, Steven A. 1981. "Analyzing Recent Trends in Prejudice toward Blacks: Insights from latent Class Models." *American Journal of Sociology* 87:130-42.

Tumin, Melvin M. 1953. "Some Principles of Stratification: A Critical Analysis." *American Sociological Review* 18:387-94.

Turk, Austin T. 1969. *Criminality and Legal Order.* Chicago: Rand McNally.

Turner, Bryan S. 1986. *Equality.* New York: Methuen.

Turner, Jonathan H. 1986. *The Structure of Sociological Theory.* Chicago: Dorsey.

Turner, Jonathan H., Leonard Beeghley, and Charles H. Powers. 1989. *The Emergence of Sociological Theory.* Chicago: Dorsey.

Turner, Jonathan H., Royce Singleton, Jr., and David Musick. 1984. *Oppression: A Socio-History of Black-White Relations in America.* Chicago: Nelson-Hall.

Turner, R. Jay, and Morton O. Wagenfeld, 1967. "Occupational Mobility and Schizophrenia: Assessment of the Social Causation and Social Selection Hypotheses." *American Sociological Review* 32:104-13.

Turner, R. Jay, and Samuel Noh. 1983. "Class and Psychological Vulnerability Among Women: The Significance of Social Support and Personal Control." *Journal of Health and Social Behavior* 24:2-15.

Turner, Ralph H., ed. 1967. *Robert E. Park: On Social Control and Collective Behavior.* Chicago: Phoenix Books.

Turner, William H. 1986. "The Black Ethnographer 'At Home' in Harlem: A Commentary and Research Response to Stephenson and Greer." *Human Organization* 45:279-92.

Tyree, Andrea, and Judith Treas. 1974. "The Occupational and Marital Mobility of Women." *American Sociological Review* 39:293-302.

Tyree, Andrea, Moshe Semyonov, and Robert W. Hodge. 1979. "Gaps and Glissandos: Inequality, Economic Development, and Social Mobility in 24 Countries." *American Sociological Review* 44:410-24.

U.S. Bureau of the Census. 1988. *Statistical Abstract*

of the United States 1988. Washington, D.C.: U.S. Government Printing Office.

U.S. Bureau of the Census. 1989. *Statistical Abstract of the United States 1989.* Washington, D.C.: U.S. Government Printing Office.

U.S. Bureau of the Census. 1990. *Statistical Abstract of the United States 1990.* Washington, D.C.: U.S. Government Printing Office.

U.S. Bureau of the Census. August 1987. *Male-Female Differences in Work Experience, Occupation, and Earnings: 1984.* Current Population Reports, Series P-70, No. 10. Washington, D.C.: U.S. Government Printing Office.

U.S. Bureau of the Census. September 1990. *Money Income and Poverty Status in the United States 1989.* Current Population Reports, Series P-60. No. 168. Washington, D.C.: U.S. Government Printing Office.

U.S. Bureau of the Census. February 1989a. *Money Income of Households, Families, and Persons in the United States: 1987.* Current Population Reports, Series P-60, No. 162. Washington, D.C.: U.S. Government Printing Office.

U.S. Bureau of the Census. February 1989b. *Poverty in the United States 197.* Current Population Reports, Series P-60, No. 163. Washington, D.C.: U.S. Government Printing Office.

U.S. Bureau of the Census. 1987. *Money Income and Poverty Status of Families and Persons in the United States: 1986.* Current Population Reports, Series P-60, No. 157.

U.S. Bureau of the Census. July 1986. *Household Wealth and Asset Ownership: 1984.* Current Population Reports, Series P-70, No. 7. Washington, D.C.: U.S. Government Printing Office.

U.S. Bureau of the Census. March 1986. *Voting and Registration in the Elections of 1984.* Current Population Reports, Series P-20, No. 405. Washington, D.C.: U.S. Government Printing Office.

U.S. Bureau of the Census. *The Social and Economic Status of the Black Population in the United States: An Historical View, 1790–1978.* Current Population Reports, Series P-23, No. 80. Washington, D.C.: U.S. Government Printing Office.

U.S. Census Office. *Statistical Atlas of the United States, 1900.* Washington, D.C.: U.S. Government Printing Office.

U.S. Congress, Committee on Ways and Means. 1988. *Background Material on Programs within the Jurisdiction of the Committee on Ways and Means.*

Washington, D.C.: U.S. Government Printing Office.

U.S. Department of Commerce and Labor, Bureau of Statistics. 1911. *Statistical Abstract of the United States 1911.* Washington, D.C.: U.S. Government Printing Office.

U.S. Department of Commerce, Office of Management and Budget. 1980. *Social Indicators III.* Washington, D.C.: U.S. Government Printing Office.

U.S. Department of Education. March 1990. *Faculty in Higher Education Institutions, 1988.* Washington, D.C.: U.S. Government Printing Office.

U.S. Department of Health and Human Services. 1985. *Health Status of Minorities and Low Income Groups.* Washington, D.C.: U.S. Government Printing Office.

U.S. Department of Health and Human Services. January 1989b. *Medicare.* SSA Publication No. 05-10043. Washington, D.C.: U.S. Government Printing Office.

U.S. Department of Health and Human Services. March 1989. *Health United States 1988.* Washington, D.C.: U.S. Government Printing Office.

U.S. Department of Health and Human Services. October 1988. *Use of Dental Services and Dental Health United States, 1986.* Washington, D.C.: U.S. Government Printing Office.

U.S. Department of Health and Human Services. September 1988. *Current Estimates from the National Health Interview Survey United States, 1987.* Washington, D.C.: U.S. Government Printing Office.

U.S. Department of Health and Human Services. January 1989a. *Disability.* SSA Publication No. 05-10029. Washington, D.C.: U.S. Government Printing Office.

U.S. Department of Housing and Urban Development. 1984. *A Report to the Secretary on the Homeless and Emergency Shelters.* Washington, D.C.: Office of Policy Development and Research.

U.S. Department of Labor, Bureau of Labor Statistics. March 1982. *Analysis of Work Stoppages, 1980.* Bulletin 2120. Washington, D.C.: U.S. Government Printing Office.

U.S. Department of Justice. 1976. *Capital Punishment 1975.* National Prisoner Statistics Bulletin, Law Enforcement Assistance Administration, National Criminal Justice Information and Statistics Service.

U.S. Department of Labor, Bureau of Labor Statistics. January 1989. *Employment and Earnings.* Washington, D.C.: U.S. Government Printing Office.

U.S. Department of Labor, Bureau of Labor Statistics. June 1989. *Current Wage Developments.* Washington, D.C.: U.S. Government Printing Office.

U.S. Department of Labor, Bureau of Labor Statistics. January 1990. *Employment and Earnings.* Washington, D.C.: U.S. Government Printing Office.

U.S. Department of Labor, Bureau of Labor Statistics. January 1991. *Employment and Earnings.* Washington, D.C.: U.S. Government Printing Office.

U.S. Department of Labor, Bureau of Labor Statistics. June 1985. *Handbook of Labor Statistics, Bulletin 2217.* Washington, D.C.: U.S. Government Printing Office.

U.S. Department of Labor, Bureau of Labor Statistics. March 1989. *Monthly Labor Review.* Washington, D.C.: U.S. Government Printing Office.

U.S. Department of Labor, Women's Bureau. 1947. *Women's Occupations Through Seven Decades.* Washington, D.C.: U.S. Government Printing Office.

Ulbrich, Patricia M., George J. Warheit, and Rick S. Zimmerman. 1989. "Race, Socioeconomic Status, and Psychological Distress: An Examination of Differential Vulnerability." *Journal of Health and Social Behavior* 30:131–46.

United Nations. 1988. *1985/86 Statistical Yearbook.* New York: Department of International Economics and Social Affairs.

Urgent Relief for the Homeless Act. February 4, 1987. *Hearing before the Subcommittee on Housing and Community Development of the Committee on Banking, Finance and Urban Affairs, House of Representatives.* Serial No. 100-3. Washington, D.C.: U.S. Government Printing Office.

Useem, Michael. 1978. "The Inner Group of the American Capitalist Class." *Social Problems* 25:225–40.

Useem, Michael. 1979. "The Social Organization of the American Business Elite and Participation of Corporation Directors in the Governance of American Institutions." *American Sociological Review* 44:553–72.

Useem, Michael. 1980. "Which Business Leaders Help Govern?" Pp. 199–225 in *Power Structure Research,* edited by G. W. Domhoff. Beverly Hills, CA: Sage.

Useem, Michael. 1984. *The Inner Circle: Large Corporations and the Rise of Business Political Activity in the U.S. and U.K.* New York: Oxford University Press.

Valentine, Charles A. 1968. *Culture and Poverty.* Chicago: University of Chicago Press.

Van den Berghe, Pierre L. 1967. *Race and Racism: A Comparative Perspective.* New York: John Wiley & Sons.

Van den Berghe, Pierre L. 1985. "Review of J. S. Chafetz's Sex and Advantage." *American Journal of Sociology* 90:1350.

Van Hasselt, Vincent B., Randall L. Morrison, Alan S. Bellack, and Michel Hersen, eds. 1988. *Handbook of Family Violence.* New York: Plenum Press.

Vanfossen, Beth E., and Robert I. Rhodes. 1974. "A Critique of Abrahamson's Assessment." *American Journal of Sociology* 80:727–32.

Vanneman, Reeve, and Fred C. Pampel. 1977. "The American Perception of Class and Status," *American Sociological Review* 42:422–437.

Vanneman, Reeve, and Lynn Weber Cannon. 1987. *The American Perception of Class.* Philadelphia: Temple University Press.

Varian, Hal R. 1978. "Economic Theories of Distributive Justice." Paper presented at the Symposium on Economic Justice, The College of Wooster, Wooster, Ohio, November 3, 1978.

Veblen, Thorstein. 1953. *The Theory of the Leisure Class.* New York: The New American Library.

Verba, Sidney, and Gary R. Orren. 1985. *Equality in America: The View from the Top.* Cambridge, MA: Harvard University Press.

Verba, Sidney, and Norman H. Nie. 1972. *Participation in America: Political Democracy and Social Equality.* New York: Harper & Row.

Verbrugge, Lois M. 1983. "Multiple Roles and Physical Health of Women and Men." *Journal of Health and Social Behavior* 24:16–30.

Verbrugge, Lois M. 1985. "Gender and Health: An Update on Hypotheses and Evidence." *Journal of Health and Social Behavior* 26:156–82.

Vesterdal, Jorgen. 1977. "Handling Child Abuse in Denmark." *Child Abuse and Neglect* 2:193–98.

Vogel, David. 1987. "Political Science and the Study of Corporate Power: A Dissent from the New Conventional Wisdom." *British Journal of Political Science* 17:385–405.

Vogel, Lise. 1983. *Marxism and the Oppression of Women.* New Brunswick, NJ: Rutgers University Press.

Vogeler, Ingolf. 1975. "American Peasantry." *Anthropological Quarterly* 48:223–235.

Wacquant, Lois J.D., and William Julius Wilson. 1989. "The Cost of Racial and Class Exclusion in the Inner City." *Annals of the American Academy of Political and Social Science* 501:8–25.

Waegel, William B. 1984. "How Police Justify the Use of Deadly Force." *Social Problems* 32:144–55.

Walby, Sylvia. 1986. *Patriarchy at Work.* Minneapolis: University of Minnesota Press.

Walinsky, Adam. 1965. "Keeping the Poor in Their Place: Notes on the Importance of Being One-up." Pp. 159–68 in *New Perspectives on Poverty,* edited by A. B. Shostak and W. Gomberg. Englewood Cliffs, NJ: Prentice-Hall.

Wall Street Journal. December 1, 1988. "Pricey Sneakers in Inner City Help Set Nations Fashion Trend." pp. A1, A6.

Wallace, Michael, and Arne L. Kalleberg. 1981. "Economic Organization, Occupations, and Labor Force Consequences: Toward a Specification of Dual Economy Theory." Pp. 77–117 in *Sociological Perspectives on Labor Markets,* edited by I. Berg. New York: Academic Press.

Wallace, Michael, Larry J. Griffin, and Beth A. Rubin. 1989. "The Positional Power of American Labor, 1963–1977." *American Sociological Review* 54:197–214.

Wallerstein, I. 1974. *The Modern World-System: Capitalist and the Origins of the European World-Economy in the Sixteenth Century.* New York: Academic.

Wallerstein, I. 1979. *The Capitalist World-Economy.* Cambridge: Cambridge University Press.

Walls, David S. 1978. "Internal Colony or Internal Periphery? A Critique of Current Models and an Alternative Formulation." Pp. 319–249 in *Colonialism in Modern America: The Appalachian Case,* edited by H. Lewis, L. Johnson, and D. Askins. Boone, NC: Appalachian Consortium Press.

Warner, W. Lloyd, with Marchia Meeker and Kenneth Eells. 1960. *Social Class in America.* New York: Harper & Row.

Warnock, John W. 1987. *The Politics of Hunger.* Toronto: Methuen.

Weber, Max. 1964. *The Theory of Social and Economic Organization,* edited by Talcott Parsons. New York: The Free Press.

Weede, Erich. 1982. "The Effects of Democracy and Socialist Strength on the Size Distribution of Income." *American Sociological Review* 23:151–165.

Weinstein, Michael M., and Eugene Smolensky. 1978. "Poverty." *Dictionary of American Economic History.*

Weir, Stanley, 1977. "U.S.A.: The Labor Revolt." Pp. 487–517 in *American Society, Inc.,* edited by M. Zeitlin. Skokie, IL: Rand McNally.

Weiss, Robert S., and David Riesman. 1966. "Work and Automation: Problems and Prospects." Pp. 553–618 in *Contemporary Social Problems,* edited by R. K. Merton and R. A. Nisbet. New York: Harcourt Brace Jovanovich.

Welch, Susan, and Michael W. Combs. 1985. "Intraracial Differences in Attitudes of Blacks: Class Cleavage or Consensus?" *Phylon* 46:91–97.

Welch, Susan, John Gruhl, and Cassia Spohn. 1984. "Dismissal, Conviction, and Incarceration of Hispanic Defendants: A Comparison with Anglos and Blacks." *Social Science Quarterly* 65:257–64.

Welch, W. P. 1985. "Regression Toward the Mean in Medical Care Costs." *Medical Care* 23:1234–41.

Welch, W. P., and R. G. Frank. 1986. "The Predictors of HMO Enrollee Populations: Results from a National Sample." *Inquiry* 23:16–22.

Weller, Jack E. 1965. *Yesterday's People: Life in Contemporary Appalachia.* Lexington, KY: University of Kentucky Press.

Werner, Paul D., and Georgina Williams LaRussa. 1985. "Persistence and Change in Sex-Role Stereotypes." *Sex Roles* 12:1089–1100.

Wertz, Richard W. and Dorothy C. Wertz. 1981. "Notes on the Decline of Midwives and the Rise of Medical Obstetricians." Pp. 165–183 in *The Sociology of Health and Illness: Critical Perspectives,* edited by P. Conrad and R. Kern. New York: St. Martin's Press.

Wheaton, B. 1980. "The Sociogenesis of Psychological Disorder: An Attributional Theory." *Journal of Health and Social Behavior* 21:100–24.

Wheaton, B. 1983. "Stress, Personal Coping Resources, and Psychiatric Symptoms: An Investigation of Interactive Models." *Journal of Health and Social Behavior* 24:208–229.

Wheeler, Stanton, David Weisburd, and Nancy Bode.

1982. "Sentencing the White-Collar Offender: Rhetoric and Reality." *American Sociological Review* 47:641–59.

Whisnant, David E. 1983. *All That Is Native & Fine: The Politics of Culture in an American Region.* Chapel Hill, NC: University of North Carolina Press.

Whitt, J. Allen. 1980. "Can Capitalists Organize Themselves?" Pp. 97–113 in *Power Structure Research,* edited by G. W. Domhoff. Beverly Hills, CA: Sage.

Wilde, William A. 1968. "Decision-Making in a Psychiatric Screening Agency." *Journal of Health and Social Behavior* 9:215–21.

Wilensky, Harold L. 1966. "Measures and Effects of Social Mobility." Pp. 98–140 in *Social Structure and Mobility in Economic Development,* edited by N. J. Smelser and S. M. Lipset. Chicago: Aldine.

Wilensky, Harold L. 1972. "Word Careers, and Social Integration." Pp. 79–92 in *Status Communities in Modern Society,* edited by Holger R. Stub. Hinsdale, IL: Dryden.

Wiley, Mary Glenn and Arlene Eskilson. 1983. "Scaling the Corporate Ladder: Sex Differences in Expectations for Performance, Power and Mobility." *Social Psychology Quarterly* 46:351–9.

Wilhite, Allen, and John Theilmann. 1986. "Women, Blacks, and PAC Discrimination." *Social Science Quarterly* 67:283–96.

Williams, Jay R., and Martin Gold. 1972. "From Delinquent Behavior to Official Delinquency." *Social Problems* 20:209–29.

Williams, Jr., Robin M. 1970. *American Society: A Sociological Interpretation.* New York: Knopf.

Williams, Kirk R. 1984. "Economic Sources of Homicide: Reestimating the Effects of Poverty and Inequality." *American Sociological Review* 49: 283–89.

Williams, Kirk R., and Robert L. Flewelling. 1988. "The Social Production of Criminal Homicide: A Comparative Study of Disaggregated Rates in American Cities." *American Sociological Review* 53:421–31.

Williams, Ted. May 8, 1987. "On the Reservation: America's Apartheid." *National Review,* pp. 28–30.

Willie, Charles Vert. 1979. *The Caste and Class Controversy.* Bayside, NY: General Hall.

Wilson, Kenneth L., and Alejandro Portes. 1975. "The Educational Attainment Process: Results from a National Sample." *American Journal of Sociology* 81:343–63.

Wilson, William J. 1970. "Race Relations Models and Explanations of Ghetto Behavior." Paper presented at the Seventh World Congress of Sociology of the International Sociological Association, September 14–19, 1970, Varna, Bulgaria.

Wilson, William J. 1973. *Power, Racism and Privilege.* New York: The Free Press.

Wilson, William J. 1978. *The Declining Significance of Race: Blacks and Changing American Institutions.* Chicago: University of Chicago Press.

Wilson, William Julius, and Kathryn M. Neckerman. 1986. "Poverty and Family Structure: The Widening Gap between Evidence and Public Policy Issues." Pp. 232–59 in *Fighting Poverty: What Works and What Doesn't,* edited by S. H. Danziger and D. H. Weinberg. Cambridge, MA: Harvard University Press.

Wilson, William Julius. 1982. "The Declining Significance of Race-Revisited but Not Revised." Pp. 399–405 in *Majority & Minority: The Dynamics of Race and Ethnicity in American Life,* edited by N. R. Yetman and C. H. Steele. Boston: Allyn & Bacon.

Wilson, William Julius. 1987. *The Truly Disadvantaged: The Inner City, the Underclass, and Public Policy.* Chicago: University of Chicago Press.

Winegarden, C. R. 1974. "The Fertility of AFDC Women: An Economic Analysis." *Journal of Economics and Business* 26:159–66.

Wolf, Wendy C. 1976. "Occupational Attainments of Married Women: Do Career Contingencies Matter?" Madison, WI: Center for Demography and Ecology Working Paper No. 76-3, University of Wisconsin.

Wolf, Wendy C., and Neil D. Fligstein. 1979. "Sex and Authority in the Workplace: The Causes of Sexual Inequality." *American Sociological Review* 44:235–52.

Wolfgang, Marvin and Marc Riedel. 1973. "Race, Judicial Discretion, and the Death Penalty." *The Annals of the American Academy of Political and Social Science* 407:118.

Wolfgang, Marvin E., and Bernard Cohen. 1970. *Crime and Race.* New York: Institute of Human Relations Press.

Wolinsky, F. D. 1980. "The Performance of Health Maintenance Organizations: An Analytic Review." *Millbank Memorial Fund Quarterly* 58:537–87.

"Women's Perception of Job Bias Grows." January/February 1987. *The Gallup Report,* p. 18.

Wooster Daily Record. May 9, 1988, p. B4.

Wright, Eik Olin, and Bill Martin. 1987. "The Transformation of the American Class Structure, 1960–1980." *American Journal of Sociology* 93:1–29.

Wright, Erik Olin, and Joachim Singelmann. 1982. "Proletarianization in the Changing American Class Structure." Pp. S176–S209 in *Marxist Inquiries: Studies of Labor, Class, and States,* edited by M. Burawoy and T. Skocpol. Chicago: University of Chicago Press.

Wright, Erik Olin, and Luca Perrone. 1977. "Marxist Class Categories and Income Inequality." *American Sociological Review* 42:32–55.

Wright, Erik Olin, Cynthia Costello, David Hachen, and Joey Sprague. 1982. "The American Class Structure." *American Sociological Review* 47:709–26.

Wright, Erik Olin. 1976. "Class Boundaries in Advanced Capitalist Societies." *New Left Review* 98:3–41.

Wright, Erik Olin. 1978. "Race, Class, and Income Inequality." *American Journal of Sociology* 83:1368–97.

Wright, Erik Olin. 1977. "Class Structure and Occupation: A Research Note." Institute for Research on Poverty Discussion Paper No. 415-77. Madison, WI: University of Wisconsin-Madison.

Wright, James D., and Julie A. Lam 1987. "Homeless and the Low-Income Housing Supply." *Social Policy* 17:48–53.

Wrong, Dennis H. 1959. "The Functional Theory of Stratification: Some Neglected Considerations." *American Sociological Review* 24:772–82.

Wrong, Dennis H. 1972. "Social Inequality Without Social Stratification." Pp. 69–79 in *Status Communities in Modern Society,* edited by H. R. Stub. Hinsdale, IL: Dryden.

Yanagisako, Sylvia Junko, and Jane Fishburne Collier. 1987. "Toward a Unified Analysis of Gender and Kinship." Pp. 14–50 in *Gender and Kinship: Essays Toward a Unified Analysis,* edited by J. F. Collier and S. J. Yanagisako. Stanford, CA: Stanford University Press.

Yancey, William L., Leo Rigsby, and John D. McCarty. 1972. "Social Position and Self Evaluation: The Relative Importance of Race." *American Journal of Sociology* 78:338–359.

Yeuell, H. Davis. 1985. *Moving Mountains: A History of Presbyterian and Reformed Faith at Work in Appalachia.* Amesville, OH: Coalition for Appalachian Ministry.

Yllo, K. 1983. "Sexual Equality and Violence Against Wives in American States." *Journal of Comparative Family Studies* 14:67–86.

Yllo, K. 1984. "The Status of Women, Marital Equality and Violence Against Wives." *Journal of Family Issues* 5:307–20.

Zastrow, Charles. 1982. *Introduction to Social Welfare Institutions: Social Problems, Services and Current Issues.* Homewood, IL: Dorsey Press.

Zeitlin, Irving. 1968. *Ideology and the Development of Sociological Theory.* Englewood Cliffs, NJ: Prentice-Hall.

Zeitlin, Maurice, ed. 1977. *American Society, Inc.* Skokie, IL: Rand McNally.

Zieger, Robert H. 1986. *American Workers, American Unions, 1920–1985.* Baltimore: The Johns Hopkins University Press.

Zigler, Edward, and Susan Muenchow. 1983. "Infant Day Care and Infant-Care Leaves." *American Psychologist* 38:91–94.

Zimmerman, Don H., and Candace West. 1975. "Sex Roles, Interruptions and Silences in Conversation." Pp. 105–29 in *Language and Sex: Difference and Dominance,* edited by B. Thorne and N. Henley. Rowley, MA: Newbury House.

Zingraff, Rhonda, and Michael D. Schulman. 1984. "Social Bases of Class Consciousness: A Study of Southern Textile Workers with a Comparison by Race." *Social Forces* 63:98–116.

Zuckerman, Alan. 1977. "The Concept 'Political Elite': Lessons from Mosca and Pareto." *The Journal of Politics* 39:324–44.

INDEX